Canadian Rockies Trail Guide

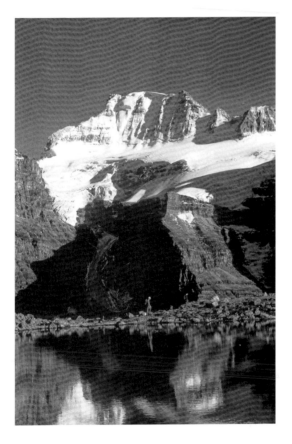

Brian Patton & Bart Robinson

Ninth Edition

Summerthought

Banff, Alberta

Canadian Rockies Trail Guide

Published by

Summerthought

Summerthought Publishing
PO Box 2309
Banff, AB T1L 1C1
Canada
www.summerthought.com

Printing History
1st Edition — 1971
9th edition — 2011, reprinted 2013, revised 2015

All photos by the authors unless otherwise noted
Front cover photo: Tonquin Valley. © John Marriott/www.wildernessprints.com
Design and production: Linda Petras
Printed in Canada by Friesens

We gratefully acknowledge the financial support of the Alberta Foundation for the
Arts for our publishing activities.

Library and Archives Canada Cataloguing in Publication

Patton, Brian, 1943-
Canadian Rockies trail guide: a hiker's guide to Banff, Jasper, Yoho, Kootenay,
Waterton Lakes, Mount Robson, Mount Assiniboine, Peter Lougheed, Elk Lakes and
Akamina-Kishinena Parks / Brian Patton & Bart Robinson. — 9th ed.

Includes bibliographical references and index.
ISBN 978-0-9811491-8-9

1. Trails — Rocky Mountains, Canadian (B.C. and Alta.) — Guidebooks.
2. Hiking — Rocky Mountains, Canadian (B.C. and Alta.) — Guidebooks.
3. Rocky Mountains, Canadian (B.C. and Alta.) — Guidebooks. I. Robinson, Bart II. Title.

FC219.P375 2011   796.5109711   C2011-900688-X

Contents

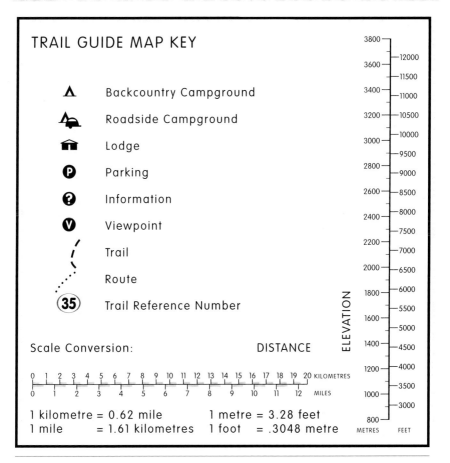

TRAIL GUIDE MAP KEY

Backcountry Campground

Roadside Campground

Lodge

Parking

Information

Viewpoint

Trail

Route

(35) Trail Reference Number

Scale Conversion: DISTANCE

0 1 2 3 4 5 6 7 8 9 10 11 12 13 14 15 16 17 18 19 20 KILOMETRES
0   1   2   3   4   5   6   7   8   9   10   11   12 MILES

1 kilometre = 0.62 mile   1 metre = 3.28 feet
1 mile   = 1.61 kilometres 1 foot = .3048 metre

ELEVATION

3800
3600 — 12000
— 11500
3400 — 11000
3200 — 10500
3000 — 10000
— 9500
2800 — 9000
2600 — 8500
— 8000
2400 — 7500
2200 — 7000
2000 — 6500
1800 — 6000
— 5500
1600 — 5000
1400 — 4500
1200 — 4000
— 3500
1000 — 3000
800
METRES   FEET

Preface

It was a different world when we set out to write the *Canadian Rockies Trail Guide* in 1970. Annual park visitation was half of what it is today. Mountain bikes, Gore-Tex©, GPS location devices, pepper spray, and water purification pumps were unknown. Backcountry campgrounds were mere suggestions, and mostly we camped where we pleased. There were no backcountry permits or fees. And there were no trail guidebooks.

The hikers you encountered on backcountry trails in the 1970s were usually from Canada (mostly Alberta) and the United States. Today you meet people from all over the world on day trips, and when you travel into the backcountry, you are as likely to encounter someone from Europe as North America.

We have worked to keep our trail guide current over the past 45 years with numerous revisions, three major expansions, and now a website dedicated to hiking in the Canadian Rockies (see opposite page for details). In this edition, we have taken a fresh look at the trails we have hiked through the years, taking into consideration that the way people travel in the backcountry keeps on evolving.

With this in mind, the ninth edition of the *Canadian Rockies Trail Guide* provides revised routes and descriptions that suggest many new approaches to old pathways. As in the past, we endeavour to be a comprehensive and reliable source of information for nearly all the trails in the mountain parks, even though many of these trails only receive a smattering of visitation each summer. And we recognize the importance of emerging technology by providing GPS coordinates for all trailheads, which should serve as a reference for previewing trips on digital maps and Google Earth, as well as helping to direct you to your hike.

Of course, one of our most important jobs is keeping up-to-date on changes to trails, landscape and parks policy since the last go-around. Some things you may discover:

Forest fires in Kootenay National Park during 2001 and 2003 burned out seven major trails in the northern half of the park, and all of these routes are still in a state of recovery. Major flooding in 2013 affected trails throughout the eastern section of Banff National Park and throughout much of Peter Lougheed Provincial Park.

Travel restrictions designed to protect wildlife and habitat have altered access and the way people hike the trails in several areas of the mountain parks. In Banff Park, there is particular emphasis on protection of grizzly bear habitat, and various seasonal restrictions have been instituted on trails around Moraine Lake and Paradise Valley, in the Spray River and Brewster Creek valleys, and on the trails to Aylmer Lookout and Pass. Caribou are a concern in Jasper Park, and several trails running through prime habitat, including the Skyline and Tonquin Valley, have been listed as "dog-free zones." And some high alpine areas, like Banff's Parker Ridge and Mount Robson's Snowbird Pass, are simply too fragile to allow early-season travel.

We take some pride in celebrating the 40th anniversary of the *Canadian Rockies Trail Guide* at the same time as the centennial of both Parks Canada and British Columbia's Provincial Park system. We all keep evolving and our purpose remains the same: to help people enjoy and appreciate our parks while leaving them unimpaired for future generations.

canadianrockiestrailguide.com

A website dedicated to Canadian Rockies hiking

One of the advantages of the digital age is the ability to provide important information immediately so you can plan your backcountry adventure. That is why we've created the website canadianrockiestrailguide.com, which contains a wide array of information designed to supplement the 454-page edition you are holding in your hands.

Highlights of the website include:

Trail Updates: When you are browsing the *Canadian Rockies Trail Guide* for short walks, day hikes or backpacking trips, and you've found something of interest, you can now go online and check the "Trail Updates" link to see if there have been any changes or disruptions to your route.

Hiking Blog: Authors Brian Patton and Bart Robinson contribute regularly to this informative blog. Subjects of their posts include personal hiking reports, seasonal news, Parks Canada policy updates, backcountry history, gear recommendations, and favourite hiking shops.

Canadian Rockies eBooks: Summerthought is developing a series of eBooks that focus on specific areas of hiking interest—day trips in various regions, popular backpacking trips, and hikes to special features (such as *Canadian Rockies Waterfall Hikes*). These books can be purchased directly from the website or major online retailers.

The website also brings a wide range of useful Canadian Rockies resources together, making searching out **webcams**, **weather forecasts**, and **trail reports** easy. It also features a section devoted to helping you plan your Canadian Rockies hiking adventure, the ability for readers to submit feedback and trip reports, and a page dedicated to the history of the *Canadian Rockies Trail Guide*.

Acknowledgements

Steve Kun, Keith Plowman, Neil Woledge, Mickey McGuire, Mac Elder, Bert Pittaway, Bill Vroom, Andy Anderson, Bob Wood, Ian Jack, Kurt Seele, and Dudley Foskett— the names of park superintendents, wardens and naturalists who helped us when we published the first edition of the *Canadian Rockies Trail Guide* in 1971. Looking back on the list today, it reads like a who's who of Parks Canada history. It was an honour for us to know these legends of the mountain parks, and we recognize our book could not have been published without their help.

There were others who were instrumental in getting that original edition off the ground, including Jim Thorsell, who suggested the idea of a trail guide and supplemented the first and subsequent editions with his description of the Great Divide Trail. Peter Steiner and Jon Whyte formed a publishing company, Summerthought, to get the finished product on bookshelves. Louise Mayer played an essential role as "associate producer" with her companionship and logistical support during the fieldwork and production of the first three editions.

Many other names come to mind as we look back over 40 years, but two have provided exceptional support that helped form subsequent editions: marathon backpacker Mike McReynolds has provided trail intelligence and photography for the past eight editions; Don Beers, dean of Rocky Mountain hikers, has not only produced the most beautifully illustrated trail guides in North America, but he has selflessly provided us with information and photography.

A record number of individuals participated in the production of this edition by reading the text and providing corrections and suggestions. From Parks Canada: Don Gorrie (Banff); Kim Baines, Roger Hostin, Kathyrn Cameron, Joel Hagen (Lake Louise, Yoho, Kootenay); Greg Horne, Al McKeeman, Michael Mitchell, Greg Slatter, Patti Walker, Mike Wesbrook (Jasper); Locke Marshall, Blandine Baritaud (Waterton). From BC Parks: Wayne Van Velzen, Hugo Mulyk (Mt Robson); Jeff Volp, Craig Gentle (Columbia-Southern Rockies). For Alberta Parks: Duane Fizor (Peter Lougheed). Their feedback was essential to the completion of this revision, and we thank them for their contributions.

As she has for past editions, Donna Nelson of Gem Trek has taken time from her never-ending map revisions to provide us with corrections and the latest scoop. Gord Stermann of White Mountain Adventures reviewed the Sunshine Village section and provided suggestions. And Andrew Hempstead went far beyond his role as publisher with his contributions to this edition.

Rhonda Allen provided trailhead photography, logistical support and companionship for Brian throughout the 2010 fieldwork season, and Pete and Jacquie Brewster of Canmore provided good humour and hospitality at their Alberta base camp. Barbara Robinson provided Bart with trailhead photography, travel companionship and superior editorial advise for his Waterton and Peter Lougheed revisions

We would also like to thank friends and colleagues who contributed photography to this edition: Don Beers, Andrew Hempstead, John Marriott, Mike McReynolds, and Cyndi Smith.

Over the past four decades, the *Canadian Rockies Trail Guide* has emerged as one of the most comprehensive guidebooks of its kind in North America. Maintaining good information for more than 225 trails can only be accomplished with outside help. As always, we welcome comments, corrections and recommendations from our readers, directed to us through our publisher at info@summerthought.com.

—Brian Patton
Bart Robinson

Introduction

In 1885, the Dominion of Canada created a 26 square km reserve near Banff to protect the Sulphur Mountain Cave and Basin hot springs from commercialization. Two years later the reserve was expanded to 673 square km and named Rocky Mountains National Park—the second national park in North America following the creation of Yellowstone in 1872. The park, which was subsequently expanded and renamed Banff, was the beginning of a system of national and provincial parks that now protects more than 30,000 square km of mountain landscape in the southern half of the Canadian Rockies.

The creation of recreational trails for hikers and horseback riders was a priority for Banff's first park superintendent. The Canadian Pacific Railway also played an early and important role in the development of hiking trails, particularly in Banff and Yoho National Parks. Other trails were blazed by outfitters, and still others were built by park wardens and trail crews for patrol and fire protection purposes. When provincial parks were established throughout the 20th century, the construction and maintenance of hiking trails was always the first priority.

Today a trail system totalling more than 3,000 km threads its way through the valleys and passes and by the lakes and glaciers of one of the world's most spectacular mountain ranges.

This book is an invitation to park visitors to experience one of North America's finest hiking areas. It has been designed as a comprehensive guide to the trails of Banff, Jasper, Yoho, Kootenay and Waterton Lakes National Parks, and Mount Robson, Mount Assiniboine, Peter Lougheed, Elk Lakes and Akamina-Kishinena Provincial Parks. We have endeavoured to describe every trail that could conceivably be of interest to hikers, ranging from short walks of an hour or less to multi-week wilderness treks.

Hiking has always been an appropriate and effective means of appreciating the natural heritage preserved within our parks. We have always believed that anyone who walks these mountain trails will come away with a better appreciation of the importance of parks and why we should continue to preserve them "unimpaired for the enjoyment of future generations."

Weather, climate and hiking season

Despite the northerly latitude of the range, the Canadian Rockies experience climate and weather patterns that compare closely with higher mountain ranges hundreds of kilometres to the south.

During mid-summer, you can expect average daytime high temperatures in valley-bottom locations like Banff and Jasper to range around 22°C (72°F) and overnight lows of 7°C (45°F). But if you're hiking or camping at higher elevations, say1980 m (6,500 ft), you can expect the temperature to range between 15°C (59°F) and 3°C (37°C). In the central Rocky Mountain parks, on average, you can expect some precipitation on 13 to 15 days of each month. (Waterton and Akamina-Kishinena Parks are noticeably drier and warmer.)

The mountain snowpack usually begins to disappear as temperatures moderate in April. By mid-May hiking is possible on a handful of low-elevation trails in the major valleys and on south-facing slopes in the Front Ranges. By the first of July most trails below treeline are open, but many are still wet and muddy. Above treeline trails open gradually from early July to early August, depending on slope exposure, snowpack and weather.

Mid-July to mid-August is considered peak hiking season. During this period we experience the warmest weeks of summer, there is usually less rainfall than June and early July, most trails are snowfree, and high country wildflowers are in bloom (this is also when trails are most heavily used and insect pests are flourishing).

NATIONAL PARKS

PROVINCIAL PARKS

High country temperatures start to fall in mid-August, and early September usually sees the first snow falling in the high country. However, these early storms are usually short-lived, and the latter weeks of September and early October are often blessed by beautiful Indian Summer weather. (Most locals consider this the best hiking season.) However, weather changes quickly and dramatically at this time of year, so autumn backpackers should be prepared for surprise storms and the possibility of some cold, snowy hiking. And on any clear night above 1980 m (6,500 ft), expect temperatures to drop below freezing.

Topographic maps

While the maps in this book provide total or partial coverage for most of the trails described, they are only designed to give you a general idea of trail location, course and surrounding topography. It's always good to have a more detailed map along to identify natural features and help dispel confusion. A good topographic map also provides an overview of trail systems, and it is a necessity when heading into more remote regions.

Canadian Government Maps. All areas in the mountain parks are covered by National Topographic System (NTS) 1:50,000 scale maps (approximately 2 cm = 1 km). These sheets provide a high degree of detail and are extremely useful for both navigation and the identification of natural features.

The most recent of these government-produced maps (released in 1996) are much improved over earlier editions. They now show many of the trails, though not always with a high degree of accuracy. Elevations are metric on most sheets, usually with a contour interval of 40 m (occasionally 20 m at lower elevations). Unfortunately, it takes over 40 of these maps to cover the mountain parks, and even shorter trails can sometimes run over two or three sheets.

Gem Trek Maps. A number of privately-produced topographic maps covering sections of the mountain parks have been published in recent years, but the most comprehensive and up-to-date series is produced by Gem Trek Publishing. While the Gem Trek series does not currently provide coverage for the more remote areas of Banff and Jasper National Parks, it does cover most of the popular hiking areas in our book.

The scale of these recreational topo maps varies from 1:35,000 to 1:100,000, and contour intervals range from 25 m to 50 m. These maps are more accurate than government maps for locations of trails, backcountry campsites, lodges, huts and other cultural features; they provide point-to-point distances; and they are updated with each printing.

Sources for government and Gem Trek maps are listed in *Sources—Books and maps*.

Digital Maps. In the world of the computer and GPS, hikers are no longer relegated to large paper maps. There are many digital topo maps available on DVD or online. Most of these digital sources can be used with GPS coordinates to locate and preview trails and even print your own customized map. This area of cartography is expanding at such a rate, it would be impossible to keep up with all the available resources. But suffice to say, you can find maps that will download to your computer, and you can use GPS coordinates in this book to locate trails and improve upon the basic maps we provide.

One online source of free digital topographical maps is Natural Resources Canada's The Atlas of Canada website (www.atlas.nrcan.gc.ca). By clicking on the Toporama topographical maps viewer, you can zoom in on any area of the Canadian Rockies and view stylized versions of NTS maps down to a scale of 1:20,000. Again, trail and cultural information won't be as accurate as Gem Trek maps, but it's a quick way to preview hikes and print your own take-along map.

Bears, bugs and other hazards

Compared to many of the world's wild regions, this is a relatively benign area when it comes to dangerous beasts and other natural hazards. Yet there are a few creatures, both great and extremely small, worthy of discussion.

Bears. The mountain parks are home to a modest population of black and grizzly bears. Most every year at least one person is injured in a bear encounter somewhere in the Rockies, usually with grizzlies and more rarely with black bears. But when you consider the tens of thousands of people who hike the trails each summer, these incidents are extremely rare. (Driving to the trailhead is far more hazardous.)

Yet it is always a good idea to be prepared for an unexpected bear encounter and, even more importantly, to follow a few basic rules to avoid the encounter in the first place:

- Check trail reports and posted warnings at park visitor centres for a listing of trails where bears have been sighted. If a bear is active on the trail you were planning to hike, you may want to go elsewhere. If you do hike the trail, be extra vigilant and make noise where visibility is poor.

- Watch for bear sign, such as fresh droppings, diggings or tracks. If you come across an animal carcass, leave the area immediately and report the location to park staff as soon as possible.

- Always stay alert. You don't want to come upon a bear suddenly at close range. You should continually scan your surroundings, and peruse the slopes and valley ahead before descending from a pass or ridge.

- Make noise in areas where bears have been seen or any prime bear habitat where visibility is limited. The occasional loud shout or whistle will alert bears to your presence. Talking loudly or singing can also be effective. Most bear bells are not loud enough to warn bears at a safe distance—unless it's a Swiss cow bell!

- Groups of three or more hikers have far less chance of being charged or attacked. Nearly all serious attacks in the Rockies have occurred when a single individual encountered a bear at close range; attacks on two hikers are less common and usually involve mother grizzlies with cubs.

- Never leave garbage or food around your camp. Seal all food and garbage and hang it from the bear poles provided at most campsites. Where bear poles are not provided, pack along 20 m of nylon cord and hang food from a strong tree well away from your campsite. (Food should be suspended at least 4 m above the ground and 1 m from the tree trunk.)

- Avoid cooking in your tent (food smells linger). Cook away from your campsite, wash cooking utensils immediately and dispose of dishwater well away from your campsite.

- If you do see a bear, stop immediately and retreat slowly from the area.

The national and provincial parks publish excellent brochures covering all aspects of avoidance, etiquette and what to do in an attack situation. Pick up one of these free pamphlets at a park visitor centre and read it thoroughly.

Other mammals. Far more people are charged and injured by elk each year than by bears. Aggressive elk are much more common in park towns and on nearby trails than elsewhere in the parks since these "urbanized" animals have lost their fear of humans. Never approach elk at any time of year, but give females with young a very wide berth during the calving season (late May and early June), and the same with bulls during the mating season (late August to early October).

There are few other mammals that pose a significant threat to hikers. There have been some incidents with cougars in recent years, but these animals are shy and very rarely seen. Warnings will be posted when there have been cougar sightings on a trail.

Of course, there are records of nearly every species having charged or chomped tourists at one time or another. (These include an irate mother spruce grouse that permanently scarred one of the authors.) The golden rule around all wildlife: always give animals room and never harass or feed them.

Insect pests. Mosquitoes are generally less of a problem in the southern Canadian Rockies than they are in the mountains and wetlands farther north. However, some summers are worse than others, and certain areas are renowned for their bloodsucking hordes. Insect repellent should be carried throughout the hiking season until early September, and headnets or bug jackets might be useful in a few infamous locales during mid-summer, like Jasper's Tonquin Valley.

Horseflies are another common nuisance during midsummer. Insect repellent has no effect on these large biting flies. While a heavy shirt and pants will protect you, horseflies are most active on warm, sunny days, when you are inclined to wear only shorts and a t-shirt. At least they're slow to bite, so you can club 90 percent of them before they take their pound of flesh.

Wood ticks. Second to bears, visitors worry about wood ticks—small, flat-bodied arachnids (related to spiders) that require a meal of mammal blood as part of their reproductive cycle. Ticks are abundant in dry grassy areas of the Rockies in the spring (early May through late June), and at elevations ranging from the lowest valley bottoms to 2130 m (7,000 ft). They cling to low-lying shrubs and grasses, waiting for a potential meal to pass by. Once on a mammal, they can spend three hours or more exploring before burying their heads in its flesh, so hikers have a good chance of discovering and removing the beasts before the feast begins.

Although ticks in the Canadian Rockies have been free of Rocky Mountain Spotted Fever and Lyme disease (so far), they can cause a potentially fatal tick paralysis if they burrow at the base of the skull. The best precaution is to wear long pants tucked into socks or gaiters and to avoid lounging about on grassy, south-facing slopes, particularly in areas habituated by mountain sheep. Always check your clothing and body carefully following a spring hike (ticks are partial to heads, armpits and crotches).

When a tick is discovered, a simple touch or gentle tug often dislodges it. If it has already burrowed into the skin, do not try to burn it with a match or coat it with some noxious liquid, like gasoline or nail polish. Instead, grasp its head as close to the skin as possible with tweezers and pull slowly. If you can't remove it, or mouthparts remain in the skin, see a doctor.

Giardia. Another addition to the list of hiker miseries is the protozoan *Giardia lamblia*, a waterborne parasite that can cause severe and prolonged gastrointestinal distress. *Giardia* is carried by many species of animals, but the human infective strain is most frequently found in beaver, domestic dogs and, of course, humans. The parasite finds its way into mountain streams and rivers through the feces of these animals, but once they've become infected, beaver are the best situated to perpetuate the parasite in wilderness water systems.

Many local hikers are willing to take their chances in the upper portions of watersheds, particularly above treeline or where they feel secure there is no beaver activity or human sources of infestation. But the only way to be totally safe is to boil your drinking water for at least a minute or use a portable water filter.

Stream crossings. The only other hazard worth noting is unbridged stream crossings, which occur on some remote backcountry trails. While the creeks and rivers of the Canadian Rockies are relatively tame compared to the thundering torrents of the Interior and Coast Ranges, they can still be dangerous at certain times of the year.

As a general rule, rivers run highest in June and July. In the Front Ranges streams are usually highest during rainy periods when runoff sluices down into drainages from bare limestone peaks; stream levels in these eastern ranges usually drop dramatically once the rain stops. In the heavily-glaciated Main Ranges, the highest runoff usually occurs during warm spells in July and August when glaciers are in full melt; these rivers are easier to cross in the morning after the flow has subsided with the cool of the night.

Any trail involving a major ford should only be attempted by river-wise backpackers. If the current is strong and water threatens to rise above your crotch, you should abandon the crossing altogether. Either look for a better place to cross, wait for water levels to subside or, if that is unlikely, retreat the way you came and live to ford another day.

Backcountry information

We recommend that all hikers stop by a park visitor centre before embarking on any serious hiking in the mountain parks. These centres provide current weather forecasts, reports on trail conditions and closures, and warnings concerning bear activity. They also dispense free park visitor guides, day hiking and backcountry camping brochures, and a variety of pamphlets relating to bear safety, mountain biking, fishing, etc.

While you can obtain information from park visitor centres in person, you can also obtain specific information by mail, phone, fax or e-mail. However, parks websites cover all aspects of park visitation and are by far the most effective way to obtain information when you are planning a trip. (See *Sources—Park information.*)

Visitor centres are located in all five national parks (see park introductions for locations). Of the provincial parks included in this guidebook, only Peter Lougheed in Alberta and Mount Robson in British Columbia have visitor centres. (The Mount Robson Visitor Centre only operates May to September 30.)

Park rangers are stationed in the core of Mount Assiniboine Provincial Park and along Mount Robson's Berg Lake trail during the summer. Information for Elk Lakes and Akamina-Kishinena Parks can be obtained through the East Kootenay Provincial Parks office in Cranbrook and on the BC Parks website. (See *Sources—Park information.*)

Camping

Due to the growth in backcountry use, most parks require that backcountry visitors stay in designated campgrounds. With only a few exceptions, these campgrounds have quotas on the number of people who can overnight there. All parks on a camping permit system require that backpackers indicate the campgrounds where they will be overnighting and the dates of occupation.

Banff, Jasper and Yoho are the only national parks were random camping is permitted, but only in specific areas where visitation is low. In selecting a campsite in a random camping zone, you must be 5 km from a trailhead, at least 50 m off the trail, and 70 m from the nearest stream or lake.

Campfires are only permitted at certain campgrounds, and only where metal fireboxes and firewood are provided.

Park visitor centres are your primary outlet for camping permits and information about backcountry campgrounds.

National parks. Parks Canada requires anyone overnighting in the backcountry to purchase a Wilderness Pass. These passes were instituted in 1994 to recover some of the costs of maintaining trails, backcountry facilities and patrols.

When you purchase a Wilderness Pass, you must specify the trails and campsites you will be using on specific nights during your trip. At the time of publication, a Wilderness Pass costs $9.80 per person/per night. An annual pass is also available, which allows for an unlimited number of nights in the backcountry ($68.70 per person/per year).

In Banff National Park a fee is charged to stay at the Bryant Creek or Egypt Lake shelters ($6.80 per person/per night) in addition to a Wilderness Pass.

National park backcountry campsites and shelters can be reserved up to 90 days in advance by phone, fax or in person at Park Visitor Centres (see *Sources—Park information*). A non-refundable fee is charged for this service.

Provincial parks. Most provincial parks have instituted camping fees on a per person/per night basis. Camping permits are required for all backcountry campgrounds in Alberta's Peter Lougheed Park and for sites on the Berg Lake trail in B.C.'s Mount Robson Park. These permits are obtained in person at park visitor centres or in advance through dedicated reservation phone lines.

Camping fees are collected on site at Magog and Og Lake Campgrounds and the Naiset Cabins in Mount Assiniboine Park, and at Lower Elk Lake and Pétain Creek Campgrounds in Elk Lakes Park. Some BC Parks campgrounds may require self-registration and fee payments. (See park chapter introductions for current fees.)

Voluntary safety registration

Anyone concerned about their safety on their backcountry trip can voluntarily register at Parks Canada visitor centres. If you do not return on the date and time indicated, a search will be initiated. While this registration is designed for individuals or groups involved in off-trail risk activities, solo backpackers journeying into remote areas can also register. While there is no charge for this service, you must report back in at a park visitor centre immediately upon your return. Regardless of whether you use this service or not, it is always best to leave a detailed copy of your itinerary with a responsible person.

Using this book

This guidebook is designed to be comprehensive, describing all trails of any significance within the mountain parks of the Canadian Rockies.

Trails are presented by regions within each park, usually oriented to the roads that provide access to the trailheads or to a central area serving as a core for several hikes. These regional sections include a map showing trails and their reference numbers.

Walks, short hikes and a few secondary routes are presented without trail summaries or distance outlines. Half-day trips, day trips and backpacks are presented with a trail summary, distance outline, descriptive text and, in many cases, a photo.

Trail summary. Beneath each trail heading is its distance in both kilometres (km) and miles (mi). Whenever a hike runs out and back on the same trail, distances are one-way. But for loop trips (circuits) and long distance trails ending at a different trailhead than point of origin, total distance is provided.

The general round trip duration of the hike is indicated as a half-day trip (usually up to four hours), day trip, or backpack.

Hiking time is the one-way number of hours or days it will take to reach your objective. (In the case of loop trips and long distance trails to another trailhead, total time is presented.) The times are estimated for a strong, steady pace with few breaks along the way. Strong hikers may "beat" listed times, while slower walkers and those who make frequent stops will take longer.

Elevation gain is the total ascent, in metres (m) and feet (ft), over the one-way course of the trail; if there is a significant loss of elevation, it is also noted. On longer trails with lots of ups-and-downs, maximum and minimum elevations are provided instead of elevation gain.

Maximum elevation is the highest point reached on the hike, often at the trail's destination.

Map references are provided for NTS 1:50,000 topo maps. Gem Trek map references are also included when a trail is covered by a map in that series with a scale of 1:70,000 or better.

Distance outlines. Trail distance outlines give you a brief, point-to-point summary of the route in kilometres. All basic directions are presented in the outline. These reference points along the route, including both natural and man-made features, can be used to calculate how far you've hiked and how far you have to go. The outlines are prefixed with important access directions for reaching the trailhead.

The authors have pushed trail wheels with odometres over most of these trails to obtain accurate distances. We have also used some distances from parks trail inventories and trustworthy outside contributors. When we have been forced to estimate distances, this is indicated by a footnote.

Trail distances in this guide seldom agree exactly with those on parks trail signs or other resources (like Gem Trek maps), but these discrepancies are usually minor.

GPS coordinates. Due to the popularity and usefulness of GPS units, we have included latitude and longitude coordinates in GPS style for every road-accessible trailhead and most backcountry trailheads. Of course, these coordinates can help direct you to the trailhead when entered into your GPS unit, though most trailheads are very well marked and easily discovered. Of more importance, these coordinates can be used to preview your hike on digital maps or Google Earth, and it seems inevitable that GPS coordinates will be used more and more in the future. You will find these coordinates beneath the trailhead reference in distance outlines, and at the end of the access entry in the shorter trail descriptions.

Trail description. The text is written to describe the trail's scenic rewards, to provide a running description of the trail, and to interpret natural features and historical points-of-interest along the way. Where applicable, optional routes and extensions are provided at the end of the main trail description.

Photos. With the exception of a few shots provided by friends and outside contributors, all photographs were taken by the authors. They have been selected to illustrate the scenic highlights of the hike.

Maps. Maps in this book provide only a general overview of trails and their location. Specific trails can be found by referring to trail numbers on the maps. (Some trails described in this book are not covered by these maps, and a notation to this effect is made at the bottom of the distance outline.)

On most of these maps land above 2300 m is shaded to give a general impression of topography, particularly major mountains and passes. Where regional elevations are lower, shading shows land above 2000 m. (See key at bottom of maps.)

Some final words

- Plan ahead. Choose trips you are in shape to handle. Allow time for unexpected weather and other events that might alter your schedule.

- Stay on the trail, even if it means muddy boots. Leaving the trail creates parallel tracks and widens existing trails. Shortcutting switchbacks causes erosion.

- Leave rocks, flowers, antlers and other natural objects undisturbed. Never pick wildflowers or other plants.

- Never feed, disturb or harass wildlife. It is illegal, harmful to the animal's health, and alters their natural behavior.

- Pack out all garbage. Carry plastic bags and, whenever possible, pack out litter that other, less-considerate hikers have left behind. Do not throw garbage into privies.

- Where facilities are not provided, your toilet duties should be carried out well away from trails, campsites, and at least 50 m from lakes and streams. Dig a small pit (15 cm maximum) and restore the ground as closely as possible to its original state. Pack out toilet paper or burn it if fire danger is low.

- All dogs on parks trails must be kept on a leash. If your dog is not well trained or is difficult to control, be considerate of other hikers and leave it at home. Also, be aware that dogs have incited grizzly attacks.

- Even where campfires are permitted in the backcountry, it is preferable to use lightweight gas stoves for cooking. If you do have a campfire at a site where fires are permitted, it should only be set in metal fireboxes utilizing firewood provided at the site or, where permitted, dead wood lying on the ground. Keep all fires small and make sure they are totally extinguished before you depart.

- Keep food, soap, toothpaste, and detergent out of lakes and streams. Dispose of wash water on well-drained soil well away from the nearest surface water. Even biodegradable soaps are pollutants.

- Be considerate of fellow hikers when sharing a campsite or backcountry shelter. Be considerate as well of horseback riders: move well off the trail (preferably downslope), remain still and be prepared to comply with the guide's requests.

- Cyclists should avoid surprising hikers, horses and wildlife. Be particularly careful on blind corners and rises. Be prepared to dismount if you encounter hikers or horseback parties on narrow, rough trails.

Banff National Park

With an area of 6,641 sq km, Banff is second in size to Jasper among the mountain parks. It is bordered by Yoho and Kootenay National Parks to the west, Jasper National Park to the north, and Mount Assiniboine, Height of the Rockies, and Peter Lougheed Provincial Parks on the south.

Banff contains more than 1500 km of trail, more than any other mountain park. Since many of these trails are near the park's world-renowned tourist centres, they are also among the most heavily travelled in the Rockies.

The park is noted for its day hiking. The trails leading into the spectacular peaks and glaciers of the Bow Range surrounding Lake Louise and nearby Moraine Lake are by far the most popular. The town of Banff and nearby Lake Minnewanka is another hiking centre, with trips ranging from short walks near the town to day trips into the hanging valleys and passes of the Front Ranges.

Many excellent hikes originate in the Bow Valley between Banff and Lake Louise, utilizing trailheads on the Trans-Canada Highway, the Bow Valley Parkway and Highway 93. Sunshine Meadows is off the beaten track 20 km southwest of Banff, but is an exceptional alpine region that is near-and-dear to day hikers. And the park's highest road, the Icefields Parkway, provides access to a variety of trails leading through its most dramatic scenery north of Lake Louise.

The park's two most popular backpacking destinations are Skoki Valley, east of Lake Louise, and Egypt Lakes, west of Banff. You can backpack to these areas in a single day and spend a day or two exploring from your campsite.

Serious backpackers focus on the longer Sawback and Bow Valley Highline Trails running along the ranges to the east and west of the Bow Valley, or the Upper Spray and Bryant Creek Valleys at the south end of the park. More adventurous souls roam the park's eastern wilderness for the ultimate in challenge and solitude.

Information and services. Park Visitor Centres are located in downtown Banff (224 Banff Avenue) and beside the Samson Mall in Lake Louise village. Roadside campgrounds are scattered throughout the park. Full service sites are available at Tunnel Mountain and Lake Louise, and showers are provided at Tunnel Mountain, Two Jack Lakeside, Johnston Canyon and Lake Louise.

Gas, groceries, restaurants and accommodation are available in the town of Banff, Lake Louise village and, in a limited fashion, at Johnston Canyon, Castle Junction and Saskatchewan River Crossing. Banff offers all the services of a major resort town, including outdoor recreation specialty shops.

Access: Banff is 130 km west of Calgary via the Trans-Canada Highway—the main east-west artery through Banff Park. The Icefields Parkway runs north 230 km from Lake Louise to Jasper. Highway 93 runs southwest from the Trans-Canada Highway to Kootenay National Park and southeastern B.C. The David Thompson Highway (Hwy 11) connects Red Deer, Alberta, with the Icefields Parkway at Saskatchewan River Crossing in the northern section of the park.

The nearest airport with scheduled flights is Calgary International. Numerous airporter buses and shuttles run between the airport and Banff every day. Greyhound buses also run east and west through the park on the Trans-Canada Highway several times a day, with scheduled stops at Banff and Lake Louise.

N

Mt Aylmer

Aylmer
Pass

(77)

(6)
Elk
Lake

River

(4) V

(3)

Lake Minnewanka

Mt▲
Brewster

(5)

Cascade Mountain

(1)

▲Mt
Inglismaldie

▲Mt
Girouard

Forty

Mile

Creek

Mt▲
Peechee

▲Mt
Edith

(16)

Mt▲
Norquay

(17)

(7)

Johnson
Lake

(2)

BANFF

(1)

(8)

(9)

Princess Margaret
▲Mtn

(11)

(10)

Sulphur Mountain

(15)

(1)

Bow

(12)

(13)

Spray

Mount Rundle

Canmore
Nordic Centre

CANMORE

Sundance
Lodge

(70)

Sundance Range

Goat

(14)

River

Creek

River

(71)

Ha Ling Pk

Land above 2300 metres

0 1 2 3 4 5 km

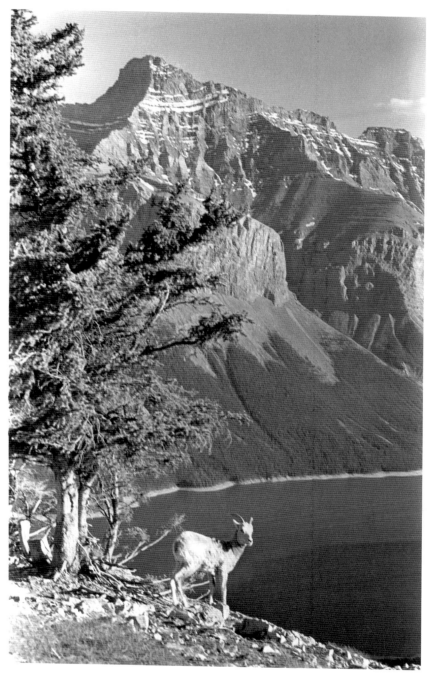

Mountain sheep at Aylmer Lookout

1 C Level Cirque

Upper Bankhead Picnic Area to C Level Cirque—3.9 km (2.4 mi)

Half-day trip

Allow 1.5 hours one way

Elevation gain: 455 m (1,500 ft)

Maximum elevation: 1920 m (6,300 ft)

Maps: Banff 82 O/4
      Banff Up-Close (Gem Trek)

Access: From the Trans-Canada Highway at the Banff East Exit interchange, follow the Lake Minnewanka Road 3.5 km (2 mi) to the Upper Bankhead Picnic Area. The trail begins at the far (west) end of the picnic area parking lot.

0.0—Trailhead (1465 m).
    N51°14.209' W115°31.194'

   —Steady uphill through forest.

1.1—Old mine building. Faint trail leads from behind building to Lake Minnewanka viewpoint (100 m).

1.8—Mine shaft vent holes.

   —Steady climb through forest.

3.9—C Level Cirque (1920 m).

The C Level Cirque trail is one of the more attractive hikes in the Banff-Lake Minnewanka vicinity. In less than 4 km it climbs past artifacts of the long-defunct Bankhead coal operation and a panoramic viewpoint for Lake Minnewanka to a high, rockbound pocket beneath the sheer east face of Cascade Mountain.

The trail begins its ascent through a pleasantly varied forest of lodgepole pine, aspen and spruce, where calypso orchids, blue clematis and many colourful violets bloom in early summer.

Within a half-hour you reach two skeletal buildings, the remnants of an anthracite coal operation that flourished in the area from 1904 to 1922. A town of nearly 1,000 inhabitants called Bankhead was spread across the valley where the trail begins, and these old buildings were a part of the "C Level" operation—the highest coal seams worked within the eastern slope of Cascade Mountain.

From behind the cement transformer building, follow a faint, overgrown trail through scrub trees 100 m to a ridge of coal tailings that provides an excellent view out to Lake Minnewanka. The Palliser Range stretches away from the northern shoreline, while Mount Inglismaldie (2965 m) and the Fairholme Range rise above the lake's southern shores. Both ranges exhibit scorched slopes from prescribed fires set in the early 1990s through 2003.

Back on the main trail, you climb above the C-Level buildings and viewpoint and soon pass by several fenced holes, which were once air vents for the mineshafts below.

The rest of the hike is a steady climb through forest until, 200 m before reaching the cirque, views open down the Bow Valley to Mount Rundle, the Three Sisters and other mountains beyond the town of Canmore.

"Cirque" is a French word used by geologists to describe a semicircular,

Lake Minnewanka from C-Level Cirque trail

bowl-shaped depression created by an alpine glacier, and C Level Cirque is a miniature example of the phenomenon. Though the glacier that produced the basin has long since disappeared, snow often lingers in the basin into mid-summer. As it retreats, a carpet of yellow glacier lilies spreads across the damp, subalpine soil near its entrance. A tiny pond below the trail provides water throughout the summer, fed by the extensive snowfield on the talus slopes above.

From the rockslide at the edge of the cirque, a faint trail continues up to the right along a sparsely-forested ridge to an even higher vantage point above the basin. However, most hikers prefer to "boot ski" the snowfield beneath Cascade's cliffs or simply relax on a convenient rock to watch the antics of the local inhabitants—hoary marmots, pikas and golden-mantled ground squirrels.

Another local resident in spring is the wood tick, so no lounging in the grass! And be sure to check your body and clothes carefully following early season outings.

Cascade Mountain from Johnson Lake

2 Johnson Lake

Johnson Lake Circuit—3.0 km (1.9 mi)

The trail around Johnson Lake is a fine walk in the early season (often snow-free by late April) and displays variety throughout the hiking season, including a succession of montane wildflowers and several species of nesting waterfowl. By hiking around the lake counter-clockwise, you will enjoy continuous views of Cascade Mountain returning along the north shore.

From the picnic area parking lot, walk downhill across a small earth-fill dam and bridge, then angle uphill to a power-line. After a brief run beneath the wires, the trail branches left into the forest and rolls along above the lake's south shore (purple calypso orchids flower here in May).

Approximately 1 km into the hike, scan the woods to the right for an old cabin—home to Billy Carver, "the Hermit of Inglismaldie", during the 1940s.

At the far end of the lake, the trail crosses an earthen dike, where you get your first good views back to Cascade Mountain.

Returning along the north shore, you cross grassy slopes, which are filled with the yellow blooms of brown-eyed Susan (gaillardia) in July, and skirt the margins of a dry Douglas fir forest. There are pockets of burned trees, remains of the Fairholme prescribed burn (2003), and some wonderful, old aspen groves as you complete the circuit back to the picnic area.

Access: Follow the Lake Minnewanka Road from the Trans-Canada Highway 1.0 km (0.6 mi) to the Lake Minnewanka-Johnson Lake road split. Turn right and continue 3.7 km (2.3 mi) to where the Johnson Lake road branches right. The Johnson Lake parking lot and picnic area are reached in 2.3 km. N51°11.966' W115°29.377' *Maps: Canmore 82 O/3; Banff Up-Close (Gem Trek).*

3 Lake Minnewanka

Lake Minnewanka Parking Area to Devil's Gap—28.9 km (18.0 mi)

Backpack

Allow 8 to 10 hours to Ghost Lakes

Elevation gain: 45 m (150 ft)

Maximum elevation: 1525 m (5,000 ft)

Maps: Canmore 82 O/3
Lake Minnewanka 82 O/6

Access: From the Trans-Canada Highway at the Banff East Exit interchange, follow the Lake Minnewanka Road 5.5 km (3.5 mi) to the parking area at the lake. Walk to the access gate leading to the tour boat concession and picnic area. Follow paved access road 0.6 km through the picnic area to the trailhead sign at road's end.

0.0— Trailhead (1480 m).
N51°15.158' W115°29.693'

0.8— Stewart Canyon bridge.

1.0— Junction. Stewart Canyon left.
Lake Minnewanka straight ahead.

2.4— Lake Minnewanka viewpoint (1525 m).

— Trail rolls along just above lakeshore.

7.2— Junction (1510 m). Aylmer Pass Junction Campground (Lm8) right 100 m. *Aylmer Lookout* left.
Lake Minnewanka ahead.

8.7— Aylmer Canyon Campground (Lm9).

10.5— Mt Inglismaldie Campground (Lm11).

18.2— Mt Costigan Campground (Lm20).

20.0— Narrows Campground (Lm22).

22.2— East end of Lake Minnewanka.

23.2— First Ghost Lake.

25.0— Ford between Ghost Lakes.

25.1— Junction. Ghost Lake Campground (Lm31) right. Devil's Gap left.

28.9— Devils Gap (1510 m). Park boundary.

Notice: Due to bear activity, travel on Aylmer Lookout and Pass trails is restricted to groups of at least four people hiking in close proximity from from July 15 until September 30. Lm8 Campground is closed during this period, but the lakeshore trail usually remains open and unrestricted. Check with the Park Visitor Centre or website for alterations to this policy.

The trail along the north shore of Banff's largest lake is attractive to early and late season backpackers since its low elevation and location in the Front Ranges usually provides dry, snow-free hiking from May until mid-autumn. Mountain bikes are also permitted along the entire length of the trail, so expect their company if you hike here.

From the boat dock and picnic area at the west end of Lake Minnewanka, the trail crosses Stewart Canyon, climbs over a low, forested ridge, then rolls along the north shore for the next 20 km with little gain or loss of elevation.

There are many fine campgrounds along the trail, and pleasant gravel beaches scattered with driftwood provide numerous opportunities to stop and relax. The most popular site is Aylmer Pass Junction Campground, where backpackers often camp and then day trip to Aylmer Lookout or Pass. (See *Aylmer Lookout.*)

Burned forest along much of the route dates between 1988 and 2003 when Parks Canada set prescribed burns to emulate the valley's prehistoric fire regime.

The landscape becomes noticeably drier near the lake's east end and the vegetation more typically montane. Limber pine is scattered among the stands of lodgepole, and western wood lilies, gaillardia, flax, harebells and other dry-land wildflowers cover grassy hillsides in early summer.

Past the east end of Lake Minnewanka, the trail skirts the shore of the first Ghost Lake to a channel connecting it with the second Ghost Lake. Cross to the opposite side (shallow or deep ford, depending on time of year), then wander eastward into the Devil's Gap or turn right and follow a 9-km trail running back to the south shore of Lake Minnewanka and the pleasantly-isolated Ghost Lakes Campground (Lm31).

4 Aylmer Lookout

Lake Minnewanka Parking Area to Aylmer Lookout—11.2 km (7.0 mi)
Lake Minnewanka Parking Area to Aylmer Pass—12.9 km (8.0 mi)

Day trip or backpack

Allow 4 to 5 hours to lookout

Elevation gain: 560 m (1,840 ft)

Maximum elevation: 2040 m (6,700 ft)

Maps: Canmore 82 O/3
Lake Minnewanka 82 O/6

Access: From the Trans-Canada Highway at the Banff East Exit interchange, follow the Lake Minnewanka Road 5.5 km (3.5 mi) to the parking area at the lake. Walk to the access gate leading to the tour boat concession and picnic area. Follow paved access road 0.6 km through the picnic area to the trailhead sign at road's end.

0.0—Trailhead (1480 m).
N51°15.158' W115°29.693'

0.8—Stewart Canyon bridge.

1.0—Junction. Stewart Canyon left. Aylmer Lookout ahead.

2.4—Lake Minnewanka viewpoint (1525 m).

— Trail rolls along just above lakeshore.

7.2—Junction (1510 m). Aylmer Pass Junction Campground (Lm8) right 100 m. *Lake Minnewanka* trail ahead. Aylmer Lookout and Pass left.

— Steep uphill.

9.5—Junction. Aylmer Pass ahead (3.4 km). Aylmer Lookout right.

— Steady climb along lookout ridge.

11.2—Aylmer Lookout site (2040 m).

Notice: Due to bear activity, travel on Aylmer Lookout and Pass trails is restricted to groups of at least four people hiking in close proximity from July 15 until September 30. Lm8 Campground is closed during this period, but the lakeshore trail usually remains open and unrestricted. Check with the Park Visitor Centre or website for alterations to this policy.

When Sir George Simpson, Governor of the Hudson's Bay Company, made the first recorded visit to Lake Minnewanka in August, 1841, he marvelled at the beauty of the lake and exclaimed that "the surrounding mountains were very grand, of every varied form...their craggy summits resembling battlements among which dizzy heights the goat and sheep delight to bound." Hikers who journey to Aylmer Lookout can retrace part of Sir George's route and visit those dizzy heights where many sheep (and wood ticks) delight to bound.

Strong hikers can reach Aylmer Lookout and return in a day, though many bound for both the lookout site and the pass prefer to camp at Aylmer Pass Junction Campground (Lm8) and day hike from there.

Though the first 7.2 km of the journey follows Lake Minnewanka's north shore over gentle, undemanding trail, you should be ready for the ordeal beyond. Forking uphill, away from the tranquility of the lake, the trail to Aylmer Lookout is strenuous indeed.

From the junction with the *Lake Minnewanka* trail, you gain nearly 300 metres over the next 2 km. Since this slope is usually snow-free in early June, and one of the hot spots in the Rockies on sunny days, you should carry an adequate supply of water to complete the ascent.

The site of the defunct Aylmer fire lookout is on the end of an open ridge below the summit of Mount Aylmer. As you labour up the steep draw leading toward Aylmer Pass, watch for the lookout trail branching right 2.3 km beyond the Minnewanka junction.

The trail to the lookout continues steeply upwards, angling southeast towards the crest of the ridge. Along the way it passes through a prescribed burn that was set on this slope in 1990.

Lake Minnewanka from Aylmer Lookout

Nearly all of Lake Minnewanka can be seen from this 2040-m viewpoint. The water, over 500 m below, is of the deepest blue, and boats look like tiny water insects skimming to-and-fro.

Across the lake stand the twin summits of Mount Inglismaldie (2965 m) and Mount Girouard (2995 m), displaying massive cliffs of Mississippian and Devonian-age limestone. Looming above the ridge, less than 3 km to the north, is Mount Aylmer (3162 m)—the highest peak in the Banff-Lake Minnewanka area. Mount Rundle and the Bow Valley near Banff can be seen to the south.

Though the lookout tower and cabin are long gone, the open ridge is often visited by herds of mountain sheep who, perhaps, have some ancestral memory of the days when fire lookouts used to live here and put out salt blocks. Another form of wildlife found here in abundance in the spring is the wood tick (check your body and clothes carefully upon returning from this trip).

Aylmer Pass. From the Aylmer Lookout trail junction at km 9.5, the left fork continues its steady climb to the park boundary and the open alpine meadows of Aylmer Pass. The pass lies well above the last forest cover and is free of snow considerably later than the lookout ridge.

From the crest of the pass, views open into the highly folded and faulted mountains of the Palliser Range. Directly above the pass to the east is the summit of Mount Aylmer, a gruelling but straightforward scramble for hikers with good boots. Like the Aylmer Lookout area, the slopes above the pass are prime mountain sheep habitat.

Backpackers with a few days to spare can continue over the pass to explore the Ghost River Wilderness Area. Good trail continues down the north side of the pass to Spectral Creek, but the descent to Ghost River and beyond is strictly for explorers who are willing to make numerous fords of Spectral Creek and the Ghost River, or else bushwhack along their banks.

5 Cascade Amphitheatre

Mount Norquay Ski Area to Cascade Amphitheatre—7.7 km (4.8 mi)

Day trip

Allow 2 to 3 hours one way

Elevation loss: 150 m (490 ft)
       gain: 640 m (2,100 ft)

Maximum elevation: 2195 m (7,200 ft)

Maps: Banff 82 O/4
      Banff Up-Close (Gem Trek)

Access: Follow the Mount Norquay Road north from the Trans-Canada Highway 6.0 km (3.5 mi) to the Mount Norquay ski area. Enter the first parking lot on the right and follow it 200 m to the day lodge at the far end. (Park well away from the gated service road and other ski area buildings).

0.0— Trailhead (1705 m).
      N51°12.190' W115°35.880'

— Walk through lodge complex and down-valley on ski area service road.

0.8— Junction. Forty Mile Creek trail (*Sawback Trail*) left. Cascade Amphitheatre ahead.

1.0— Trail descends into forest.

2.9— Junction. Lower Forty Mile Creek trail left. Cascade Amphitheatre right.

3.1— Forty Mile Creek bridge (1555 m).

— Steady uphill.

4.3— Junction. *Elk Lake* ahead. Cascade Amphitheatre right.

— Steady switchbacking climb.

6.6— Cascade Amphitheatre entrance.

— Gradual uphill through meadows.

7.7— Amphitheatre headwall (2195 m).

One of the longer and more strenuous day trips near Banff leads up the western flank of Cascade Mountain to a large natural amphitheatre at just over 2100 m. This hanging valley, enclosed by the limestone cliffs of the mountain's summit ridges, features lush subalpine wildflower meadows and immense rock-slides inhabited by marmots and pikas.

The hike begins at the Mount Norquay ski area's day lodge. Continue through the lodge plaza and straight down-valley on the main service road.

The first kilometre can be a bit confusing as you work your way past the base stations of a number of ski lifts, but stay on the service road and ignore branch trails into the forest on the right. At 0.8 km, in the middle of a ski run, the trail to Mystic Pass and upper Forty Mile Creek branches left. Stay right and, 200 m further along, the service road ends at the last ski lift and a broad forest trail begins.

After a steady descent through lush, flower-filled forest, the trail reaches Forty Mile Creek, turns right and soon crosses the creek on a substantial bridge.

Just beyond the bridge, the forest opens to a view of the sheer 390-m face of Mount Louis—one of the most demanding rock climbs in the Rockies. The rugged summit of Mount Edith, another popular climb, can be seen south of Louis and behind Mount Norquay.

The last trail fork on the trip appears 1.2 km beyond the Forty Mile Creek bridge, where the Amphitheatre trail branches uphill to the right from the *Elk Lake* trail. A relentless series of switch-backs transport you upwards through a dense forest of spruce and lodgepole pine for 2.3 km to the cool, subalpine forest at the mouth of the amphitheatre.

From the amphitheatre entrance, the trail extends for just over a kilometre to a headwall created by the mountain's main summit ridge. The moist meadows along

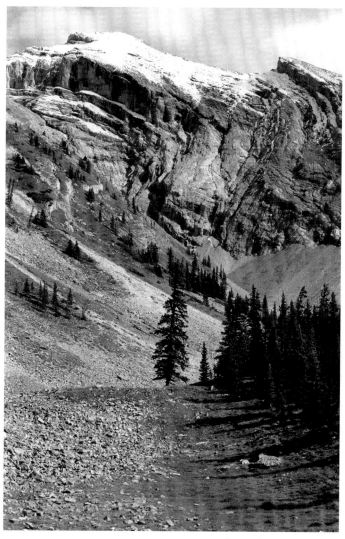

Cascade Amphitheatre

the way are carpeted with wildflowers throughout much of the summer, beginning with white-flowered western anemone and nodding yellow glacier lilies along the edges of receding snow banks in late June.

Two small sink lakes also appear in the meadows with the spring snowmelt, but these usually disappear by early July. Rockslides enclosing the upper end of the cirque are home to hoary marmots and pikas as well as the occasional white-tailed ptarmigan.

While the ascent of Cascade Mountain from the amphitheatre is not particularly difficult, the route is tricky and can be dangerous at certain times of the year. If you want to go for the summit, pick-up a copy of *A Scrambler's Guide to Cascade Mountain* at the Park Visitor Centre in Banff.

6 Elk Lake

Mount Norquay Ski Area to Elk Lake — 13.5 km (8.4 mi)

Day trip or backpack

Allow 4 to 5 hours one way

Elevation loss: 150 m (490 ft)
       gain: 610 m (2,000 ft)

Maximum elevation: 2165 m (7,100 ft)

Maps: Banff 82 O/4
     Castle Mountain 82 O/5

Access: Follow the Mount Norquay Road north from the Trans-Canada Highway 6.0 km (3.5 mi) to the Mount Norquay ski area. Enter the first parking lot on the right and follow it 200 m to the day lodge at the far end. (Park well away from the gated service road and other ski area buildings).

0.0— Trailhead (1705 m).
     N51°12.190' W115°35.880'

   — Walk through lodge complex and down-valley on ski area service road.

0.8— Junction. Forty Mile Creek trail (*Sawback Trail*) left. Elk Lake ahead.

1.0— Trail descends through forest.

2.9— Junction. Lower Forty Mile Creek trail left. Elk Lake right.

3.1— Forty Mile Creek bridge (1555 m).

   — Steady uphill.

4.3— Junction. *Cascade Amphitheatre* right. Elk Lake ahead.

   — Gradual uphill through forest.

6.8— Trail enters subalpine meadows.

11.5— Elk Summit and Junction (2055 m). Elk Lake Summit Campground (Ek13). Cascade Valley and Stony Creek ahead (9.5 km). Elk Lake left.

   — Steady uphill through forest followed by a short descent to lake.

13.5— Elk Lake (2120 m).

Mount Brewster, visible from Banff between Mount Norquay and Cascade Mountain, is the southern end of a 20-km-long massif that runs due north into the eastern wilderness of Banff Park. Along the eastern face of this unbroken chain of peaks are numerous amphitheatres, some containing small lakes. Almost a third of the way down the range is Elk Lake, the largest and most scenic of these tarns.

Elk Lake can be visited as a long day hike or an easy overnight trip, and the trail continuing north from Elk Summit to the Cascade River is a key route for backpacking trips into Banff's Front Ranges.

The first 4.3 km of trail follows the same route as the *Cascade Amphitheatre* hike, cutting down through the Mount Norquay ski area, across Forty Mile Creek, and up the western flank of Cascade Mountain. At the *Cascade Amphitheatre* junction, it stays to the left and continues northward through a forest of lodgepole pine, Engelmann spruce and alpine fir. The path is wide and well defined throughout.

Two hours or so into the hike, you enter an extensive subalpine meadow, characterized by few trees, low willows, dwarf birch, shrubby cinquefoil, and a profusion of wildflowers. The vale is dominated by Mount Brewster (2859 m) and its subsidiary peaks to the west. (The mountain is named for John Brewster, an early Banff settler who opened the town's first dairy in 1887.)

The trail continues through this open forest for the next 5 km—a beautiful stretch where an occasional over-the-shoulder glance reveals a long, unobstructed view down-valley to Mount Norquay, Sulphur Mountain, and a section of the Sundance Range.

You eventually reach Elk Summit and its campground at km 11.5. Just beyond the campground the trail to Elk

Elk Lake and Mount Brewster

Lake branches left from the main trail over the summit. It gradually ascends a forested ridge for just over 1.0 km before dropping into the amphitheatre containing Elk Lake. The high point on the ridge (2165 m) offers an excellent, unobstructed view back down the length of the approach valley to Mount Norquay and points south.

Elk Lake lies beneath a 500-m wall of limestone, and since it is located very near treeline, its environment differs markedly from the lush meadows along the approach from Forty Mile Creek. The forest above the lake is predominantly alpine larch, and the boggy meadows leading to its shores support a number of wildflowers typical of saturated tundra regions, such as globeflower, marsh marigold, elephant-head and mountain laurel. The nearby rockslides are inhabited by hoary marmots and pikas.

Since there is no campsite at the lake, backpackers should set camp at the Elk Lake Summit Campground.

In addition to Elk Lake, the ridges and slopes of Cascade Mountain to the east are gentle and open, offering numerous opportunities for day trips from the campground.

Cascade Valley. Backpackers bound for the remote Front Ranges of the park can follow the trail north from Elk Summit to reach the Cascade Valley near the mouth of Stony Creek—a distance from Elk Summit of 9.5 km.

The trail descends 475 vertical metres through a narrow, forested valley from Elk Summit. It follows a well-defined if sometimes muddy track then, when it reaches the Cascade Valley, crosses fords over the Cascade River and Stony Creek just before reaching the broad trail running along the Cascade River. (See *Cascade Fire Road.*)

7 Stoney Squaw

Mt Norquay Ski Area to Stoney Squaw Summit — 2.1 km (1.3 mi)

Like Tunnel Mountain, across the valley, Stoney Squaw is not really a mountain, just an 1884-m promontory extending east from the slopes of Mount Norquay. It is one of the highest, easily reached viewpoints above Banff, and though there are a lot of trees to contend with, a few openings provide "windows" to the town and the Bow Valley far below.

This moderately graded but steady uphill trail is enclosed in a dense forest of lodgepole pine and spruce most of the way, but within 200 m of the top you begin to catch glimpses of the Banff environs. The Bow Valley and the town of Banff lie immediately below, and Tunnel Mountain, Mount Rundle, and Sulphur Mountain are all visible beyond.

At the summit, nearby Cascade Mountain rises to the north and the Bow Valley stretches away to the southeast.

You can make a slightly-longer loop back to the trailhead by descending northwest from the summit on a faint path that soon turns into good trail. This track descends through a dense, mossy forest on the cool north side of Stoney Squaw.

When you reach the top of a clearing, walk down the slope to the ski area service road, turn left and follow it to the day lodge and main parking lot.

Access: From the Trans-Canada Highway at the Banff West Exit, follow the Mount Norquay Road north, climbing 6 km (3.5 mi) to the Mount Norquay ski area. Turn right at the main parking lot and watch for the trail sign just inside the entrance to the right. N51°12.040' W115°35.714' *Maps: Banff 82 0/4; Banff Up-Close (Gem Trek).*

8 Fenland Trail

Fenland Circuit — 2.1 km (1.3 mi)

This flat, easy loop trail near downtown Banff leads you through forest at the eastern edge of the Vermilion Lakes marshland. The trail runs beside the peaceful waters of Echo and Forty Mile Creeks and through a spruce forest carpeted with bunchberry and a green cloud of horsetails. With the exception of periods following heavy snowfalls, it can be hiked year round.

Follow the trail from the rear of the Forty Mile Picnic Area, cross a bridge over the creek, and continue 100 m to a trail split. You can either turn left or right at this point, since the trail makes an elongated loop through the forest and returns to this junction in just under 2 km. (Walking from town, access the loop via a trail branching left as soon as you cross the railway tracks.)

The trail can also be used as access to Vermilion Lakes Drive, where you can extend your walk another 4 km along one of the best wetland environments in the Bow Valley (watch for a branch trail part way around the loop that immediately crosses a bridge to the road).

Female elk have used the Fenland area as a calving ground for a number of years, and the trail is usually closed from late May through early June when these protective new mothers can be very aggressive.

Access: Follow Mount Norquay Road from downtown Banff, cross the railway tracks, and continue 0.3 km to the Forty Mile Picnic Area. N51°11.051' W115°34.959' *Maps: Banff 82 0/4 (trail not shown); Banff Up-Close (Gem Trek).*

© Andrew Hempstead *Banff and the Bow Valley from Tunnel Mountain*

9 Tunnel Mountain

St. Julien Road to Tunnel Mountain summit — 2.3 km (1.4 mi)

The Tunnel Mountain hike is short and readily accessible from downtown Banff. The summit, 300 m above the town, offers excellent views of the Banff environs, the north ridge of Mount Rundle, and a 30-km stretch of the Bow Valley. The trail is one of the oldest in the park and a popular outing for Banff residents.

After climbing 0.4 km from the St. Julien Road trailhead, the trail crosses Tunnel Mountain Road at a viewpoint-parking area (an optional starting point if you want to shorten the hike).

Above the road a series of sweeping switchbacks make a gradual but steady ascent through a thick forest of lodge-pole pine and Douglas fir. There are occasional glimpses of the town and valley, culminating at a good viewpoint beside a series of limestone slabs near the summit ridge.

On the summit ridge, the trail doubles back and runs above the mountain's sheer east-facing cliffs. Views along the ridge extend over the Banff Springs Golf Course and down-valley to the park's eastern boundary.

The trail ends on the sparsely-forested 1690-m summit, which was once the site of a fire lookout tower. Limestone outcrops just west of the summit provide the best views of Banff, the Vermilion Lakes and Massive Range.

Access: Drive or walk from downtown Banff on Wolf St. to St. Julien Road. Follow St. Julien 0.3 km to the trailhead parking area. N51°10.523' W115°33.708' *Map: Banff 82 O/4 (trail not shown); Banff Up-Close (Gem Trek).*

10 Sulphur Mountain

Upper Hot Springs to Banff Gondola Upper Terminal—5.5 km (3.4 mi)

Half-day trip

Allow 2 hours one way

Elevation gain: 700 m (2,300 ft)

Maximum elevation: 2281 m (7,486 ft)

Maps: Banff 82 O/4
Banff Up-Close (Gem Trek)

Access: Follow Sulphur Mountain Drive from downtown Banff 3.5 km to its termination at the Banff Gondola and Upper Hot Springs parking lots. Park in the Upper Hot Springs lot and walk back to the trailhead just above the entrance to the parking area.

0.0— Trailhead (1580 m).
N51°08.971' W115°33.564'

— Follow broad trail uphill through forest. Steady ascent via long switchbacks.

2.4— Trail passes within 200 m of waterfall.

2.7— Old trail shelter site (1890 m).

— Steady switchbacks continue, passing back and forth beneath gondola line.

5.5— Gondola Upper Terminal (2281 m).
N51°08.661' W115°34.471'

For those who disdain using a gondola lift to reach a mountaintop, the 5.5-km trail from the Upper Hot Springs is the preferred route to the summit ridge of Sulphur Mountain. While the trail gains 700 m from bottom to top, 28 switchbacks keep the grade reasonable and ease the strain of the ascent. And once you get to the top, if you don't really want to hike back down the trail, you can ride the gondola down in eight minutes flat! (One-way tickets are only available for the downhill ride and must be purchased at the gondola ticket office in advance.)

The track is wide and grades are moderate as the trail climbs the heavily-forested east slope of the mountain, though views do open briefly as it passes just north of a waterfall.

At km 2.7, a short side trail branches right to the site of an old trail shelter (removed in 2002). Prior to the completion of the gondola in 1959, a tractor and wagon transported visitors up the trail to this point, which is the halfway point on the hike.

The grade is steeper near the summit as you switchback back and forth beneath the gondola line. A scattering of alpine larch in the forest heralds your arrival at the summit ridge and the upper gondola terminal with its restaurant and much-needed refreshments.

Sanson's Peak. No hike, or ride, up Sulphur Mountain would be complete without continuing north from the upper terminal to a promontory known as Sanson's Peak. The route follows what is most certainly the most lavish alpine trail in Canada—a 0.6-km boardwalk, complete with viewing platforms, that leads to a stone weather observatory constructed in 1903. (The 2337-m peak is named for park meteorologist Norman Sanson, who hiked up the mountain over 1,000 times until his retirement in

Banff and Cascade Mountain from Sanson's Peak

1931.) While views of Banff, the Bow Valley and Lake Minnewanka are even more expansive than from the upper terminal, you will be accompanied by the throngs who have ridden up on the gondola.

South Ridge. Another trail runs south along the ridge for 0.8 km to steeply-tilted limestone slabs and views of the Sundance Range and Valley (look for the trail sign 60 m south of the upper terminal). The track is a bit rocky and rough, but it allows you to enjoy the forest and inhabitants of the summit ridge (mountain sheep, golden-mantled ground squirrels, and a variety of birds) in a peaceful setting away from the crowds.

Cosmic Ray Station Road. This abandoned road on Sulphur Mountain's west slope receives its colourful name from the days when it serviced the Cosmic Ray Station, constructed on Sanson's Peak as part of Canada's contribution to the 1957-58 International Geophysical Year. The lofty laboratory studied the bombardment of the earth's atmosphere by high-energy galactic particles until 1978,

and the building and its equipment were removed in 1981.

While you can climb Sulphur Mountain on this road, we like to hike from the top down, enjoying open, subalpine forest on the upper slopes and unimpeded views of the Bow Valley and the Sundance and Massive Ranges nearly to the bottom (the lower forest is the site of several tree-thinning operations). In addition to views, you pass beside numerous slabs of steeply-tilted limestone chock-full of fossils.

Follow the Sanson's Peak boardwalk 0.3 km to a signed junction. Descend the broad, moderately-steep roadbed for 5.6 km to an intersection with the *Sundance Canyon* trail. At this junction, turn right and walk 2.2 km on flat pavement to the Cave and Basin (see *Sundance Canyon*).

Regardless of whether you hike up or down, you will want to arrange transportation between the Upper Hot Springs and Cave and Basin parking areas.

11 Sundance Canyon

Cave and Basin to Sundance Canyon — 4.3 km (2.7 mi)

Half-day trip

Allow 1.5 hours

Elevation gain: 135 m (440 ft)

Maximum elevation: 1545 m (5,070 ft)

Maps: Banff 82 O/4
      Banff Up-Close (Gem Trek)

Access: From the intersection at the south end of the Bow River bridge in Banff, follow Cave Avenue 1.2 km to the parking area for the Cave and Basin National Historic Site. A paved walkway leads to the Cave and Basin complex and continues 200 m beyond to the trailhead kiosk.

0.0— Trailhead (1410 m).
      N51°10.118' W115°35.683'

   — Gradual descent on broad paved trail through forest.

0.7— Junction. Marsh Loop right; Sundance Canyon ahead.

   — Flat walking beside Bow River.

1.8— Trail leaves open valley and climbs into forest.

2.2— Junction. Sulphur Mtn summit (5.6 km) left; Brewster Creek (2.9 km) and Sunshine Road (4.6 km) right; Sundance Canyon ahead.

2.7— Junction. Sundance Pass left; Sundance Canyon ahead.

3.1— Sundance Canyon Picnic Area.

3.3— End of paved trail. Bike stands.

   — Foot trail climbs into Sundance Canyon, moderate to steep grades.

4.3— Top of Sundance Canyon (1545 m). Trail loops back through forest to the end of the paved trail.

Throughout most of its long history, the short 2-km loop trail at Sundance Canyon was accessible by road from the town of Banff. In the mid-1980s, the road beyond the Cave and Basin was converted to a paved walking and cycling path, which made the trip longer but more scenically varied. Many people bike to the canyon on the broad, asphalt trail, but the first half of the trip is an open and pleasant route for walkers as well.

From the trail kiosk beyond the Cave and Basin complex, the trail descends gradually through forest to the Bow River. For the next 1.5 km it follows along the river and its side channels with views of the rugged peaks to the north, including the sharp spire of Mount Edith. (The experience is tempered somewhat by the scent of a well-used horse trail that follows beside the pavement.)

The final stretch to the canyon climbs gradually through forest. The paved trail passes the Sundance Canyon Picnic Area and ends just beyond, where foot trail continues into the canyon proper (no bikes are permitted beyond the pavement). This is the original Sundance Canyon loop trail, a 2.1-km circuit that climbs beside Sundance Creek for 1.0 km before circling right through dense forest and descending back to the end of the paved trail. In addition to the canyon with its mini-cascades, you pass a viewpoint for the Massive Range at the 1.4-km mark, but the vista is more obscured by trees than when the trail was constructed many decades ago.

Marsh Loop. This 1.6-km trail circling the Cave and Basin marsh is a popular nature walk that provides an alternate view of the unique, warm-spring wetland, and if you're returning from Sundance Canyon, this diversion makes an interesting way to end your trip.

Follow the paved Sundance Canyon trail 0.7 km, where it comes abreast of the

Mount Edith from Sundance Canyon trail

Bow River, then turn right onto a broad, dirt path and follow it downstream beside the river. You soon emerge on the north side of the marsh, looking back across to the viewing platforms and the Cave and Basin complex. There are often signs of beaver and muskrat activity along this shoreline, and waterfowl on both the river and marsh can be easily identified with binoculars.

At the east end of the marsh, turn right and cross an earthen dike back to the Cave and Basin parking area.

Cosmic Ray Station Road. At km 2.2, a well-defined roadbed branches uphill into the forest on the left. This road serviced the Cosmic Ray Station on Sulphur Mountain's summit ridge during the International Geophysical Year, 1957-58, and until the station was decommissioned and removed in 1981. Today, the 5.6-km roadbed serves as an alternate route to the summit, though it's a steep, steady slog (you start nearly 200 m lower than the more popular 5.5-km trail from the Upper Hot Springs). But for those who arrange transportation between the Cave and Basin and Upper Hot Springs

parking lots, it can be an interesting way of traversing this popular and highly-scenic summit, which includes a mid-trip break at the Banff Gondola summit restaurant. (See also *Sulphur Mountain.*)

Healy Creek. This roadbed branches right from the Sundance Canyon trail at 2.2 km, directly opposite the Cosmic Ray Station Road, and rolls through forest along the south side of the Bow Valley to Brewster Creek junction (2.9 km) and the Sunshine Road (4.6 km). The smooth, broad track is of more interest to mountain bikers than hikers. (See also *Brewster Creek.*)

12 Mount Rundle

Banff Springs Golf Course to Trail's End—4.7 km (2.9 mi)

Half-day or day trip

Allow 1.5 to 2 hours to trail's end

Elevation gain: 470 m (1,550 ft)

Maximum elevation: 1830 m (6,000 ft)

Maps: Banff 82 O/4
Banff Up-Close (Gem Trek)

Access: From downtown Banff, cross the Bow River bridge and turn left onto Spray Avenue. Continue on Spray Avenue 0.8 km to Bow Falls Ave. Turn left and follow it downhill to the Bow Falls parking area. Continue around the parking area and across the Spray River bridge on the Golf Course Road. Park in a small parking area on the right 150 m past the bridge and walk along the road another 200 m to where a trail branches right at a "hiker" symbol sign.

0.0— Trailhead (1360 m).
N51°09.906' W115°33.183'

— Trail skirts behind golf course green.

0.2— Junction. Stay left.

1.0— Junction. Mt Rundle trail branches left from the Spray River east side trail.

— Trail climbs and switchbacks through pine forest.

3.9— Junction. Scrambler's track to 1st peak of Mt Rundle branches uphill to left. Mt. Rundle trail ahead.

4.7— Trail's end (1830 m). Route to main peak of Mt Rundle continues across major gully.

The trail up the southwest slope of Mount Rundle is steep and mostly enclosed by forest. While it does offer occasional views of the Spray Valley and the town of Banff, its primary function is as an approach route to the mountain's 2949-m summit—the most popular climb in Banff Park.

The first 1.0 km follows along the east arm of the Spray River Circuit. The trail strikes off from the golf course access road just beyond the first green on the right, skirts behind it and, at a junction, branches left on a broad track leading up into the forest. This old access road climbs well above the Spray River on its ascent along the east side of the valley.

Just 0.8 km beyond the golf course, the Mount Rundle trail branches left from the Spray River trail and begins its steady climb up the mountain's southwest slope. You are enclosed by forest for 2.4 km, where the trail finally switchbacks onto open slopes and there are good views of Banff and the Spray Valley.

The trail contours along the slope until it eventually ends at the edge of a major gully. Looking up this gully, you can see the limestone slabs and talus slopes leading to the top of the mountain.

The climb to the summit can be made by fit scramblers, but the peak lies a gruelling 1120 m above. The correct route follows across the gully and up the ridge on the opposite side (ascending the gully itself leads to serious problems). Anyone continuing beyond the end of the trail should pick up a copy of the pamphlet *A Scrambler's Guide to Mount Rundle* at the Park Visitor Centre in Banff, or download it from the Banff National Park website.

The trail and the mountain slopes beyond are bone dry, so be sure to carry water on the hike or the climb.

13 Spray River Circuit

Spray River Circuit—12.4 km (7.7 mi)

Half-day trip

Allow 3 to 4 hours round trip

Elevation gain: 75 m (250 ft)

Maximum elevation: 1435 m (4,700 ft)

Maps: Banff 82 O/4
       Banff Up-Close (Gem Trek)

Access: From downtown Banff, cross the Bow River bridge and turn left onto Spray Avenue. Continue on Spray Avenue 0.8 km to Bow Falls Ave. Turn left and follow it downhill to the Bow Falls parking area. Continue around the parking area and across the Spray River bridge on the Golf Course Road. Park in a small parking area on the right 150 m past the bridge and walk along the road another 200 m to where a trail branches right ("hiker" symbol sign).

0.0— Trailhead (1360 m).
      N51°09.906' W115°33.183'

     — Trail skirts behind golf course green.

0.2— Junction. Spray River Circuit trail split. Stay right.

0.4— Spray River.

     — Follow trail upstream.

1.2— Spray River footbridge.

1.4— Junction with Spray River trail at km 0.7. Turn left.

6.4— Junction and picnic area (1435 m). Spray River and *Goat Creek* ahead. Spray River Circuit east side left.

6.5— Spray River footbridge.

7.3— Mt Rundle Campground (Sp6).

11.0— Banff Springs Hotel viewpoint.

11.4— Junction. *Mt Rundle* right. Continue ahead.

12.2— Junction. Spray River Circuit trail split. Turn right.

12.4— Trailhead (1360 m).

This popular loop trip runs up one side of the Spray River and back down the other from the Banff Springs Golf Course. Though it follows abandoned park fire roads most of the way, it is a pleasant outing—a favourite trip for cyclists in summer and cross-country skiers in winter.

From the "hiker" sign on the right side of the road, follow a broad, dirt track that skirts behind a green and fairway for 200 m to a signed junction. From this point you can hike the circuit clockwise by turning left or, our preference, counter-clockwise by keeping right. Either way, you will return to this junction at the completion of the circuit.

By staying right, you climb over a forested rise to the Spray River and follow the trail leading upstream. At km 1.2 you reach a footbridge beside an old limestone quarry (the "Rundle Rock" used to construct the Banff Springs Hotel). Cross the bridge, where there is a view back to the hotel, and follow the trail up through the forest to the Spray River trail.

Turn left and follow the broad track of this old fire road up-valley for the next 5 km. Views are limited, but the river is a constant companion as you near the south end of the circuit.

At km 6.4, you arrive at a junction and picnic area on open flats beside the river. Turn left and cross the footbridge to return down the east side of the valley.

The trail is a bit more pleasant and varied along the east side, rolling through forest, passing a campground and climbing gradually to an open benchland overlooking the river and the Banff Springs Hotel, which rises from the forest like a medieval castle. From this viewpoint, a short, gradual descent brings you back to the 0.2-km trail junction beside the golf course fairway.

14 Goat Creek

Spray Lakes Road to Banff Springs Golf Course—19.4 km (12.1 mi)

Day trip

Allow 5 hours

Elevation loss: 300 m (985 ft)

Maximum elevation: 1660 m (5,450 ft)

Maps: Canmore 82 O/3
Banff 82 O/4

Access: The trailhead is on the Spray Lakes Road (Hwy 742) 9 km (5 mi) from downtown Canmore. Follow the road west from Canmore to Whiteman's Gap (steep gravel road after passing the Canmore Nordic Centre). The road skirts a lake in the gap and descends a hill to the Goat Creek parking area on the right.

0.0— Trailhead (1660 m).
N51°03.706' W115°25.110'

1.0— Park boundary.

— Gradual descent near creek.

7.2— Goat Creek bridge.

9.0— Spray River bridge.

9.3— Junction with Spray River trail. Turn right.

— Follow downstream on roadbed.

13.4— Junction. Straight ahead to Spray Avenue trailhead (5.7 km) and Banff Springs Hotel. Stay right for Spray River east side trail and golf course.

13.5— Spray River footbridge.

14.3— Mt Rundle Campground (Sp6).

18.0— Banff Springs Hotel viewpoint.

18.4— Junction. *Mt Rundle* trail right. Golf course ahead.

19.4— Trailhead (1360 m). Golf course road.
N51°09.906' W115°33.183'

Notice: The decommissioned Spray Fire Road continues south from its junction with the Goat Creek trail for another 29 km to Spray Lakes Reservoir, but travel has been restricted from April through November for over a decade to preserve the upper valley for grizzly bears.

The Goat Creek trail connects the decommissioned fire road along the Spray River to the Spray Lakes Road (Hwy 742) just beyond the park boundary in Spray Valley Provincial Park. However, it is usually travelled from south to north as a day trip from the Spray Lakes Road to Banff. Since it loses elevation gradually but steadily (300 m over 19.4 km), the trip is very popular with cyclists in summer and cross-country skiers in winter. It is a long hike, though pleasant and undemanding, which is often near the rushing waters of Goat Creek and the Spray River.

From the parking area beside Spray Lakes Road, you can look down the long corridor you will be travelling to Banff, contained by Mount Rundle on the right and Goat and Sulphur Mountains on the left. Soon after passing the park boundary, the trail comes abreast of Goat Creek and follows near it for the next 5 km.

Bridges that span Goat Creek at km 7.2 and Spray River at km 9.0 appear suddenly at the bottom of short, steep grades, so cyclists and skiers should control their speed as they near these crossings.

Turn right when you reach the Spray River trail and follow the broad track of this old fire road downstream along the west side of the Spray. When you reach a trail split on an open flat beside the river at km 13.4, you have a choice: stay left on the Spray River trail to reach the south end of Spray Avenue and the Banff Springs Hotel; or stay right and immediately cross a bridge to the east side of the river to another old roadbed leading to the Banff Springs Golf Course (see *Spray River Circuit*). We prefer the latter, though it is marginally longer.

Unless you are a cyclist making a circuit around Mount Rundle, you will want to arrange transportation between the two distant trailheads.

15 Rundle Riverside

Banff Springs Golf Course Road to Canmore Nordic Centre—14.6 km (9.1 mi)

Day trip

Allow 3.5 hours hiking

Elevation gain: 135 m (450 ft)
loss: 60 m (200 ft)

Maximum elevation: 1490 m (4,880 ft)

Maps: Banff 82 O/4
Canmore 82 O/3

Access: Drive to Bow Falls below the Banff Springs Hotel. Continue past the falls parking area and across the Spray River bridge onto the golf course loop road. Continue along this road 4.4 km, keeping right at a road split, to the small, trailhead parking area on the right side of the road.

The south end of the trail is at the Canmore Nordic Centre, 4 km from downtown Canmore on the Spray Lakes Road (Hwy 742). Follow the "Banff Trail" from the Nordic Centre.

0.0— Trailhead (1355 m).
N51°10.180' W115°30.726'

0.4— Trail comes abreast of Bow River.

— Gentle, rolling trail near river.

2.7— Rock outwash.

4.9— Trail angles away from river.

5.7— Rock outwash.

7.5— Rock-mud outwash.

7.8— Moderate climb through rooty forest.

8.4— Park boundary.

— Steady uphill on wide gravel trail.

8.8— Trail enters Nordic Centre trail network.

— Follow gravel trail ("Banff Trail").

11.9— Trail summit (1490 m).

— Steady downhill.

14.6— Canmore Nordic Centre (1430 m).
N51°05.433' W115°23.164'

The Rundle Riverside trail reaches the Bow River in less than 15 minutes—a peaceful spot with a nice view of the Fairholme Range. Past this idyllic spot, the trail has little attraction for hikers beyond a few more riverside viewpoints. However, it is the most direct trail between Banff and Canmore and popular with mountain bikers.

The trail runs from the end of the Banff Springs Golf Course loop road to the Canmore Nordic Centre beyond the park boundary. It is rough, forest-enclosed, and sometimes very rocky (it crosses three major outwashes).

You reach the Bow River at km 0.4 and stay close to its bank for the next 4 km. There are numerous opportunities to stop and relax beside the river, and the massive buttresses of Mount Rundle, visible through the trees, are constant companions.

The last access to the river is at km 4.9, where the trail angles off to the right and starts climbing to the park boundary.

After crossing the boundary at km 8.4, the trail becomes a wide gravel track that rises steeply into the midst of the Nordic Centre ski-trail network. This smooth roadbed leads you through the maze of trails (follow signs indicating "Banff Trail" and "Stadium" at trail intersections).

The highest elevation on the trip, 180 m above the Bow Valley, is reached in the middle of a large, grassy clearing (an old strip mine scar from the dying days of the Canmore coal industry in the 1970s). If you are on a bike, this viewpoint is followed by a quick downhill run to the Nordic Centre lodge and stadium, where the 1988 Winter Olympic Nordic events were staged.

Some cyclists return to Banff on the paved Legacy Trail along the Trans-Canada Highway or via the *Goat Creek* trail. One-way hikers and cyclists will need to arrange transportation between the two trailheads.

Land above 2300 metres

0 1 2 3 4 5 km

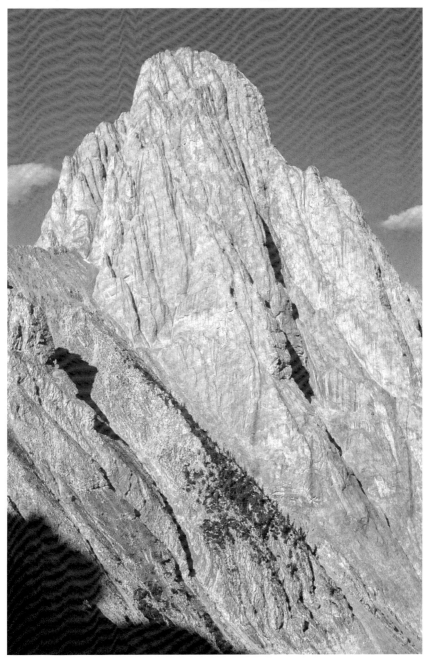

Mount Louis from Cory Pass

16 Cory Pass—Mount Edith Circuit

Fireside Picnic Area to Cory Pass—5.8 km (3.6 mi)
Mount Edith Circuit—13.0 km (8.1 mi)

Day trip

Allow 3 hours to Cory Pass

Elevation gain: 915 m (3,000 ft)

Maximum elevation: 2350 m (7,700 ft)

Maps: Banff 82 O/4
      Banff Up-Close (Gem Trek)

Access: Follow the Trans-Canada Highway west 5.5 km from Banff's west exit interchange to the Bow Valley Parkway exit. Continue on Bow Valley Parkway 0.3 km to the Fireside Picnic Area access road. Follow the road 1.0 km to the picnic area. A bridge spanning the creek to the picnic area is the starting point for the trail.

0.0—Trailhead (1435 m).
    N51°10.443' W115°39.267'
    —Trail angles away from the rear of the picnic area on an old roadbed.

0.2—Trail cuts left into forest from roadbed.

1.1—Junction. Edith Pass trail straight ahead, Cory Pass uphill to left.
    —Stiff uphill climb.

1.7—Cory Knoll viewpoint.
    —Extremely steep uphill.

2.4—Crest of narrow forested ridge.
    —Trail follows ridge crest then climbs steeply across open slope to pass.

5.8—Cory Pass (2350 m).
    —Steep, rocky descent to Gargoyle Valley.

6.8—Exit Gargoyle Valley. Keep right up steep talus slope.

7.1—Trail contours southeast on slopes above Edith Pass.

8.2—Trail descends avalanche slope.

9.0—Junction with Edith Pass trail.
    —Steady descent through heavy forest.

11.9—Junction. Cory Pass-Edith Pass trail junction.

13.0—Trailhead (1435 m).

Cory Pass is the most spectacular hike near Banff. The 2300-m gap frames the monolithic south face of Mount Louis to create a view that is usually reserved for mountaineers. And after gaining almost a vertical kilometre in elevation to get there, you will feel like a mountaineer.

Whether you simply hike to the pass and return or complete the 13-km loop trip around Mount Edith, you are in for a good workout. (Caution: do not underestimate the physical exertion that this hike requires. The trail is also hazardous when the ground is frozen or there is snow and ice on sections of the route.)

From the Fireside Picnic Area the trail runs through coniferous forest and pleasant aspen groves to a junction at km 1.1. (If you complete the Mount Edith Circuit, you will return to this junction...someday!) The trail to Cory Pass cuts uphill to the left at this split and begins a heart-pounding climb on an open, south-facing slope. After a brief respite on a grassy knoll overlooking the Bow Valley, it continues its relentless ascent for another 1.3 km to a forested ridge and the first views of your objective—the lofty notch of Cory Pass.

You climb along this rocky, sparsely forested ridge for another kilometre or so to the top of a small cliff band, which requires that you down-climb through an obvious but steep break in the rock (nothing serious, but you'll need to use your hands to steady yourself).

The trail picks up again at the base of this cliff and, a few moments later, emerges from the trees and ascends across a long open slope to the pass (take care if snow is lingering in the steep gullies traversed by the trail).

Cory Pass can be a very cold and windy place. Sandwiched between the cliffs of Mounts Edith (2555 m) to the east and Cory (2800 m) to the west, this high, rockbound gap might more

Mount Louis from the Edith Pass high route

appropriately be considered a col—a French term for a high gap between two peaks. However, the views are worth any discomforts of trail or pass, highlighted by the towering slabs of grey limestone that form the 500-m face of Mount Louis. This forbidding, unapproachable mountain has been a popular objective for rock climbers ever since it was first ascended by the Austrian guide Conrad Kain and Albert H. MacCarthy in 1916.

Mount Edith Circuit. Instead of going back the way you came (a knee-jarring experience), you can descend the north side of the pass and make a loop around Mount Edith via the Edith Pass high trail.

Barring lingering snow in early summer, a vague trail leads down the steep talus slope beyond the pass and into Gargoyle Valley, named for the rock pinnacles just north of the summit. After a quick loss of elevation, a rocky but defined track traverses to the right beneath Mount Edith's cliffs and just above the floor of the valley—an incredible, rock-filled sanctuary dominated by Mount Louis's imposing south face.

The rocky trail leads you through the mouth of the Gargoyle Valley to an open rockslide and a view of the broad Forty Mile Valley. Hikers sometimes lose the trail here, so look for the long scree slope leading up to the right. A faint trail climbs directly up this rocky slope for approximately 300 m and, near the top, branches left off the scree and into stunted trees.

The route continues as a high traverse across lightly-forested slopes beneath Mount Edith's cliffs, where there are impressive views back to Mount Louis and down to the summit of Edith Pass.

The trail eventually plunges down the mountainside on an avalanche slope, re-enters the forest, and intersects the main Edith Pass trail 0.6 km south of its summit (see also *Edith Pass via Forty Mile Creek*).

The loop is completed by following a lively little stream down through mossy-floored forest and back to the 1.1-km junction with the Cory Pass trail. Total distance for the loop is 13 km, and taking into account the steep climbs and descents, it makes for a very strenuous day.

17 Edith Pass via Forty Mile Creek

Mt Norquay Ski Area to Fireside Picnic Area—12.8 km (8.0 mi)

Day trip

Allow 3.5 to 4 hours

Elevation loss: 90 m (300 ft)
       gain: 335 m (1,100 ft)

Maximum elevation: 1950 m (6,400 ft)

Maps: Banff 82 O/4
      Banff Up-Close (Gem Trek)

Access: From the Trans-Canada Highway at the Banff West Exit, follow the Mount Norquay Road north from the Trans-Canada Highway 6.0 km (3.5 mi) to the Mount Norquay ski area. Enter the first parking lot on the right and follow it 200 m to the day lodge at the far end. (Park well away from the gated service road and other ski area buildings).

The Fireside Picnic Area trailhead is reached by following the Trans-Canada Highway west 5.5 km from Banff's west exit interchange to the Bow Valley Parkway exit. Continue on Bow Valley Parkway 0.3 km to the Fireside Picnic Area access road and follow it 1.0 km to the picnic area parking area and trailhead.

0.0—Trailhead (1705 m).
     N51°12.190' W115°35.880'
     —Walk through lodge complex and down-valley on ski area service road.

0.8—Junction. *Cascade Amphitheatre* and *Elk Lake* ahead. Forty Mile Creek and Edith Pass left.

4.0—Forty Mile Creek bridge (1615 m).
     —Trail follows upstream along creek.

6.0—Junction. *Sawback Trail* ahead. Cross bridge left to Edith Pass.
     —Steep climb south toward pass.

8.3—Edith Pass (1950 m).
     —Descent into forest.

8.8—Junction. Mount Edith Circuit intersects from right. Stay ahead.
     —Steady descent through forest.

11.7—Junction. *Cory Pass* right. Stay ahead.

12.8—Fireside Picnic Area (1435 m).
     N51°10.443' W115°39.267'

While you can hike directly to Edith Pass by following the descent route on the Mount Edith Circuit, it's a steady 4.6-km climb through heavy forest with little scenic reward. A more interesting approach is the way we first hiked it many years ago, from Mount Norquay Ski Area to Fireside Picnic Area, with the first 6.0 km following the *Sawback Trail*. Highlights include a lush forest filled with arnica and other wildflowers (July), a mid-trip interlude beside Forty Mile Creek, and the ever-beckoning spire of Mount Louis, one of the most impressive rock walls in western Canada.

You will want to arrange transportation between the two distant trailheads, and starting from the much higher Mount Norquay is certainly preferable. From the ski area day lodge, follow the service road down past the base stations of several ski lifts. At 0.8 km, in the middle of a ski run, the trail to Edith Pass branches left from the *Cascade Amphitheatre* and *Elk Lake* trail.

The trail climbs steeply into the forest from the ski runs and then makes a lengthy descent to Forty Mile Creek along the heavily-forested north slope of Mount Norquay.

The bridge crossing Forty Mile Creek at km 4.0 affords excellent views back to Cascade Mountain. As the trail follows upstream, the magnificent towers of Edith, Louis and Fifi appear—three striking monuments that dominate the scene for the next two km.

At km 6.0, you branch left from the *Sawback Trail*, cross Forty Mile Creek (bridged) and make a very stiff 2.3-km ascent to Edith Pass (snow often lingers here into late spring). Mount Louis is a constant companion, with Mount Edith towering just beyond. From scattered forest on the summit, the trail descends to join the Mount Edith Circuit and finishes on that route down to the Fireside Picnic Area (see *Cory Pass-Mount Edith Circuit*).

Castle Mountain and Bow Valley from Muleshoe trail meadows

18 Muleshoe

Muleshoe Picnic Area to Muleshoe Meadows — 0.9 km (0.6 mi)

This short trail gains 255 heart-pounding metres up the steep, southwest slope of Mount Cory. At the top you discover lush montane meadows and expansive views of the Bow Valley stretching up-valley to Castle Mountain and Mount Temple near Lake Louise.

Starting from the trail sign across the road from Muleshoe Picnic Area parking lot, a narrow path climbs through a stand of aspen and into a fire-blackened Douglas fir forest. (This fire was a pre-scribed burn set by Parks Canada in May 1993.)

After traversing steeply to the right across the slope, the trail turns straight uphill and becomes extremely steep. You finally struggle out of partially burned forest and into a meadow, angling left to the edge of a large gully filled with burned trees. The trail levels out briefly here, and you have the best viewpoint for the valley.

The trail receives its name from the horseshoe-shaped lake beside the picnic area below. The small lake was once a channel of the Bow River, but was isolated from the main flow by railway construction.

A steep but well-defined track continues upwards along the gully, climbing another 2 km to a lofty promontory. This extension is not worthwhile since it stays mainly in the forest and views are limited.

While the Muleshoe is an ideal spring hike, the slope is infested with wood ticks early in the season. Be sure to check yourself over carefully after the hike.

Access: Follow the Bow Valley Parkway west from its eastern intersection with the Trans-Canada Highway 5.5 km (3.4 mi) to Muleshoe Picnic Area. The trailhead is directly across the road from the parking area. N51°10.808' W115°43.201' *Maps: Banff-Egypt Lake (Gem Trek).*

19 Johnston Canyon—Ink Pots

Johnston Canyon Resort to Upper Falls—2.7 km (1.7 mi)
Johnston Canyon Resort to Ink Pots—5.8 km (3.6 mi)

Half-day trip

Allow 45 minutes to Upper Falls
　　2 hours to Ink Pots

Elevation gain: 320 m (700 ft)
　　　　loss: 105 m (350 ft)

Maximum elevation: 1750 m (5,750 ft)

Maps:　Banff 82 O/4
　　　　Castle Mountain 82 O/5
　　　　Banff-Egypt Lake (Gem Trek)

Access: Follow the Bow Valley Parkway
west from its eastern interchange with the
Trans-Canada Highway 17.5 km (11 mi) to
Johnston Canyon. The parking area is on
the east side of Johnston Creek. From the
rear of the parking area, follow the trail
leading across a footbridge to the lodge and
trailhead on the west side of the creek.

0.0— Trailhead (1430 m).
　　　N51°14.815' W115°50.445'

1.1— Lower Falls.

2.7— Upper Falls (1565 m).

3.2— Junction. Intersection with Moose
　　　Meadows trail (see *Sawback Range
　　　Circuit*). Keep right.

　— Steady climb.

4.5— Trail summit (1750 m).

5.3— Trail narrows .

　— Gradual descent to Johnston Creek
　　　meadows.

5.8— Ink Pots (1645 m).

The trail to the waterfalls of Johnston Canyon has to be the busiest in the Canadian Rockies. Nearly every day throughout the summer, hundreds of visitors follow its canyon-clinging catwalks and cliff-mounting staircases to the gorge's Lower and Upper Falls. While the canyon and its unique trail are certainly worthy of a visit, you'll have to do the hike in the evening or very early in the morning to avoid the hordes.

The trail begins immediately behind the main building at Johnston Canyon Resort. After a short climb through the forest, it descends and stays close to Johnston Creek all the way to Lower Falls. Along the way you pass over sturdy iron catwalks attached beneath overhanging canyon walls, where the turbulent waters of the creek flow beneath your feet.

Lower Falls is reached at km 1.1. A bridge across the creek serves as a viewpoint for the thundering cataract, and a short tunnel through the canyon bedrock allows passage to an even more intimate vantage point (albeit a wet one).

Back on the main trail, you continue up the canyon via more catwalks and broad, well-graded trail. There are many viewpoints overlooking the canyon and a small waterfall.

Throughout the journey, scan the creek and its banks for dippers. Also known as water ouzels, these solitary, slate-grey birds are often seen bouncing up and down on streamside rocks.

At the 30-metre-high Upper Falls, there are two viewpoints: the bottom of the falls is reached by a side-trail and catwalk leading to a viewing platform; a short steep climb on the main trail takes you to the top of the falls and another viewing platform, which hangs out over the gorge above the waterfall.

While the rock slabs near the brink of the falls are fenced, people still clamber through to be near the creek. Be

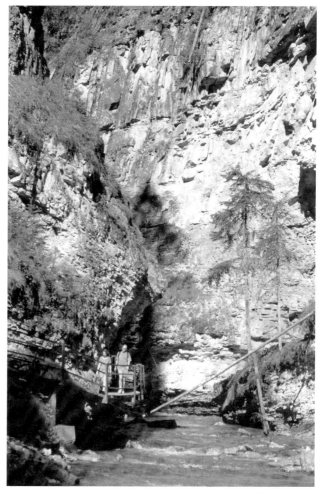

Johnston Canyon

forewarned: if you slip into the stream, you will be swept over the falls! (Always stay on the trail and keep children under control.)

Ink Pots. A small percentage of those who hike to Upper Falls continue another 3 km to the Ink Pots—seven cold mineral springs bubbling to the surface in the open meadows beside Johnston Creek. For most who extend the hike, it is a welcome relief from the bustling canyon.

Above Upper Falls, the trail climbs out of the canyon to join the trail from Moose Meadows. After 1.3 km of steady climbing from the Moose Meadows junction, it descends to the meadows and springs, located on the right side of the trail not far from the creek.

While these springs are unique (they have a constant temperature of 4 degrees C. and their basins are composed of quicksand), the wild setting, open, willow meadows of the Johnston Creek valley and views of the Sawback Range are the main reward.

20 Sawback Trail

Mount Norquay Ski Area to Lake Louise Ski Area—72.6 km (45.1 mi)

Backpack

Allow 4 to 6 days

Maximum elevation: 2450 m (8,040 ft)

Minimum elevation: 1615 m (5,300 ft)

Maps: Banff 82 O/4
     Castle Mountain 82 O/5
     Lake Louise 82 N/8

Access: Travelling from south to north, start at the Mount Norquay ski area (see *Cascade Amphitheatre* access description). Travelling from north to south, start from the Fish Creek parking area at the Lake Louise ski area (see *Boulder Pass-Skoki Valley* access description).

0.0— Mount Norquay day lodge (1705 m). N51°12.190' W115°35.880'

0.8— Junction. *Cascade Amphitheatre* and *Elk Lake* right. Sawback Trail left.

4.0— Forty Mile Creek bridge (1615 m).

6.0— Junction. *Edith Pass* left 2.3 km. Sawback Trail ahead.

8.2— Mt Cockscomb Campground (Fm10).

15.9— Junction (1845 m). Mystic Jct Campground (Fm19) and Forty Mile Summit ahead. Sawback Trail left.

16.0— Mystic Patrol Cabin.

18.6— Mystic Valley Campground (Ml22).

19.1— Junction. Mystic Lake left 0.5 km; Sawback Trail and Mystic Pass ahead.

22.7— Mystic Pass (2285 m).

29.3— Johnston Creek Junction (1680 m). Larry's Camp Campground (Jo9), Johnston Canyon and Moose Meadows left. Sawback Trail right.

33.0— Johnston Creek Patrol Cabin.

37.9— Johnston Creek bridge to west bank.

38.0— Junction. Johnston Creek Campground (Jo18). Luellen Lake and Campground (Jo19) left 1.0 km. Sawback Trail ahead.

39.4— Johnston Creek ford to east bank.

43.3— Junction (2025 m). Badger Pass and Sawback Range Circuit right. Sawback Trail ahead.

The Sawback Trail is a name we coined for an extended backpack running from Banff to Lake Louise. The route travels through the jagged limestone peaks of the Sawback Range and over three 2300-m passes—Mystic, Pulsatilla and Boulder. Along the way it utilizes trails in the Forty Mile Creek valley and the upper reaches of Johnston and Baker Creeks. It is an exceptional wilderness trip that usually takes four to six days to complete and is one of the more popular long distance backpacks in Banff Park.

Mount Norquay Ski Area to Johnston Creek Junction—29.3 km. We prefer to start this trip from the Banff end since there is a steady improvement in scenery travelling toward Lake Louise. Departing from the Mount Norquay ski area, the first portion of the trip makes a gradual descent around the heavily forested northern flank of Mount Norquay to Forty Mile Creek.

After crossing Forty Mile Creek at 4.0 km, the trail proceeds upstream along its eastern side, with sporadic views of Mount Brewster to the east and Mount Louis ahead. (Since this trail is used for commercial horse trips, expect muddy conditions and rough track as far as Mystic Lake.)

A junction at km 15.9 marks the point where you cross back to the west side of Forty Mile Creek and begin the climb toward Mystic Pass. (The trail is plagued by rocks and roots beyond the Mystic Patrol Cabin.) At km 18.6, it crosses the creek below a large avalanche path and passes the Mystic Valley Campground. In a few minutes you reach the junction for the 0.5-km side-trail to Mystic Lake—a serene body of water contained by the massive cliffs of Mount Ishbel.

Though the origin of the lake's name is somewhat obscure, it likely dates back to around 1891 when the Stoney Indian William Twin guided 11-year-

Pulsatilla Lake and Wildflower Creek valley from Pulsatilla Pass

43.8—Badger Pass Jct. Campground (Jo29).

47.2—Pulsatilla Pass (2345 m).

48.3—Pulsatilla Lake.

53.6—Baker Creek Junction (1830 m).
Wildflower Creek Campground (Ba15).
Sawback Trail right.

58.9—Junction. Red Deer Lakes ahead.
Sawback Trail left.

59.6—Baker Lake and Campground (Sk11).

62.1—Junction (2450 m). Intersection with
Boulder Pass-Skoki Valley trail at km
10.5. Deception Pass-Skoki Valley to
right. Continue ahead.

64.0—Boulder Pass (2345 m).

65.5—Junction. Halfway Hut. Hidden Lake
Campground (Sk5) and Hidden Lake
to right. Continue ahead.

68.7—Temple Lodge (2010 m).

   —Temple access road.

72.6—Fish Creek Parking Area (1690 m).
N51°26.411' W116°09.097'

old Bill Brewster and his nine-year-old brother Jim to the lake. The Banff boys, who would later create an outfitting and tourist transportation empire, are reputed to be the first white folks to visit the lake.

Mystic Pass is a 3.6 km climb from Mystic Lake junction. The trail over this 2285-m summit runs through beautiful alpine meadows flanked by outcrops and sweeping layers of Devonian limestone.

East of the pass, the trail drops through the heart of the Sawback Range, traversing some spectacular rockslides and avalanche paths and passing delicate waterfalls. At km 29.3 it emerges into the Johnston Creek valley at an intersection with the trail running up-valley from Johnston Canyon and Moose Meadows. (See *Johnston Canyon-Ink Pots* and *Sawback Range Circuit*.)

Johnston Creek Junction to Baker Creek Junction—24.3 km. From the junction, turn right and begin a gradual, mostly forested ascent along the east side of Johnston Creek. At 37.9 km the hiker's trail branches left and crosses the creek to Johnston Creek Campground and the

Luellen Lake trail junction. This side trail reaches Luellen Lake and Campground in 1.0 km. Since the lake is a must-see feature, these campgrounds should be considered as potential overnight stops.

Luellen is a long, narrow lake contained by the cliffs of Helena Ridge and a forest of Engelmann spruce and alpine fir. Whether viewed beneath evening shadow or the first rays of morning sun, it is a remarkably peaceful body of water. While the lake hasn't been stocked for many years, it still provides anglers and a resident osprey family with sporadic success.

Continuing beyond Luellen Lake junction, the trail soon crosses back to the east side of Johnston Creek, where it enters open willow meadows with views of the jagged summits of the Sawback Range to the east.

Badger Pass junction is reached at km 43.3. A campground 500 m beyond the junction is a good base for a side trip to 2545-m Badger Pass, one of the highest trail-accessible passes in the Canadian Rockies. The pass, which is reached following a steady 5 km climb, serves as a gateway to the remote headwaters of the Cascade River (see *Sawback Range Circuit*).

Just 1.4 km beyond Badger Pass Junction the trail swings across the creek one last time (easy ford) and begins its ascent to Pulsatilla Pass. Beware of side trails leading off to the right, but instead stay left beneath the glacier-draped cliffs of Pulsatilla Mountain and follow the trail climbing straight ahead to the obvious low notch.

The view beyond the 2345-m summit is one of the classic wilderness scenes in the Rockies—the sparkling waters of Pulsatilla Lake perfectly framed between mountain chains marching away to the north. Pulsatilla is an old genus designation for western anemone, just one of a myriad of wildflowers that spread over the alpine-meadow headwaters of the appropriately named Wildflower Creek in mid-summer.

The trail descends northward from the pass, skirts the shores of Pulsatilla Lake, then drops sharply down the narrow Wildflower Creek valley to Baker Creek and the Wildflower Creek Campground. (A rough trail down Baker Creek once provided an optional exit to the Bow Valley Parkway, but it is no longer maintained and using it is discouraged to minimize disturbance to wildlife that range in the valley.)

Baker Creek Junction to Fish Creek Parking Area—19.0 km. Boulder Pass is the last and highest pass on your journey. While it is a gem, you will suffer a bit over the next 5 km to attain this sublime summit.

After crossing Wildflower Creek at its confluence with Baker Creek (hopefully there is a log bridge so you can avoid the wade), climb through forest and across avalanche paths on rough trail along the east side of the creek. After 2 km, the trail descends into a boggy meadow, where it becomes indistinct and difficult to follow. At the north end of the meadow, cross a side-stream and rocky outwash, followed by a short steep climb over rough, rocky and often muddy trail.

You finally emerge into pleasant subalpine meadows and cross to the west side of the creek. At km 58.9, turn left at a junction onto the trail leading west to Baker Lake.

From Baker Lake Campground, the trail travels along the lake's north shore and then climbs to Ptarmigan Valley and an intersection with the *Boulder Pass-Skoki Valley* trail just below Deception Pass.

You are on a popular trail now and traversing one of the finest summits in the Rockies. The trail rolls along above Ptarmigan Lake, with little gain or loss of elevation, to the crest of Boulder Pass, where views stretch across the Bow Valley to Mount Temple and the Valley of the Ten Peaks.

From Boulder Pass, you complete your trip by following the *Boulder Pass-Skoki Valley* trail down Corral Creek to the Lake Louise ski area and Fish Creek parking area.

21 Sawback Range Circuit

Badger Pass-Flint's Park-Mystic Pass Circuit—72.5 km (45.0 mi)

Backpack

Allow 4 to 6 days

Maximum elevation: 2545 m (8,350 ft)

Minimum elevation: 1430 m (4,700 ft)

Maps: Castle Mountain 82 O/5

Access: Follow the Bow Valley Parkway to the Moose Meadows parking area, located on the north side of the highway 2.3 km (1.4 mi) west of Johnston Canyon and 4 km (2.5 mi) east of Castle Junction. The parking area is situated 100 m off the Parkway.

0.0—Moose Meadows trailhead (1430 m). N51°15.423' W115°51.424'

2.7—Junction. *Johnston Canyon-Ink Pots* trail intersects from right.

5.3—Ink Pots.

5.6—Johnston Creek bridge to east bank.

7.4—Junction and bridge (1680 m). Larry's Camp Campground (Jo9). Mystic Pass right. Sawback Range Circuit ahead.

11.1—Johnston Creek Patrol Cabin.

16.0—Johnston Creek bridge to west bank.

16.1—Junction and Johnston Creek Campground (Jo18). Luellen Lake and Campground (Jo19) left 1.0 km. Sawback Range Circuit ahead.

17.5—Johnston Creek ford to east bank.

21.4—Junction (2025 m). Badger Pass Junction Campground (Jo29) 0.5 km and Pulsatilla Pass 3.9 km ahead. Sawback Range Circuit right.

26.4—Badger Pass (2545 m).

33.4—Block Lakes Jct Campground (Cr37).

38.8—Junction. *North Fork Pass* left. Sawback Range Circuit ahead.

38.9—Junction (1830 m). *Flint's Park* and *Cascade Fire Road* ahead. Turn right across Cascade River bridge for Sawback Range Circuit.

43.7—Junction. Sawback Lake Campground (Fm29) 1.4 km and Sawback Lake 2.2 km to right. Sawback Range Circuit ahead.

45.7—Forty Mile Summit (2150 m).

The Sawback Trail connecting Banff and Lake Louise is a fairly popular long-distance backpacking route. However, you can sample some of the region's best scenery by making a loop trip through the heart of the range via Johnston Creek, Badger Pass, Flint's Park, Forty Mile Summit and Mystic Pass.

The Sawback Range Circuit passes through some of the highest and wildest country in the Front Ranges, covers the same distance as the Sawback Trail, and conveniently brings you back to where you started.

Some cautionary notes: sections of trail on the east side of the Sawback Range are utilized by a commercial horse operation, so expect the mud and muck of a heavily-used horse trail; much of this circuit travels through prime grizzly bear habitat, particularly between Badger Pass and Forty Mile Summit, so follow all the rules for safe travel in bear country; and a major snow cornice on the eastern lip of Badger Pass may cause difficulties early in the season.

Moose Meadows to Badger Pass Junction—21.4 km. The Sawback Range Circuit starts and ends at the Moose Meadows parking area on the Bow Valley Parkway—the trailhead for most trips into the Johnston Creek valley. From the parking area, you climb through forest and, soon after passing the intersection with the Johnston Canyon trail, emerge into open willow-dwarf birch meadows at the Ink Pots. After crossing to the east side of Johnston Creek just beyond the cold mineral springs, the trail remains near the creek and makes a gradual, straightforward ascent of the valley.

At just over 7 km you pass Larry's Camp Campground and, a few moments later, arrive at a bridged side stream and the junction for Mystic Pass. This junction is the trail split for your round-trip circuit through the Sawback Range.

© Mike McReynolds — *Bonnet Peak from Badger Pass*

51.4—Junction at Mystic Junction Campground (Fm19). Forty Mile Creek ahead. Sawback Range Circuit right.

51.8—Junction (1845 m) at Mystic Patrol Cabin. Forty Mile Creek left; Mystic Lake and Sawback Range Circuit right.

54.4—Mystic Valley Campground (Ml22).

54.9—Junction. Mystic Lake left (0.5 km). Mystic Pass ahead.

58.5—Mystic Pass (2285 m).

65.1—Johnston Creek Junction (1680 m). Larry's Camp Campground (Jo9). Moose Meadows trailhead left.

72.5—Moose Meadows trailhead (1430 m).

Here you must decide whether to follow the loop in a counter-clockwise direction by heading toward Mystic Pass or clockwise by continuing along Johnston Creek. Our preference is clockwise (as described here), since the approaches to both Badger and Mystic Passes are more gradual.

As you continue up Johnston Creek, you are following the central section of the Sawback Trail, reaching the Luellen Lake Junction at km 16.1 and Badger Pass junction at km 21.4 (see *Sawback Trail*, km 29.3 to km 43.3).

If you arrive at Badger Pass junction early in the afternoon, consider pitching camp in the campground 0.5 km north of the junction. From there you can side-trip north along the Sawback Trail 3.4 km to the alpine meadows of Pulsatilla Pass—a magnificent viewpoint over-looking Pulsatilla Lake and the upper reaches of the Wildflower Valley.

Badger Pass Junction to Flint's Park—17.5 km. At Badger Pass junction you leave the Sawback Trail, turning north-east to begin the steady ascent to Badger Pass—one of the highest trail-accessible points in Banff Park. The climb to the pass is moderate to steep, and you cross the creek draining its western slope twice as you climb through forest-fringed meadows. Once you emerge above the last trees, the trail is faint to non-existent through rocky, alpine meadows and along talus slopes, but the route to the pass is always obvious ahead.

Badger Pass (2545 m) is about as wild and remote a place as you could imagine. The summit is surrounded by a sea of peaks typical of the Front Ranges, composed of steeply-tilted layers of limestone and shale; Bonnet Peak (3234 m), one of the highest mountains in the Sawback Range, rises immediately to the north. On warm, sunny days the pass is a wonderful place to relax and enjoy the high point on your journey, but if the weather is poor, you won't want to linger on this exposed summit.

Continuing eastward, you may have to circumnavigate a snow cornice before beginning the descent to the headwaters of the Cascade River (the big drift often lingers into late July). It is a dramatic drop over steep, broken rock and through a boulder-filled basin, where you will likely lose the track. (Persevere through the rocks until you pick up the trail again.)

Approximately 7 km beyond the pass, you arrive at Block Lakes Junction Campground, situated on the flats where two tributary streams flow into the Cascade from Bonnet Peak to the north and Block Mountain to the south. The trail continues eastward along the north side of the Cascade River, rolling through forest and along willow flats on the wide track of an old fire road.

At km 38.9, just 100 m west of the Flint's Park Patrol Cabin, you reach a junction and bridge crossing to the south side of the Cascade River. While the main valley trail continues eastward for 8 km to intersect the Cascade Fire Road (see *Flint's Park*), you turn south, cross the bridge, and begin your ascent of Sawback Creek.

Flint's Park to Mystic Junction—12.5 km. The route up Sawback Creek follows a much-used horse trail, so expect mud and sloppy hiking until you reach Forty Mile Summit. A welcome break, and the major attraction on this leg of the journey, is Sawback Lake—a 2.2-km side trip that should be included in your itinerary. The lake, set beneath the eastern wall of the Sawback Range, has been popular with fishermen since the early years of the 20th century. A campground 0.8 km before you reach the lake is worth considering as a spot to overnight.

Continuing to Forty Mile Summit from Sawback Lake junction, you have a good viewpoint back to Sawback Lake as you crest the pass. At 2150 m, Forty Mile Summit is still below treeline, but you do pass through a long meadow bordered with alpine larch. Watch for the hiker's trail, which splits left from the horse trail on the pass and leads down along Forty Mile Creek to Mystic Lake junction.

Mystic Junction to Moose Meadows—21.1 km. At Mystic Lake Junction Campground, the hiker trail rejoins the horse trail and crosses to the west side of Forty Mile Creek. You are joined by a cut-off trail from lower Forty Mile Creek in less than a kilometre. Now you are headed west on the last leg of the circuit, which follows the same route as the Sawback Trail past Mystic Lake, over Mystic Pass and down the west side of the Sawback Range to the 7.4 km junction near Larry's Camp Campground in the Johnston Creek valley (see *Sawback Trail*, km 15.9 to km 29.3). From there, you retrace your steps down Johnston Creek valley to the Moose Meadows trailhead.

22 Rockbound Lake

Bow Valley Parkway to Rockbound Lake—8.4 km (5.2 mi)

Day trip

Allow 2.5 to 3 hours one way

Elevation gain: 760 m (2,500 ft)

Maximum elevation: 2210 m (7,250 ft)

Maps: Castle Mountain 82 0/5
    Banff-Egypt Lake (Gem Trek)

Access: Follow the Bow Valley Parkway
(Hwy 1A) to Castle Junction, 30 km
(18.5 mi) west of the town of Banff. The
paved parking area for the trail is on the
north side of the Parkway 200 m east of the
intersection and Castle Mountain Chalets.

0.0— Trailhead (1450 m).
     N51°16.142' W115°54.948'

— Follow old roadbed track.

0.3— Junction. Silverton Falls right 0.6 km;
     Rockbound Lake ahead.

— Gradual to moderate uphill grades.

5.0— Old roadbed narrows to single track.

5.3— Boggy and wet conditions during
     early season and rainy periods.

7.7— Tower Lake (2120 m).

— Trail skirts to right of lake and
  switchbacks up headwall.

8.4— Rockbound Lake (2210 m).

This rigorous hike to a high valley hidden behind the massive cliffs of Castle Mountain visits two distinctly different lakes; Tower is a placid, green mirror fringed by open subalpine forest and lush wildflower meadows; Rockbound is true to its name—a cold, grey sheet contained by steep talus slopes and massive, tumbled boulder-fields. Both lakes are overshadowed by the impressive Eisenhower Peak tower and the limestone cliffs of Castle Mountain.

The trail starts on an old access road, which provides little scenic interest as it climbs gradually along the southern flank of Castle Mountain for the first 2.4 km. Eventually it gains sufficient elevation to provide glimpses of the Bow Valley and the mountains to the west. Prominent are pyramid-shaped Copper Mountain and, to the south, Pilot Mountain, which served as a landmark to CPR surveyors charting the line of the railway down the valley in 1881. The trail, still following the old roadbed, continues its traverse around the end of Castle Mountain and finally enters the high valley running northwest between its ramparts and Helena Ridge.

At 5.0 km the trail narrows to a single track and, just a bit farther on, views open to the Eisenhower Tower on Castle Mountain, a 2752-m limestone pinnacle rising in front of the main body of the mountain. The trail beyond this point can be rather messy, particularly early in the season when the entire area is soggy from the melting snow.

An extensive meadow leads to Tower Lake, a small body of water set within a semicircle of rock. This appears to be the end of the journey, but the trail continues to the right of the lake and climbs steeply up the headwall beyond.

At the top of the cliff you catch your first view of Rockbound Lake and immediately appreciate the aptness of the name. It is totally enclosed by rock.

Rockbound Lake

Cathedral Formation limestone contains the bed of the lake, while Stephen and Eldon Formation limestone creates the high walls of the cirque. The lake lies precisely in the centre of a major down-fold in the strata—the Castle Mountain Syncline, which starts here and runs all the way to Mount Kerkeslin in Jasper Park, some 260 km to the northwest.

From the scattered forest of Engelmann spruce, alpine fir and larch at the top of the headwall, you can spend a full day exploring the Rockbound basin: huge boulders beyond the southern shore provide a playground for novice rock climbers; the slopes of Helena Ridge to the east are easily ascended for a better perspective of the amphitheatre; and experienced scramblers can ascend the main peak of Castle Mountain from the slopes beyond the lake's north shore (see Alan Kane's *Scrambles in the Canadian Rockies*).

Silverton Falls—0.9 km. A 50-m stair-case-style waterfall hidden in the forest off the Rockbound Lake trail near Castle Junction. Though this impressive waterfall is less than a kilometre from the Bow Valley Parkway, it is a natural feature few people know about or visit. The creek and falls are named for the nearby mining town of Silver City (Silverton was a name proposed for the town), which boomed briefly in 1883-84 then disappeared.

The short hike starts on the Rockbound Lake trail and branches right from that route at 0.3 km. Another 0.6 km through dense forest brings you to a viewpoint near the top of the falls. Total elevation gain for the trip is only 90 m.

23 Castle Lookout

Bow Valley Parkway to Castle Lookout—3.8 km (2.4 mi)

Half-day trip

Allow 1.5 to 2 hours one way

Elevation gain: 550 m (1,800 ft)

Maximum elevation: 2010 m (6,600 ft)

Maps: Castle Mountain 82 O/5
       Banff-Egypt Lake (Gem Trek)

Access: Follow the Bow Valley Parkway 4.8 km (3.0 mi) west from Castle Junction to the paved, trailhead parking area—set back in the forest on the north side of the road. The trail begins at the upper end of the parking area.

0.0— Trailhead (1460 m).
      N51°17.611' W115°58.468'

   — Steady moderate to steep uphill on old roadbed.

1.5— Old cabin.

2.2— Broad trail narrows to single track.

   — Moderate to steep uphill via switchbacks.

3.8— Castle Lookout (2010 m).

This short, steep trail up the slopes of Castle Mountain leads to the site of the old Mount Eisenhower fire lookout and an excellent panorama of the Bow Valley stretching from the grey limestone peaks near Banff to the glacier-capped summits near Lake Louise. Since it climbs along a slope with a southwesterly exposure, it is one of the earliest trails at this elevation to be free of snow in the spring (early to mid-May) and one of the latest to remain snowfree in autumn.

From the parking area, follow a steep, wide pathway upward through forest of lodgepole pine, spruce and occasional Douglas fir. The dense forest allows only a few glimpses of the Bow Valley over the first 2 km, but an old dilapidated cabin offers a stop of interest at 1.5 km (the collapsing structure possibly dates to the short-lived mining boom in this part of the valley circa 1884).

The broad trail eventually reverts to single-track 0.7 km beyond the cabin and traverses out onto the steep, sparsely forested slopes overlooking the Bow Valley. In early summer this open forest produces a colourful array of wildflowers, including Indian paintbrush, columbine, and heart-leaved arnica.

As you gain elevation, views up and down the Bow Valley improve. Finally the trail twists up through a cliff band, enters a stand of whitebark pine, and contours to the right above the precipice for 100 m to the old lookout site.

All that remains at the site is the foundation of the lookout cabin, which was constructed by labourers from the park's conscientious objector camps in the autumn of 1942. It was abandoned by Parks Canada in the mid-1970s and accidentally burned by visiting hikers in 1983.

Check yourself over closely for wood ticks after any early season trip to the lookout.

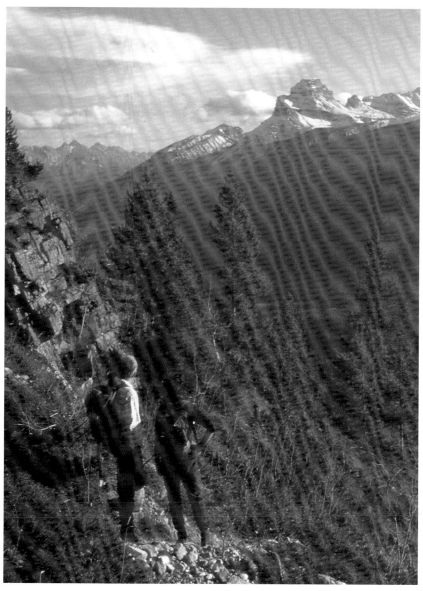

Pilot Mountain from the Castle Lookout trail

24 Bourgeau Lake

Trans-Canada Highway to Bourgeau Lake—7.5 km (4.6 mi)
Trans-Canada Highway to Harvey Pass—9.7 km (6.0 mi)

Day trip
Allow 2.5 to 3 hours to lake
Elevation gain: 725 m (2,380 ft)
Maximum elevation: 2160 m (7,100 ft)
Maps: Banff 82 O/4
      Banff-Egypt Lake (Gem Trek)

Access: Follow the Trans-Canada Highway (Hwy 1) to the Bourgeau Lake trailhead parking area, 2.8 km (1.7 mi) west of the Sunshine Village interchange. The parking area is set back in the forest on the southwest side of the twinned highway. (A cross-over road provides access from westbound lanes.)

0.0— Trailhead (1435 m).
      N51°10.086' W115°43.895'
    — Steady uphill via switchbacks, moderate.

1.6— Switchbacks end, trail climbs along southeast side of valley.

3.7— Tributary stream bridge.

5.5— Wolverine Creek crossing. Cascades.
    — Steep switchbacks.

6.8— Trail levels out into meadows.

7.5— Bourgeau Lake (2160 m).
    — Trail veers away from northwest side of lake and climbs steeply to obvious notch due west.

8.8— Small unnamed lake in alpine bowl.
    — Veer left and climb to pass.

9.7— Harvey Pass and Lake (2454 m).

Set within an amphitheatre carved from the limestone walls of the Massive Range, Bourgeau Lake exhibits a variety of subalpine and alpine scenery, flowers and wildlife. Its waters are bordered by alpine fir and larch stands, meadows and barren talus slopes, where ptarmigan, marmots and pikas pursue their daily chores. In spring, avalanches thunder down over Mount Bourgeau's cliffs and goats stroll placidly along the slopes of Mount Brett to the north. These attractions, coupled with some spectacular scenery on Harvey Pass above the lake, make this an outstanding full day's outing.

Striking off from a parking area beside the Trans-Canada Highway, the trail quickly buries itself in a forest of lodgepole pine and spruce, and after quickly gaining elevation via a series of switchbacks, climbs steadily along the southeast side of the Wolverine Creek valley. At km 2.4 views open back to the Bow Valley and the sharp, serrated peaks of the Sawback Range. The broad summit of Mount Brett (2984 m), the highest mountain in the Massive Range, dominates the scene ahead.

At km 5.5 the trail crosses Wolverine Creek, where the stream descends from the Bourgeau Lake cirque in a series of cascades. The foot of the waterfall is a good spot for rest and refreshment before tackling the steep switchbacks that complete the climb to a long, streamside meadow leading to the lake.

The amphitheatre containing the lake is carved into the northwest side of Mount Bourgeau (2930 m). Like other peaks in the range, its cliffs are formed by Devonian and Mississippian limestones and shales—formations bearing fossils of brachiopods, corals, and other examples of early ocean life. Dr. James Hector named the mountain for the French botanist Eugene Bourgeau, his

Bourgeau Lake

comrade-in-exploration with the Palliser Expedition during the summer of 1858.

Snowbanks often linger in the meadows bordering the lake until mid-July, their meltwaters feeding a wide variety of subalpine wildflowers. White-tailed ptarmigan are sometimes seen along the lake's outlet stream or in the nearby talus slopes, their mottled summer plumage making them all but invisible among the piles of broken rock. Pikas, golden-mantled ground squirrels and chipmunks scurry back and forth through the boulders, closely watching passing hikers for a possible handout.

Harvey Pass. You can explore above the lake to an alpine basin and pass, which lies 2.2 km beyond and 295-vertical metres higher up. A path follows above the forested north shore of Bourgeau Lake then climbs steeply toward the obvious notch where a stream drops from between Mounts Bourgeau and Brett. After some strenuous climbing, the track skirts a small, rockbound lake and emerges into an open alpine bowl complete with small ponds.

While this lofty cirque is quite pleasant, you will want to continue climbing south to the obvious pass at the foot of Mount Bourgeau's long summit ridge. In less than 15 minutes you crest Harvey Pass (2454 m) and are greeted with an exceptional view south to the towering pyramid of Mount Assiniboine. Harvey Lake is a small tarn cradled on the summit and, like the pass, is named for Ralph Harvey, who was a manager for Banff's Brewster Transport Co. and involved in the development of skiing at nearby Sunshine Village.

If you are a very strong hiker and got an early start, you can cap your day's outing by climbing the long ridge to the summit of Mount Bourgeau—one of the easiest 2900-m-plus peaks in the Rockies.

Sunshine Meadows

The Sunshine Meadows region is unique in the Canadian Rockies. Unlike most of the Great Divide, which is composed of glaciated peaks and towering limestone and quartzite walls, the 15-km stretch of the divide between Citadel Pass and Monarch Ramparts is a mixture of rolling subalpine and alpine meadowland. Pacific weather systems flowing in from the west add their moisture to create a vast, rolling rock garden with an incredible variety of wildflowers, some of which appear nowhere else in the range.

In the centre of this exceptional landscape is the Sunshine Village ski area—a lofty 2200-m (7,218-ft) starting point for all hikes leading into Sunshine Meadows and along the crest of the Great Divide. Of several popular trips, the 1.8-km trail to Rock Isle Lake is the shortest and most popular, the Sunshine Meadows Loop (and its options) provides the best panoramas and wildflowers, and the 18.6-km round-trip to Citadel Pass is the longest and most demanding. Most of the hikes can be comfortably completed in five hours or less, and all have fine views of Mount Assiniboine, "the Matterhorn of the Rockies."

In winter, Sunshine is reached via a 5-km-long gondola lift, but the gondola doesn't run during the summer and most visitors use the shuttle bus that makes hourly trips on the 6-km service road between the gondola base parking area and the ski area day lodge. You can also hike or bike the service road, but it is a long, arduous approach for day-hikers and a steep climb for cyclists (bikes are only allowed as far as the day lodge).

The day lodge contains a deli and gift shop. During foul weather, the lodge is a welcome refuge, while on a warm afternoon the deck is a pleasant place to relax at day's end while awaiting the shuttle.

You also have the option of camping in the meadows. Backpackers can bus or hike up the access road then follow the Citadel Pass trail another 5.8 km to Howard Douglas Lake Campground (Su8). From this base camp, you can make easy day trips to Citadel Pass, Rock Isle Lake and other points of interest.

All trails in the following Sunshine Meadows section are described for the majority of hikers who use the shuttle bus and start from Sunshine Village.

Access: Follow the Trans-Canada Highway to the Sunshine Village interchange, 9 km (5.5 mi) west of the town of Banff. Continue on the Sunshine Road for another 9 km to the parking area at the gondola base station (N51°06.922' W115°45.771'). The access road to Sunshine Village starts at a gate to the left of the gondola base station, and the *Healy Pass* trail begins from the parking area to the right, immediately behind the base station.

Shuttle buses to Sunshine Village depart from the gondola base station throughout the morning and afternoon. Return trips to the parking area follow a similar schedule throughout the morning and afternoon until 5:30 p.m. There is also direct service from downtown Banff at additional cost.

As of 2015, adult round-trip fares are $27, and fares for children (3-12 years) $16. Backpackers hiking to Assiniboine and other destinations, or arriving from those distant locales, can purchase a one-way fare for $16. Reservations for shuttle services should be made in advance by contacting White Mountain Adventures (see *Sources—Backcountry access* for contact information).

Pilot Mtn▲

N

1A

18

Lake Louise

Creek

1

Banff

▲Mt
Brett

24

Wolverine

Bourgeau
Lake

Mt▲
Bourgeau

Sunshine Road

Brewster

Harvey Pass

70

Creek

P
Gondola

Creek

Healy

Access Road

Eagle
Mtn▲

33
Egypt Lake

Healy
Pass

Mt▲
Howard Douglas

ALBERTA

BRITISH COLUMBIA

28

27

Sunshine
Village

BR T

Twin
Cairns

V

Lookout
▲Mtn

25

Grizzly
Lake

Rock Isle
Lake

Eohippus
Lake

Larix
Lake

The ▲
Monarch

26

MOUNT

Quartz
▲Hill

Howard
Douglas Lake

ASSINIBOINE

Fatigue
▲Mtn

71

Simpson

Citadel
Pass

PARK

Citadel Pk

Fatigue
Pass

River

Assiniboine

212

Land above 2300 metres

0   1   2   3   4   5km

25 Sunshine Meadows Loop

Sunshine Village to Rock Isle Lake Viewpoint—1.8 km (1.1 mi)
Sunshine Meadows Loop—6.3 km (3.9 mi)

Half-day trip

Allow 40 minutes to Rock Isle Lake

Elevation gain: 105 m (350 ft)
loss: 25 m (80 ft)

Maximum elevation: 2305 m (7,560 ft)

Maps: Banff 82 O/4
Banff-Egypt Lake (Gem Trek)

Access: Travel to Sunshine Village as described in the Sunshine Meadows area introduction. From the trail sign above the day lodge, follow a gravel road leading uphill to the southeast.

0.0—Trailhead (2200 m).
N51°04.712' W115°46.942'

—Gravel road leading uphill.

0.1—Junction. Trail branches left from road immediately above Avalanche Control cabin.

—Steady uphill through meadows.

1.2—Great Divide (2305 m). Alberta-B.C. boundary.

1.3—Junction. Citadel Pass trail left; Rock Isle Lake ahead.

1.8—Rock Isle Lake viewpoint (2280 m).

—Trail continues around lake to right.

2.0—Junction. Rock Isle Lake outlet and Grizzly-Larix Lakes left; stay right for Standish Viewpoint and Twin Cairns-Meadow Park.

—Steady climb along Standish Ridge.

2.4—Junction. Standish Viewpoint right 0.3 km; Twin Cairns-Meadow Park trail ahead.

—Gradual climb through alpine meadows.

4.6—Junction. Wawa Summit (0.3 km) and *Simpson Pass-Healy Meadows* to left. Sunshine Village via Meadow Park trail right.

—Steady descent via meadows, ski run and forest.

6.3—Sunshine Village day lodge (2180 m).
N51°04.812' W115°46.937'

In the early morning, the waters of Rock Isle Lake are often a mirror reflecting its rocky island and shoreline. There is a peacefulness and natural symmetry in the scene, including distant peaks in British Columbia that has attracted artists and photographers for many decades.

While the trip to the Rock Isle Lake viewpoint and back can be completed in little more than an hour, most hikers extend their outing by hiking all or part of the Sunshine Meadows Loop, which circles back between Standish Ridge and Twin Cairns peak to the Meadow Park trail. There are several variations possible along this circuit: most consider the climb to 2400-m Standish Viewpoint and its unparalleled panorama of the meadows a must; another popular add-on is the short loop trip down into the lush wildflower meadows surrounding Grizzly and Larix Lakes; and if you do make it to Meadow Park, you'll want to make the 0.3-km side-trip to Wawa Summit (aka Monarch Viewpoint). The entire loop, with all the options, encompasses a total distance of only 12 km and what is certainly one of the finest day trips in the Rockies.

The trail to Rock Isle Lake is usually very busy, as are the options to Grizzly-Larix Lakes and Standish Viewpoint that lie beyond. Following a broad gravel track from the centre of Sunshine Village, you make a steady but brief climb to the Great Divide, passing through the last scattered stands of alpine fir into a treeless alpine landscape. (Columbian ground squirrels will greet you as you climb, bounding through fields of tall, fuzzy western anemones gone-to-seed.) On the 2300-m summit, views stretch south across the vast Sunshine Meadows to the distant pyramid of Mount Assiniboine (a scene somewhat diminished by the presence of ski lifts).

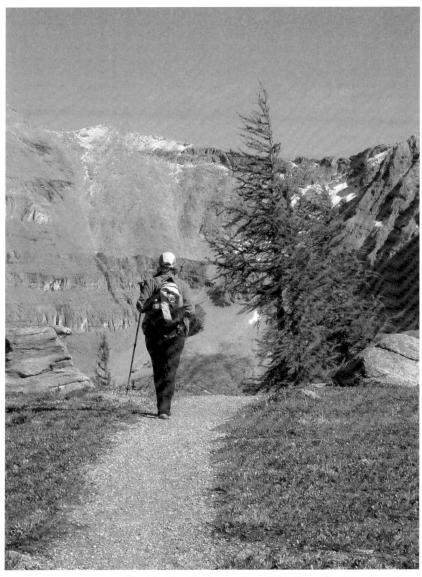

The Meadow Park section of the Sunshine Meadows Loop

West of the divide, you enter British Columbia and Mount Assiniboine Provincial Park, passing the *Quartz Hill-Citadel Pass* trail junction and descending to Rock Isle Lake viewpoint. Meadow, limestone outcrops and a few islands of alpine fir surround the lake, which serves as a perfect window across the north end of Mount Assiniboine Park to the sharp peaks that form the eastern boundary of Kootenay National Park. Benches at this contained viewpoint are a good place to rest and contemplate your next move.

Beyond this classic overlook of the lake, the trail narrows and follows above the shoreline to the right. Just 0.3 km

Rock Isle Lake

past the viewpoint, you reach a junction, where you must make a decision—stay left on the trail to Grizzly and Larix Lakes or go right and climb to Standish Viewpoint and the Twin Cairns-Meadow Park trail. And as many do, you can do both options.

Grizzly-Larix Lakes Loop. Most hikers include these two meadow-fringed lakes in their itinerary, even though it means they lose 55 m of elevation from Rock Isle Lake and add 3.5 km to their day's total. After passing the junction for the Standish Viewpoint/Twin Cairns-Meadow Park trail at km 2.0, the trail climbs over a low, rocky hill to where the Rock Isle's outlet stream plunges down steep limestone slabs. From this wonderful natural waterslide, you see Larix and Grizzly Lakes below and, across the Simpson Valley, the distant peaks of Kootenay Park.

Continuing beyond the lake's outlet, the trail drops through open forest and lush meadows filled with wildflowers. Soon the trail splits to begin a 2.5-km loop around Grizzly and Larix Lakes. Keep right and descend to Grizzly Lake

in 0.5 km. From the lake's inlet bridge, the trail turns left and contours the lip of the basin to a fine viewpoint for the Simpson Valley.

Larix, the largest of the two lakes, is just beyond the viewpoint. The lake lies between meadow and larch forest (the Latin botanical name for alpine larch is *Larix lyallii*, hence the lake's name.) You follow the shoreline for nearly a kilometre before climbing back to the loop split and returning to Rock Isle Lake.

Standish Viewpoint. Another popular side-trip from Rock Isle Lake is Standish Viewpoint, which provides an unparalleled panorama of the Sunshine Meadows region. Follow the Twin Cairns-Meadow Park trail, which branches uphill from the 2.0-km junction above the northwest corner of Rock Isle Lake. Climb 0.4 km through thinning forest to Standish Viewpoint junction and then another 0.3 km to the viewing platform near the top of 2420-m Standish Ridge.

Rock Isle, Larix and Grizzly Lakes lie below the viewpoint to the south, while the route to Citadel Pass can be traced

Looking down to Rock Isle Lake from Standish Viewpoint

across the vast meadows to the southeast to Quartz Hill and Citadel Peak. The distinctive summit of Mount Assiniboine (3618 m) rises beyond Quartz Hill, and to the west a sea of peaks form the ranges of Kootenay National Park.

Wildflowers on this windswept ridge, like alpine forget-me-not and moss campion, are adapted to the harsh dry conditions on this windswept slope, and white-tailed ptarmigan with chicks are sometimes seen along the trail.

Twin Cairns-Meadow Park. Though the majority of hikers return to Sunshine Village via Rock Isle Lake following their climb to Standish Viewpoint, we usually continue along the less-travelled trail running beneath Twin Cairns peak to Meadow Park. Back on the main trail below the viewpoint, you continue north and immediately enter the shallow alpine valley between Standish Ridge and Twin Cairns. The trail runs over this flat, open meadow for nearly 2 km to a junction with the Simpson Pass trail, passing beside small pools fringed with the white-tufts of cotton grass and crossing several small streams. Grizzly bears

have visited this vale in recent years, digging up the landscape in search of tasty ground squirrels.

At the junction with the Simpson Pass trail, you should make the 300-m detour to the Wawa Summit, a shallow pass between Twin Cairns and Wawa Ridge. Known by some locals as Monarch Viewpoint, it is just that, a wonderful vantage point for the impressive pyramid-peak called The Monarch to the southwest and the long ridge of Monarch Ramparts leading to Healy Pass to the west.

As you descend back to Sunshine Village on the Meadow Park trail, there are more expansive views out across Sunshine Meadows toward Quartz Ridge and Mount Assiniboine. Ahead, directly across the valley, is Lookout Mountain (2730 m), identified as Brewster Rock on topo maps; its summit forms the border between Alberta and British Columbia, and the Continental Divide Quad Chairlift that runs to a point just below the peak is Canada's highest ski lift.

Views dwindle as you make a steep descent along a ski run and then a forest trail back to the day lodge.

26 Quartz Hill—Citadel Pass

Sunshine Village to Quartz Hill—5.2 km (3.2 mi)
Sunshine Village to Citadel Pass—9.3 km (5.8 mi)

Day trip or backpack

Allow 2.5 to 3 hours to Citadel Pass

Elevation gain: 195 m (640 ft)
loss: 115 m (375 ft)

Maximum elevation: 2395 m (7,850 ft)

Maps: Banff 82 O/4
Banff-Egypt Lake (Gem Trek)

Access: Travel to Sunshine Village as described in the Sunshine Meadows area introduction. From the trail sign above the day lodge, follow a gravel road leading uphill to the southeast.

0.0— Trailhead (2200 m).
N51°04.712' W115°46.942'

— Gravel road leading uphill.

0.1— Junction. Trail branches left from road immediately above Avalanche Control cabin.

— Steady uphill through meadows.

1.2— Great Divide (2305 m). Alberta-B.C. boundary.

1.3— Junction. *Rock Isle Lake* ahead 0.5 km; Citadel Pass left.

— Flat followed by gradual descent across open meadows.

4.7— Trail begins climb over east ridge of Quartz Hill.

5.2— Quartz Hill east ridge (2395 m).

— Steep descent.

5.8— Howard Douglas Lake and Campground (Su8).

7.4— Citadel Lake (150 m off-trail to right).

— Gradual climb through meadows.

9.3— Citadel Pass (2360 m). Junction.
Fatigue Pass left 2.5 km;
Mt Assiniboine ahead 18.2 km.
(See *Mount Assiniboine via Citadel Pass*.)

The trail to Quartz Hill and Citadel Pass is one of the most scenic hikes from Sunshine Village. Rolling up and down through the heart of the Sunshine Meadows, it crosses and recrosses the Great Divide, weaving back and forth between Alberta and British Columbia. Highlights include wildflower meadows, which are justifiably renowned as some of the finest in the Rockies, and views of Mount Assiniboine and countless ranges to the south and west.

If you use the shuttle bus to and from Sunshine Village, it is a real whirlwind trip to reach Citadel Pass and then get back to catch the last bus down in the late afternoon. Most hikers only go as far as the east ridge of Quartz Hill, the highest point on the trail and a good viewpoint for the southern reaches of the meadows. If you do decide to continue to the pass, you may have to walk down the access road in the evening, which makes for a long 25-km day. Another option is to camp at Howard Douglas Lake, which allows for a more leisurely day trip to both Citadel and Fatigue Passes.

The trail starts from the centre of Sunshine Village and follows the same route as the *Rock Isle Lake* hike for the first 1.3 km. Just beyond the 2305-m summit on the Alberta-B.C. boundary, the Citadel trail branches left from the Rock Isle route (Rock Isle Lake viewpoint is only 0.5 km beyond the junction and a worthwhile side-trip).

From the junction you cross a vast alpine meadow for more than 1.0 km before invisibly re-entering Alberta and gradually descending into scattered forest. The trail flattens out briefly across a meadow then ascends steeply through stands of alpine fir and larch to Quartz Hill's east ridge.

This high vantage point is a good destination for those lacking time or energy to continue farther. Howard Douglas

Descending from Quartz Hill to Sunshine Meadows

Lake lies below the ridge to the southeast, and a long line of meadows and scattered forest stretches away beyond the lake to Citadel Pass, cradled between Citadel Peak and Fatigue Mountain.

Quartz Hill was described by boundary surveyor A.O. Wheeler in 1913 as "a prominent hill, with a crest of broken blocks of quartz, falling very steeply on the south west side to form the valley of the Simpson River." It is one of several rocky promontories rising from the Sunshine Meadows.

Continuing beyond the summit, the trail drops sharply to the shores of Howard Douglas Lake. The campground near its outlet is quite scenic and, with the exception of the mosquitoes, a good base for exploring the surrounding meadows and ridges.

Another small lake, Citadel, lies off to the right of the trail less than 2 km beyond Howard Douglas, its basin set beneath in a gap that serves as a window to Mount Assiniboine. This is one of the best views of this famous 3618-m "horn" peak from the Sunshine Meadows trail system. Though the summit seems to loom near, it is over 15 km away.

Citadel Pass offers several options if you have the time and a yen for exploration. One of the most interesting is the climb to Fatigue Pass—a 2395-m crest to the southeast, which can be reached in an hour or less. A trail runs to this high summit, but the junction on Citadel Pass is vague, so scan the slopes above for the obvious track leading across the scree to the pass. (See also *Fatigue Creek.*)

The main trail continues over Citadel Pass and back into British Columbia's Mount Assiniboine Provincial Park. This is one of the popular access routes to Lake Magog at the base of Mount Assiniboine, and at this point you are one-third of the way there. (See *Mount Assiniboine via Citadel Pass*, Mount Assiniboine Park chapter.)

27 Simpson Pass—Healy Meadows

Sunshine Village to Healy Meadows Junction—7.6 km (4.7 mi)
Healy Meadows Junction to Sunshine Parking Lot—7.7 km (4.8 mi)

Day trip

Allow 2 hours to Healy Meadows

Elevation gain: 180 m (590 ft)
      loss: 225 m (740 ft)

Maximum elevation: 2360 m (7,750 ft)

Maps: Banff 82 O/4
      Banff-Egypt Lake (Gem Trek)

Access: Travel to Sunshine Village as described in the Sunshine Meadows area introduction. Walk downhill from the day lodge to the trailhead, located to the left at the base of the Wawa quad chairlift.

0.0—Trailhead (2180 m).
      N51°04.812' W115°46.937'

  —Steady uphill along open ski run.

1.6—Junction. Twin Cairns-Meadow Park trail left. Simpson Pass ahead.

1.9—Wawa Ridge summit (2360 m).

  —Gradual descent.

5.6—Simpson Pass (2135 m).

  —Steep uphill.

6.0—Junction. Eohippus Lake left 3.2 km. Healy Meadows ahead.

  —Trail levels out into Healy Meadows.

7.6—Junction (2180 m). Intersection with *Healy Pass-Egypt Lake trail*. Healy Pass left 1.5 km; Sunshine Parking Lot right 7.7 km.

While Simpson Pass and the Healy Meadows can be reached by ascending Healy Creek from the Sunshine Parking Lot, the shortest, easiest and most scenic approach is from Sunshine Village via Wawa Ridge. It is a route that can be used by day hikers looking for a scenically varied trip from Sunshine Village or as a highline option by backpackers bound for Healy Pass and Egypt Lake (see *Bow Valley Highline Trail*).

Ascending the most northerly ski run on Wawa Ridge, the first 1.9 km climbs directly through the upper fringes of subalpine forest to the treeless summit of the ridge—the route's highest elevation and best viewpoint. The panorama includes the Citadel Pass region and Mount Assiniboine to the southeast, and the massive pyramid of The Monarch to the southwest. Small ponds fringed with cotton grass dot the meadows and, like many open areas in the Sunshine region, the ridge is a wildflower-lover's dream.

Beyond Wawa Ridge the trail descends back into stands of alpine fir and larch. After following beneath a low escarpment for nearly 2 km, it drops into a small meadow on the summit of Simpson Pass. Here a trail from Healy Creek intersects from the right—an optional route of descent to the Sunshine Parking Lot.

The pass was crossed by Sir George Simpson, governor of the Hudson's Bay Company, in the summer of 1841. It was a disappointment as an improved route for the company's fur brigades bound for the Oregon territory, but Sir George did linger long enough to allow his guide to carve their initials and the date in a tree. The artifact was discovered and salvaged by local outfitter Jim Brewster in 1904 and now resides at the Banff Park Museum.

From the Simpson Pass meadow, the trail stays on the Alberta side of the divide

The Monarch and Healy Meadows from near Healy Pass

and begins its climb to the Healy Meadows. Just before reaching the meadows, 0.4 km beyond the pass, a trail branches left to Eohippus Lake—an interesting 3.2-km side-trip for strong hikers who have time and energy to spare.

Just beyond the Eohippus junction, you reach the southeastern edge of the Healy Meadows beside a small lake. This lake was once the hideout of legendary outfitter and park warden Bill Peyto, and the remains of his cabin lie hidden in the forest beyond the lake's north shore. (If you find it, please leave this important historic site undisturbed!)

The trail continues for another kilometre through lake-studded meadows beneath the long ridge of the Monarch Ramparts. If you hike here from mid-July to mid-August, you will be greeted by one of the most luxuriant wildflower gardens in the Rockies—a vast snowbed community filled with the blooms of western anemone, Indian paintbrush, valerian, fleabane, ragwort, globe flower, marsh marigold and many, many more.

At km 7.6 you reach an intersection with the Healy Pass trail. While you can turn around here and hustle back to Sunshine to catch the last shuttle back to the lower parking lot, we prefer to walk back to the parking area on the Healy Pass trail (it is the same distance and all downhill). But first, we usually take the 1.5-km side-trip up to Healy Pass (2330 m), where we enjoy more wildflowers and a panoramic overview of the Egypt Lake region. And some energetic hikers even follow the crest of the Monarch Ramparts (faint trail and cairns) to Eohippus Lake before returning to Sunshine or the lower parking area.

Healy Meadows-Simpson Pass Circuit. If you don't want to bus to Sunshine Village, you can follow the Healy Pass trail from the Sunshine Parking Lot to access the Healy Meadows and Simpson Pass. (See *Healy Pass-Egypt Lake*.)

28 Healy Pass—Egypt Lake

Sunshine Parking Lot to Healy Pass—9.2 km (5.7 mi)
Sunshine Parking Lot to Egypt Lake Campground—12.4 km (7.7 mi)

Day trip or backpack

Allow 2.5 to 3 hours to Healy Pass
3 to 4 hours to Egypt Lake

Elevation gain: 655 m (2,150 ft)
　　　　　loss: 335 m (1,100 ft)

Maximum elevation: 2330 m (7,650 ft)

Maps: Banff 82 O/4
　　　Banff-Egypt Lake (Gem Trek)

Access: Follow the Trans-Canada Highway to the Sunshine Village interchange, 9 km (5.5 mi) west of the town of Banff. Continue on the Sunshine Road for another 9 km to the parking lot at the gondola base station. Stay right to the Healy Pass trailhead parking area, immediately behind the base station.

0.0— Trailhead (1675 m).
　　　N51°06.895' W115°45.890'

　　— Follow broad track uphill.

0.8— Junction. Sunshine Village ahead; Healy Pass right.

3.1— Healy Creek bridge.

5.2— Old cabin foundation.

5.5— Healy Creek Campground (E5).

5.9— Junction. Simpson Pass left 1.3 km; Healy Pass ahead.

　　— Trail begins to climb.

7.7— Junction (2180 m). *Simpson Pass* left 2.0 km; Healy Pass ahead.

　　— Steady climb through Healy Meadows.

9.2— Healy Pass (2330 m).

　　— Steady downhill.

12.1— Junction. Egypt Lake Patrol Cabin right 50 m. Keep left.

12.2— Junction. Talc Lake left 4.2 km; campground and shelter ahead across bridge and meadow.

12.4— Egypt Lake Campground (E13) and Shelter (1995 m). Intersection with *Pharaoh Creek* trail.

Healy Pass and the vast wildflower meadows leading to its summit are a popular destination for hikers who are up for a full day of wandering and exploration. Though the pass is not exceptionally high, views are as rewarding as any in the park—a panorama of nearly every peak along a 70-km stretch of the Great Divide from Mount Assiniboine to Storm Mountain. The trail is also the favourite access route to Banff's most popular backcountry campground at Egypt Lake.

Climbing from the parking lot behind the Sunshine gondola base station, the trail follows a wide, bulldozed track for nearly a kilometre before cutting off onto a more aesthetic forest path. Gradually, but steadily, the trail ascends the Healy Creek valley, rising from a dense canopy of Engelmann spruce and alpine fir to subalpine meadows where wildflowers bloom in lush profusion from mid-July to late August.

The climb finally culminates among the last scattered alpine larch on Healy Pass. Since there are no nearby mountains blocking the view, this 2330-m pass at the north end of the Monarch Ramparts ridge offers an excellent overview of the surrounding landscape.

The block of peaks beyond the ridge to the northeast is the Massive Range, dominated by Mount Brett on the left and Mount Bourgeau to the right. Nearly 30 km to the southeast, rising high above all its neighbouring peaks, is the 3618-m "horn" of Mount Assiniboine—the highest mountain in the Canadian Rockies south of the Columbia Icefield. Less than 6 km away, at the south end of the Monarch Ramparts, is the massive pyramid called The Monarch. Due west of the pass, stacked beneath the Pharaoh Peaks, are Egypt and Scarab Lakes.

Eohippus Lake and Mount Assiniboine from Monarch Ramparts

Egypt Lakes. Most backpackers travel to the Egypt Lakes area by way of Healy Pass since it is both the shortest and most scenic approach. Continuing northwest over the summit of the pass, the trail drops rapidly through the forest to Pharaoh Creek in just over 3 km. Just 50 m past a right-hand spur trail to the Egypt Lake Patrol Cabin, you reach the creekside Talc Lake trail junction and a bridge. Cross the bridge to the campground and shelter on the rise ahead.

Since all major trails for the area radiate from the campground, it is ideally situated as a base camp for short half-day trips. (See *Egypt Lakes* introduction.)

Monarch Ramparts-Eohippus Lake. If you day-hiked to Healy Pass, and your legs are up for a 24-km day, you can spend another couple hours in the alpine by following the crest of the Monarch Ramparts south approximately 7 km to Eohippus Lake in Mount Assiniboine Provincial Park. (There is faint trail and cairns, but the route is open and obvious.) From this fine, flower-bordered lake, follow good trail back across the divide to Simpson Pass and follow the connector trail down to the 5.9-km junction on Healy Creek trail.

Or if you'd like a bit of variety without so many extra kilometers, return to the 7.7-km junction and follow the Healy Meadows-Simpson Pass trail south through the meadows and down to Simpson Pass and then the connector trail down to the 5.9-km junction on the Healy Creek trail. This option only adds 1.5 km to the trip back from the pass. (See also *Simpson Pass-Healy Meadows*.)

29 Egypt Lake via Pharaoh Creek

Trans-Canada Highway to Egypt Lake Campground—19.2 km (11.9 mi)

Backpack

Allow 5 to 6 hours one way

Elevation gain: 595 m (1,950 ft)

Maximum elevation: 1995 m (6,550 ft)

Maps: Banff 82 O/4
     Banff-Egypt Lake (Gem Trek)

Access: Follow the Trans-Canada Highway (Hwy 1) to the Redearth Creek parking area, located on the south side of the highway 20 km (12.5 mi) west of Banff or 10.5 km (6.5 mi) east of Castle Junction. (A crossover road provides access from westbound lanes.) The trail begins at a step-up gate through the wildlife control fence at the rear of the parking area.

0.0— Trailhead (1400 m).
     N51°13.206' W115°48.227'

   — Broad gravel trail through forest.

0.4— Trail joins old roadbed.

6.9— Redearth Creek bridge. Lost Horse Creek Campground (Re6).

10.5— Junction. Shadow Lake right 3.5 km; Pharaoh Creek ahead.

10.7— Redearth Creek Patrol Cabin.

   — Trail makes gradual ascent of Pharaoh Valley.

14.7— Pharaoh Creek Campground (Re16).

18.7— Junction. Pharaoh Lake right; Egypt Lake ahead.

19.2— Egypt Lake Campground (E13) and Shelter (1995 m). Intersection with the Bow Valley Highline and Healy Pass trails.

Hiking to the Egypt Lakes area by way of Redearth and Pharaoh Creeks is longer and not nearly as scenic as the popular approach over Healy Pass. However, this valley-bottom route is usually snow-free a week or two earlier in the season than the pass. The trail is sometimes used as an exit from Egypt Lakes (downhill all the way!) by those who arrange transportation between the Redearth Creek and Healy Pass trailheads. It also serves as the first (or last) leg of the Egypt Lakes-Shadow Lake circuit trip (see below).

Starting from the Redearth Creek trailhead on the Trans-Canada Highway, the route follows up the Redearth Valley at an easy grade to the Pharaoh Creek junction at km 10.5 (see *Redearth Creek-Shadow Lake*). From the junction, you pass the Redearth Patrol Cabin and immediately enter the Pharaoh Creek valley. Continue to gain elevation gradually, before reaching the Pharaoh Creek Campground. Over the last few kilometres to Egypt Lake Campground, there are open meadows with views of the Pharaoh Peaks.

Egypt Lakes-Whistling Pass-Shadow Lake Circuit. This loop trip samples some of the best scenery on the Bow Valley Highline Trail without the hassle of arranging transportation between distant trailheads. The clockwise approach follows the Pharaoh Creek route to Egypt Lakes, the Bow Valley Highline over Whistling Pass to Shadow Lake, and Redearth Creek back to your starting point. (There are no particular disadvantages to doing the circuit counterclockwise.) This three- to four-day trip covers a total distance of 46 km. (See also *Bow Valley Highline Trail* and *Redearth Creek-Shadow Lake*.)

Land above 2300 metres

0 1 2 3 4 5km

Egypt Lakes

"After thirty years of exploration, surveys and mapping of the main ranges of the Canadian Rockies, the writer can safely say that outstanding among them for scenic charm and interest may be classed the group of peaks, lakes and alpine meadows of the Egypt Lake area...."

—A.O. Wheeler, 1939

Pretty strong words coming from the founder of the Alpine Club of Canada and the man who surveyed the Great Divide. With that sort of endorsement, it is little wonder the Egypt Lakes area is the most popular backpacking destination in Banff Park.

The area is located near the Great Divide just 25 km west of the town of Banff. Though there is only one Egypt Lake, the names of other nearby lakes—Scarab, Mummy, Pharaoh and Sphinx—have resulted in the term Egypt Lakes being applied to the area. In fact, A.O. Wheeler was responsible for naming all of the lakes when he surveyed this section of the Alberta-British Columbia boundary in 1913; the two pyramid-shaped Pharaoh Peaks overlooking the lakes had already been named, so he decided to stick with the Egyptian theme.

The Egypt Lake Campground, situated in a meadow 0.8 km from Egypt Lake, is the only campground in the core area and the primary destination for most backpackers. There is also a shelter cabin that accommodates 12 overnight guests; opened in 1969, it is one of only two such shelters ever constructed by Parks Canada in the mountain parks. The campground is perfectly situated as a base for half-day trips to all of the aforementioned lakes and Talc (Natalko) Lake, just over the divide in British Columbia. (All of these hikes are described on the following pages.)

This is all very nice, but the campground and shelter are very popular, and because of this popularity, site quotas are often filled. To insure a campsite or space in the shelter, you can reserve up to 3 months before your trip by contacting the Banff Visitor Centre (see *Sources—Park information*). There is an additional fee for staying at the shelter.

Of course, you don't have to stay at the central campground-shelter. The Pharaoh Creek (Re16) and Ball Pass Jct (Re21) Campgrounds are within easy reach of Egypt Lake and Whistling Pass, allowing backpackers to move through the area and still sample some of the best side trips (see Egypt Lakes-Whistling Pass-Shadow Lake Circuit described in *Egypt Lake via Pharaoh Creek* trail). And guests at Shadow Lake Lodge and Campground (Re14), travelling light, can complete a 25-km loop in a single day from there.

Access: There are three possible routes to the Egypt Lakes: the shortest and most scenic approach is the 12.4-km trail running over Healy Pass from the Sunshine Parking Lot at end of the Sunshine Road (see *Healy Pass-Egypt Lake*); a route following Redearth and Pharaoh Creeks is longer (19.2 km) and travels along valley bottoms, but there is less elevation gain and the ascent is gradual (see *Egypt Lake via Pharaoh Creek*); and backpackers hiking the Bow Valley Highline Trail from north to south, descend into the area from Whistling Pass (see *Bow Valley Highline Trail*).

Egypt Lake

Egypt Lakes Area Hikes

All of the following hikes are described from the Egypt Lake Campground.

Egypt Lake—0.8 km. The lowest of the Egypt Lakes at 2025 m, the area's namesake is a placid, green body of water bordered by forest and backed by a low, cone-shaped peak unofficially called Sugarloaf Mountain. Egypt Lake is usually the first place campers visit, often as an after-dinner stroll, following the day's backpack to Egypt Lake Campground.

This short, flat walk begins on the Whistling Pass trail, which runs southwest from the campground. Follow the trail through the forest for 0.5 km to where the 0.3-km side trail to Egypt Lake branches left.

Whistling Pass—3.3 km. No trip to Egypt Lakes is complete without visiting the Whistling Valley—a 2300-m pass providing far-reaching views along the eastern escarpment of the Great Divide. Along the way, you will want to include the 1.4-km side-trip to Scarab and Mummy Lakes—two tarns cradled in glacier-carved basins just above Egypt Lake. The round trip to Whistling Pass, including Scarab and Mummy, is 9.4 km, and can easily be completed in a half-day from the campground.

Follow the trail running southwest from the campground. After passing the Egypt Lake junction at 0.5 km, the trail switchbacks steeply upward through forest and over rockslides before descending into a larch-fringed meadow. In the middle of this meadow, at km 1.9, the trail to Scarab and Mummy Lakes branches left from the Whistling Valley trail.

Beyond Scarab-Mummy junction, the main trail continues upwards and bends northwest into the pass—a narrow rocky gap sandwiched between Haiduk Peak and Pharaoh Peaks. Views north extend over Haiduk Lake and Valley to glacier-crowned Mount Ball (3311 m), while Scarab Lake sparkles back to the south. And if they haven't become jaded by the continual passage of hikers, you will hear the long, shrill whistle of the resident hoary marmots, which gives the pass its name.

If you are backpacking through the Egypt Lakes region on the Bow Valley Highline route, Whistling Pass will be part of your itinerary. (See *Bow Valley Highline Trail*.)

Scarab-Mummy Lakes—3.3 km. From the 1.9-km junction on the Whistling Pass hike, the Scarab-Mummy Lakes trail descends through scattered stands of alpine larch and wildflower meadows for 0.6 km to the shore of Scarab Lake. The lake is bordered by subalpine forest and backed by scree slopes and cliffs, and its outlet stream makes a spectacular leap over a 100-m cliff to Egypt Lake below.

Continue to Mummy Lake by crossing at Scarab's outlet and scrambling up a short, steep track to a trail split beneath a cliff. The right branch ascends a 10-m escarpment to a meadow overlooking the lake's north end; the left branch takes a longer but somewhat easier route to the lake's east shore.

Mummy's setting is as high and wild as any lake in the Rockies—surrounded by alpine meadow, talus, cliffs and, at its far end, a gap in the divide that serves as a window to distant mountains in British Columbia.

Pharaoh-Black Rock Lakes—2.4 km. This trail climbs to a pair of cirque lakes high on the eastern slope of the Pharaoh Peaks. It is one of the shortest trips from Egypt Lake Campground, but you gain 240 m of elevation in less than 2 km if you go all the way to Black Rock Lake.

Follow the Pharaoh Creek trail 0.5 km downstream from the campground to the Pharaoh Lake trail junction. The trail branches left and immediately begins a steep 0.8-km climb to Pharaoh Lake. While the lake's east end is densely forested with fir and larch, the cliffs of the

Haiduk Lake and Valley from Whistling Pass

south Pharaoh Peak create a dramatic backdrop.

Black Rock Lake lies 1.1 km beyond Pharaoh Lake via a rocky and rooty trail that climbs steeply through stands of alpine larch. It is appropriately named for the sharp, shadowy cliff of the north Pharaoh Peak, which looms above its southwest shore.

Talc (Natalko) Lake—4.4 km. Just across the Great Divide in Kootenay National Park, Talc Lake sits at 2180 m in a rocky bowl fringed by stands of alpine larch.

From the junction below Egypt Lake Campground, follow the trail running due south to Redearth Pass. At a point 2.3 km from the junction, and just 0.5 km short of the park boundary on this brushy and unremarkable pass, the Talc Lake trail branches right. The lake is a stiff 1.9 km climb from this intersection.

Though shown on most maps as Talc Lake, we like the original name, which commemorates one of the most unlikely wilderness enterprises in the Rockies. In 1917, park warden Bill Peyto filed a claim on the talc deposits at the lake. In the late 1920s, the National Talc Company (hence Natalko) took over the claim. The company built a wagon road to haul the talc down Pharaoh Creek to the rail line—a distance of over 20 km! The claim was worked sporadically, but without any substantial production, into the 1940s. Scattered remnants of the operation and two cabins are near the lakeshore.

Experienced scramblers can traverse the high col northwest of Talc to Mummy Lake. This option allows you to loop back to Egypt Lake Campground via Mummy and Scarab Lakes. The traverse has been so popular over the past couple decades, a track is forming through the scree, so well-shod hikers with a topo map should have little problem finding the route. Total distance for the loop is approximately 9 km.

30 Redearth Creek—Shadow Lake

Trans-Canada Highway to Shadow Lake—14.0 km (8.7 mi)

Day trip or backpack
Allow 3.5 to 4.5 hours one way
Elevation gain: 440 m (1,450 ft)
Maximum elevation: 1840 m (6,050 ft)
Maps: Banff 82 O/4
        Banff-Egypt Lake (Gem Trek)

Access: Follow the Trans-Canada Highway to the Redearth Creek parking area, located on the south side of the highway 20 km (12.5 mi) west of Banff or 10.5 km (6.5 mi) east of Castle Junction. (A cross-over road provides access from westbound lanes.) The trail begins at a step-up gate through the wildlife control fence at the rear of the parking area.

  0.0— Trailhead (1400 m).
        N51°13.206' W115°48.227'
        — Broad gravel trail through forest.

  0.4— Trail joins old roadbed.

  6.9— Redearth Creek bridge. Lost Horse Creek Campground (Re6).

 10.5— Junction. *Pharaoh Creek* ahead; Shadow Lake right.
        — Moderate uphill on single-track trail.

 12.7— Shadow Lake Campground (Re14).

 12.9— Shadow Lake Lodge.

 13.0— Junction. Gibbon Pass right 3.1 km; Shadow Lake ahead.

 14.0— Shadow Lake (1840 m). Outlet bridge.
        — Trail continues along Haiduk Creek to Ball Pass (7.0 km), Haiduk Lake (7.5 km) and Whistling Pass (9.7 km).

Situated beneath the massive cliffs of Mount Ball, Shadow Lake is one of the more impressive lakes along the Great Divide. A few people hike to the lake and back in a day, or they bike-and-hike, since mountain bikes are permitted as far as Pharaoh Creek junction. Others prefer to overnight at Shadow Lake Lodge or the nearby campground and then day trip to several scenic backcountry locales, including Ball Pass, Haiduk Lake or Gibbon Pass.

The first three-quarters of the trip follow the broad track of the old talc-mining road constructed up Redearth and Pharaoh Creeks in the late 1920s. The hiking is somewhat tedious, but the climb is gradual and it is easy to make good time.

At 10.5 km the Shadow Lake trail branches right from the roadbed and climbs into the forest. (Mountain bikes are not permitted beyond this junction, and a rack is provided for lock-up.) From the junction it is only 2.2 km to Shadow Lake Campground and another 0.2 km to the lodge. The trail to Shadow Lake continues up-valley beyond the lodge and reaches the lake's eastern end at a bridge spanning the outlet stream.

Shadow Lake is large compared with most subalpine lakes, stretching for over 2 km to the base of Mount Ball (3311 m). Carved from Cambrian limestone and quartzite formations and draped with glaciers, the mountain provides a photo-genic backdrop.

The trail continues around the lake's south shore for a kilometre before breaking away up Haiduk Creek, bound for such destinations as Ball Pass, Haiduk Lake and Whistling Valley. (See *Bow Valley Highline Trail* and trail descriptions on following pages.)

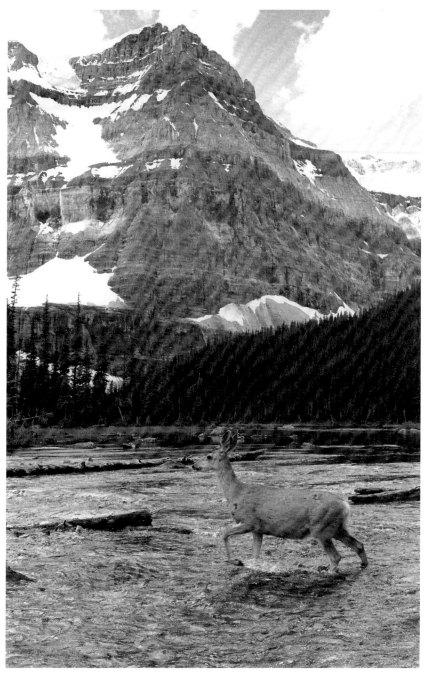

Mule Deer at Shadow Lake's outlet and Mount Ball

Shadow Lake Area Hikes

Day trips in and around Shadow Lake originate at Shadow Lake Lodge or Campground. As of this writing, there are only 5 tent sites at the campground, so you should consider making reservations with Parks Canada if you plan to stay there.

The core of the Shadow Lake Lodge complex is the restored CPR rest cabin, which was built on the site in 1929-30. The cabin was used sporadically until the 1990s, when the Brewster family of Banff redeveloped the site into a lodge. Today there are a dozen log guest cabins scattered along the margin of the meadow, a kitchen-dining room cabin, and the original CPR cabin, which serves as a guest lounge. In addition to summer accommodation, the lodge is currently operating in February and March for skiers. (For contact information, see *Sources— Backcountry lodges.*)

Following are half-day and day trips from the campground and lodge.

Gibbon Pass—3.1 km. Gibbon Pass is the best short hike from Shadow Lake. The 2300-m summit is carpeted with wildflowers in summer and bordered by extensive stands of golden larch in mid-September. The pass is also an exceptional viewpoint for a long stretch of the Great Divide extending from the peaks near Lake Louise south to Mount Assiniboine.

The trail branches north from the Shadow Lake trail at 13 km, a few metres beyond the lodge junction. It climbs steeply through subalpine forest and soon emerges into alpine meadows on the pass.

You can continue over the pass to Twin Lakes, reaching Lower Twin Lake at km 6.0. While the hike to Twin Lakes is still a reasonable day trip from Shadow Lake, you will have to climb over Gibbon Pass again on the return.

If you have arranged transportation, you can exit from the Shadow Lake environs via Gibbon Pass and Twin Lakes.

From Twin Lakes you can either continue over Arnica Summit to Highway 93 via the *Arnica Lake-Twin Lakes* trail, or descend to Castle Junction on the Twin Lakes trail. (See also *Bow Valley Highline Trail.*)

It's interesting to note that many lodge guests and campers prefer to hike to Shadow Lake on the more-scenic Bow Valley Highline Trail from Highway 93, even though it is slightly longer (15 km) and a bit more arduous. By arranging transportation, they then use Redearth Creek as an exit.

Ball Pass—8.1 km. Ball Pass is a rocky 2210-m gap on the crest of the Great Divide between Mount Ball and Haiduk Peak. While it can be reached in a long day from Highway 93 in Kootenay Park, the trail from Shadow Lake is shorter and not nearly as steep.

After hiking to Shadow Lake's outlet bridge, follow the trail continuing around the south shore and then along Haiduk Creek to Ball Pass Junction and Campground—a distance of 4.3 km from the outlet. Stay right at this junction and climb to the pass in another 2.7 km of steady uphill slogging.

The pass lies atop the Great Divide and is a passageway through the Ball Range just south of Mount Ball. The northern edge of the pass is filled with rockslides, but the remainder of the summit is composed of small meadows and stands of alpine fir and larch. A close-up view of Mount Ball's glacier-topped summit (3311 m) is the scenic highlight of the trip.

From the pass the trail continues down the Hawk Creek valley another 10.1 km to Highway 93 in Kootenay Park. (See *Hawk Creek-Ball Pass*, Kootenay Park chapter.)

Haiduk Lake—8.1 km. The rugged buttress of Haiduk Peak provides a dramatic backdrop for this peaceful lake at the foot of Whistling Pass. The hike to

Gibbon Pass

the lake and back is one of the longer trips from Shadow Lake, and even longer if you decide to extend the trip to or beyond Whistling Pass.

Follow the Haiduk Creek trail south from the Shadow Lake outlet for 4.3 km to Ball Pass Junction and Campground. Turn left and continue south for another 2.7 km, climbing steeply at first, then gradually through subalpine forest. You reach Haiduk Lake just after crossing to the east side of the creek.

Boundary surveyor A.O. Wheeler named the lake in 1913 "from a Polish word meaning 'lively, vigorous,' and when first seen with the sun, like diamonds, sparkling on its wind-blown ripples the name seemed to apply." (However, some Polish-speaking people dispute the meaning of the word.)

The trail travels briefly along the lake's east shore then makes a steep ascent in less than 2 km to the summit of Whistling Pass.

Strong hikers can make a long day trip from Shadow Lake and return by continuing over Whistling Pass to Egypt Lake and then returning to Shadow via the Pharaoh Creek and Shadow Lake trails. Total distance for the loop is 25 km. (See also *Bow Valley Highline Trail* and *Pharaoh Creek*.)

Shadow Lakeshore—3.0 km. This short hike follows rough and sometimes indistinct trail to the west end of Shadow Lake.

Follow the Shadow Lake trail to the lake from the campground or lodge. The lakeshore trail branches right from the Shadow Lake trail just before the lake's outlet bridge.

Rough trail rolls up and down through heavy forest above the north shore for 1.9 km before descending to a point near the shoreline. From there you can explore along the lake to its west end beneath the cliffs of Mount Ball.

The Ball Glacier and its ice caves were once an attractive if somewhat rigorous extension to this hike. However, one of the ice caves has collapsed and a major avalanche in 1999 covered much of the approach route with deadfall. The trip is hardly worth the effort.

31 Twin Lakes

Altrude Creek Parking Area to Lower Twin Lake—8.1 km (5.0 mi)

Day trip or backpack

Allow 2 to 3 hours one way

Elevation gain: 605 m (2,000 ft)

Maximum elevation: 2055 m (6,750 ft)

Maps: Castle Mountain 82 O/5
      Banff 82 O/4
      Banff-Egypt Lake (Gem Trek)

Access: Follow the Trans Canada Highway to the Castle Junction interchange, 30 km (18.5 mi) west of Banff and 26 km (16 mi) east of Lake Louise junction. Exit westbound to Radium on Highway 93 and watch for an access road just west of the Trans-Canada overpass branching south through the animal control fence. Follow this gravel road down into the forest 0.4 km to a parking area beside Altrude Creek and the trailhead kiosk.

0.0— Trailhead (1450 m).
    N51°15.666' W115°55.940'

   — Cross bridge. Stay right at junction on old access road.

0.2— Junction. *Smith Lake* left 1.5 km. Twin Lakes ahead.

0.5— Roadbed narrows to single track.

0.8— Altrude Creek bridge.

2.4— Uphill grade steepens.

4.0— Grade moderates.

   — Rocky, rooty trail with boggy sections.

6.3— Trail enters meadow.

   — Track often faint following along stream.

7.9— Junction. Intersection with *Bow Valley Highline Trail*. Gibbon Pass left 2.9 km. Upper Twin Lake and Twin Lakes Campground (Tw7) right 0.8 km. Lower Twin Lake ahead.

8.1— Lower Twin Lake (2055 m).

"The Twin Lakes lie at the base of the scarped and nearly vertical front of the watershed range, which rises above them in stupendous cliffs, in the rifts and hollows of which, snow remains throughout the year."

Geologist George M. Dawson penned this apt description following a visit to the lakes on August 5, 1884.

Two trails of near equal length access Twin Lakes: our favourite, and the most scenic, runs from Highway 93 via Arnica Lake, but a lot of elevation is lost and gained en route (see *Arnica Lake-Twin Lakes*); the trail from Altrude Creek is scenery-poor, but there is less elevation gain and its all downhill on the return.

From Altrude Creek the trail climbs through uninspiring forest most of the way. At km 6.3 it emerges into meadows with views to Dawson's "stupendous cliffs." In these meadows the track becomes boggy and indistinct as it follows near the stream from Lower Twin Lake.

Just 0.2 km from Lower Twin you reach a junction: Upper Twin Lake and Campground are to the right; the Gibbon Pass trail crosses the outlet stream to the left; 200 m ahead is Lower Twin Lake—a wonderful foreground to the cliffs of Storm Mountain beyond.

You will also want to pay a visit to Upper Twin Lake—located in a near identical setting to Lower Twin. A pleasant campground is located just south of the lake's outlet meadow. Beyond Upper Twin Lake the trail continues north over Arnica Summit to Arnica Lake.

Gibbon Pass—2.9 km. Our favourite half-day hike from the campground climbs from the junction below Lower Twin to stands of alpine larch, wildflower meadows and distant views. (See also *Bow Valley Highline Trail*.)

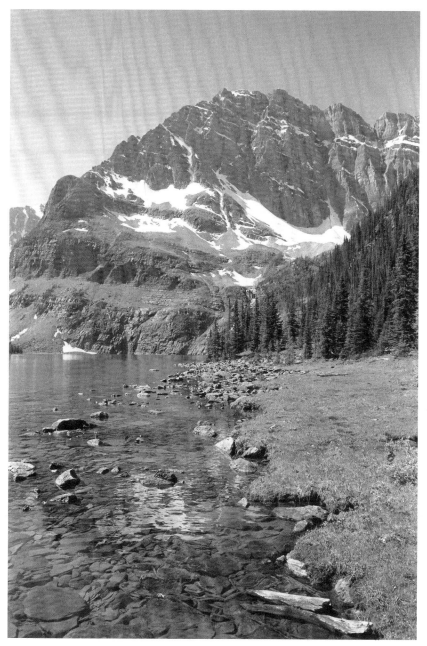

Lower Twin Lake

32 Arnica Lake—Twin Lakes

Vista Lake Viewpoint to Arnica Lake—5.0 km (3.1 mi)
Vista Lake Viewpoint to Upper Twin Lake—7.2 km (4.5 mi)

Half-day to day trip

Allow 1.5 to 2 hours to Arnica Lake

Elevation gain: 580 m (1,900 ft)
loss: 120 m (400 ft)

Maximum elevation: 2150 m (7,050 ft)

Maps: Mount Goodsir 82 N/1
Banff 82 O/4
Banff-Egypt Lake (Gem Trek)

Access: Follow the Banff-Radium Highway to the Vista Lake viewpoint, 8 km (5 mi) west of Castle Junction and 2 km (1.2 mi) east of the Banff-Kootenay Park boundary at Vermilion Pass. The viewpoint and trailhead are at a broad, paved pull-off on the south side of the highway overlooking Vista Lake and the Altrude Creek valley.

0.0— Trailhead (1690 m).
N51°14.476' W116°02.131'

— Steady downhill through old burn.

1.4— Vista Lake outlet (1570 m).

— Steady uphill moderate to steep.

4.0— Trail enters subalpine forest.

4.2— Small pond.

— Steady climb.

4.6— Trail levels off.

5.0— Arnica Lake (2150 m).

5.8— Arnica Summit (2285 m).

— Steady downhill.

7.2— Upper Twin Lake (2090 m).
Twin Lakes Campground (Tw7).

8.0— Junction. *Twin Lakes* trail from Altrude Creek left. Gibbon Pass ahead. Lower Twin Lake right.

8.2— Lower Twin Lake (2055 m).

Though the distance to Arnica Lake is not great, the hike is somewhat arduous—you start out by losing over 100 m of elevation, then gain nearly 600 m over the last 3.6 km. Yet, despite all its ups-and-downs, the hike to this tarn nestled against the imposing east face of Storm Mountain is a popular day trip and well worth the effort. You can also make a full day trip—and a four-lake grand slam—by continuing to Twin Lakes.

Starting at Vista Lake viewpoint on the Highway 93, the trail descends steadily through an old burn (1968) that is filling in with lodgepole pine. It soon reaches its lowest elevation beside Vista Lake, a peaceful green body of water that is a pleasant destination for less energetic hikers. You will want to spend some time here relaxing and enjoying the scene before tackling the steep climb ahead.

From the lake's outlet bridge, the trail climbs eastward across the lower slopes of Storm Mountain. Views along this stretch were quite open for a couple of decades after the 1968 Vermilion Pass burn, but like the descent to Vista Lake, pine forest is enclosing the trail once more.

At km 4.0 you enter a mature subalpine forest, and not long after passing a small pond you reach the shores of Arnica Lake.

The lake is backed against the sheer cliffs of Storm Mountain and enclosed on three sides by a typical upper subalpine forest of Engelmann spruce and alpine fir with a scattering of larch. Its name comes from the yellow-flowered arnica, which blooms in this cool, moist forest during early summer.

From the lake's outlet the trail climbs for another 0.8 km to the summit of a forested ridge extending northeastward from Storm Mountain. By leaving the trail and climbing along the ridge to the southwest, you are rewarded with

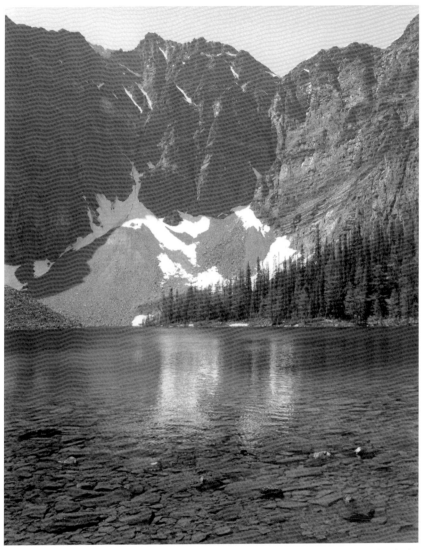

Arnica Lake

extensive views north and south along the Bow Valley.

Twin Lakes. The trail continues over Arnica Summit to Twin Lakes, reaching Upper Twin Lake and Twin Lakes Campground after a steady 1.4-km descent. We prefer this approach to Twin Lakes over the more direct route from Altrude Creek because it is more open and scenic, and the distance is virtually the same. However, we often arrange transportation between the two trailheads and hike down to the Altrude Creek trailhead at Castle Junction on the way out, thereby avoiding all the ups-and-downs of returning via Arnica and Vista Lakes. (See also *Twin Lakes* and *Bow Valley Highline Trail*.)

33 Bow Valley Highline Trail

Sunshine Village to Highway 93—40.3 km (25.0 mi)

Backpack

Allow 3 to 4 days

Maximum elevation: 2360 m (7,750 ft)

Minimum elevation: 1570 m (5,150 ft)

Maps: Banff 82 O/4
       Mount Goodsir 82 N/1
       Banff-Egypt Lake (Gem Trek)

Access: To reach the southern end of the Highline Trail, travel to Sunshine Village as described in the Sunshine Meadows area introduction. Start from the *Simpson Pass-Healy Meadows* trailhead, below the day lodge at the base of the Wawa chairlift.

To reach the northern end, follow Highway 93 to the Vista Lake viewpoint, 8 km (5 mi) west of Castle Junction and 2 km (1.2 mi) east of the Banff-Kootenay Park boundary at Vermilion Pass (see *Arnica Lake-Twin Lakes* trail description).

    0.0— Sunshine Village (2200 m).
        N51°04.812' W115°46.937'

    1.6— Twin Cairns-Meadow Park Junction.

    1.9— Wawa Ridge summit (2360 m).

    5.6— Simpson Pass (2135 m) and Junction.

    6.0— Eohippus Lake Junction.

    7.6— Healy Meadows Junction.

    9.1— Healy Pass (2330 m).

  12.3— Egypt Lake Campground (E13) and Shelter (1995 m). Pharaoh Creek Junction.

  12.8— Egypt Lake Junction.

  14.2— Scarab-Mummy Lakes Junction.

  15.6— Whistling Pass (2300 m).

  17.8— Haiduk Lake.

  21.0— Ball Pass Junction and Campground (Re21).

  25.3— Shadow Lake.

  26.3— Shadow Lake Lodge Junction (1820 m).

  29.4— Gibbon Pass (2300 m).

  32.3— Lower Twin Lake Junction (2055 m).

The dream of a highline trail running along the southwest side of the Bow Valley from Banff to Lake Louise was hatched in August 1915, when Banff outfitter Jim Brewster, parks commissioner J.B. Harkin and two CPR officials rode north along the proposed route from the Sunshine Meadows. As reported in the Banff Crag and Canyon "the officials were more than delighted with the magnificent views of mountains, lakes and watersheds the section of the country traversed afforded, and firmly convinced of the desirability of such a trail being constructed...."

The CPR promoted and expanded the idea over the next 25 years and, in 1929-30, built "rest house" cabins for hikers and horseback riders at Sunshine and Shadow Lake. In 1929, the Trail Riders of the Canadian Rockies rode the southern half of "the long-wished-for High Line Trail from Banff to Lake Louise" for the first time. Ten years later the Trail Riders followed the northern half of the route to Moraine Lake.

Though it is not officially designated as the Highline Trail today, the historic name seems appropriate. While the northern section is no longer signed and has virtually disappeared, the 40-km stretch from Sunshine Village to Highway 93 is a much-travelled route linking the popular hiking destinations of Egypt Lakes, Shadow Lake and Twin Lakes. This attractive three-to-four-day trip passes beneath the eastern escarpment of the Great Divide, over four 2300-m summits, near a dozen high lakes, and through vast wildflower meadows and stands of alpine larch.

The hike's only drawback is the popularity of the areas it passes through. There are only four campgrounds en route, so consider making advance reservations, particularly on long, holiday weekends. However, it is possible to complete the trip without a tent by overnighting at

Egypt Lakes from Healy Pass

Haiduk Lake and Peak

Parks Canada's Egypt Lake Shelter and the commercially operated Shadow Lake Lodge (two opposite extremes in back-country accommodation!).

The Highline Trail follows several trails described in more detail over the preceding pages of this section, starting from the south end on the *Simpson Pass-Healy Meadows* trail and finishing up on the *Arnica Lake-Twin Lakes* trail. Though we describe this trip from south to north, the direction it was travelled by the Trail Riders in 1929 and 1939, there is no disadvantage to hiking it in the opposite direction.

Sunshine Village to Egypt Lake—12.3 km. The first 7.6 km of the Highline route follows the *Simpson Pass-Healy Meadows* trail to an intersection with the *Healy Pass-Egypt Lake* trail. (You can also hike the *Healy Pass-Egypt Lake* trail to this junction, but you will miss some wonderful alpine scenery on Wawa Ridge.)

At that junction, stay left and continue over Healy Pass and down to Egypt Lake Campground. Highlights of the trip are views from the summits of Wawa Ridge and Healy Pass and the wildflowers of Healy Meadows.

Backpackers usually travel from Sunshine Village or Sunshine Parking Area to Egypt Lake Campground on the first day, and often spend a day there partaking of one or two of the area's excellent half-day hikes. (See descriptions for *Simpson Pass-Healy Meadows*, *Healy Pass-Egypt Lake* and *Egypt Lakes Hikes*.)

Egypt Lake to Shadow Lake—14.1 km. From Egypt Lake Campground, the trail climbs steeply through forest and across rockslides to the intersection with the Scarab and Mummy Lakes trail—a short, worthwhile detour to a pair of very scenic lakes (see *Egypt Lakes Hikes*).

Beyond the junction, you climb into the open meadows and rockslides of Whistling Valley and over 2300-m Whistling Pass. The valley was named for the resident hoary marmots, who provide ample warning of approaching hikers with a long, shrill whistle. The vale is also home to a healthy population of pikas, which can be seen darting over the rockslides near the trail.

As you near Whistling Pass there are views back to Scarab Lake and, when you crest the summit, an even more expansive vista north to Haiduk Lake and the escarpment of the Ball Range stretching to Mount Ball and Storm Mountain.

The trail drops rapidly from the pass to the shores of Haiduk Lake. After passing along the east shore of this sparkling lake with its Haiduk Peak backdrop, it crosses to the true left side of Haiduk Creek just below the outlet.

The trail makes a gradual descent of the valley through scattered forest and then drops steeply to Ball Pass Junction and Campground. Ball Pass is a worthwhile 2.7-km side-trip from this intersection, particularly if you camp here. (See Ball Pass description, *Shadow Lake Hikes*.)

The final 4.3 km to Shadow Lake is a rather humdrum stroll through forest and willow meadow; Shadow Lake Lodge and Campground lie just over a kilometre beyond the lake's outlet bridge. (For more details, see *Redearth Creek-Shadow Lake*.)

Shadow Lake to Highway 93—14.0 km. The Highline Trail route continues north from a junction just a few metres west of Shadow Lake Lodge. The trail climbs steeply through subalpine forest and into meadows scattered with alpine larch on the summit of Gibbon Pass—3.1 km from the junction.

Since there are no nearby peaks blocking views to the north and southeast, the vista from the pass is quite remarkable. The most notable landmark is Mount Assiniboine (3618 m), which rises high above its neighbouring peaks 40 km to the southeast.

A cairn with a bronze plaque at Gibbon Pass commemorates its naming for John Murray Gibbon, an author and CPR publicist who helped establish the Trail Riders of the Canadian Rockies in 1924 and Sky Line Hikers in 1933. Gibbon, who was a promoter of the Highline Trail and other long-distance trails in the Rockies, rode over this pass with the Trail Riders in 1929 and accompanied the crew that blazed the northern section of the trail prior to the 1939 trail ride.

While the trail over the pass is indistinct in places, you should have no trouble finding it again as you descend the northern slope. Just before re-entering dense forest there are views to your next objective—Lower Twin Lake.

You intersect the Twin Lakes trail 2.9 km from Gibbon Pass, just 0.2 km below Lower Twin Lake. After visiting the lake, return to the junction and climb to nearby Upper Twin Lake and Twin Lakes Campground—the last campground on the Highline route.

The final 7.2 km of the Highline Trail crosses Arnica Summit to Arnica Lake, plunges down to Vista Lake, and then makes one last brief climb to Highway 93 at the Vista Lake Viewpoint. (See *Arnica Lake-Twin Lakes*.)

34 Boom Lake

Boom Creek Picnic Area to Boom Lake—5.1 km (3.2 mi)

Half-day trip

Allow 1.5 hours one way

Elevation gain: 175 m (575 ft)

Maximum elevation: 1895 m (6,210 ft)

Maps: Mount Goodsir 82 N/1
Lake Louise 82 N/8
Lake Louise & Yoho (Gem Trek)

Access: Follow Highway 93 to the Boom Creek Picnic Area, located on the north side of the highway 7 km (4.5 mi) west of Castle Junction. The trail begins from the bridge at the rear of the picnic area.

0.0—Trailhead (1720 m).
N51°14.951' W116°01.455'

—Steady gradual to moderate uphill on broad track.

5.0—Trail narrows to footpath.

5.1—Boom Lake (1895 m).

The Boom Lake trail is an easy 5-km walk to a beautifully formed lake contained by a massive 600-m limestone wall and glacier-mantled peaks. The trail is often snow-free (but still wet) in early June, which makes it a popular early season outing. It is also fun to visit the lake in late spring and early summer when the snow pack on Boom Mountain is breaking up and where, on a sunny day, you can see numerous avalanches cascading down the mountain's north face.

For most of its length the trail is a wide, bulldozed track that climbs at a moderate grade well above the creek. In the spring many small streams make the trail a bit sloppy, but the runoff redeems itself by creating a well-watered forest with lush undergrowth and wildflowers.

Just before the trail reaches the lake it narrows to a traditional footpath, and 100 m beyond it ends abruptly at a rockslide that has tumbled down from the slope to the north into the eastern end of the lake. A bit of rock-hopping will get you to the water's edge.

The broad north face of Boom Mountain soars above the lake's south shore, and the glaciated spires of Quadra Mountain (3173 m) and Bident Mountain (3084 m) rise beyond its far end.

The Alpine Club of Canada held its annual camp at nearby Vermilion Pass in 1912, and later documented how Boom Lake received its name: "Boom Lake is so called from the fact that near its eastern extremity an old moraine, at one time the bounding wall of the lake, now just touches the surface which has overflowed it. It spans the lake in a crescent, some distance from the eastern end, and intercepts the driftwood floating down the lake. The appearance created is that of a lumber boom, and hence the name."

Boom Lake

35 Smith Lake

Altrude Creek Parking Area to Smith Lake—1.8 km (1.1 mi)

This peaceful little lake hidden in the forest on the south slope of the Bow Valley is not well known nor frequently visited. Despite the lake's relatively low elevation (1600 m), the trail to it climbs steadily and gains 150 m over the course of the journey. Views from its shores are limited to glimpses of Copper and Castle Mountains.

From the Altrude Creek trailhead cross the bridge spanning the creek and, from a junction 50 m beyond, follow the Twin Lakes trail to the right. The Smith Lake trail branches left in another 100 m.

Though you mainly travel through valley-bottom forest for the remainder of the journey, there are occasional meadows where a wide variety of wildflowers bloom in mid-July.

At 1.7 km the trail crests a forested rise where you get your first view of the lake, then descends steeply for 100 m to its shore.

The lake was named for Joe Smith, Banff Park's most famous hermit. Smith was the lone resident of the nearby ghost town of Silver City from around 1884 until 1937. He did a lot of prospecting and trapping in the area over the years and undoubtedly visited this lake many times.

Access: Follow the Trans-Canada Highway (Hwy 1) to the Castle Junction interchange, 30 km (18.5 mi) west of Banff. Exit westbound to Radium on Highway 93 and watch for an access road immediately west of the Trans-Canada overpass bridge, which branches south through the animal control fence. Follow this gravel road 0.4 km to a parking area beside Altrude Creek and the trailhead kiosk. N51°15.666' W115°55.940' *Maps: Castle Mountain 82 O/5.*

36 Taylor Lake

Trans-Canada Highway to Taylor Lake—6.6 km (4.1 mi)

Day trip

Allow 1.5 to 2 hours one way

Elevation gain: 585 m (1,920 ft)

Maximum elevation: 2065 m (6,780 ft)

Maps: Lake Louise 82 N/8
       Lake Louise & Yoho (Gem Trek)

Access: Follow the Trans-Canada Highway (Hwy 1) to the Taylor Lake trailhead parking area, located on the southwest side of the highway 7.9 km (4.9 mi) west of Castle Junction or 17.5 km (11.0 mi) east of Lake Louise Junction. (A cross-over road provides access from westbound lanes.) The trail begins at a gate through the wildlife-control fence at the rear of the parking area.

0.0— Trailhead (1480 m).
     N51°18.310' W116°01.270'

   — Trail parallels wildlife-control fence.

0.3— Trail bends left.

1.3— Taylor Creek bridge.

   — Steady uphill.

6.1— Taylor Creek bridge.

6.4— Junction. O'Brien Lake left 2.1 km. Taylor Lake ahead.

6.6— Taylor Lake (2065 m).

6.7— Taylor Lake Campground (Ta6). Trail to Panorama Ridge meadows branches uphill from rear of campground.

Taylor Lake is one of the most accessible of several hanging-valley lakes along the southwest side of the Bow Valley between Banff and Lake Louise. It is every bit as scenic as its sister lakes and offers the added bonus of two attractive side-trips from its shores.

The hike used to begin at the pleasant Taylor Creek Picnic Area, but that site was removed when the Trans-Canada Highway was twinned through this section of the valley. Now it begins from a parking area 0.4 km east of the creek.

The first section of trail follows near the highway's wildlife-control fence, then bends west and comes abreast of Taylor Creek. The rest of the trip to the lake is straightforward and not particularly inspiring, travelling over a broad track that switchbacks steadily up the side of the valley through a closed forest of lodgepole pine and spruce. As the trail nears the lake, it is often quite muddy.

The goal is well worth the drudgery of the climb, however, as the trail suddenly emerges into meadow near the lake's outlet—a moist area carpeted with western anemone, marsh marigold, buttercups, and mountain laurel through much of the summer. Fringing the meadow and much of the lakeshore is a typical upper-subalpine forest of alpine fir and Engelmann spruce dotted with the pale green, summer foliage of alpine larch (golden in September).

The north face of Mount Bell rises abruptly from the south shore of the lake, forming a 750-m wall. The low notch of Taylor Pass to the west separates Mount Bell from Panorama Ridge and serves as a rock scrambler's route to the Consolation Valley and Moraine Lake.

A small, five-site campground lies within the forest margin at the east end of the lake—an easy destination for anyone who wants to spend a night out without travelling a great distance.

Taylor Lake

O'Brien Lake. This lake is located in a smaller cirque 2.1 km to the south. With a more lavish display of wildflowers along its shore and more alpine larch in the surrounding forest, it can be even more charming than Taylor.

To reach the lake cross Taylor Creek at the trail sign 0.2 km below Taylor Lake. Follow the rocky but well-travelled track that drops below Mount Bell's cliffs and then climbs steeply to the level of the O'Brien cirque. Watch for a sign indicating the junction where the O'Brien trail branches to the right. The 0.5-km side-trail all but disappears in the boggy meadows, but by staying along the left side of the lake's outlet stream you soon reach your destination.

While views are more limited than at Taylor Lake, the lush margins along its south shore are filled with moisture-loving flowers, including the beautiful, magenta-hued variation of Indian paintbrush.

Panorama Ridge Meadows. By following the trail leading north from the rear of the Taylor Lake Campground for 0.5 km (a steep, steady climb), you can visit one of the great wildflower meadows and larch forests in the Rockies. The snow-streaked cliffs of Panorama Ridge serve as a backdrop to this long, gently rising meadow, which in summer is quite verdant and filled with the tall showy blooms associated with snowbed plant communities. In mid-September, the surrounding forest is awash with gold as the larch trees reach their autumn colour peak.

The meadow and scattered larch forest extend uphill for well over a kilometre. While the trail disappears at the lower end of the meadow, you can wander and explore uphill for an hour or more and, by following along the meadow's outlet stream, discover three small lakes at the head of the basin.

Part way up along the right side of the meadow, the old Panorama Ridge trail branches into the forest. It soon emerges onto open slopes overlooking the Bow Valley and at the ruins of an old miner's cabin, which likely dates back to the mid-1880s.

Lake Louise—Moraine Lake

There are few hiking areas that can rival the Lake Louise-Moraine Lake region. Compressed within 100-sq km are seven major hikes and a variety of options—over 70 km of trail traversing some of the most rugged alpine scenery on the continent.

Lake Louise is the birthplace of recreational hiking in the Canadian Rockies. Soon after the erection of the first rustic chalet on the lake's shoreline in 1890, manager Willoughby Astley began clearing trails to scenic points above the lake. In 1893, a pair of young adventurers from the eastern U.S., Walter Wilcox and Samuel Allen, began a systematic exploration of the region. The following summer, they discovered and explored Paradise Valley, Sentinel Pass and the upper end of the Valley of the Ten Peaks, and completed the first ascent of Mount Temple. In 1899, Wilcox and a companion made the first recorded visit to Moraine Lake and nearby Consolation Valley.

Wilcox and Allen named many local features, and their explorations led to further trail construction by the CPR. As these trails became popular, the CPR built teahouses and shelters at strategic locations. In fact, hotel staff maintained much of the trail system through the mid-20th century.

Today these trails are some of the most heavily used in the Canadian Rockies. The most popular from Lake Louise are Lake Louise Lakeshore, Lake Agnes, Plain of the Six Glaciers and Saddleback, all starting from the lakeshore near the Chateau Lake Louise. Nearby Moraine Lake lies at the entrance to the Valley of the Ten Peaks and is the departure point for hikes to Consolation Lakes, Larch Valley-Sentinel Pass, and Eiffel Lake-Wenkchemna Pass. In between Lake Louise and Moraine Lake is Paradise Valley, with its trail leading to Lake Annette and Giant Steps.

Access: From the Trans-Canada Highway (Hwy 1) interchange, the road to Lake Louise and Moraine Lake immediately passes through Lake Louise Village. A small shopping mall and the Park Visitor Centre are in the village core, and service stations, restaurants, hotels and a hostel are nearby. Lake Louise Campground, one of the park's largest, is just over a km from the village centre.

Lake Louise Drive climbs west from the village for 5.5 km to Lake Louise, where parking is available in one of several large lots just south of the Chateau. The Moraine Lake Road branches south from Lake Louise Drive 3 km from the village and rolls along the west side of the Bow Valley 12 km to a parking area at Moraine Lake Lodge and the north end of lake. The Paradise Valley trail begins at a parking area on the right side of the Moraine Lake Road at km 2.5.

At present, there is no shuttle bus service to either Lake Louise or Moraine Lake, so most people drive there in their own vehicles. Be forewarned, parking lots at both Louise and Moraine overflow during the summer, so expect bumper-to-bumper vehicles, tour buses, crowds and a general atmosphere of mayhem.

Important Notice: Whenever grizzly bears take up residence in the Moraine Lake-Paradise Valley environs, special restrictions are enacted requiring hikers and climbers to travel in a tight group of four or more. These restrictions have been commonplace since 1999, usually from late June/mid July until closure of the Moraine Lake Road in mid-October. Restrictions apply to Consolation Lakes, Larch Valley, Sentinel Pass, Wasatch Pass, Eiffel Lake, Wenkchemna Pass, Sheol and Paradise Valleys.

While it is usually not too difficult to connect with other hikers to form a group of four at Moraine Lake trailheads, never consider a trip into Paradise Valley unless you organize a group in advance and all members agree to the itinerary. And whenever the group-of-four requirement is in effect, Paradise Valley Campground is closed.

Field

1

93

48

49

47

N

Ross
Lake

Lake Louise
Ski Area

?

LAKE
LOUISE

Mt St Piran
Teahouse

V

Château

Mt
Niblock

Lake
Agnes

39

V

37

Lake Louise

38

1A

Bow

Narao
Pk

Popes
Pk

Mt
Whyte

Fairview
Mtn

41

Saddleback

River

40

Teahouse

Banff

1

BRITISH COLUMBIA

ALBERTA

Plain-of-the-Six Glaciers
Victoria Glacier

Haddo
Pk

Sheol
Mtn

Creek

Moraine Lake Road

Mt
Aberdeen

Mt
Victoria

42

Valley

Abbot Pass

Mt
Lefroy

The
Mitre

Giant Steps

Paradise

Paradise

Lake
Annette

Creek

Lake
Oesa

Yukness
Mtn

Ringrose
Pk

Horseshoe Glacier

Mt
Temple

Moraine

Hungabee
Mtn

Pinnacle Mtn

Sentinel
Pass

43

Larch
Valley

Moraine Lake
Lodge

P

Eiffel Pk

Mt
Biddle

Wenkchemna Pk

44

Eiffel Lake

46

Moraine Lake

45

Curtis
Pk

Wenkchemna
Pass

Valley of the Ten Peaks

Consolation
Lakes

Neptuak
Mtn

Wenkchemna Glacier

Mt
Babel

YOHO NATIONAL PARK
KOOTENAY NATIONAL PARK

Tokumm

Deltaform Mtn

Mt Tuzo

Mt
Bowlen

Mt Fay

Mt
Allen

Quadra
Mtn

Bident
Mtn

Creek

Land above 2300 metres

0   1   2   3   4   5km

Lake Louise Lakeshore trail

37 Lake Louise Lakeshore

Chateau Lake Louise to Lake Louise west end—1.9 km (1.2 mi)

Believe it or not, we have actually walked to the west end of Lake Louise and back on the very popular lakeshore trail and not met another soul. (Admittedly it was early in the season and very late afternoon.) Yet, even when the trail is busy, there are worse ways to spend an hour than strolling along this broad, flat trail with its ever-changing views of great peaks.

The walk starts from the trail sign just west of the Chateau and follows along the north shoreline to where the silty waters from Victoria Glacier feed into the lake. Away from the crowds surrounding the hotel, you can better appreciate the description by British mountaineer James Outram shortly after the turn of the 20th century: "At every season, every hour, it is wonderful.... As a gem of composition and of colouring it is perhaps unrivalled anywhere."

At the far end of the lake the trail climbs over a low rise and traverses beneath quartzite cliffs, which are often decorated by the colourful ropes of Lycra-clad rock climbers. And if you sit down to have a snack, you'll undoubtedly be greeted by other "head-of-the-lake" inhabitants—golden-mantled ground squirrels, chipmunks, Clark's nutcrackers and grey jays.

Back across the lake's distant shore, the Chateau floats like the *Titanic*, with the ski-run-laced slopes of Whitehorn Mountain rising beyond. It's enough to make a person want to keep on hiking. (See *Plain of the Six Glaciers*.)

Access: Follow the paved shoreline trail in front of Chateau Lake Louise north 200 m to the trail sign for the Lake Louise Lakeshore and Plain of the Six Glaciers trails. Follow the broad, shoreline path. N51°25.044' W116°13.160' Maps: *Lake Louise 82 N/8; Lake Louise & Yoho (Gem Trek); Best of Lake Louise (Gem Trek.)*

© Andrew Hempstead

Chateau Lake Louise from Fairview Lookout

38 Fairview Lookout

Lake Louise to Fairview Lookout—1.0 km (0.6 mi)

This short, moderately steep hike from the lakeshore near the Chateau Lake Louise takes you through the cool Engelmann spruce-alpine fir forest above the lake and provides a pleasant escape from the busyness of the lakeshore. The view of the Chateau and the east end of the lake from the wooden observation platform at the top is partially obscured by trees and, as advertised, only fair.

From the shoreline viewpoint near the boathouse, follow the *Saddleback* trail. At 0.3 km, branch right onto the Fairview trail. The remaining 0.7 km follows a smooth track, climbing steadily through mossy forest to the viewing platform, 140 m above lake level.

Access: The trailhead is at the exhibit area just south of the lake's outlet bridge and 70 m north of the boathouse. N51°24.969' W116°12.964' *Maps: Lake Louise 82 N/8; Lake Louise & Yoho (Gem Trek); Best of Lake Louise (Gem Trek).*

39 Lake Agnes

Lake Louise to Lake Agnes—3.5 km (2.2 mi)

Half-day to day trip

Allow 1 to 1.5 hours to Lake Agnes

Elevation gain: 405 m (1,330 ft)

Maximum elevation: 2135 m (7,000 ft)

Maps: Lake Louise 82 N/8
Lake Louise & Yoho (Gem Trek)
Best of Lake Louise (Gem Trek)

Access: Follow the paved shoreline trail in front of Chateau Lake Louise north 200 m to the trail sign for the Lake Louise Lakeshore, Plain of the Six Glaciers and Lake Agnes trails. Follow the Lake Agnes trail leading uphill to the right.

0.0— Trailhead (1730 m).
N51°25.044' W116°13.160'

— Steady uphill on broad track.

1.7— Switchback. View to Lake Louise.

2.5— Junction. Intersection with horse trail.

2.7— Mirror Lake (2025 m). Junction. Lake Agnes highline trail and Plain of the Six Glaciers left. Lake Agnes right.

— Steady climb via switchbacks.

3.2— Junction. Little Beehive right (1.2 km); Lake Agnes ahead.

3.5— Lake Agnes and Teahouse (2135 m).

3.6— Junction. Little Beehive (0.9 km) and Mt St. Piran (2.5 km) uphill to right. Lake Agnes shoreline and Big Beehive ahead.

Lake Agnes is hidden in a hanging valley high above Lake Louise. It has been one of the Rockies' most popular hikes ever since Lady Susan Agnes Macdonald, wife of Prime Minister Sir John A. Macdonald, hitched up her skirt and scrambled to its shores in 1890. In addition to its own charms, which include a teahouse, the lake and the nearby Beehives provide breathtaking views of Lake Louise and a broad stretch of the Bow Valley. While Lake Agnes and its teahouse are the main attraction on this short hike, you can easily spend a full day following the trails leading to higher viewpoints like Little Beehive, Big Beehive and Mount St. Piran, or even cross over the Big Beehive ridge to include the Plain of the Six Glaciers in your itinerary.

The first half hour from the shore of Lake Louise follows a broad, moderately graded trail through dense subalpine forest. At 1.7 km the first switchback marks a break in the trees where you have a clear view down to the pale turquoise waters of Lake Louise.

Another 0.8 km brings you to Mirror Lake—a tiny sink lake that takes its name from its round looking-glass appearance. The dark, layered cliffs of Big Beehive loom above, and, in the gap to the right, the roof of Lake Agnes Teahouse is barely visible.

By taking the Plain of the Six Glaciers highline trail to the left at the Mirror Lake junction, you can make a direct ascent to Lake Agnes via a steep trail that traverses the rockslide beneath Big Beehive. (This short cut branches right from the highline trail 150 m beyond this junction.) But if this steep trail is wet, icy or snowy, avoid it and follow the traditional route that branches right at Mirror Lake (it's only 200 metres longer).

Regardless of which option you choose, the journey to Lake Agnes is completed on one of two steep, wooden staircases that surmount a cliff band

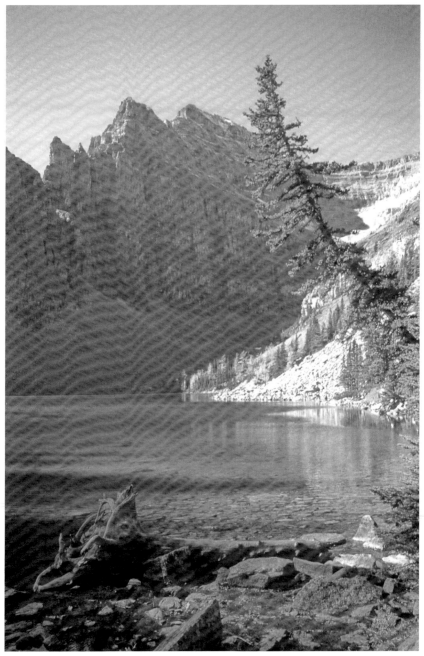

Lake Agnes

beside the waterfall created by the lake's outlet stream.

Arriving at the narrow opening where Lake Agnes tumbles from its basin, the entire length of the lake suddenly appears, stretching westward to a jagged backdrop created by Mounts Whyte (2983 m) and Niblock (2976 m). The teahouse sits atop the cliff on the north side of the outlet stream, just a few metres from the lake.

The original Lake Agnes Teahouse was constructed shortly after the turn of the 20th century. The present-day version was built in 1981. It serves refreshments and light snacks from mid-June to early October and is one of the attractions for many who do this hike. While its covered porch is a relaxing place to sit and admire the view, it is usually a very busy place. (We like to stop there shortly after it opens at 10 am or just before 6 pm closing to avoid the crowds.)

The area surrounding Lake Agnes abounds with wildlife of the upper subalpine forest, especially those species that like to be where people are eating. Least chipmunks, golden-mantled ground squirrels, Clark's nutcrackers and grey jays congregate around the teahouse porch and beg for food. (Don't feed them! They do well enough from the crumbs they find on the ground.) The hoary marmots and pikas, who whistle and cheep from the rocky slopes above the lakeshore, are somewhat less corrupted by humanity.

Many hikers end their day with a stroll along the shore of Lake Agnes to its boulder-strewn western end, only 0.8 km beyond the teahouse. But there are options for more energetic souls, including side-trips to the summits of Little Beehive and Big Beehive. You can also complete a full day circuit by crossing over the Big Beehive to the Plain of the Six Glaciers.

Lake Agnes to Little Beehive—0.9 km. The Little Beehive is the most popular short hike beyond Lake Agnes. Though not as high as the nearby Big Beehive, it provides better views of both Lake Louise and the Bow Valley, and you won't work as hard to get there.

The trail branches uphill from the Lake Agnes shoreline trail 50 m beyond the teahouse. It climbs steadily to the northeast through alpine fir and larch and across avalanche slopes. Along the way there are a number of rocky viewpoints overlooking Lake Louise, the hanging valley containing Lake Agnes, and Mount Aberdeen and the glacier-crowned peaks of Mounts Lefroy and Victoria. Stands of larch become thicker as you climb, making this a very rewarding trip in the last two weeks of September when their needles turn to gold.

The trail ends at the 2225-m Little Beehive summit and the foundation of the old fire lookout cabin. Views are quite impressive, including a panorama of the Bow Valley that stretches from the mountains near the headwaters of the Bow River to the peaks surrounding Banff to the south. Across the way, the Pipestone Valley stretches north into some of the wildest country in Banff Park. (You will want to bring a map to appreciate all the landmarks visible from this vantage point.)

Lake Agnes to Mt. St. Piran—2.5 km. The 2650-m summit of Mount St. Piran is one the best viewpoints overlooking the Lake Louise environs and the Bow Valley (second only to nearby Fairview Mountain). For strong hikers who would escape the crowds on the more popular routes, and who don't mind a good stiff climb, this side-trip from the Little Beehive trail is an excellent option.

Follow the Little Beehive trail from Lake Agnes for 0.5 km to where the St. Piran trail branches uphill to the left. A narrow but obvious footpath climbs steeply through stands of larch and then switchbacks up steep, open slopes to the summit. The track disappears on the summit ridge, but the route is obvious— UP!

Lake Louise from the Little Beehive

While views from the summit to Lake Louise are obscured, you can look down on Lake Agnes to the south and tiny Minewakun Lake in the forested valley to the north. This lofty viewpoint also provides an exceptional perspective of nearby peaks and distant landscapes.

Lake Agnes to Big Beehive—1.6 km. Another popular trip beyond Lake Agnes Teahouse is the hike to the 2255-m summit of Big Beehive.

The trail to Big Beehive continues around the far end of the lake and climbs a steep series of switchbacks to a junction on the Beehive summit ridge. Traverse eastward along the rocky, lightly forested ridge to a gazebo-style shelter on the northeast edge of the promontory.

Though somewhat obscured by trees, there are views over the Bow Valley and down to Lake Louise, over 500 m below. (Do not attempt to shortcut down from the gazebo viewpoint in any direction; there are dangerous cliffs on all sides. Return back along the ridge the way you came.)

Lake Agnes-Plain of the Six Glaciers Circuit—14.5 km. Hikers looking for a full day's outing can include the Plain of the Six Glaciers in their itinerary after visiting Lake Agnes and the Big Beehive.

Cross the Big Beehive's summit ridge at the viewpoint trail junction and follow a steep trail down the south side. In just over a kilometre you reach an intersection with the highline trail running up-valley from Mirror Lake. Turn right and follow this trail as it descends across the lower slopes of Devil's Thumb to an intersection with the Plain of the Six Glaciers trail.

Continue up-valley toward the imposing, glacier-topped summits of Mounts Lefroy and Victoria for another 1.4 km to the Plain of the Six Glaciers Teahouse. After visiting the teahouse and, perhaps, the Abbot Pass viewpoint farther along, you return to Lake Louise on the *Plain of the Six Glaciers* trail.

40 Plain of the Six Glaciers

Lake Louise to Plain of the Six Glaciers Teahouse—5.5 km (3.4 mi)

Half-day to day trip

Allow 1.5 hours one way

Elevation gain: 340 m (1,115 ft)

Maximum elevation: 2070 m (6,800 ft)

Maps: Lake Louise 82 N/8
       Lake Louise & Yoho (Gem Trek)
       Best of Lake Louise (Gem Trek)

Access: Follow the paved shoreline trail in front of Chateau Lake Louise north 200 m to the trail sign for the Lake Louise Lakeshore, Plain of the Six Glaciers and Lake Agnes trails.

0.0— Trailhead (1730 m).
     N51°25.044' W116°13.160'

     — Follow Lake Louise Lakeshore trail.

1.9— West end of Lake Louise.

2.4— Steady climb begins.

3.3— Junction. Big Beehive shortcut right.

     — Steady, moderate climb along avalanche paths.

4.1— Junction. Highline route to Mirror Lake-Big Beehive intersects from right.

     — Grade steepens through glacial moraines and along valley slope.

5.5— Plain of Six Glaciers Teahouse (2070 m).

     — Gradual to moderate climb from meadow and along ridge of lateral moraine.

6.8— Talus slope. Abbot Pass viewpoint (2195 m).

The Plain of the Six Glaciers trail transports you into the heart of the Canadian Rockies' most famous postcard view and sets you down beneath the glacier-capped summits of Mounts Victoria and Lefroy. And if scenery isn't enough, you can stop for a spot of tea on the sheltered verandah of one of the Rockies' oldest backcountry teahouses. However, don't expect much solitude on one of Banff's most popular trails.

Starting from the trail sign just beyond the Chateau, follow the busy lakeshore trail to the far end of Lake Louise. Beyond the lake's silty inlet, the crowds thin as the trail climbs steadily through subalpine forest and across the occasional avalanche path. Eventually it emerges into a landscape scoured by the Victoria Glacier, where views open to Mounts Victoria and Lefroy.

After passing the intersection with the highline trail from Mirror Lake and the Big Beehive, you ascend along the edge of old glacial moraines. A final series of steep switchbacks lead up through a band of alpine fir and larch to the teahouse.

The Plain of the Six Glaciers Teahouse was constructed by the Canadian Pacific Railway in the mid-1920s. Refreshments and light snacks are served throughout the summer season, and its verandah is an ideal vantage point for the frequent avalanches thundering off Mounts Lefroy and Victoria in the early summer.

If the teahouse is overflowing with visitors, as it often is, you can relax in the clearing below the teahouse and scan the nearby boulder-field for hoary marmots and pikas.

The trail continues up-valley beyond the teahouse for another 1.3 km. Along the way it traverses the crest of a lateral moraine—a steep ridge of debris formed during the last advance of the Victoria Glacier, which reached its zenith during the mid-1800s. Today it provides

Mount Victoria from the Plain of the Six Glaciers trail

an excellent viewpoint for the rock and boulder-covered ice of the Victoria Glacier below.

Beyond the moraine, the trail fizzles out on a steep talus slope. While this slope is a rather precarious resting spot, it is the best viewpoint for 2922-m Abbot Pass between the towering summits of Mount Victoria (3464 m) and Mount Lefroy (3441 m). You can see the Abbot Pass Hut on the summit skyline— a substantial stone structure constructed by CPR Swiss guides in 1922 as an overnight shelter for mountaineers. Today it is operated by the Alpine Club of Canada and is Canada's highest National Historic Site.

The pass is named for the American alpinist Philip Stanley Abbot, who fell to his death while attempting the first ascent of Mount Lefroy in 1896—the first mountaineering fatality in North America. The steep, ice-filled couloir rising from the Victoria Glacier to the pass is known as "The Death Trap", so-named by early mountaineers because avalanches frequently fall into it from the cliffs above. (Don't even dream of heading in that direction unless you are

an experienced, well-equipped mountaineer and have checked with Parks Canada about current route conditions.)

Lake Agnes-Plain of the Six Glaciers Circuit—14.5 km. Strong hikers looking for a full day's outing can return to Lake Louise via the Big Beehive and Lake Agnes. From the trail junction 1.4 km below the teahouse, follow the highline route toward Mirror Lake for 2 km, branch left on the Big Beehive trail and cross over its summit ridge to Lake Agnes. This option adds approximately 4 km to the normal 11 km round trip to the Plain of the Six Glaciers Teahouse and includes a very strenuous climb over Big Beehive (2255 m).

This classic loop allows you to visit the two most famous destinations above Lake Louise in one day. However, we prefer to go to Lake Agnes first and then cross Big Beehive to Plain of Six Glaciers, since this approach seems somewhat less arduous and the views more rewarding. (See *Lake Agnes.*)

41 Saddleback

Lake Louise to Saddleback—3.7 km (2.3 mi)

Half-day to day trip

Allow 1 to 2 hours to Saddleback

Elevation gain: 600 m (1,970 ft)

Maximum elevation: 2330 m (7,650 ft)

Maps: Lake Louise 82 N/8
Lake Louise & Yoho (Gem Trek)
Best of Lake Louise (Gem Trek)

Access: The trailhead is located at the exhibit area just south of the lake's outlet bridge and 70 m north of the canoe-rental boathouse.

0.0— Trailhead (1730 m).
N51°24.969' W116°12.964'

— Follow broad trail up through dense subalpine forest.

0.3— Junction. *Fairview Lookout* right 0.7 km.

0.4— Junction. Moraine Lake-Paradise Valley left. Saddleback right.

1.1— Avalanche path.

— Steady moderate to steep uphill.

2.7— Trail climbs through stands of alpine larch.

3.7— Saddleback (2330 m). Fairview Mtn right 1.3 km. Sheol Valley ahead.

Notice: Any travel beyond Saddleback into Sheol Valley may require a group of four people hiking in close proximity to one another if special restrictions concerning grizzly bears are in place. See "Important Notice" in Lake Louise-Moraine Lake introduction, page 88.

To see Mount Temple in its noblest grandeur I would take you to the Saddleback. This is a broad green alp, nearly 2000 feet above Lake Louise, a very favourite hour's ascent by trail, between Mount Fairview and the projecting 'horn' of the Saddle Peak. Crossing the plateau to the tree-fringed brink of the abyss beyond, our gaze is carried straight across the chasm, 1500 feet in depth, to the huge peak.

This description of Saddleback published by British mountaineer James Outram in 1905 sums up the glories of this short, strenuous hike from Lake Louise. The trail is also one of the best places to view golden-needled alpine larch in late September, and it is the approach to a spectacular viewpoint atop Fairview Mountain.

In its early stages the trail climbs steadily through the forest. At the end of the first kilometre it crosses a major avalanche path on Fairview's northeast slopes, where you have a view back to the Chateau and distant Mount Hector. Farther along, the trail angles up to the southwest and begins the final steep, switchbacking ascent to the pass.

Views improve just below the summit, stretching down the length of the Bow Valley to the mountains near Banff. You also pass through a stand of unusually large and very old, alpine larch (core samples from similar trees in nearby Larch Valley reveal ages of more than 400 years).

Saddleback is a pleasant upland meadow where buttercups, western anemone, alpine speedwell and many other wildflowers bloom in early summer. And as Outram noted, the towering north wall of Mount Temple (3544 m) dominates the view south of the pass.

The best view of Temple, looming over tiny Lake Annette and Paradise Valley, is obtained by descending southeast

Mount Victoria from Fairview Mountain summit

approximately 200 m along the summit ridge. Follow a faint path through scrub alpine fir to an open promontory overlooking Sheol Valley—a classic alpine viewpoint that has even been exploited by Hollywood (John Barrymore gripped his leading lady Camilla Horn in a passionate embrace here during the filming of *Eternal Love* in August, 1928).

From Saddleback summit, you can scramble to Saddle Peak for even better views of Mount Temple and Paradise Valley. But many hikers are willing to expend more effort to reach the grandiose views atop Fairview Mountain.

Fairview Mountain—1.3 km. With the glacier-crowned summits of Mount Victoria, Mount Temple and Sheol Mountain close by, and the turquoise waters of Lake Louise a vertical kilometre below, the 2745-m summit of Fairview Mountain offers a true alpine experience. The peak is arguably the highest trail-accessible point in the mountain parks, though the 1.3 km track scratched up its rocky slope many decades ago has largely disappeared.

Follow faint trail northwest from Saddleback summit to begin the ascent. Continue upwards on often vague, switchbacking track, or simply scramble over loose rock towards the obvious summit. (You may have to skirt snow-banks early in the season.)

Sheol Valley Option. You can extend your journey by continuing over Saddleback and down through the Sheol Valley. You pass through several lush meadows on the 4.1-km descent to Paradise Valley, where it intersects that trail at km 4.2 (see *Paradise Valley*).

42 Paradise Valley

Moraine Lake Road to Lake Annette—5.7 km (3.5 mi)
Moraine Lake Road to Giant Steps—10.3 km (6.4 mi)*

Half-day to day trip
Allow 1.5 to 2 hours to Lake Annette
2.5 to 3 hours to Giant Steps
Elevation gain: 385 m (1,250 ft)
Maximum elevation: 2105 m (6,900 ft)
Maps: Lake Louise 82 N/8
Lake Louise & Yoho (Gem Trek)

Access: Follow Lake Louise Drive from Lake Louise Village 3 km (1.9 mi) to the junction with the Moraine Lake Road. Follow Moraine Lake Road 2.5 km (1.5 mi) to the Paradise Valley parking area, in the forest on the right side of the road.

0.0—Trailhead (1720 m).
N51°23.763' W116°10.306'
1.1—Junction. Moraine Lake left. Paradise Valley right.
1.3—Junction. Lake Louise ahead (4.0 km). Paradise Valley left.
3.4—Paradise Creek bridge.
3.9—Paradise Creek bridge.
4.2—Junction. *Saddleback* via Sheol Valley right 4.1 km.
5.1—Paradise Creek bridge.
5.7—Lake Annette (1965 m).
6.5—Trail summit (2105 m).
8.4—Junction. Sentinel Pass ahead 2.7 km. Giant Steps right.*
9.1—Paradise Creek bridge, junction. Horseshoe Meadows left. Giant Steps ahead.*
9.5—Junction. Horseshoe Meadows left. Giant Steps ahead.*
10.1—Junction. Paradise Valley Campground left (0.2 km). Giant Steps ahead.*
10.3—Giant Steps (2000 m).*
*Distances approximate.

Note: Travel on this trail may require a group of four people hiking in close proximity to one another if special restrictions concerning grizzly bears are in place. (See "Important Notice" in Lake Louise-Moraine Lake introduction, page 88.) If so, never consider a trip into the valley unless you organize a group in advance. And whenever the group-of-four requirement is in effect, Paradise Valley Campground is closed.

When Walter Wilcox and his companions climbed to the summit of Mitre Pass from Lake Louise in 1894, they looked into "a valley of surpassing beauty, wide and beautiful, with alternating open meadows and rich forests." They named it Paradise.

Today a 10.3-km trail runs up the valley from the Moraine Lake Road to the Giant Steps cascades. While it's possible to hike to the Giant Steps and back in a long day, most opt for a more modest and scenic objective, Lake Annette beneath the imposing north wall of Mount Temple.

The first 3 km of trail are forest-enclosed, but at the first Paradise Creek bridge, views open to Mount Temple. In another kilometre, you cross back to the northwest side of the creek and pass the Sheol Valley-Saddleback junction. At km 5.1, the trail crosses the creek once more followed by a short but strenuous ascent to Lake Annette.

Lake Annette's rocky surroundings are typical of many subalpine tarns, but its backdrop is extraordinary—the ice-capped, 1200-m north face of Mount Temple. This wall is one of the most difficult ascents in North America and remained unclimbed until 1966. And if you see one of the massive avalanches that sweep the face, you will understand one reason why.

The trail continues southwest from Lake Annette, climbing through stands of alpine larch at the base of Mount Temple. Even if you don't plan on hiking to the Giant Steps, it's worthwhile continuing another 15 minutes or so beyond the lake to the trail's summit atop a major rockslide. Here views open to the valley headwall—Hungabee Mountain, Ringrose Peak, and Horseshoe Glacier—scenery that is blithely ignored by the marmots and pikas inhabiting the surrounding boulder field.

Paradise Valley

Giant Steps. Nearly 2 km beyond the trail summit, you reach a cutoff trail to the Giant Steps. This trail descends to a bridge over Paradise Creek then angles directly across the valley to the Giant Steps and Paradise Valley Campground. Sections of old trail loop further up-valley to the head of the Horseshoe Meadows, but there seems little reason to hike this slightly longer route unless you're bound for Sentinel Pass (see below).

Nearing the Giant Steps, you pass the branch trail to Paradise Valley Campground. Stay right and, just 200 m beyond this junction, reach the Giant Steps—a remarkable staircase waterfall on the north fork of Paradise Creek. The falls have been photographed many times over the years, but some of the earliest images were made by members of the Alpine Club of Canada, who held their second annual camp here in 1907.

Anyone who hiked here before 2006, will remember a section of trail running down-valley along Paradise Creek from near the Giant Steps to the 5.1-km bridge. This trail allowed hikers to complete a loop around the upper half

of the valley. However, this section was removed to provide more elbowroom for grizzly bears that sometimes feed on Mount Aberdeen's avalanche slopes. So today the only option is to return the way you came. Or you can exit the valley by climbing the steep trail over Sentinel Pass to Larch Valley and Moraine Lake.

Sentinel Pass. At the 8.4-km junction, take the left branch that continues along the southeast side of the valley. In another 0.4 km, you reach Sentinel Pass junction. The pass lies a very steep and rocky 2.3 km up to the left. Most hikers find it less strenuous to climb to Sentinel Pass from Moraine Lake and then descend to Paradise Valley. This 17-km traverse between Moraine Lake and the Paradise Valley trailhead is fairly popular with parties who can arrange transportation. (See *Larch Valley-Sentinel Pass* description.)

43 Larch Valley—Sentinel Pass

Moraine Lake to Larch Valley—2.4 km (1.5 mi)
Moraine Lake to Sentinel Pass—5.8 km (3.5 mi)

Half-day to day trip
Allow 2 hours to Sentinel Pass
Elevation gain: 724 m (2,376 ft)
Maximum elevation: 2611 m (8,566 ft)
Maps: Lake Louise 82 N/8
       Lake Louise & Yoho (Gem Trek)

Access: Follow Lake Louise Drive from
the village of Lake Louise 3 km (1.9 mi) to
the junction with the Moraine Lake Road.
Continue on the Moraine Lake Road 12.5 km
(7.5 mi) to the parking area at Moraine Lake.
Walk to the lakeshore and continue to the
trail sign below the lodge.

0.0— Trailhead (1887 m).
     N51°19.673' W116°10.899'

  — Follow *Moraine Lakeshore* trail.

0.2— Junction. *Moraine Lakeshore* ahead.
     Larch Valley and Eiffel Lake right.

1.1— Switchbacks begin.

  — Steady uphill climb.

2.4— Junction. *Eiffel Lake-Wenkchemna
     Pass* ahead. Larch Valley-Sentinel
     Pass right.

  — Trail climbs into Larch Valley
     meadows.

4.5— Upper Minnestimma Lake.

4.7— Switchbacks begin up steep talus
     slope.

5.8— Sentinel Pass (2611 m).

  — Very steep descent through boulders
     and talus to Paradise Valley.

8.1— Junction (2100 m). Horseshoe
     Meadows loop trail. Keep right.

8.5— Junction with *Paradise Valley* trail at
     km 8.4.

**Notice: Travel on these trails may
require a group of four people hiking
in close proximity to one another if
special restrictions concerning grizzly
bears are in place. See "Important
Notice" in Lake Louise-Moraine Lake
introduction.**

Larch Valley is one of the most heavily
visited trail destinations in the mountain
parks. And no wonder. This meadowland above Moraine Lake, with its dense
stands of alpine larch and panoramic
overview of the Ten Peaks, is exquisite.
And above the valley, amid stark pinnacles of rock, is Sentinel Pass—the highest point reached by a major trail in the
mountain national parks.

From Moraine Lake the trail climbs
through a forest of Engelmann spruce
and alpine fir, following a steadily
ascending series of switchbacks much
of the way. At km 2.4 the trail branches right from the Eiffel Lake trail and
immediately enters the lower meadows
of Larch Valley.

This high valley is the main focus
for most hikers who walk the trail, and
in late September, when alpine larch
needles have turned to gold, it is one of
the most visited trails in the Rockies. In
mid-summer, however, the larch needles
are a pale green and the meadows are
carpeted with wildflowers.

The trail continues to climb through
larch and meadows, and by the time it
emerges above the last trees, there are
fine views back to the rugged Ten Peaks,
the ice-capped summit of Mount Fay
(3235 m) being the most prominent
and striking. The small lakes that dot
the upper meadows of the valley were
named Minnestimma, a Stoney word
meaning "sleeping water," by the pioneer
alpinist Samuel Allen.

Ahead, between the rugged walls
of Pinnacle Mountain on the left and
Mount Temple on the right, is the 2611-
m summit of Sentinel Pass. After passing
the uppermost Minnestimma Lake, the
trail begins a switchbacking climb of the
steep, open slope leading to the pass—a
vertical rise of nearly 200 m that weeds
out many Larch Valley hikers.

Mount Fay from Larch Valley's Minnestimma Lakes

The rock formations surrounding Sentinel Pass lie nearly horizontal, and erosion of these layers has created the weird spires immediately north of the summit. The pass receives its name from these towers, the tallest of which is called the Grand Sentinel.

The pass was first ascended in 1894 by Samuel Allen and Yandell Henderson, members of a group of American mountain climbers exploring the Lake Louise region. A few days later they returned to the pass with their companions and climbed Mount Temple (3544 m), which was the first ascent in Canada above 11,000 feet.

Paradise Valley. Strong hikers who have arranged transportation between trailheads at Moraine Lake and Paradise Valley can continue north over Sentinel Pass and descend into Paradise Valley.

The trail down the north slope of the pass is extremely steep for more than a kilometre, switching back and forth through a field of boulders where good footwear and balance are necessary. (Route-finding is difficult on this precipitous descent, and trail-obscuring snowfields often linger into late summer near the bottom of the slope. The trail should be avoided entirely when the boulders near the pass are snow or ice-covered.)

It is 2.7 km and a vertical descent of 500 m from Sentinel Pass to the junction with the main Paradise Valley trail. (Ascending the pass from the Paradise Valley side is a brutal grunt.)

At the Paradise Valley trail junction, stay right and hike to Lake Annette and points east, eventually emerging at the Paradise Valley trailhead on the Moraine Lake Road. Total distance from Moraine Lake to the Paradise Valley trailhead is 16.9 km. (See also *Paradise Valley*.)

44 Eiffel Lake—Wenkchemna Pass

Moraine Lake to Eiffel Lake—5.6 km (3.5 mi)
Moraine Lake to Wenkchemna Pass—9.7 km (6.0 mi)

Half-day to day trip

Allow 1.5 to 2 hours to Eiffel Lake

3 hours to Wenkchemna Pass

Elevation gain: 733 m (2,405 ft)

Maximum elevation: 2620 m (8,595 ft)

Maps: Lake Louise 82 N/8
      Lake Louise & Yoho (Gem Trek)

Access: Follow Lake Louise Drive from
the village of Lake Louise 3 km (1.9 mi) to
the junction with the Moraine Lake Road.
Continue on the Moraine Lake Road 12.5 km
(7.5 mi) to the parking area at Moraine Lake.
Walk to the lakeshore and the trail sign
below the lodge.

0.0— Trailhead (1887 m).
     N51°19.673' W116°10.899'

    — Follow *Moraine Lakeshore* trail.

0.2— Junction. *Moraine Lakeshore* ahead.
     Larch Valley and Eiffel Lake right.

1.1— Switchbacks begin.

    — Steady uphill climb.

2.4— Junction. *Larch Valley-Sentinel Pass*
     right. Eiffel Lake-Wenkchemna Pass
     ahead.

    — Trail levels out, contouring across
     open slopes.

5.6— Eiffel Lake Viewpoint (2360 m).
     Trail traverses talus slope high
     above lake.

    — Moderate but steady uphill over
     alpine meadows and talus slopes.

9.7— Wenkchemna Pass (2600 m).

**Notice: Travel on these trails may
require a group of four people hiking
in close proximity to one another if
special restrictions concerning grizzly
bears are in place. See "Important
Notice" in Lake Louise-Moraine Lake
introduction.**

Following their explorations to Wenkchemna Pass and the upper end of the Valley of the Ten Peaks in 1894, Walter Wilcox and his companions were so overwhelmed by the stark, boulder-filled landscape they named it Desolation Valley. In its deepest and most desolate heart lies Eiffel Lake.

The Eiffel Lake trail follows the same course as the Larch Valley trail for the first 2.4 km, switchbacking upward through closed forest from the north end of Moraine Lake. Splitting near the lower edge of Larch Valley, the Eiffel Lake trail continues along the north side of the Valley of the Ten Peaks. It soon emerges onto open slopes where all of the ten summits are revealed across the valley as well as the brilliant blue waters of Moraine Lake far below.

As the trail continues through flower-filled meadows, the Wenkchemna Glacier is barely discernible in the valley below. Heavy rockfall from the cliffs above the glacier has completely covered most of its surface, shielding the ice from the sun's rays and accounting in part for the glacier's relatively small recession over the past century.

At km 5.6 the trail passes across a steep scree slope above Eiffel Lake. Reflecting upon one of his first visits to the lake, Walter Wilcox wrote: "It would be difficult to find another lake of small size in a wilder setting, the shores being of great angular stones, perfectly in harmony with the wild range of mountains beyond. Except in one place where a green and inviting slope comes down to the water, this rough ground is utterly unsuitable for vegetation and nearly devoid of trees."

Eiffel's rugged surroundings were created by a massive rockslide that broke away from Neptuak Mountain in the distant past and spread rock debris across the valley. In fact, the lake undoubtedly

Eiffel Lake and the Valley of the Ten Peaks

formed after the slide, which created a natural dam for water flowing from the snowfields at the head of the valley.

Immediately above the lake to the north is Eiffel Peak (3085 m), named for a rock pinnacle near its summit that resembles the famous Parisian tower. Looking at the peak from this angle, you can see the striking contrast between the grey limestone composing its summit and the orange-red quartzite of the lower cliffs.

If you don't want to labour down over 200 m of broken rock to reach Eiffel Lake, you can enjoy an overview of both lake and the Ten Peaks by continuing west along the trail to a sheltering grove of larch trees—Wilcox's "green and inviting slope."

Wenkchemna Pass. You can hike beyond Eiffel Lake for another 4 km to one of the highest trail-accessible points in the mountain national parks and an outstanding viewpoint for the Valley of the Ten Peaks.

The trail continues due west across rolling alpine meadows, then climbs over moraine and along the rocky south ridge of Wenkchemna Peak before descending to the windswept gap between Wenkchemna Peak and Neptuak Mountain. (Sections of the trail may be obscured by snowfields before late July.)

Standing on the crest of the Great Divide, you overlook the entire length of the Valley of the Ten Peaks. On the west side of the divide is the rocky Eagle's Eyrie region of Yoho Park and, further south, the forested headwaters of Tokumm Creek in Kootenay Park.

The elevation of Wenkchemna Pass is listed on most maps as being 2600 m, or 11 m lower than nearby Sentinel Pass. Yet you lose at least 20 m as you descend to its summit. So, who knows, this may qualify as the highest maintained trail in the Canadian Rockies.

45 Consolation Lakes

Moraine Lake to Lower Consolation Lake—2.9 km (1.8 mi)

Half-day trip

Allow 45 minutes one way

Elevation gain: 65 m (215 ft)

Maximum elevation: 1950 m (6,400 ft)

Maps: Lake Louise 82 N/8
      Lake Louise & Yoho (Gem Trek)

Access: Follow Lake Louise Drive from the village of Lake Louise 3 km (1.9 mi) to the junction with the Moraine Lake Road. Continue on the Moraine Lake Road 12.5 km (7.5 mi) to the parking area at Moraine Lake. Walk down to the bridge over Moraine Creek, just below the lake outlet.

0.0— Trailhead (1885 m).
      N51°19.703′ W116°10.872′
      — Trail climbs over rockslide.

0.1— Junction. Spur trail right to Rockpile viewpoint (0.3 km).
      — Gradual climb into forest.

2.3— Open meadow.

2.9— Lower Consolation Lake (1950 m).

Notice: Travel on this trail may require a group of four people hiking in close proximity to one another if special restrictions concerning grizzly bears are in place. See "Important Notice" in Lake Louise-Moraine Lake introduction.

The hike to Lower Consolation Lake is short and relatively flat, but the rugged scenery is as rewarding as that found on many of Banff's longer and more-demanding trails.

After crossing the Moraine Creek bridge just below the parking area, the trail passes over a substantial rockslide, which is the natural dam that created Moraine Lake. A short trail branches to the top of the "Rockpile", where you are greeted by the classic view of Moraine Lake and the Valley of the Ten Peaks.

Beyond the rockslide, the trail enters a forest of spruce and fir and climbs gradually along the west side of Babel Creek. Just beyond the halfway point to the lake, the trail levels out along a meadow—a section that is often quite muddy.

A large rockslide blocks direct access to the north end of Lower Consolation Lake, but you still have a magnificent view of the lake and the glacier-capped summits of Bident and Quadra beyond. Mount Temple commands the view back down-valley to the north—at 3544 m, the third highest mountain in Banff Park and the highest in the Lake Louise-Moraine Lake vicinity.

Upper Consolation Lake. If you are visiting Consolation after the high-water period (June to mid-July) and want to spend a little more time in the area, you can visit Upper Consolation Lake. Cross Babel Creek below Lower Consolation Lake on rickety log booms and then follow a rough, muddy track along the lake's eastern shore. At the far end, climb over a ridge of rock debris separating the two lakes. (Good boots are required for this option.)

Bident and Quadra Mountains from Lower Consolation Lake

46 Moraine Lakeshore

Moraine Lake Lodge to Moraine Lake inlet—1.2 km (0.7 mi)

In 1899, Walter Wilcox and Ross Peacock set out to explore the lower reaches of "Desolation Valley", which Wilcox had surveyed from the summit of Mount Temple five years earlier. After a hard bushwhack into the valley, Wilcox came to a "massive pile of stones" blocking the way ahead. He climbed to the top and, behold, "there lay before me one of the most beautiful lakes that I have ever seen."

Today, thousands climb to Wilcox's viewpoint to photograph the classic view of the lake. However, the trail down its west shoreline, away from the crowds milling about the parking lot, lodge and viewpoint, offers a different perspective for what many visitors feel is one of the most beautiful lakes they've ever seen.

From the trail sign just below Moraine Lake Lodge, continue on the lakeside trail. The trail remains flat and close to the shoreline all the way to the lake's inlet at its southwest end. Along the way, you have continuous views across the lake to the rugged summits of the first five of the Ten Peaks rising from its eastern shore. Most impressive is Peak #1, Mount Fay, with its prominent summit glacier.

Access: Follow Lake Louise Drive from the village of Lake Louise 3 km (1.9 mi) to the junction with Moraine Lake Road. Continue on Moraine Lake Road 12.5 km (7.5 mi) to the parking area at Moraine Lake. Walk to the lakeshore and the trail sign below the lodge. N51°19.673' W116°10.899' *Maps: Lake Louise 82 N/8; Lake Louise & Yoho (Gem Trek).*

Boulder Pass and Skoki Valley

Hidden behind the Lake Louise ski area are the high valleys, passes and lakes of the Slate Range—an area of over 200 sq km that is one of the exceptional hiking areas in the Canadian Rockies.

Despite the area's proximity to Lake Louise, it was not visited or explored to any extent before the first decade of the 20th century. After A.O. Wheeler conducted the first topographical survey of the region in 1906, pioneer mountain adventurers, like Walter Wilcox and Mary Schäffer, began to visit the range and explore its many wonderful features.

James Foster Porter, a mountaineer from Winnetka, Illinois, visited the region in 1911 and named many of the natural features, including the Skoki Valley. "Skokie", as he spelled it, is a Potawatomi (Ojibwa) word meaning "swamp", which probably refers to the well-watered Merlin Meadows. (Porter would use the name again many years later when the Chicago suburb of Skokie was being created.)

Skoki Lodge was built in the valley by a group of Banff ski enthusiasts in 1930. It began operation as one of the first backcountry ski lodges in the Canadian Rockies in 1931 and was enlarged to its present dimensions in 1936. Designated a National Historic Site in 1992, it continues to provide hikers and skiers with cozy accommodation and meals.

The main access route, the *Boulder Pass-Skoki Valley* trail, starts at the Fish Creek parking area at the base of Whitehorn mountain and follows a ski area access road up Corral Creek valley to Temple Lodge (a day lodge during ski season). From there, it reverts to a standard trail running to Boulder Pass, through the Ptarmigan Valley, across Deception Pass, and down into the Skoki Valley.

While this is the core access trail, there are many side trails and countless options for both day hikers and backpackers. You should have 1:50,000 scale maps with you on any trip into this region; study them before you depart so you understand all the possibilities and can customize the outing to fit your party's tastes and abilities.

The trail is also an access point for more serious wilderness adventures, including trips into the remote Red Deer Valley and along the Sawback Trail between Lake Louise and Banff. (See *Sawback Trail*.)

Boulder Pass–Ptarmigan Valley. A lofty treeline-alpine region that is noted for its high lakes surrounded by lush wildflower meadows. In essence it encompasses the area south and east of Deception Pass on the *Boulder Pass-Skoki Valley* trail, and much of it can be accessed by strong hikers in a long day. But since there are a number side-trips to places like Hidden Lake, Redoubt Lake and Baker Lake, you may prefer to backpack to the Hidden Lake Junction or Baker Lake Campgrounds and explore in a more leisurely manner.

Skoki Valley. Deception Pass (2475 m) is the highest point on the *Boulder Pass-Skoki Valley* trail. Everything north of the pass is considered part of the Skoki Valley area.

Skoki Lodge is in the heart of the valley. The rustic lodge with outlying cabins provides accommodation and meals for guests throughout the summer and winter months. (See *Sources—Backcountry lodges*.)

Strong hikers can visit the Skoki Valley in a long day, but most visitors overnight at Skoki Lodge or the nearby Merlin Meadows Campground. Merlin Lake is the best day hike from Skoki Lodge and the campground.

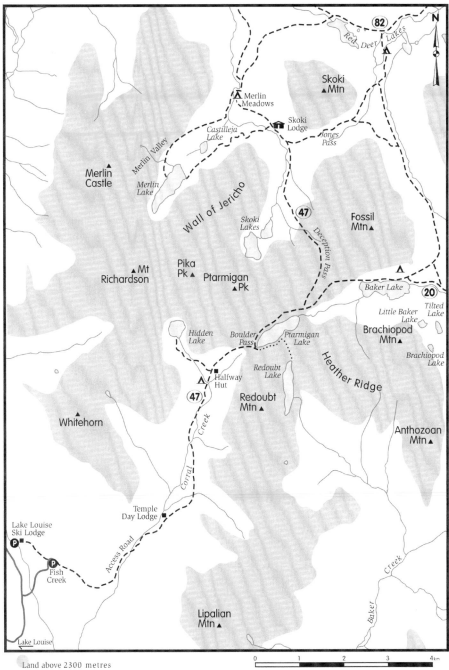

Land above 2300 metres

0   1   2   3   4 km

47 Boulder Pass—Skoki Valley

Fish Creek Parking Lot to Boulder Pass—8.6 km (5.3 mi)
Fish Creek Parking Lot to Skoki Lodge—14.4 km (8.9 mi)

Day trip or backpack
Allow 2 to 3 hours to Boulder Pass
3.5 to 5 hours to Skoki Valley
Elevation gain: 785 m (2,575 ft)
Maximum elevation: 2475 m (8,120 ft)

Maps: Lake Louise 82 N/8
　　　 Hector Lake 82 N/9
　　　 Lake Louise & Yoho (Gem Trek)

Access: From the Trans-Canada Highway interchange at Lake Louise, follow Whitehorn Road uphill toward the Lake Louise ski area. At 1.7 km turn right onto the gravel Fish Creek Road and follow it 1.0 km to the Fish Creek Parking Area. Restricted Access Road sign and gate marks the start of the hike.

0.0— Trailhead (1690 m).
　　　 N51°26.411' W116°09.097'

　　 — Follow Temple access road.

3.9— Temple Lodge (2015 m). Chairlift base stations.

　　 — Trail climbs across ski slope for 200 m and enters forest.

6.3— Corral Creek meadow.

7.1— Junction. Left 0.1 km to Hidden Lake Campground (Sk5) and Hidden Lake (1.3 km). Halfway Hut right 100 m. Boulder Pass ahead.

　　 — Steady uphill.

8.6— Boulder Pass (2345 m). Ptarmigan Lake (west end).

10.5— Junction. Baker Lake ahead 1.3 km. Deception Pass and Skoki Valley left.

　　 — Steep uphill over open terrain.

11.0— Deception Pass (2475 m).

　　 — Steady downhill.

13.9— Junction. Red Deer Lakes Campground right 4.6 km. Skoki Lodge ahead.

14.4— Skoki Lodge (2165 m).

15.6— Merlin Meadows Campground (Sk18).

This is the main access trail running to Skoki Valley in the heart of the Slate Range. Boulder Pass-Ptarmigan Valley is a spectacular destination for day hikers, highlighted by Ptarmigan Lake, wildflower meadows, rugged mountains and views to the distant peaks of Lake Louise. Backpackers usually travel on over Deception Pass to Skoki Valley, where they use Skoki Lodge or the Merlin Meadows Campground as base camps for halfday to day long trips to nearby points of interest.

The trail begins at the Fish Creek Parking Area, located at the bottom of the 4 km-long service road to the Temple day lodge and ski lifts. The hike up the gravel access road will not bring joy to your heart, but it is the fastest way to the sublime landscape beyond. (Mountain bikes are currently permitted to the end of the access road, and Skoki Lodge guests are transported up the road by van to begin their hike to the lodge.)

Once past the ski lifts at Temple, the road reverts to trail, which climbs steeply across a ski run and into a pleasant subalpine forest of spruce and fir with a scattering of alpine larch. The trail is wide and moderately graded, but since it is used for commercial horse trips and pack trains supplying Skoki Lodge, it is often quite muddy.

You soon reach the Corral Creek meadows, where there are views ahead to Boulder Pass and the rugged summits of Mount Richardson, Pika Peak and Ptarmigan Peak—the mountains that form the core of the Slate Range. Back to the southwest, 15 km away, glacier-topped Mount Temple (3544 m) dominates the skyline. The meadow is filled with a wide variety of colourful wildflowers in midsummer, and slate-coloured dippers are often seen flying from rock to rock along nearby Corral Creek.

At km 7.1 you reach the junction for

Redoubt Mountain and Ptarmigan Valley from Deception Pass

the 1.3 km trail running north to Hidden Lake Campground and Hidden Lake. Halfway Hut sits on a low bluff just south of the junction. The log cabin received its name during the early days of skiing when it served as an overnight stop for skiers—halfway between the Lake Louise railway station and Skoki Lodge. Today it is a day-use-only shelter for hikers.

Beyond Hidden Lake junction, the trail climbs through scattered forest to the summit of Boulder Pass and the west end of Ptarmigan Lake. At an elevation of 2345 m, this unique, lake-filled pass is at the upper limits of tree growth. There are open views down the lake to the distant peaks of Mount Douglas and Mount St. Bride, and the surrounding meadows and rockslides are well-populated with hoary marmots, pikas and white-tailed ptarmigan.

The trail continues along the slopes above the north shore of Ptarmigan Lake. Near the east end of the lake, at Baker Lake junction, it branches left and climbs to the summit of Deception Pass.

This rocky, alpine pass was named by Skoki ski pioneer Cyril Paris because he always thought its summit was closer than it really was when he was crossing it. From this lofty 2475 m vantage point, there is an all-encompassing view over the Ptarmigan Valley to Redoubt Mountain and through Boulder Pass to the distant mountains near Lake Louise. The pass is the best viewpoint on the trail and usually the farthest point reached by day hikers.

From Deception Pass the trail drops steadily northward towards the Skoki Valley. Views to the west include Ptarmigan Peak and the turquoise Skoki Lakes—Myosotis and Zigadenus (genus names for the forget-me-not and camas lily). After descending over rocky slopes and alpine meadows, the trail passes through scattered alpine larch and re-enters the forest.

You reach Skoki Lodge 3.4 km beyond the pass, and Merlin Meadows Campground (Sk18) is just over a kilometre beyond the lodge.

Boulder Pass Area Hikes

Strong day hikers can include a short side-trip to one of three high lakes just off the Boulder Pass trail. Any of these diversions add no more than 2.6 km to your day's total. If you stay at Hidden Lake (Sk5) or Baker Lake (Sk11) Campgrounds, you can visit any of these destinations on an easy half-day trip from your campsite.

Hidden Lake—1.3 km. This diminutive lake is embraced by the walls of Mount Richardson, Pika Peak and Ptarmigan Peak and surrounded by some of the finest wildflower meadows in Banff Park. The lake is reached by a short trail running north from the Boulder Pass trail at km 7.1 (100 m north of Halfway Hut).

From the junction, you immediately pass the Hidden Lake Campground and begin a steady climb up a shallow vale leading to the lake. The forest thins out during the ascent, giving way to stands of alpine larch and, finally, to lush, treeless meadows surrounding the lake.

Redoubt Lake—1.1 km. This high lake is hidden above Ptarmigan Lake beneath the east-facing cliffs of Redoubt Mountain. The short side-trip begins at the west end of Ptarmigan Lake on the summit of Boulder Pass.

The trail to Redoubt Lake is not well defined, but with a little perseverance you should reach the lake in 20 minutes or so from Boulder Pass. Follow close along the south shore of Ptarmigan Lake for 0.8 km, skirting (and sometimes clambering through) a major boulder field. Then cut straight up over open slopes to the obvious gap between Redoubt Mountain and Heather Ridge.

Once you reach the lake, continue down along the east side to its outlet, where you have a fine overview of larch forest, lush meadows and the Baker Creek valley to the southeast.

Baker Lake Campground—2.5 km. Baker Lake lies in marshy meadows just east of and 120 m below the Ptarmigan Valley. Though it is only a short side-trip off the Boulder Pass-Skoki Valley trail, it is often visited as an overnight destination rather than an extension to the Boulder Pass day hike.

The trail to Baker Lake branches right from the Boulder Pass-Skoki trail at km 10.5. From this junction on the open slopes beneath Deception Pass, it descends at a gradual to moderate grade to the lakeshore in just over a kilometre. Continue east along the north shoreline to reach Baker Lake Campground near the lake's outlet.

Anyone camping at Baker Lake should be extra fastidious in storing food. Not only are you in prime grizzly country, but the campground has a past history of camp-robbing wolverines.

Fossil Mountain Circuit—12.3 km. While most visitors to Skoki Valley camp there or stay at the lodge, others like to overnight in the high country at Baker Lake. However, it is still possible to sample the best of Skoki on a full day circuit around Fossil Mountain from Baker Lake Campground, including a side-trip to Merlin Lake.

Stay left at a junction just east of Baker Lake Campground and descend northeast gradually for 2 km to the open meadows of Cotton Grass Pass. The trail continues north through the pass for another kilometre, passing beneath the eastern slopes of Fossil Mountain to a junction where the trail to the Skoki Valley branches left (main trail continues north for another 2 km to Red Deer Lakes).

The Skoki branch bends west and runs between Fossil and Skoki Mountains for 3 km to intersect the Boulder Pass-Skoki Valley trail at km 13.9—500 m south of Skoki Lodge. You complete the loop by returning to Baker Lake via Deception Pass. (See *Boulder Pass-Skoki Valley.*)

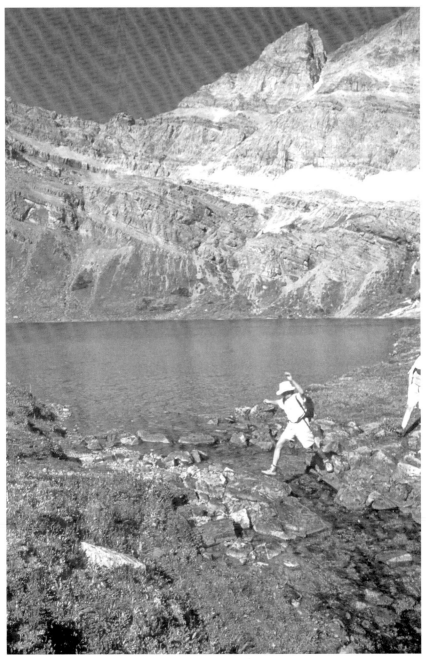

Hidden Lake

Skoki Valley Area Hikes

Skoki Lodge and Merlin Meadows Campground (Sk18) serve as base camps for a handful of half-day and full day trips in the Skoki Valley and to points of interest in adjacent valleys. Following are three of the more popular routes that utilize designated trails (*indicates distance approximate).

Skoki Lodge to Merlin Lake–3.1 km. Set between the colourfully-named Wall of Jericho and Merlin's Castle, Merlin Lake is one of the little-known gems of the Rockies. However, it is well known to anyone staying in the Skoki Valley and is the most popular hike from Skoki Lodge and Merlin Meadows Campground.

The high trail to the lake starts at the footbridge in front of Skoki Lodge. The trail was designed and partially constructed in the 1940s by mountaineer and master trail-builder Lawrence Grassi. Like other Grassi trails, it takes you through high boulder-fields, in this case along the Wall of Jericho, and allows you to traverse this tumbled slide with relative ease.

Emerging from the boulders, the trail skirts above Castilleja Lake and, following cairns and more recently constructed sections of trail, climbs to the cliff immediately below the Merlin Lake cirque. To ascend the cliff, pick the line of least resistance via the scree gully on the left side—a steep scramble over loose rock. From the top of the cliff, you descend through meadow and stunted trees to the lakeshore.

Massive Mount Richardson provides the backdrop for the lake, while Merlin's Castle contains its western shores. James Porter named the latter peak in 1911 for a "picturesque cluster of tower-like rocks" near the summit, which reminded him of a castle Merlin the Magician might have inhabited.

Merlin Meadows Campground to Merlin Lake—2.6 km*. You can also reach Merlin Lake via a horse trail along the northwest side of Merlin Valley. While this is a shorter and more direct route from Merlin Meadows Campground, escaping the meadows is a bit messy.

Cross Skoki Creek just below the campground (look for a makeshift log bridge), then follow indistinct trail upstream. Watch for a defined track branching right from the meadows.

This trail switchbacks up along the northwest side of the valley toward the Merlin cirque. In circumnavigating the cliff beneath the lake, it climbs above the cirque, then drops through scrub forest to the lake's north shore. (We prefer to hike to the lake via Grassi's highline route and return on the horse trail.)

Skoki Lodge to Natural Bridge–9.5 km*. The Red Deer Lakes and Campground can be reached over good trail branching east from the Boulder Pass-Skoki Valley trail near Skoki Lodge. The three Red Deer Lakes lie in low marshy terrain with willow meadows, and trails between the campground and lakes are many and muddy.

The most compelling reason to hike this trail is to continue down the Red Deer River to Natural Bridge—an impressive cataract that thunders through a hole in limestone bedrock. However, the hike is a rather long, messy adventure that requires two leg-chilling fords.

From the junction 0.5 km south of Skoki Lodge, follow the trail running due east between Skoki and Fossil Mountains—a gap known locally as Jones Pass. As the trail emerges from the pass and bends north around Skoki Mountain, trails from Baker Lake and Cotton Grass Pass intersect from the right (stay left at all intersections).

Merlin Lake and Mount Richardson

At the Red Deer Lakes Campground junction, you can stay left and make a short side-trip to Upper Red Deer Lake—the largest and most scenic of the three Red Deer Lakes.

To continue down the Red Deer Valley to Natural Bridge, follow the trail leading to Red Deer Lakes Campground. Continue on the hiker's trail leading east from the campground. This alternative to the horse trail runs 0.3 km to a bridge across the headwaters stream that forms the Red Deer River. On the opposite side you intersect the Red Deer River trail 200 m west of Cyclone Patrol Cabin.

Turn right and continue down-valley along the north side of the Red Deer 2.3 km to the Natural Bridge junction. Follow the Natural Bridge trail right to a ford of the Red Deer (usually calf deep).

The trail continues south up a narrow side-valley between Oyster Peak and Mount Douglas for 2 km to Natural Bridge, but before you reach the falls, you must make yet another soaking ford of the valley's main stream.

Little Pipestone Creek. The trails running down Little Pipestone Creek to the Pipestone River are tempting for many who are staying in the Skoki Valley or at Red Deer Lakes Campground. However, both routes consist of multiple tracks that are brushy, vague, muddy and cut-up by horse traffic, and the route down Skoki Creek from Merlin Meadows requires a ford of Little Pipestone Creek. And if that isn't enough, views are limited until you reach the Pipestone River.

We can only recommend these trails to curious explorers or backpackers bound for Molar Pass or the upper Pipestone River valley (see *Pipestone River* and *Molar Pass*).

48 Pipestone River

Pipestone Parking Area to Pipestone Pass—36.2 km (22.5 mi)*

Backpack

Allow 2 to 3 days to Pipestone Pass

Elevation gain: 894 m (2,933 ft)

Maximum elevation: 2449 m (8,036 ft)

Maps: Lake Louise 82 N/8
Hector Lake 82 N/9

Access: Follow the Trans-Canada Highway west 1.1 km from the Lake Louise exit overpass to Slate Avenue (intersection marked by "Pipestone" trail sign). Follow this paved road uphill 0.2 km to another intersection. Follow "Pipestone" trail sign to right 100 m to the trailhead parking area beside a horse corral.

0.0— Trailhead (1555 m).
N51°26.014 W116°11.125'

0.9— Junction. Mud Lake right 0.8 km.

3.0— Trail comes abreast of Pipestone River.

7.0— End of bicycle access.

14.5— Pipestone River ford. Major crossing to east bank.

17.5— Little Pipestone River ford.

18.0— Junction (1850 m). Little Pipestone Patrol Cabin. Red Deer Lakes and Skoki Valley right. Pipestone River trail fords river to west bank.

18.1— Junction. Molar Pass left. Pipestone Pass right.

27.0— Singing Meadows (old campsite). Pipestone River ford to east bank.

28.0— Junction. Fish Lakes-North Molar Pass left. Pipestone Pass ahead.

36.2— Pipestone Pass (2449 m). Trail continues north down Siffleur River. See also *North Molar-Pipestone-Dolomite Circuit.*

*Distances approximate

(Trail not fully shown on maps in this book.)

The Pipestone River trail is broad, well-graded and a popular bike route for the first 7 km. Beyond that point it is a rather grim, uninspiring journey over heavily-used horse trail. A serious ford of the Pipestone makes all of this tedium seem rather silly. There are better ways to reach the upper Pipestone Valley (see *North Molar-Pipestone-Dolomite Circuit*). But if you must persevere, here are the details:

From the parking area, the trail climbs quickly past Mud Lake junction and onto a forested plateau. The broad, solid track flattens out and soon comes abreast of the Pipestone River. At the 7-km mark bike access ends and so does the good trail. A rough, muddy horse trail leads onward along the west side of the river.

At approximately 14.5 km, the track swings across the Pipestone's multi-channels to the east bank. While this ford has been navigated by hikers, it can be hazardous during high runoff.

Further upstream there are fords across Little Pipestone Creek and, at Little Pipestone Patrol Cabin, back across the Pipestone to its west bank (usually mid-calf to thigh deep over slippery rocks). Two trails intersect at this crossing: the Little Pipestone trail from Skoki on the east side and the Molar Creek trail on the west.

The remainder of the trip to Pipestone Pass is relatively open and scenic. You enter Singing Meadows around 24 km and, at the north end of the meadows, pass an old campsite to a relatively easy ford to the east side of the river. After passing the Fish Lakes junction, the trail climbs to open subalpine forest and wildflower meadows.

The final 2 km to the pass is steep, rocky and windswept. The high route from Fish Lakes intersects from the left near the summit. (See *North Molar-Pipestone-Dolomite Circuit.*)

49 Mud Lake

Pipestone Parking Area to Mud Lake—1.7 km (1.1 mi)

For anyone in search of an escape from the bustling village of Lake Louise, Mud Lake is a pleasant if not overly spectacular destination. The lake is just over 500 m in length and encircled by a dense forest of lodgepole pine, but the lakeshore is open enough to allow views to Whitehorn and Lipalian Mountains.

The short hike begins from the Pipestone trailhead on the opposite side of the Trans-Canada Highway from Lake Louise Village. Beyond the trailhead kiosk and access gate, you follow a gravel service road that climbs gradually into dense pine forest. At 0.4 km, the Mud Lake and Pipestone River trails branch left from the road. In another 0.5 km, the Mud Lake trail forks uphill to the right from the broad Pipestone track. From this final junction, it is an easy 0.8 km ascent to the lakeshore.

Access: Follow the Trans-Canada Highway west 1.1 km from the Lake Louise exit overpass to Slate Avenue (intersection also marked by "Pipestone" trail sign). Follow this paved road uphill 0.2 km to another intersection. Follow "Pipestone" trail sign to right and continue another 100 m to the trailhead parking area beside a horse corral. N51°26.014 W116°11.125' *Maps: Lake Louise 82 N/8; Lake Louise & Yoho (Gem Trek).*

Icefields Parkway

The 230-km Icefields Parkway (Hwy 93) between Lake Louise and Jasper is undeniably one of Canada's most scenic highways. More importantly for hikers, the road's southern section, running through the northern part of Banff Park and into southern Jasper Park, is the highest stretch of road in Canada. Many hikes originating from the Parkway, particularly in the vicinity of Bow Summit (2069 m) and Sunwapta Pass (2035 m), get you into the alpine quicker than elsewhere in the mountain parks. On the Banff Park section of the Parkway, there are three trails that reach treeline in less than 5 km—Helen Lake, Bow Summit Lookout and Parker Ridge.

There are also a number of low elevation trails in the North Saskatchewan Valley near Saskatchewan River Crossing—Mistaya Canyon, Howse River Flats, Warden Lake and Glacier Lake—which are usually snowfree by early June. And trails running over North Molar and Dolomite Passes travel through vast alpine expanses and are the most direct routes to the park's remote northeast wilderness.

BANFF ICEFIELDS PARKWAY — SOUTH

Land above 2300 metres

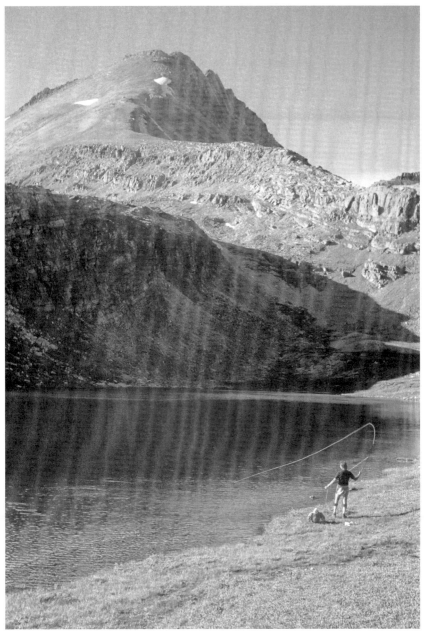

Helen Lake

50 Molar Pass

Icefields Parkway to Molar Pass—10.5 km (6.5 mi)

Day trip or backpack
Allow 3 hours one way
Elevation gain: 510 m (1,675 ft)
Maximum elevation: 2340 m (7,675 ft)
Maps: Hector Lake 82 N/9

Access: Follow the Icefields Parkway north from the Trans-Canada Highway 24 km (15 mi) to the Mosquito Creek Campground. The trail is across the highway from the campground entrance at the northeast corner of the Mosquito Creek bridge. (A parking area is on the west side of road beside the entrance to the Mosquito Creek Hostel).

0.0— Trailhead (1830 m).
     N51°37.801' W116°19.711'

     — Short, steep climb followed by gradual uphill on rooty, rocky trail.

3.3— Side stream (bridged).

3.5— Side stream (bridged).

4.1— Major side stream (bridged).

5.0— Mosquito Creek Campground (Mo5). Bridge to south side of Mosquito Creek 150 m past campground.

6.8— Bridge to north side of Mosquito Creek.

7.4— Junction. *North Molar Pass—Fish Lakes* trail left. Molar Pass right.

     — Steady climb toward pass.

10.2— Trail crests Molar Pass meadows.

10.5— Molar Pass summit (2340 m).

When you hike the trail up Mosquito Creek, you have a choice of two high routes near the headwaters—Molar Pass or North Molar Pass. While both possess expansive views and some of the finest wildflower meadows in Banff Park, most day hikers find Molar Pass a more reasonable goal. Beyond Molar Pass, the trail continues down the Molar Creek valley, providing backpackers with an optional, if somewhat lacklustre and muddy, route to the Pipestone Valley.

Through its first 7 km, the trail rises gradually along open willow flats and subalpine forest near Mosquito Creek. The track is rocky and rooty most of the way, and there are numerous wet sections that can be particularly messy during wet summers or when a horse party has preceded you.

Three small tributary streams (all bridged) are crossed in the first 4 km. At km 5.0 you pass Mosquito Creek Campground—a good base for a more leisurely day trip to either Molar or North Molar Pass.

Beyond the campground you immediately cross Mosquito Creek and then recross it 1.8 km farther along. At km 7.4, you reach the junction where the North Molar Pass route branches left from the Molar Pass trail. The Molar trail is a bit indistinct over the next kilometre, but horse tracks and churned-up meadow span the brief gaps.

As the forest opens up, you get your first views of Molar Pass ahead. There are also numerous lush meadows sporting showy wildflowers, such as western anemone, globe flower, marsh marigold, purple fleabane, valerian, and ragwort.

Over the last 2 km the trail climbs out of the trees and ascends across the valley's steep headwall to the crest of the pass. Another 300 m of nearly flat, alpine meadow brings you to the true summit.

The Molar Pass meadows are just as impressive as those beneath nearby North Molar Pass, though the flowers are smaller, ground-hugging alpine varieties. The pass also offers an excellent view of twin-peaked Molar Mountain (3022 m), rising above the meadows to the southeast. Farther off in that direction, across the Pipestone Valley, are the rugged peaks of the Slate Range, which contain the Skoki region. The glacier-crested summits of the Mount Hector massif rise immediately above the pass to the west and south.

Molar Pass is so extensive it invites exploration and aimless wandering. Another option is to visit Mosquito Lake and the meadows beneath North Molar Pass on your way back by hiking up that branch trail for 3 km; or you can traverse due north across open meadows to intersect with the North Molar trail near tiny Mosquito Lake. However, either of these options makes for a rather strenuous day trip. Visiting both passes in one day is far more reasonable from the Mosquito Creek Campground. (See also *North Molar Pass-Fish Lakes.*)

Molar Creek. The Molar Creek trail runs southeast from the summit of Molar Pass for another 14 km to the Pipestone River trail. From that junction you can either ford the Pipestone and ascend Little Pipestone Creek to Skoki Valley or turn left toward Pipestone Pass and Fish Lakes. The trail also serves as an optional last leg for the Clearwater-Red Deer Circuit (see *Clearwater River*).

Be forewarned, however, that the trail down Molar Creek is rough, very wet, and has been a disappointment to most people who have hiked it.

51 North Molar Pass—Fish Lakes

Icefields Parkway to North Molar Pass—11.9 km (7.4 mi)
Icefields Parkway to Fish Lakes Campground—15.2 km (9.5 mi)

Day trip or backpack

Allow 5 hours to Fish Lakes

Elevation gain: 760 m (2,500 ft)
         loss: 365 m (1,200 ft)

Maximum elevation: 2590 m (8,500 ft)

Maps: Hector Lake 82 N/9

Access: Follow the Icefields Parkway north from the Trans-Canada Highway 24 km (15 mi) to Mosquito Creek Campground. The trail is across the highway from the campground entrance (parking available on west side of road beside the entrance to Mosquito Creek Hostel).

- 0.0—Trailhead (1830 m).
   N51°37.801' W116°19.711'

   —Short, steep climb followed by gradual uphill on rooty, rocky trail.

- 3.3—Side stream (bridged).

- 3.5—Side stream (bridged).

- 4.1—Major side stream (bridged).

- 5.0—Mosquito Creek Campground (Mo5). Bridge to south side of Mosquito Creek 150 m past campground.

- 6.8—Bridge to north side of Mosquito Creek.

- 7.4—Junction. Molar Pass right 3.1 km. North Molar Pass left.

   —Trail climbs above trees and levels out into alpine meadows.

- 9.2—Mosquito Lake.

- 10.9—Steep climb to North Molar Pass begins.

- 11.9—North Molar Pass (2590 m).

   —Short steep descent levelling out into alpine meadow.

- 15.2—Fish Lakes Campground (Mo18) and Upper Fish Lake (2225 m).

- 15.4—Junction. Fish Lakes Patrol Cabin and Pipestone Pass highline route left. Lower Fish Lake ahead.

- 16.1—Lower Fish Lake.

The trail running up Mosquito Creek from the Icefields Parkway leads to one of the most extensive alpine meadows in Banff Park. While it is possible to day hike to the best of this meadow, or even lofty North Molar Pass, most folks prefer to backpack over North Molar to Fish Lakes Campground. From there they can spend days exploring the lakes and meadows above the Pipestone Valley. In addition, the trail provides the easiest and most direct route to Pipestone and Clearwater Passes.

The first 7.4 km of the trail follows the same route as Molar Pass (see *Molar Pass*). At a junction near the Mosquito Creek headwaters, the North Molar trail branches east and climbs through verdant subalpine meadows—an exceptional wildflower garden dominated by the showy purple blooms of fleabane during late July and early August.

Sharp fingers of rock and steep talus slopes form a huge amphitheatre that encloses the treeless upper meadows. To the west the glacier-clad ramparts of Mount Hector create a rugged backdrop for tiny Mosquito Lake.

Near the 11-km mark, the rolling meadows are left behind and the stiff climb to North Molar Pass begins. Near the pass views extend westward to the mountains of the Bow Valley.

At 2590 m, this rockbound notch is the third highest trail-accessible pass in Banff Park. Winds whistle through the gap throughout the year, and these prevailing westerlies form a snowdrift on the east side of the summit that can be a bit of an obstacle early in the season.

The drop to Upper Fish Lake from the pass is rapid and steep, passing through an alpine landscape constricted by vertical walls and rockslide debris. The lake is seen from above long before it is reached, cradled in a pretty basin overlooking the Pipestone Valley. Just over 3 km below the pass, the trail finally reaches the open shoreline and campground—a peaceful spot but for the occasional cascade of rock falling from cliffs on the opposite shore.

The campground is an excellent base for wandering and exploration. It is just under a kilometre to Lower Fish Lake— a much smaller body of water bordered by one of the most northerly stands of alpine larch in North America. By contouring south along the slope of Molar Mountain from the lower lake, you can reach another small lake after approximately 2 km of trail-less hiking.

Pipestone Pass. One of the most popular destinations beyond Fish Lakes is the Pipestone Pass region. The pass can be reached as a day trip from the campground or by extending your backpack to the north. (See *North Molar-Pipestone-Dolomite Circuit.*)

While it is possible to descend directly from Lower Fish Lake to the Pipestone River trail via a rough, steep 2-km trail, most people prefer a more direct approach to Pipestone Pass via a highline route that contours around to the

northwest from Upper Fish Lake. This trail stays at or above treeline throughout its 9-km journey to the pass. At last report, the trail is reasonably well defined with occasional marshy sections, but where the track is indistinct, the route to the pass is quite obvious in this open country.

The trail branches north near the Upper Fish Lake outlet and runs to the nearby patrol cabin. On the opposite side of a small stream flowing behind the cabin, pick up the trail again as it begins its contour around to the northwest.

Just over 2 km from the patrol cabin the trail passes below Moose Lake (unnamed on the topo map) and, 2.5 km farther along, skirts another small unnamed lake. The route continues high to the northwest along open slopes and meadows, intersecting with the Pipestone River trail on the 2449-m summit of the pass.

52 Helen Lake—Dolomite Pass

Icefields Parkway to Helen Lake—6.0 km (3.7 mi)
Icefields Parkway to Dolomite Pass—8.9 km (5.0 mi)

Half-day to day trip

Allow 1.5 to 2 hours to Helen Lake

Elevation gain: 550 m (1,800 ft)

Maximum elevation: 2500 m (8,200 ft)

Maps: Hector Lake 82 N/9
Bow Lake-Sask Crossing
(GemTrek)

Access: Follow the Icefields Parkway north from the Trans-Canada Highway 33 km (20.5 mi) to the Crowfoot Glacier Viewpoint. The short spur road to the Helen Lake trail parking area is on the opposite side of the highway from the viewpoint.

0.0— Trailhead (1950 m).
N51°39.848' W116°26.307'

— Moderate to steep climb through subalpine forest.

2.4— Avalanche slope with open views.

2.9— Open views for remainder of hike.

3.4— Trail turns north at end of ridge.

— Grade moderates, trail contours into Helen Lake cirque.

4.5— Rockslide.

5.0— Helen Creek crossing.

6.0— Helen Lake (2405 m).

— Steep switchbacking ascent.

6.9— Cirque Peak south ridge (2500 m).

— Steep descent.

8.1— Katherine Lake (2375 m).

8.9— Dolomite Pass (2395 m). Trail continues down Dolomite Creek (see *North Molar-Pipestone-Dolomite Circuit*).

Wildflower meadows, lofty lakes and castellate peaks provide a constant change of scene that draws you onward to a remarkable panorama of a vast, alpine landscape. The Helen Lake meadows are also home to an amazing number of hoary marmots, who seem to have nothing better to do than sit in the sun and count passing hikers. However, when the weather is deteriorating in the Bow Valley, it is absolutely vile on these exposed highlands.

The trail climbs steadily through forest along the west-facing slopes of the Bow Valley for the first 3 km and then emerges onto steep mountainside meadows. Views open across the valley to Crowfoot Mountain and Glacier, and the sharp summit of Mount Hector (3394 m), down-valley to the southeast.

The trail reaches the south end of a long ridge at km 3.4, where a scattering of whitebark pine indicate that you are nearing treeline. Here it switches around 180 degrees and contours into the amphitheatre containing Helen Lake.

After another kilometre of gradual ascent through lightly forested meadows, you drop beneath the toe of a relatively recent rockslide. The pile of tumbled boulders is surrounded by a lush snowbed plant community filled with the colourful blooms of purple fleabane, paintbrush, ragwort and valerian. Beyond the slide the trail climbs above the last trees and remains above treeline to Dolomite Pass and beyond.

Helen Lake is bordered by open alpine meadows and scree slopes beneath the summit of Cirque Peak. It is a great place to kick-back and enjoy the scene, which is animated by the antics of the resident hoary marmots and, occasionally, by the over-flight of a golden eagle.

Helen Lake would be an above average destination on most hikes, but you shouldn't end your day there. Gather

Katherine Lake and Dolomite Pass from trail summit

your strength and continue for at least another 0.9 km up a steep series of switchbacks to the rocky ridge extending south from Cirque Peak.

The 2500-m ridge is the highest point on the trail, and it provides an outstanding overview of Katherine Lake and Dolomite Pass to the east and Helen Lake and its meadows back to the southwest. By leaving the trail and hiking to the southeast end of this ridge, you gain another 50 m of elevation and unobstructed views south along the Great Divide.

For most day hikers the ridge is a good spot to turn for home, but strong hikers can reach even better views by scrambling up the broken scree slopes to the north leading to the summit of Cirque Peak (2993 m), one of the most easily-ascended mountains in the park. Or, if you don't mind climbing back over this ridge at the end of the day, you can descend to Katherine Lake and Dolomite Pass.

The trail drops nearly 100 m to the north end of Katherine Lake, which stretches beneath the castellate cliffs of Dolomite Peak. An opening beyond the south end of the lake serves as a window to the southern half of Banff Park, and on a clear day the sharp horn of Mount Assiniboine is visible 100 km away.

Though the trail is not well defined beyond Katherine Lake, it is an easy climb over spongy alpine meadows to a small lake on the crest of Dolomite Pass.

Katherine and Helen Lakes were both named for the daughters of the Rev. Harry P. Nichols, who was with a party of wayward mountaineers who stumbled across the pass in July 1898. Dolomite Peak received its name because it reminded the alpinists of the European Dolomites.

Dolomite Creek–Isabella Lake. Backpackers can continue over Dolomite Pass and down Dolomite Creek to Isabella Lake, 13.4 km north of the pass. The trail is rugged and reserved for experienced hikers who don't mind fording swift-flowing streams. (See *North Molar-Pipestone-Dolomite Circuit.*)

Mosquito Creek to Crowfoot Glacier Viewpoint—68.9 km (42.8 mi)*

Backpack
Allow 4 to 5 days
Maximum elevation: 2590 m (8,500 ft)
Minimum elevation: 1830 m (6,000 ft)
Maps: Hector Lake 82 N/9
       Siffleur River 82 N/16

Access: Southern access to the circuit is from the Icefields Parkway opposite the Mosquito Creek Campground (see *North Molar Pass-Fish Lakes*). Northern access is from the Helen Lake parking area opposite the Crowfoot Glacier viewpoint (see *Helen Lake-Dolomite Pass*).

0.0—Mosquito Creek trailhead (1830 m).
     N51°37.801' W116°19.711'

5.0—Mosquito Creek Campground (Mo5).

7.4—Junction. *Molar Pass* ahead 3.1 km.
     North Molar Pass left.

9.2—Mosquito Lake.

11.9—North Molar Pass (2590 m).

15.2—Upper Fish Lake (2225 m). Fish Lakes
      Campground (Mo18).

15.4—Junction. Pipestone Pass left.

18.0—Moose Lake.

24.0—Pipestone Pass (2449 m).
      Intersection with the *Pipestone River*
      trail.

27.0—Junction. Clearwater Pass right
      1.0 km.

36.2—Siffleur River Campground (Sf).

39.4—Siffleur River ford.

43.2—Dolomite Creek ford.

43.3—Junction (1800 m). Park boundary
      right 1.5 km. Dolomite Pass left.

46.6—Isabella Lake (1830 m).

51.9—Dolomite Creek ford.

55.2—Dolomite Creek ford.

56.5—Waterfall.

60.0—Dolomite Pass (2395 m).

62.0—Cirque Peak south ridge (2500 m).

62.9—Helen Lake.

68.9—Helen Lake trailhead (1950 m).
      N51°39.848' W116°26.307'

*distance approximate

This four-to-five day backpack traverses one of Banff Park's prime wilderness regions. The trail crosses three high passes, and approximately 32 km of the circuit is at or above treeline. It is an exceptional trip, but you should be comfortable fording swift streams, since there are three crossings of Dolomite Creek that can be tricky when water levels are high. And, you're in prime grizzly country, so be observant and keep a clean camp.

We prefer to start this circuit from the North Molar Pass trailhead at Mosquito Creek and hike it in a counter-clockwise direction. By travelling in this direction it is easier to follow the high traverse from Fish Lakes to Pipestone Pass than visa versa, and you save most of the fords until the latter part of the trip.

Since the circuit doesn't make a complete loop, you must arrange transportation or plan on hitchhiking between the Mosquito Creek and Helen Lake trailheads.

Mosquito Creek trailhead to Pipestone Pass—24.0 km. The first leg of the journey follows the trail up Mosquito Creek and over North Molar Pass to Fish Lakes—the usual first night destination. From Fish Lakes Campground, you follow the highline route northwest past Moose Lake and another small, unnamed lake to the summit of Pipestone Pass. (See *North Molar Pass-Fish Lakes*.)

From Pipestone Pass views open to the northwest, carrying the eye down the Siffleur Valley nearly as far as the Kootenay Plains. This is a very exposed viewpoint, a long way from the nearest trees, and a grim place in a storm.

Pipestone Pass to Isabella Lake—22.6 km. North of the pass the trail continues into the Siffleur Valley. Approximately 3 km beyond the pass the trail to Clearwater Pass branches right. The junction is not obvious and the track to the pass is

Upper Pipestone Valley from Pipestone Pass

poorly defined, but the route is straightforward across meadows and rocky open terrain. If the weather is reasonable, you should consider a side-trip to the pass (1.0 km) and the Devon Lakes (2.6 km).

Beyond Clearwater junction the trail steps its way down from the alpine into heavy forest, where conditions are often boggy. Lower down it enters willow meadows and passes the Siffleur River Campground.

Approximately 15 km north of Pipestone Pass, the trail fords the Siffleur River to its west bank (usually knee-deep and straightforward). Nearly 4 km farther along, after crossing a low, forested ridge, there is yet another ford—a more difficult wade of Dolomite Creek that can be treacherous during high water. On the opposite side, the Dolomite Creek trail intersects from the south. Turn left and begin the long ascent of Dolomite Creek to Dolomite Pass.

After passing an abandoned cabin, you reach the south end of Isabella Lake and a primitive campsite in just under 3 km. While random camping is allowed in the Dolomite Valley, this is as good a spot to overnight as any.

Isabella Lake to Helen Lake trailhead—22.3 km. Continuing up-valley from Isabella Lake, you immediately encounter erratic track along multi-channeled mudflats (follow the forest margin on the west side and watch for the trail's reappearance). Less than 2 km beyond these flats, you make a knee-to-thigh-deep crossing to the east side of Dolomite Creek. After a series of switchbacks and a mudslide traverse, you recross to the west side of the creek—another swift, moderately-difficult ford during periods of high runoff.

The last 5 km to Dolomite Pass climbs steeply beside a waterfall and across a rockslide before emerging into the stark treeless landscape at the creek's headwaters. The trail is faint below Dolomite Pass, but the route to its summit is obvious—veering up to the right across open, rolling alpine meadow.

From Dolomite Pass, the final 8.9 km climbs over a 2500-m ridge to Helen Lake and descends to the Helen Lake trailhead on the Icefields Parkway. (See *Helen Lake-Dolomite Pass.*)

54 Bow Glacier Falls

Bow Lake Parking Area to Bow Glacier Falls—4.7 km (2.9 mi)

Half-day trip

Allow 1.5 hours one way

Elevation gain: 95 m (310 ft)

Maximum elevation: 2055 m (6,740 ft)

Maps: Hector Lake 82 N/9
       Bow Lake-Sask Crossing
       (Gem Trek)

Access: Follow the Icefields Parkway north from the Trans-Canada Highway 36 km (22.5 mi) to the Num-Ti-Jah Lodge access road at Bow Lake. Follow the gravel road 0.4 km to the public parking area and washrooms. The trailhead kiosk is at the west end of the parking area.

0.0— Trailhead (1960 m).
      N51°40.727' W116°27.886'

   — Trail follows Bow Lake shoreline.

0.3— Trail sign at lodge parking area.

   — Trail angles across willow flats to lake's north shore.

1.9— Bow Lake inlet.

   — Trail follows along stream.

2.7— Broad gravel flats.

3.4— Bottom of canyon.

   — Steep uphill along canyon for 200 m.

3.6— Bow Glacier basin viewpoint.

   — Trail descends and crosses basin to falls.

4.7— Bow Glacier Falls (2055 m).

The Bow Glacier basin has been a popular half-day trip for travellers ever since the tourist-explorer Walter Wilcox visited it in 1896. The glacier, which filled much of the basin in Wilcox's day, has retreated above the headwall, leaving a 120-m waterfall as the only hint of the icefield hidden above.

A broad pathway skirts along Bow Lake from the trailhead parking area to a secondary trailhead just beyond the lodge parking lot. From there, it launches off across willow flats to the lake's northern shoreline. A more modest track, often muddy and sometimes flooded in spots, follows along the lake for more than a kilometre to the alluvial flats at its inlet. Views over the first 2 km include Crowfoot Mountain across the lake and the leaning spire of Mount St. Nicholas rising from the white expanse of the Wapta Glacier on the skyline ahead.

The route beyond the lake is mainly flat, with an occasional brief climb, and follows near the silty, glacier-fed steam draining the basin. At 3.4 km you reach a narrow canyon and make a short, steep climb along its rim (this section is hazardous when wet, icy or snow-covered). As described by Wilcox: "Where the canyon is deepest an immense block of limestone about twenty-five feet long has fallen down, and with either end resting on the canyon walls, it affords a natural bridge over the gloomy chasm."

The trail does not cross the natural bridge, but continues up along the gorge to the sparsely-forested crest of a terminal moraine. From this viewpoint the glacial basin lies beneath you, and Bow Glacier Falls pours off the headwall beyond.

The trail continues another kilometre across the rocky basin to the base of the falls, which is fed by a small meltwater lake near the toe of the Bow Glacier. The waterfall is most impressive during the warmest days of summer.

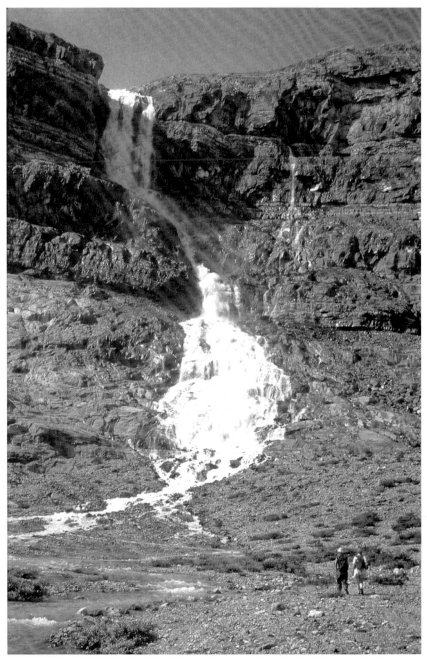

Bow Glacier Falls

55 Bow Summit Lookout

Bow Summit Parking Area to Bow Summit Lookout—3.1 km (1.9 mi)

Half-day trip

Allow 1 hour one way

Elevation gain: 230 m (760 ft)

Maximum elevation: 2315 m (7,600 ft)

Maps: Blaeberry River 82 N/10
  Bow Lake-Sask Crossing
  (Gem Trek)

Access: Follow the Icefields Parkway to Bow Summit, 41 km (25.5 mi) north of its junction with the Trans-Canada Highway. Follow the viewpoint access road branching west from the Parkway 0.5 km (0.3 mi) and turn right at the road split into the Bow Summit parking area. (The road leading to the upper parking area is reserved for tour buses and the disabled.) The trail begins at the far end of the parking area.

0.0— Trailhead (2085 m).
  N51°43.022' W116°29.982'
  —Steady uphill on paved trail.

0.6— Peyto Lake Viewpoint (2120 m).
  —Follow paved trail branching uphill (right-hand option).

0.7— Junction. Follow middle trail angling uphill to left from interpretive sign.

0.9— Junction (unsigned). Paved nature trail turns right. Follow old roadbed ahead.
  —Steady uphill on roadbed.

2.4— Descent into basin.

2.6— Stream crossing.
  —Steep climb.

3.1— Bow Summit Lookout (2315 m).

The paved trail leading to Peyto Lake viewpoint is the most popular short walk along the Icefields Parkway. However, after you visit this teeming overlook, leave the crowds behind and continue upwards to the Bow Summit fire lookout site. There you will find peace, sublime alpine meadows and a lofty viewpoint for the Bow Summit environs.

From the Bow Summit parking area, follow the paved nature trail uphill to the viewing platform overlooking Peyto Lake. Take the obligatory photo, then escape on the right-hand of two paved trails leading uphill.

In 100 m you arrive at a three-way junction at an interpretive sign. Continue on the middle branch angling uphill to the left of the sign—an arm of the upper Bow Summit nature trail loop. In a few minutes the paved trail turns right, but you continue straight ahead on the old fire lookout service road.

The roadbed soon switchbacks over a rise with views back to Peyto Lake. Just in case you think you are entering little-known territory at this point, be aware that this thinly-forested knoll was where Hollywood movie stars Alan Ladd and Jay Silverheels (aka Tonto) galloped on horseback during filming of the motion picture *Saskatchewan* in 1953.

From the rise, the trail turns southeast and climbs steadily along the mountain slope. Views over Bow Summit continue to improve throughout the ascent. As you climb, you enter the *kruppelholz* zone—an area where islands of altitude-stunted alpine fir dwindle into treeless alpine meadow.

Wildflowers bloom in profusion throughout this section in July and August, dominated by white-flowered valerian and white, pink and magenta varieties of Indian paintbrush. Higher up the lush growth is replaced by fields of ground-hugging white mountain avens, and white and pink mountain heather.

Mistaya Valley from Bow Summit Lookout

At km 2.4 the trail drops into a draw and crosses a small stream beneath a huge rockslide. We call this Marmot Basin, since we have often encountered curious hoary marmots bounding along the stream and sunning themselves on the nearby boulders. The stream is bordered with moisture-loving flowers, including yellow ragwort and red-stemmed saxifrage.

The roadbed climbs steeply beside a great mound of rock rubble over the final 0.5 km to the alpine knoll where the Bow Summit lookout cabin once stood. (Until it was removed in the 1970s, it was the highest fire lookout in Banff Park.)

From the lookout site you have open views of the Icefields Parkway crossing Bow Summit and the entire Mistaya Valley, including Waterfowl Lakes, to the north. By following a steep footpath for another 200 m beyond the knoll, you reach the best viewpoint for Bow Lake and the glaciated peaks to the south.

The mountain rising directly above you is Mount Jimmy Simpson, named for the pioneer guide and outfitter who began the development of Num-Ti-Jah Lodge on the shores of Bow Lake in 1922. He lived there until his death in 1972 at age 95.

56 Peyto Lake South

Bow Summit Parking Area to Peyto Lake—2.8 km (1.7 mi)

Though many travellers admire the turquoise waters of Peyto Lake from the viewpoint at Bow Summit, few walk to its shore. And that, for most, is fortunate, since the 2.2-km trail connecting the viewpoint to the lakeshore drops 275 m—a formidable hole that might prove the undoing of many idle tourists.

Two trails lead to Peyto's shores. The trail descending from the viewpoint, while being the most strenuous, is probably the most interesting since it allows hikers to explore the vast alluvial fan at the lake's south end or continue on towards Peyto Glacier.

After hiking from the Bow Summit parking area to the Peyto Lake viewing platform, follow the right of two paved trails leading uphill. Just 40 m above the viewpoint, beyond the end of the guardrail, the unmarked trail to the lake plunges into the forest.

After switchbacking madly downward through dense forest for 2 km, the trail emerges onto the alluvial flats southeast of Peyto Lake's inlet. From here you can roam across the flats to the lakeshore or head off in the direction of Peyto Glacier to the south.

Access: Follow the Icefields Parkway to Bow Summit, 41 km (25.5 mi) north of its junction with the Trans-Canada Highway. Follow the viewpoint access road branching west from the Parkway 0.5 km (0.3 mi) and turn right at the road split into the Bow Summit parking area. The trail starts from the far end of the parking area. N51°43.022' W116°29.982' *Map: Blaeberry River 82 N/10; Bow Lake-Saskatchewan Crossing (Gem Trek).*

57 Peyto Lake East

Icefields Parkway to Peyto Lake—1.4 km (0.9 mi)

A short, seldom-travelled trail descends through dense forest to a shallow bay on the east shore of Peyto Lake. There are good views south from this shoreline to the Peyto Glacier and surrounding peaks, and across the lake to Caldron Peak and Mount Patterson.

From the lower edge of the parking area entrance, follow a steep, overgrown path downhill 100 m to the old Banff-Jasper Highway roadbed. Turn left and continue on a gradual descent of the old roadbed for 0.3 km to where an unsigned footpath branches left into dense spruce-pine forest.

Another 1.0 km of rooty, occasionally muddy, mostly downhill trail brings you to the lakeshore. Elevation loss from the parking area is 85 m.

If you arrive on the shores of Peyto Lake early in the season, you will likely be pinned against the shore by high water levels. However, later in the season, when lake levels are lower, it is possible to walk south along a pleasant gravel beach for 400 m or more.

While you lounge on the beach, you might commune with the spirit of pioneer guide and outfitter Bill Peyto, the lake's reclusive namesake. Legend says when Peyto guided clients here at the turn of the 20th century, he would leave the "dudes" in camp on Bow Summit and hike to the lake to spend the night away from the campfire chatter.

Access: Follow the Icefields Parkway north 2.4 km (1.5 mi) from Bow Summit and watch for the trailhead parking area on the west side of the highway. The unsigned trail departs from the north edge of the parking area. N51°44.377' W116°30.714' *Maps: Blaeberry River 82 N/10; Bow Lake-Saskatchewan Crossing (Gem Trek).*

N

Nigel Pk

Nigel Pass

Cataract Pass

65

Nigel Creek

Sunwapta Pass

JASPER NATIONAL PARK

Mt Athabasca

66 **69**

68

Saskatchewan Glacier

Cirrus Mtn

Mt Stewart

WHITE GOAT WILDERNESS AREA

Cataract Creek

Cline River

Minster Mtn

Castleguard Meadows

Terrace Mtn

Mt Saskatchewan

93

North

Mt Coleman

Pinto Lake

Sunset Pass

64

V

67

Castleguard River

Alexandra

River

Saskatchewan

Mt Amery

Mt Wilson

Mt Alexandra

Mt Lyell

LYELL ICEFIELD

River

The Crossing Resort

11

62

Mt Erasmus

Survey Pk

Sullivan Pk

63

Glacier Lake

61

60

House

59

Mt Sarbach

Kaufmann Peaks

Bush Mtn

BRITISH COLUMBIA

ALBERTA

Mons Pk

Mt Forbes

Mt Outram

River

Howse Pass

Land above 2300 metres

0 2 4 6 8 10 km

58 Chephren Lake—Cirque Lake

Waterfowl Lakes Campground to Chephren Lake—3.5 km (2.2 mi)
Waterfowl Lakes Campground to Cirque Lake—4.2 km (2.6 mi)

Half-day or day trip

Allow 1 hour to Chephren Lake

Elevation gain: 105 m (345 ft)
loss: 42 m (140 ft)

Maximum elevation: 1755 m (5,750 ft)

Maps: Mistaya Lake 82 N/15
Bow Lake-Sask Crossing
(Gem Trek)

Access: Follow the Icefields Parkway to
Waterfowl Lakes Campground, 58 km
(36 mi) north of the Trans-Canada Highway
or 19 km (12 mi) south of the David
Thompson Highway (Hwy 11) junction.
Follow the campground access road 100 m
to a split. Bypass the campground entrance
kiosk and continue ahead on a service road
200 m to a parking area on the left. Follow
a trail from this parking area around the
south boundary of the campground for
0.4 km to the trailhead kiosk at the Mistaya
River bridge. (Registered campers can follow
a trail along the Mistaya River at the west
edge of the campground to the trailhead.)

0.0—Mistaya River bridge (1650 m).
N51°50.448' W116°37.393'

—Moderate uphill through subalpine
forest.

1.3—Junction. Cirque Lake left 2.9 km.
Chephren Lake right.

—Flat through forest with muddy
sections.

1.6—Meadow to left of trail (1755 m).
View of Howse Peak.

3.5—Chephren Lake (1713 m).

While you can admire the rugged mountains on the west side of the Mistaya Valley from roadside pull-outs at Lower Waterfowl Lake, they are best appreciated from the shores of Chephren or Cirque Lakes, which lie at the very foot of the escarpment. Either lake can be visited in a half-day from Waterfowl Lakes Campground, or you can hike to both and return in three or four hours.

The hike begins at the Mistaya River footbridge at the rear of Waterfowl Lakes Campground. (If you are not registered at the campground, use the 0.4 km trail from the campground service road to reach the bridge.)

After crossing the Mistaya bridge, you climb quickly through forest to a trail junction at km 1.3. Chephren Lake, the most popular destination, is to the right, Cirque Lake to the left. There is little gain or loss of elevation from the junction to Chephren Lake, but the trail is often a muddy mess. Views en route are limited to a brief glimpse of Howse Peak at a trailside meadow.

Two great peaks rise above Chephren Lake: the imposing, glaciated mountain to the south is Howse Peak, site of frequent avalanches in spring and early summer; Mount Chephren (pronounced kefren) forms the west shore and is named for the second of the three great pyramids of Egypt.

Cirque Lake. Because it is a bit smaller and the approach a bit longer and steeper, Cirque Lake is less frequently visited than Chephren.

From the 1.3 km junction, the trail soon reaches Cirque's outlet stream, then climbs beside it through heavy subalpine forest to the lake. Midway, Stairway and Aries Peaks create the 800-m wall rising beyond its far shore.

If you visit both lakes on your trip, the total round trip distance is 12.8 km.

Chephren Lake and Howse Peak

59 Howse River

Icefields Parkway to Howse River Flats—4.5 km (2.8 mi)
Icefields Parkway to Howse Pass—26.8 km (16.7 mi)

Day hike or backpack

Allow 2 days to Howse Pass

Elevation loss: 85 m (280 ft)
gain: 150 m (500 ft)

Maximum elevation: 1585 m (5,200 ft)

Maps: Mistaya Lake 82 N/15
Bow Lake-Sask Crossing
(Gem Trek)

Access: Follow the Icefields Parkway to the Mistaya Canyon parking area, located on the west side of the highway 31 km (19 mi) north of Bow Summit and 5.2 km (3.2 mi) south of David Thompson Highway (Hwy 11) junction. Trailhead is located at the lower end of the parking area.

0.0— Trailhead (1520 m).
N51°56.492' W116°43.037'

0.5— Mistaya Canyon bridge (1480 m).

0.7— Junction. *Sarbach Lookout* left.
Howse River ahead.

— Gradual descent through forest.

4.3— Junction. Horse trail to Icefields Parkway right. Howse River left.

4.5— Howse River flats (1435 m).

— Trail rolls through sandy, sparsely forested hills.

6.2— Trail re-enters forest.

15.5— Trail emerges briefly on river flats.

— Gradual climb through dense forest.

24.0— Junction. Howse River Patrol Cabin right. Howse Pass ahead (ford stream).

— Trail climbs above Conway Creek.

26.5— Stream crossing (ankle-deep).

26.8— Howse Pass (1527 m). Historic plaque, Alberta-B.C. boundary marker.

31.7— Lambe Creek bridge.

34.8— Tributary stream (log bridge).

39.2— Cairnes Creek (single log bridge).

39.5— Cairnes Creek parking area.

Howse Pass was the first fur trade route across the Great Divide, and the valley leading to it is nearly as wild today as when David Thompson used it in 1807. Despite its historical significance, the trek up this broad, mostly-forested valley is tedious and difficult—strictly for experienced wilderness travellers and good route-finders.

However, if you aren't going to the pass, you can day-trip to pleasant, open flats near the confluence of the Howse and North Saskatchewan Rivers. This section is snowfree early in the season and the grassy river flats are awash with the colourful blooms of montane wild-flowers in early summer.

Howse River Flats. After crossing Mistaya Canyon (0.5 km), the trail immediately passes the Sarbach Lookout junction and makes a gradual descent through forest to the Howse River.

At four km, you emerge onto river flats just south of the North Saskatch-ewan-Howse River confluence. For the next 2 km travel is flat along sandy hills and meadows with open views across the Howse River to massive Mount Wilson (3261 m).

Where the Howse makes a bend to the northwest, and a grassy slope rises across the river, you are at the furthest point David Thompson reached by canoe in June 1807. His party camped here for two weeks, until the snow melted on Howse Pass, before making their first crossing into today's British Columbia.

Howse Pass. The trail re-enters forest at km 6.2—the furthest point day hikers will want to travel. While the trail is maintained for another seven km or so, up to the Glacier Lake horse ford, it is not a worthwhile route. And since the trail beyond that junction is not maintained, anyone continuing to the

Conway Creek near its confluence with Howse River

pass will have a more difficult trip than David Thompson.

The track of the old trail continues in the trees for the rest of the journey. It is rough, rooty and depressing, and most recent reports indicate the section from Glacier Lake junction to km 24.0 is covered with deadfall and nearly impassible. Up to km 15.5, the trail often runs close to the river and is flooded early in the season and during warm weather. Some backpackers wade in the river, others bushwhack through trackless forest, all have a wretched time.

If you manage to reach the 24.0-km junction, most of your troubles are over. At this intersection, a short 1.3-km trail branches due west to the Howse River Patrol Cabin on open alluvial flats at the confluence of Conway, Freshfield and Forbes Creeks. With excellent views to the surrounding peaks, the flats are one of the best places to camp in the valley. (One knee-to-thigh deep ford of Conway Creek is required to reach the flats.)

From the 24.0-km junction, the trail to the pass continues, immediately crosses a tributary stream and climbs through forest above Conway Creek canyon to the summit of Howse Pass. While more open than much of the upper valley, views from the pass are unexceptional. A historic plaque and provincial boundary marker are the only indication you are atop the Great Divide.

Though the track was easily followed when we last passed that way, expect some overgrowth as you continue onto the headwaters of B.C.'s Blaeberry River. The trail passes through meadows and beside small pools before reaching the west bank of the Blaeberry River. At last report, major tributary streams at Lamb and Cairnes Creeks were bridged as the trail descended along the Blaeberry to a clearcut 300 m south of Cairnes Creek (see trail distance outline). At this point, you are 55 km north of the Trans-Canada Highway via the forestry road, but this road has been subject to washouts and closures, which means the Mummery Creek Recreation Site, 10 km further south, may be the nearest point to arrange transportation. (Contact the Ministry of Forests, Mines and Lands office in Revelstoke for the latest report.)

60 Sarbach Lookout

Icefields Parkway to Sarbach Lookout—5.2 km (3.2 mi)

Half-day or day trip

Allow 1.5 to 2 hours one way

Elevation loss: 40 m (130 ft)
      gain: 595 m (1,950 ft)

Maximum elevation: 2075 m (6,800 ft)

Maps: Mistaya Lake 82 N/15
     Bow Lake-Sask Crossing
     (GemTrek)

Access: Follow the Icefields Parkway to the Mistaya Canyon parking area, located on the west side of the highway 31 km (19 mi) north of Bow Summit and 5.2 km (3.2 mi) south of David Thompson Highway (Hwy 11) junction. Trailhead is located at the lower end of the parking area.

  0.0— Trailhead (1520 m).
      N51°56.492' W116°43.037'

  0.5— Mistaya Canyon bridge (1480 m).

  0.7— Junction. *Howse River* ahead; Sarbach Lookout left.

   — Gradual ascent through forest.

  3.1— Moderate to steep grades begin.

  5.2— Sarbach Lookout (2075 m).

The steep trail to the old Sarbach fire lookout site is hardly worth the effort—the climb is steep and steady, and views at the top are mostly obscured by trees. But if you are willing to scramble upslope for another 45 minutes or so, there are panoramic views encompassing the confluence of three rivers and a sea of massive peaks and glaciers.

From the Icefields Parkway, the trail descends and crosses the Mistaya Canyon bridge. At a junction 200 m beyond the bridge, the Sarbach trail cuts back sharply to the left from the *Howse River* trail.

Soon you begin a steady, steep switchbacking ascent that continues all the way to the lookout. Scattered forest limits views from the spot where Banff's only wooden fire tower and a small cabin once stood, but with a bit more effort you can obtain a scenic reward.

Old trails, constructed by a former fire lookout, continue behind the site (bordered by rocks in their early stages). One contours to the left across the slope and, in 200 m, reaches an avalanche path with open views across the valley to Mount Murchison.

A higher trail climbs through the forest and provides a head start for a steep scramble to a rocky viewpoint at the end of Mount Sarbach's north ridge. From this vantage point, 300 vertical metres above the lookout site, you see Glacier Lake and the sprawling glaciers of the Lyell Icefield to the west. The confluence of the North Saskatchewan, Howse and Mistaya Rivers is immediately below the ridge to the north. Mounts Wilson and Murchison are quite massive from this prospect, the latter rising 1900 m above the valley floor.

Mount Sarbach was named for the Swiss guide Peter Sarbach, who completed the first ascent of the peak via this ridge with J. Norman Collie and George P. Baker in 1897.

61 Mistaya Canyon

Icefields Parkway to Mistaya Canyon—0.5 km (0.3 mi)

This limestone slot canyon compares favourably with the better-known canyons of Maligne in Jasper and Marble in Kootenay. Though not as heavily visited as its sister canyons, the short downhill walk is still a popular diversion for many travellers along the Icefields Parkway.

Follow an old roadbed leading gradually downhill through the forest for 10 minutes to reach the canyon. A bridge spans the canyon at its narrowest point, where you can peer down into its depths.

The canyon has been carved from limestone bedrock by the Mistaya River, which originates in Peyto Lake, 28 km to the southeast. The river flows through open willow meadows just upstream from the bridge, and rock slabs near the point where it plunges into the abyss are a pleasant place to relax and enjoy the upstream view.

Avoid the temptation of looking into the canyon from anywhere except the bridge. Unfenced, canyon-rim viewpoints below the bridge are very dangerous, particularly when conditions are wet or snowy.

Just 200 m beyond the bridge, trails branch to Sarbach Lookout and the Howse Valley. (See *Sarbach Lookout* and *Howse River.*)

Access: Follow the Icefields Parkway to the Mistaya Canyon parking area, on the west side of the highway 31 km (19 mi) north of Bow Summit and 5.2 km (3.2 mi) south of David Thompson Highway (Hwy 11) junction. Trailhead is at the lower end of the parking area. N51°56.492' W116°43.037' *Maps: Mistaya Lake 82 N/15; Bow Lake-Saskatchewan Crossing (Gem Trek).*

62 Warden Lake

Icefields Parkway to Warden Lake—2.2 km (1.4 mi)

Although it passes through the blackened remains of the 2014 Spreading Creek wildlife, this trail remains a nice evening stroll for anyone camping or lodging near Saskatchewan River Crossing. The trail is flat and undemanding, and the views along the North Saskatchewan River are open and wonderful. The lake itself is a peaceful body of water where waterfowl are often seen swimming in the reflection of mighty Mount Murchison. Moose are often seen in this section of the valley (watch for tracks).

The trail begins by skirting along the south side of the patrol station, then traverses fire-ravaged flats to come abreast of the North Saskatchewan River on an old road track.

The track continues beside the river for nearly a kilometre before breaking away to the right along a marshy meadow. The roadbed reverts to single-track trail and passes a small pond at km 1.9. Moments later, you emerge on the lake's north shore.

Access: Follow the Icefields Parkway to the Saskatchewan River Crossing Patrol Station, 2.0 km (1.2 mi) south of the David Thompson Highway (Hwy 11) junction. A gravel access road across the highway from the station leads to a parking area for the trail. The trailhead is 100 m south of the station on the east side of the highway. N51°58.081' W116°42.893' *Maps: Mistaya Lake 82 N/15; Bow Lake-Saskatchewan Crossing (Gem Trek).*

63 Glacier Lake

Icefields Parkway to Glacier Lake—8.9 km (5.5 mi)

Day trip or backpack

Allow 2.5 to 3 hours one way

Elevation gain: 210 m (700 ft)
       loss: 225 m (750 ft)

Maximum elevation: 1660 m (5,450 ft)

Maps: Mistaya Lake 82 N/15
     Bow Lake-Sask Crossing
     (Gem Trek)

Access: Follow the Icefields Parkway to the trailhead parking area, located in an old roadside gravel pit on the west side of the highway 1.2 km (0.7 mi) north of the David Thompson Highway (Hwy 11) junction.

0.0—Trailhead (1450 m).
    N51°58.386' W116°45.581'
   —Flat followed by a sharp descent to river.

1.1—North Saskatchewan River bridge.
   —Brief steep climb followed by flat.

2.3—Howse River viewpoint (open benchland to left of trail).
   —Trail descends to Howse River flats then begins a long climb over a forested ridge.

8.9—Glacier Lake (1435 m).

9.2—Glacier Lake Campground (Gl9).
   —Rough trail follows north shore of lake.

12.6—Glacier Lake west end.

14.4—Trail becomes indistinct along meadow and braided stream channels.

In June 1807, David Thompson and a party of North West Company fur traders entered the Howse Valley on their way across the Rockies to build the first trading post on the Columbia River. While camped on the Howse River, Thompson wandered into a side valley and discovered a large lake. He marvelled that "all the Mountains in sight from the end of the Lake are seemingly of Ice." The lake was named Glacier 51 years later when Dr. James Hector, geologist with the Palliser Expedition, camped by its shores.

Today the lake can be visited over good trail. Because of its relatively low elevation, it can be hiked earlier and later in the season than many of the park's trails. Some folks hike to Glacier Lake and back in a day, while others backpack to the campsite near the lake's east end. Less energetic souls only travel as far as the bridge across the North Saskatchewan River canyon (1.1 km) or the benchland overlooking the Howse River (2.3 km).

The trail to Glacier Lake begins its journey in a forest of lodgepole pine—regrowth following one of Banff Park's big forest fires, the Survey Peak burn of 1940. As you near the end of the first kilometre, the trail plunges down to the North Saskatchewan River, which is crossed on a deluxe bridge where the river funnels through a short canyon.

After climbing from the gorge, you continue through pine trees for another kilometre to where the trail skirts the end of an open, grassy bluff—an outstanding viewpoint for the valley leading to historic Howse Pass. This is a great place to take a break, enjoy the silence, and think about the first fur traders, led by David Thompson, who camped here for two weeks in 1807.

Dropping from the bench, the trail passes close to a bend in the Howse River then cuts inland from the braided flats to begin the long, forested climb over a ridge to Glacier Lake. The high point of

Division Mountain and Southeast Lyell Glacier from Glacier Lake

hike, approximately 1660 m, is reached around 7 km. From there the trail plunges down to the east end of the lake.

Glacier Lake is 3 km in length and nearly 1 km wide—one of the largest backcountry lakes in Banff Park. A campground not far from the lake's outlet is a good base for explorations along the north shore and to the Southeast Lyell Glacier beyond.

Lakeshore-Southeast Lyell Glacier. A rough trail continues along the north shore for 3.4 km to the brushy Glacier River flats at the west end of the lake. The river is the lake's major tributary, and you can follow along the north side of its braided channels for another 5 km to terminal moraines beneath the Southeast Lyell Glacier.

The trail is indistinct along the meanders and shifting gravels of the alluvial plain, and you are forced to do a bit of bushwhacking where river channels force you into the willows. However, the route stays to the right of the river and is obvious.

Scramble to the top of the steep moraines at the end of the valley for a fantastic view of the Southeast Lyell Glacier icefall and a small meltwater lake.

64 Sunset Pass

Icefields Parkway to Sunset Lookout—4.5 km (2.8 mi)
Icefields Parkway to Sunset Pass Viewpoint—8.2 km (5.1 mi)
Icefields Parkway to Pinto Lake—13.7 km (8.5 mi)

Day trip or backpack

Allow 2.5 to 3 hours Sunset Pass

Elevation gain: 725 m (2,380 ft)

Maximum elevation: 2165 m (7,100 ft)

Maps: Cline River 83 C/2
       Bow Lake-Sask Crossing
       (Gem Trek)

Access: Follow the Icefields Parkway to the trailhead parking area, located on the east side of the highway 16.8 km (10.4 mi) north of the David Thompson Highway (Hwy 11) junction.

0.0—Trailhead (1440 m).
       N52°04.139' W116°54.602'

   —Moderate uphill grade.

0.6—Grade becomes steep.

1.0—Norman Creek gorge viewpoint.

   —Steady uphill via switchbacks.

2.9—Junction. Sunset Lookout site left 1.6 km. Sunset Pass ahead.

4.0—Trail levels out into extensive meadow.

4.4—Norman Lake Campground (No5).

   —Flat to rolling through open meadow.

6.7—Trail climbs moderate to steep through open forest.

8.2—Sunset Pass (2165 m). Park boundary.

8.7—Pinto Lake Viewpoint.

   —Steep descent.

13.7—Pinto Lake Campground (1750 m).

The Sunset Pass trail travels through extensive meadows beneath the cliffs of Mount Coleman to a high viewpoint overlooking Pinto Lake, the remote Cline River valley, and the sea of peaks comprising Alberta's White Goat Wilderness Area.

Since a day hike to Sunset Pass and back doesn't leave much time for exploration, some folks backpack to Norman Lake or Pinto Lake Campground and explore from there. Or you can simply hike 4.5 km to the old Sunset fire lookout site for its overview of the North Saskatchewan and Alexandra River valleys.

A steep climb from the Icefields Parkway makes any itinerary an arduous one. The first 3 km rise at an excruciating grade over a trail that is forest-enclosed and dry (make sure to pack sufficient water). The only scenic respite on this ascent is a brief glimpse of the Norman Creek gorge.

After you pass the Sunset Lookout junction, the grade moderates somewhat. A kilometre further along the trail levels out and drops into the Norman Creek meadows, which extend unbroken for the next 2.5 km.

Norman Lake Campground is located in a grove of large spruce trees on the eastern edge of the meadow. While it is nearly 500 m distant from the marshy lake on the meadow's western margin, it is still a very pleasant site with open views to Mount Coleman.

The trail continues flat through the meadow, but it is often muddy and there are minor streams you must hop across. At the north end of the meadow, you climb through scattered trees to the park boundary and, 0.5 km beyond, emerge onto a high open ridge.

The ridgetop viewpoint is actually higher than the true summit of Sunset Pass, which lies nearly 2 km away to the

Pinto Lake from Sunset Pass summit

southeast. By detouring off the trail to the precipitous edge of the ridge, fantastic views open down to Pinto Lake and the Cline River valley.

Day hikers turn back at the viewpoint, but backpackers can continue to a primitive campground at the northwest corner of Pinto Lake—a steep descent of 415 m in just over 5 km.

Many place names along the trail commemorate the first recorded traverse of the pass by geologist Arthur P. Coleman in 1893. Mount Coleman was named in his honour in 1903, and Pinto Lake immortalizes one of the expedition's most troublesome packhorses.

Sunset Lookout. The trail to Sunset Lookout branches left from the Sunset Pass route at km 2.9. This side trail climbs northwest for more than a kilometre along the forested slopes of Mount Coleman before descending to a fine viewpoint on the lip of a sheer limestone cliff 450 m above the Icefields Parkway and North Saskatchewan River.

The small, one-room Sunset Lookout cabin was built here during the summer of 1944 and was demolished in 1977 after Parks Canada abandoned its fire lookouts. In addition to the massive summits of Mount Amery (3329 m) and Mount Saskatchewan (3342 m), the lookout commanded a view directly up the Alexandra River to the ice-covered peaks of the Great Divide over 18 km away.

There is no water on the trail to the lookout site, so remember to pack enough to quench your thirst for the duration of the trip.

65 Nigel Pass

Icefields Parkway to Nigel Pass—7.2 km (4.5 mi)

Day trip

Allow 2 hours one way

Elevation gain: 335 m (1,100 ft)

Maximum elevation: 2195 m (7,200 ft)

Maps: Columbia Icefield 83 C/3
    Columbia Icefield (Gem Trek)

Access: Follow the Icefields Parkway to the Nigel Creek parking area, located on the northeast side of the highway 8.5 km (5.5 mi) south of the Banff—Jasper Park boundary at Sunwapta Pass. The parking area and trail kiosk are at a barrier gate just below the highway. Follow gravel roadbed downhill from gate for 150 m to a trail sign on the right.

0.0— Trailhead (1860 m).
    N52°11.250′ W117°04.227′

— Footbridge to northeast side of Nigel Creek.

2.1— Old Camp Parker.

— Ascent along east side of Nigel Creek valley.

5.1— Trail enters open meadows.

— Steady ascent to park boundary.

7.2— Nigel Pass (2195 m). Banff-Jasper Park boundary. Trail crosses Brazeau River headwaters and continues down Brazeau Valley (see *Jonas Pass–Brazeau Lake Loop* and *South Boundary Trail*, Jasper Park chapter).

Nigel Pass is one of the most rewarding day trips in the Columbia Icefield vicinity. The trail climbs moderately through scattered forest and flower-filled meadows to a point above the true pass. Atop this open, rocky ridge on the boundary of Banff and Jasper Parks, there are expansive views back to rugged, glaciated peaks near the Icefield and north into Jasper's remote Brazeau River valley.

You start your hike on the roadbed for the old Banff-Jasper Highway and, 150 m below the parking area, turn right into the forest and cross a bridge over Nigel Creek. The trail contours across avalanche paths as it follows upstream along the creek.

At km 2.1 the site of old Camp Parker is passed in a stand of large Engelmann spruce. This area was used as a campsite by native hunters before the arrival of the white man, and mountaineers exploring the Columbia Icefield region at the turn of the 20th century continued the tradition. The carvings on the surrounding trees record the visits of many of these early campers, though most date to the period following the opening of the Banff-Jasper Highway in 1940.

At Camp Parker the trail turns north and begins the ascent to Nigel Creek's headwaters. Throughout this section there are good views back to Parker Ridge and Hilda Peak—a sharp subpeak of Mount Athabasca. Nigel Pass is seldom out-of-sight ahead.

The trail climbs more seriously over the last kilometre to the trail summit, attained on a rocky ridge where a cairn marks the boundary between Banff and Jasper Parks. (The true summit of Nigel Pass lies just over a kilometre to the northeast.) Forest cover is very sparse and stunted on this 2195-m ridge, an indication of the upper limit of tree growth in this latitude.

Back down-valley to the south, the ice-clad summit of Mount Saskatchewan

Nigel Pass

(3342 m) rises beyond Parker Ridge. To the north is the wild Brazeau River valley and the maze of peaks comprising the southern region of Jasper Park. Directly west of the pass, rising above a large cirque, is Nigel Peak (3211 m), named in 1898 by British mountaineers Hugh Stutfield and Norman Collie for their packer Nigel Vavasour.

You can discover more views by continuing north into Jasper Park another kilometre or so. A short 0.4-km descent brings you to the south fork of the Brazeau River (an easy rock-hop crossing). Continue down across a rocky slope to a large, marshy meadow where there are even better views of the Brazeau Valley and back to the north side of Nigel Pass—a fine rock wall featuring several small waterfalls.

Strong hikers will find the descent of the valley as far as Boulder Creek Campground (3.5 km beyond Nigel Pass) quite rewarding. (See *Jonas Pass-Brazeau Lake Loop*, Jasper Park chapter.)

Cataract Pass. This high pass at the headwaters of the south fork of the Brazeau River lies approximately 6 km southeast of Nigel Pass. While no defined trail leads in this direction, energetic explorers with a topo map can strike out from Nigel Pass and pick a route through the rocky, open terrain to a small lake at the foot of Cataract Pass.

Backpackers can continue over Cataract Pass to Pinto Lake. After crossing its 2485-m summit, descend to the headwaters of Cataract Creek. Trail reappears near treeline on the east side of the creek, which is followed down-valley to a junction with the Cline River trail just below Pinto Lake.

This trip is best reserved until late in the season since snowbanks often cover the very steep approaches to Cataract Pass into August. There are also fords of Cataract Creek near its confluence with the Cline River and at Huntington Creek; both may present some difficulty during periods of high runoff.

The distance from Nigel Pass to Pinto Lake is approximately 26 km. (See also *Sunset Pass*.)

66 Parker Ridge

Icefields Parkway to Saskatchewan Glacier Viewpoint—2.7 km (1.7 mi)

Half-day trip
Allow 1 hour one way
Elevation gain: 250 m (820 ft)
Maximum elevation: 2250 m (7,380 ft)
Maps: Columbia Icefield 83 C/3
      Columbia Icefield (Gem Trek)

Access: Follow the Icefields Parkway to the Parker Ridge parking area, located on the west side of the highway 4.0 km (2.5 mi) south of the Banff-Jasper Park boundary at Sunwapta Pass.

0.0— Trailhead (2000 m).
    N52°11.491' W117°06.943'
— Steady, switchbacking ascent through open forest.

1.1— Trail emerges onto open alpine slopes.
— Switchbacks continue across open slopes.

2.1— Parker Ridge summit (2250 m).
— Trail contours left across south side of ridge.

2.5— First Saskatchewan Glacier viewpoint.

2.7— Second Saskatchewan Glacier viewpoint (2235 m).

The Parker Ridge hike is a short, highly rewarding excursion into the alpine life zone. The northernmost trail in Banff Park rises quickly above the treeline and crosses a high, open ridge to a spectacular view of the Saskatchewan Glacier—the Columbia Icefield's longest outlet valley glacier. However, as one of the most scenic and well-publicized short trails in the Rockies, it is also one of the most heavily used, particularly on sunny mid-summer days.

The lower section of trail switchbacks steadily upward through scattered stands of alpine fir and open meadows created by snowslides. Wildflowers in this section are protected from the elements and nourished by abundant moisture from snowmelt. Tall, showy flowers, like paintbrush, valerian, purple fleabane, and fringed grass-of-Parnassus, bloom from early July through mid-August.

Halfway up the north-facing slope, at an elevation of 2100 m, you emerge above treeline into the alpine zone—a region of tiny ground-hugging plants. In this harsh, wind-scoured environment the blooms of moss campion, white mountain avens, rock jasmine, and forget-me-nots last only a couple of weeks.

After passing above an extensive talus slope (domain of pikas), the trail makes its final switchbacking ascent to the 2250-m crest of the ridge. From this summit it veers left and makes a slight descent to the first of two viewpoints for the 9 km-long Saskatchewan Glacier.

While many hikers stop at the first viewpoint, another one 0.2 km farther along provides the most rewarding prospect of the glacier and the uppermost limits of the North Saskatchewan River valley. A rocky promontory at the viewpoint is filled with fossil coral and covered by orange foliose (*Xanthoria*) lichen.

Saskatchewan Glacier from Parker Ridge

The ridgetop is also a rich area for alpine wildlife and birds. It is frequently visited by both mountain sheep and goat, and occasionally a grizzly bear wanders through. Rosy finches and horned larks nest here in summer, white-tailed ptarmigan are year-round residents, and golden eagles and hawks patrol the meadows around the glacier viewpoints for Columbian ground squirrels.

The Parker Ridge trail was built in the 1960s, and it was designed with a series of gradually ascending switchbacks. Unfortunately, this encouraged people to shortcut straight downhill on their return from the summit. A number of barriers and "official" shortcuts (staircases) were constructed to discourage this slope-damaging practice. Be considerate of this fragile, easily eroded environment and stay on the designated trail or staircases.

Because the trail ascends a north-facing slope, snowbanks often cover the route into early July. To help preserve the fragile meadows, Parks Canada usually keeps the area closed until the track is snow-free. You should check on the trail's status at a park visitor centre if you plan on hiking it before mid-July.

67 Castleguard Meadows

Icefields Parkway to Castleguard Meadows—35.1 km (21.8 mi)

Backpack
Allow 2 days one way
Elevation gain: 535 m (1,750 ft)
Maximum elevation: 2060 m (6,750 ft)
Maps: Cline River 83 C/2
        Columbia Icefield 83 C/3

Access: Follow the Icefields Parkway to an unmarked pull-off on the west side of the highway, 24.4 km (15.2 mi) north from the David Thompson Highway (Hwy 11) junction and 1.3 km (0.8 mi) north of the Coleman Picnic Area. Park at this pull-off and walk north along the highway 80 m to where an unmarked but well-defined trail leads downhill 180 m to a bridge across the North Saskatchewan River.

0.0— N. Saskatchewan River bridge (1525 m).
N52°07.256' W116°59.035'

— Flat to gently rolling on abandoned fire road.

5.8— Road bends west into Alexandra Valley.

10.9— Road comes abreast of river flats.

11.7— Road crosses river flats. Unbridged Alexandra River channel. End of bicycle access.

— Road crosses unbridged river channels. Thigh deep fords or worse.

13.5— Terrace Creek crossing. Old campsite.

20.5— Road reverts to trail, enters forest.

20.9— Castleguard Patrol Cabin (1555 m).

21.4— Old campsite.

— Gradual to moderate climb up Castleguard Valley.

30.6— Major stream crossing (log bridge?).

31.9— Outram's Shower Bath Falls.

— Steep climb.

35.1— South edge of Castleguard Meadows (2060 m). Castleguard Campground (Cs).

Located on the edge of the Columbia Icefield in the remote northwest corner of Banff National Park, the Castleguard Meadows lie between Castleguard and Terrace Mountains—a pass between the headwaters of the North Saskatchewan and Castleguard Rivers. But what a pass! As Dalton Muir and Derek Ford have aptly described in their book *Castleguard*, "so many natural features compete for attention that the senses become saturated."

Like many remote trails in Banff Park, this trail is not maintained. It is long, gruelling, and plagued with deadfall. The main obstacles are hazardous crossings of the unbridged Alexandra River channels during periods of high water. We recommend hiking this trail in late summer when water levels are lower.

The trip starts on an old fire road running up the Alexandra River to the Castleguard Patrol Cabin. While the road is slowly becoming overgrown, the first section is straightforward and open for mountain biking. However, at km 11.7 the road descends onto the Alexandra River flats and your troubles begin. Bridges that once spanned the wandering river channels have long since washed away. When warm weather brings high water, these crossings are dangerous.

When the river is running high, hikers abandon the road and follow along the forest margin on the north side of the river flats. The main difficulties are thrashing through mostly untracked forest and fording side streams, particularly Terrace Creek, which is tricky at high water.

The road ends near the confluence of the Alexandra and Castleguard Rivers, just a short distance before the patrol cabin. Here it reverts to single-track and turns northwest up the Castleguard Valley.

Rocky and rooty trail follows the northeast side of the Castleguard for just

© Mike McReynolds

Castleguard Meadows

over 10 km (tributary streams must be forded if log bridges are not in place).

After passing the trail branching west to Watchman Lake and Thompson Pass, you make a steep 3-km climb through the forest to a campground on the southern edge of the Castleguard Meadows. Here the trail ends and the meadows are yours to explore at your leisure.

The meadows comprise a narrow corridor running north from the campsite for 4 km to a 2250-m pass overlooking the Saskatchewan Glacier. Ascending this broad vale, you pass from well-watered, marshy meadows bordered by stands of alpine fir, through extensive alpine meadows dotted with islands of kruppelholz (dwarfed and stunted trees), and finally emerge onto the barren, windswept pass.

The climb through the meadows is quite gradual. The dominant feature throughout is glacier-draped Castleguard Mountain (3090 m) looming above to the west. Nearly as impressive is Terrace Mountain, which rises on the east side of the valley. Though they have long since retreated to higher levels, glaciers descended from both of these

peaks, leaving great terminal moraines along the valley margins.

The view from the summit is quite amazing. The Saskatchewan Glacier flows at your feet—the longest outlet valley glacier descending from the Columbia Icefield. Directly across the valley, tributary glaciers tumble down the slopes of Mount Andromeda (3450 m). And, off to the west, peeking over the white expanse of the Icefield, is Mount Columbia—the highest point in Alberta at 3747 m.

Saskatchewan Glacier Route. For experienced climbers equipped with rope and ice axe, the most direct route to the meadows is over the Saskatchewan Glacier. This journey entails a 7-km hike to the toe of the glacier followed by a 5-km ascent up the centre of the glacier to a point where you traverse across to the northern edge of the meadows. (At last report, climbing onto the toe of the glacier is very treacherous.) Anyone attempting this route should inquire at the Lake Louise Visitor Centre for a report on current conditions and a detailed route description.

68 Saskatchewan Glacier

Icefields Parkway to Saskatchewan Glacier Basin—6.0 km (3.7 mi)

During World War II, an access road was built to the Saskatchewan Glacier so U.S. Army engineers could test over-snow vehicles that would be used for Alaska Highway construction. However, the glacier has receded over a kilometre since then, and the road now ends far short of the ice. This old track to the glacier basin is of marginal interest, except for experienced glacier-travellers bound for the Castleguard Meadows. (See *Castleguard Meadows*.)

Cross the concrete bridge at the trailhead and turn right immediately onto a rough forest path. The path joins the old army road in 0.5 km.

The road climbs over a forested ridge and descends to the glacier's outwash plain at km 2.6. Sections of road on the flats have been washed away by the river, but rough trails through brushy spruce detour these washouts and bring you back to the roadbed.

Around km 6.0 the road ends in a hummocky moonscape of recessional moraines. The glacier is visible far ahead, and some hikers continue beyond this point in an attempt to reach it. However, steep ice-cored moraines and extreme hazards await the foolhardy who would attempt the final scramble to its surface.

Access: Follow the Icefields Parkway to the Big Bend—a point where the highway makes a 180-degree switchback on open gravel flats, 11 km (7 mi) south of the Banff-Jasper boundary at Sunwapta Pass. An old concrete bridge just below the highway 0.7 km (0.4 mi) south of the Big Bend pull-out is the trailhead. A small parking area at the bridge accommodates 2 or 3 vehicles, otherwise, park at the Big Bend and walk from there. N52°10.352' W117°03.852' *Maps: Columbia Icefield 83 C/3; Columbia Icefield (Gem Trek).*

69 Panther Falls

Icefields Parkway to Panther Falls Viewpoint—0.5 km (0.3 mi)

Mary Schäffer and her companions came upon this waterfall in July, 1907: "As we later found a panther (or wild-cat) had followed in our footsteps for a considerable distance along this special bit of trail, we named them the Panther Falls."

This 60-m waterfall is one of Banff's highest and suitably impressive, mainly for the volume of water that Nigel Creek funnels over the abyss, and it is only a short walk from the Icefields Parkway.

At the viewpoint for Bridal Veil Falls (another fine waterfall across the valley), walk downhill to the trail sign atop an earthen barrier at lower end of the lengthy pull-off. The trail drops into the forest on the opposite side of the

earthwork and, after a few switchbacks, arrives at a muddy, spray-soaked slope, which serves as the viewpoint at the base of the falls. (This slope can be hazardous, particularly for those with smooth-soled shoes.)

Do not visit the top of this falls. The smooth rocks at the lip of the abyss make it an incredibly dangerous place.

Access: Follow the Icefields Parkway to the Bridal Veil Falls viewpoint, a long pull-out on the east side of the highway 9.0 km (5.5 mi) south of the Banff-Jasper Park boundary at Sunwapta Pass. N52°10.807' W117°03.391' *Maps: Columbia Icefield 83 C/3; Columbia Icefield (Gem Trek).*

N

Nasswald Pk

Halfway
Lodge

BRITISH COLUMBIA
ALBERTA

212

70 Allenby
Pass

Og
Mtn

Cave
Mtn

Nublet

Assiniboine
Pass

Assiniboine
Lodge

Mt
Cautley

Lake
Magog

Wonder Pass

73

Lake
Gloria

Mt
Assiniboine

Mt
Gloria

Aye
Mtn

Marvel
Pass

Marvel Lake

Marvel
Pk

74

Owl
Lake

Aurora
Mtn

Mt
Byng

Mt
Alcantara

Red Man
Mtn

76

Mt
Brussilof

White
Man
Pass

White Man
Mtn

Mt
Soderholm

Forestry Road

Sundance Range

Mt
Allenby

Mt
Mercer

72

Bryant Creek

72

Mt
Turner

Mt
Morrison

Mt
Currie

Mt
Warre

Mt
Vavasour

Spray River

75

Forestry Road

Leman
Lake

Mt
Leman

Mt
King Albert

Goat Range

Banff

Spray River

Mt
Turbulent

Spray Range

SPRAY VALLEY

PROVINCIAL

PARK

Mt
Nestor

Lakes

Reservoir

Smith Dorrien / Spray Trail

The
Three
Sisters

742

Mt
Buller

Mt
Engadine

Mt
Shark

Mt
Smuts

Mt
Birdwood

P

P

Burstall
Pass

209

Mt
Burstall

PETER LOUGHEED

PROVINCIAL PARK

Mt
Sir Douglas

Mt
French

Palliser
Pass

Land above 2300 metres

0 1 2 3 4 5 km

70 Brewster Creek—Allenby Pass

Sunshine Road to Allenby Pass—27.0 km (16.8 mi)
Sunshine Road to Bryant Creek—32.8 km (20.4 mi)

Backpack
Allow 2 days to Allenby Pass
Elevation gain: 1020 m (3,350 ft)
Maximum elevation: 2440 m (8,000 ft)
Maps: Banff 82 O/4
     Mount Assiniboine 82 J/13

Access: Follow the Trans-Canada Highway to the Sunshine Road exit, 9 km (5.5 mi) west of the Banff town west exit. Follow the Sunshine Road to the trailhead parking area, located on the left side of the road 0.3 km (0.2 mi) beyond the Trans-Canada Highway overpass.

- 0.0— Trailhead (1420 m).
  N51°09.234' W115°41.107'
  —Healy Creek footbridge.
- 0.6— Junction. *Sundance Canyon* trail ahead 4.6 km. Brewster Creek right.
- 3.3— Junction (1570 m). Intersection with Brewster Creek trail. *Sundance Canyon* left; Brewster Creek right.
- 8.7— Sundance Lodge.
- 10.3— Junction (1630m). Brewster Creek Campground (Bw10) and *Fatigue Creek* right. Allenby Pass ahead.
- 13.2— Brewster Creek bridge to west side.
- 23.0— Halfway Lodge (1950 m).
  —Trail crosses creek south of cabin.
- 24.0— Steep switchback ascent to Allenby Pass begins.
- 27.0— Allenby Pass (2440 m).
  —Moderate to steep descent south from pass.
- 31.7— Junction. Intersection with *Og Pass* trail. Right to Og Pass (5.5 km) and Mt Assiniboine Lodge (11.0 km). Bryant Creek trail ahead.
- 32.6— Junction. Og Pass shortcut right. Bryant Creek ahead.
- 32.8— Junction. Intersection with *Bryant Creek* hiker's trail at km 18.0.

The Brewster Creek trail has long been a major access route to the Bryant Creek area in the south part of Banff Park. It was also the original route used by skiers between Banff and Mount Assiniboine Lodge starting in 1928, and soon thereafter it became a primary route for Assiniboine-bound horse parties in the summer.

While Allenby Pass, at the head of the Brewster Valley, is a fine destination, regular horse use and a long forested approach discourage many backpackers from hiking the trail. In recent years, mid-summer restrictions due to grizzly activity has decreased the trail's use even further (see notice below).

While it is possible to reach Brewster Creek directly from the town of Banff by way of the Sundance Canyon trail and the old Healy Creek access road, the shortest approach is from the Sunshine Road.

From the Sunshine Road trailhead you immediately cross a footbridge over Healy Creek and follow the broad track of the old Healy Creek road 0.6 km to the shortcut trail branching right to Brewster Creek. (Cyclists and skiers will find a wider, smoother track and less demanding grades by continuing another 1.3 km on the Healy Creek road to where the Brewster Creek access road branches right, a detour that adds 2.2 km.)

The shortcut climbs steeply through dense forest on rocky, muddy horse trail to km 3.3, where it intersects the access road from the Sundance Canyon trail. This broad track rolls southward into the Brewster Creek valley and follows along the east side of the creek to Sundance Lodge.

The lodge's primary function is as an overnight destination for horse parties. Like Halfway Lodge, which lies farther up-valley, it provides accommodation for hikers when there are empty beds, usually early or late in the season.

The historic Ten Mile Cabin, built by the CPR in the 1920s, is located beside the lodge. It was one of several back-country shelters constructed by the company along the Great Divide between Assiniboine and Lake Louise to encourage hiking and horseback recreation. For 50 years it operated as a way station between Banff and Mount Assiniboine Lodge by lodge owner and ski pioneer Erling Strom.

Beyond Sundance Lodge the smooth access road reverts to heavily-travelled horse trail, which continues up-valley through heavy forest with occasional views of the Sundance Range to the east. At km 10.3 the Fatigue Creek trail branches right to Brewster Creek Campground, the valley's only campsite.

Nearly 3 km beyond Fatigue Creek junction you cross a bridge to the west side of Brewster Creek and continue the long, uneventful ascent of the valley. A short distance before arriving at a side-stream ford, views open southeast to the Brewster Glacier—one of the valley's scenic highlights.

After sloshing across a main tributary flowing into Brewster Creek from the southwest, the trail begins to climb at a moderate but steady grade. Soon after passing Brewster Creek Patrol Cabin, it bends south into a side-valley and climbs to Halfway Lodge—so-called because it was used as the halfway overnight stop for skiers and horse parties travelling between Banff and Mount Assiniboine.

Just beyond the lodge, you make one final stream crossing before starting the steep climb to Allenby Pass—a vertical ascent of 450 m to this spectacular defile composed of rockslides and alpine meadows.

Beyond the pass you can descend to the Bryant Creek trail in another 5.8 km (see *Bryant Creek*), or take the Og Pass cutoff to Mount Assiniboine Provincial Park (see *Og Pass-Windy Ridge*, Mount Assiniboine Park chapter).

Notice: Due to seasonal grizzly bear activity near Allenby Pass, a special group permit is required from August 1 until September 30 for travel through the pass or on trails between its summit and the Bryant Creek trail. Check the Park Visitor Centre or website for specific details and an update if you plan on travelling in this area.

71 Fatigue Creek

Brewster Creek to Fatigue Pass—10.9 km (6.8 mi)
Brewster Creek to Citadel Pass—13.4 km (8.3 mi)

The Fatigue Creek trail links Brewster Creek to the Citadel Pass trail via Fatigue Pass—a 2395-m summit with marvelous views of the southern Sunshine Meadows. The trail is rough, wet and seldom used by hikers, but the track is well-defined thanks to regular horse trips from Sundance Lodge in the Brewster Valley.

From the 10.3-km junction on the *Brewster Creek-Allenby Pass* trail, you branch west to the valley's only campground. Immediately beyond the campground the trail crosses Brewster Creek—the first of many foot-soaking fords.

The Fatigue Creek valley is narrow, forcing the trail to swing back and forth across the creek six times in the first 5 km—all unbridged crossings. Above the last ford you climb steadily and steeply onto the alpine meadows of Fatigue Pass.

Beyond the pass, the trail descends northwest across the rocky, open slopes of Fatigue Mountain for another 2.5 km to the crest of Citadel Pass. (See *Citadel Pass.*)

Access: To reach the north end of the trail, follow the Brewster Creek-Allenby Pass trail to the Fatigue Creek trail junction, 1.6 km south of Sundance Lodge. The south end of the trail is accessed from a junction on the crest of Citadel Pass (see *Citadel Pass*). *Maps: Banff 82 O/4.*

72 Bryant Creek—Assiniboine Pass

Mt Shark Parking Area to Marvel Lake Campground—13.6 km (8.5 mi)
Mt Shark Parking Area to Mount Assiniboine Lodge—25.3 km (15.7 mi)

Backpack

Allow 3.5 to 4 hours to Marvel Lake

Elevation loss: 65 m (215 ft)
    gain: 460 m (1,510 ft)

Maximum elevation: 2165 m (7,100 ft)

Maps: Spray Lakes Reservoir 82 J/14
    Mount Assiniboine 82 J/13

Access: Follow the Spray Lakes Road and Smith-Dorrien/Spray Trail (Hwy 742) west from the town of Canmore 38 km (23.5 mi) to the Mount Shark Road junction. Follow the Mount Shark Road 5.3 km (3.3 mi) to its termination at the trailhead parking area.

  0.0— Trailhead (1770 m).
    N50°51.557' W115°22.748'

  3.7— Junction. Watridge Lake left 150 m. Bryant Creek ahead.

  5.9— Spray River bridge.

  6.0— Junction (1705 m). *Upper Spray River-Palliser Pass* left. Bryant Creek right.

  6.6— Bryant Creek bridge.

  6.7— Junction. Trail Centre. Bryant Creek left.

  9.6— Big Springs Campground (Br9).

  12.0— Junction. *Owl Lake-Marvel Pass* trail left.

  13.0— Junction. Left 0.6 km to Marvel Lake Campground (Br13) and Marvel Lake (1.6 km).

  13.6— Junction. Bryant Creek Shelter left 0.2 km.

  14.2— Junction. McBride's Camp Campground (Br14) right 0.2 km.

  14.3— Junction. Bryant Creek Patrol Cabin. *Wonder Pass* trail left; Assiniboine Pass ahead.

  17.3— Allenby Junction Campground (Br 17).

  17.5— Junction. Assiniboine Pass horse trail left (stream crossing); hiker trail right.

  18.0— Junction. Allenby Pass right. Assiniboine Pass left.

When many hikers think of the Bryant Creek trail, they only think of the most direct route to Mount Assiniboine. Yet, the valley's campgrounds and shelter cabin serve as base camps for a number of fine day trips. Worthwhile destinations include Assiniboine Pass, Wonder Pass, Owl Lake, Marvel Pass and Allenby Pass—all within a day hike of your camp.

Starting from the Mount Shark parking area in Spray Valley Provincial Park, a broad, well-graded trail runs due west and descends to a bridge across the Spray River. Follow the Spray River trail right 0.7 km to Trail Centre junction.

The ascent of the Bryant Creek valley begins at Trail Centre on a broad track—a straightforward if uninspiring trek. Owl Lake junction is passed at km 12.0, and 1.0 km farther along, the trail to Marvel Lake Campground and the east end of Marvel Lake.

At km 13.6 you reach the Bryant Creek Shelter. Lying just off the trail to the left, the shelter is popular with tent-less hikers. Because of this popularity, you should make reservations through the Banff Visitor Centre if you plan on staying there.

Another kilometre brings you to the junction to McBride's Camp Campground and, just beyond, the Wonder Pass trail junction and Bryant Creek Patrol Cabin. McBride's is a good centrally-located campground for backpackers who don't want to stay at the shelter.

Assiniboine Pass. The Bryant Creek trail continues up-valley beyond the patrol cabin and immediately enters an extensive meadow covered with shrub willow and dwarf birch.

At km 17.3 you reach the valley's last campground, Allenby Junction. This is another good base camp, particularly for day trips to Allenby, Og and Assiniboine

Bryant Creek Patrol Cabin

22.4—Junction. Horse trail rejoins hiker trail.

—Steady uphill switchbacks.

23.0—Assiniboine Pass (2165 m). Banff–
Mt. Assiniboine Park boundary.

24.8—Junction. Og Pass, Og Lake, Citadel
Pass right. Lake Magog ahead.

25.1—Junction. Lake Magog Campground
ahead 1.6 km. Mt. Assiniboine Lodge,
Naiset Cabins and Mt. Assiniboine
Park Headquarters Cabin left.

25.3.—Mount Assiniboine Lodge (2180 m).

**Notice: Due to seasonal grizzly bear
activity near Allenby Pass, a special
group permit is required from August 1
until September 30 for travel between
the Bryant Creek-Assiniboine Pass
trail and Allenby Pass. Check the Park
Visitor Centre or website for specific
details and an update if you plan on
travelling in this area.**

Passes. If you shoulder your backpack
past this point, you are likely bound for
Mount Assiniboine via Assiniboine Pass.

A hiker's trail branches right from the
old horse trail just beyond the campground. While this trail stays on higher
and drier ground on the north side of
the valley, and eliminates an immediate
ankle-deep crossing of Bryant Creek, it
adds approximately 1.5 km to the distance to Assiniboine Pass.

The hiker's trail soon reaches the
junction for Allenby Pass. Keep left and
continue up-valley to the last series of
switchbacks leading to Assiniboine Pass.

While the subalpine meadows of the
pass would be a pleasant destination
on many other trails, hikers who take
the trouble of climbing to its summit
are inevitably bound for Lake Magog
at the foot of Mount Assiniboine, just
2.5 km beyond (see Mount Assiniboine
chapter).

Marvel Lake from the Wonder Pass trail

Marvel Lake. Ringed by heavy subalpine forest, Marvel is one of Banff Park's largest backcountry lakes and the shortest hike from the Bryant Creek campgrounds and shelter. The lake's main attraction is not the scenery but the fishing, and its deep waters have been known to produce large trout. (Contact Parks Canada for current fishing regulations.)

The east end of the lake can be reached via the 1.6-km trail that branches from the Bryant Creek trail at km 13.0 (only 1.0 km beyond Marvel Lake Campground). It can also be reached in 1.6 km from McBride's Campground via the *Wonder Pass* trail

The west end of the lake is accessed from the *Wonder Pass* and *Owl Lake-Marvel Pass* trails.

Allenby Pass. This lofty, rockbound pass can be reached in a day from any of the campgrounds or the shelter in the Bryant Creek valley.

At the 17.5-km junction, just beyond Allenby Junction Campground, keep right on the hiker's trail leading to Assiniboine Pass. At the next junction,

0.5 km farther along, stay right for Allenby Pass.

The trail climbs steadily for 5.8 km to the 2440-m summit, traversing some delightful wildflower meadows and alpine larch stands along the way. One-way distance to the pass from Allenby Junction Campground is 6.5 km. (See also *Brewster Creek-Allenby Pass.*)

Bryant Creek Options. In addition to the short hike to Marvel Lake and the day trip to Allenby Pass, you can also day trip to Wonder Pass, Owl Lake and Marvel Pass from the Bryant Creek Shelter and valley campgrounds.

Longer loop trips can also be completed into Mount Assiniboine Park from Bryant Creek campgrounds and shelter using Assiniboine, Og and Wonder Passes.

73 Wonder Pass

Bryant Creek Junction to Wonder Pass—8.9 km (5.5 mi)
Bryant Creek Junction to Mount Assiniboine Lodge—12.0 km (7.5 mi)

Backpack
Allow 3 hours to Wonder Pass
Elevation gain: 550 m (1,800 ft)
Maximum elevation: 2395 m (7,850 ft)
Maps: Mount Assiniboine 82 J/13

Access: Follow the *Bryant Creek-Assiniboine Pass* trail to the 14.3-km junction in front of the Bryant Creek Patrol Cabin. The Wonder Pass trail branches southwest (left) at this junction. (The trail can also be accessed by connector trails running northwest from Marvel Lake Campground and Bryant Creek Shelter.)

0.0—Bryant Creek Junction (1845 m).
  N50°54.079′ W115°31.338′
  — Trail crosses large meadow.

0.3—Junction. Bryant Creek bridge.
  Bryant Creek Shelter left 0.5 km.
  Wonder Pass ahead.
  — Trail enters forest.

1.1—Junction. Left to Marvel Lake (0.5 km)
  and Marvel Lake Campground
  (1.5 km).

2.0—Avalanche path.
  — Contour across avalanche paths.

5.6—Junction. Left to Marvel Pass and
  Marvel Lake (0.5 km).
  — Steady switchbacking ascent.

7.3—Enter scattered subalpine forest.
  — Moderate climb through meadows.

8.9—Wonder Pass (2395 m). Intersection
  with *Wonder Pass* trail from Lake
  Magog (see *Assiniboine Park*
  chapter).

10.5—Gog Lake.

11.5—Naiset Cabins—Mt. Assiniboine Park
  Headquarters Cabin.

12.0—Mount Assiniboine Lodge (2180 m).

13.5—Lake Magog Campground (2165 m).

Wonder Pass is one of the most scenic day hikes from the campgrounds and shelter on Bryant Creek. In addition to its outstanding views of Marvel Lake, the pass overlooks the vast meadows leading down to Mount Assiniboine's Lake Magog region.

The pass can also be used to access the core area of Assiniboine Park, however, the trail is a kilometre longer and steeper than the more popular Assiniboine Pass route. Most backpackers use Assiniboine Pass on the way in and Wonder Pass on the way out.

Starting from the 14.3-km junction on the Bryant Creek trail, the Wonder Pass trail runs west across a meadow to a bridge over Bryant Creek. Trails from the Bryant Creek Shelter and Marvel Lake Campground intersect from the left at km 0.3 and 1.1, providing access to the trail from either of those sites. The latter trail also leads 0.5 km to the east end of Marvel Lake.

The main trail continues up-valley, contouring well above the lake across the lower slopes of Wonder Peak. Numerous avalanche paths between km 2.0 and 5.3 provide views of Marvel Lake and the glaciated summits of Aye Mountain, Eon Mountain and Lunette Peak at the head of the valley.

At km 5.6 you pass a side-trail leading down to the west end of Marvel Lake (see *Owl Lake–Marvel Pass*) and a viewpoint for Lakes Gloria and Terrapin at the head of the valley.

Beyond the junction the trail makes a steep ascent to the pass. However, the scenery near the summit more than compensates for the struggle.

If you are continuing into Assiniboine Park, it is a 3.1-km descent through meadows and larch forest to Mount Assiniboine Lodge. (See *Wonder Pass*, Assiniboine Park chapter.)

74 Owl Lake—Marvel Pass

Bryant Creek Trail Junction to Owl Lake—3.5 km (2.2 mi)
Bryant Creek Trail Junction to Marvel Pass—9.3 km (5.8 mi)

Backcountry day hike

Allow 1 hour to Owl Lake

Elevation gain: 150 m (500 ft)

Maximum elevation: 1890 m (6,200 ft)

Maps: Mount Assiniboine 82 J/13

Access: Follow the *Bryant Creek-Assiniboine Pass* trail to the 12.0-km junction. The Owl Lake trail branches southwest (left) at this junction.

0.0—Bryant Creek Junction (1770 m).

—Gradual descent.

0.3—Bryant Creek bridge.

1.9—Trail crests rise above Owl Lake basin.

3.4—Junction. South end of Owl Lake and Marvel Pass ahead. North end of Owl Lake left 100 m.

3.5—Owl Lake (1890 m).

5.0—Owl Lake south end.

5.4—Old campsite in meadow.

—Trail climbs through forest and across avalanche paths.

9.3—Marvel Pass (2200 m).

Owl Lake is a charming blue-green body of water set in the central portion of a valley contained by Marvel Peak and Mounts Byng, Morrison and Turner. Its pleasant subalpine setting makes it a worthy destination or a scenic waypoint on an extended journey to Marvel Pass.

Owl Lake is usually visited as a day hike from one of the Bryant Creek valley campgrounds. Marvel Lake Campground and the Bryant Creek Shelter are both within 1.8 km of Owl Lake junction; McBride's Camp and Big Springs Campgrounds are 2.4 km from the junction.

From its junction with the Bryant Creek trail at 12.0 km, the trail to Owl Lake gradually descends to the valley bottom and swift-flowing Bryant Creek (crossed on a bridge 200 m upstream from the horse ford). Beyond the creek it climbs moderately for a little over 1.5 km to the Owl Lake basin.

Once the basin is reached you traverse some intriguing meadows, characterized by low ridges of peculiarly jumbled rock. This section of twisted and broken terrain also provides a good opportunity to take your bearings on the surrounding country.

At km 3.4 the trail splits, the left branch descending to the north end of Owl Lake in 100 m, the right contouring above the lake's western shore to the south end in another 1.5 km. With Mount Byng and Aurora Mountain serving as a backdrop, the view from the north shore is quite scenic, particularly in early morning.

Marvel Pass. Lying 4.3 km beyond and 300 m above the southern end of Owl Lake, Marvel Pass is an interesting option for experienced hikers. Located at the apex of three high alpine valleys on the Great Divide, the pass is a wonderful destination in an area celebrated for its scenic wonders.

Mount Alcantara from Marvel Pass

The pass is sometimes visited as part of a 23-km loop trip from the campgrounds or shelter near the east end of Marvel Lake, approaching from Owl Lake and returning via the west end of Marvel Lake and the Wonder Pass trail. However, this is a demanding trip requiring some route-finding skills, and you should be armed with a 1:50,000 topo map.

From the south end of Owl Lake an obvious trail runs 0.4 km to an old campsite in a broad meadow. Watch for cairns leading out of the meadow and up along the northwest side of the Owl Creek drainage.

The remainder of the trip to the pass climbs beneath the south-facing slopes of Marvel Peak and its lush avalanche paths. This approach and the pass itself are prime grizzly habitat (bears are frequently seen here), so travel with care and make noise when visibility is limited.

A small lake on the pass, known unofficially as "Cabin Lake", provides a pleasant rest stop and is also a bit of a curiosity. Though its waters drain west into British Columbia, it was mistakenly mapped as part of Alberta and as being within Banff National Park. A small log cabin sits on the lake's north shore. It was constructed by two Alberta residents in the early 1960s who felt it was safe to do so in this jurisdictional no-man's-land.

You can complete the loop trip by continuing north down Marvel Creek. The route from the pass runs down the east side of the Marvel Creek valley to the west end of Marvel Lake, then climbs steeply to the Wonder Pass trail. However, there is deadfall, some rather sketchy sections across boggy meadows, and a double ford just above Marvel Lake (look for log bridges). It is a trip reserved for good route finders.

Distance from Marvel Pass to the Wonder Pass trail is 6.2 km. (See also *Wonder Pass.*)

75 Upper Spray River—Palliser Pass

Mt Shark Parking Area to Palliser Pass—26.7 km (16.6 mi)

Backpack

Allow 2 days to Palliser Pass

Elevation loss: 65 m (200 ft)
gain: 400 m (1,300 ft)

Maximum elevation: 2105 m (6,900 ft)

Maps: Spray Lakes Reservoir 82 J/14
Kananaskis Lakes 82 J/11
Canmore-Kananaskis (Gem Trek)
Kananaskis Lakes (Gem Trek)

Access: Follow the Spray Lakes Road and Smith-Dorrien/Spray Trail (Hwy 742) west from the town of Canmore 38 km (23.5 mi) to the Mount Shark Road junction. Follow the Mount Shark Road 5.3 km (3.3 mi) to its termination at the trailhead parking area.

0.0— Trailhead (1770 m).
N50°51.557' W115°22.748'

— Broad well-marked trail.

3.7— Junction. Watridge Lake left 150 m.

5.9— Spray River bridge.

6.0— Junction (1705 m). *Bryant Creek* trail right; Palliser Pass left.

9.2— Junction. Spray River bridge. *White Man Pass* trail right: Palliser Pass ahead (across bridge).

12.8— Junction. South cutoff to White Man Pass right.

15.2— Birdwood Campground (Us15).

15.8— Birdwood Creek. Palliser Patrol Cabin.

19.3— Stay left on bench trail above river.

19.8— Junction. *Burstall Pass* trail left.

20.0— Junction. Right 0.3 km to Burstall Campground (Us18) and Leman Lake (1.3 km).

24.6— Steep ascent to Palliser Pass begins.

25.9— Belgium Lake.

26.7— Palliser Pass (2105 m). Park boundary.

The upper Spray River valley forms the extreme southern end of Banff Park—a wild, scenic region contained by rugged limestone peaks and home to a wide variety of wildlife, including moose and grizzly bear.

The trail running up the valley receives only moderate use during the summer. With Palliser Pass as a primary destination, you can spend several days exploring, taking side trips to White Man Pass, Leman Lake or Burstall Pass. Burstall Pass also serves as an optional route of access or exit to the upper end of the valley, and is the preferred trail for many backpackers.

The first 6 km of the hike follows the same route as the *Bryant Creek-Assiniboine Pass* trail. This section, which mostly lies within Spray Valley Provincial Park, tends to be very busy, particularly on weekends when families are strolling to Watridge Lake and mountain bikers are out in force. But once you cross the Spray River and begin your ascent of the valley proper, things become quite peaceful.

From the Spray River bridge junction, the trail runs up-valley through a stretch of heavy forest before emerging into open willow meadow. At km 9.2 the White Man Pass trail branches west (see *White Man Pass*), and the Spray River trail crosses a bridge back to the east side of the river.

At 15.2 km you pass Birdwood Campground and, 0.6 km farther along, the Palliser Patrol Cabin. Beyond the cabin the trail crosses an extensive meadow, revealing mountains at the upper end of the valley, including Mount Leman. After traversing a long stretch of meadow, it angles left onto higher and drier ground along the forest margin.

The Burstall Pass trail intersects from the left at 19.8 km, and just 200 m farther along the trail to Burstall Campground and Leman Lake branches right across

Mount Leman from the Upper Spray Valley

the river. This campground is only 0.3 km off the main trail and well situated as a base for day trips to upper-valley destinations, including Palliser Pass, Burstall Pass and nearby Leman Lake.

The trail to Palliser Pass continues up-valley along the eastern side of the Spray. After sloshing across two small streams, the steep, final ascent to the pass begins.

Emerging from the forest at the top of the grade, the trail flattens out across subalpine meadows beside Belgium Lake and, less than a kilometre beyond, the summit of Palliser Pass. Back and Palliser Lakes lie beyond the pass (off-trail to the right) in British Columbia's Height of the Rockies Provincial Park, and serve as possible campsites.

Leman Lake—1.3 km. This forest-encircled lake lies between Mounts Leval and Leman just east of Spray Pass and the Alberta-B.C. boundary. It is a short hike from Burstall Campground.

From the 20.0-km junction, cross bridges spanning Spray River and Leman Creek. The trail passes Burstall Campground and climbs steeply

through forest before making a final, quick descent to the lakeshore.

Leman is a peaceful lake that reflects its namesake mountain to the south. It is also a place where we have always seen or heard loons.

A path continues along the west shoreline for just over 1.0 km to the park boundary at Spray Pass—a forested gap with no views. A brief descent into B.C. brings you to the end of a forestry road extending up the Albert River. (The condition of this road dictates whether people can easily reach the lake from the B.C. side.)

Burstall Pass. This 12-km trail running from the Smith-Dorrien/Spray Lakes Trail (Hwy 742) in Peter Lougheed Provincial Park is often used as an optional access or exit route for Upper Spray Valley backpackers. The pass is also a rewarding 5.3-km day trip from Burstall Campground. (See *Burstall Pass*, Peter Lougheed Provincial Park chapter.)

76 White Man Pass

Mount Shark Parking Area to White Man Pass—16.9 km (10.5 mi)

Backpack

Allow 4 to 5 hours one way

Elevation loss: 65 m (230 ft)
gain: 445 m (1,460 ft)

Maximum elevation: 2150 m (7,050 ft)

Maps: Spray Lakes Reservoir 82 J/14
Canmore-Kananaskis (Gem Trek)
Kananaskis Lakes (Gem Trek)

Access: Follow the Spray Lakes Road and Smith-Dorrien/Spray Trail (Hwy 742) west from the town of Canmore 38 km (23.5 mi) to the Mount Shark Road junction. Follow the Mount Shark Road 5.3 km (3.3 mi) to its termination at the trailhead parking area.

0.0— Trailhead (1770 m).
N50°51.557' W115°22.748'

3.7— Junction. Watridge Lake left 150 m.

5.9— Spray River bridge.

6.0— Junction (1705 m). *Bryant Creek* right; Upper Spray River and White Man Pass left.

9.2— Junction. *Upper Spray River–Palliser Pass* ahead (across bridge); White Man Pass right.

10.5— Currie Creek ford.

10.8— White Man Creek ford.

— Gradual climb.

13.1— Junction. South cutoff to Palliser Pass trail left; White Man Pass right.

14.8— Begin steep ascent to pass.

16.4— Small unnamed lake.

16.9— White Man Pass (2150 m).

Whatever White Man Pass may lack in scenery, it more than compensates with a rich and colourful past. This is the pass that James Sinclair led the Red River emigrants and their livestock through on the way to the Oregon Territory in 1841. Beside a small lake just east of the pass, the Métis guides of Jesuit missionary Father Pierre DeSmet erected a wooden cross in his honour in 1845. Two British officers, Henry James Warre and Nigel Vavasour, crossed the pass the same year, bound for Oregon to spy on the Americans. But despite its exciting history, the trail attracts very little use today.

The trip to the pass utilizes the same approach as the *Upper Spray River–Palliser Pass* hike. Starting from the Mount Shark trailhead, the trail leads 6 km to the Spray River bridge. On the opposite side of the bridge, you arrive at a junction with the trail leading up the Spray Valley, which you follow south for 3.2 km.

The White Man Pass trail branches right from the Upper Spray-Palliser route at km 9.2. Entry into the White Man Creek valley is not without its toll—a knee-deep ford of Currie Creek 1.3 km from the Upper Spray junction followed by an ankle-deep crossing of White Man Creek 0.3 km beyond.

The remainder of the ascent to the pass is straightforward and uneventful, travelling through a mix of meadow and subalpine forest for 4 km before starting a strenuous 2 km climb to the divide.

White Man Pass is a forested summit with few views, but the tiny lake just east of the pass, where Father DeSmet's guides erected the cross, makes a fine place to rest and contemplate the pioneers who passed this way.

Latter-day explorers can continue this historic journey by venturing down the Cross River headwaters to the end of the B.C. forestry road 6 km beyond the pass.

Land above 2300 metres

0   5   10   15km

77 Cascade Fire Road

Upper Bankhead Picnic Area to Bighorn Creek—83.0 km (51.6 mi)

Backpack

Allow 3 to 5 days one way

Maximum elevation: 2255 m (7,400 ft)

Minimum elevation: 1465 m (4,800 ft)

Maps: Banff 82 O/4
       Castle Mountain 82 O/5
       Barrier Mountain 82 O/12

Access: Northbound hikers begin from the Upper Bankhead Picnic Area, located on the west side of the Lake Minnewanka Road 3.5 km (2.2 mi) north of the Trans-Canada Highway interchange (Banff east exit). Trail begins at the north corner of the picnic area parking lot.

Southbound hikers start at Ya-Ha-Tinda Ranch just beyond Banff Park's eastern boundary. Follow Highway 1A east from Canmore 59 km (37 mi) to Highway 940 junction. Continue north 81 km (50 mi) on Highway 940. Turn left onto the Ya-Ha-Tinda road immediately after crossing the Red Deer River bridge. Follow this road west 23 km (14 mi) to Ya-Ha-Tinda Ranch. The Bighorn Creek parking area is 2.6 km (1.6 mi) past the ranch entrance gate, opposite the entrance to Bighorn Campground.

  0.0— Upper Bankhead Picnic Area (1465 m).
       N51°14.220' W115°31.146'

    — Follow trail across open meadow and into forest.

  1.2— Junction. Trail joins roadbed. Turn left.

  6.4— Cascade River bridge (1555 m).
       Cascade Bridge Campground (Cr6).

13.3— Junction. Stony Creek Patrol Cabin left.

14.2— Junction. Stony Creek Patrol Cabin rejoins from left.

14.7— Junction. Elk Summit trail left.

14.8— Stony Creek crossing (ford).
       End of mountain bike access.

15.0— Junction. Stony Creek Campground (Cr15) left. *Dormer Pass* right.

23.1— Junction. *Flint's Park* trail left.

33.0— Wigmore Summit (2010 m).

The track of the old Cascade Fire Road traverses the park's remote Front Ranges and two major valleys, the Cascade and Red Deer. While there are no alpine passes on the trail, there is plenty of wild, rugged scenery, and with the exception of the route's southern end, there are no designated campgrounds. It is a region reserved for experienced, self-reliant wilderness travellers who are well schooled in how to travel and camp safely in prime grizzly bear habitat.

The Cascade Fire Road was completed during the late 1930s after large forest fires swept the region. Until 1984 the road was utilized by Parks Canada vehicles, but when two bridges collapsed, it was allowed to revert to foot and horse trail.

The roadbed remains one of the primary access routes into the Front Ranges and is the core for the park's eastern trail system. While the track is broad and well-graded, the removal of bridges and culverts in 1990 left a number of unbridged streams (the Cascade and Red Deer Rivers are the only waterways still bridged). The most formidable crossing is the Panther River, and any trips over the central section of the trail are best postponed until later in the summer when the Panther's waters have subsided.

Starting from the southern trailhead at Upper Bankhead Picnic Area, the trail ascends the Cascade Valley for 23 km before breaking away to cross Wigmore and Snow Creek Passes to the Red Deer Valley. It then follows along the north side of the Red Deer to the park's eastern boundary and the historic Ya-Ha-Tinda Ranch, where Parks Canada's horses are billeted during the winter.

Few people hike the trail end-to-end, since arranging transportation between the two distant trailheads is a time-consuming enterprise. Most prefer to explore the country and side trails that can

Cascade River

39.1— Junction (1875 m). Windy Patrol Cabin and *Panther River* right.

39.3— Junction. *North Fork Pass* left.

39.4— Panther River crossing (major ford). Panther Falls right (0.4 km).

49.3— Snow Creek Summit (2255 m).

57.5— Junction. Scotch Camp Patrol Station left.

58.2— Red Deer River bridge (1740 km).

58.4— Junction. *Upper Red Deer River* trail left.

62.9— Tyrrell Creek crossing (ford).

69.3— Park boundary (1660 m).

81.4— Scalp Creek crossing (ford).

81.6— Ya Ha Tinda Ranch Road Junction. Turn right.

83.0— Bighorn Creek parking area (1580 m). N51°44.159' W115°32.400'

be easily accessed from either the south or north trailheads.

The first 15 km beyond the southern trailhead is the most heavily used section. Since mountain bikes are permitted as far as Stony Creek, much of this visitation comes from cyclists. (The road's surface has been churned-up by commercial horse parties, so cycling is not as smooth and speedy as you might expect.) The trail's only two designated campgrounds are located on this section—a very pleasant site at the Cascade River bridge (6.4 km) and at Stony Creek (15.0 km).

Except for the occasional horse party, you are not likely to encounter many travellers between Flint's Park junction and the park's eastern boundary. Random camping is permitted on this section, which means you can camp anywhere as long as your site is at least 50 m off the trail and 70 m from the nearest water source.

You will pass by a number of recently burned slopes along the way. Most of these fires date to the 1990s and were intentionally set by the Parks Canada to improve wildlife habitat.

Following is a brief summary of the Cascade Fire Road, travelling from south to north:

Upper Bankhead to Flint's Park Junction—23.1 km. Starting from the southern trailhead at Upper Bankhead Picnic Area, the trail climbs over a low divide adorned by a marshy willow meadow, then descends sharply to the Cascade River bridge at km 6.4. Beyond the Cascade bridge, there is little elevation gain for 7 km as the old roadbed follows upvalley along the Cascade River to Stony Creek.

After passing two side roads to Stony Creek Patrol Station, you arrive at Stony Creek bridge. Just south of the bridge a trail branches west to Elk Summit (see *Elk Lake*); on the north side of the bridge, Stony Creek Campground lies to the left and the trail to *Dormer Pass* strikes off to the right.

The trail continues its gradual ascent along the east side of the Cascade River from Stony Creek to Flint's Park Junction. At this intersection, the Flint's Park trail branches west to link up with trails leading over Badger Pass and Forty Mile Summit (see *Flint's Park* and *Sawback Range Circuit*).

Flint's Park Junction to Red Deer River—35.1 km. From Flint's Park Junction, the trail branches north up Cuthead Creek to Wigmore Summit. At 30.1 km, Cuthead Creek flows down from Cuthead Lake to the west. (Reaching that lake is a difficult journey for off-trail explorers, as is Bighorn Lake across the valley to the east.) Wigmore Summit is a long pass with a small lake at its north end.

North of the pass the trail descends to Panther River and the Windy Patrol Cabin. One of the earliest warden cabins in the park was constructed on this site in 1915. (This original Windy Cabin now sits on the grounds of Banff's Whyte Museum). The present cabin was constructed in the 1950s with all the modern amenities of the day—including a furnace and a nuclear bomb shelter!

After splashing across the Panther River (quite difficult during high water), you climb to Snow Creek Summit (2255 m)—the trail's highest elevation. Harrison, Snowflake and Grouse are enticing lakes in the hanging valleys west and east of the trail, but again, these are routes reserved for off-track explorers.

The trail drops steadily beyond Snow Creek Summit to the Scotch Camp Patrol Station and the Red Deer River.

Red Deer River bridge to Bighorn Creek—24.8 km. The Red Deer Valley has been used as a route between the mountains and the Foothills for many centuries. A number of archaeological sites have been discovered in the valley, including 600 to 2800-year-old house-pit depressions associated with the Salish tribes of British Columbia's Interior Plateau.

After crossing the bridged Red Deer River, the trail turns east and climbs along the southern slopes of Mount Tyrrell for a kilometre or so before descending to open valley-bottom and Tyrrell Creek. Following this calf-deep ford, it follows along the Red Deer for 2 km before bending northeast to exit the park and the Front Ranges between Wapiti Mountain and Warden Rock.

Throughout the descent of the valley, you will notice sections of dead forest north of the trail—slopes that were burned during a major prescribed fire in the autumn of 1994.

East of the park boundary, the final 12.5 km rolls into the foothill parklands comprising Parks Canada's Ya-Ha-Tinda Ranch. (Mountain bikes are permitted on this section to the park boundary.)

Just beyond a calf-deep ford of Scalp Creek, you reach the Ya-Ha-Tinda Ranch access road. While vehicles are permitted on the road, parking is not, so you should turn right and follow the ranch road another 1.4 km to the Bighorn Creek bridge. A parking area is on the east side of the bridge, opposite the entrance to Bighorn Campground.

78 Flint's Park

Cascade Fire Road to Flint's Park Junction—7.8 km (4.8 mi)*

Backpack
Allow 2.5 hours one way
Elevation gain: 85 m (280 ft)
Maximum elevation: 1820 m (5,970 ft)
Maps: Castle Mountain 82 O/5

Access: Follow the Cascade Fire Road to km 23.1 to reach the trail's east end, or the *Sawback Range Circuit* to km 38.9 for the west end of the trail.

0.0— Cascade Fire Road Junction (1735 m). N51°24.290' W115°40.607'

— Trail follows old roadbed.

0.3— Cuthead Creek bridge and junction. Cuthead Patrol Cabin right; Flint's Park ahead.

— Flat to rolling trail north of Cascade River.

4.0— Junction. Shortcut trail from Cascade Fire Road (upper Cuthead Creek) intersects from right; Flint's Park ahead.

4.5— Junction. Outfitter's camp left; Flint's Park ahead.

7.5— North Cascade River bridge. Flint's Park Campground (Cr 31).

7.7— Flint's Park Patrol Cabin.

7.8— Junction (1820 m). Intersection with *Sawback Range Circuit* at km 38.9. Forty Mile Summit left; Badger Pass and *North Fork Pass* ahead.

*All distances approximate.

Flint's Park, which is situated near the confluence of Sawback Creek and the Cascade and North Cascade Rivers, has long been a popular camping area and centre of operation for horseback parties. Lying beneath the twin summits of Flints Peak, its open meadows and sparkling waters make a pleasant base camp for backpackers as well. More importantly, it is a hub for several interesting excursions.

Though the well-travelled track (horses) is relatively flat and humdrum, it is an important east-west link through Banff's Front Ranges. The route follows an old roadbed branching from the Cascade Fire Road at km 23.1 and, at the Cuthead Creek bridge, passes the junction to the historic Cuthead Patrol Cabin.

After crossing Cuthead Creek, it rolls westward through forest to the north of the Cascade River. Just past the halfway point, a well-trodden horse trail branches left to an outfitter's camp (keep ahead on the less-pounded track).

Flint's Park Campground and the North Cascade River bridge are reached at km 7.5. The junction with the Sawback Range Circuit lies 300 m west of the bridge near the Flint's Park Patrol Cabin. The campground is a good base for trips to local attractions, such as Sawback Lake, and also serves as a waypoint for extended trips over Forty Mile Summit or Badger Pass (see *Sawback Range Circuit*).

All trails in this area are subject to heavy horse use and are often churned-up during rainy periods. And remember, you will be camping in prime grizzly country, so take extra care at your campsite and while travelling the trails.

79 Dormer Pass

Cascade Fire Road to Dormer Pass—12.5 km (8.0 mi)*

Backpack

Allow 4 to 6 hours to Dormer Pass

Elevation gain: 730 m (2,400 ft)

Maximum elevation: 2375 m (7,800 ft)

Maps: Castle Mountain 82 O/5
Barrier Mountain 82 O/12

Access: Trail branches from the Cascade Fire Road at km 15.0, just north of the Stony Creek bridge and opposite the Stony Creek Campground (Cr15).

0.0—Cascade Fire Road Junction (1630 m). N51°20.946' W115°35.923'

1.3—Stony Creek ford to east bank.

6.5—Stony Creek ford to west bank.

6.8—Stony Creek ford to east bank.

9.0—Junction. Stony Pass ahead (5.5 km). Dormer Pass left.

9.1—Stony Creek ford.

12.0—Washed out section of trail

12.5—Dormer Pass (2375 m).

18.5—Junction. Dormer Patrol Cabin left; Dormer River trail fords to east bank ahead.

—Trail follows east side of river.

18.6—Junction. Stony Pass trail intersects from right.

24.5—Junction (1770 m). Park boundary ahead (6.0 km). *Panther River* via Dormer-Panther Divide left (7.5 km).

*All distances approximate.

The trail running up Stony Creek to Dormer Pass was severely affected by the 2013 floods (especially the headwaters of Stony Creek), but remains passable. It is a lengthy side-trip from the Cascade Fire Road, but one with scenic rewards. In addition to the 2375-m pass, which breaks through the limestone walls of the Palliser Range in spectacular fashion, there are optional trips to nearby Stony Pass or over the Dormer-Panther Divide to the Panther River.

The trail to Dormer Pass is well-defined throughout, but there are a number of unbridged streams along the way. The first of these is at 1.3 km, where the trail swings to the east side of Stony Creek—a troublesome ford during periods of high runoff. Three fords of the creek farther up-valley are less demanding.

At km 9.0 the trail to Stony Pass stays right while the Dormer Pass trail branches left. The Dormer option immediately crosses Stony Creek and makes a steep ascent to the pass. Around 3.0 km from the junction, a section of trail was washed on in 2013 flooding, but the route is still obvious.

Dormer Pass is a long, narrow corridor with an extensive alpine meadow—a wonderful area for alpine wildflowers in late July and early August. The pass is within the range of a large population of mountain sheep and frequently visited by grizzly bear.

Beyond the summit, the trail switch-backs down to a tributary and meadows leading to the Dormer River. Just above the Dormer Patrol Cabin, you reach the river and cross to the east side. Stay on the east side for the next 6 km, passing through open meadows with fine views of the surrounding peaks.

At km 24.5 a junction is reached. The trail ahead continues down the Dormer River to the park boundary and points east; the left branch fords the river and

© Cyndi Smith

Dormer Meadows from Dormer Pass

runs north to the Panther River via the Dormer-Panther Divide.

Dormer–Panther Divide. Backpackers who continue down the Dormer River beyond the Dormer Patrol Cabin junction are inevitably bound for the Panther River via the Dormer-Panther Divide trail. While the trip provides little worthwhile scenery, it does take you into remote wilderness that is considerably more challenging than following the Cascade Fire Road.

The 7.5-km-long Dormer–Panther Divide trail branches west from the Dormer River trail at 24.5 km. You immediately ford the Dormer River and make a steady climb north through mixed forest for nearly 4 km before cresting an unremarkable divide and then descending to the Panther River.

To return to the Cascade Fire Road, follow the Panther River trail back upstream. (See *Panther River*.)

Stony Pass. This 2330-m pass lies east of Dormer Pass on the opposite side of a block of unnamed limestone peaks. The pass is seldom visited, the trail is not maintained and is vague to non-existent most of the way. But the route is shown as a trail on topo maps and remains a scenic option to Dormer Pass for off-trail explorers. If you take this detour, you leave the Dormer trail at km 9.0 and return to it at km 18.6.

80 Panther River

Cascade Fire Road to Park Boundary—15.2 km (9.4 mi)*

Backpack

Allow 5 hours to park boundary

Elevation loss: 140 m (450 ft)

Maximum elevation: 1875 m (6,150 ft)

Maps: Barrier Mountain 82 O/12

Access: Eastbound backpackers can reach the west end of the trail by following the Cascade Fire Road to the Windy Patrol Cabin at km 39.1 (the trail departs from the meadow behind the cabin). Westbound travellers usually approach from the south via the Dormer-Panther Divide trail (see *Dormer Pass* trail description), intersecting with the Panther River trail at km 12.0, approximately 3 km west of the park boundary.

- 0.0—Windy Patrol Cabin (1875 m). N51°32.297' W115°43.839'
- 1.5—Panther River ford to north bank (mid-calf to knee deep).
  - —Flat to rolling trail.
- 6.0—Junction. Elkhorn Summit left (poorly marked). Main trail crosses Panther River to south side (ford).
- 7.5—Large meadow and campsite.
- 12.0—Junction (1770 m). Dormer-Panther Divide trail right. Panther River trail ahead.
- 12.5—Barrier Patrol Cabin.
- 15.0—Park boundary (1735 m).

*All distances approximate.

Panther River is one of the least-visited valleys in eastern Banff Park. It does not contain the spectacular mountains or views found elsewhere in the Front Ranges, but it is a worthy destination for experienced backpackers seeking solitude and can be used to create a circuit with Dormer Pass.

The trail branches east from the Cascade Fire Road at Windy Patrol Cabin. It immediately enters a gorge then crosses to the north side of the river (normally a calf-deep ford). Once through this defile, good trail leads downstream along the north side of the river and views open to a valley scorched by two prescribed burns (north of the river 1990, south 1999).

At 5.7 km the charred remains of a cabin are passed, and just beyond a creek flows into the Panther from the north. The trail to Elkhorn Summit branches north on the east side of this stream, but more importantly, the main trail crosses to the south side of the Panther River (ford).

The trail remains mostly on the south side of the river to the Dormer-Panther Divide trail junction (follow most obvious track and ford when necessary). At this junction (km 12.0), most backpackers head south to Dormer River and Pass. The main trail continues downstream beyond the park boundary to The Corners (the confluence of the Panther and Dormer Rivers)—a difficult route used almost exclusively by horse parties.

Elkhorn Summit. From its junction with the Panther River trail at km 6.0, this 13.5-km trail runs north along the east side of the Bare Range to the Red Deer River. Highlights include a 2200-m divide and extensive meadows; the lowlight is a difficult ford of the Red Deer River at the north end to reach the Cascade Fire Road at km 62.9.

81 North Fork Pass

Cascade Fire Road to North Fork Pass—12.0 km (7.5 mi)*
Cascade Fire Road to Flint's Park Junction—20.5 km (12.5 mi)

Backpack
Allow 4 hours to North Fork Pass
Elevation gain: 550 m (1,800 ft)
Maximum elevation: 2425 m (7,950 ft)
Maps: Barrier Mountain 82 O/12
       Castle Mountain 82 O/5

Access: To reach the north end of the trail, follow the Cascade Fire Road to 39.3 km, where the trail branches west less than 100 m south of the Panther River crossing. Access to the south end of the trail is from a junction near the west end of the Flint's Park trail (100 m west of the Cascade River bridge junction).

0.0— Cascade Fire Road (1875 m).
      N51°32.359' W115°43.948'

0.4— Panther River ford to north bank (mid-calf deep).

   — Flat valley-bottom trail.

5.2— Panther River ford to south bank.

   — Trail climbs then swings south toward pass.

10.7— Steep climb begins.

   — Trail ascends left side of bowl toward pass.

12.0— North Fork Pass (2425 m).

   — Steep descent south of pass.

14.0— Grade moderates.

   — Intermittent trail through deadfall.

16.3— Good trail reappears on east side of creek.

18.0— Cross to west side of creek.

   — Steady, gradual downhill.

20.5— Flint's Park Junction (1830 m). Intersection with *Sawback Range Circuit* at 38.8 km and west end of *Flint's Park* trail.

*All distances approximate.

This 2425-m divide between the headwaters of the Panther River and the Cascade River's north fork is probably one of the least hiked trail-accessible passes in Banff Park. The pass can be reached as a day trip from Flint's Park Campground (Cr31) to the south or a random campsite on the Cascade Fire Road near Windy Patrol Cabin to the north. You can also use the pass as part of an extended backpack through Banff's Front Ranges.

Starting from its intersection with the Cascade Fire Road (on the south side of the Panther River just 200 m from the Windy Patrol Cabin), the trail runs a short distance upstream along the south side of the Panther before crossing to the north side.

Near the 5-km mark the trail crosses back to the south side, climbs over a shoulder, and then turns south into a narrow valley, where it begins its ascent to North Fork Pass. Nearly 400 m are gained en route to the summit, most of it over the last 1.5 km.

The narrow gap of North Fork Pass provides excellent views due south across Forty Mile Summit to Mounts Edith, Louis and Fifi and the peaks south of Banff. Nearby, you are circled by the steeply-tilted limestone summits of the Sawback Range.

South from the pass the trail descends steeply and enters the weathered remains of a major fire that swept this slope in 1936. The trail promptly disappears into deadfall and is intermittent for the next 2 km. By persevering down the east side of the stream, you should come upon it again where it reappears as a well-defined track.

You soon swing to the west side of the stream and complete the remainder of the descent to the Cascade River and the Flint's Park junction on a broad obvious path. (See *Sawback Range Circuit* and *Flint's Park*.)

82 Upper Red Deer River

Cascade Fire Road to Cyclone Patrol Cabin Junction—26.7 km (16.6 mi)

Backpack

Allow 8 hours

Elevation gain: 365 m (1,200 ft)

Maximum elevation: 2105 m (6,900 ft)

Maps: Hector Lake 82 N/9
Barrier Mountain 82 O/12

Access: Reach the east end of the trail by hiking the Cascade Fire Road to the 58.4 km junction—200 m north of the Red Deer River bridge.

Access the west end of the trail at Cyclone Patrol Cabin by hiking the Skoki Lodge-Natural Bridge trail from Skoki Valley to the junction with the Upper Red Deer trail at the patrol cabin, 400 m beyond Red Deer Lakes Campground.

0.0—Cascade Fire Road Junction (1740 m).
N51°40.108' W115°49.517'

—Follows old roadbed.

1.4—Divide Creek crossing (rock-hop or ankle-deep ford).

1.6—Junction. *Divide Creek–Peters Creek* trail right.

—Gradual to rolling ascent along north side of Red Deer Valley.

6.1—McConnell Creek ford (calf-deep).

10.4—Junction. Horseshoe (Skeleton) Lake left.

12.3—Red Deer River gorge and waterfall.

14.1—Tributary creek crossing (on logjam).

14.5—Red Deer Patrol Cabin.

20.3—Junction. Douglas Lake left 3.0 km.

22.2—Drummond Creek ford (calf-deep).

24.9—Junction. Natural Bridge left 2.5 km.

26.7—Junction. Cyclone Patrol Cabin. Red Deer Lakes Campground (Sk19) left 0.4 km. (See Skoki Lodge to Natural Bridge, *Skoki Valley Area Hikes*.)

The Red Deer Valley is one of the great wilderness valleys in Banff Park. Most hikers only know the valley's headwaters, which is often visited on day trips from the Skoki Valley. Yet the entire valley offers fine scenery, interesting side-trips, and lots of solitude.

The lower valley is traversed by the Cascade Fire Road and usually accessed from the Ya-Ha-Tinda Ranch just east of the park boundary (see *Cascade Fire Road*). The upper valley trail branches from the Cascade trail 200 m north of the Red Deer River bridge.

The first 1.6 km follows an old roadbed, but after crossing Divide Creek and passing the *Divide Creek-Peters Creek* trail junction, it reverts to single track. Following a calf-deep ford of McConnell Creek at km 6.1, the trail traverses open meadows interspersed with sections of forest.

At 10.4 km a short side trail crosses the Red Deer to Horseshoe Lake (aka Skeleton Lake). While the lake has a reputation for good trout fishing, fording the river at this point can be difficult.

A more interesting side-trip is Douglas Lake, which branches left at a signed junction on riverside flats at km 20.3. After wading the Red Deer's braided channels, continue to the north end of the lake in 3 km. There is no trail beyond this large, scenic lake, but you can camp here and then explore south to the head of the Valley of Hidden Lakes.

After another calf-deep ford at Drummond Creek (good views northwest to Drummond Glacier), you pass the trail to Natural Bridge and reach the Cyclone Patrol Cabin. At the junction just beyond the cabin, most hikers turn south to the Red Deer Lakes Campground en route to the Skoki Valley (see Skoki Lodge to Natural Bridge, *Skoki Valley Area Hikes*).

83 Divide Creek—Peters Creek

Red Deer River Junction to Clearwater River Junction—25.7 km (16.0 mi)

Backpack

Allow 8 hours

Elevation gain: 625 m (2,050 ft)
loss: 655 m (2,150 ft)

Maximum elevation: 2395 m (7,850 ft)

Maps: Barrier Mountain 82 O/12
Forbidden Creek 82 O/13

Access: Reach the south end of the trail from the junction at km 1.6 on the *Upper Red Deer River* trail. Reach the north end at the *Clearwater River* trail junction 2.4 km east of the park boundary in the Clearwater Valley.

0.0—Red Deer River Junction (1770 m).

— Steady climb above Divide Creek canyon.

6.6—Trail begins sharp descent.

8.0—Divide Creek ford (ankle-deep).

8.4—Divide Patrol Cabin.

— Steady climb into alpine.

11.6—Divide Summit (2395 m).

— Descend north side of pass.

13.0—Peters Creek crossing to east side.

— Valley narrows. Numerous side scree slopes.

18.8—Walk along river bed for 1.0 km.

20.8—Steep climb away from creek begins.

22.4—Steep descent to Clearwater Valley.

24.0—Clearwater Valley meadows.

24.9—Old outfitter camp.

25.3—Clearwater River ford to north bank (thigh-deep and swift).

25.7—Junction (1740 m). Intersects the *Clearwater River* trail.

This horse trail branches north from the *Upper Red Deer River* trail 1.6 km west of its junction with the Cascade Fire Road. A well-used route for horse parties, it crosses the lofty and scenic Divide Summit to link the Red Deer and Clearwater Valleys.

From its junction with the *Upper Red Deer River* trail, the trail climbs a steep, grassy bluff and begins a steady ascent along a mountainside west of the precipitous Divide Creek canyon. After reaching an elevation of nearly 2285 m, it plunges 150 m in less than 2 km and crosses Divide Creek just below the Divide Patrol Cabin.

The trail eases its way up through open meadows from the patrol cabin to the remarkably scenic Divide Summit—a 2395-m pass with fine views south across the Red Deer Valley.

Trail descends north from the pass to the east of upper Peters Creek. Near the base of Mount Peters, a section of trail was washed out by 2013 floods; hikers must now walk along the creek bed for approximately 1.0 km (calf-deep fords required). The transition back to the original trail is obvious, after which it traverses scree slopes and makes a final climb over the northeast shoulder of the mountain to an old outfitter's camp in a meadow near the Clearwater River.

The ford of the Clearwater is wide and challenging, but usually straightforward after water levels drop in August. Once you've crossed the river, which serves as the park boundary, follow the trail north 0.4 km to an intersection with the Clearwater River trail. From this junction most backpackers turn west and follow the Clearwater Valley back into Banff Park (see *Clearwater River*).

84 Clearwater River

Peters Creek Junction to Clearwater Pass—30.5 km (19.0 mi)
Clearwater–Red Deer Circuit—145 km (90 mi)

Backpack

Allow 8 to 9 hours

Elevation gain: 590 m (1,950 ft)

Maximum elevation: 2330 m (7,650 ft)

Maps: Forbidden Creek 82 O/13
Siffleur River 82 N/16
Hector Lake 82 N/9

Access: Reach the east end of the Clearwater River trail via the *Divide Creek-Peters Creek* trail. Access the west end of the trail 3 km north of Pipestone Pass on the *North Molar-Pipestone-Dolomite Circuit*.

0.0—Peters Creek Junction (1740 m).

—Follow west along old roadbed.

2.4—Park boundary. Road reverts to single-track.

3.4—Indianhead Lodge Patrol Cabin.

3.5—Indianhead Creek ford (ankle-deep).

4.2—Junction. *Whiterabbit Pass* trail right.

7.5—Malloch Creek ford (rock-hop or calf-deep).

13.1—Trident Lake.

14.4—Junction. Martin Creek waterfalls left.

14.6—Martin Lake. Martin Creek ford at lake outlet (knee to thigh-deep).

17.1—Clearwater Lake (1905 m).

19.6—Clearwater Lakes Patrol Cabin.

—Steady climb to Clearwater Pass.

28.9—Upper Devon Lake.

30.5—Clearwater Pass (2330 m).

31.6—Junction. Intersection with *North Molar-Pipestone-Dolomite Circuit* at 27.0 km (3.0 km north of Pipestone Pass).

The Clearwater is the most remote valley in Banff Park. The valley is traversed by good trail, but getting to either end of it usually takes two days. Yet this isolation preserves it as one of the last unspoiled regions in Banff Park.

The trail can be reached from the west via Pipestone Pass and the headwaters of the Siffleur River (see *North Molar-Pipestone-Dolomite Circuit*). However, the valley unfolds more dramatically when it is ascended from the park's east boundary to its scenic climax on Clearwater Pass.

The most common approach to the east end of the trail is from the Red Deer Valley via the *Divide Creek-Peters Creek* trail. This route requires a sometimes-demanding ford of the Clearwater River just prior to intersecting the Clearwater trail 2.4 km east of the park boundary. This junction can also be reached by long approach trails from Ya-Ha-Tinda Ranch or Alberta's Cutoff Creek Recreation Area.

From Peters Creek junction, the trail runs due west along the north side of the Clearwater into Banff Park. A kilometre beyond the boundary it passes Indianhead—one of the park's most isolated patrol cabins.

The gradual ascent of the valley continues, entering mixed forest and extensive meadows near Malloch Creek, and nearby slopes bear the scars of a 2009 wildfire.

As the trail skirts north of Trident Lake, two waterfalls are heard—one across the valley on Roaring Creek and the other just below Martin Lake (a short spur trail leads to the latter).

The trail crosses Martin Creek just below Martin Lake. (The creek is best forded by hiking upstream and wade through the shallows at the lake's outlet where the current is less swift.) After this deep, soaking ford, the trail rolls along

© Mike McReynolds

Upper Devon Lake

to Clearwater Lake, where there are fine views to the head of the valley.

After passing the historic Clearwater Lakes Patrol Cabin, the ascent to Clearwater Pass begins, gradually at first, then more steeply over the last 6 km.

Clearwater Pass is a long, curving alpine summit highlighted by the Devon Lakes. The lakes are bordered by rolling meadows and overshadowed by the cliffs of Devon Mountain. Mount Willingdon (3373 m), one of the highest mountains in the Front Ranges, rises to the north.

The trail passes beside the largest of the Devon Lakes. While the meadow near the lake is a pleasant place to camp, few will want to linger here when conditions are foul. If you are westbound, you face a long journey before you regain forest cover and protection from the elements.

From the summit of Clearwater Pass, vague trail descends across rocky, alpine meadows to a junction with the Siffleur Valley trail 3 km north of Pipestone Pass. At this point you can descend the Siffleur Valley to the north or head south over Pipestone Pass to Fish Lakes. (See *North Molar-Pipestone-Dolomite Circuit*.)

Clearwater-Red Deer Circuit—145 km (90 mi). This is a grand but demanding wilderness tour that crosses five passes ranging in elevation from 2330 m to 2590 m. On one section, from Mosquito Creek meadows to the upper Clearwater, you are at or above treeline for 25 km. There is plenty of low elevation travel, too, along two of the most remote and scenic valleys in Banff Park—the Clearwater and Red Deer.

The circuit is not frequently hiked since it is not as well maintained or appointed as better known wilderness trips. Much of the journey travels though areas where random camping is allowed. There are numerous fords, including difficult crossings of the Clearwater and Pipestone Rivers (its best to do this trip in August or early September). The full circuit should only be considered by experienced wilderness backpackers who are comfortable in remote backcountry for 10 days or so.

The circuit can be hiked as a loop, starting and finishing at the Mosquito Creek trailhead on the Icefields Parkway. You can travel clockwise or counterclockwise. While the latter option saves

Land above 2300 metres

0   5   10   15 km

the best scenery until the end of the trip, we prefer to hike clockwise. This allows the option of bailing out near the end of the journey at Red Deer Lakes by hiking out to Lake Louise via the *Boulder Pass-Skoki Valley* trail. (You can plan this itinerary in advance and arrange transportation between the Mosquito Creek and Boulder Pass trailheads.)

Follow the circuit clockwise by hiking the *North Molar Pass-Fish Lakes* trail to Fish Lakes. Continue on the *North Molar-Pipestone-Dolomite Circuit* from Fish Lakes to Pipestone Pass and the Clearwater Pass junction. Traverse Clearwater Pass and descend the Clearwater River trail to Peters Creek junction. Head south over Divide Summit to

the Red Deer River via the *Divide Creek-Peters Creek* trail. Ascend the *Upper Red Deer River* trail to the Red Deer Lakes junction just beyond Cyclone Patrol Cabin.

At this point you have two options: follow the Red Deer Lakes trail back to the *Boulder Pass-Skoki Valley* trail and out to the Fish Creek trailhead at Lake Louise; or complete the loop by descending Little Pipestone Creek to the Pipestone River crossing, fording the river, and then following the *Molar Creek* trail over Molar Pass and back to the Mosquito Creek trailhead. (The Boulder Pass-Skoki Valley option reduces total distance for the trip by 15 km.)

85 Whiterabbit Pass

Clearwater River Junction to Whiterabbit Pass—12.7 km (7.9 mi)

Backpack
Allow 4 hours to pass
Elevation gain: 470 m (1,550 ft)
Maximum elevation: 2270 m (7,450 ft)
Maps: Siffleur River 82 N/16

Access: Follow the *Clearwater River* trail to the junction at 4.2 km, 0.7 west of the Indianhead Creek ford. Trail angles off to northwest from Clearwater River.

0.0— Clearwater River Junction (1800 m).

— Gradual to moderate uphill to northwest.

3.4— Trail turns due north, begins steep climb.

6.1— Ridge summit (2165 m).
Begin descent to Indianhead Creek.

7.9— Trail levels off above Indianhead Creek, begins ascent to pass.

10.7— Cross to east side of Indianhead Creek (rock-hop).

12.7— Whiterabbit Pass (2270 m).
Park boundary.

— Trail descends to Headwaters Cabin (6.0 km beyond pass) and follows horse trail down Whiterabbit Creek. It eventually emerges at the North Saskatchewan suspension bridge at Kootenay Plains and David Thompson Highway (Hwy 11) 36.8 km from pass.

The Whiterabbit trail is an old outfitter's route connecting the Clearwater Valley with the Kootenay Plains to the north. It is still commonly used by horse parties, but seldom by backpackers, even though it is quite passable and scenic.

From its junction with the Clearwater River trail, 0.8 km west of the Indianhead Patrol Cabin, the trail climbs over a 2165-m ridge and descends into the Indianhead drainage.

Much of the ascent of Indianhead Creek is through open meadows. The climb culminates on 2270-m Whiterabbit Pass—a broad, grassy summit with good views north into the Ram River valley.

While Whiterabbit Pass is a worthy objective for backpackers camped in the Clearwater Valley, you can continue north beyond the Banff Park boundary and through provincial forest to the Kootenay Plains.

North of the pass the trail makes an easy descent to the south branch of the Ram River. The river is forded to its west bank 4.7 km beyond the pass, but the horse trail is often difficult to follow due to numerous all-terrain-vehicle tracks.

Just over a kilometre beyond the Ram River ford is the abandoned Headwaters Cabin, which sits on a bluff commanding one of the most scenic viewpoints in the Front Ranges.

Follow the horse trail northwest from the cabin, over a low divide and down onto the headwaters of Whiterabbit Creek (beware of intersecting ATV trails). The Whiterabbit is a long, straight valley marked by heavy forest.

When Whiterabbit Creek runs out onto the floor of the North Saskatchewan Valley, the trail enters an area of old logging roads. Keep left at all junctions until the Siffleur River bridge is crossed. From this bridge it is a short walk to the suspension bridge across the North Saskatchewan River and the trailhead parking area on Highway 11.

Jasper National Park

With an area of 10,878 sq km, Jasper is the largest of Canada's Rocky Mountain national parks. Lying along the eastern slope of the Rockies in western Alberta, the park is bordered on the west by the Great Divide and British Columbia's Mount Robson and Hamber Provincial Parks and on the south by Banff National Park.

Jasper's trail system totals more than 1200 km. The largest concentration of half-day and day trips is near the town of Jasper, but these are mostly low elevation hikes to forest-enclosed lakes. The park's most popular day trips are Cavell Meadows, beneath Mount Edith Cavell; Bald Hills and Opal Hills at Maligne Lake; Sulphur Skyline, above Miette Hot Springs; and Wilcox Pass, overlooking the Athabasca Glacier.

Jasper is best known for its backpacking trail system, and it may well be the premier area for remote wilderness hiking in North America. The North and South Boundary Trails offer solitary rambles of over 160 km; the 80-km Jonas Pass-Brazeau Lake Loop is the most popular circuit trip; and the park's most accessible and popular backcountry areas, the Skyline Trail and Tonquin Valley, are undeniably two of the most scenic backpacking destinations in Canada.

Like all other mountain national parks, Jasper has a quota for all its backcountry campgrounds. Sites on the Skyline Trail, the Jonas Pass-Brazeau Lake Loop, and in the Tonquin Valley are the busiest, particularly in July and August. If you are planning on camping along these trails, or any others in the park, you can reserve campsites up to three months prior to departure.

Information and services. Park Visitor Centres are located in downtown Jasper at 500 Connaught Drive (year around) and at the Icefield Centre (summer only). Both dispense Wilderness Passes and the latest information on trail conditions, bear sightings, weather reports, etc., but the downtown centre's trail desk is by far the most useful for anyone setting out on overnight trips.

Scattered throughout the park are 10 road-accessible campgrounds. The two largest, Whistlers and Wapiti, are just south of the town of Jasper. They are both full-service campgrounds and the only ones with showers.

The town of Jasper provides the full gamut of visitor services, including hotels, banks, restaurants, gas stations, grocery stores and numerous retail outlets catering to tourist clientele, including shops specializing in hiking gear. Food services and accommodation are also available during the summer months at the Icefield Centre, Sunwapta Falls, Miette Junction (Pocahontas) and Miette Hot Springs.

Access: The Yellowhead Highway (Hwy 16) is the east-west access route through the park, and a connector to the nearest city, Edmonton, Alberta (370 km east of Jasper). The Icefields Parkway connects Jasper with Banff National Park to the south (230 km from Jasper to Lake Louise).

The primary means of public transportation to Jasper Park is bus. Jasper is serviced by east and westbound Greyhound buses that run daily between Alberta and British Columbia on the Yellowhead Highway.

While the nearest international airport is in Edmonton, there is also a daily bus service between Calgary International Airport and Jasper via Banff and the Icefields Parkway in the summer.

Several east and westbound VIA Rail passenger trains make scheduled stops at the Jasper station each week throughout the summer season.

N

Mt Colin

The Palisade

Buttress Mtn

Celestine Lake Road

Edmonton

Athabasca

114

Palisade Lookout 90

Mt Zengel

Pyramid Mtn

River

16

Mt Kinross

Pyramid Lake

113 Maligne Canyon

Maligne Lake

Mt Henry

Mt Kerr

Cairngorm

Lake Edith

92

High Lakes

Patricia Lake

Lake Annette

Elysium Pass

88

Saturday Night Lake

Riley Lake 87

89

Jasper Park Lodge

Minnow Lake

Christine Lake

Mina Lakes

86

116

91

Dorothy Lake

88

Hibernia Lake

Cabin Lake

JASPER

Skyline

Virl Lake

Yellowhead Pass

16

Miette

Caledonia Lake

Marjorie Lake

River

16

Old Fort Point 94

Signal Mtn

Muhigan Mtn

Jasper Tramway

93

The Whistlers

Valley of Five Lakes

95

Indian Ridge

93

Marmot Basin Ski Area

Icefields

Wabasso Lake

Marmot Mtn

Manx Pk

96

Majestic Mtn

Peveril Pk

99

Portal Creek

93A

Astoria River

Parkway

Maccarib Pass

Lectern Pk

Mt Edith Cavell

Land above 2300 metres

0   1   2   3   4 km

86 Discovery Trail

Discovery Trail Circuit—8.3 km (5.2 mi)

The Discovery Trail loops around the town of Jasper, providing an interesting introduction to the town and surrounding wilderness. From the museum parking area, take the right fork uphill and cross Pyramid Lake Road. The trail then descends gradually through a mixed forest, with filtered views across the town for 1.4 km. After crossing Connaught Dr., a paved section loops south back to town beside the rail line. There are unobstructed views southeast to the Maligne Range, and Mt Edith Cavell is easily identified to the south. Beyond Jasper Railway Station, the trail crosses Hazel Ave. and continues to parallel the rail line to the western edge of town. It then crosses to the north side of Connaught Ave., from where it is 3.2 km of easy walking through open forest to the museum trailhead, with one steep section leading to a junction with the *Mina Lakes-Riley Lake Circuit.*

Access: The Discovery Trail can be accessed from many points around the town of Jasper, including the train station on Connaught Drive. Our favourite starting point is beside the Jasper Yellowhead Museum at the corner of Bonhomme St. and Pyramid Lake Rd., where the trail passes by the far corner of the parking area. N52°52.799' W118°05.208' *Maps: Jasper 83 D/16; Best of Jasper (Gem Trek).*

87 Mina Lakes—Riley Lake Circuit

Pyramid Lake Drive to Upper Mina Lake—2.0 km (1.2 mi)
Mina Lakes-Riley Lake Circuit—9.0 km (5.6 mi)

Mina and Riley Lakes can be reached in less than an hour from the western edge of the town of Jasper. Though the lakes are a fairly popular destination, their setting in a mixed forest of lodgepole pine, white spruce, Douglas fir and poplar gives them a feeling of isolation and a certain charm.

From the trailhead parking area, follow trail #8 up across the slope to the left and into the forest. After a kilometre of steady uphill, the trail crosses the Cabin Lake Road (a restricted-access service road leading to Cabin Lake).

Grades moderate beyond the Cabin Lake Road crossing, and the trail soon comes abreast of tiny Lower Mina Lake, a mere pond. A short distance beyond you reach the larger Upper Mina Lake and follow its northern shore.

At 3.5 km, just beyond Upper Mina Lake, you arrive at a trail junction.

Follow trail #8 to the right another 2.0 km to reach Riley Lake.

If you are doing a short walk, turn around at Riley and return the way you came. But if you are up for the complete Mina-Riley circuit, continue on trail #8 to Cottonwood Slough and its trailhead parking area on the Pyramid Lake Road. Follow trail #2 south from the parking area back to the Mina-Riley Lakes trailhead on Pyramid Lake Drive.

Access: The trailhead parking area is on the western edge of the town of Jasper at the corner of Pyramid Lake Rd. and Bonhomme St. The large, paved parking area is opposite the Jasper Activity Centre and adjacent to the Jasper Yellowhead Museum. The trail begins near the forest margin at the far rear corner of the parking area. N52°52.799' W118°05.208' *Maps: Jasper 83 D/16; Best of Jasper (Gem Trek).*

88 Saturday Night Lake Circuit

Saturday Night Lake Circuit—24.6 km (15.3 mi)

Day trip or backpack

Allow 7 to 9 hours return

Elevation gain: 540 m (1,800 ft)

Maximum elevation: 1640 m (5,400 ft)

Maps: Jasper 83 D/16
    Best of Jasper (Gem Trek)

Access: Follow Miette Avenue southwest from downtown Jasper and turn right onto Cabin Creek Road. Cabin Creek Road continues along the edge of town and enters a mobile home residential area. Watch for a gravel road branching steeply uphill to the right. Follow this branch 50 m to the trailhead parking area and kiosk.

0.0— Trailhead (1100 m).
    N52°52.293' W118°06.049'

2.3— Marjorie Lake.

2.6— Junction. Hibernia Lake right 400 m.

4.2— Caledonia Lake.

9.2— Junction. Minnow Lake Campground left 300 m.

12.4— Junction. High Lakes Campground right 200 m.

12.9— Cascade (1640 m). Trail turns back down-valley.

18.0— Junction. Saturday Night Lake Campground left 500 m.

21.4— Cabin Lake (west end).

22.3— Junction. Upper Mina Lake left 400 m.

22.5— Junction. Cabin Lake (east end). Access road to *Mina Lakes-Riley Lake* trail and Jasper ahead. Turn right across landfill dam.

23.4— Cabin Creek bridge.

24.6— Trailhead (1100 m).

This trail through the hill country west of Jasper is also known as the Pyramid Bench or Twenty Mile Loop, though it is not nearly that long. It visits several small lakes and can be hiked as a long day or overnight trip. Or you can make a shorter trip by going only as far as Marjorie, Hibernia and Caledonia Lakes.

While most of the journey is through heavy forest with limited views, it is an excellent nature walk where you will encounter a wide variety of wildflowers, waterfowl, beaver workings and, perhaps, black bear.

Mountain bikes are also permitted on the trail, though the track is rough and steep with muddy sections west of Caledonia and Cabin Lakes.

From the trailhead on the west edge of town, the broad path immediately crosses Cabin Creek and climbs onto a low bluff with a brief view up the Athabasca Valley. Marjorie Lake appears through the forest to the left at 2.3 km, and just beyond the short side trail to Hibernia Lake branches up to the right.

A quick look at a map shows that the lakes and ridges in this rolling country tend to be elongated in an east-west direction. This landscape was partly created by a valley glacier, which once advanced down the Miette to the Athabasca Valley. Large boulders and other glacial detritus are found throughout the area.

At 4.2 km the trail skirts the north shore of Caledonia Lake, where western wood lilies and wild roses bloom in early summer. Beyond Caledonia there is a long section of forest-enclosed trail with steady uphill grades. Many forest wildflowers grow along the trail, including bunchberry, single's delight, arnica, calypso orchids and Indian paintbrush; also watch for scattered patches of red columbine—a rare flower on the east slope of the Rockies.

Cabin Lake

At 9.2 km, you reach the junction for the 300-m branch trail leading to Minnow Lake and its campground, which some feel is the nicest site with the best views of the loop's three campgrounds. After passing the Minnow Lake junction, the trail climbs along forested ridges to the High Lakes Campground junction. The campground is located beside a tiny lake, which is the most westerly of several small lakes contained within the Saturday Night Lake loop.

The main trail reaches the foot of a large cascade on Cabin Creek at km 12.9, where it turns back to the east and begins the return journey. The descent along the north arm of the loop is steady through a forest of spring-fed streams and beaver swamps. At 18.0 km a short, steep trail branches north to Saturday Night Lake and the last of the circuit's three campgrounds.

From Saturday Night Lake junction it is just over 3 km to the west end of Cabin Lake—the largest lake on the loop. At the east end of Cabin Lake, cross the landfill dam to the right and follow the access road leading down through the forest.

After crossing Cabin Creek 0.6 km below the lake, the trail crests an open bluff overlooking the Athabasca Valley (the best viewpoint on the circuit), then descends through forest back to the trailhead parking area.

This entire area is frequented by black bears, so backpackers should keep a clean camp and use the bear poles provided at campsites.

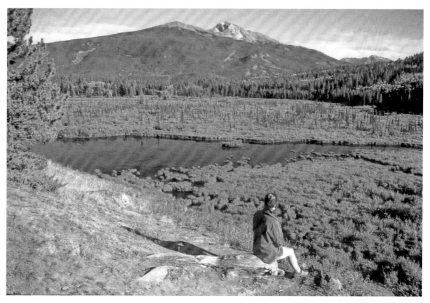

Cottonwood Slough

89 Cottonwood Slough

Cottonwood Slough Circuit—4.1 km (2.5 mi)

Despite its boggy name, Cottonwood Slough is quite a pleasant place. The short loop hike around this marshland, which cradles a small lake, is one of the most rewarding in the Jasper vicinity, particularly for birdwatchers. The montane slopes overlooking marsh and lake are dotted with wildflowers in spring and early summer, and there are good views across the Athabasca Valley to Signal Mountain and Mount Tekerra. Due to its low elevation, you can hike here much of the year.

The circuit starts on trail #8 and stays close to the south shoreline of the lake for 0.9 km. After passing beneath a powerline spanning the marsh, the trail climbs through forest to a junction at 1.6 km. (At this intersection, you can make a short side trip to Riley Lake by following trail #8 left for 10 minutes.)

Turn right on trail #8d to continue around the circuit. At km 1.9 you cross

Cottonwood Creek and intersect trail #6, which you follow to the right.

The trail quickly climbs to grassy slopes overlooking Cottonwood Slough. This dry, south-facing slope dotted with large Douglas fir trees provides distant views to the southeast and is a good place to scan the lake below for waterfowl.

At 3.0 km you reach a junction where trail #6 veers left toward the riding stables; stay right and descend trail #6a into aspen groves. When you reach Pyramid Lake Road, turn right and follow it back to the trailhead parking area.

Access: Follow Pyramid Lake Road 1.9 km (1.2 mi) from the west edge of the town of Jasper. The trailhead parking area is on the left side of the road near the bottom of a short downhill grade. N52°53.531′ W118°05.494′ *Maps: Jasper 83 D/16; Best of Jasper (Gem Trek).*

90 Palisade Lookout

Pyramid Lake to Palisade Lookout Site—10.8 km (6.7 mi)

Day trip

Allow 3-4 hours one way

Elevation gain: 840 m (2,750 ft)

Maximum elevation: 2020 m (6,650 ft)

Maps: Jasper 83 D/16

Access: Follow Pyramid Lake Road from the west edge of the town of Jasper 6.5 km (4 mi) to Pyramid Lake. Continue around the lake to the right until the road ends at a parking area near a locked access gate.

0.0— Trailhead (1180 m).
    N52°55.550' W118°05.618'

   — Follow gravel roadbed east along Pyramid Lake.

1.1— Pyramid Lake outlet bridge.

   — Road makes a steady climb north along The Palisade ridge.

6.5— Bridged stream.

7.6— Junction. Pyramid Mtn access trail left. Palisade Lookout right.

10.8— Palisade Lookout site (2020 m).

Views from the summit of The Palisade escarpment are among the most rewarding in the Jasper vicinity. From the sheer precipice where the Palisade Lookout cabin once stood, there is a broad panorama of the Athabasca Valley from Roche Miette and Jasper Lake to the snowy summit of Mount Edith Cavell. However, the hike is a long, steady uphill grind over a broad roadbed, and there are few views until you reach the top. It is popular with Jasper mountain bikers and hikers who are willing to endure the long climb.

From the access gate at the end of Pyramid Lake Road, follow the roadbed as it skirts the shore of Pyramid Lake to the Pyramid Creek outlet bridge. After crossing the bridge, the relentless climb of the The Palisade begins.

At km 7.6 the road forks, the right spur leading to the lookout site, the left 4 km to the base of Pyramid Mountain climber's route. Beyond the junction, the roadbed gets rougher and a bit brushy.

Though the lookout cabin was removed in the early 1980s, the site still commands outstanding views to the north and east. In fact, the entire Athabasca Valley from Jasper to the east park gate is spread beneath you like a map—peaks, rivers, wetlands, the railway and highway. Across the Athabasca Valley are the sharp, sawtooth peaks of the Colin Range, while Roche Miette, a distinctive butte-like mountain, juts out beyond Jasper Lake to the northeast.

Remember to pack sufficient water to complete this trail, because it is long, dry and south-facing.

91 Dorothy, Christine and Virl Lakes

Yellowhead Highway to Christine Lake — 4.4 km (2.7 mi)

Half-day trip

Allow 1.5 to 2 hours one way

Elevation gain: 250 m (820 ft)

Maximum elevation: 1340 m (4,400 ft)

Maps: Jasper 83 D/16 †
      † full trail not shown

Access: Follow the Yellowhead Highway (Hwy 16) west from the Icefields Parkway (Hwy 93) junction 11 km (7 mi) to the Meadow Creek bridge. The trailhead kiosk and parking area are just past the west end of the bridge on the north side of the highway. The hike begins on the railway service road beyond the locked access gate.

0.0— Trailhead (1220 m).
      N52°52.036' W118°15.108'

   — Follow service road 150 m. Trail branches right and crosses railroad tracks.

0.2— Miette River bridge.

   — Gradual climb west above river.

1.0— Trail bends right and climbs over ridge.

2.3— Minaga Creek bridge.

2.7— Junction. *Elysium Pass* ahead. Dorothy, Christine and Virl Lakes right.

3.7— Junction. Virl Lake right 0.4 km. Dorothy and Christine Lakes ahead.

4.1— Dorothy Lake (1340 m).

4.4— Christine Lake.

Of the many lakes in the rolling, heavily wooded country west of the town of Jasper, Dorothy, Christine and Virl are personal favourites. Though views from their shores are limited, these lakes provide more solitude than those nearer to town or the more popular high elevation hikes elsewhere in the park. In addition, the lakes' low elevation makes them ideal for early and late season hiking.

After clambering over the railroad right-of-way and crossing the Miette River bridge, you head up-valley above the Miette River briefly before veering right and climbing over a forested ridge. The trail descends to cross Minaga Creek at km 2.3, then makes a gradual ascent for the next 1.4 km to Virl Lake junction. A short spur trail leads to the shore of this tiny, elongated lake and views of Indian Ridge and Muhigan Mountain across the Miette Valley.

Just 400 m beyond Virl Lake junction, the main trail reaches Dorothy Lake, the largest of the three sisters. Dorothy is tightly embraced by forest and quite similar in appearance to Virl, except for a lack of distant views. Another 0.4 km brings you abreast of Christine Lake with its unique rock peninsulas and islands.

If you look at a map, you will see how these three lakes, and others west of Jasper, are all contained by low, parallel ridges running in a west-northwest to east-southeast direction. The sedimentary bedrock creating these ridges is primarily gritstone (coarse sandstone) alternating with shale. These rocks are part of the 600 million-year-old Middle Miette Formation—one of the oldest in the mountain parks—and numerous faults running through this section of the valley contributed to the formation of the ridges.

If you visit all three of the lakes, your round trip distance will be 9.6 km.

© Andrew Hempstead

Christine Lake

94 Old Fort Point

Old Fort Point Road to Old Fort Point summit — 0.8 km (0.5 mi)
Old Fort Point Circuit — 3.8 km (2.4 mi)

Half-day trip

Allow 1.5 hours for circuit

Elevation gain: 135 m (445 ft)

Maximum elevation: 1165 m (3,820 ft)

Maps: Jasper 83 D/16
     Best of Jasper (Gem Trek)

Access: Follow Hazel Avenue (Hwy 93A) south from its intersection with Connaught Drive (Jasper's main street). Cross the railway tracks to an intersection with the Yellowhead Highway (Hwy 16). Continue across the Yellowhead Highway 100 m to the Old Fort Point/Lac Beauvert Road junction. Turn left and follow this road 1.0 km and across the Athabasca River bridge to the trailhead parking area, on the right at the foot of a rocky bluff.

0.0— Trailhead (1030 m).
      N52°52.270' W118°03.720'

   — Old Fort Point Circuit: follow trail #1 from information kiosk at the rear of parking area.

0.9— Junction. Trail #7a to Lac Beauvert left.

1.6— Junction. Trail #1a ahead. Old Fort Point right.

1.8— Steep climb through forest and cliffs.

2.1— Junction. Trails #1a and #9 to *Valley of the Five Lakes* left. Old Fort Point ahead.

   — Steady uphill.

2.5— Junction. Unsigned side trail 200 m to Old Fort Point southeast summit.

   — Gradual descent.

2.8— Trail begins climb to northwest summit.

3.1— Old Fort Point Junction (1165 m). Spur trail ahead through rock bluffs to summit viewpoint (100 m).

   — Steady downhill with steep sections.

3.7— Junction. Trail #9c intersects from left. Heritage River monument 20 m ahead.

   — Stairs to parking area.

3.8— Trailhead parking area (1030 m).

Old Fort Point rises across the Athabasca River from the town of Jasper. It is named for a fur trade post which was constructed a short distance downstream by William Henry in 1812. While Old Fort Point is little more than a hill, its position in the middle of the Athabasca Valley provides a 360-degree panorama that includes all the important points of interest: the town stretches beyond the Athabasca River to the northwest; Lac Beauvert and Jasper Park Lodge lie immediately below to the north; Mounts Hardisty and Kerkeslin, rise up-valley; and the snowy summit of Mount Edith Cavell dominates the southern skyline.

The shortest route to the top of Old Fort Point is only 0.8 km. This direct route begins on a staircase beside the parking area. At the top of the stairs you arrive at a monument honouring the historical importance of the Athabasca River and your first viewpoint—the confluence of the Athabasca and Miette Rivers.

Stay left at the junction just beyond the monument and climb steeply up open slopes and through stands of Douglas fir until you crest the summit ridge. Just beyond a pair of stone monuments, branch left through rock outcrops to the northwest summit viewpoint.

Old Fort Point Circuit. While the trail up the northwest slope of Old Fort Point is the shortest, we prefer the longer, less direct route—sneaking up on the viewpoint from behind.

The Old Fort Point Circuit is a loop trip, which includes both the southeast and northwest summits. This hike is quite rewarding in spring and early summer when meadows are filled with wildflowers, or in late September when the numerous aspen groves turn to gold.

Follow trail #1 into heavy forest from the kiosk at the rear of parking area.

Pyramid Mountain and the Athabasca Valley from Old Fort Point

(Though there are a number of intersecting trails on the circuit, you stay on course by always following the yellow #1 trail markers.)

The trail is flat to gradual uphill for the first 1.5 km, passing through pleasant groves of cottonwood and aspen poplar. This section is followed by a short climb to the crest of the Old Fort Point ridge, where the trail turns back to the northwest. Here you encounter more aspen stands and montane wildflowers, including blue flax, harebells, blue-eyed grass and gaillardia.

An unsigned trail branches right onto open slopes at 2.5 km. This is Old Fort Point's southeast summit, which is virtually the same elevation as the northwest summit. While views are more limited on this promontory, it is a wonderful place for flowers.

Continuing along the main trail to km 3.1, you reach the rock outcrops marking the northwest summit viewpoint. Complete the circuit by descending the steep, direct route to the staircase and parking area.

Old Fort Point to Valley of the Five Lakes. This branch trail from the Old Fort Point Circuit rolls up-valley to the Valley of the Five Lakes. It passes through numerous aspen groves and along open wetlands, which are excellent locales for birdwatching.

Though the trail is often used by mountain bikers (a demanding route with many ups-and-downs), it is also a pleasant half-day hike for those who can arrange transportation between Old Fort Point and the Valley of the Five Lakes trailhead on the Icefields Parkway.

Follow trail #9 south from its junction with the Old Fort Point Circuit at km 2.1. Continue up-valley 4 km to where trail #9a splits left from #9. Stay on #9a to the Valley of the Five Lakes. You will intersect the trail from the Icefields Parkway at the far end of the first lake.

Total distance from the Old Fort Point Circuit trailhead to the parking area on the Icefields Parkway is approximately 11.5 km. (See *Valley of the Five Lakes.*)

Wabasso Lake and Mount Kerkeslin

95 Valley of the Five Lakes

Icefields Parkway to Valley of the Five Lakes—2.0 km (1.2 mi)

These five lakes on the floor of the Athabasca Valley vary in size from just over a kilometre in length at First Lake to the tiny pond of Third Lake. While the hike to the valley and back can be completed in less than two hours, you can easily spend a half-day or more wandering about the lakes' circuit.

From the parking area, the first 0.5 km of trail is mainly flat through a forest of lodgepole pine. At 0.8 km the trail descends to a boardwalk across Wabasso Creek. This is followed by a brief climb to open meadow and a junction with trail #9—the valley trail running from Old Fort Point to Wabasso Lake. Continue ahead on #9a to a split, where you begin the circuit that loops around the five lakes (you can go right on #9a or left on #9b, which is our preference).

By staying on #9b you descend from the ridge and pass between First and Second Lake, where you are reunited with

#9a. Turn right and follow it along the northeast shore of Second and Fourth Lakes to the northwest end of Fifth Lake. Stay right on #9a to complete the loop.

More ambitious hikers can travel southeast to Wabasso Lake or northwest to Old Fort Point via trail #9—both trips ideally completed by arranging transportation at those trailheads. (See *Old Fort Point* and *Wabasso Lake*.)

Access: Follow the Icefields Parkway (Hwy 93) south 9 km (5.5 mi) from its intersection with the Yellowhead Highway (Hwy 16). The trailhead parking area is located on the east side of the highway. N52°48.507' W118°01.402' Maps: Jasper 83 D/16; Best of Jasper (Gem Trek).

96 Wabasso Lake

Icefields Parkway to Wabasso Lake—3.2 km (2.0 mi)

Half-day trip

Allow 1 hour to Wabasso Lake

Elevation gain: 50 m (165 ft)

Maximum elevation: 1150 m (3,775 ft)

Maps: Medicine Lake 83 C/13

Access: Follow the Icefields Parkway (Hwy 93) to the Wabasso Lake parking area, located on the east side of the highway 14.5 km (9.0 mi) south of the Yellowhead Highway (Hwy 16) intersection.

0.0— Trailhead (1100 m).
     N52°46.174' W117°58.781'

   —Rolling forested terrain.

2.3— Ridge viewpoint.

3.2— Wabasso Lake (1150 m).

   — Trail skirts north end of lake.

4.2— Junction. *Valley of the Five Lakes* and *Old Fort Point* left (trail #9). *Skyline Trail* ahead.

   — Steep switchbacking climb through pine forest.

13.0— Grade moderates.

14.1— Shovel Pass Lodge.

14.2— Curator Campground.

   — Steep ascent.

15.0— Junction (2200 m). Intersection with the *Skyline Trail* at 19.5 km. Curator Lake left 0.9 km. Big Shovel Pass right 2.0 km.

Notice: Due to possible conflicts with caribou, dogs are not permitted on the section of trail beyond the 4.2-km junction at Wabasso Lake to the Skyline Trail.

This short trail leads to a small but very pretty lake on the floor of the Athabasca Valley. Though Wabasso is the Cree word for "rabbit," you are more likely to see muskrat along the lake's marshy shores.

The hike begins with a brief climb from the Icefields Parkway, then it rolls through lodgepole pine forest. At km 1.4 it crosses a stream and climbs onto an open ridge—a fine viewpoint for all the major peaks to the south.

From the ridgetop, it is less than a kilometre to the marsh at the southeast corner of Wabasso Lake. The trail continues around the lake's north shore, where you have the best views of the lake, its tiny island, and the impressive summits of Mounts Kerkeslin, Christie and Brussels Peak rising far to the south.

Wabasso Lake to the Skyline. The Wabasso trail continues beyond the lake and up the side of the Maligne Range for another 11 km to an intersection with the Skyline Trail. It is most often used by pack trains supplying Shovel Pass Lodge.

Since the trail is steep and forest-enclosed, it has little attraction as an approach to the Skyline, but it can provide a quick exit during inclement weather. It can also be linked with the Watchtower Basin trail via Big Shovel Pass to create a 30-km traverse across the Maligne Range. (See *Watchtower Basin.*)

After passing Wabasso Lake, the trail branches into the forest to a junction at km 4.2. The Skyline option stays right and runs briefly through mixed forest before starting the long, gruelling climb.

The forest eventually thins to open views of the Athabasca Valley, and the grade moderates near the lodge and Curator Campground. From the campground it is a short, steep climb to the Skyline Trail junction. (See *Skyline Trail* and *Sources: Backcountry lodges* for Shovel Pass Lodge.)

N

Marmot
Basin
Ski Area

Marmot
Mtn

Manx
Pk

Peveril
Pk

Lectern
Pk

(99)

Franchère Pk

Oldhorn
Mtn

(100)

Throne
Mtn

Blackhorn
Pk

Chevron
Mtn

Needle
Pk

(102)

Divergence
Pk

Alnus
Pk

Tonquin Valley

Maccarib
Pass

Tonquin Valley

Outpost Lake

Whirlpool

Middle

Jasper

(95)

Valley of Five Lakes

Amber Mtn

Skyline Trail

The
Notch

(116)

Lodge

Curator Mtn

Wabasso Lake

(96)

Antler Mtn

93

93A

Astoria River

Edith Cavell Road

Hostel

Cavell
Lake

(97)

(98)

Mt
Edith Cavell

Cavell
Meadows

Moab
Lake

Athabasca

Icefields

93A

Mt
Hardisty

Geraldine Road

River

Geraldine
Lookout

Athabasca
Falls

93

Mt
Kerkeslin

Parkway

Lower
Geraldine
Lake

(103)

Geraldine
Lakes

Columbia
Icefield

River

Whirlpool

River

Mt
Fryatt

(104)

Creek

Fryatt

Fryatt
Lake

Mt
Lapensee

Mt
Belanger

Fryatt
Valley

Brussels Pk

ACC Hut

Athabasca Pass

Land above 2300 metres

0   2   4   6   8km

Angel Glacier from the Path of the Glacier trail

97 Path of the Glacier

Path of the Glacier Loop—1.6 km (1.0 mi)

The Path of the Glacier trail travels through a rocky glacial basin to the tiny but exquisite Cavell Pond at the toe of Cavell Glacier. The pond's dark blue waters are highlighted by drifting icebergs, and its shoreline is one of the best vantage points for viewing the Angel Glacier and the towering cliffs of Mount Edith Cavell. Signs along the trail describe the glacial events that have shaped this dramatic landscape.

While we would rank this as one of the most spectacular short trails in the Canadian Rockies, it is not a place where you're likely to find solitude. With the exception of early morning or late evening, it is a steady parade of humanity.

Begin the hike by ascending the stairwell above the parking area and then climbing steadily on paved trail along a lateral moraine for 0.5 km. From the end of pavement, the trail descends into the rockbound basin containing the lake.

From the lakeshore, Mount Edith Cavell rises an incredible 1600 m (a vertical mile) to the highest peak in this area of the park. Angel Glacier clings to its wall, though it doesn't resemble an angel these days since its toe and wings have receded. Meanwhile, Cavell Glacier sprawls along the lake's southern shore and calves icebergs into its placid waters.

The return trail to the parking area travels beside Cavell Creek, where willows and other plants are slowly recolonizing a rocky valley bottom that was covered by ice 150 years ago.

Access: Follow the Icefields Parkway (Hwy 93) south from Jasper 7 km (4.5 mi) to Highway 93A. Continue south on 93A for 5.5 km (3.5 mi) to the Cavell Road and follow it 14.5 km (9 mi) to its terminus at the parking area beneath Mount Edith Cavell. The trail starts at the upper edge of the parking area. N52°41.228' W118°03.309' *Maps: Amethyst Lakes 83 D/9.*

98 Cavell Meadows

Cavell Meadows Loop—6.1 km (3.8 mi)

Half-day trip
Allow 2 hours round trip
Elevation gain: 400 m (1,300 ft)
Maximum elevation: 2165 m (7,100 ft)
Maps: Amethyst Lakes 83 D/9

Access: Follow the Icefields Parkway
(Hwy 93) south from Jasper 7 km (4.5 mi) to
Highway 93A. Continue south on 93A for
5.5 km (3.5 mi) to the Cavell Road and follow
it 14.5 km (9 mi) to its terminus at the
parking area beneath Mount Edith Cavell.
The trail starts at the upper edge of the
parking area.

0.0— Trailhead (1765 m).
   N52°41.228' W118°03.309'
   — Follows paved trail along a lateral
   moraine.

0.5— Junction. *Path of the Glacier* trail
   ahead. Cavell Meadows uphill to left.
   — Trail climbs over and along the lateral
   moraine.

1.5— Trail begins switchbacking ascent
   through forest.

2.2— Junction. Trail split for Cavell
   Meadows loop. Keep right.

2.4— Angel Glacier viewpoint.
   — Trail climbs into meadows.

3.0— Junction (2120 m). South end of
   meadow loop. Branch trail continues
   ahead 100 m to a viewpoint.
   — Trail turns left and continues climb
   across meadows.

3.2— Junction (2165 m). Branch trail to high
   viewpoint right (0.9 km); meadows
   loop ahead.
   — Steep descent to loop trail split.

3.9— Junction. Return to trail split for
   Cavell Meadows loop at km 2.2.

6.1— Trailhead (1765 m).

**Notice: Due to possible conflicts with
caribou, dogs are not permitted on the
Cavell Meadows trail or in adjacent
alpine meadows.**

The lush, flower-filled Cavell Meadows
would be a worthy destination in their
own right, but they are also an outstanding viewpoint for Angel Glacier and the
sheer north wall of Mount Edith Cavell
(3363 m), one of the highest mountains
in the Canadian Rockies. It's not surprising that the loop trail through the meadows is one of Jasper's most popular, and
unless you hike in the evening or early
morning, expect to have company.

The hike begins on the paved *Path
of the Glacier* trail. After 500 m it
branches left and climbs over a ridge of
lateral moraine. It continues along the
moraine (watch for hoary marmots on
the rockpiles), then switchbacks up into
subalpine forest—a woodland that is
carpeted with glacier lilies, marsh mari-
golds and globe flowers in early summer.

At 2.2 km, the trail splits for the loop
through the meadows lying above. By
staying right, and hiking the loop counter-
clockwise, the ascent is more gradual.
Soon, you're past the last scattered trees,
and views of Angel Glacier and Mount
Edith Cavell emerge on the right.

The trail continues its climb above
treeline to the southern end of the
meadows loop, where an extension
continues 100 m to a rocky viewpoint.
Turning back to the north, you continue
your climb for another 200 m to a junction. While views at this alpine intersection are remarkable, a branch trail to
the right leads to an even loftier 2290-m
vantage point.

Climbing straight up the slope to the
east, you gain a breathless 150 m or so
in just under a kilometre. This is true
alpine terrain, where ground-hugging
plants, like moss campion and white
mountain avens, eke out a meagre living in the harshest of environments. As
with so many sections of this trail, the
rocky summit viewpoint is home hoary
marmots, who seem unconcerned about
either climate or hikers.

© Andrew Hempstead   *Angel Glacier and Cavell Pond from Cavell Meadows trail*

Whether you visit the summit view-point, or simply continue ahead on the meadows loop, you eventually plunge down through lush meadows on the north arm of the loop and complete the circuit back at the original 2.2-km trail split.

Major rehabilitation and trail rebuilding have been carried out over the past decade to guard these meadows from damage by the many thousands who hike here each summer. Do your part and stay on designated trails.

Tonquin Valley

J. Monroe Thorington, an American mountaineer and historian who devoted most of his life to rambling about the Canadian Rockies, wrote eloquently of the Tonquin Valley and how its "unique combination of lake, precipice, and ice...presents itself with a singular beauty almost unequalled in alpine regions of North America."

Anyone who has visited the valley at the end of summer when the air is crisp and clear would undoubtedly support his appreciation. But in the midst of summer, when the rain is pelting down, the mosquitoes and horseflies are swarming, and the trails have been churned to mush by horses, it can resemble a backpacker's definition of hell.

The Tonquin Valley is actually a 5 km-long pass whose broad crest cradles the Amethyst Lakes—a pair of beautiful connected lakes set at the base of a 1000-m wall of Precambrian quartzite called The Ramparts. The Ramparts are composed of ten spectacular castellate peaks, which are worthy of such names as Bastion, Drawbridge, Redoubt, Dungeon and Paragon. They form a glowering collection of towers and turrets that natives once believed to be inhabited by huge, supernatural beasts.

While no horrible beasts have been sighted in the valley in recent years (except for the pesky midsummer bugs), it is home to a variety of wildlife. Two celebrity species always in residence are caribou (seen most everywhere) and grizzly bear (expect posted warnings at campgrounds).

A few kilometres west of the north Amethyst Lake are Moat Lake and the twin passes of Moat and Tonquin. Chrome Lake and the heavily glaciated spires of the Eremite Valley lie just south of the Tonquin Valley. Both areas are prime day-trip destinations from the valley's campsites and lodges.

Two trails of almost equal length lead into the valley—one running up the Astoria River from the Cavell Road, the other via Portal Creek and Maccarib Pass from the Marmot Basin Road. Maccarib Pass is considered the most scenic approach, while the Astoria River is the shortest route to campgrounds at the south end of the Amethyst Lakes and the Alpine Club of Canada hut at Outpost Lake. If you arrange transportation between trailheads, you can hike in on one of the trails and out on the other. (See *Maccarib Pass* and *Astoria River*.)

Four campgrounds are located in the valley and three others on the approach trails, and campfires are not permitted at any of these sites. While use of the campgrounds is modest, you can assure a site by making reservations up to 3 months in advance of your trip.

In addition to campgrounds, there are two lodges in the valley:

Tonquin-Amethyst Lake Lodge is on the east side of Amethyst Lakes near the Narrows. The rustic Brewster Chalet, which serves as the centrepiece for the cabin camp, was built by Jasper's pioneer outfitter Fred Brewster, who first developed the site in 1939. While the lodge books horse trips throughout the summer season, it reserves 40% of its space for hikers.

Tonquin Valley Backcountry Lodge is at the north end of the lakes just off the Moat Lake trail. At present it is more oriented to guided horse parties, though it does have special rates for walk-in guests. (See *Sources—Backcountry lodges*.)

Camping is not permitted in the Eremite Valley region, but the Alpine Club of Canada's Wates-Gibson Hut on the shores of Outpost Lake can accommodate up to 30 people at quite reasonable rates. (See *Sources—Huts*.)

Notice: Due to possible conflicts with caribou, dogs are not permitted on any trails in the Tonquin Valley area or approach routes via Portal Creek and Astoria River.

Land above 2300 metres

99 Maccarib Pass

Marmot Basin Road to Amethyst Campground—22.9 km (14.2 mi)
Marmot Basin Road to Clitheroe Campground—26.3 km (16.3 mi)

Backpack

Allow 7 to 8 hours

Elevation gain: 730 m (2,400 ft)
loss: 235 m (770 ft)

Maximum elevation: 2210 m (7,250 ft)

Maps: Jasper 83 D/16
Amethyst Lakes 83 D/9

Access: From its intersection with the
Yellowhead Highway (Hwy 16), follow the
Icefields Parkway (Hwy 93) south 7 km
(4.5 mi) to the 93A Highway junction.
Continue south on Highway 93A for 2.5 km
(1.5 mi) to the Marmot Basin Road junction.
Follow the Marmot Basin Road 6.5 km (4 mi)
to the Portal Creek bridge and parking area.

0.0— Trailhead (1480 m).
  N52°46.855' W118°04.609'

0.5— Portal Creek bridge to north side of
  creek.

  — Ascend Portal Creek canyon.

4.0— Circus Creek bridge.

5.0— Trail emerges into open rockslides.

8.7— Portal Creek Campground.

10.1— Trail begins steep ascent toward
  pass.

12.4— Maccarib Pass (2210 m).

12.9— First views into Tonquin Valley.

  — Gradual descent.

19.5— Maccarib Campground and Maccarib
  Creek bridge.

20.4— Junction. Tonquin Valley Backcountry
  Lodge (1.5 km) and Moat Lake
  (3.5 km) ahead. Amethyst Lakes
  east shore left.

  — Flat trail running south.

21.3— Amethyst Lakes-north end.

22.9— Amethyst Campground.

24.0— Tonquin-Amethyst Lake Lodge (1975 m).

  — Trail climbs east from lodge junction.

26.2— Junction. Astoria River trail ahead
  (see *Astoria River*). Clitheroe
  Campground (0.1 km), Surprise Point
  Campground (2.3 km) and Eremite
  Valley to right (see *Eremite Valley*).

Of the two main trails into the Tonquin Valley, Maccarib Pass is slightly
longer and more arduous. However, it
holds a definite scenic advantage over
the Astoria River trail. The descent of a
6-km-long meadow west of Maccarib
Pass is the scenic highlight, disclosing
ever-improving views of The Ramparts
and Amethyst Lakes as you approach the
valley.

Starting from the Marmot Basin Road
parking area, the trail climbs into the
narrow canyon known as The Portal.
It traverses high onto the north side of
the valley and crosses rockslides below
Peveril Peak, and you soon have excellent
views to the head of the valley and the
peaks surrounding the pass.

After descending back to the valley floor, the trail makes a 5-km climb
through an open subalpine forest of
Engelmann spruce and alpine fir. Shortly
after passing Portal Creek Campground,
it emerges above treeline and makes its
final climb to the pass.

While the approach to Maccarib Pass
offers some fine views, particularly to
the jagged summit of Old Horn Mountain, the trail's true reward lies on the
descent west from its pass. From the first
glimpse of The Ramparts and Moat Pass,
obtained just beyond the pass, each suc-
ceeding kilometre across alpine meadows brings better views of the Tonquin
Valley and its surrounding peaks. The
open slopes stretching on either side of
the trail are a good place to see caribou.

After passing the scenically situated
Maccarib Campground at 19.5 km, the
trail reaches the floor of the Tonquin
Valley at a junction just north of the
Amethyst Lakes. The right branch leads
to the north end of the lakes and Tonquin
Valley Backcountry Lodge, the left runs
south along the east shore of the lakes to
the Tonquin-Amethyst Lake Lodge and
three of the valley's campgrounds.

Amethyst Lakes and The Ramparts from the Maccarib Pass trail

Following the valley trail south from the junction, you come abreast of the north Amethyst Lake in less than a kilometre. The trail runs flat through scattered forest for another 1.6 km to Amethyst Campground—the most centrally located of the valley's four campgrounds.

The trail continues south for another kilometre to Tonquin-Amethyst Lake Lodge. From the lodge it climbs onto higher, drier ground along the east side of the valley to the Clitheroe Campground junction. At this intersection the Astoria River trail continues left and the trail to Surprise Point at the south end of the lakes branches down to the right (see *Astoria River* and *Eremite Valley*).

Campfires are not permitted at any of the campgrounds on the Portal Creek-Maccarib Pass trail or at sites in the Tonquin Valley. And special care should be taken when handling and storing food, since the area is often visited by grizzlies.

Moat Lake. The trail around the north end of Amethyst Lakes to Moat Lake is an obvious day trip from Maccarib and Amethyst Campgrounds. It is 3.5 km to the lake from its intersection with the Maccarib Pass trail at km 20.4, though the trail is not maintained past the Tonquin Valley Backcountry Lodge.

From Maccarib junction, the trail runs across rocky, open meadows before entering forest. A spur trail cuts left at km 1.3 and leads to the Tonquin Valley Backcountry Lodge at the north end of Amethyst Lakes—a very pretty viewpoint for the lakes and The Ramparts. (If you don't want to return to the main trail, you can continue toward Moat Lake on a trail running west from the lodge.)

From the lodge junction, the trail continues west into a vast, boulder-strewn meadow, and it is often vague over the final kilometre to the lake's east end. The perpendicular cliffs of The Ramparts, specifically Drawbridge and Bastion Peaks, rise above the lake's southern shoreline, while the lake stretches for more than a kilometre toward the twin passes of Moat and Tonquin on the Alberta-B.C. boundary. (A vague trail follows along the north side of the lake in that direction.)

100 Astoria River

Cavell Road to Clitheroe Campground—17.2 km (10.7 mi)
Cavell Road to Amethyst Campground—20.4 km (12.7 mi)

Backpack

Allow 6 to 7 hours

Elevation gain: 445 m (1,450 ft)
     loss: 130 m (420 ft)

Maximum elevation: 2105 m (6,900 ft)

Maps: Amethyst Lakes 83 D/9

Access: Follow the Icefields Parkway
(Hwy 93) south from Jasper 7 km (4.5 mi)
to Highway 93A. Continue south on 93A
for 5.5 km (3.5 mi) to the Cavell Road and
follow it 12.5 km (8 mi) to the Tonquin Valley
parking area. Follow trail downhill from sign
at parking area.

0.0— Trailhead (1740 m).
     N52°42.152' W118°03.598'

0.3— Cavell Lake outlet bridge (1720 m).

    — Descent through forest along north
      slope of Mt. Edith Cavell.

5.3— Astoria River bridge to north side
     (1660 m).

7.1— Astoria Campground.

8.5— Junction. Chrome Lake (6.5 km) and
     Eremite Valley left. Tonquin Valley
     ahead.

    — Steep switchbacks up lower slopes
      of Oldhorn Mtn.

13.2— Maximum elevation (2105 m).
      Open subalpine meadows.

13.6— Junction. Switchback Campground
      left 0.2 km.

17.1— Junction. Left to Clitheroe
      Campground (0.1 km), Surprise Point
      Campground (2.3 km), and Eremite
      Valley (see *Eremite Valley*). Tonquin-
      Amethyst Lake Lodge and Amethyst
      Lakes east shore ahead.

19.3— Tonquin-Amethyst Lake Lodge
      (1975 m).

20.4— Amethyst Campground. *Maccarib
      Pass* trail ahead.

Though the hike to Amethyst Lakes via
the Astoria River is not much shorter
than the Maccarib Pass trail, the elevation gain is markedly less. And if you are
bound for the Alpine Club of Canada
hut at Outpost Lake or the campgrounds
near the south end of Amethyst Lakes,
the Astoria trail is by far the quickest
option.

From the trailhead on the Cavell
Road, the trail descends to the Cavell
Lake outlet bridge and a great view of
Mount Edith Cavell. Beyond Cavell Lake,
it makes a long, gradual descent through
forest along Mount Edith Cavell's north
slope. At km 5.3, you reach the Astoria
River, cross to the north side, and begin
a steady ascent of the valley.

At km 8.5 the trail to Chrome Lake
branches left across the Astoria on a log
bridge (this bridge washed out late 2010,
so check with Visitor Information on its
status). The main trail continues along
the north side and soon begins a strenuous switchbacking climb alongside a
massive rockslide on the south slope of
Oldhorn Mountain. You reach the trail's
maximum elevation near the 13-km
mark, where the trail levels off across the
west slope of Oldhorn Mountain. At this
point you are greeted by the first views of
The Ramparts and Amethyst Lakes.

It was from the slopes of nearby
Mount Clitheroe that topographical
surveyor Morrison P. Bridgland first
photographed the valley in 1915 and
subsequently revealed its glories to the
world. The area drew a steady procession
of visitors over the ensuing years, including photographers and artists: Banff
photographer Byron Harmon shot the
first motion picture footage of the valley
from the slopes of Clitheroe in 1918;
Group of Seven artists Lawren Harris
and A.Y. Jackson painted in the valley in
1924; and in 1928 the famous American
landscape photographer Ansel Adams

Amethyst Lakes and The Ramparts

visited the valley with members of California's Sierra Club.

At km 17.1 the trail splits. The right branch descends to Tonquin-Amethyst Lake Lodge and Amethyst Campground, while the left runs downhill to the outlet for the southern lake beneath Surprise Point (Clitheroe Campground is 100 m below the junction).

Many backpackers who reach the Tonquin Valley via Astoria River stay at Clitheroe or Surprise Point Campgrounds. Both have fine views of The Ramparts and are good base camps for day trips into the Eremite Valley (see *Eremite Valley*). And remember, no campfires are permitted at any campsites on the Astoria River trail or in the Tonquin Valley region.

Chrome Lake via Astoria Valley. This old trail serves as a direct route from the Astoria River to Chrome Lake, Eremite Valley, and the Alpine Club's Wates-Gibson Hut at Outpost Lake. It also saves 2 km and a lot of climbing for those heading to the Surprise Point Campground. (Check on the status of the bridge at 8.5 km before taking this route.)

The trail branches from the Astoria River route at 8.5 km, crosses a bridge over the river, and follows up the south side of the valley, reaching Chrome Lake in 6.5 km. The trail is not well maintained and tends to be narrow, rough and, with the exception of a few meadows, forest-enclosed. (You wouldn't want to run into a grizzly bear here. Stay alert and make noise when visibility is limited.)

Once you reach Chrome Lake, stay on the trail leading around its north side for 0.3 km to an intersection with the *Eremite Valley* trail. This junction is 1.9 km south of Surprise Point Campground.

Maccarib Pass-Astoria River Circuit. If you are willing to arrange transportation between trailheads, you can complete a circuit by entering the Tonquin Valley on one of the access trails and exiting via the other. (Our preference is to approach the valley via Maccarib Pass and return on the Astoria River trail.) Total distance for the circuit is 43 km. (See *Maccarib Pass*.)

101 Eremite Valley

Clitheroe Campground Junction to Arrowhead Lake—8.9 km (5.5 mi)

Day trip

Allow 2 to 3 hours one way

Elevation loss: 320 m (1,050 ft)
gain: 200 m (650 ft)

Maximum elevation: 2130 m (6,980 ft)

Maps: Amethyst Lakes 83 D/9

Access: Trail begins at the Clitheroe Campground junction on the *Astoria River* trail (km 16.8). If starting from Surprise Point Campground or the Wates-Gibson Hut at Outpost Lake, subtract 2.3 km and 3.6 km respectively from the total distance to Arrowhead Lake.

0.0– Clitheroe Campground Jct (2130 m).
     N52°41.703' W118°14.373'

0.1– Clitheroe Campground.

   –Steady descent.

1.0– Amethyst Patrol Cabin.

1.8– Bridge across Amethyst Lakes outlet stream.

2.3– Surprise Point Campground.

   – Trail runs south, descending steadily on rough, rocky track.

4.2– Junction (1810 m). Left to Chrome Lake north shore (0.3 km) and Astoria River shortcut trail. Outpost Lake and Eremite Valley right.

4.7– Junction. Outpost Lake and Wates-Gibson Hut right 1.1 km. Eremite Valley stay left.

   – Trail runs through open meadows west of Chrome Lake.

7.0– Trail climbs onto rockslide. Track vague and intermittent.

8.9– Arrowhead Lake (2010 m).

While Amethyst Lakes and The Ramparts are the centrepiece of the Tonquin Valley region, the nearby Eremite Valley is another scenic highlight. Chrome Lake lies at the entrance to the valley, and the rugged, glaciated mountains surrounding tiny Arrowhead Lake at the headwaters are every bit as spectacular as the better-known Ramparts. It is little wonder that these peaks have attracted alpinists ever since the first Alpine Club camps were held in the Tonquin Valley in 1926 and at Chrome Lake in 1934.

The trail into the valley from the south end of Amethyst Lakes is the most popular and worthwhile day trip from campgrounds and lodges in the Tonquin Valley. While the distance is not far, particularly from Clitheroe and Surprise Point Campgrounds, you will want to reserve a full day for the outing so you can explore the upper end of the Eremite Valley. Less energetic hikers can complete a shorter trip by only going as far as Chrome and Outpost Lakes.

Our description of the trail begins at the 16.8-km junction on the Astoria River trail, just 100 m from Clitheroe Campground. From the junction the trail descends past the campground and onwards to the south end of Amethyst Lakes, crossing the lakes' outlet to Surprise Point Campground.

The trail continues south from the Tonquin Valley as a rough, rocky track to a large meadow containing Penstock Creek. At the meadow's first junction, you can take a 300-m side trail left through forest to the best shoreline viewpoint for Chrome Lake—a small but beautiful turquoise lake reflecting the mountains surrounding the head of the Eremite Valley. (This trail continues to a bridge over Chrome Lake's outlet and down-valley to connect with the *Astoria River* trail at km 8.5.)

The main trail continues right 0.5 km to another junction just a short distance

Chrome Lake

above Penstock Creek. The right-hand branch follows Penstock Creek upstream to Outpost Lake, while the main valley trail stays left, attaches itself to Eremite Creek and follows it south for another 4 km to its headwaters. Beyond the 7-km mark, the track is rough and vague, but the route is obvious and the destination well worth the effort.

The head of the Eremite Valley is a spectacular alpine region where glaciers crown most every peak. The most dramatic of these are Mount Erebus and Eremite Mountain, rising above Eremite Glacier to the west. The valley surrounding Arrowhead Lake is filled with rockslides and glacial moraines and offers unlimited opportunities for scrambling and exploration.

Outpost Lake—1.1 km. From the junction at km 4.7, just west of Chrome Lake, the Outpost Lake trail follows Penstock Creek upstream. It crosses to the south side of the creek at the foot of a steep forested slope and then climbs to the shores of tiny Outpost Lake. While the lake is ringed by forest, the sharp prow of Outpost Peak provides a fine backdrop.

The Wates-Gibson Hut, operated by the Alpine Club of Canada, is on the lake's north shore. This substantial log structure was constructed in 1963. It accommodates 30 people and provides a good base for anyone who wants to spend more time in the Eremite Valley region. For information and rates, contact the Alpine Club of Canada (see *Sources—Huts*).

Chrome Lake–Outpost Lake via Astoria Valley. The entrance to the Eremite Valley can be reached directly without the need of detouring through the Tonquin Valley. At km 8.5 on the Astoria River trail, the short-cut trail branches left and crosses a bridge to the south side of the river (check on the status of this bridge). It continues along that side of the valley, ascending to Chrome Lake and the junction with the Eremite Valley trail in another 7.6 km. This route is of most interest to those staying at the Alpine Club's hut on Outpost Lake. (See also *Astoria River*.)

102 Athabasca Pass

Moab Lake Parking Area to Athabasca Pass—49.1 (30.5 mi)

Backpack

Allow 2 to 3 days to Athabasca Pass

Elevation gain: 545 m (1,780 ft)

Maximum elevation: 1755 m (5,750 ft)

Maps: Athabasca Falls 83 C/12
Amethyst Lakes 83 D/9
Athabasca Pass 83 D/8

Access: From the junction of the Icefields Parkway and Highway 93A at Athabasca Falls, follow the 93A north 9 km (5.5 mi) to the Moab Lake Road junction. Continue on the Moab Lake Road 7 km (4.5 mi) to the access gate and parking area.

0.0— Trailhead (1210 m).
N52°40.166' W117°57.269'

—Route follows restored fire road.

0.3— Junction. Moab Lake right 200 m.

6.6— Whirlpool Campground.

8.6— End of roadbed.

—Single-track trail continues along west side of Whirlpool River.

11.2— Tie Camp Campground.

15.0— Simon Creek Campground.

19.8— Middle Whirlpool River crossing.

20.3— Middle Forks Patrol Cabin.

21.1— Middle Forks Campground.

25.8— Scott Gravel Flats north end.

30.9— Scott Camp Campground.

38.8— Whirlpool River bridge to east side.

40.9— Kane Creek ford (difficult thigh-deep).

41.0— Kane Meadows Campground (1585 m).

—Trail crosses Kane Meadows then bends south-southwest to the pass.

48.5— Athabasca Pass Campground (0.4 km left).

49.1— Athabasca Pass (1755 m). Historical marker and park boundary near north shore of Committee Punch Bowl.

During the winter of 1811, fur trader David Thompson made the first recorded crossing of Athabasca Pass. For the next 40 years, the pass was the main trade route across the Canadian Rockies.

Today the long trail up the Whirlpool River to the pass is about as lonely as it was during the first half of the 19th century. It is a great place to commune with the spirits of fur traders and imagine their awe as they first wandered through this corridor of ice-clad peaks.

The first 8.6 km follows an old fire road along the west side of the Whirlpool Valley. After the roadbed reverts to trail, you pass Tie Camp Campground and, a short distance further along, encounter the remains of the Otto brothers' Tie Camp, where timber was cut and floated down the Whirlpool and Athabasca Rivers to be used for railway ties during the early part of the 20th century. (Please respect the historic artifacts at this site and leave them for others to enjoy.)

Near the 20-km mark, you cross the Middle Whirlpool River and then pass the Middle Forks Patrol Cabin. After a long stretch of forest hiking, you emerge onto the northern end of the extensive Scott Gravel Flats. Follow a hiker's trail that splits right from the horse trail—a detour that avoids fords of the ever-meandering channels of the Whirlpool.

Travel continues over and along the Scott Gravel Flats for 5 km to Scott Camp Campground, which is at the southern end of the flats. This is one of the most scenic campsites on the Athabasca Pass trail, providing a dramatic view south up the Scott Creek valley to the tumbled icefalls of Scott Glacier—a tongue of the Hooker Icefield. To this point the trail is fairly straightforward as it swings back and forth from gravel flats to forest.

Below Kane Meadows, a footbridge crosses to the east side of the Whirlpool. Another 2 km brings you to the lower end of Kane Meadows at Kane Creek.

© Don Beers

Scott Glacier and Mount Hooker from Scott Gravel Flats

Follow cairns upstream to the best fording location. The silty creek is fed by the Kane Glacier and is the most difficult stream crossing on the trail. Kane Meadows Campground lies on the opposite side.

After fording a tributary stream a kilometre beyond Kane Meadows Campground, you complete the ascent to the pass on a defined track that swings back and forth between forest and meadow (often wet and muddy).

At the pass there is a historic marker commemorating this important fur trade route, and a small pond called the Committee Punch Bowl. Here, on the crest of the continent, fur traders would stop and drink a toast to the officers of the Hudson's Bay Company.

The pass is contained by McGillivray Ridge to the east and glaciated Mount Brown to west. The latter peak was supposedly climbed by botanist David Douglas in May 1827. Douglas estimated the elevation of the mountain and nearby Mount Hooker to be 15,000 feet high, a figure which was later published on maps of the region. Many decades later mountaineers searched in vain for these two giants, not realizing that Douglas had been grossly misled concerning the base elevation of the Rockies.

103 Geraldine Lakes

Geraldine Lakes Fire Road to Second Geraldine Lake—5.0 km (3.1 mi)

Half-day trip or backpack

Allow 2 hours one way

Elevation gain: 410 m (1,340 ft)

Maximum elevation: 1890 m (6,200 ft)

Maps: Athabasca Falls 83 C/12

Access: From the junction of the Icefields Parkway and Highway 93A at Athabasca Falls (31 km south of the town of Jasper), follow the 93A north 1.1 km (0.7 mi) to the Geraldine Lakes Fire Road. Follow this gravel road 5.5 km (3.5 mi) to an access gate. The parking area and trailhead lie 50 m below the gate at the last bend in the road.

0.0— Trailhead (1480 m).
      N52°37.706' W117°54.868'

   — Moderate climb.

1.8— Lower Geraldine Lake.

   — Trail skirts west shore of the lake.

2.7— Southern end of Lower Geraldine Lake.

   — Steep 90 m climb. At the top, follow markers left to east side of valley.

4.2— Waterfall.

   — Very steep 150 m climb.

5.0— Viewpoint overlooking Second Geraldine Lake.

   — Trail contours above east shore of lake.

6.2— Second Geraldine Campground (1890 m).

Sandwiched between the steep slopes of Mount Fryatt and Whirlpool Peak, the Geraldine Lakes offer hiking options ranging from a one hour walk to a full day or more of scrambling and exploration. The first lake lies 1.8 km from the trailhead via easy trail; the trail to the second lake is boulder-strewn with steep pitches; the third and fourth lakes, and the high pass at the head of the valley, are for well-shod, off-trail explorers.

The short hike to Lower Geraldine Lake follows a moderately graded, well-travelled, root-laced trail. While the serene, forest-encircled lake beneath the flanks of Mount Fryatt is pleasant enough, it only whets the appetite for what lies beyond. And what lies beyond is not for casual walkers.

The trail gets rougher as it follows the lake's west shore. Beyond the lake the track becomes very rocky and rooty as it climbs steeply beside a 90-m waterfall cascading over rock steps.

At the top of the falls you enter a short valley. Here the trail angles left (watch for markers), crosses Geraldine Creek (beneath the rocks), and skirts a small pond in the midst of a large boulderfield. At the end of this rock-choked valley there is yet another steep, rough scramble beside a very impressive waterfall.

From a rocky crest above the falls there are good views back down-valley and your first glimpse ahead to Second Geraldine Lake—the largest in the chain. From this vantage point you can appreciate the staircase nature of the Geraldine Valley and how the higher lakes feed into the lower. The lakes and their basins were created as a glacier receded up the valley, creating a geological feature called paternoster lakes (resembling the chain of beads in a rosary).

Although this crest viewpoint will be a good turn-around for many hikers, rough trail continues along the rocky east shore of the second lake to its inlet

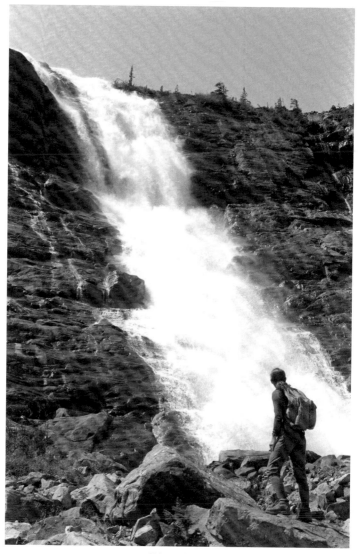

Waterfall below Second Geraldine Lake

and the Geraldine Lake Campground (no campfires). This site is a good base for further exploration up-valley.

While no formal trail exists beyond the south end of Second Geraldine Lake, experienced scramblers can follow trail snippets, cairns, and their noses for another 4 km up the valley staircase to higher lakes set beneath the 1000-m northwest wall of Mount Fryatt. You can also scramble to a 2220-m pass at the head of the valley that overlooks two unnamed lakes and the Divergence Creek valley.

Much of the travel in this valley is over broken rock, which can make for hazardous walking when wet or following a snowstorm.

104 Fryatt Valley

Geraldine Lakes Fire Road to Upper Fryatt Valley—23.2 km (14.4 mi)

Backpack
Allow 7 hours one way
Elevation gain: 820 m (2,700 ft)
Maximum elevation: 2040 m (6,700 ft)
Maps: Athabasca Falls 83 C/12†
Fortress Lake 83 C/5†
† last 3.7 km not shown

Access: From the Icefields Parkway–Highway 93A junction at Athabasca Falls 31 km (19 mi) south of the town of Jasper, follow the 93A north 1.1 km (0.7 mi) to the Geraldine Lakes Fire Road. Follow this gravel road 2.1 km (1.3 mi) to the small parking area and trail sign on the left side of the road.

0.0— Trailhead (1220 m).
N52°38.925' W117°53.988'
—Route follows old roadbed.

1.9— Bridges across Geraldine Creek channels.

7.2— Trail comes abreast of Athabasca River.
— Trail climbs away from river.

11.6— Lower Fryatt Campground (1280 m). End of bike access. Fryatt Creek bridge to east bank.
— Trail climbs east side of Fryatt Valley.

15.9— Fryatt Creek bridge to west bank.

17.7— Brussels Campground.
— Trail climbs over alluvial fan.

18.7— Fryatt Lake (1715 m).
— Trail follows along west shore of lake.

19.5— Southwest end of Fryatt Lake.
— Trail winds and climbs through forest.

21.1— Headwall Campground (1780 m).
— Steep scramble up Headwall.

21.9— Top of Headwall.

22.0— Sydney Vallance (Fryatt) Hut (2000 m).
— Trail runs through meadows and over forested moraine.

23.2— Unnamed lake (2040 m).

The Fryatt Valley trail is a rather long, tedious grunt, and the final climb up the Headwall to the upper valley is steep and rough. But this tiny hanging valley tucked into one of Jasper's great mountain ranges is a jewel that rewards all your efforts.

Mountain bikes are permitted on the first 11.6 km of the trail, which makes a day trip to Upper Fryatt Valley somewhat feasible. However, we suggest you leave the bikes at home and complete the hike over three days: one day to hike in and set a base camp, one day for exploring the upper valley, and one day to hike out.

The first 7 km from the Geraldine Lakes Fire Road trailhead is flat and enclosed by forest. The trail finally comes abreast of the Athabasca River near the site of an old cable car crossing, where you will have the dubious pleasure of seeing the Icefields Parkway 200 m away on the opposite side of the river (experienced canoeists do make this crossing on occasion). From this point the trail veers south and begins its climb to the mouth of the Fryatt Valley.

Fryatt Creek is crossed at Lower Fryatt Campground (end of bike access), where you enter the valley proper—a narrow gorge between the towering peaks of Mounts Fryatt and Christie. The climb along the east side of the valley is steady for the next 4 km, mostly through heavy forest. At km 15.9 the track crosses to the west side of the creek and continues along open gravel flats, where the first views open out to the sharp, glaciated peaks at the head of the valley.

You climb over a major alluvial fan at km 17.7, but the summit of the rocky fan provides a fine view of Fryatt Lake. After descending to the lake, the trail becomes rocky and rooty along the northwest shore.

Beyond the lake you climb through forest to the foot of the Headwall. Here,

Fryatt Lake and the Headwall Falls below Upper Fryatt Valley

at the base of the impressive Headwall Falls, the last act in the Fryatt Valley drama unfolds—an extremely steep scramble that gains 200 m of elevation over the next 0.8 km.

The top of the Headwall will silence your curses. Suddenly the upper valley opens into view—ice-clad peaks and subalpine meadowland. Back to the north the lower valley stretches out beneath you and the peaks of the Maligne Range rise beyond the broad Athabasca Valley. A small waterfall dropping into a large pool ("Roman Bath") near the top of the Headwall makes a fine place to rest on a warm day, and the Sydney Vallance (Fryatt) Hut lies less than 100 m farther along.

The hike to the lake at the head of the upper valley is short and scenic. The trail, which is wet and not always well defined, crosses wildflower meadows, and climbs a rocky, sparsely forested moraine where the creek plunges briefly into an underground passage.

The route finally descends through stands of stunted alpine fir to the shore of a small lake fed by the meltwaters of the nearby Belanger Glacier. From the lakeshore you have an unobstructed view of a crowd of rugged peaks and glaciers enclosing the head of this fine hanging valley.

From this point you can explore beyond the trail, particularly onto the slopes to the north. (Experienced scramblers can ascend to the high col between Mounts Fryatt and Belanger.)

Camping is not permitted in the Upper Fryatt Valley, but the Sydney Vallance (Fryatt) Hut is operated by the Alpine Club of Canada and accommodates 12 (see *Sources—Huts*).

However, most backpackers prefer to camp at Headwall or Brussels Campgrounds and commute to the upper valley without the burden of a full pack.

105 Fortress Lake

Sunwapta Falls to Fortress Lake—24.0 km (15.0 mi)*

Backpack

Allow 7 to 9 hours one way

Elevation loss: 60 m (200 ft)

Maximum elevation: 1400 m (4,600 ft)

Maps: Athabasca Falls 83 C/12
Fortress Lake 83 C/5

Access: Follow the Icefields Parkway
(Hwy 93) to the Sunwapta Falls junction,
54.5 km (34 mi) south of the town of Jasper
and 49 km (30.5 mi) north of the Icefield
Centre. The Sunwapta Falls Road leads
0.6 km to the falls parking area. The
trail begins on the opposite side of the
viewpoint bridge spanning Sunwapta Falls
Canyon.

0.0— Trailhead (1400 m).
N52°31.911' W117°38.674'

— Gradual descent to Athabasca River.

7.8— Big Bend Campground (right 200 m).

— Flat to rolling along the east side of
Athabasca River.

12.2— Junction. Long Lake and Chaba Patrol
Cabin right. Stay left.

14.6— Athabasca Crossing Campground.

15.2— Athabasca River bridge.

— Trail runs south above Chaba River.

21.4— Chaba River ford (calf to thigh deep)
to west side.

— Trail along west side of river flats.

23.4— Fortress Pass (1340 m).

23.8— Junction. Fortress Lake and East End
Campground left 0.2 km. Rough trail
continues right along north lakeshore
for approximately 3 km.

*All distances approximate.

(Trail not shown on maps in this book.)

Fortress Lake is one of the largest lakes along the Great Divide. Though it lies in B.C.'s Hamber Provincial Park, the only trail to the lake is from Jasper Park. Because it is such a major feature, and surrounded by spectacular mountains, you would expect it to be a popular destination. However, a ford of the Chaba River discourages all but the most dedicated.

The installation of a bridge across the Athabasca River in 1985 eliminated one of the most harrowing fords in the Rockies. However, the Chaba channels are difficult during high water, usually late June through mid-August (the trip is best hiked in late summer).

The trail rolls due south Sunwapta Falls through heavy forest on the east side of the Athabasca River. The first 15 km follows old fire road, which can be traversed by mountain bike.

At km 15.2, the roadbed ends and single-track trail crosses the Athabasca River suspension bridge just upstream from its confluence with the Chaba River. From the bridge, continue south along a plateau above the east side of the Chaba for approximately 6 km. The trail eventually descends to the river and crosses to the west side (multi-channels, usually thigh-deep). The track continues south along the broad, alluvial gravel flats on the west side of the Chaba for approximately 2 km to the Alberta-B.C. boundary.

You reach the boundary at Fortress Pass and another 0.6 km brings you to East End Campground, appropriately located at the east end of Fortress Lake. Trail continues along the north shore for approximately 3 km to two other campgrounds, but East End offers the best views.

There is also a commercial fishing camp at the mouth of Chisel Creek on the lake's south shore, but this facility is used primarily by fly-in fishermen and is not trail-accessible.

106 Lower Sunwapta Falls

Sunwapta Falls Parking Area to Lower Sunwapta Falls—1.3 km (0.8 mi)

While thousands of tourists stop along the Icefields Parkway to view Sunwapta Falls each summer, only a few make the trip to a series of cataracts 1.3 km beyond the main falls.

Lower Sunwapta Falls is composed of three major waterfalls spread over approximately 150 m of the Sunwapta River. In our opinion, the combination of solitude and open views to the surrounding mountains make this hike as rewarding an experience as the upper falls.

From the Sunwapta Falls parking area, follow the main viewing trail above the falls to the right. Continue past the falls viewpoint to where the paved trail ends and begin a gradual descent through lodgepole pine forest to the lower falls.

At km 0.6 the trail emerges from the forest to open views across the Sunwapta River to the upper Athabasca Valley and the glaciated summit of Mount Quincy.

Lower Sunwapta Falls have formed where the river is cutting through a narrow canyon similar to the one containing the upper falls, but a staircase waterfall has formed instead of a single cataract.

Access: Follow the Icefields Parkway (Hwy 93) to the Sunwapta Falls junction, 54.5 km (34 mi) south of the town of Jasper and 49 km (30.5 mi) north of the Icefield Centre. The Sunwapta Falls Road leads 0.6 km to the falls parking area. N52°31.895' W117°38.735' *Maps: Athabasca Falls 83 C/12 (trail not shown).*
(Trail not shown on maps in this book.)

107 Beauty Creek

Icefields Parkway to Stanley Falls—1.6 km (1.0 mi)

Before the old Banff-Jasper Highway was rerouted across the Sunwapta River flats, one of the popular roadside stops was Beauty Creek canyon, where a trail climbed past a series of cataracts to Stanley Falls. This trail is a bit removed from the present highway, and few visitors even know that there is something special up this unremarkable, forested gorge.

From the small roadside parking area, follow trail along the crest of a gravel, water diversion dike into an arm of forest. On the opposite side of this narrow band of trees, you emerge onto the old Banff-Jasper Highway. Turn right and follow the roadbed 0.6 km to where a bridge once spanned Beauty Creek.

The trail branches left from the road and follows along the north side of a

narrow limestone canyon, climbing steadily through dense forest and passing a number of small waterfalls. The last and highest of these cataracts, Stanley Falls, is reached at 1.6 km. Beyond this fine waterfall the trail fades and the canyon opens out into a forested valley.

Access: Follow the Icefields Parkway north from the Icefield Centre 15.5 km (9.5 mi). Two km south of the Beauty Creek Hostel, while crossing broad alluvial flats beside the Sunwapta River, watch for a small pull-out on the east side of the highway at the end of gravel water diversion dike. N52°19.675' W117°19.797' *Maps: Sunwapta Peak 83 C/6.*

Maligne Mtn

Southesk Lake

Southesk River

124

N

Mt Paul

Maligne Lake

112
Mt Mary Vaux

Mt Warren

Mt Brazeau

Maligne Lake

Mt Henry MacLeod

Sawtooth Mtn

Replica Pk

Coronet Mtn

110

Jasper

Maligne Pass

Sunwapta Station

Poboktan

Le Grand Brazeau

Poboktan Mtn

Chocolate Mtn

Mt Aztec

Brazeau Lake

South Boundary

122

Waterfall Peaks

112 111

Creek

Sunwapta

Jonas

Creek

Poboktan Pass

Jonas Shoulder

John-John Creek

109

Gong Pk

River

Sunwapta Pk

Marble Mtn

109

Jonas Pass

109

107

Beauty

112

Afternoon Pk

Diadem Pk

Mt Woodley

Creek

Tangle Ridge

112 109

Mt Alberta

Stutfield Pk

Wilcox Pass

108

93

Nigel Pass

North Twin

Icefield Centre

Sunwapta Pass

65

South Twin

Mt Kitchener

COLUMBIA ICEFIELD

Snow Dome

Mt Athabasca

Lake Louise

Land above 2300 metres

0   5   10   15km

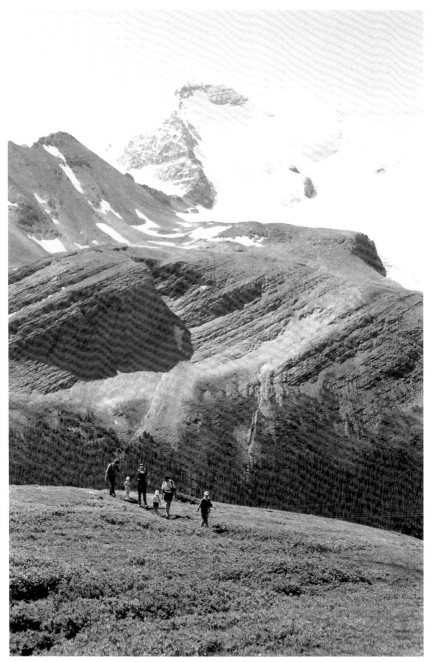

Mount Athabasca from the Wilcox Pass trail

108 Wilcox Pass

Wilcox Creek Campground to Wilcox Pass—4.0 km (2.5 mi)
Wilcox Creek Campground to Tangle Falls—11.2 km (7.0 mi)

Half-day to day trip

Allow 1.5 hours to Wilcox Pass

Elevation gain: 335 m (1,100 ft)

Maximum elevation: 2375 m (7,800 ft)

Maps: Columbia Icefield 83 C/3
Sunwapta Peak 83 C/6

Access: Follow the Icefields Parkway (Hwy 93) to the Wilcox Creek Campground, on the east side of the highway 2.8 km (1.7 mi) south of the Icefield Centre or 1.9 km (1.2 mi) north of the Banff-Jasper boundary at Sunwapta Pass. The trailhead parking area is on the left side of the campground access road, 50 m from the highway.

0.0—Trailhead (2040 m).
N52°13.098' W117°11.104'

— Steep climb through subalpine forest.

1.8—Trail emerges above treeline.

— Grade moderates.

2.5—Athabasca Glacier viewpoint.

— Short, steep climb to flat alpine meadows.

4.0—Wilcox Pass Summit (2375 m).

— Route continues north across pass. Track often vague.

7.2—North edge of pass (watch for markers or cairns).

— Steep descent into forest.

8.8—Trail crosses to left of creek. Track becomes more defined.

— Moderate to steep descent on slope south of Tangle Creek.

11.2—Tangle Creek trailhead (1860 m). Icefields Parkway 200 m south of Tangle Falls and 10 km north of Wilcox Creek trailhead.

Wilcox Pass is a high alpine valley due east of the Icefield Centre and Athabasca Glacier. Beginning close to treeline, the trail quickly rises to extensive meadows and views of the Athabasca Glacier and its surrounding peaks, which are some of the highest and most dramatic in the Canadian Rockies. It is quite justifiably recognized as one of the finest day hikes in Jasper Park.

From the entrance to Wilcox Creek Campground, Canada's highest roadside campground, the trail climbs directly through a mature subalpine forest. This initial stretch is steep, gaining 120 m in less than a kilometre.

The grade moderates as you break out of the trees and emerge onto an open ridge overlooking the Icefields Parkway and the Athabasca Glacier. The Rockies' most famous valley glacier is the centrepiece of an exceptional panorama, which includes such ice-covered giants as Mount Athabasca (3491 m), Snow Dome (3460 m), and Mount Kitchener (3511 m).

Beyond the viewpoint, the trail climbs steeply along the edge of a gully containing a small stream. After this short, stiff ascent, it levels out across alpine tundra and heads northwest into the long U-shaped pass between Wilcox and Nigel Peaks. Here the lush, tall wildflowers of treeline are replaced by ground-hugging alpine plants, like forget-me-not, white mountain avens, and moss campion.

As soon as you reach the summit meadows, scan the nearby slopes and ridges for bighorn sheep. Mature rams hang together here each summer, leaving flocks of ewes, lambs and immature males to feed in the valley below. Wilcox Pass is one of the most reliable places to see bighorns at close range in a backcountry setting.

The official summit is reached at 4.0 km, though the pass is so long and flat

Wilcox Pass

it is difficult to recognize it as the highest point. (A large rock cairn beside the trail marks the spot.) Though you have left the best views of the Icefield region behind, the heavily-glaciated north face of Mount Athabasca is still visible back across the meadows to the south.

Wilcox Peak and Pass are named for American mountaineer Walter Wilcox, whose horseback party first crossed the pass in 1896. The pass became the standard route north following Wilcox's trip since it avoided the rugged Sunwapta Gorge and the Athabasca Glacier, which nearly blocked the valley below.

The rising meadows and ridges to the west and east of the summit are an open invitation to wander. However, any off-trail travel should be undertaken with care and sensitivity for the environment. Avoid crossing wet, marshy areas, and always walk abreast of one another rather than single-file, since this lessens damage to fragile alpine vegetation.

One of our favourite off-trail side-trips is the climb to the crest of the ridge just south of Wilcox Peak—an amazing aerial viewpoint overlooking the Athabasca Glacier. From this lofty ridgetop, you can contemplate the ant-sized people scurrying around Ice Explorer buses on the glacier and at the Icefield Centre far below.

Another favourite excursion climbs around the end of Nigel Peak's northwest ridge to 2470-m Wilcox Lake—lying in a rockbound cirque beneath the mountain's west face. Use a topo map to locate the lake, then climb to the obvious sheep trails on the high talus slopes northeast of Wilcox Pass and follow the most-defined track in a northerly direction around the end of the ridge. Continue over rock ridges until you reach a point immediately above the lake's northwest shore.

Tangle Creek. You can continue northwest through the pass and descend Tangle Creek back to the Icefields Parkway, 7 km beyond Wilcox Pass summit. Though the trail often disappears on the tundra and rocky terrain near the northern end of the pass, a marker indicates where the descent to the Tangle Creek valley begins. As you drop into the forest a defined trail gradually takes shape. The trail emerges onto the highway at Tangle Falls, 10 km north of the Wilcox Creek Campground trailhead.

–Brazeau Lake Loop

Pass—23.8 km (14.8 mi)
oop—81.4 km (50.6 mi)

)0 ft)
) ft)

....d 83 C/3

Sunwapta Peak 83 C/6

Access: Follow the Icefields Parkway to the Nigel Creek parking area, on the northeast side of the highway 8.5 km (5.5 mi) south of the Banff-Jasper Park boundary at Sunwapta Pass. The parking area and trail kiosk are at a barrier gate just below the highway. Follow gravel roadbed downhill from gate for 150 m to a trail sign on the right.

0.0— Trailhead (1860 m).
N52°11.250' W117°04.227'

7.2— Nigel Pass (2195).

7.6— Brazeau River south fork ford.

10.6— Brazeau River bridge to west side.

10.7— Boulder Creek Campground.

11.4— Boulder Creek bridge.

13.8— Four Point Campground.

14.0— Junction (1915 m). *South Boundary Trail* and Brazeau Lake ahead. Jonas Pass left.

18.4— Trail emerges above treeline.

23.8— Jonas Pass Summit (2320 m).

29.6— Jonas Shoulder Summit (2470 m).

32.7— Jonas Cutoff Campground (no campfires).

32.9— Junction (1810 m). Poboktan Creek bridge. Intersection with *Poboktan Creek* trail at km 21.3. Poboktan Pass right.

35.9— Poboktan Pass (2300 m).

40.2— John-John Creek Campground.

44.4— John-John Creek bridge.

48.1— Northwest Brazeau River bridge.

48.2— Junction (1810 m). Brazeau Lake and Brazeau Lake Campground left 0.9 km. Brazeau River trail right.

The Jonas Pass-Brazeau Lake Loop is one of Jasper's most popular backpacking trips. Little wonder. The circuit includes one of the park's largest backcountry lakes and an extraordinary 13 km alpine traverse culminating on the park's second highest trail-accessible summit. Along the way there are glaciated peaks, lush wildflower meadows, and opportunities to view a wide variety of alpine wildlife ranging from hoary marmots to caribou. It is "the grand tour" of Jasper's southern ranges.

Most backpackers take four or five days to complete the loop. However, if you only go as far as Jonas Pass, you can visit the circuit's scenic highlight and return in three days—an option which allows you to explore the pass environs with a light day pack instead of a full backpack.

Be aware that sections of the Jonas Pass trail are occasionally covered with snow into late July, particularly on the leeward side of Jonas Shoulder. Check on trail conditions at a park visitor centre before embarking on this trip.

Nigel Pass trailhead to Four Point Junction—14.0 km. The hike begins in Banff National Park and follows the 7.2-km Nigel Pass trail to the Jasper Park boundary (see *Nigel Pass*, Banff Park chapter). While Nigel Pass provides a quick scenic reward, the descent along the upper Brazeau River is very attractive as well. After hopping across the river's headwaters 400 m beyond the park boundary, you make a steep descent through rockslides to the first of several lush meadows—marshy, cottongrass flats fed by a large waterfall.

After crossing to the west side of the Brazeau at the lower end of the meadow, you pass Boulder Creek Campground and descend through 3 km of subalpine forest to another plateau with an

Jonas Pass

50.2— Junction (1720 m). Intersection with *South Boundary Trail* at km 136.3. Nigel Pass to right across Northwest Brazeau River bridge.

50.3— Brazeau River Campground.

53.5— Brazeau River bridge to east side.

58.8— Wolverine South Campground.

61.1— Brazeau River bridge to west side.

64.8— Four Point Creek Crossing.

65.6— Junction (1915 m). Close Jonas Pass-Brazeau Loop. Jonas Pass right. Nigel Pass ahead.

65.8— Four Point Campground.

68.9— Boulder Creek Campground.

72.4— Nigel Pass (2195 m).

79.6— Nigel Pass trailhead (1860 m).

Notice: Due to possible conflicts with caribou, dogs are not permitted on the Jonas Pass and Poboktan Pass trails above the Brazeau River trail and Brazeau Lake Campground.

extensive meadow. At km 13.8 you reach Four Point Campground and, 200 m beyond, the trail split for the Jonas Pass-Brazeau Lake Loop.

Since Four Point Campground is a favourite first-night destination, and the base camp for those who are day hiking to Jonas Pass, it is usually the busiest campground on the circuit.

At Four Point you can continue down the Brazeau Valley and hike the loop counterclockwise, or strike off for Jonas Pass and complete the circuit in a clockwise direction. Most people register to hike the loop clockwise as described here.

Four Point Junction to Jonas Cutoff Junction—18.9 km. Regardless of whether you are day hiking from Four Point Campground to Jonas Pass or backpacking over the pass, you have a long day ahead.

The journey starts with a vigorous climb along the west side of the Four Point Valley, rising 200 m in less than 2 km to open forest. A series of small streams descending from the left herald the approach of treeline, and within a few minutes the trail levels off and leaves the last stunted alpine fir behind. (We know a number of hikers who have encountered grizzly bears here. Stay alert!)

The trail continues its gradual ascent up the southwest side of the long, narrow vale, staying just above the creek. Jonas Pass is as long as it is beautiful, and you are nearly 10 km from Four Point Junction before you reach its crest.

You maintain elevation for the next 1.5 km, bypassing a small tarn, then descending gradually to the north. After passing beneath a large rockslide the trail swings right and begins to climb towards Jonas Shoulder. The first portion of the climb is steep and the trail is sketchy in places, but the track becomes more obvious as you gain elevation.

The scenery on the Jonas Shoulder climb is spectacular, and frequent stops with map and camera are rewarding. Hoary marmots and pikas inhabit nearby rockslides, and we have seen caribou on the meadows below the trail.

From the 2470-m summit of Jonas Shoulder views open out over the Poboktan Pass meadows and the forested Poboktan Valley stretching away to the northwest. Beyond the summit, the trail plunges northward to the upper Poboktan, descending a steep talus slope and spongy meadows, then angling to the east side of a major gully. Less than a kilometre after reaching treeline, you reach Jonas Cutoff Campground and, 200 m further along, the junction with the *Poboktan Creek* trail.

Jonas Cutoff Junction to Brazeau Lake—16.2 km. Poboktan Pass and Brazeau Lake are the two major features on the third leg of the trip.

From the junction with the Poboktan Creek trail 200 m below Jonas Cutoff Campground, you climb southeast from the timbered Poboktan Valley onto the broad alpine meadows of Poboktan Pass in just 3 km.

The pass and valley were named by A.P. Coleman in 1892, Poboktan being the Stoney name for the owls the party saw in the valley. The pass is sometimes visited by caribou, and grizzly bear are

occasionally seen in the distance across the open tundra.

From the pass the trail drops sharply onto John-John Creek—a narrow valley composed of rockslides and open gravel flats. At the mouth of the valley you emerge onto a large slide overlooking Brazeau Lake. (Park warden Charlie Matheson was stunned to discover the trail and phone line to his Brazeau Lake cabin buried beneath this massive slide shortly after it slumped into the valley in July 1933.) From this viewpoint it is just over 2 km to Brazeau Lake junction and the side trail leading to Brazeau Lake Campground at the southeast end of the lake.

Surrounded by forest, and with the ice-covered summits of Le Grande Brazeau Range rising beyond, this peaceful 5-km-long body of water is one of the largest wilderness lakes in Jasper Park.

Brazeau Lake to Four Point Junction—18.3 km. After visiting or camping at Brazeau Lake, follow the 2-km trail down the Northwest Brazeau River to an intersection with the *South Boundary Trail* in the Brazeau Valley. Here you turn for home, following the Brazeau River back to Four Point Junction and Nigel Pass.

While the ascent of the Brazeau may look a bit humdrum on the map, the valley is quite pleasant and open. Wolverine South Campground, nestled in a grove of trees on the river's east bank, is one of our favourite sites—a place where you can truly appreciate the solitude of a fine wilderness valley. (See also *South Boundary Trail*.)

Four Point Junction to Nigel Pass trailhead—14.0 km. From Four Point Junction, complete your journey back to civilization on the approach trail over Nigel Pass.

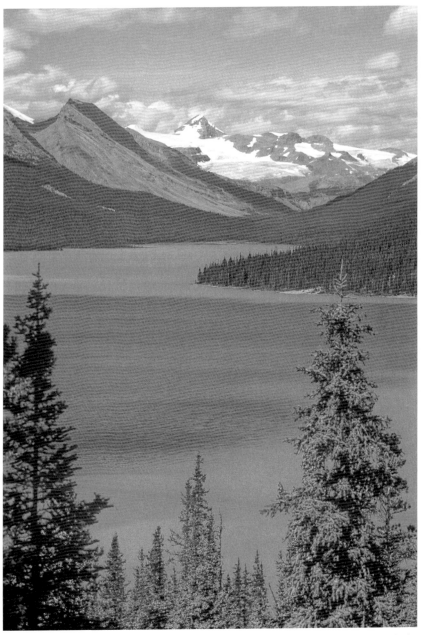

Brazeau Lake

110 Maligne Pass

Icefields Parkway to Maligne Pass—14.7 km (9.1 mi)*

Day trip or backpack

Allow 1 to 3 days

Elevation gain: 760 m (2,500 ft)

Maximum elevation: 2300 m (7,550 ft)

Maps: Sunwapta Peak 83 C/6

Access: Follow the Icefields Parkway (Hwy 93) to Parks Canada's Sunwapta Station, 31.5 km (19.5 mi) north of the Icefield Centre or 71.5 km (44.5 mi) south of the town of Jasper. Continue on the highway 100 m south of the station (south side of Poboktan Creek) to an access road branching east into a parking area. The trailhead is at the rear of Sunwapta Station, so walk back across Poboktan Creek on the highway and through the station grounds to the trail sign.

- 0.0— Trailhead (1540 m).
  N52°27.030' W117°26.534
- 6.2— Junction (1760 m). *Poboktan Creek* ahead. Maligne Pass left.
  - — Trail climbs along Poligne Creek (several crossings).
- 11.2— Avalanche Campground.
  - — Trail emerges into alpine meadows, often boggy and indistinct.
- 14.7— Maligne Pass (2300 m).

*Distances beyond 6.2 km approximate.

Notice: Due to possible conflicts with caribou, dogs are not permitted on the Maligne Pass trail.

Maligne Pass is an outstanding alpine summit, comprised of rolling alpine meadows and numerous small lakes. It is historically significant as the pass Mary Schäffer and her party used in 1908 when they discovered Maligne Lake.

A surprising number of hikers travel to the pass and back in a day, albeit a very long one. Our preference is to camp at Avalanche Campground, but you'll need to book early as only one group can camp here at a time (reducing pressure on prime grizzly habitat). And you may also discover that, like many of the higher passes in the Rockies, Maligne is buried under snow until mid-July.

From the parking area on the south side of Pooktan Creek, walk back along the highway to Sunwapta Station. The trail begins from a sign at the rear of the station compound and begins a steady ascent along the north side of the valley. You gain 210 m of elevation over the next 6 km to Maligne Pass junction. At the junction, branch north from the *Poboktan Creek* trail and begin what can be a long, wet climb to Maligne Pass.

The trail up the Poligne Valley crosses back and forth over the creek several times in less than 5 km as it climbs steadily through heavy spruce-pine forest. Though these crossings were bridged in the past, maintenance of the trail may be reduced, so check at the visitor centre for an update.

Beyond Avalanche Campground, the trail reaches treeline and the climb moderates. Throughout this section the track is often indistinct as it traverses boggy meadows.

At km 14.7, the trail reaches the eastern shore of a one-kilometre-long lake on the crest of Maligne Pass (2300 m). Vast meadows rise gradually northwest and southeast from the lake, inviting further exploration to more than half-a-dozen smaller lakes nestled against the escarpment of the Endless Chain Ridge.

© Don Beers

Maligne Pass

Beyond the pass views open to glacier-crowned Mount Mary Vaux and a long line of peaks stretching northward along the upper Maligne River valley, a view described by Mary Schaffer on July 6, 1908: "I think I never saw a fairer valley. From our feet it swept away into an unbroken green carpet as far as the eye could see… and then the cavalcade made a quick descent of about a thousand feet, tramping under foot thousands of blossoms of the trollius [globeflower] and pulsatilla [western anemone] which covered the way."

Maligne Pass to Maligne Lake—33.0 km. Despite Mary Schäffer's poetic waxings, the trail north from Maligne Pass to Maligne Lake is a rather long, gloomy trudge. And it is even more dismal now that Parks Canada has decommissioned it.

In an effort to preserve the upper Maligne Valley for bears and other wildlife, Parks Canada no longer maintains the trail, has not replaced the Maligne River bridge 20 km north of the pass, and is planning to remove all the campgrounds. This means you will encounter dense, 3-4m tall willows, deadfall, and a significant ford on the Maligne River. (The trail can be very difficult to find in the sections of willow.) Experienced backpackers can still hike the trail, but should treat it as a wilderness route and follow the rules of random camping. And make sure to make lots of noise, since this is prime grizzly habitat.

111 Poboktan Creek

Icefields Parkway to Jonas Cutoff Campground—21.3 km (13.2 mi)
Icefields Parkway to Poboktan Pass—24.3 km (15.1 mi)

Backpack

Allow 6 to 7 hours to Jonas Cutoff Jct.

Elevation gain: 580 m (1,900 ft)

Maximum elevation: 2120 m (6,950 ft)

Maps: Sunwapta Peak 83 C/6

Access: Follow the Icefields Parkway (Hwy 93) to Parks Canada's Sunwapta Station, 31.5 km (19.5 mi) north of the Icefield Centre or 71.5 km (44.5 mi) south of the town of Jasper. Continue on the highway 100 m south of the station (south side of Poboktan Creek) to an access road branching east into a parking area. The trailhead is at the rear of Sunwapta Station, so walk back across Poboktan Creek on the highway and through the station grounds to the trail sign.

0.0— Trailhead (1540 m).
N52°27.030' W117°26.534'

6.2— Junction (1760 m). *Maligne Pass* left. Poboktan Creek ahead.

6.4— Poligne Creek bridge.

7.5— Poboktan Creek Campground.

12.0— Waterfalls Campground.

13.8— Waterfalls Patrol Cabin.

21.3— Junction (2120 m). Intersection with *Jonas Pass-Brazeau Lake Loop* at km 32.9. Turn right for Jonas Cutoff Campground (0.2 km) and Jonas Shoulder (3.3 km); Poboktan Pass ahead 3.0 km.

Notice: Due to possible conflicts with caribou, dogs are not permitted on the Poboktan Creek trail.

The trail up Poboktan Creek and over Poboktan Pass to Brazeau Lake was constructed during the summers of 1921 and 1922 by a crew supervised by Park Warden J.M. Christie. It was the first trail to the park's remote south boundary and has served as an important patrol route ever since. It also serves hikers as the most direct trail to the Poboktan Pass-Jonas Shoulder environs, an optional route to Brazeau Lake, and the link between the Jonas Pass and Maligne Pass sections of the *Glacier Trail*.

The first 6.2 km of the hike follows the same route as the *Maligne Pass* trail. Beyond Maligne Pass junction, the trail crosses Poligne Creek and continues along the north side of Poboktan Creek. After passing Poboktan Creek Campground, it bends southeast and begins a long, steady ascent of the upper Poboktan Valley.

As you travel up-valley, you discover some of the difficulties Warden Christie faced in building the trail in the early 1920s—boggy terrain that is frequently muddy and churned-up by horse use (corduroy and alternate hiker detours help you over and around the worst spots). The cataract at Waterfalls Campground and another waterfall 2 km farther up-valley provide welcome relief from the drudgery of mud and pine-spruce forest.

At km 21.3 you descend into a pleasant little ravine at Jonas Cutoff Junction. Jonas Cutoff Campground (200 m to the right) is conveniently situated as a base camp for day trips to both Poboktan Pass (3.2 km) and Jonas Shoulder (3.1 km). Whether you extend your trip south over Jonas Shoulder and Pass or southeast to Brazeau Lake, you will be following the *Jonas Pass-Brazeau Lake Loop*. (See also *Glacier Trail*.)

112 Glacier Trail

Sunwapta Station to Nigel Creek—54.2 km (33.7 mi)

Backpack
Allow 3 to 4 days
Maximum elevation: 2470 m (8,100 ft)
Minimum elevation: 1540 m (5,050 ft)
Maps: Sunwapta Peak 83 C/6
Columbia Icefield 83 C/3

Access: Travelling from north to south, start from the Poboktan Creek trailhead at Parks Canada's Sunwapta Station (see *Poboktan Creek* and *Maligne Pass*). Northbound hikers start from the *Nigel Pass* trailhead in Banff Park (see also *Jonas Pass-Brazeau Lake Loop*).

 0.0— Sunwapta Station trailhead (1540 m).
N52°27.030' W117°26.534

 6.2— Junction (1760 m). *Maligne Pass* left.
Poboktan Creek (*Glacier Trail* south) ahead.

 7.5— Poboktan Creek Campground.

12.0— Waterfalls Campground.

21.3— Jonas Cutoff Junction (2120 m).
Poboktan Pass ahead.
Jonas Shoulder (*Glacier Trail* south) right.

21.5— Jonas Cutoff Campground.

24.6— Jonas Shoulder Summit (2470 m).

30.4— Jonas Pass Summit (22320 m).

40.2— Junction (1915 m). South Boundary Trail and Brazeau Lake left.
Nigel Pass (*Glacier Trail* south) right.

40.4— Four Point Campground.

43.5— Boulder Creek Campground.

47.0— Nigel Pass (2195 m).

54.2— Nigel Pass trailhead (1860 m).
N52°11.250' W117°04.227

*Distances approximate.

Notice: Due to possible conflicts with caribou, dogs are not permitted on the Glacier Trail.

In 1924, before construction of the Banff-Jasper Highway, Jasper outfitter Jack Brewster initiated one of the most scenic pack trips in the Rocky Mountains—a three-week journey by horseback from Jasper to Lake Louise via the Columbia Icefield. Brewster called it "The Glacier Trail." Though most of the historic trail has been replaced by the Maligne Lake Road and Icefields Parkway, the section from Maligne Lake to Nigel Creek is still intact and can be hiked in a week or less.

The route runs between Maligne Lake and the Nigel Pass trailhead in Banff Park, crossing three passes—Maligne, Jonas and Nigel—along the way. However, Parks Canada has recently decommissioned the most northerly Maligne Pass section, so we are only recommending the full route to experienced wilderness travellers who are willing to ford the unbridged Maligne River and randomly camp in the upper Maligne Valley (see *Maligne Pass*).

Instead, we are now describing a slightly truncated version of the original route we first published in 1986. For most backpackers, we suggest starting the trip from the Poboktan Creek trailhead. This trail intersects the Glacier Trail route at 6.2 km, and if you can camp at nearby Poboktan Creek Campground, you can still visit Maligne Pass on a day trip from there.

Continuing up Poboktan Creek, you branch right at 21.3 km and climb over the highly scenic Jonas Shoulder, traverse the vast alpine meadows of Jonas Pass, and descend to the upper Brazeau Valley. The last leg of the trip follows up the Brazeau River to its headwaters and crosses Nigel Pass to the Icefields Parkway.

The Glacier Trail utilizes sections of three trails presented in this chapter (see *Maligne Pass*, *Poboktan Creek*, and *Jonas Pass-Brazeau Lake Loop* for details on each section).

Roche Jacques

Hwy 16

Emir Mtn

Jacques Pass

Mt Colin

Rocky River

Mt Merlin

Merlin Pass

122

Roche Bonhomme

Mt Dromore

Sirdar Mtn

South Boundary Trail

113

Jacques Lake

121

Maligne River

Summit Lakes

Signal Mtn

116

Beaver Lake

Mt Tekarra

Medicine Lake

Amber Mtn

The Watchtower

The Notch

115

Maligne

Curator Lake

Wabasso Lake

Shovel Pass Lodge

Shovel Pass

96

Curator Mtn

River

Antler Mtn

116

Snowbowl

Opal Pk

Opal Hills

120

Little Shovel Pass

Mona Lake

117

Lorraine Lake

Pass

Athabasca River

93

93A

119

Bald Hills

Maligne Lake

Moose Lake

118

Mt Hardisty

Land above 2300 metres

0   1   2   3   4 km

113 Maligne Canyon

Sixth Bridge Picnic Area to Maligne Canyon Parking Area—3.7 km (2.3 mi)

Maligne Canyon is the Rockies' most impressive limestone slot canyon. The trail along the upper canyon is usually overrun, but few ever hike its entire length. By starting below the canyon, you can enjoy peaceful sections of the Maligne River and, as the canyon gradually unfolds, gain a better appreciation of how it was formed.

Begin at Sixth Bridge Picnic Area, near the confluence of the Maligne and Athabasca Rivers, and climb gradually along the north side of the Maligne River through a forest of spruce, pine, poplar and birch. At km 1.6 you pass Fifth Bridge, which crosses the river to a parking area. Above Fifth Bridge the trail steepens and the ascent along the canyon begins.

Fourth Bridge is passed at km 2.9, and you cross Third Bridge to the south side of the canyon at km 3.1. This is the deepest (55 m) and most spectacular section, so narrow that a person could spread their arms and touch both walls.

From Third Bridge to First Bridge, you cross water-polished bedrock and overlook potholed canyon walls. The trail ends at the usually-busy upper parking area, and a café-gift shop.

Access: From its intersection with the Yellowhead Highway, follow Maligne Lake Road 2.3 km (1.4 mi) to the Sixth Bridge access road. Turn left and follow it 1.6 km (1.0 mi) to Sixth Bridge Picnic Area. Walk across the bridge to the north side of the Maligne River to begin the hike. N52°56.019' W118°01.772' *Maps: Jasper 83 D/16; Best of Jasper (Gem Trek).*

114 Overlander Trail

Sixth Bridge Picnic Area to Cold Sulphur Spring—15.5 km (9.6 mi)

The Overlander Trail follows the east side of the Athabasca Valley from the Maligne River to the Cold Sulphur Spring pull-out on the Yellowhead Highway. The trail receives its name from the Overlanders—adventurous emigrants who travelled up-valley in 1862 to British Columbia's Cariboo gold fields. It is a pleasant outing that passes through prime montane habitat and by an early valley homestead.

The trail is often hiked by arranging transportation between the two trailheads. It can also be cycled, though some sections are quite demanding.

Cross the Maligne River at Sixth Bridge and follow the left branch downstream past the river's confluence with the Athabasca. Continue north along the Athabasca River briefly before angling inland to rejoin the cycling trail. For the next 14 km you enjoy many open views of the valley and the Colin Range.

At km 6.5 you reach the remains of the John Moberly homestead (1898-1910) in a grassy meadow. Beyond the homestead the trail passes through a prescribed burn and above a sulphur spring (km 9.0). After traversing Morro Peak's steep, rocky slopes, it descends to the Cold Sulphur Spring on Highway 16.

Access: From the Yellowhead Highway, follow Maligne Lake Road 2.3 km (1.4 mi) to the Sixth Bridge road. Turn left and follow it 1.6 km (1.0 mi) to Sixth Bridge Picnic Area. Walk across the Maligne River bridge to begin the hike. N52°56.021' W118°01.787'.

Cold Sulphur Spring trailhead is at a pull-out on the east side of the Yellowhead Highway, 18.5 km (11.5 mi) north of the town of Jasper's east exit. N53°02.631' W118°05.041' *Maps: Jasper 83 D/16; Snaring 83 E/1.*

115 Watchtower Basin

Maligne Lake Road to Watchtower Campground—9.8 km (6.1 mi)
Maligne Lake Road to Big Shovel Pass—13.2 km (8.2 mi)*

Day trip or backpack

Allow 3 hours to Watchtower Campground

Elevation gain: 610 m (2,000 ft)

Maximum elevation: 2000 m (6,550 ft)

Maps: Medicine Lake 83 C/13

Access: From its junction with the Yellowhead Highway (Hwy 16) 5 km (3 mi) north of the town of Jasper, follow the Maligne Lake Road 18.5 km (11.5 mi) to the Watchtower Basin trailhead. The parking area is reached via a short gravel access road.

0.0—Trailhead (1390 m).
　　N52°52.763' W117°50.169'

0.1—Maligne River bridge.

　—Trail climbs steeply through forest.

0.5—Trail angles southeast, gradual to moderate uphill.

5.6—Trail turns south into meadows along Watchtower Creek.

　—Gradual ascent along west side of creek.

9.6—Ford to east side of creek (rock-hop).

9.8—Watchtower Campground (2000 m).

　—Trail climbs along east side of creek.

12.3—Trail climbs talus slope beneath headwall col.

12.8—Watchtower Col (2375 m).

　—Trail contours left across open slopes to Big Shovel Pass.

13.2—Big Shovel Pass Junction (2320 m). Intersection with *Skyline Trail* at km 17.6.

*Distances approximate beyond 9.8 km.

Notice: Due to possible conflicts with caribou, dogs are not permitted on the Watchtower trail.

Watchtower Basin is one of our favourite long day hikes in Jasper Park since it allows access to the renowned meadows and lofty alpine ridges of the Maligne Range without having to book campsites on the popular Skyline Trail.

Many prefer a more leisurely visit and stay at Watchtower Campground. From the campground you can hike to Big Shovel Pass on the Skyline Trail in an hour or so and still have lots of time to explore the vast wildflower meadows and open slopes that comprise this attractive alpine valley. But be forewarned, the campground and the approach trail are mosquito-ridden throughout much of the summer.

From the parking area off the Maligne Lake Road, the trail immediately crosses a bridge over the Maligne River. Beyond the river it makes a short, steep climb up the heavily-forested north slope of The Watchtower. After it has gained enough elevation to leave most hikers slightly winded, it angles off to the southeast. You climb more gradually for the next 2 km but are forced to navigate a number of marshy areas.

At km 5.6 the trail gradually veers back to the south, comes abreast of Watchtower Creek and climbs gradually through meadows and open subalpine forest (boggy, brushy and vague stretches). You follow along the west side of Watchtower Creek until km 9.6, where you rock-hop to the stream's east side and, a few minutes later, reach Watchtower Campground. The campground is sheltered in a stand of alpine fir and Engelmann spruce and is the site of the old Watchtower Cabin, which served as a base for Jasper ski enthusiasts in the 1930s (the cabin was destroyed by fire in the late 1970s).

One of the easiest side trips from the campground is to a small lake less than a kilometre to the west, and 150 m higher

Watchtower Basin

up, on the lower slopes of The Watchtower. While there is no trail to this pretty tarn, finding your way across the meadows is no problem. The rockslides surrounding the lake are home to pikas and white-tailed ptarmigan.

Watchtower Col. The trail up-valley from the campground stays along the east side of the creek and soon rises above the last scattered islands of stunted trees into the alpine meadows of the upper Watchtower Basin. (Track is faint in places—watch for markers.) At the end of the valley, a defined trail across the headwall scree slope leads up to the 2375-m pass on the crest of the Maligne Range.

From this lofty col, approximately 3 km beyond the campground, views open out over the scenic heart of the range— Big Shovel Pass, Curator Lake and The Notch.

Beyond the summit the trail angles southeast across rocky slopes for another 0.4 km to Big Shovel Pass, where it intersects with the *Skyline Trail*. Backpackers can continue their journey onto the Skyline by turning northwest toward Curator Lake and The Notch or southeast toward Little Shovel Pass and Maligne Lake.

You can also descend to Curator Campground and follow the Wabasso Lake trail to the Athabasca Valley. Total distance for this traverse of the Maligne Range, from the Maligne Lake Road to the Icefields Parkway, is 30 km. (See *Wabasso Lake* trail description.)

116 Skyline Trail

Maligne Lake to Signal Mountain trailhead—44.1 km (27.4 mi)

Backpack

Allow 2 to 3 days

Elevation gain: 820 m (2,700 ft)
          loss: 1350 m (4,450 ft)

Maximum elevation: 2510 m (8,200 ft)

Maps: Athabasca Falls 83 C/12
      Medicine Lake 83 C/13

Access: Follow the Maligne Lake Road to Maligne Lake. Continue past the day lodge-boat tour complex on the main road for another 0.5 km, crossing the lake's outlet bridge to the picnic area and parking area at road's end. The trailhead is at the upper edge of the parking area, 50 m to the right of the Bald Hills trailhead kiosk.

0.0—Maligne Lake trailhead (1690 m).
     N52°43.569' W117°38.732'

2.1—Junction. Lorraine Lake left 0.2 km.

2.4—Junction. Mona Lake right 0.2 km.

4.8—Evelyn Creek Campground and bridge.

8.3—Little Shovel Campground.

10.3—Little Shovel Pass (2240 m).

12.2—Snowbowl Campground.

17.5—Big Shovel Pass (2320 m).

17.6—Junction. Intersection with Watchtower Basin trail at km 13.2.

19.5—Junction. Intersection with Wabasso Lake trail at km 15.0. Curator Campground and Shovel Pass Lodge left 0.8 km.

20.4—Curator Lake.

22.1—The Notch (2510 m).

28.3—Centre Lakes.

30.4—Tekarra Campground (2060 m).

35.6—Junction. Signal Mtn lookout site left 0.5 km.

35.7—Signal Campground.

44.1—Maligne Lake Road trailhead (1160 m).
      N52°54.855' W118°00.080'

Notice: Due to possible conflicts with caribou, dogs are not permitted on the Skyline Trail.

The Skyline Trail is one of the exceptional backpacking routes in the Rockies. Following along the rolling crest of the Maligne Range, with 25 of its 44 km at or above treeline, it is the highest trail in Jasper Park. Along the way there are vast meadows, barren windswept ridges, and expansive views that extend over much of the park.

There are a few considerations before you set off on the journey. Due to the trail's high, unprotected situation, you may be exposed to severe conditions if the weather turns foul (snow can fall anytime during the summer). Five of six campgrounds along the trail lie above 2000 m, so the temperature can drop to near freezing on clear nights, particularly in late August and September. The trail has a relatively short season, and the steep section between Curator Lake and The Notch is often blocked by the previous winter's snow well into July. It is also one of the most popular backpacking trips in the Canadian Rockies, and since Parks Canada limits the number of hikers on the trail at any given time, it is advisable to reserve campsites in advance of your trip.

Though trail runners have completed the Skyline in a day, most backpackers schedule three days for the journey. Shovel Pass Lodge near the midway point is also an attractive alternative for those who like a light pack and enjoy creature comforts on their trek.

The logical direction to hike the Skyline Trail is from Maligne Lake, starting 530 m higher than the northwest trailhead near Maligne Canyon. From Maligne Lake, the trail strikes off through lodgepole pine forest and gains little elevation over the first 5 km. At km 4.8 you cross Evelyn Creek and begin a switch-backing ascent to Little Shovel Pass. Views continue to improve, particularly back to the peaks surrounding Maligne Lake, as you climb through subalpine

The Snowbowl near Little Shovel Pass

meadows with scattered stands of alpine fir to the treeless crest of the pass.

From Little Shovel Pass the trail drops into the lush, sprawling meadows of the Snowbowl. Even during the driest summers fresh streams tumble through the meadows, adding to the sogginess of the terrain. Ascending from the Snowbowl, the trail reaches the crest of Big Shovel Pass at km 17.5.

Shovel Pass was named in 1911 when Jasper's Otto brothers packed Mary Schäffer and a boat over the range to Maligne Lake via this improbable route. When the party encountered deep snow near the pass, the Ottos carved a pair of wooden shovels from trees below and scratched out a trail through the drifts for their horses. The shovels were erected near the summit and stood for several years as monuments to the arduous journey. (You can view the original shovels at the Jasper Yellowhead Museum in the town of Jasper.)

Near the pass the trail from Watchtower Basin intersects from the right. A 0.4 km side trip to Watchtower Col provides an overview of this high, subalpine basin.

Two km below Big Shovel Pass you reach the Wabasso Lake trail junction. Less than a kilometre down this trail is Curator Campground and Shovel Pass Lodge. The Watchtower Basin and Wabasso Lake trails both serve as optional routes to and from the heart of the Skyline, and the Wabasso Lake trail is occasionally used as an escape route during vile weather. (See *Watchtower Basin* and *Wabasso Lake*).

From Wabasso junction the trail climbs quickly to the shores of Curator Lake—a peaceful tarn in the midst of a wild, treeless landscape. Here you begin the steep ascent to The Notch—the high col leading to the summit ridge of Amber Mountain.

The Notch (2510 m) is considered the high point on the Skyline, even though the trail contours northwest for another 2 km at virtually the same elevation. This barren divide is an extraordinary viewpoint for the Athabasca Valley and Mount Edith Cavell, and on clear days Mount Robson is visible 80 km away to the northwest.

Just beyond the summit of Amber Mountain the trail makes a switchbacking descent to Centre Lakes, then levels

© Mike McReynolds

Curator Lake and The Notch

off down a narrow vale to Tekarra Lake. Crossing the outlet stream below the lake, you enter scattered stands of alpine fir and begin your contour around to the northern slopes of Mount Tekarra. Views gradually open ahead to the Colin Range, Pyramid Mountain and other familiar peaks near the town of Jasper.

At km 35.6, the trail intersects the Signal Mountain fire road, just 0.5 km below the mountain's old fire lookout site (a worthwhile side trip for improved views over the Athabasca Valley). The Skyline's most northerly campground, Signal Campground, lies 100 m below the junction.

From the campground, the broad roadbed runs steadily and tediously downhill through forest for the final 8.4 km to the trailhead parking area on the Maligne Lake Road 0.8 km west of the upper parking area at Maligne Canyon.

Shovel Pass Lodge is adjacent to Curator Lake Campground and more-or-less midpoint along the Skyline Trail. Located in a meadow at 2060 m (6,750 ft), it offers an alternative for hikers who want to travel light. It also provides a more comfortable base for an extra day or two of exploration in this alpine region.

When it was rebuilt in 1991, the lodge was designed for both guided horse parties and hikers, but 90 percent of current guests are hikers. The complex comprises seven guest cabins and a main chalet with a dining room. In addition to the usual services found in a staffed, backcountry facility, the lodge's pack trains will transport up to seven kg (15 lb) of personal duffel for its hiker guests. (See *Sources—Backcountry lodges.*)

117 Lorraine and Mona Lakes

Maligne Lake Picnic Area to Mona Lake—2.6 km (1.6 mi)

Escape the hubbub at the busy north end of Maligne Lake by hiking the first 2.4 km of the Skyline Trail to a pair of peaceful forest-encircled lakes. Mona Lake is the more substantial of the pair, and from its shore the rounded summits of the Opal Hills rise above the forest to the north.

From the picnic area parking lot, follow the *Skyline Trail* through thick lodgepole pine forest for 2.1 km and watch for the trail branching left to Lorraine Lake. Continue on the main trail another 0.3 km to a side trail branching right to Mona Lake. Both lakes are less than 200 m from the main trail.

Mona Lake is named for Mona Harragin, a tough, self-reliant lady who worked for outfitter Fred Brewster at the Maligne Lake tent camp in 1927. In 1928 Mona and her sister Agnes became the first licensed women trail guides in the mountain parks. Two years later Mona married park warden Charlie Matheson, and the couple shared a number of wilderness adventures while living at the Maligne Lake Warden Cabin.

Access: Follow the Maligne Lake Road to Maligne Lake. Continue past the day lodge-boat tour complex for another 0.5 km and cross the lake's outlet bridge to the picnic area and parking area at road's end. The trailhead is at the upper edge of the parking area, 50 m to the right of the Bald Hills trailhead access gate. N52°43.569' W117°38.732' *Maps: Athabasca Falls 83 C/12.*

118 Moose Lake

Moose Lake Circuit—2.7 km (1.7 mi)

If you are overwhelmed by the crush of vehicles, tour buses, and snap-shooting tourists at the north end of Maligne Lake, the Moose Lake loop offers a short walk-in-the-woods where you will find a little solitude. The hike follows a section of the *Maligne Pass* trail before cutting off into the forest to this quiet little tarn surrounded by pine and spruce; on the return trip you follow along a short section of the Maligne Lake shoreline.

From the access gate at the upper edge of the Maligne Lake Picnic Area, follow the broad Bald Hills trail 300 m to the Maligne Pass junction. Turn left and continue along the Maligne Pass trail for another kilometre to Moose Lake junction. Follow this branch left 100 m to the lake (Samson Peak rises above the trees to the southeast).

Finish your loop trip by following the trail running east from Moose Lake to Maligne Lake at km 2.4, then along the shoreline for 0.3 km to the parking area.

Access: Follow the Maligne Lake Road to Maligne Lake. Continue past the day lodge-boat tour complex for another 0.5 km and cross the lake's outlet bridge to the picnic area and parking area at road's end. The walk begins at the Bald Hills trail kiosk opposite the parking area entrance. N52°43.542' W117°38.731' *Maps: Athabasca Falls 83 C/12.*

119 Bald Hills

Maligne Lake Picnic Area to Bald Hills Lookout—5.2 km (3.2 mi)

Half-day to day trip

Allow 1.5 to 2 hours one way

Elevation gain: 480 m (1,575 ft)

Maximum elevation: 2170 m (7,120 ft)

Maps: Athabasca Falls 83 C/12

Access: Follow the Maligne Lake Road to Maligne Lake. Continue past the day lodge-boat tour complex for another 0.5 km and cross the lake's outlet bridge to the picnic area and parking area at road's end. The hike begins at the trail kiosk beside an access gate near the parking area entrance.

0.0—Trailhead (1690 m).
N52°43.542' W117°38.731'

0.3—Junction. *Moose Lake* and *Maligne Pass* left. Continue ahead.

—Steady uphill on moderately graded roadbed.

2.5—Junction. Bald Hills Shortcut left.

3.2—Junction. Evelyn Creek right.

5.2—Bald Hills Lookout site (2170 m).

Notice: Due to possible conflicts with caribou, dogs are not permitted on the Bald Hills trail.

The Bald Hills provide an exceptional overview of Maligne Lake and its surrounding peaks. The subalpine meadows on this open ridgeline are carpeted with wildflowers in July and early August, and the gentle terrain is an open invitation to hike to even higher viewpoints beyond the old lookout site.

While the hike to Bald Hills is one of the best half-day trips in Jasper Park, it involves a rather uninspiring trudge up an old fire road. And make sure you have an adequate supply of water for this dry trip.

The trail starts its climb to Bald Hills in a fire-succession forest of lodgepole pine. Near km 2.5 the slope becomes pronouncedly subalpine with open meadows and stands of stunted alpine fir and Engelmann spruce.

The roadbed ends near the site of the old Bald Hills fire lookout—a cabin that was removed by the park service in the early 1980s. The old lookout site provides your first good view of Maligne Lake. Five hundred metres below, the lake stretches southeast to The Narrows—the gateway to the upper lake. Leah Peak (2801 m) and Samson Peak (3081 m) rise on the opposite side of the valley; the prominent glaciated summits rising above the meadows to the south are Mounts Unwin and Charlton, both well over 3000 m above sea level.

In 1908, Mary Schäffer, the Rockies' first lady of exploration, and her companions reached Maligne Lake—recording the first non-native visit since the lake's accidental discovery by a railway surveyor in 1875. After constructing a raft, the party journeyed down the lake to The Narrows, where "there burst upon us that which, all in our little company agreed, was the finest view any of us had ever beheld in the Rockies... Yet there it lay, for the time being all ours—those miles and miles of lake, the unnamed peaks rising above us, one

Maligne Lake from Bald Hills

following the other, each more beautiful than the last." Mary returned three years later and provided most of the names for the mountains surrounding the lake, including Bald Hills and Samson Peak, who she named for Samson Beaver, the Stoney who drew the map that led her to Maligne Lake.

While it is easy to hike to the lookout site and return in a half-day, we usually set aside a full day and wander the ascending ridge of the Bald Hills to the south. Follow a steep footpath leading beyond the end of the roadbed for another kilometre to a large cairn. Continue south through wildflower meadows and over two 2300-m promontories for another 2 km to even better views.

Bald Hills Shortcut. While we prefer to follow the easier grades of the fire road on the ascent to Bald Hills, there is also a footpath to the site that branches left from the roadbed at km 2.5. This single-track trail is shorter and steeper than the road, so it is an alternative on the way down. Watch for it branching downslope just beyond the lookout.

120 Opal Hills

Maligne Lake Upper Parking Area to Opal Hills Summit—3.2 km (2.0 mi)

Half-day trip

Allow 1 to 1.5 hours one way

Elevation gain: 460 m (1,500 ft)

Maximum elevation: 2160 m (7,100 ft)

Maps: Athabasca Falls 83 C /12

Access: Follow the Maligne Lake Road to Maligne Lake. Turn left into the main parking area just before the day lodge-boat rental concession and keep left to the third and uppermost parking lot. The trailhead is at the upper left corner of the parking lot.

0.0— Trailhead (1700 m).
   N52°43.856' W117°38.075'

0.2— Junction. Mary Schäffer trail right. Stay left.

— Very steep uphill.

1.6— Junction. Opal Hills Loop trail split. Stay right.

2.6— Trail emerges into meadow.

3.2— Trail summit (2160 m). Trail levels out into meadows behind hills.

4.7— Trail emerges from behind hills and descends into forest.

6.6— Junction. End of Opal Hills Loop. Connect back into approach trail at km 1.6.

8.2— Maligne Lake parking area (1700 m).

Notice: Due to possible conflicts with caribou, dogs are not permitted on the Opal Hills trail.

Like Bald Hills across the valley, the Opal Hills boast views of Maligne Lake and lots of wildflowers. But if you want the best views of the lake, go to Bald Hills, and for the best wildflowers, stick with Opal Hills. However, the lush meadows that make this area a wildflower-lover's paradise are also popular with grizzly bears, so plan for posted warnings and closures.

While the trail is shorter than Bald Hills, it is a lot steeper. From the upper parking lot at Maligne Lake, the trail dips briefly and then heads grimly upward through dense lodgepole pine forest with nary a switchback, gaining elevation at a heart-pounding rate. It can also be slippery and treacherous when wet.

The trail's upper loop begins at a junction 1.6 km into the hike. Either branch will bring you to the same point, but the right-hand option reaches the meadows in less time.

Staying right at the trail split, you remain in subalpine forest for another kilometre before suddenly emerging into open meadow.

Soon after reaching the meadow, the trail levels off, angles left through a draw, and circles into a basin behind low hills. Climb to the top of the first knoll on the left for the best view of Maligne Lake, and if it's a warm day, you'll be happy to fall back on the grassy, south-facing slope to relax in the sun.

Though the view isn't as expansive as from Bald Hills, much of lower Maligne Lake is visible, as are the twin peaks of Mounts Unwin (3268 m) and Charlton (3217 m) beyond its western shore. The rounded, red-hued ridge of the Opal Hills, named by Maligne Lake pioneer Mary Schäffer, rise above the trail to the east.

The trail traverses the vale behind the hills and passes through the best of the wildflowers before returning to the forest and completing a moderately steep descent back to the loop split.

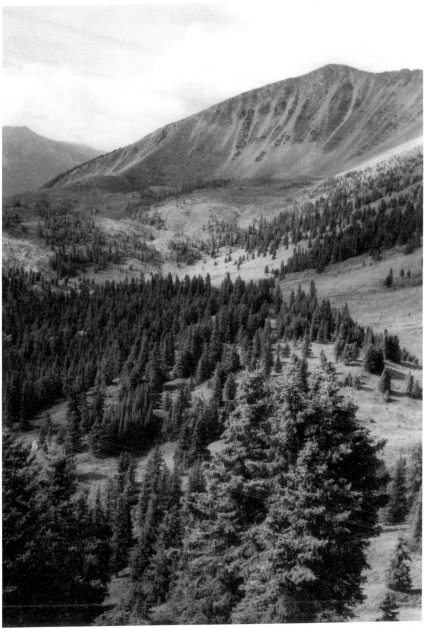

Opal Hills

121 Jacques Lake

Maligne Lake Road to Jacques Lake Campground—12.2 km (7.6 mi)

Day trip or backpack

Allow 3 to 4 hours one way

Elevation gain: 90 m (300 ft)
loss: 45 m (150 ft)

Maximum elevation: 1540 m (5,050 ft)

Maps: Medicine Lake 83 C/13

Access: From its junction with the Yellowhead Highway (Hwy 16), follow the Maligne Lake Road 28 km (17.5 mi) to the Beaver Creek Picnic Area, on the left side of the road opposite the southeast end of Medicine Lake. Trail sign is at an access gate at the north edge of the picnic area.

0.0—Trailhead (1450 m).
N52°50.960' W117°43.315'

—Follow roadbed beyond access gate.

1.6—Beaver Lake.

4.8—First Summit Lake. Foot trail branches right into forest.

6.0—Second Summit Lake (1540 m). Trail follows through forest to right of lake.

7.4—Trail skirts to left of small lake.

—Section with numerous stream crossings.

11.6—Jacques Lake (southwest end).

12.2—Jacques Lake Campground (1495 m).

—Trail crosses outlet stream at north end of lake.

12.5—Jacques Lake Patrol Cabin. *South Boundary Trail* continues to northeast.

The trail to Jacques Lake is unique. It travels through a narrow mountain valley, skirts four lakes, and crosses a watershed divide—all in less than 12 km and with little gain or loss of elevation. The undemanding approach makes it a worthwhile destination for a long day hike and a good early season backpack when the high country is still choked with snow.

The trail is open to mountain bikes as far as Jacques Lake, and an old roadbed on the initial 5 km to Summit Lakes makes for easy cycling. However, the narrow, muddy single-track trail beyond Summit Lakes is rough and quite demanding.

From the access gate at Beaver Creek Picnic Area, the route follows the flat roadbed north through dense forest bordering the creek. At km 1.6 you reach the first point of interest, Beaver Lake. This pleasant, green lake, which is often inhabited by loons and other waterfowl, is a popular destination for birdwatchers, fishermen and anyone looking for a rewarding short walk.

The roadbed narrows to a broad, smooth pathway as it continues into more open terrain beyond Beaver Lake, and views open out to the north end of the Queen Elizabeth Range—a saw-toothed series of peaks eroded from steeply-tilted slabs of grey Devonian limestone.

At km 4.8 you reach the first Summit Lake—a small sink lake ringed by spruce, lodgepole pine and cottonwood poplar. Here the broad path reverts to single-track trail, which continues northwest through forest and meadow to the second Summit Lake—yet another sink with no visible outlet.

The final section of trail to Jacques Lake travels through dense forest filled with streams, and the rooty track is often quite muddy.

Jacques Lake

Though strong hikers can make the round trip to the lake and back in a day, Jacques Lake's peaceful setting deserves more than a hit-and-run visit. There are nice views across the lake to the Queen Elizabeth Ranges from the small campground near the north end, though the patrol cabin 0.3 km beyond occupies the prime real estate—overlooking the full length of the lake from a buttercup-filled meadow.

The lake is named for the mountain range to the northwest, which was named for Jacques Cardinal—a colourful Métis mountain man who began his storied career in the 1820s as a horse-keeper in the Athabasca Valley.

The trail continues beyond the north end of the lake and then heads northeast down Breccia Creek. This is the route followed by South Boundary Trail travellers, but there is little worthwhile scenery that can be reached on a day trip from the lake. (See *South Boundary Trail*.)

Merlin Pass–Jacques Pass. Though the trail from Jacques Lake to Highway 16 via Merlin and Jacques Passes is shown on maps, and even indicated by a trail sign at km 11.2, it is no longer maintained and its campgrounds have been removed. It was always a grim trek, but now it is not even worthy of consideration. (And just in case you're still tempted, a Parks Canada source estimates major deadfall across the trail at a thousand or more trees since trail clearing was curtailed years ago.)

122 South Boundary Trail

Maligne Lake Road to Nigel Pass trailhead—165.7 km (103.0 mi)

Backpack

Allow 7 to 10 days

Maximum elevation: 2255 m (7,400 ft)

Minimum elevation: 1360 m (4,450 ft)

Maps: Medicine Lake 83 C/13
      Mountain Park 83 C/14
      Southesk Lake 83 C/11
      George Creek 83 C/10
      Job Creek 83 C/7
      Sunwapta Peak 83 C/6
      Columbia Icefield 83 C/3

Access: Travelling from north to south, start from the *Jacques Lake* trailhead on the Maligne Lake Road. Northbound backpackers start at the *Nigel Pass* trailhead on the Icefields Parkway in Banff Park.

0.0—Beaver Creek Picnic Area (1450 m). N52°50.960' W117°43.315'

1.6—Beaver Lake.

4.8—First Summit Lake.

6.0—Second Summit Lake (1540 m).

12.2—Jacques Lake Campground (1495 m).

25.0—Grizzly Campground (1360 m).

31.0—Grizzly Patrol Cabin.

33.9—Rocky River suspension bridge.

37.6—Climax Campground.

39.7—Gretna Lake.

42.6—Rocky Falls.

47.9—Rocky Forks Campground (1590 m).

56.8—Medicine Tent Campground.

57.0—Rocky Pass Junction (1700 m). *Rocky Pass* left 4.4 km.

60.9—Medicine Tent Patrol Cabin.

66.1—Lagrace Campground.

70.5—Medicine Tent Lakes.

74.1—Cairn Pass (2255 m).

76.1—Cairn Pass Campground.

79.1—Cairn River Patrol Cabin.

86.2—Cairn River bridge.

The South Boundary Trail is no spectacular, high country trek—there are only two alpine passes and much of the trail travels through lowland forest. But whatever the trail may lack in flashy scenery, it makes up in a feeling of total isolation. It is a long, uncompromising journey, there are unbridged stream crossings, and some days will pass without another human encounter. Added to the mix are two major forest fires that burned large parts of the trail in 2003 and 2006, improving views but confronting backpackers with deadfall and, as revegetation occurs, overgrown sections where the track is disappearing.

Once you pass Jacques Lake at the trail's north end, or the Brazeau Lake junction near the south end, there is a sense of total commitment to the trip. The only escape route between those two points is the Rocky Pass trail, which brings you out onto the Cardinal River Road just below Cardinal River Divide— a very remote location indeed. (See *Rocky Pass* for optional access onto the trail and a more direct route to the scenic Cairn Pass region.)

So after discussing current conditions at the Park Visitor Centre, and if you're still determined to complete the journey, take your pick as to which direction you hike it. Since the best scenery lies on the southern half of the route, we opt to start in the north and hike southwards toward the improving views.

Beaver Creek to Rocky Pass Junction—57.0 km. You could not ask for an easier start to a major trek than the gentle Jacques Lake trail, and Jacques Lake Campground at km 12.2 makes a good first night destination (see *Jacques Lake*).

The trail is not so civilized beyond Jacques Lake. The track gets rougher and hikers are few and far between as you work your way northeast down the

Mount Dalhousie from Cairn River

narrow Breccia Creek gorge, crossing the stream four times on footbridges. After the final crossing, the trail climbs out of the Breccia canyon and enters the 2003 Rocky River burn. Not long after, it turns southeast and descends to the Rocky River at Grizzly Campground. This 12.5 km stretch from Jacques Lake to Rocky River is much more open and scenic than it was pre-fire, but staying on track due to deadfall and revegetation may be a problem.

Grizzly Campground was spared by the 2003 burn and is quite a pleasant site on a bank above the sparkling waters of the Rocky River. (The historic Grizzly Warden Cabin and its more recent companion cabin were destroyed in the

88.6— Southesk Lake Junction.
Southesk Lake right 21.7 km.
88.8— Cairn River ford (calf to knee-deep).
88.9— Cairn River Campground (1675 m).
93.0— Park boundary.
95.2— Southesk River suspension bridge.
Park boundary.
95.9— Junction. Cardinal River left.
97.5— Southesk Campground (1610 m).
97.8— Junction. Dowling Ford left.
110.0— Isaac Creek ford (calf-deep).
110.2— Isaac Creek Campground (1585 m).
111.3— Junction. Isaac Creek Patrol Cabin
left.
123.1— Arete Patrol Cabin.
123.7— Arete Campground.
132.4— Hole-in-the-Wall Springs.
135.9— Brazeau Patrol Cabin.
136.3— Junction and Northwest Brazeau
River bridge (1720 m). Intersection
with *Jonas Pass-Brazeau Lake
Loop* at km 50.2. Brazeau Lake and
Poboktan Pass right.
136.4— Brazeau Campground.
144.9— Wolverine South Campground.
151.7— Four Point Junction. Jonas Pass
right.
151.9— Four Point Campground.
155.0— Boulder Creek Campground.
158.5— Nigel Pass (2195 m). Banff-Jasper
Park boundary.
165.7— Nigel Pass trailhead (1830 m).
N52°11.250' W117°04.227'

**(Trail not fully shown on maps in this
book)**

blaze, and a makeshift patrol cabin was
erected on the site.)

The trail carries on up-valley along
the river's southwest side and soon
passes back into unburned forest. While
the track is well defined, there is an unexpected calf-deep ford of a side stream
at km 33.4. Views are limited until you
cross the Rocky River suspension bridge
at km 33.9 and emerge onto open willow flats on the northeast side of the
river (the bridge is 200 m upstream from
where the horse trail crosses the river).

Continuing up-valley from the bridge,
you stay in the forest, though there are
openings out to the steeply-tilted limestone peaks of the Front Ranges. At
km 42.6, you suddenly emerge onto an
overlook above Rocky Falls—a waterfall
staircase that creates an impressive diversion along this otherwise lacklustre
section.

At km 47.9, just beneath the westward
dipping limestone slabs of Mount Lind-
say, you arrive at Rocky Forks Campground. Just over a kilometre beyond the
campground, a horse trail branches right
and crosses the Medicine Tent River to
the horse campground and the Rocky
Forks Patrol Cabin, but the hiker's trail
continues straight ahead and maintains
its southeast course up along the Medicine Tent.

The horse trail fords the Medicine
Tent at km 53.9, but watch for a hiker's
trail branching left 100 m before the
crossing. The horse trail swings back
across the river to rejoin the hiker's track
at the Medicine Tent Campground.

Just 200 m beyond the campground,
the Rocky Pass trail intersects from the
north. This is an important junction,
since it is the only reasonable escape
route from the South Boundary Trail
along its entire length. This 11.4-km trail
climbs steeply to Rocky Pass and crosses
the park boundary to the Cardinal River
Road (see *Rocky Pass*).

**Rocky Pass Junction to Dowling Ford
Junction—40.8 km.** As you continue
up the Medicine Tent Valley from Rocky
Pass Junction, the forest becomes more
open and views improve. Beyond Lagrace

Southesk River Bridge

Campground, the trail begins its climb to the summit of Cairn Pass. The Medicine Tent Lakes are passed in an open alpine meadow at km 70.5 and, after a short steep climb through the last stands of alpine fir, you reach the pass.

At 2255 m, Cairn Pass is the high point of the trip in more ways than one. The view back down the Medicine Tent to the Rocky River valley is spectacular, allowing the first good overview of the country you've been hiking through for the past couple of days. Alpine meadows stretch out on both sides of the pass. Dotted with numerous small lakes, they are about as extensive and beautiful as any in Jasper Park. The summit is also inhabited by scores of hoary marmots, who aren't that accustomed to seeing people.

Immediately above the pass to the west is the low, cone-shaped peak named Southesk Cairn (2575 m). If you look closely, you can see the giant rock cairn that was erected on its summit by James Carnegie, the ninth Earl of Southesk, when he passed this way on a hunting trip in 1859. (In 2009, the 13th Earl of Southesk, David Carnegie, traveled to the pass, scrambled to the peak and stood beside the cairn built by his great-great grandfather 150 years before.)

Beyond Cairn Pass the trail continues its southeasterly course, descending through alpine and subalpine meadows for the next 5 km. Southesk Cairn and the pass remain visible all the way to the Cairn River Patrol Cabin junction. The trail bypasses the cabin, which lies on the opposite side of the Cairn River, and drops down into the forested Cairn Valley, staying along the river's northeast bank for the next 7 km.

At km 86.2, you ford to the south side of the Cairn. After traversing a forested rise, the trail returns to the river and crosses it again just above its confluence with the Southesk River (both of these fords are normally calf-deep). Just 200 m before the second ford, the 22.4-km trail to Southesk Lake branches right (see *Southesk Lake*).

Cairn River Campground is scenically situated on the east side of the second ford, with fine views south along the river to Mount Dalhousie (2947 m). The trail turns east at this point and less than 2 km beyond the campground, it breaks out of the forest and into the 2006 Southesk River burn. Views for the next seven km or so improve greatly over what they once were, but following the route might not be as easy.

Soon after entering the burn, the horse trail comes abreast of the Southesk River and crosses to the south bank. In order to avoid this demanding ford, a hiker's trail continues east and climbs a ridge above the river. At km 93.0, the trail crosses the park boundary and into Alberta's Rocky Mountains Forest Reserve. Just 0.6 km beyond, it intersects a broad seismic line. Turn left and follow this cut for 100 m to where the trail branches right into the forest. Another seismic line is encountered 100 m farther along. Follow this cut to the left for yet another 100 m and watch for the point where the trail exits to the right again. (Hopefully, there will be some directional markers or flagging to help you through this maze.)

Following this brief encounter with Alberta's seismic-line network, you switchback down into a canyon containing the Southesk River. A suspension bridge spans the gorge and, on the opposite side, you return to the sanctity of the park. After taking a break on the rock slabs of this pleasant canyon, climb 0.3 km to rejoin the horse trail.

All of this wandering about has taken you out of the Front Ranges and into the fringes of the Foothills. Less than a kilometre east of Southesk Campground, you reenter unburned forest on a flat, unremarkable trail. Southesk Campground is on a point of land overlooking a sink lake, where you have a fine perspective of the surrounding countryside, comprised of great expanses of flat, forested terrain overlooked by the dramatic multiple-summits of Mount Dalhousie to the southwest.

Dowling Ford Junction to Nigel Pass trailhead—67.9 km. Just beyond Southesk Campground you reach the junction with a horse trail from Dowling Ford. This is significant since it is the point where the South Boundary Trail turns south and re-enters the mountains via the Brazeau Valley.

The trail runs through a rocky and rooty forest as it makes its ascent of the Brazeau, but the grade remains flat, as it has been ever since the Southesk suspension bridge. With the exception of some sink lakes at km 100.4, which allow open views south to Tarpeian Rock, this is a long, tedious section running through a dense forest of lodgepole pine.

The scenery in the Brazeau Valley begins to improve at Isaac Creek. Here, on the rocky, dryas-covered flats near the mouth of the Isaac Creek canyon, there is a fine view of the mountains across the valley, again dominated by the sheer 1300-m face of Tarpeian Rock.

As you follow up the Brazeau, the trail alternates between sections of forest and grassy meadows that slope down to the river. In midsummer these meadows are covered with montane wildflowers, including brown-eyed Susans, western wood lilies, harebells, and shrubby cinquefoil.

At km 132.4 there is a surprise—several large springs gushing from the base of a cliff and cascading down to the trail. Known as the Hole-in-the-Wall Springs (aka Big Springs), they create a minirainforest environment in the midst of a semi-arid valley and provide cool refreshment on hot summer days.

The trail runs through the grounds of the Brazeau Patrol Cabin at km 135.9 and, 0.5 km farther along, reaches Brazeau Lake Junction. Brazeau Lake is just over 2 km northwest of this intersection, and you may want to hike to the lake—the largest along the South Boundary route. (See *Jonas Pass-Brazeau Lake Loop*.)

At Brazeau Lake Junction, you return to more-travelled ways. The solitude of the past several days disappears as you enter the popular Jonas Pass-Brazeau Lake circuit, and you can expect to encounter more hikers over the final 30 km of your journey. This last leg to the Brazeau River headwaters and Nigel Pass is one of the most scenic on the entire trip, and it provides a fitting climax to your South Boundary adventure. (See also *Nigel Pass*, Banff Park chapter.)

123 Rocky Pass

Cardinal River Road to South Boundary Trail—11.4 km (7.1 mi)*

Day trip or backpack

Allow 3 to 4 hours to Medicine Tent River

Elevation gain: 120 m (390 ft)
loss: 260 m (850 ft)

Maximum elevation: 1960 m (6,430 ft)

Maps: Mountain Park 83 C/14

Access: Follow the Yellowhead Highway (Hwy 16) east from Jasper Park East Gate 22 km (13.5 mi) to junction with Highway 40S, 1.5 km west of Hinton. Follow Highway 40S west 48 km (30 mi) to its junction with the Cadomin road. Turn right and continue south, through the hamlet of Cadomin, 23 km (14 mi) to Cardinal Divide on the Grave Flats Road (passing through a major coal strip-mining operation en route). Continue beyond Cardinal Divide on the Cardinal River Road another 1.7 km to a pullout at the southern boundary of Wildhorse Wildland Provincial Park. A spur road leads right 160 m to the trailhead parking area.

0.0— Trailhead (1840 m).
   N52°53.423' W117°13.949'

   — Route follows seismic line southwest.

2.2— Junction. Trail branches left from seismic line.

4.4— Cardinal River fords (calf-deep).

   — Steep climb toward pass.

7.0— Rocky Pass (1960 m). Park boundary.

   — Contouring climb south from pass.

9.0— Steep switchbacking descent begins.

11.4— Junction (1700 m). Intersection with *South Boundary Trail* at km 57.0. Medicine Tent Campground right 0.2 km.

*all distances approximate.

(Trail not shown on maps in this book)

For hikers who want to access, or escape from, the heart of the South Boundary Trail quickly, the trail over Rocky Pass from Cardinal Divide is the only option. Rocky Pass (aka Cardinal Pass) is also a scenic and worthwhile objective as a day trip, though the long, rough drive to this remote trailhead beyond Jasper's eastern boundary will likely take as long as the hike itself.

Departing from the trailhead parking area 1.7 km east of Cardinal Divide, the trail follows a seismic line southwest. Continue until you reach a meadow around km 2.2, where the trail branches left from the broad, arrow-straight seismic path.

Once you leave the seismic line, and beat your way through a section of willow, the horse trail to the pass is obvious running across a meadow. You skirt two small lakes, pass a campsite and then descend to the first of three quick fords of the Cardinal River.

From the last ford, you begin a steep climb to the pass. Grades moderate before the trail crosses into Jasper Park on a slope just east of the true summit.

The pass is true to its name—a rocky, windswept gap overlooking the wild Medicine Tent Valley. Day hikers can continue another 2 km or so beyond the pass to even higher views as the trail contours and climbs along open, west-facing slopes.

The final descent to the Medicine Tent Valley is quick, plunging downward along the east side of a canyon. After passing beneath a series of punchbowl waterfalls, it reaches the South Boundary Trail at a junction 200 m south of the Medicine Tent Campground. (See *South Boundary Trail*.)

If you are using the Rocky Pass trail as an exit from the South Boundary Trail, you should realize that traffic on the Cardinal River Road is sparse. However, those who do travel it are usually sympathetic to hitchhikers.

124 Southesk Lake

South Boundary Trail to Southesk Lake Campground—22.0 km (13.7 mi)*

Backpack

Allow 6 to 7 hours one way

Elevation gain: 170 m (560 ft)

Maximum elevation: 1850 m (6,070 ft)

Maps: George Creek 83 C/10
Southesk Lake 83 C/11

Access: Hike the *South Boundary Trail* to the Southesk Lake trail junction—88 km from Beaver Creek on the Maligne Lake Road; 77 km from the Icefields Parkway at Nigel Creek; or 43 km from the Cardinal River Road via *Rocky Pass* and the *South Boundary Trail*.

0.0—Southesk Lake Junction (1680 m).

—Rolling trail above Southesk River.

4.3—Junction. Dean Pass Horse Campground left via river ford.

—Descent to north bank of river. Muddy sections and stream fords.

21.7—Southesk Lake (1850 m).

22.0—Southesk Lake Campground.

—Trail continues along north shore of lake.

*All distances approximate.

(Trail not fully shown on maps in this book.)

If Southesk Lake isn't the most remote spot in Jasper Park, it certainly feels like it. The lake is tucked away in the park's southeast wilderness and only accessible via a 22 km trek up the Southesk Valley from the South Boundary Trail.

Backpackers hiking the South Boundary Trail end-to-end seldom, if ever, visit the lake as a side trip. The handful who do visit it usually start their trip on the Cardinal River Divide and hike over Rocky Pass to the South Boundary Trail, then follow the South Boundary over Cairn Pass to Southesk Lake Junction. Total distance to the lake via this route is 65.5 km. (See *Rocky Pass* and *South Boundary Trail*.)

The trail branches west from the South Boundary Trail at km 88.6—300 m west of Cairn River Campground. Horse parties are the most frequent trail users, so the track up the north side of the river is often muddy and cut-up.

The ascent of the valley is pleasant, open and quite gradual all the way to the lake. Beyond the Dean Pass Campground junction, there are a number of stream crossings that will cost you time as you fuss about to find the best fording point.

After passing the campground (hiker-horse) at the east end of Southesk Lake, the trail continues along the north shore and beyond the lake towards Southesk Pass.

The lake is contained by unnamed peaks both north and south, which create a very wild and romantic setting. The most impressive is glaciated Maligne Mountain (3225 m), rising near the head of the valley to the west.

Horse parties often travel up-valley from the lake to Southesk Pass, then continue north down the Rocky River to Rocky Forks Campground. Though we know backpackers who have completed this loop, it is a long, rough trail (sometimes vague) with numerous stream crossings.

N

WILLMORE WILDERNESS PARK

Grande Cache

40

WILLIAM A
SWITZER
PROVINCIAL
PARK

Rock
Lake

40

129

ROCK LAKE-
SOLOMON CREEK
WILDLAND PARK

128

Moosehorn
Lakes

Willow Creek

Wolf
Pass

Boshe Range

Athabasca River

Hinton

BRÛLÉ

Brûlé Lake

Snake Indian
Falls

Snake

De Smet Range

128

16

Moosehorn Creek

Indian River

Celestine
Lake

Mt
Haultain

Princess
Lake

127

Roche
Miette

Fiddle

Mystery
Lake

P

Roche de
Smet

Miette
Hot Springs

Miette River

125

Vine Creek

Jasper Lake

Talbot
Lake

ROAD

126

Snaring River

CELESTINE

16

Miette Range

Snaring
Mtn

Jacques
Pass

Mt
Colin

Jacques Range

114

Merlin
Pass

Jasper

Land above 2000 metres

0   5   10   15km

125 Sulphur Skyline

Miette Hot Springs to Sulphur Skyline Summit—4.0 km (2.5 mi)

Half-day trip

Allow 1.5 hours one way

Elevation gain: 700 m (2,300 ft)

Maximum elevation: 2070 m (6,790 ft)

Maps: Miette 83 F/4

Access: From its junction with the Yellowhead Highway (Hwy 16) 7 km (4 mi) west of Jasper Park East Gate, follow the Miette Hot Springs Road south 17 km (11 mi) to its termination at the Miette Hot Springs pool parking area. Walk to the entrance of the pool complex on the right side of the building. Follow the sidewalk right 30 m to the trailhead.

0.0—Trailhead (1370 m).
    N53°07.768' W117°46.197'

  —Steady uphill on paved trail and then roadbed.

0.8—Roadbed narrows to single-track trail.

  —Steady ascent through old burn.

2.2—Shuey Pass Junction (1660 m). Fiddle River canyon ahead 2.3 km. Sulphur Skyline right.

  —Steep switchbacking ascent.

3.4—Trail emerges above treeline.

4.0—Sulphur Skyline Summit (2070 m).

The trail to the summit of Sulphur Ridge from Miette Hot Springs is one of the better half-day trips in Jasper Park. The ridge overlooks several remote wilderness valleys—the most prominent being Fiddle River, which snakes away to the southwest for over 24 km to its headwaters on Whitehorse Pass.

This hike is particularly nice in late spring and early summer when Front Range wildflowers are in bloom, and we've often encountered bighorn sheep on the way. But be sure to pack water—this is a steep, dry hike.

The trail begins as a broad paved path, but soon reverts to roadbed and then single-track. The climb is steady for 2.2 km to a junction on the crest of Shuey Pass, where you turn right and begin an even more serious climb to the ridge.

The trail switchbacks steadily upward through scattered forest and across open, grassy slopes before reaching the ridge summit, where a wonderful 360-degree panorama unfolds.

In addition to views south to Fiddle River and the rocky pyramid of Utopia Mountain, there are impressive valleys and mountains to the north, including the multi-summits of Ashlar Ridge—layers of steeply-tilted limestone that have been eroded into a series of sawtooth peaks.

Mystery Lake—10.5 km. This forest-encircled lake lies just beyond the park's east boundary. It is a long, rough day trip from Miette Hot Springs, and not much fun as a backpack either.

From the junction on Shuey Pass, descend (steeply) to the Fiddle River canyon. Ford the river 0.3 km below the point of first contact (difficult during high water), then follow rough trail downstream for 2 km before climbing overgrown track to the lake.

Our recommendation: avoid the ford, and the lake, and only go as far as Fiddle River canyon (km 4.5).

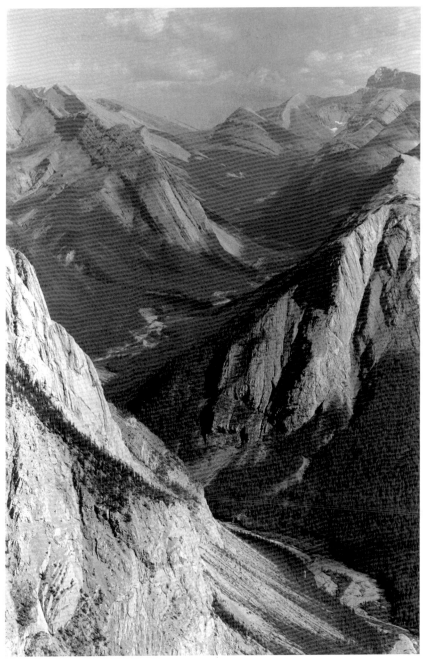

Fiddle River Valley from Sulphur Skyline

126 Fiddle River

Miette Hot Springs to Fiddle Pass—25.0 km (15.5 mi)*

Backpack

Allow 2 days to pass

Elevation gain: 1025 m (3,350 ft)
         loss: 260 m (850 ft)

Maximum elevation: 2135 m (7,000 ft)

Maps: Miette 83 F/4
       Cadomin 83 F/3
       Mountain Park 83 C/14

Access: From its junction with the Yellowhead Highway (Hwy 16) 7 km (4 mi) west of Jasper Park East Gate, follow the Miette Hot Springs Road south 17 km (11 mi) to Miette Hot Springs pool parking area. Start the hike from the trail kiosk on paved pathway just south of the parking lot entrance.

0.0— Trailhead (1370 m).
      N53°07.759' W117°46.376'
      —Descend paved trail.

0.3— Miette Aquacourt (1938-1984).
      —Boardwalk.

0.6— Miette source spring.

0.7— Forest trail begins.

3.0— Utopia Pass (1645 m).

4.6— Junction. Fiddle River horse trail left. Stay right.

4.7— Fiddle River (1400 m).

6.1— Utopia Creek ford (ankle-to mid-calf-deep). Utopia Creek Campground.

8.8— Junction. Fiddle River Patrol Cabin left across river. Continue ahead.

13.4— Slide Creek Campground.

13.7— Fiddle River ford to northeast bank.

20.7— Fiddle Campground.

23.0— Trail enters alpine meadows.

25.0— Fiddle Pass (2135 m).
      — Trail descends into Whitehorse Wildland Park.

38.2— Whitehorse Creek Recreation Area (1600 m).
      N52°59.073' W117°21.131'

*distances beyond km 4.7 approximate

(Trail not fully shown on maps in this book.)

Fiddle Pass, formerly known as Whitehorse Pass, is a wild alpine summit straddling Jasper Park's eastern boundary. Backpackers can trek to the pass from Miette Hot Springs via the 25-km Fiddle River trail, or they can reach it over a 13.2-km trail from Alberta's Whitehorse Creek Recreation Area. Wherever they start, many arrange transportation and make a complete traverse from one trailhead to the other.

The first section from Sulphur Creek to the Fiddle River is frequently visited from Miette Hot Springs. However, the trail becomes more primitive as it proceeds up-valley along the southwest side of Fiddle River. The first of several fords occurs at Utopia Creek, just prior to reaching Utopia Creek Campground.

Soon after crossing a massive rockslide, you reach Slide Creek Campground, and just beyond the trail swings to the northeast side of the Fiddle—a crossing that ranges from dry to knee-deep depending on the season. Farther along the horse trail crosses back to the southwest bank briefly, but hikers stay on the northeast side. Throughout this section, the trail alternates between rockslides, forest and gravel flats, and there are many open views.

Two more easy crossings of the Fiddle are made just prior to reaching Fiddle Campground. Here the trail angles up the river's north tributary and makes a quick ascent to Fiddle Pass on the park boundary. In addition to its fine alpine meadows, which start 2 km below the pass, there are good views back down the Fiddle Valley to the rugged peaks of the Nikanassin Range.

You can continue on through the pass and into Whitehorse Wildland Park. Follow horse trail to Whitehorse Creek, then old roadbed to the trailhead at the west end of the Whitehorse Creek Recreation Area campground, just off the Grave Flats Road 6 km south of the town of Cadomin.

Celestine Lake Road

The Celestine Lake Road runs for 27 km (17 mi) along the west side of the Athabasca Valley from the Yellowhead Highway (Hwy 16) to the Snake Indian Valley. The last 23 km is gravel, and some spots are rough and narrow, but the road is kept open to motor vehicles from May through September because it provides access to some wonderful montane landscape on that side of the valley and trails leading up the Snake Indian River, including *Devona Lookout* and the *North Boundary Trail*. The road itself is an excellent trip for mountain bikes and general hiking at any time of year, whenever it's snow-free.

Vehicle travel over the last 13.5 km to road's end at a parking area and barrier above the Snake Indian River, is controlled by one-way access restrictions. The control point is at a pull-out and sign 1.3 km beyond the Snaring Patrol Cabin. From this point on traffic alternates between north (inbound) and south (outbound) on a strict schedule (two-way traffic permitted outside these hours), which is listed on a sign at the pull-out. The schedule is as follows:

Inbound (north):	Outbound (south):
8:00 am to 9:00 am	9:30 am to 10:30 am
11:00 am to 12:00 noon	12:30 pm to 1:30 pm
2:00 pm to 3:00 pm	3:30 pm to 4:30 pm
5:00 pm to 6:00 pm	6:30 pm to 7:30 pm

This information is also posted where the paved road turns to gravel 1.3 km beyond Snaring Campground. To be safe, check this sign or at the Park Visitor Centre in Jasper to make sure the times have not been altered.

While this road can be navigated by most any vehicle, it is narrow and rocky in spots. Extreme caution should be exercised. You should adhere strictly to the listed times, but be wary on blind corners—someone else might not be following the schedule. During periods of heavy rainfall, check with the Park Visitor Centre concerning conditions, since muddy sections and high water at the Corral Creek crossing could cause problems for vehicles with low clearance. No trailers are permitted on the road.

Access: Follow the Yellowhead Highway (Hwy 16) to the Snaring Campground junction, 9 km east of the town of Jasper's eastern exit. Follow this road 6.3 km, past Snaring Campground and across the Snaring River bridge, to where the paved road ends and the gravel Celestine Lake Road branches left. The Celestine Lake Road continues along the west side of the Athabasca Valley, past the Ewan Moberly Homestead historic site and the Snaring Patrol Cabin, to the one-way access pull-out at 13.5 km (all distances from Highway 16).

Continuing on the one-way section beyond the access sign, the road crosses the wooden Corral Creek sluiceway and begins to climb along the west side of the valley. Vine Creek is crossed at km 15.0 and a gated branch road to Devona Flats is passed at km 23.5. After crossing over two high points of land, the road descends to a locked access gate and parking area at km 27.0.

127 Devona Lookout

Celestine Lake Road to Celestine Lake—6.8 km (4.2 mi)
Celestine Lake Road to Devona Lookout—9.4 km (5.8 mi)

Day trip or backpack

Allow 2.5 to 3 hours to lookout site

Elevation gain: 325 m (1,070 ft)

Maximum elevation: 1405 m (4,610 ft)

Maps: Snaring 83 E/1

Access: Drive the Celestine Lake Road to the parking area at road's end—as described in the *Celestine Lake Road* introduction. The hike begins on the roadbed beyond the access barriers.

0.0—Trailhead (1080 m).
    N53°09.490' W118°02.281'

  —Follow roadbed downhill.

0.5—Snake Indian River bridge.

  —Moderate uphill on roadbed.

5.2—Junction. *North Boundary Trail* ahead. Celestine Lake and Devona Lookout right.

6.5—Princess Lake.

6.8—Celestine Lake and Campground.

  —Moderate, steady uphill on old fire road.

8.7—Road crests open ridge.

9.4—Devona Lookout site (1405 m).

The hike to Devona Lookout is a long but rewarding day trip from the end of the Celestine Lake Road. In addition to passing two pretty lakes, Princess and Celestine, the old lookout site at the end of the trail overlooks a broad swath of the Athabasca Valley stretching from near Jasper townsite to the hills beyond the park's eastern boundary. But despite its scenic rewards, you will likely find the drive to the trailhead more exciting than the hike itself.

Before the Snake Indian River bridge was decommissioned in 1993, you could drive 5 km farther on the Celestine Lake Road than you can today. That left a short walk to Princess and Celestine Lakes, and the hike to Devona Lookout could be completed in a half-day. Now the trip to the lakes and the lookout site is a full day from the end of the road.

Since mountain bikes are permitted on this section of the *North Boundary Trail*, time for the trip can be shortened by biking the first 5.2 km to the Celestine Lake-Devona Lookout junction (a bit of a grunt on the way up; a nice brisk ride down). Or you can backpack to Celestine Lake Campground and hike to the lookout from there.

From the parking area at the end of the Celestine Lake Road, you descend immediately to an iron bridge across the Snake Indian River. (Erosion of the bridge foundation on the far side caused its closure to vehicles.) From the bridge there is a short, moderately steep uphill along the northeast side of the canyon. However, grades soon moderate as the road turns northwest and climbs steadily for another 4 km to the junction where the Celestine Lake-Devona Lookout fire road turns right from the North Boundary Trail.

From the road split, it is a short, easy walk through the forest to Princess and Celestine Lakes. Both lie off the trail to the

Roche Miette and the Athabasca Valley from Devona Lookout

left and are substantial lakes surrounded by spruce forest and with views of the Beaver Bluffs and Bosche Range to the north. Both have long been popular with fishermen, though somewhat less so since the road closure at Snake Indian bridge.

The trail turns southeast beyond Celestine Lake. Once upon a time it was a broad track used to service the Devona Fire Lookout, but the forest has encroached from both sides to create a narrow path climbing gradually along the ridge leading to the lookout site. At km 8.7 it breaks out of the forest onto the crest of the ridge, where you get your first views of the Athabasca Valley.

The grassy, south-facing slopes are typical of the montane life zone—covered with the blooms of western wood lilies, Indian paintbrush, camus lilies and purple vetch from mid-June through mid-July, and brown-eyed Susans, harebells and purple asters in late July and August.

At km 9.4 you reach the site of the Devona Lookout—a fire tower that was dismantled in the mid-1980s. Continue another 150 m to the end of the ridge for your best views of the Athabasca Valley.

Jasper Lake lies directly beneath the viewpoint, and the distinctively shaped Pyramid Mountain is seen off to the south near the town of Jasper. To the northeast the Athabasca River flows through the last of the Front Ranges into the forested foothills beyond the park's eastern boundary.

By far the most impressive mountain is Roche Miette, rising across the valley beyond Jasper Lake. The mountain is composed of the massive, cliff-forming Palliser limestone—an Upper Devonian formation. As an early traveller on the Athabasca Trail recounted, Miette's Rock "derives its appellation from a French voyageur, who climbed its summit and sat smoking his pipe with his legs hanging over the fearful abyss."

128 North Boundary Trail

Celestine Lake Road to Berg Lake Parking Lot—179.4 km (111.5 mi)

Backpack

Allow 7 to 14 days

Maximum elevation: 2020 m (6,625 ft)

Minimum elevation: 850 m (2,790 ft)

Maps: Snaring River 83 E/1
       Rock Lake 83 E/8
       Blue Creek 83 E/7
       Twintree Lake 83 E/6
       Mount Robson 83 E/3

Access: Westbound hikers follow the Celestine Lake Road to the parking area at road's end—as described in the *Celestine Lake Road* introduction. Eastbound hikers start from the *Berg Lake* trailhead in Mount Robson Provincial Park.

0.0— Celestine Lake Road trailhead (1080 m).
      N53°09.490' W118°02.281'

0.5— Snake Indian River bridge.

5.2— Junction. Celestine Lake and *Devona Lookout* right.

17.3— Shalebanks Campground.

25.0— Seldom Inn Campground.

26.5— Snake Indian Falls (left 200 m).

27.3— Junction. Trail branches right from road. Seldom Inn Horse Campground left (200 m).

35.6— Horseshoe Campground.

37.4— Willow Creek Junction (1355 m). *Willow Creek* trail right to Rock Lake trailhead (13.9 km). Stay left.

37.9— Willow Creek Campground (hiker-horse).

43.5— Mud Creek Junction. Rock Creek trail right.

46.5— Deer Creek Junction (1395 m). Little Heaven, *McLaren Pass* and *Glacier Pass* right.

46.9— Deer Creek.

49.7— Junction. Welbourne Falls left 0.4 km.

50.6— Welbourne Campground and Patrol Cabin.

55.3— Milk Creek.

In the summer of 1910, a party of European alpinists exploring the slopes of Mount Robson heard of an old trail leading down the Smoky River, over a high pass and eastward along the Snake Indian River to the Athabasca Valley. Thinking the route might offer a quick and interesting exit from the mountains, they set off under the guidance of outfitter John Yates and completed the first recorded traverse of today's North Boundary Trail.

The North Boundary Trail remains one of the more popular long-distance trails in the Rockies. Except for Mount Robson and a brief interval on Snake Indian Pass, the trail does not offer spectacular alpine scenery. Yet, this trail across the northern end of Jasper Park possesses its own unique and subdued brand of beauty—a wilderness of broad valleys and distant views that is inhabited by moose, caribou, bear and wolves.

Though once known as the 100-Mile North Boundary Trail, we calculate today's distance at 111.5 miles, or 179.4 km (measured by trail wheel with adjustments for more recent alterations). The traditional eastern trailhead for this lengthy trek is the end of the Celestine Lake Road, approximately 36 km north of the town of Jasper, while the western terminus is Mount Robson's Berg Lake trailhead.

You can shorten the trip by hiking the 13.9-km Willow Creek trail (see *Willow Creek*) from Rock Lake-Solomon Creek Wildland Park on Jasper's northeast boundary to its intersection with the traditional route at km 37.4. This option may be the most popular way to start or finish the North Boundary Trail since it saves a day or more of rather tedious hiking in the lower Snake Indian Valley. However, it misses Snake Indian Falls, one of the trail's highlights. Regardless of which route you use for your eastern terminus, the hiking options in such a

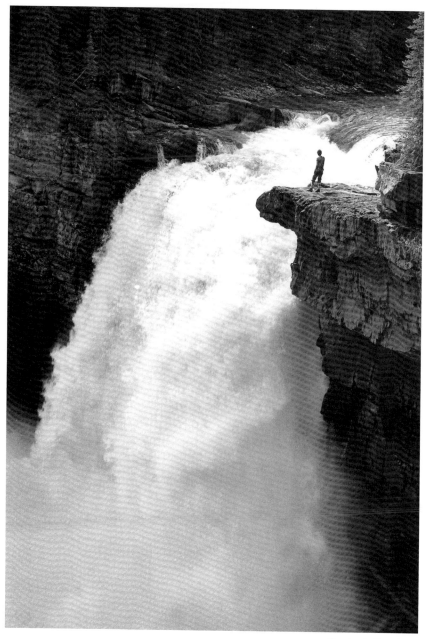

Snake Indian Falls

57.4— Nellie Lake.

61.6— Blue Creek Patrol Cabin.

62.5— Blue Creek Campground.

62.8— Blue Creek Junction (1495 m).
Blue Creek and McLaren Pass right.

63.0— Ford of Blue Creek required
(difficult early in the season).

74.8— Three Slides Patrol Cabin.

77.5— Three Slides Campground.

85.7— Hoodoo Patrol Cabin (left 200 m).

90.2— Oatmeal Camp Campground.

96.5— Snake Indian Pass (2020 m).

102.4— Byng Campground.

102.8— Byng Patrol Cabin.

110.7— Twintree Lake (1558 m).

111.9— Twintree Patrol Cabin.

113.6— Twintree Campground.

115.8— Twintree Creek bridge.

122.9— Donaldson Creek Campground.

125.5— Smoky River bridge.

126.0— Smoky River Junction (1385 m).
Stay left.

126.4— Lower Smoky Patrol Cabin.

130.1— Chown Creek Campground and
bridge. Bess Pass trail right.

137.2— Wolverine Patrol Cabin.

138.3— Carcajou Creek.

141.2— Wolverine Campground.

151.3— Junction. *Moose Pass* trail left.

153.7— Adolphus Patrol Cabin.

154.1— Adolphus Campground.

155.9— Adolphus Lake.

156.7— Robson Pass (1652 m). Jasper-
Mount Robson Park boundary.
Connects with *Berg Lake* trail at
km 22.7.

179.4— Berg Lake trailhead (850 m).
N53°03.047' W119°12.870'

vast region are endless. Many backpackers only penetrate this wilderness for a day or two before retracing their steps. Strong cyclists can travel to Snake Indian Falls and back in a day, while other cyclists tackle the full day-trip from the Rock Lake trailhead to the Celestine Lake Road (biking is permitted on the lower Snake Indian River and Willow Creek trails.) Others use the trail to reach destinations such as McLaren Pass, Glacier Pass, Blue Creek, or the Willmore Wilderness Park. But to most the attraction lies in traversing the entire trail from end to end.

While some hike the North Boundary from west-to-east, our preference is from east-to-west. Travelling in this direction provides a gradual improvement in scenery day by day, culminating at spectacular Mount Robson. Elevation gain is spread out over many kilometres on the east-to-west option and is hardly noticeable, whereas eastbound travellers face two long, gruelling climbs on the first half of their trip and an uninspiring 27-km fire road at the end.

Going east-to-west will require that you plan your trip carefully. Unless you hike from Adolphus Lake Campground (just east of Robson Pass) to the Berg Lake trailhead in a day, you will have to reserve campsites on the popular Berg Lake trail before you begin your trek. (See *Berg Lake*, Mount Robson Park chapter.)

Celestine Lake Road Gate to Willow Creek Junction—37.4 km. Starting from the access gate on the Celestine Lake Road, you follow roadbed downhill to an iron bridge over the Snake Indian River. For the next 27 km this well-graded road follows upstream along the northeast side of the river. Travel is rather uninspiring along this section except for Snake Indian Falls—one of the most impressive and photogenic waterfalls in the Rockies.

Just beyond the falls, the road splits. Stay on the more substantial roadbed leading left and, a short distance beyond, follow the trail branching right.

At km 34 the trail runs out into broad

Upright Mountain from Three Slides

meadows as it nears the point where the Snake Indian Valley bends to the west and Willow Creek flows in from the north. The country surrounding this junction is quite sublime, with expansive views up-valley and north to Daybreak Peak.

Willow Creek Junction to Blue Creek Junction—25.9 km. At km 37.4 the Willow Creek trail intersects from the north. From this junction, the North Boundary Trail turns westward, passes Willow Creek Campground, and begins its long journey toward the Great Divide. The country remains pleasant and open as the trail winds through stands of aspen and lodgepole pine and skirts meadows covered with dwarf birch, willow and shrubby cinquefoil.

Near the Deer Creek–Little Heaven trail junction (see *Glacier Pass*), you travel through windfall created by a storm that swept this section of the valley in 1978. The tornado-like winds, which struck in the early spring, blew due east and uprooted all but the youngest and slimmest lodgepole pines. Trees were hurled into parallel piles like giant jackstraws, cutting a swath approximately 3-km long and 300-m wide.

The valley narrows as you approach the rugged peaks forming the gateway to Blue Creek and the upper Snake Indian Valley. At km 57.4 the trail passes beside Nellie Lake, and the reflection of Mount Simla in this pretty backwater provides the most inspiring view along this section. From here on there is a true sense of having entered the mountains.

Blue Creek is a significant landmark: it serves as the gateway to some very remote and scenic country on the park's northern boundary; for the westbound hiker, it is the beginning of more strenuous mountain travel; and like much of the upper Snake Indian Valley, it is an area that can be plagued with mosquitoes when the conditions are right.

Blue Creek Junction to Snake Indian Pass—33.2 km. The trail continues west from Blue Creek Campground and, over the next kilometre, passes the Blue Creek trail junction and then crosses Blue Creek via an unbridged crossing that can be difficult until late in the season (see *Blue Creek*).

The 6-km stretch beyond Blue Creek is quite scenic, with frequent open views across the Snake Indian River and its marshy, lake-dotted overflow plain.

At Three Slides Campground the first major glacier of the trip is seen on the slopes of Upright Mountain, rising at the head of the valley to the south. (Don't be misled into believing it is Mount Robson; you've got a long way to go before you reach that prize.)

At km 85.7 you pass the Hoodoo Patrol Cabin and begin the climb to Snake Indian Pass. The moderate but steady uphill lifts you above treeline at km 92, where you receive your first unobstructed views ahead to the narrow gap of the pass.

Snake Indian Pass (2020 m) is set in rolling alpine meadows and contained by low, gentle ridges. Steeply tilted slabs of limestone form the most prominent peaks to the north—Snake Indian and Monte Cristo Mountains.

Snake Indian Pass to Smoky River Junction—29.5 km. West of the pass the trail descends steadily for 6 km to Byng Campground. The campground is not particularly attractive, but it is a site where many travellers end up after crossing Snake Indian Pass—a boon to local porcupines who delight in passing the night chewing on boots, pack straps and other backpacking paraphernalia.

The descent continues to the shores of Twintree Lake—the largest lake on the North Boundary. The lake received its name in 1910, when John Yates guided his party up Twintree Creek and discovered "a very beautiful lake in our side valley with two infinitesimal islands, on each of which was one fir tree." Meltwater from glaciers on Swoda Mountain and Calumet Peak flow into the lake from the south, filling its waters with glacial silt.

From the lake you continue down Twintree Creek for a short distance before crossing it and climbing over the north end of Twintree Mountain (aka Vimy Ridge). Beyond the forested crest of this ridge, you make a stiff 300-m descent over the next 8 km to the Smoky River bridge. It is a rocky, rooty and often boggy track—easily the toughest section on the entire trip.

Smoky River Junction to Robson Pass—30.7 km. You enter a new world once you reach the Smoky River—a region of rocky river flats and rugged, glacier-topped mountains. The valley of Chown Creek, running away to the west at km 130, is particularly scenic, dominated by the grey ramparts of 3216-m Mount Bess.

The climb up the Smoky is relatively gradual, though the track is often rough and rocky. Scenery continues to improve and, at km 144, the trail passes beneath the Mural Glacier and begins a steady, gradual ascent toward Robson Pass.

Weather permitting, your first close-up view of Mount Robson is gained from the open meadow below Adolphus Lake. The lake lies about 1.5 km into the trees beyond this willow-covered meadow, but its western shore opens out onto the broad flats of Robson Pass, where the monarch of the Rockies towers in all its majesty.

Robson Pass to Berg Lake trailhead—22.7 km. When you reach the Mount Robson Park boundary on Robson Pass, you have returned to civilization. Within the space of a few kilometres you pass from a relatively peaceful and primitive landscape into one of the busiest backcountry areas in the mountain parks. However, when the weather cooperates, the scenery is exceptional. (For a detailed description of this final stretch, see *Berg Lake* in the Mount Robson Park chapter.)

North Boundary Options. While the North Boundary Trail as described here is the itinerary of choice for most backpackers, trails branching from the route allow for a great variety of trips. Some of these options are described over the following pages. (See *Willow Creek, Glacier Pass-McLaren Pass, Blue Creek* and *Moose Pass*.)

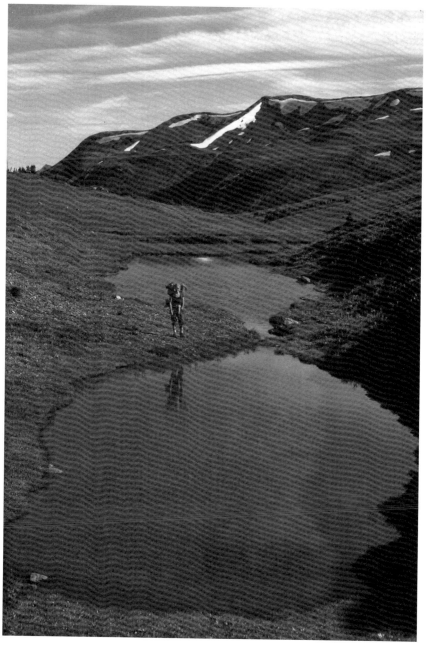

Snake Indian Pass

129 Willow Creek

Rock Lake to North Boundary Trail—13.9 km (8.6 mi)

Backpack
Allow 4 hours one way
Elevation loss: 140 m (450 ft)
Maximum elevation: 1495 m (4,900 ft)
Maps: Rock Lake 83 E/8

Access: Follow the Yellowhead Highway (Hwy. 16) east from Jasper Park East Gate 20 km (12.5 mi) to the junction with Highway 40 (4 km west of Hinton). Follow Highway 40 north 40 km (25 mi) to the Rock Lake Road junction. Turn left and follow the Rock Lake Road 2 km (1.2 mi) to a junction beyond Moberly Creek bridge. Turn left and continue on the most defined road for 27 km (16.5 mi) to Rock Lake-Solomon Creek Wildland Park, keeping right at major intersections. Keep right at the campground entrance and subsequent intersections, climbing around and above the north side of Rock Lake for 4.3 km (2.7 mi) to road's end at an access gate and parking area at the Wilmore Wilderness Park boundary.

0.0— Trailhead (1495 m).
N53°27.579' W118°17.591'

— Follow roadbed west.

1.8— Junction. Willow Creek trail branches left from road.

— Gradual descent through lodgepole pine forest.

4.8— Willmore-Jasper Park boundary.

6.5— Rock Creek (double-channel ford).

8.5— Junction. Wolf Pass left.

— Trail follows open valley and crosses boggy willow flats.

12.0— Willow Creek Patrol Cabin.

13.9— Junction (1355 m). Intersection with *North Boundary Trail* at km 37.4.

The Willow Creek trail is an important access route into Jasper Park's North Boundary country. As an optional starting point for the North Boundary Trail, it saves 24 km on the trek to Mount Robson and a lot of tedious fire road walking. It is also the best access trail for loop trips north from the North Boundary Trail. The trail's only disadvantages are the lengthy drive to the Rock Lake trailhead and the Rock Creek ford.

From the access gate beyond Rock Lake, hike along the old road into Willmore Wilderness Park. Branch left from the road at km 1.8 and follow trail downhill through a fire-succession forest of lodgepole pine.

Shortly after crossing into Jasper Park, you reach Rock Creek, where there are two channels to cross. Since maintaining bridges here is difficult, expect a double ford (usually ankle-deep, but thigh-deep during high run-off).

South of Rock Creek, the trail is mostly flat and sometimes boggy as it crosses open willow meadows. It passes through the grounds of the Willow Creek Patrol Cabin at km 12.0 and, 2 km beyond, intersects the North Boundary Trail near the Willow Creek Campground (see *North Boundary Trail*, km 37.4).

Mountain biking is permitted on the Willow Creek trail and the first 37.4 km of the North Boundary Trail to the end of the Celestine Lake Road.

Wolf Pass. This 12 km trail branches east from the Willow Creek trail 2 km south of Rock Creek crossing. It skirts the north end of the Boshe Range, then turns southeast and ascends a long forested valley to the summit of Wolf Pass. Though there is a campground just north of the pass, this rough track is of limited interest for hikers. It is mainly used by horse parties and Parks Canada patrols.

Land above 2000 metres

130 Glacier Pass–McLaren Pass

North Boundary Trail to Glacier Pass—29.4 km (18.3 mi)
North Boundary Trail to McLaren Pass—19.7 km (12.2 mi)

Backpack

Allow 2 days to Glacier Pass

Elevation gain: 705 m (2,300 ft)

Maximum elevation: 2100 m (6,900 ft)

Maps: Rock Lake 83 E/8
Blue Creek 83 E/7

Access: Follow the *North Boundary Trail* to
Deer Creek Junction at km 46.5 (0.4 km east
of Deer Creek).

0.0— Deer Creek Junction (1395 m).

5.0— Ascent of Deer Creek canyon begins.

8.8— Junction. Rock Creek via lower
Mowitch Creek right.

8.9— Junction. Little Heaven Campground.
McLaren Pass left 10.8 km.

9.0— Little Heaven Patrol Cabin (1690 m).

11.0— Mowitch Creek fords (3) next 200 m
(calf to knee deep).

— Trail ascends north side of Mowitch
Creek.

19.5— Spruce Tree Campground.

20.3— Junction. Desolation Pass right.

22.6— Vega Patrol Cabin.

24.6— Glacier Pass Campground.

27.4— Trail bends north and begins final
ascent to pass.

29.4— Glacier Pass (2100 m). Jasper-
Willmore Wilderness Park boundary.

The Glacier Pass trail takes you to spectacular alpine meadows and magnificent wilderness scenery on Jasper Park's boundary with the Willmore Wilderness Park. However, the approach is long, sometimes overgrown and confusing, and there are unbridged stream crossings. Most backpackers will want to use this trail to reach McLaren Pass—a more user-friendly trail to an equally high and scenic alpine pass, and one that doesn't require nearly so much time or trouble.

Glacier Pass. The trip to Glacier Pass is for experienced wilderness travellers who don't mind sloshing across streams and beating through willow brush. Arm yourself with current 1:50,000 topo maps, but realize that these maps do not always represent trails accurately.

The trail branches northwest from the North Boundary Trail at km 46.5 and runs north of Deer Creek for 5 km to the mouth of Deer Creek canyon. You climb over 150 m in the canyon before emerging into the meadows of Little Heaven (traditionally, a heavenly pasture for horses). Little Heaven Patrol Cabin is on a promontory overlooking this pastoral scene, and the hiker campground and junction for the McLaren Pass trail are reached 100 m before the cabin.

The Glacier Pass trail exits the meadows 2 km north of the patrol cabin and crosses to the north side of Mowitch Creek. It makes two more fords over and back across the creek in rapid succession, or you can avoid these by staying on the north side and bushwhacking upstream for 200 m. (Okay, you're boots are already wet, so why bushwhack?)

The trail remains on the north side of Mowitch Creek as it follows it upstream beneath the Starlight Range. Expect boggy, overgrown sections over the next 16 km, until you turn north and make the final ascent to Glacier Pass.

© Mike McReynolds

Glacier Pass

A small lake on the grassy summit is a good spot to relax and scan the open slopes for bighorn sheep and caribou. It's also a good place to contemplate your next move, which may be a circuit around the north end of the Ancient Wall to the Blue Creek valley. (See *Blue Creek.*)

McLaren Pass. This is the most attractive and least demanding excursion north from the Snake Indian Valley. A broad alpine meadow crowns McLaren Pass, and views to the southwest are exceptional—including the Snake Indian Valley, the glaciated summit of Upright Mountain, and Mount Robson, 45 km in the distance.

You can use McLaren Pass as an optional and more scenic alternative to the North Boundary Trail between Deer Creek and Blue Creek—a detour that only adds 10.6 km to your trip.

The pass is also a reasonable objective from the Willow Creek trailhead. Distance to the pass via Willow Creek, the North Boundary Trail and Deer Creek is 43 km. From there you can complete a loop by descending to Blue Creek and

returning east along the North Boundary Trail.

The trail branches west from the Glacier Pass trail at Little Heaven Campground and, after a brief descent, joins Deer Creek and follows it upstream. There are crossings of Deer Creek and other streams along this 3-km section of valley, which may or may not be bridged (reasonable fords if not).

Around km 6.5, the trail branches due west from Deer Creek and, after a short, steady ascent, turns south and climbs through open meadows to reach the 2120-m pass at km 10.8. Vertical ascent from Deer Creek to the pass is 350 m.

South of the pass the trail drops steeply for just over 3 km to an intersection with the Blue Creek trail. While you can turn right and ascend Blue Creek from this junction, you'll likely turn left and follow the trail downstream 4.5 km to the North Boundary Trail near the Blue Creek Campground. (See *North Boundary Trail*, km 62.8.)

131 Blue Creek

North Boundary Trail to Azure Lake—33.0 km (20.5 mi)

Backpack

Allow 2 to 3 days to Azure Lake

Elevation gain: 470 m (1,550 ft)

Maximum elevation: 1965 m (6,450 ft)

Maps: Blue Creek 83 E/7
Twintree Lake 83 E/6

Access: Follow the *North Boundary Trail* to the junction with the Blue Creek trail at km 62.8.

0.0— Blue Creek Junction (1495 m).

— Trail climbs gradually on northeast side of Blue Creek.

4.0— Junction. *McLaren Pass* right 3.2 km. Stay left.*

— Trail enters series of willow meadows.

11.9— Ancient Wall horse campground.

14.7— Topaz Patrol Cabin.

16.0— Topaz Campground.

21.1— Natural Arch Horse Campground.

22.7— Natural Arch viewpoint.

23.8— Caribou Inn Campground.

— Short, steep climb to upper meadows. Trail becomes sketchy.

33.0— Azure Lake (1965 m).

— Route to Hardscrabble Pass climbs steeply along slopes north of lake.

35.0— Park boundary.*

36.0— Hardscrabble Pass (2270 m).*

*distances approximate

Blue Creek is one of the most scenic side trips from the North Boundary Trail. Starting near the Blue Creek river crossing, the trail runs northwest up the 33-km valley to Azure Lake on the Jasper Park-Willmore Wilderness boundary. Along the way you can visit Topaz Lake and the Caribou Lakes—noted for their fine scenery and fishing. Azure Lake is set in open meadows astride the park boundary, and an hour or so beyond is the rocky summit of Hardscrabble Pass.

While you can include Blue Creek in your North Boundary Trail itinerary, this adds three or four days to an already long journey. It is more attractive as a destination in itself. The round trip to the Azure Lake-Hardscabble Pass environs from the Willow Creek trailhead is 146 km—substantially less than hiking the North Boundary Trail end-to-end and, some would say, more rewarding.

The first section of trail from Blue Creek Junction runs through forest on the northeast side of the creek, passing the junction for McLaren Pass around the 4-km mark. (See *Glacier Pass-McLaren Pass*.) A few kilometres further along, you enter extensive meadows, which dominate the valley for the remainder of the trip.

At Topaz Campground, you can make a 1.7-km side trip to Topaz Lake—a 3-km-long lake set beneath the ramparts of Monte Cristo and Snake Indian Mountains. To reach the lake, continue beyond the campground on the main trail approximately 0.4 km and ford Blue Creek. There is no defined trail on the other side, but you can backtrack downstream and pick-up occasional horse tracks and blazes leading over a rise to the lake.

As you continue up Blue Creek, the sawtoothed limestone peaks of The Ancient Wall march away to the northwest ahead of you. Just before Caribou Inn

Hardscrabble Pass

Campground, you arrive at a viewpoint for the Natural Arch—a huge, hollowed-out up-fold in the wall beneath the summit of Mount Perce.

From Caribou Inn Campground you can side-trip to Caribou Lakes, which are similar in setting to Topaz Lake. Cross the bridge over Blue Creek to Caribou Inn Patrol Cabin and pick-up the rough, often-vague, 2.5-km track to the lower lake.

If you are planning on returning down Blue Creek, you may want to camp at Caribou Inn and complete the journey to Azure Lake and Hardscrabble Pass as a day hike. The trail is sketchy in the upper valley, but since the meadows are dry and open, the walk to Azure Lake is quite straightforward and pleasant.

Shortly before arriving at the east end of the lake, find your own route to Hardscrabble Pass by angling up along the open grassy meadows on the north side of the valley. Then traverse a series of rock ledges around the west end of Sunset Peak to this broad alpine summit with its numerous small lakes.

Glacier Pass. By continuing into the Willmore's Sulphur Valley from Hardscrabble Pass (good trail reappears north of the pass), you can reach the South Sulphur River and return to Jasper Park by following it upstream to Glacier Pass. (Horse trails are fairly well defined on this route, but one 8-km section on the South Sulphur River requires you to ford the river over 20 times.)

Though reserved for experienced wilderness backpackers, the Blue Creek-Glacier Pass-Little Heaven loop is one of the most rewarding trips along Jasper's northern boundary. (See *Glacier Pass-McLaren Pass*.)

132 Moose Pass

North Boundary Trail to Moose Pass—9.5 km (5.9 mi)

Backpack

Allow 3 hours one way

Elevation gain: 410 m (1,350 ft)

Maximum elevation: 2025 m (6,650 ft)

Maps: Mount Robson 83 E/3

Access: Follow the *North Boundary Trail* to the junction with the Moose Pass trail at km 151.3 (2.8 km north of Adolphus Campground).

0.0—Moose Pass Junction (1615 m).

0.1—Smoky River bridge.

0.4—Yates Torrent bridge. Junction. Coleman Glacier trail right. Moose Pass stay left.

  —Trail climbs over forested ridge.

3.5—Calumet Creek.

  —Follow along south side of creek.

6.5—Calumet Campground.

  —Steady climb to open meadows.

9.5—Moose Pass (2025 m). Intersection with *Moose River* trail at km 48.9 (see Mount Robson chapter).

Moose Pass is the most attractive side-trip from the North Boundary Trail. Its vast wildflower meadows are renowned as some of the best in the Rockies, and views of heavily-glaciated mountains along the approach are an inspiring bonus.

While the pass can be hiked as a side-trip from the North Boundary Trail, it is also an attractive extension from Berg Lake in Robson Park (from Berg Lake, you can pack to Calumet Campground and then day-trip to the pass). You can also cross the pass and descend the Moose River to the Yellowhead Highway, but this is a tough trek reserved for experienced wilderness travellers. (See *Moose River*, Robson Park.)

From the North Boundary Trail junction, the Moose Pass trail immediately crosses the creek-sized Smoky River on a bridge. The turbulent, silt-choked Yates Torrent, fed by nearby Coleman Glacier, is just beyond (look for a bridge 300 m upstream from the horse ford, and consider abandoning the trip at this dangerous stream if the bridge is not in place).

After these crossings, the trail climbs eastward over a forested ridge to Calumet Creek. Just over 3 km beyond Yates Torrent, you emerge onto flowery alluvial flats and continue upstream beside Calumet Creek. (Expect overgrown trail with muddy stretches all the way to Calumet Campground.)

Calumet Campground is a good base for a day trip to the pass. As you continue up-valley from the campground, you gradually emerge into lush meadows with fine views of Calumet Peak and Glacier.

You reach the summit of the pass at km 9.5. Even if you are not backpacking on through, it is worth exploring 3 or 4 km farther along the rocky corridor to a pair of small lakes overlooking the upper Moose Valley.

133 Miette River

Decoigne Road to Miette Lake—24.2 km (15.0 mi)*

Backpack

Allow 7 to 8 hours to Miette Lake

Elevation gain: 930 m (3,050 ft)

Maximum elevation: 2050 m (6,725 ft)

Maps: Jasper 83 D/16
       Rainbow 83 D/15
       Resplendent Creek 83 E/2

Access: Follow the Yellowhead Highway (Hwy. 16) to Parks Canada's Decoigne Station access road, 21 km (13 mi) west of the town of Jasper and 0.2 km east of Jasper Park West Gate. Follow the access road north across railway tracks and Miette River bridge 0.4 km to a T-intersection. Continue left 0.5 km, past the Parks Canada station entrance, to the access gate and parking area.

0.0— Trailhead (1120 m).
     N52°53.154' W118°23.852'
     — Trail follows roadbed due west.
4.4— Junction. Miette trail branches right.
     — Ascent along east side of Miette Valley.
14.0— Rink Cabin site.
19.5— Mt Bridgland tributary ford (knee-deep).
22.0— Miette Lake Campground.
     — Trail crosses Miette twice (knee-deep).
24.0— Junction. Miette Lake and campsite right 150 m. Centre Pass ahead.
     — Trail fords Miette River to west bank. Steady climb to Centre Pass. Trail disappears in meadows.
26.0— Centre Pass (2050 m).
     — Defined track re-emerges west of pass and contours high above Grant Brook.
34.0— Grant Pass (1935 m).
     — Descent to Snaring River headwaters.
36.8— Colonel Pass Campground.
37.0— Colonel Pass (1890 m).
     — Descend north side of Colonel Creek through burn.
43.5— Moose River ford. Junction (1395 m). Intersection with *Moose River* trail at km 24.7 (see Robson Park chapter).
*all distances approximate after 4.4 km.

(Trail is not shown on maps in this book.)

The Miette River trail runs northwest along Jasper Park's west boundary from near Jasper Park West Gate to Miette Lake and Centre Pass. While the country is wild and scenic at the lake and pass, the trail is long and muddy, and there are several fords in the upper valley.

Follow the track of an abandoned railway roadbed along the north side of the Miette River marshes for 4.4 km. The Miette River trail branches right from the roadbed 100 m before it ends where a railway bridge once spanned the river.

The trail up-valley climbs to the east, then rolls through forest. Views are limited and travel is tedious, particularly where the trail is overgrown with alder. The site of the old Rink Warden Cabin is passed at km 14, and the clearing makes a good campsite.

After fording a tributary descending from between Mounts Bridgland and Moren, the horse trail crosses and re-crosses the Miette (the hikers' trail stays on the east side).

Near km 22, you reach Miette Lake Campground, approximately 2 km below the lake. You have to ford the Miette twice before you reach the short side trail to a campsite overlooking Miette Lake's southern shore.

Immediately beyond the junction, slosh across the Miette one last time, then climb westward into the Centre Pass meadows. The route crosses an open slope north of the true summit.

Though the trail disappears on the pass, a defined track reappears high on the west side (near bluffs) and leads onward to Grant Pass and Colonel Pass.

The trail (route) descends into Robson Park along Colonel Creek, passing through the tumbled remains of a 1998 forest fire, to a ford of the Moose River and an intersection with the *Moose River* trail (see Mount Robson Park).

Yoho National Park

Yoho National Park lies on the western slope of the Great Divide in British Columbia, bordered by Banff Park on the east and Kootenay Park on the south. Covering 1310-sq km of rugged mountain terrain, it is the smallest of the four contiguous national parks.

Yoho's 400-km trail system extends into nearly every corner of the park. While a few trails lead to remote areas, Yoho is best known as a day hiker's park. Most of this activity occurs in three areas—Lake O'Hara, the Yoho Valley and the Emerald Lake basin. The overwhelming popularity of these areas is the result of spectacular terrain coupled with excellent trail systems.

The Trans-Canada Highway (Hwy 1) runs through the centre of the park, sharing its main valley with the Kicking Horse River and the Canadian Pacific Railway. The highway provides access to a number of short, scenic hikes, the most popular being Sherbrooke Lake, Paget Lookout and Wapta Falls. Longer but infrequently-travelled trails ascend the Amiskwi, Otterhead, Ottertail and Ice River Valleys.

Trails to the world famous Burgess Shale and Mt. Stephen fossil beds are closed to independent hikers; these sites can only be visited on guided interpretive walks with Parks Canada or the Burgess Shale Geoscience Foundation (see *Sources—Guided walks*.) Additionally, there are two short interpretive walks from the Kicking Horse Campground, Centennial Trail and Walk-in-the-Past (not described in this book).

Backpackers must obtain a Wilderness Pass at the Park Visitor Centre before setting out on any overnight trip. Since campgrounds have quotas, popular areas are often filled during the peak season. If you haven't reserved in advance, keep several options in mind. (There are no designated campgrounds in the Amiskwi, Otterhead and Ice River Valleys, where random camping is allowed.)

Information and services. The Park Visitor Centre is beside the Trans-Canada Highway at the entrance to the village of Field. It provides a wide range of information on the park, including current trail reports, weather forecasts, schedules for interpretive programs and guided walks, and access information for Lake O'Hara. The visitor centre also houses a park "Friends" retail outlet, which sells books, maps and other park-oriented souvenirs. (See *Sources—Parks information*.)

The most central of the park's four road-accessible campgrounds are Monarch and Kicking Horse Campgrounds, located side-by-side 5 km east of Field on the Yoho Valley Road. Hoodoo Creek and Chancellor Peak Campgrounds are along the Trans-Canada Highway not far from the park's west boundary. Additionally, the Takakkaw Falls Campground at the north end of the Yoho Valley Road provides 35 walk-in sites for those willing to ferry their gear 300 m from the parking area.

The village of Field is the park's only service centre, but those services are limited to a post office, a pottery studio, a couple of restaurants, a lodge, a hostel and 20 or so guest houses. Additionally, there is a service station-general store at the intersection of the village access road and the Trans-Canada Highway. The Yoho National Park administration office is in the village, as is the office for the Burgess Shale Geoscience Foundation.

Access: The only highway access to Yoho Park is the Trans-Canada Highway (Hwy 1). The nearest towns east of Field are Lake Louise (27 km) and Banff (84 km) in Alberta; Golden, B.C. lies 57 km to the west. The nearest international airport is in Calgary, Alberta, 210 km to the east.

While there is no formal bus depot in the park, the Field intersection beside the Park Visitor Centre is a recognized flag stop for east and westbound Greyhound buses.

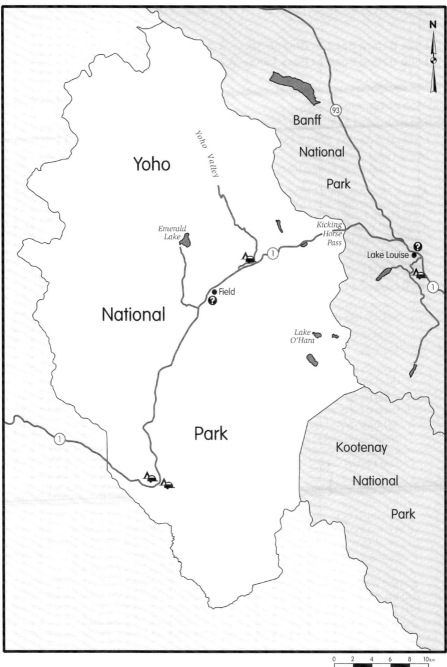

136 Paget Lookout

Wapta Lake Picnic Area to Paget Lookout—3.5 km (2.2 mi)

Half-day trip

Allow 1 to 2 hours one way

Elevation gain: 520 m (1,700 ft)

Maximum elevation: 2135 m (7,000 ft)

Maps: Lake Louise 82 N/8
      Lake Louise & Yoho (Gem Trek)

Access: Follow the Trans-Canada Highway to the Wapta Lake Picnic Area, 5.5 km (3.5 mi) west of the Alberta-B.C. border and 11 km (7 mi) east of Field, B.C. The unsigned picnic area is on the north side of the highway just west of Wapta Lake. The trailhead is upslope from the shelter at the far end of the picnic area.

0.0— Trailhead (1615 m).
     N51°26.424' W116°21.317'

0.2— Junction. Trail intersects from right. Switchback to left.

— Steady uphill through forest.

1.4— Junction. *Sherbrooke Lake* ahead 1.7 km. Paget Lookout right.

— Steady, steep ascent.

3.5— Paget Lookout (2135 m).

The lookout cabin high on the side of Paget Peak hasn't been manned for many years, but anyone who visits the site will realize why it was considered a crucial vantage point when fire lookouts were being built throughout the mountain parks in the 1940s. Not only does the site overlook the historic Kicking Horse Pass and Valley, but it provides excellent views of the Lake O'Hara environs and the Bow Valley near Lake Louise. However, like most fire lookout trails, it is steep and dry, so be sure to carry water.

The first half-hour climbs through heavy forest along the southern flank of Paget Peak. At 1.4 km, the Sherbrooke Lake trail continues straight ahead and the Paget Lookout option branches right.

After contouring across an avalanche slope, the trail starts gaining altitude again. Though you are climbing at over 1800 m, the dry south-facing exposure displays vegetation normally found at much lower elevations, such as common juniper. A few minutes later, as the exposure becomes more westerly, you encounter subalpine species like whitebark pine. As you navigate a series of steep switchbacks, there are glimpses of the pale turquoise waters of Sherbrooke Lake far below.

The trail reaches the lookout cabin following a final 0.8 km of steep uphill. Perched near the edge of a cliff overlooking Wapta Lake, the lookout is not as high as the 2375 m shown on government topo maps, but it is still lofty enough for some pretty dramatic views. Banff Park's Bow Valley lies to the east beneath the Slate Range and Mount Richardson (3086 m); the Cataract Brook valley runs south to the glacier-mantled peaks of the Lake O'Hara region; and to the southwest the braided river flats of the Kicking Horse Valley are framed between Mounts Stephen and Field.

There is no better vantage point for one of Canada's most important

Kicking Horse Valley from Paget Lookout

mountain passes, the Kicking Horse, which lies 5 km east and 485 m beneath the lookout. The pass was discovered by the Palliser Expedition's Dr. James Hector on September 2, 1858, a few days after he was rendered senseless by a kick from his packhorse. In 1884, the CPR's tracks were laid through the pass.

As you overlook the rails plunging into the Kicking Horse Valley, you might wonder if the railway builders couldn't have found a better route. The "Big Hill" remained a dangerous and expensive grade until the Spiral Tunnels were completed inside Mount Ogden and the Cathedral Crags in 1909.

Unlike other mountain parks, Yoho has preserved several of its old lookout cabins as historic reminders of the days when fire suppression was a management priority. The door to the cabin is always open and provides a welcome refuge for hikers on cold, windy days. On warm, sunny days, limestone bluffs above the cabin make wonderful viewpoints where you can relax, dry out sweaty clothing and hydrate after the stiff climb.

A rough trail leads upwards from the lookout, beckoning strong hikers

to follow in the footsteps of the Reverend Dean Paget of Calgary, a founding member of the Alpine Club of Canada who climbed the mountain in 1904. The 2565-m summit lies 430 m above the lookout and can be reached in less than an hour of steady scrambling over loose rock.

Sherbrooke Lake. If you still have energy to burn on your return from the lookout, the 1.7-km side trip to Sherbrooke Lake makes a rewarding finale to the day. (See *Sherbrooke Lake*.)

Lake O'Hara

When veteran hikers get together to reminisce, the name Lake O'Hara comes up early and fondly. It is easy to understand why it is considered such a special place. Within a 5-km radius of Lake O'Hara there are 25 named lakes, numerous high, rugged mountains, and one of the most extensive and well-maintained trail systems in the mountain parks.

The trails, built over a period of nearly 50 summers by Dr. George Link, Carson Simpson and Lawrence Grassi, radiate from Lake O'Hara like spokes from a hub. Hiking options on these trails range from a simple stroll around Lake O'Hara to a challenging traverse high above the lake's basin. Hikers can follow a different trail every day and return to the campground, lodge or Alpine Club hut each evening, making the area an ideal destination for a hiking vacation.

O'Hara's scenery is dominated by the same peaks that form the impressive backdrop for Lake Louise—the Great Divide summits of Mounts Lefroy (3423 m) and Victoria (3464 m). The two mountains also rise above one of the area's four distinct hiking areas—the Lake Oesa cirque. A second area is the Opabin Plateau, located between Yukness Mountain (2847 m) and Mount Schäffer (2693 m). Lake McArthur, set between Schäffer Ridge and Park Mountain makes a third. And the Duchesnay Basin, which cradles Linda, Morning Glory, Cathedral and Odaray Lakes is the fourth.

The Lake O'Hara region was first spotted from the summit of Mount Stephen by J.J. McArthur, a government surveyor working along the CPR line in 1887. Lieutenant-Colonel Robert O'Hara, an Irishman who heard about the area from McArthur, visited it shortly thereafter and was so impressed he returned repeatedly to explore its lakes, creeks and mountains.

In 1894, American mountaineer Samuel E.S. Allen completed a marathon day trip to the area from Paradise Valley near Lake Louise via Wastach, Wenkchemna and Opabin Passes. From this trip, and a subsequent visit, he provided the Stoney names for many of the local peaks.

The Alpine Club of Canada held one of its earliest mountaineering camps at Lake O'Hara in 1909, and by 1911 the region was popular enough among alpinists to warrant construction of a cabin, Wiwaxy Lodge, in the Alpine Meadow just west of the lake. The CPR constructed the Elizabeth Parker Hut in the meadow in 1919 and soon after added a number of small cabins to accommodate the growing number of visitors. During the winter of 1925-26 Lake O'Hara Lodge was constructed on the lakeshore, and all of the Alpine Meadow cabins, except the Elizabeth Parker Hut, were moved to the site.

Today, a number of facilities support the many hikers and climbers who visit the area each summer:

Lake O'Hara Campground, a 30-site Parks Canada campground, is 0.6 km north of the lake on the west side of the O'Hara access road. While few people hike to the campground, it operates the same as any backcountry campground—a Wilderness Pass is required. One small tent is allowed per site and only two sites can be occupied by a group (no more than six people in a group).

Campers may reserve sites for the campground up to three months prior to their visit by calling the O'Hara reservation line at 250-343-6433. A $12 reservation fee is charged along with the cost of the Wilderness Pass, bus service to the campground and the nightly campground fee (all fees payable by VISA, Mastercard or American Express when you make the reservation).

Land above 2300 metres

Le Relais is across the access road from the Parks Canada patrol cabin at the northwest corner of the lake. This log hut sells beverages, snacks, publications and area trail maps. It also serves as a shelter and bus stop for day hikers travelling to and from the area. It is also a good place to visit for current trail conditions.

Lake O'Hara Lodge is 200 m beyond Le Relais at road's end. It is one of the most delightful and well-appointed backcountry lodges in the Rockies. Guests are accommodated in the main lodge and in outlying cabins. The lodge is very popular and usually booked a year or more in advance. For information and reservations, see *Sources—Backcountry lodges.*

Elizabeth Parker Hut is in the Alpine Meadow, 0.7 km west of Le Relais by trail. Operated by the Alpine Club of Canada, the large cabin accommodates 24. The popular hut is booked via a lottery system, and applications for a summer stay at the hut should be filed the previous autumn. For more information on the lottery and forms, connect with Alpine Club of Canada (see *Sources—Huts*).

Abbot Pass Hut was constructed by the CPR in 1922 as the first high altitude climbers' hut in Canada. It is located on the crest of the Great Divide between Lake O'Hara and Lake Louise and is reached via an extremely steep 2-km scramble (see *Lake Oesa*). While it is still used primarily by climbers, strong hikers who are experienced rock scramblers often make the climb from Lake O'Hara and overnight there. The hut, which accommodates 24, is operated by the Alpine Club of Canada (see *Sources— Huts*).

Access: Trips to Lake O'Hara begin from the parking area at the bottom of the O'Hara access road. The parking lot is reached by following the Trans-Canada Highway to its junction with the Lake O'Hara access road, 3.2 km (2 mi) west of the Alberta-B.C. boundary and 1.6 km (1 mi) east of Wapta Lake. Follow the paved road across the railway tracks and turn right onto the 0.8-km gravel road leading down to the parking lot. N51°26.690' W116°19.724'.

Most visitors travel to Lake O'Hara on the shuttle bus, which makes several round trips on the gravel access road each day during the hiking season (third week of June to early October). In order to protect the fragile meadows in the area and reduce the impact on wildlife, a quota limits the number of people who can access the area by bus. Most of this quota is filled by those with reservations at the campground, lodge and Alpine Club huts.

A limited number of seats on the bus are available for day users, who can reserve online (www.pc.gc.ca/yoho) or by telephone (250-343-6433), with reservations opening in mid-April (check the website for the exact date). Reservations for campsites are taken up to three months in advance, but as sites are in high demand, be sure to call exactly three months prior to your planned visit (phone lines open daily at 8 am). At the time of publication, the following bus schedule was in effect: Inbound leaving the parking area at 8:30 am, 10:30 am, 3:30 pm, 5:30 pm; outbound leaving Lake O'Hara at 9:30 am, 11:30 am, 2:30 pm, 4:30 pm, 6:30 pm. The bus operates on an abbreviated schedule in early October. (Note: Lake O'Hara is in the Mountain Time Zone, not Pacific, so all times are MDT.) This schedule is subject to change, so always double-check when you reserve.

You may also hike to the lake on the 11-km access road, but it is a long day trip and leaves little time for exploration (although those who hike up the access road can pay a one-way fee and utilize an outbound shuttle bus without reservation). Cyclists are not permitted on the access road.

The 13.5-km Cataract Creek trail, which once served as an optional access-exit route, is no longer maintained by Parks Canada, and the bridge over the creek at km 1.5 is no longer in place. Parks Canada does not recommend the route due to possible disturbance to wildlife.

Since both day and overnight trips to Lake O'Hara require advance planning, we suggest you download the "Exploring Lake O'Hara" brochure from the Yoho Park website (see *Sources—Park information*) for a more complete discussion of the above.

Lake O'Hara

137 Lake O'Hara Circuit

Lakeshore Circuit—2.8 km (1.7 mi)

The Adeline Link Circuit is another name for the footpath that loops around the Lake O'Hara shoreline. Dr. George Link and his wife Adeline, along with a few other Lake O'Hara regulars, began work on the trail in 1943. Adeline died of a stroke the following autumn at her home in Chicago, and the trail was completed and dedicated to her memory in 1946.

As you might expect, this walk along the shore of one of the Rockies' most beautiful lakes is a very special experience, particularly in the evening when the last rays of sun are illuminating the O'Hara basin. The trail is also the starting point for trips to Wiwaxy Gap (*Alpine Circuit*), *Lake Oesa* and the *Opabin Plateau*—trails branching upwards at various points along the circuit.

Starting from the Cataract Creek outlet bridge, follow the trail east along the north shoreline. Trails to Wiwaxy Gap

and Lake Oesa branch left at km 0.2 and 0.8 respectively. At km 1.2, the rolling path passes beneath the beautiful Seven Sisters Falls (aka Seven Veils Falls).

Along the lake's south shore, the Opabin Plateau East and West Circuits branch upslope at km 1.8 and 2.1. Lake O'Hara Lodge is reached at km 2.4, and from there it is a short 400-m walk along the access road to the northwest corner of the lake where you began.

Access: Travel to Lake O'Hara as described in the *Lake O'Hara* introduction. Walk to the trailhead at the Cataract Creek bridge, located at the northwest corner of Lake O'Hara, 150 m north of the Le Relais hut and the Parks Canada patrol cabin. N51°21.486' W116°20.309' *Maps: Lake Louise 82 N/8; Lake O'Hara (Gem Trek); Lake Louise & Yoho (Gem Trek).*

139 Opabin Plateau

Lake O'Hara Lodge to Opabin Lake—3.2 km (2.0 mi)
Opabin Plateau Circuit—5.9 km (3.7 mi)

Half-day trip

Allow 1 to 1.5 hours one way

Elevation gain: 250 m (820 ft)

Maximum elevation: 2285 m (7,500 ft)

Maps: Lake Louise 82 N/8
Lake O'Hara (Gem Trek)
Lake Louise & Yoho (Gem Trek)

Access: Travel to *Lake O'Hara* as described in the Lake O'Hara introduction. From Lake O'Hara Lodge, pick-up the trail south beyond the shoreline cabins.

0.0—Lake O'Hara Lodge (2035 m).
N51°21.340' W116°20.163'

  —Follow *Lake O'Hara Circuit* trail south.

0.3—Junction. Opabin West Circuit right.

0.4—Junction. Big Larches trail right.

0.5—Mary Lake.

  —Steep climb beneath cliffs.

1.6—Junction. *Alpine Circuit*-All Souls Prospect right. Opabin Prospect left (50 m).

  —Grade levels out.

1.9—Junction. Trails to Opabin Prospect and Opabin Plateau Highline left.

2.6—Junction. Opabin Plateau Highline rejoins from left.

  —Trail skirts Hungabee Lake west shore then climbs to head of valley.

3.2—Opabin Lake (2285 m). Opabin East Circuit descends to left.

3.5—Hungabee Lake east shore.

3.6—Junction. *Alpine Circuit*–Yukness Ledge right.

4.2—Steep descent into forest.

5.3—Junction. Intersection with *Lake O'Hara Circuit* at km 1.8. Lodge left.

5.9—Lake O'Hara Lodge (2035 m).

The Opabin Plateau Circuit is one of the classic hikes of the Rockies. While the main loop trail to the head of the plateau and back is fairly short, you can easily spend a full day exploring and photographing its larch-fringed meadows and numerous small lakes. It is little wonder Opabin was a favourite locale for a number of Canadian landscape artists.

The circuit makes an elongated loop, which runs up one side of the plateau and down the other. The west and east side trails are known as the Opabin Plateau West Circuit and the Opabin Plateau East Circuit. Because it is the shortest route to the top of the plateau, the West Circuit is usually used on the approach from Lake O'Hara. Along the way several trails branch to scenic points within the loop. One of the Lake O'Hara area trail maps is essential to understanding all the options (available at Le Relais and the lodge).

Starting from Lake O'Hara Lodge, follow the O'Hara lakeshore circuit in a counterclockwise direction, heading south along the lake's west shore. Just 300 m beyond the lodge complex, the West Circuit trail branches right. After passing Mary Lake, it climbs steeply through cliffs forming the northern escarpment of the plateau.

The trail reaches the top of the cliff at km 1.6, where a short trail branches left to Opabin Prospect—an outstanding cliff-top viewpoint overlooking Lake O'Hara, the Cataract Valley and the distant summit of Cathedral Mountain.

Beyond the Opabin Prospect junction, the trail enters the plateau meadows, passes along the west shore of Hungabee Lake and ascends a rocky benchland to the head of the valley and Opabin Lake. (The Opabin Highline Trail branches left at km 1.9, traverses the crest of a rocky ridge leading up-valley, and rejoins the main trail at km 2.6.) Until you reach

Odaray and Cathedral Mountains from Opabin Plateau

Opabin Lake at the top of the valley, you are continually passing through stands of alpine larch—a photographer's dream in mid-September when their needles have turned to gold.

From the alpine shores of Opabin Lake you have fine views in all directions. Great, glowering walls rise above the head of the valley, the most impressive being Hungabee Mountain (3492 m) and Mount Biddle (3319 m), which guard Opabin Pass and Glacier to the south. Hungabee means "the chieftain" in Stoney, while Opabin means "rocky"; both were named by the American mountaineer Samuel Allen following his solo journey into the area via Opabin Pass in August, 1894.

From Opabin Lake, you complete the circuit by returning to Lake O'Hara on the East Circuit trail. The trail descends through alpine meadow and a scattering of stunted larch trees as it skirts great rockslides beneath Yukness Mountain. (Watch for hoary marmots and pikas.)

Soon after passing the east shore of Hungabee Lake, the trail drops into forest and descends steeply to Lake O'Hara. You reach the lakeshore trail just 300 m east of the West Circuit junction. You can complete the Opabin Circuit by turning left and walking back to the lodge, or go right and continue around the lake to the O'Hara access road near the Le Relais hut.

Yukness Ledge Alpine Route. This section of the Alpine Circuit branches from the Opabin East Circuit at km 3.6 beside the east shore of Hungabee Lake. By following this route across the rockslides and ledges of Yukness Mountain, you can complete a highline traverse to Lake Oesa. An Opabin Plateau-Lake Oesa loop trip makes a good full-day outing.

All Souls Prospect Alpine Route branches from the Opabin West Circuit at km 1.6 and is the western end of the Alpine Circuit. This rugged, 1.8-km alpine route crosses All Souls Prospect to Schäffer Lake and the Lake McArthur trail. (See *Alpine Circuit* for descriptions of both alpine routes.)

140 Lake McArthur

Lake O'Hara to Lake McArthur—3.5 km (2.2 mi)

Half-day trip

Allow 1 to 1.5 hours one way

Elevation gain: 310 m (1,025 ft)
loss: 95 m (310 ft)

Maximum elevation: 2345 m (7,700 ft)

Maps: Lake Louise 82 N/8
Lake O'Hara (Gem Trek)
Lake Louise & Yoho (Gem Trek)

Access: Travel to *Lake O'Hara* as described in the Lake O'Hara introduction. The hike begins from the trailhead beside Le Relais hut on the O'Hara access road, 0.6 km south of the campground and 0.2 km north of the lodge.

0.0— Trailhead (2035 m).
N51°21.454' W116°20.337'

— Trail climbs to Alpine Meadow.

0.3— Junction. Big Larches Route to Schäffer Lake left. Keep right.

— Trail crosses Alpine Meadow.

0.6— Elizabeth Parker Hut Junction. Linda Lake right. Keep left.

— Moderate to steep uphill.

1.5— Junction. Big Larches Route rejoins from left.

1.6— Schäffer Lake Junction. McArthur Pass right. Stay left for Lake McArthur high route.

— Trail climbs shoulder of Mt. Schäffer and skirts rockslide.

2.4— Junction (2210 m). McArthur Pass-Odaray Highline right. Lake McArthur left.

— Moderate to steep uphill along cliffs and boulder fields.

3.0— Trail summit (2345 m).

— Gradual descent to lake.

3.5— Lake McArthur (2250 m).

Lake McArthur is the largest and deepest lake in the O'Hara area. The 85-m depth of the lake contributes to its deep blue colour, which contrasts with the brilliant white of the Biddle Glacier beyond its far shore. The pyramid-shaped summit of Mount Biddle rises above the lake and glacier, adding symmetry to a scene that has attracted artists and photographers for decades.

From the trailhead at the Le Relais hut, hike to the Alpine Meadow and the junction beside the Elizabeth Parker Hut. Stay left and climb southwest through dense subalpine forest to Schäffer Lake.

Just 50 m beyond the Schäffer Lake outlet bridge, the high trail to Lake McArthur branches left from the McArthur Pass trail. While you can reach the lake by staying on the right-hand option to McArthur Pass, we prefer the more scenic high option. This high route skirts around the lake's south shore, climbs steeply through alpine larch to the shoulder of Mount Schäffer, and follows the edge of a rock band for a short distance. Here you are greeted with good views north to Cathedral Mountain.

At km 2.4 you pass the junction for the short connector trail down to McArthur Pass and the Odaray Highline-Grandview Prospect route (see below). Stay left and continue around the west ridge of Mount Schäffer, climbing along cliffs and boulder fields to the trail summit and your first view of Lake McArthur. The final 0.5 km descends through meadows and rocky ridges to the lake.

Big Larches Route. This alternate trail branches south from the Lake McArthur trail at km 0.3, on the eastern edge of the Alpine Meadow. It runs 0.3 km toward Mary Lake, then branches right and climbs steeply along a rockslide beneath Mount Schäffer's cliffs. You pass through stands of giant alpine larch on the ascent

Lake McArthur and Mount Biddle

and then rejoin the main trail at km 1.5 on the shores of Schäffer Lake. This option is only 300 m longer than the main trail, but since it is very steep and rocky in places, it is usually hiked on the return from Lake McArthur. (See also *Alpine Circuit*).

Odaray Highline-Grandview Prospect. This optional side-trip from the Lake McArthur trail follows the Odaray Highline and Grandview Prospect trails north from McArthur Pass to a 2535-m viewpoint on the east slope of Odaray Mountain. Odaray Grandview overlooks much of the O'Hara basin, including Lake O'Hara and nearly all of its outlying lakes. Along the way you also have a "grand view" of the Goodsirs, Yoho's highest peaks, across the Ottertail Valley to the south.

While you can reach the Odaray Highline by hiking directly to McArthur Pass from Schäffer Lake, we also use the Lake McArthur high-route (it's a bit longer but more open and scenic).

From the high-route junction at km 2.4, descend to McArthur Pass and pick-up the Odaray Highline trail running north (see restrictions below). At a junction 1.1 km beyond McArthur Pass, the Grandview trail branches uphill to the left. The last 1.0 km is more alpine route than trail, mostly following paint marks and cairns up a very steep slope. A large cairn atop a moraine marks the Grandview Prospect summit viewpoint.

Restrictions: Parks Canada has identified McArthur Pass and the Odaray Plateau as a narrow wildlife corridor used by grizzly bears and other species travelling between McArthur Creek and the Cataract Valley. As a result, it has closed traditional trails on Odaray Plateau and asks that no more than four groups per day use the Odaray Highline route. A logbook has been placed in McArthur Pass at the start of the route, and everyone hiking the trail should sign-in there. Check the logbook when you arrive there, and if four groups have already signed it for the day, you should turn around and go elsewhere. (Check at the Le Relais hut for the latest update on this route.)

141 Linda Lake—Cathedral Basin

Lake O'Hara Campground to Linda Lake—3.7 km (2.3 mi)
Lake O'Hara Campground to Cathedral Basin—7.4 km (4.6 mi)

Day trip

Allow 2 to 3 hours to Cathedral Basin

Elevation gain: 305 m (1,000 ft)

Maximum elevation: 2315 m (7,600 ft)

Maps: Lake Louise 82 N/8
Lake O'Hara (Gem Trek)
Lake Louise & Yoho (Gem Trek)

Access: Travel to *Lake O'Hara* as described in the Lake O'Hara introduction. From near the last campsite on the north edge of the O'Hara Campground, follow the trail leading into the forest.

0.0— Lake O'Hara Campground (2010 m).
N51°21.721' W116°20.615'

— Gradual descent through forest.

1.9— Junction. O'Hara access road right.
Linda Lake left.

2.4— Morning Glory Creek bridge.

2.7— Junction. Morning Glory Lakes and
Alpine Meadow left. Linda Lake ahead.

3.7— Linda Lake Junction (2090 m).
Keep right.

— Trail circles north side of Linda Lake.

4.5— Junction. Linda Lake south shore left.
Cathedral Basin right.

— Gradual uphill.

5.6— Cathedral Lakes.

— Gradual to moderate uphill.

6.1— Junction. Duchesnay Pass and
Last Larch Prospect left.
Cathedral Basin right.

— Steep uphill via forest and rockslide.

6.6— Uphill ends.

— Trail contours right.

7.1— Cathedral Platform Prospect
(2315 m).

7.4— Cathedral Basin and Monica Lake.

The trail to Linda Lake and the Cathedral Basin is the longest hike from Lake O'Hara. It is also the least crowded. Pleasant subalpine lakes along the way, coupled with a spectacular overview of the O'Hara basin from Cathedral Platform Prospect, make it a very rewarding trip.

Starting from the north end of O'Hara Campground, the trail descends through forest for 1.9 km to a broad trail running west from the O'Hara access road. Turn left and continue 1.8 km to Linda Lake. Stay right on the lake's north shoreline trail and follow it to fine views back across the lake to distant Hungabee Mountain, Mount Biddle, and other peaks beyond Lake O'Hara.

If you are looking for a short, easy hike, Linda Lake is sufficient reward. But the real glory of this area is the Cathedral Basin, 3.7 km farther along and 225 m higher up.

To reach the Cathedral Basin, continue around Linda Lake and follow the trail branching west at the far end of the lake. This trail climbs gradually through subalpine forest interspersed with meadows. At km 5.6, it crosses a bridge between the first and second Cathedral Lakes. The lower lake, also known as Vera Lake, is situated in a meadowy area overlooked by the north wall of Odaray Mountain. Just 0.4 km beyond, the Last Larch Prospect junction is passed, and the steep ascent to Cathedral Basin begins.

The last 1.3 km follows rough, rocky trail, which is frequently more route than track. After climbing through a major rockslide, the trail contours east to the mouth of the Cathedral Basin.

Views on the ascent are outstanding, but they reach their pinnacle at the lip of the cirque—the Cathedral Platform Prospect. No other viewpoint gives quite so complete an overview of the Lake O'Hara region. High on the side

Linda Lake

of Cathedral Mountain, you are viewing the area much as surveyor J.J. McArthur did when he first saw it from the summit of nearby Mount Stephen in 1887. The upper Cataract Valley stretches southeast to Lake O'Hara and its surrounding peaks. The meadows and lakes of the Duchesnay Valley lie immediately below, backed by the north face of Odaray Mountain.

A short stroll down through alpine meadow from the Prospect brings you to tiny Monica Lake in the heart of the Cathedral Basin cirque.

Linda Lake via Alpine Meadow—4.7 km. If you are staying at Lake O'Hara Lodge or the Elizabeth Parker Hut, we suggest you follow the trail running north from the Alpine Meadow to Linda Lake. While this alternate route to the lake is slightly longer, it passes by the second Morning Glory Lake and is a bit more interesting than the trail from the campground.

If you are starting from Lake O'Hara, hike the *Lake McArthur* trail 0.6 km from the Le Relais hut trailhead to the junction in front of the Elizabeth Parker

Hut. Keep right and continue on the trail leading north, skirting a small pond at the far end of the Alpine Meadow and entering the forest beyond.

The trail contours through dense subalpine forest for 1.8 km and then descends to cross Morning Glory Creek at the inlet to the second Morning Glory Lake. The shortcut to Linda Lake branches left just beyond the stream crossing.

The shortcut from Morning Glory Lakes is very rocky and rooty. It makes a moderately steep ascent through forest and then descends to the south shore of Linda Lake. Turn left to reach the junction with the standard route (km 4.5) at the west end of the lake. Stay left to continue on to Cathedral Basin, or turn right to skirt back along the lake's north shore.

Lake O'Hara Alpine Circuit—11.8 km (7.3 mi)

Day trip

Allow 4 to 5 hours

Minimum elevation: 2035 m (6,675 ft)

Maximum elevation: 2530 m (8,300 ft)

Maps: Lake Louise 82 N/8
     Lake O'Hara (Gem Trek)
     Lake Louise & Yoho (Gem Trek)

Access: Travel to Lake O'Hara as described in the *Lake O'Hara* introduction. Walk to the trailhead at the Cataract Creek bridge, located at the northwest corner of Lake O'Hara 150 m north of the Le Relais hut and the Parks Canada patrol cabin.

0.0— Trailhead (2035 m).
     N51°21.486' W116°20.309'

  —Follow lakeshore trail.

0.2— Junction. Wiwaxy Gap left.

  —Very steep, steady uphill.

2.1— Wiwaxy Gap (2530 m).

  —Steep descent to southeast.

4.1— Junction (2275 m). Cross *Lake Oesa* trail at km 3.0. Lake Oesa left 0.2 km.

  —Cross Oesa outlet and traverse Yukness Ledge Route.

6.4— Junction. Intersection with *Opabin Plateau* trail at km 3.6. Follow Opabin East Circuit left.

6.8— Opabin Lake (2285 m). Follow Opabin West Circuit right.

8.4— Junction. Opabin Prospect right. Follow All Souls' Route to left at junction 50 m ahead.

  —Steep, rocky ascent.

9.3— All Souls' Prospect (2475 m).

  —Extremely steep descent (loose rock and ledges).

10.2— Junction. Big Larches trail right. Schäffer Lake left.

10.3— Schäffer Lake Junction. Intersection with *Lake McArthur* trail at km 1.5.

11.8— Lake O'Hara (2035 m).

The Alpine Circuit traverses high above the Lake O'Hara basin and allows you to survey much of the region's best scenery on a single outing. However, most of this circuit is not over traditional trail, but instead follows rough paths, paint marks and cairns across steep slopes, through rockslides, and along exposed ledges. The circuit was once called the "Alpinist's Traverse", an appropriate name when stormy weather or lingering snow transforms the hike into a hazardous expedition (we do not recommend this hike when the route is covered with fresh snow).

Yet, when the weather is fine, and the route is bare and dry, the scramble around this inspired route is surprisingly straightforward. But even under the best conditions, it should only be undertaken by fit hikers who are not bothered by exposed heights.

Starting the circuit by climbing to Wiwaxy Gap is more strenuous than by heading to Schäffer Lake and All Souls' Prospect first and then moving around the basin counterclockwise. But by labouring up Wiwaxy first, you put the toughest climb behind you early in the day, and if you can scamper to this lofty col without undue fear or suffering, you'll know you're tough enough for the trip.

Start at O'Hara's outlet bridge and follow the lakeshore trail 0.2 km to where the Wiwaxy trail branches uphill to the left. The distance to the gap is just under 2 km, but it will seem twice as far. In addition to wiggling straight up through forest and across scree, the narrow path skirts exposed ledges—wide enough to walk comfortably but just a step away from lots of air.

Wiwaxy Gap is a grand viewpoint for the O'Hara basin. In addition to views back across the lake, the col looks north to the lower Cataract Valley and the mountains near Kicking Horse Pass.

Lake O'Hara from All Souls' Prospect

From the gap the route makes a descending traverse along the south slope of Mount Huber to Lake Oesa, which is frequently visible ahead. Its all ledges and steep rockslides, but paint marks and cairns keep you on-route.

The Alpine Circuit crosses the Oesa trail on a rocky knoll 200 m west of the lake, and if you made an early start, it is a fine place to stop for lunch.

Beyond this bluff a new traverse begins (watch for paint marks), descending to cross the Oesa outlet stream and then climbing west to the tumbled cliffs of the Yukness Ledge Alpine Route. This traverse, which skirts around Yukness Mountain and drops you onto the Opabin Plateau, is very steep, rocky and demanding (watch carefully for paint marks and cairns).

After intersecting the Opabin East Circuit, walk the well-graded Opabin Plateau trail to the head of the valley. From Opabin Lake descend the opposite side of the plateau on the Opabin West Circuit. The short detour to Opabin Prospect on the northern lip of the plateau is a worthwhile diversion, and when you return to the Opabin West Circuit,

you are just 50 m from the next important junction—the trail to All Souls' Prospect.

The All Souls' Alpine Route is the last traverse and, in some respects, the most demanding. The ascent from the Opabin Plateau is quick and steep as you climb across rockslides beneath Mount Schäffer via a narrow track to All Souls' Prospect—a natural platform on the mountain's north ridge. The view across Lake O'Hara from this splendid viewpoint allows you to retrace the entire Alpine Circuit—an appropriate finale to the day.

From All Souls' Prospect there is one last very steep descent (paint marks and cairns again) to the Big Larches trail near Schäffer Lake. If you are still feeling your oats, return to Lake O'Hara via the steep but scenic Big Larches trail (see *Lake McArthur*). Otherwise, continue left 100 m to Schäffer Lake and shuffle down the Lake McArthur trail to the Alpine Meadow and Lake O'Hara.

Yoho Valley—Emerald Lake

Emerald Lake was discovered by pioneer outfitter Tom Wilson in 1882 while he was packing for the CPR survey. Having lost some horses, he followed their tracks up the Emerald Valley from the Kicking Horse River to this hidden gem.

Despite the early discovery of Emerald Lake, the nearby Yoho Valley wasn't explored until 1897 when the German alpinist Jean Habel reached the valley from Emerald Lake via Yoho Pass. Habel reported on the valley's exceptional features, which included an impressive array of glaciated peaks, extensive icefields, and the stunning 254-m Takakkaw Falls.

Edward Whymper, conqueror of Switzerland's Matterhorn, explored the region for the Canadian Pacific Railway in 1901. Though he was 61 years old, he climbed and hiked throughout the Yoho Valley area, photographing all the major mountains and valleys. From his long experience in Europe, he saw the recreational potential of the Yoho and recommended the construction of several trails.

In 1903, the CPR opened its first backcountry chalet at Emerald Lake—the forerunner of today's Emerald Lake Lodge. Three years later the area gained further notoriety when the Alpine Club of Canada based its first annual mountaineering camp at Yoho Lake.

Today Emerald Lake, Yoho Valley, and the adjacent Little Yoho Valley constitute one of the Canadian Rockies' major backcountry recreation areas. Many of the trails in the region interconnect, creating hiking options that can be tailored to the strength and available time of almost any hiking party.

Emerald Lake is reached from the Trans-Canada Highway via an 8.5-km paved road, which is open year-round to service the historic Emerald Lake Lodge. The lake is connected to the Yoho Valley by the Yoho Pass trail, yet most people hike it as a separate area. The circuit around Emerald Lake is a favourite with families and lodge guests both summer and winter. The Wapta Highline Circuit, which makes a high traverse along Wapta Mountain between Yoho and Burgess Passes, is the most popular day trip from the lake. Emerald Basin and Hamilton Lake are both rewarding half-day hikes.

Yoho Valley trails are reached via a narrow, paved road that runs 13 km from the Trans-Canada Highway to Takakkaw Falls (the road is open from late-June to early October, weather permitting, but switchbacks do not allow for trailers or long motorhomes). The valley's most popular hike is the Iceline Trail, which along with the valley-bottom Yoho River trail provides access to valley's best features—Twin Falls, Little Yoho Valley, and Whaleback. Strong hikers can reach all of these locales on long day trips, but many prefer to overnight in the valley and make shorter outings.

In addition to a walk-in campground 300 m beyond the Takakkaw Falls parking area, there are four backcountry campgrounds in the upper valley. All are popular sites, so reserve ahead and keep your itinerary flexible.

Two historic log structures are located in the upper valley backcountry. Twin Falls Chalet, a National Historic Site at the end of the Twin Falls trail, provides accommodation and meals for a limited number of guests throughout the summer (hikers can drop-in for afternoon tea). The Alpine Club of Canada's Stanley Mitchell Hut, another historic log structure near the head of Little Yoho Valley, accommodates 28 self-sufficient guests. See *Sources—Backcountry lodges* and *Huts.*

The only road-accessible accommodation in the upper Yoho is Hostelling-International's Whiskey Jack Hostel, one kilometre south of Takakkaw Falls on the Yoho Valley Road. The Iceline and Yoho Lake hikes start from the hostel's parking area, but non-guests must park at Takakkaw Falls and hike the 0.6-km connector trail back to the trailhead. See *Sources—Hostels.*

N

Isolated Pk▲

Glacier Des Poilus

Whaleback Mtn▲

Twin Falls

Yoho Glacier

(143)

WAPUTIK ICEFIELD

(146)

Laughing Falls

Mt▲ Pollinger

ACC Hut

(145)

Lake Duchesnay

Yoho

Celeste Lake

Kiwetinok Pass

River

Mt▲ Niles

▲Mt Kerr

PRESIDENT RANGE

▲The Vice President

(144)

The▲ President

Takakkaw Falls

Mt▲ Marpole

Michael ▲Pk

Hostel

Hidden Lake

Emerald Basin

Yoho Lake

(147)

(150)

(151)

Mt▲ Carnarvon

Yoho Valley Road

Yoho

Emerald ▲Pk

Hamilton Lake

Wapta Mtn▲

River

(149)

(151)

Emerald Lake

(148)

Hamilton Falls

(151)

Mt▲ Field

Burgess Pass

Lake Louise

(152)

▲Mt Burgess

(1)

(153)

Emerald River

Emerald Lake Road

Amiskwi

Amiskwi Pass

(154)

River

Mt▲ Stephen

?●FIELD

Land above 2300 metres

0   1   2   3   4   5km

143 Twin Falls

Takakkaw Falls Parking Area to Twin Falls—8.2 km (5.1 mi)

Day trip or backpack

Allow 2 to 3 hours one way

Elevation gain: 290 m (950 ft)

Maximum elevation: 1800 m (5,900 ft)

Maps: Lake Louise 82 N/8
Hector Lake 82 N/9
Blaeberry River 82 N/10
Lake Louise & Yoho (Gem Trek)

Access: Follow the Trans-Canada Highway to the Yoho Valley Road junction 3.7 km (2.3 mi) east of Field. Follow the Yoho Valley Road north 13 km (8 mi) to its termination at the Takakkaw Falls parking area. Park in the day-use parking area and walk north 300 m to the overnight parking area. The trailhead is at the north end of this parking area.

0.0— Trailhead (1510 m).
N51°29.953' W116°29.137'

— Follow old roadbed north.

0.3— Takakkaw Falls Campground.

0.5— Trail sign on north edge of campground.

— Trail runs across alluvial plain and into scattered forest.

2.2— Junction. Angel's Staircase viewpoint right. Point Lace Falls left 0.2 km.

3.6— Junction. Duchesnay Lake left 0.2 km.

4.2— Laughing Falls and Campground.

4.3— Junction. *Little Yoho Valley trail* left. Stay right.

4.7— Twin Falls Creek bridge.

6.4— Junction. Yoho Glacier right.

6.6— Twin Falls Campground.

— Steady switchbacking climb.

8.1— Junction. *Whaleback* right. Twin Falls Chalet left.

8.2— Twin Falls Chalet (1800 m). Twin Falls Creek and base of Twin Falls 100 m ahead.

The trail along the Yoho River from Takakkaw Falls to Twin Falls was originally cut by a CPR trail crew in 1901. Today it is one of the most frequently hiked trails in the Yoho Valley. While it is not particularly inspiring, it does pass a number of fine waterfalls and is the fastest route to Twin Falls. It is also popular because it provides access to two very scenic trails, Whaleback and Little Yoho Valley, both of which link with the Iceline Trail to allow a complete circuit of the valley.

The trail is flat and straightforward nearly all the way to Twin Falls. The first 2.2 km follows a road-width track that skirts the Takakkaw Falls walk-in campground, crosses a rocky alluvial wash, and runs up-valley through a forest of pine and spruce. Three waterfalls are passed along the way—Angel's Staircase Falls and Point Lace Falls at km 2.2, and the impressive, 30-m Laughing Falls at km 4.2. Beyond Point Lace Falls junction, the wide track reverts to a single-file path.

At km 3.6, a 200-m trail branches left to Lake Duchesnay—a shallow green lake that slowly dries up to the size of a pond by early autumn. Just beyond Duchesnay junction another short trail branches right to the edge of the Yoho River, where you can observe the explosive action of this glacial torrent cutting its channel. Across the river are the ice-covered Waputik Mountains, dominated by the sharp peak of Trolltinder Mountain (2917 m).

After passing Laughing Falls Campground and Little Yoho Valley junction, the trail crosses Twin Falls Creek and continues its northerly course through heavy forest with occasional glimpses of Twin Falls through the trees. At the Yoho Glacier trail junction, the main trail stays left and begins its final ascent to Twin Falls.

The Yoho Valley trail ends at Twin Falls Chalet, where you can view the double falls leaping 80 m (260 ft) off a massive cliff of Cathedral limestone. Twin Falls is formed by a stream from Glacier des Poilus, which splits into two branches just above the precipice.

Around the time the current Twin Falls Chalet was constructed by the CPR, the left falls often dwindled to a trickle or shut off altogether. As a result, CPR employees were dispatched to the stream above the falls to correct this scenic problem—with dynamite! (The name "Canadian Pacific Rockies" on some early maps may not have been all that inappropriate.)

Twin Falls Chalet was constructed by the CPR in 1923 and first opened for business the following year. The rustic Swiss-style log building has been operated by Fran Drummond of Calgary since 1962. It provides accommodation and meals for a limited number of guests throughout the summer, as well as afternoon tea for both guests and hikers. (See *Sources—Backcountry lodges.*)

Twin Falls Options. From Twin Falls, you have several excellent hiking options.

The trail over Whaleback strikes off from the junction 100 m north of the chalet and climbs to some of the best views of the upper Yoho Valley. You can also connect with the Iceline Trail by following the Marpole Lake and Celeste Lake trails south from the chalet for 7.5 km, which is by far the most scenic route back to Takakkaw Falls. (See *Whaleback, Little Yoho Valley,* and *Iceline Trail* descriptions.)

Yoho Glacier—2.3 km. This short trail branches north from the Twin Falls trail at km 6.4. It travels through dense forest and across relatively level terrain to the edge of a cutbank overlooking the Yoho River and the snout of the Yoho Glacier. It is often hiked as a half-day trip from Twin Falls Campground or the chalet.

Twin Falls

144 Iceline Trail

Yoho Valley Road to Iceline Summit—6.4 km (4.0 mi)
Yoho Valley Road to Little Yoho Campground—10.8 km (6.7 mi)

Day trip or backpack

Allow 2 hours to Iceline Summit

Elevation gain: 690 m (2,250 ft)

Maximum elevation: 2210 m (7,250 ft)

Maps: Lake Louise 82 N/8
Blaeberry River 82 N/10
Lake Louise & Yoho (Gem Trek)

Access: Follow the Trans-Canada Highway to the Yoho Valley Road junction 3.7 km (2.3 mi) east of Field. Follow the Yoho Valley Road north 13 km (8 mi) to its termination at the Takakkaw Falls parking area. Follow the broad trail leading downstream (south) from the parking area to a junction at the Yoho River bridge. Stay right and follow the 0.6-km connector trail leading up to the Yoho Valley Road and HI-Yoho/Whiskey Jack Hostel parking area. The trailhead sign is at the north end of the hostel parking area.

0.0— Trailhead (1520 m).
N51°29.471' W116°28.923'
— Steady uphill.

1.1— Junction. Hidden Lakes left 0.3 km.

1.3— Junction. *Yoho Lake* ahead.
Iceline right.
— Steady uphill across avalanche slopes.

2.5— Junction. Yoho Lake left 2.4 km.
Iceline right.
— Steady climb into rocky terrain.

4.6— Lake outlet stream (rock-hop).

5.6— Lake outlet stream (rock-hop).

5.7— Junction. Celeste Lake and Twin Falls right. Iceline ahead.

6.4— Iceline Summit (2210 m).

7.4— Lake outlet (rock-hop).
— Trail descends into subalpine forest.

10.2— Junction. Kiwetinok Pass left (2.5 km). Stay right.

10.4— Little Yoho River bridge.

10.5— Stanley Mitchell Hut. Intersection with the *Little Yoho Valley trail* at km 5.2. Little Yoho Campground left 0.3 km.

The Iceline Trail is the Yoho Valley's most scenic and popular day hike. Designed in the late 1980s as a replacement for the Highline and Skyline Trails, the Iceline takes you much higher than the old trails to expansive views of the Yoho Valley and the edge of the Emerald Glacier.

Some hikers approach the Iceline from the north after trekking to the head of the Little Yoho Valley, but most attack it in a more direct fashion from the trailhead at the HI-Yoho/Whiskey Jack Hostel. You can hike to Yoho Lake and begin the Iceline traverse from there (see *Yoho Lake*), or, as most people do, take the direct route and save 4 km.

By either route, you will arrive at a junction high on the open avalanche slopes of the President Range. This is where the real glories of the Iceline begin as it climbs over the terminal and ground moraines of the Emerald Glacier. The glacier is a constant companion above the trail from km 3.5 to 8.0, and the first of three small rockbound lakes is passed at km 4.6.

While the trail appears to be contouring northwestward, rolling up and down over glacial debris, it is actually climbing relentlessly. But the continually improving views of the Yoho Valley help to conceal the effort of the ascent. Finally, at km 6.4, the trail reaches its highest point on the crest of a moraine.

While some turn for home on this summit, many are tempted to continue to the Little Yoho Valley. The trail descends to one last lake and crosses the last ridge of glacial debris to the open subalpine forest of the Little Yoho. The twin pyramids of The Vice President and The President rise above the trail to the south, and Isolated Peak and the long ridge of the Whaleback are across the valley to the north.

Once you reach the forest, you descend gradually for 2.2 km along the

Emerald Glacier from Iceline Trail summit

route of the old Skyline Trail to the Little Yoho River. Follow the trail downstream for 200 m to a bridge that crosses to the Stanley Mitchell Hut and a junction with the Little Yoho Valley trail. (The campground is 300 m up-valley from the ACC hut.)

Strong day hikers can continue down the north side of the valley to the main Yoho Valley (*Twin Falls*) trail, or take the Marpole Lake connector to Twin Falls, or climb to the crest of the Whaleback. Backpackers will likely wash ashore for the night at the Little Yoho Campground or the Stanley Mitchell Hut. (See *Little Yoho Valley*.)

Twin Falls Option. If you are doing a day-trip loop of the upper Yoho Valley, you won't likely want to add kilometres by continuing to the upper Little Yoho Valley. The most direct route to Twin Falls branches downhill from the Iceline Trail at km 5.7— 0.7 km south of the Iceline Summit.

This branch, known as the Celeste Lake trail, descends into the forest, skirts the shores of tiny Celeste Lake, and contours north to an intersection with the Little Yoho Valley trail. At this juncture you turn right and follow the Little Yoho trail 0.7 km to the Marpole Lake trail junction. Continue north on the Marpole trail, which crosses a rockslide at the foot of the Whaleback to Marpole Lake and Twin Falls Chalet. Total distance from the Iceline junction to Twin Falls is 7.5 km—mostly downhill or flat walking through dense subalpine forest.

You can also take the scenic route to Twin Falls from the Little Yoho trail by crossing over the Whaleback, but this adds kilometres and a very stiff climb to your day.

From Twin Falls, you complete your Yoho Valley loop by returning to the Takakkaw Falls parking area on the *Twin Falls* trail. Total distance for this valley circuit is 22.5 km.

145 Little Yoho Valley

Laughing Falls Junction to Little Yoho Campground—5.5 km (3.4 mi)

Day trip or backpack

Allow 1.5 hours to Little Yoho
Campground

Elevation gain: 460 m (1,500 ft)

Maximum elevation: 2075 m (6,800 ft)

Maps: Blaeberry River 82 N/10
      Lake Louise & Yoho (Gem Trek)

Access: From the trailhead at the Takakkaw
Falls parking lot, follow the *Twin Falls* trail
to the 4.3 km junction at Laughing Falls. The
Little Yoho Valley trail branches uphill to left.

- 0.0—Laughing Falls Junction (1615 m).
  N51°31.856' W116°30.462'

  —Steep uphill switchbacks.

- 1.6—Junction. Twin Falls ahead.
  Little Yoho Valley left.

  —Steady uphill, moderate grades.

- 2.2—Junction (1905 m). *Whaleback* trail
  right.

- 2.3—Junction. Left to Celeste Lake
  (1.5 km). Stay right.

- 5.2—Stanley Mitchell Hut, Junction.
  Iceline Trail and Kiwetinok Pass left.
  Campground ahead.

- 5.5—Little Yoho Campground (2075 m).

The Little Yoho Valley is the most popular destination for backpackers in the Yoho Valley region. The campground at the head of the valley and the nearby Stanley Mitchell Hut are ideally situated as base camps for short excursions to such worthy objectives as Whaleback and Kiwetinok Pass. And the Iceline Trail, which contours high along the President Range, connects nicely with the Little Yoho trail to create a scenic loop trip.

Many visitors to the Little Yoho Valley are backpackers looking for the most direct route to the campground or the Stanley Mitchell Hut. That route follows the Twin Falls trail up the Yoho Valley 4.3 km from Takakkaw Falls to its junction with the Little Yoho Valley trail at Laughing Falls (see *Twin Falls*). From this intersection, the trail begins its ascent along the north side of the Little Yoho River.

Over the first 2 km, the trail climbs steeply through the forest via a series of switchbacks. On one of these switchbacks, at km 1.6, the Marpole Lake trail from Twin Falls intersects (keep left at this confusing junction or you will find yourself at Twin Falls in a half-hour or so). The Whaleback trail branches right at the 2.2-km mark, and just 100 m farther along, the Celeste Lake trail branches left across the river.

The forest becomes progressively more subalpine and open as you continue up-valley to the Stanley Mitchell Hut, located on the edge of a large meadow at km 5.2. The Little Yoho Campground lies 300 m farther along.

While the head of the valley is enclosed by impressive mountains, the most dramatic and dominating are the glaciated peaks of the President Range, which rise above the meadow to the south.

The log Stanley Mitchell Hut was constructed by the Alpine Club of Canada in 1939. It accommodates 28 and is one of

The President Range from the summit of Kiwetinok Pass

only a few Alpine Club huts accessible by trail (see *Sources—Huts*).

Iceline Trail Option. The popular and highly-scenic Iceline Trail runs from the Whiskey Jack Hostel parking area to a junction with the Little Yoho trail at the Stanley Mitchell Hut. Since the distance is only a kilometre longer than the Yoho Valley approach from Takakkaw Falls, it serves as an optional route to the upper Little Yoho Valley. It is a lot more strenuous, however, particularly if you are shouldering a full backpack. But if you've hiked into the hut or the campground via the low route, the Iceline is the most scenic return route down-valley. In fact, strong hikers often complete this 20-km circuit in a single day. (See *Iceline Trail*.)

Kiwetinok Pass—2.8 km. This short, steep trail climbs to the headwaters of the Little Yoho Valley on the 2450-m summit of Kiwetinok Pass—a rocky, windswept col that cradles a small lake. The pass provides fine views of both the Little Yoho Valley to the east and the Kiwetinok Valley to the west. It is usually hiked as a half-day trip from the Little Yoho Campground or the Stanley Mitchell Hut.

The trail starts at the junction in front of the Stanley Mitchell Hut, where it immediately crosses the Little Yoho River and follows the Iceline Trail for 200 m before branching right to begin its westerly ascent to the pass. The last half of the trip is very steep and the track is often vague (watch for cairns).

The pass is sandwiched between the slopes of Mounts Pollinger and Kerr, and mostly filled by the waters of Kiwetinok Lake. It can be a cold bleak spot when the weather is foul, and the lake often remains ice-covered into July.

146 Whaleback

Twin Falls Chalet to Little Yoho Junction—6.6 km (4.1 mi)

Day trip or backpack

Allow 1.5 hours to Whaleback Summit

Elevation gain: 410 m (1,350 ft)
loss: 305 m (1,000 ft)

Maximum elevation: 2210 m (7,250 ft)

Maps: Blaeberry River 82 N/10
Lake Louise & Yoho (Gem Trek)

Access: From the trailhead at the Takakkaw Falls parking lot, follow the *Twin Falls* trail 8.1 km to the Whaleback trail junction, 100 m north of Twin Falls Chalet. The south end of the Whaleback traverse is accessible from the 2.2-km junction on the *Little Yoho Valley* trail.

0.0—Twin Falls Junction (1800 m).
N51°32.751' W116°32.005'

—Trail climbs steeply via long switchbacks.

2.7—Twin Falls Creek near top of falls.

2.8—Unmarked junction.
Waterfall Valley right.

2.9—Twin Falls Creek suspension bridge.

—Steady climb.

4.5—Whaleback ridge summit (2210 m).

—Steep switchbacking descent.

6.6—Junction (1905 m). Intersection with *Little Yoho Valley* trail at km 2.2.

One of the highest and most scenic trails in the Yoho Valley runs across the Whaleback ridge between Twin Falls Chalet and the Little Yoho Valley. The trail summit provides an exceptional view of the entire headwaters of the Yoho Valley and the vast expanse of the Wapta Icefield.

Though we have hiked the Whaleback as part of a full day loop trip via the Iceline Trail, upper Little Yoho and Yoho River trails, the 26-km distance makes for a strenuous outing. Most hikers prefer to visit the Whaleback as a day trip from Twin Falls Chalet, the Stanley Mitchell Hut, or campgrounds in the Yoho and Little Yoho Valleys. This allows more time for exploration, including a side trip into the Waterfall Valley.

The north end of the Whaleback traverse intersects the Yoho Valley trail 100 m north of Twin Falls Chalet (see *Twin Falls*). From this junction, the trail switchbacks up through the rock bands that create the precipice for Twin Falls. After gaining 250 m of elevation to the plateau above the cliff, the trail descends to Twin Falls Creek at the very brink of the falls—a viewpoint that is not for the faint of heart. (Stay clear of Twin Falls Creek near the lip of the falls! This dangerous area has claimed one life.)

From the top of the falls, the trail climbs to a suspension bridge spanning Twin Falls Creek. (The bridge is removed in winter, so early and late-season hikers should check at the visitor centre to make sure it is in place.) Beyond the bridge the ascent continues across the flank of the Whaleback. The trail runs close to treeline where there are excellent views north to the Yoho Glacier, upper Waterfall Valley, and the white expanse of the Glacier des Poilus.

The high point of the trip, for both elevation and views, comes at km 4.5, where the trail turns the corner of the Whaleback ridge. Marked by a stone cairn and brass plaque commemorating

Mont des Poilus from the Whaleback

an avalanche fatality, the viewpoint provides one of the most commanding overviews of the upper Yoho Valley of any trail-accessible point in the region. Many nearby peaks were named by British mountaineer Edward Whymper when he visited the valley in 1901, including The President, The Vice President, Mount Kerr, Mount Pollinger, Isolated Peak, and the Whaleback itself.

From the viewpoint, the trail descends 300 m in 2.1 km to join the Little Yoho Valley trail. At this junction you can follow either the Celeste Lake shortcut or the Little Yoho Valley trail to the Iceline Trail. By turning left, you descend the Little Yoho trail to the Yoho River at Laughing Falls junction, or use the Marpole Lake connector trail to contour back around the end of the Whaleback to Twin Falls. (See *Little Yoho Valley*.)

Waterfall Valley—2.0 km. This sublime side trip from the Whaleback trail follows tributaries of Twin Falls Creek through alpine meadows to an excellent viewpoint for the striking white pyramid of Mont des Poilus and the vast Glacier des Poilus. (The Poilus name was applied to these features at the end of World War I, using a common term of endearment for the French infantry that translates literally as the *hairy ones.*)

The unsigned track up the vale branches right from the Whaleback trail just below the Twin Falls Creek suspension bridge. After passing an old campsite, the trail climbs steadily through meadows and beside small streams to an old morainal ridge near the head of the valley. (The trail is indistinct in its upper reaches, so watch for cairns.) From the top of this moraine you have the best view of the Glacier des Poilus region.

147 Yoho Lake

Yoho Valley Road to Yoho Lake—3.7 km (2.3 mi)

Half-day trip

Allow 1 to 1.5 hours to Yoho Lake

Elevation gain: 290 m (950 ft)

Maximum elevation: 1815 m (5,950 ft)

Maps: Lake Louise 82 N/8
      Lake Louise & Yoho (Gem Trek)

Access: Follow the Trans-Canada Highway to the Yoho Valley Road junction 3.7 km (2.3 mi) east of Field. Follow the Yoho Valley Road north 13 km (8 mi) to its termination at the Takakkaw Falls parking area. Follow the broad trail leading downstream (south) from the parking area to a junction at the Yoho River bridge. Stay right and follow the 0.6-km connector trail leading up to the Yoho Valley Road and HI-Yoho/Whiskey Jack Hostel parking area. The trailhead sign is at the north end of the hostel parking area.

0.0—Trailhead (1520 m).
     N51°29.471' W116°28.923'

— Steady uphill.

1.1—Junction. Hidden Lakes left 0.3 km.

1.3—Junction. *Iceline Trail* right.
     Yoho Lake left.

3.7—Yoho Lake (1815 m).

— Trail skirts south end of lake.

4.0—Junction. Iceline Trail right.
     Yoho Pass left.

4.6— Yoho Pass (1815 m). Intersection with *Wapta Highline Circuit* at km 6.4. Burgess Pass left. Emerald Lake ahead.

This is one of the shortest hikes in the Yoho Valley. Though the lake is historically interesting as the site of the Alpine Club of Canada's first annual camp in 1906, it is forest-enclosed and rather unremarkable. However, the lake and nearby Yoho Pass can be linked with other trails to create a number of rewarding day trips.

From the HI-Yoho/Whiskey Jack Hostel parking area, the trail immediately switchbacks up a major avalanche path and into dense subalpine forest. At km 1.1, a short side trail branches left to Hidden Lakes—two tiny ponds appropriately hidden in the forest.

Just 200 m beyond Hidden Lakes junction, the Iceline Trail branches right (you will return down this trail if you make the loop trip north from Yoho Lake). Stay left and continue your steady climb through the trees for another 2.4 km to the lake.

Though this small, green lake is surrounded on three sides by forest, its western shoreline is bordered by a lush meadow that is filled with wildflowers for much of the summer.

From a junction on the west side of the lake, you can branch left and continue through meadow and trees for another 0.6 km to Yoho Pass—a trail junction in the midst of forest. From this point you can turn left and follow a high trail south along Wapta Peak to Burgess Pass, or stay right and descend to Emerald Lake (see *Wapta Highline Circuit*).

Yoho Lake Loop. The most scenic route back to the Whiskey Jack Hostel trailhead follows the trail running north from the lake. After climbing through forest, you emerge on high open slopes overlooking the Yoho Valley and Takakkaw Falls. Intersect the Iceline Trail 2.4 km from the lake and follow it downhill to the 1.3 km junction on the Yoho Lake trail. Total round trip distance for the loop is 8.9 km.

148 Emerald Lake Circuit

Emerald Lakeshore Circuit—5.2 km (3.2 mi)

Half-day trip

Allow 1.5 hours

Elevation gain: nil

Maximum elevation: 1300 m (4,250 ft)

Maps: Golden 82 N/8
        Lake Louise & Yoho (Gem Trek)

Access: Follow the Trans-Canada Highway to its intersection with the Emerald Lake Road, 2 km (1.2 mi) west of the village of Field intersection. Follow the Emerald Lake Road north 8.5 km (5.3 mi) to its termination at the Emerald Lake parking area. The trailhead kiosk is at the north end of the parking area beside the bridge to Emerald Lake Lodge.

0.0— Trailhead (1300 m).
     N51°26.378' W116°32.500'

   — Follow paved trail through picnic area and around southwest corner of lake.

0.3— Avalanche path. End of paved trail.

   — Trail runs north along lake's west shoreline.

1.5— Junction. Intersection with horse trail.

1.6— Junction. *Emerald Basin* left.

1.7— Junction. Yoho Pass-*Wapta Highline Circuit* left.

   — Cross open alluvial plain along lake's north shore.

2.2— Inlet bridge.

   — Follow through dense forest along east shore.

3.8— Junction. Burgess Pass left. Lakeshore trail bends right.

4.3— Junction. Peaceful Pond cutoff to parking area left.

4.6— Junction. Emerald Lake Lodge complex. Turn left for parking area.

   — Cutoff trail runs behind lodge complex.

5.2— Emerald Lake parking area (1300 m).

The trip around Emerald Lake's shoreline requires no more than two hours of easy walking. It is surprisingly scenic, with many open views to Mount Burgess and the President Range, and an excellent place to experience the vegetation of this mild and moist western slope forest. Trails to Emerald Basin, Yoho Pass and Burgess Pass also branch from the circuit.

You can hike the circuit clockwise or counterclockwise, but for some reason we always go clockwise. Following the paved trail leading from the north end of the Emerald Lake parking area, you soon turn the northwest corner of the lake and enter a large avalanche path. Here you get your first good view across the lake—the much-photographed scene of Emerald Lake and Mount Burgess. The pavement ends beyond avalanche path but the trail remains wide, and there are a number of log benches at lakeside.

After joining the horse trail, you bend right and pass two junctions in rapid succession—trails continuing north to Emerald Basin and Yoho Pass. The circuit continues across an alluvial plain, where there are views south across the lake to the lodge and the distant Ottertail Range. At the far side of the alluvial flats, you cross the inlet bridge and turn south along the eastern shoreline.

The east shore is quite different from the west. It is heavily forested, moist and cool, and dominated by lush vegetation, including thimbleberry, bunchberry, alder, western red cedar, and fallen spruce trees covered with feather moss. (We always find moose droppings on this section of trail.)

The trail bends right at the lake's southeast corner and climbs into forest above the south shore back to the lodge. At km 4.3 you can take the Peaceful Pond cutoff back to the parking area or continue ahead to the lodge.

149 Hamilton Lake

Emerald Lake to Hamilton Lake—5.5 km (3.4 mi)

Day trip

Allow 1.5 to 2 hours one way

Elevation gain: 850 m (2,800 ft)

Maximum elevation: 2150 m (7,050 ft)

Maps: Golden 82 N/8
Lake Louise & Yoho (Gem Trek)

Access: Follow the Trans-Canada Highway to its intersection with the Emerald Lake Road, 2 km (1.2 mi) west of the Field intersection. Follow the Emerald Lake Road north 8.5 km (5.3 mi) to its termination at the Emerald Lake parking area. The trailhead is located at the entrance to the parking area on the west side of the road.

  0.0—Trailhead (1300 m).
      N51°26.301' W116°32.460'

  0.2—Junction. Emerald River trail left.
      Stay ahead.

    —Moderate uphill through forest.

  0.8—Hamilton Falls.

    —Steady switchbacking ascent.

  3.9—Emerald Lake viewpoint.

    —Grade moderates.

  5.5—Hamilton Lake (2150 m).

This steep trail climbs densely forested slopes to a small tarn tucked into a hanging valley between Mount Carnarvon and Emerald Peak. While Hamilton Lake is blessed by a remarkable setting and far-reaching views, many hikers seem to avoid it, probably because of the steep, relentless approach.

The trail escapes the busy Emerald Lake parking area with little fanfare, slipping quickly into the forest from a simple trail sign at the parking lot entrance.

A short distance into this mature subalpine forest you encounter Hamilton Falls—a more popular destination than the lake above. This cascade drops down a steep limestone staircase, where the action of the water has smoothed and dissolved bedrock to form numerous pothole depressions. At a switchback a short distance up the trail, there is a fine view of the upper falls as well.

The route is closed-in and arduous beyond the falls, and there are no open views until the 4-km mark, where a short side trail leads through the trees to a viewpoint overlooking Emerald Lake. Beyond the viewpoint the grade moderates somewhat, and the trail soon emerges onto open slopes overlooking the Kicking Horse Valley.

Just as you are relegating yourself to another half-hour or so of steep slogging, the trail suddenly cuts upward and pops into the Hamilton Lake cirque.

Beautiful as it is unexpected, the lake extends to the very lip of its amphitheatre, its water riffled by the occasional down-slope breeze. By stepping across the outlet, you can continue along the west shore to a pleasant knoll and look back through the cirque's entrance to the Kicking Horse Valley. In the far distance, and framed perfectly through the opening, is glacier-capped Mount Vaux and the twin towers of Mount Goodsir—the highest summits in Yoho Park.

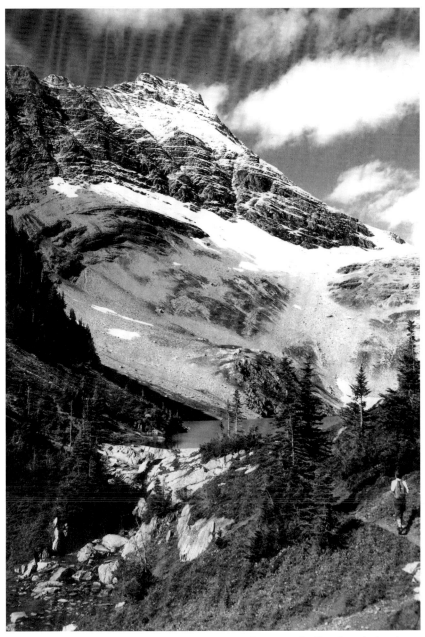

Entering the Hamilton Lake cirque

150 Emerald Basin

Emerald Lake to Emerald Basin—4.6 km (2.9 mi)

Half-day trip

Allow 1.5 hours one way

Elevation gain: 225 m (740 ft)

Maximum elevation: 1525 m (5,000 ft)

Maps: Golden 82 N/8
Lake Louise & Yoho (Gem Trek)

Access: Follow the Trans-Canada Highway to its intersection with the Emerald Lake Road, 2 km (1.2 mi) west of the Field townsite intersection. Follow the Emerald Lake Road north 8.5 km (5.3 mi) to its termination at the Emerald Lake parking area. The trailhead kiosk is located at the north end of the parking area beside the bridge to Emerald Lake Lodge.

0.0— Trailhead (1300 m).
N51°26.378' W116°32.500'

— Trail follows *Emerald Lake Circuit* around west shore of lake.

1.6— Junction. Lake circuit right. Emerald Basin left.

2.3— Junction. Yoho Pass ahead. Emerald Basin left.

— Steep ascent on rocky, rooty trail.

2.8— Trail flattens out above gorge.

3.8— Avalanche path.

4.1— Trail drops to floor of Emerald Basin.

— Trail follows up valley bottom.

4.6— Emerald Basin cairn (1525 m). End of official trail.

Emerald Basin is a rocky, avalanche-swept amphitheatre carved from the imposing cliffs of The President Range. The short trail branching up to the basin from the north end of Emerald Lake is a bit rough, and it is the least-travelled of the area's trails.

The trail follows the Emerald Lake shoreline circuit around the west side of the lake for 1.6 km to the first of two junctions just beyond the lake's north shore. Turn left and continue north through scattered lodgepole pine for 0.7 km to another junction, where the trail to Emerald Basin branches uphill to the left.

There is a short, steep climb as the rocky and rooty trail begins its ascent along the canyon below Emerald Basin. The grade moderates once you reach the edge of the deep gorge, where views open across the chasm to Michael Peak.

Another kilometre through a cool, moist forest of western hemlock and red cedar brings you to a major avalanche path, where the trail descends to the stream on the valley floor. A rough, rocky trail continues up-valley to a large rock cairn—the end of official trail in the midst of the Emerald Basin.

Though the basin is well below treeline, avalanches have cleared much of the forest cover from the surrounding slopes (snow from these slides often lingers in the basin through mid-summer). Views are totally open to the steep slopes and massive cliffs that tightly embrace the basin, including an impressive limestone wall at the head of the valley, which forms the end of The President's south ridge. Views extend back down-valley to Wapta Mountain, Mount Burgess and the lofty summit of Mount Stephen beyond Burgess Pass.

You can follow snippets of trail upstream for another kilometre or so to the head of the valley, where a pair of waterfalls plunge from the cliffs. This is also a good area for spying mountain goats.

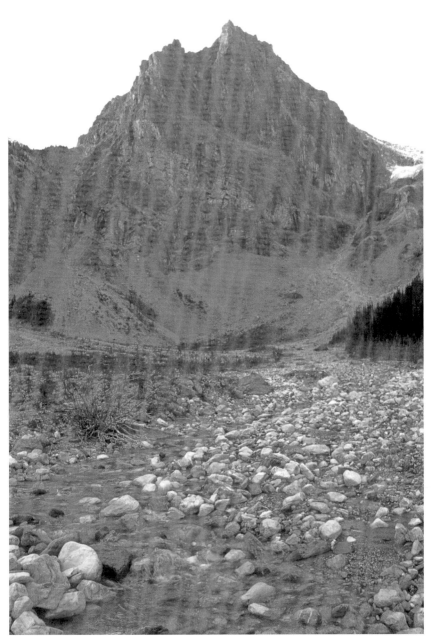

Emerald Basin

151 Wapta Highline Circuit

Yoho Pass-Burgess Pass Loop from Emerald Lake—19.7 km (12.2 mi)

Day trip

Allow 5 to 6 hours

Elevation gain: 880 m (2,890 ft)

Maximum elevation: 2180 m (7,160 ft)

Maps: Lake Louise 82 N/8
       Golden 82 N/8
       Lake Louise & Yoho (Gem Trek)

Access: Follow the Trans-Canada Highway to its intersection with the Emerald Lake Road, 2 km (1.2 mi) west of the Field townsite intersection. Follow the Emerald Lake Road north 8.5 km (5.3 mi) to its termination at the Emerald Lake parking area. The trailhead kiosk is located at the north end of the parking area beside the bridge to Emerald Lake Lodge.

0.0—Trailhead (1300 m).
     N51°26.378' W116°32.500'

— Trail follows *Emerald Lake Circuit* around west shore of lake.

1.6—Junction. *Emerald Basin* left. Keep right.

1.7—Junction. Emerald Lake Circuit ahead. Yoho Pass left.

3.5—Major stream. Trail begins to climb.

4.4—Falls viewpoint.

6.4—Yoho Pass Junction (1815 m). *Yoho Lake* ahead 0.6 km. Burgess Pass right.

— Trail climbs south along Wapta Mtn.

12.5—Burgess Pass Junction (2180 m). Intersection with *Burgess Pass* trail at km 7.6 . Kicking Horse Valley left. Emerald Lake right.

— Trail switchbacks down through forest.

18.3—Junction. Intersection with *Emerald Lake Circuit* at km 3.8. Keep left.

18.8—Junction. Peaceful Pond and Emerald Lake parking area left. Lodge ahead.

19.1—Emerald Lake Lodge Junction. Stay left for parking area.

19.7—Emerald Lake parking area (1300 m).

There aren't many good loop trips for day hikers in the Canadian Rockies, but the Wapta Highline Circuit is one of the best. You travel beside the shores of Emerald Lake, visit two passes, and make a high traverse across Wapta Mountain, where you overlook the lake and all its surrounding peaks. All of this in the space of 20 km and without having to backtrack. If you can only do one hike at Emerald Lake, and you are up for a fairly long day, this is the one to consider.

We always hike this circuit in a clockwise direction since it provides a gradual approach to the circuit's highest point on Burgess Pass. The hike departs from the north end of the Emerald Lake parking area and follows the Emerald Lake shoreline circuit around the west side of the lake for the first 1.7 km.

At the north end of the lake the Yoho Pass route breaks away from the lakeshore trail and crosses a sparsely forested alluvial fan—an extensive outwash of silt and gravel from the President Range's Emerald Basin. Beyond the flats you begin the steep climb to Yoho Pass. Views back to Emerald Lake improve as you gain elevation, and there is a fine waterfall to the north below Michael Peak.

There is little to indicate your arrival at Yoho Pass other than a moderation of the uphill grade and a trail junction in the forest. This is the first corner on the triangular circuit, where you stay to the right and head south to Burgess Pass. However, a short walk of 0.6 km on the left-hand branch leads to Yoho Lake—a small lake bordered by a lush wildflower meadow. This is the approach to the Yoho Valley taken by the German alpinist Jean Habel on his journey of discovery in 1897, and the route followed by members of the Alpine Club of Canada to their first annual camp at Yoho Lake in 1906. (See also *Yoho Lake*.)

The trail to Burgess Pass gains 300 m along the slopes of Wapta Mountain

The President Range from the slopes of Wapta Mountain

over the next 6 km. This is the Wapta Highline section of the hike, and despite the steady ascent, the beauty of this traverse dispels any sense of drudgery. Open wildflower meadows are scattered along the way, and there are impressive views down to Emerald Lake and back to the heavily-glaciated President Range.

As you near Burgess Pass, you encounter a well-defined trail branching uphill toward the col between Wapta Mountain and Mount Field. This steep track leads to the site of the world-famous Burgess Shale Beds, where paleontologists have laboured for many summers, unearthing many new and wonderful Middle Cambrian fossils. As a sign at the junction indicates, hikers are not permitted to go there except on guided tours led by Parks Canada or the Yoho-Burgess Shale Foundation. (See *Sources—Guided walks.*)

The second corner of the circuit triangle is reached at a junction on Burgess Pass. By hiking a short distance on the left-hand branch, you can look down to the Kicking Horse Valley and across to Mount Stephen—the highest and most impressive peak near the village of Field.

This trail also serves as an optional route between Burgess Pass and the Kicking Horse Valley. (See *Burgess Pass.*)

The trail back to Emerald Lake cuts downhill to the right from Burgess Pass junction. There are a few more good views before the trail plunges down into a cool, moist forest quite unlike what you'd normally encounter in the Rockies—a micro-environment dominated by western red cedar.

The steady, steep, switchbacking descent ends at an intersection with the *Emerald Lake Circuit* 5.5 km below Burgess Pass. The route back to the lodge and parking area stays left and follows the lake's southern shore.

152 Burgess Pass

Burgess Pass trail parking area to Burgess Pass—7.3 km (4.5 mi)

Day trip

Allow 2.5 hours one way

Elevation gain: 930 m (3,060 ft)

Maximum elevation: 2180 m (7,160 ft)

Maps: Lake Louise 82 N/8
Lake Louise & Yoho (Gem Trek)

Access: Follow the Trans-Canada Highway to the access road for the Burgess Pass trail, on the north side of the highway 1.2 km (0.7 mi) east of the village of Field intersection. Follow the access road (keep left at split) 0.4 km to the parking area.

0.0— Trailhead (1250 m).
N51°24.291' W116°28.984'

— Trail climbs gradually to west above highway.

0.7— Trail begins steep climb toward pass.

3.0— Forest begins to thin.

3.8— Open rockslide.

— Steady uphill via switchbacks.

7.0— Trail crosses steep, open slope.

7.6— Burgess Pass Junction (2180 m). Intersection with *Wapta Highline Circuit* at km 12.5. Emerald Lake left. Yoho Pass right.

We used this trail on our first ever trip to Burgess Pass many years ago. We were pleased with the views from the top, but it was a hot day and the steady climb up the south-facing slope was gruelling.

We've since visited the pass several times by less strenuous routes—the *Wapta Highline Circuit* from Emerald Lake, and as a through-hike from Yoho Valley via Yoho Pass and then down the Burgess Pass trail to the Kicking Horse Valley trailhead. But if you'd like the workout, you can still approach it from the Kicking Horse trailhead just off the Trans-Canada Highway east of Field.

The trail runs west through the forest above the Trans-Canada for nearly a kilometre before it turns north and begins the relentless climb to the pass. Views are limited by forest for the first 3 km, but beyond that point the trees begin to thin, and you catch occasional glimpses of Mount Stephen. An open rockslide at km 3.8 provides an unfettered view of Stephen, the Cathedral Crags, and the Kicking Horse Valley running away to the southwest.

There is a giddy view over a sharp cliff into the Emerald Lake basin when you reach the pass. However, the best views back over the Kicking Horse Valley are achieved by leaving the trail and traversing eastward through stands of alpine fir and larch to the highest point on the summit ridge.

From the junction on Burgess Pass, the trail to Emerald Lake branches down to the left, or you can stay right and traverse the open slopes of Wapta Mountain to Yoho Pass. (See *Wapta Highline Circuit*.)

And remember what we said at the outset: this is a steep, dry hike, so make sure you have a good supply of water along.

153 Emerald River

Natural Bridge to Emerald Lake—9.1 km (5.7 mi)

Half-day trip

Allow 2.5 to 3 hours one way

Elevation loss: 60 m (200 ft)
        gain: 180 m (590 ft)

Maximum elevation: 1340 m (4,400 ft)

Maps: Golden 82 N/8
      Lake Louise & Yoho (Gem Trek)

Access: Follow the Trans-Canada Highway to its intersection with the Emerald Lake Road, 2 km (1.2 mi) west of the Field intersection. Follow the Emerald Lake Road north 2 km (1.2 mi) to the Natural Bridge parking area. The hike begins at the barricaded entrance to the Kicking Horse Fire Road at the west edge of the parking area.

From the north end of the trail, begin the hike at the *Hamilton Lake* trailhead near the entrance to the Emerald Lake parking area.

0.0—Natural Bridge trailhead (1220 m).
     N51°22.949' W116°31.879'

  — Trail descends on broad, gravel fire road.

0.8—Mineral lick.

1.4—Emerald River bridge and junction (1160 m). *Amiskwi River* trail ahead. Emerald River trail right.

  — Trail climbs above Emerald River gorge.

2.9— Trail comes abreast of Emerald River.

3.6— Bridge foundations (1200 m).

5.2— Trail veers away from river.

  — Dense forest with occasional small stream crossings (bridged or rock-hop).

7.2— Trail summit (1340 m).

  — Gradual descent.

8.8— Junction. Horse corrals and Emerald Lake Road right 150 m. Stay ahead.

8.9— Junction. *Hamilton Lake* left. Emerald Lake parking area right.

9.1— Emerald Lake trailhead (1300 m).
     N51°26.301' W116°32.460'

This forest-enclosed trail running north from the Kicking Horse River to Emerald Lake has limited appeal. You are only along the Emerald River for 4 km or so, and the last half is simply a walk in the woods. However, at the south end of the trail, the open flats surrounding the confluence of the Amiskwi, Emerald and Kicking Horse Rivers are a worthwhile destination.

From the Natural Bridge parking area, follow the gradually descending fire road 1.4 km to the Emerald River bridge (watch for moose in a muddy mineral lick below the road at 0.8 km). On the opposite side of the bridge, the signed Emerald River trail branches right, but you'll likely want to linger at this scenic river confluence—the Amiskwi River bridge is 150 m further along, and the Kicking Horse flows south towards the Ottertail Range. (See also *Amiskwi River*.)

To continue the journey, follow the trail climbing into pine forest from the west end of the Emerald River bridge. You stay in contact with the river through this first section and, in just over 2 km, arrive at old, wooden bridge foundations where a road to the Amiskwi Valley once crossed the river. A clearing here is a good spot for a break, and a good turnaround point if you don't have transportation awaiting you at Emerald Lake.

If you continue north, the trail soon breaks away from the river and climbs through rooty spruce forest and along dry, pine-covered slopes (2 or 3 small stream crossings). It reaches its highest point in a dense forest carpeted with ferns and feather moss, then makes a short, gradual descent to corrals and intersecting trails near the Emerald Lake parking area.

The Kicking Horse Fire Road is open to bikes, but the trail north beyond the 1.4-km junction is not.

Natural Bridge to Amiskwi Pass—39.6 km

Backpack

Allow 2 days to Amiskwi Pass

Elevation gain: 820 m (2,700 ft)

Maximum elevation: 1980 m (6,500 ft)

Maps: Golden 82 N/8
       Blaeberry River 82 N/10

Access: Follow the Trans-Canada Highway to its intersection with the Emerald Lake Road, 2 km (1.2 mi) west of the Field townsite intersection. Follow the Emerald Lake Road north 2 km (1.2 mi) to the Natural Bridge parking area. The hike begins at the barricaded entrance to the Kicking Horse Fire Road at the west edge of the parking area.

   0.0— Trailhead (1220 m).
        N51°22.949' W116°31.879'

   — Trail descends on broad, gravel fire road.

   0.8— Mineral lick.

   1.4— Emerald River bridge and junction.
        Emerald River right.
        Amiskwi River trail ahead.

   1.6— Amiskwi River bridge.

   1.7— Junction (1160 m).
        Kicking Horse Fire Road left.
        Amiskwi River right.

   — Track narrows. Steady climb for 2 km.

   18.6— Fire Creek bridge.

   20.6— Otto Creek bridge and junction.
        Otto Creek Warden Cabin left.
        Stay right across bridge.
        (End of bike access.)

   28.1— Amiskwi River crossing
        (calf-deep ford).

   33.0— End of old roadbed.*

   35.5— Amiskwi Falls.*

   39.6— Amiskwi Pass (1980 m).

   41.0— Amiskwi Lodge parking area (1900 m).
        N51°37.122' W116°40.826.

*Approximate distance.

(Trail not fully shown on maps in this book.)

The meadows above Amiskwi Pass provide wonderful views of the heavily-glaciated peaks of the Mummery Group. However, the hike up the Amiskwi Valley to the pass is one of the longest and most remote wilderness trips in Yoho Park. Of course, if you want to cheat, you can reach Amiskwi Pass in less than a half hour from the Ensign Creek logging road (see below).

Despite following an old access road for 29 km and passing through extensive sections of fire-scarred landscape, the trek up-valley provides many peaceful and scenic moments. The road is also open to cyclists as far as the Otto Creek bridge, and random camping is permitted throughout the valley.

After descending from Natural Bridge on broad, gravel road, you cross the Emerald and Amiskwi River bridges and reach the Kicking Horse-Amiskwi junction at km 1.7. A rock barricade has kept vehicles off the Amiskwi trail for many years, so the roadbed is growing inwards to a single path, which climbs steadily for 2 km before leveling off well above the river.

The roadbed traverses high along the west side of the valley until Fire Creek, where it begins to descend to the river. Between Fire Creek and Otto Creek you traverse the open slopes of the appropriately named Burnt Hill, which provide good views across the valley to the President Range.

After reaching the valley floor, the road rolls through burned and unburned sections of forest. It crosses the unbridged Amiskwi (knee-deep ford) and continues up the east side of the river for another 5 km to its termination at an old mill site. Single-track trail continues to the pass.

After passing beneath Amiskwi Falls, ford the Amiskwi River (calf-deep) and enter unburned forest for the final stretch to the pass. Views from the pass

© Don Beers   *The Mummery Group from the Amiskwi Lodge meadows*

are limited, but 1.3 km beyond the summit and park boundary, you reach the end of the Ensign Creek logging road and the parking area for Amiskwi Lodge.

Just beyond a fenced parking area, the trail to Amiskwi Lodge (1.0 km) branches uphill to the right, where you will find alpine meadows and glorious views of the Mummery Group and its massive glaciers.

Amiskwi Pass via Ensign Creek. This may be the easiest way to reach Amiskwi Pass, but it is undoubtedly the longest and toughest drive to a short hike in the Rockies. Much of the approach is over unsurfaced forestry road and steep, rough logging roads, so a vehicle with high clearance is required. (The Blaeberry River forestry road has been subject to washouts in the past, so check with the Columbia Forest District in Revelstoke, B.C., before attempting this approach.)

Follow the Trans-Canada Highway west 11 km from the Highway 95 intersection at Golden, B.C., and turn right onto the Moberly Branch Road. Continue 2.2 km to the Golden-Donald Road

and turn left. Follow 1 km to the Oberg-Johnson Road and turn right. Continue 1.7 km to the Moberly School Road and turn left. The Moberly School Road becomes the Blaeberry Road in less than 1 km and leads up the Blaeberry Valley.

Forestry road markers lead you the rest of the way up-valley near the Blaeberry River. Just 300 m beyond the 34-km marker, the logging road to Ensign Creek branches right and immediately crosses a bridge to the east side of the river. Follow this road to a split 0.9 km beyond the bridge, and stay left on the less-defined road. Continue up this steep, switchbacking branch to another split at 7.7 km. Stay right and climb steadily south along the Ensign Creek valley for another 7.6 km to road's end in an old clearcut below Amiskwi Pass.

A fenced parking area protects vehicle tires from resident porcupines. Just beyond, signs indicate the trail up a densely wooded vale to Amiskwi Pass (1.3 km) and, to the left, the steep 1.0-km trail to Amiskwi Lodge and the alpine meadows. Accommodation at the lodge is by reservation only. (See *Sources—Backcountry lodges.*)

155 Ottertail River

Trans-Canada Highway to McArthur Creek Campground—14.9 km (9.3 mi)

Backpack

Allow 4 to 5 hours one way

Elevation gain: 285 m (935 ft)

Maximum elevation: 1480 m (4,850 ft)

Maps: Lake Louise 82 N/8
Golden 82 N/8
Lake Louise & Yoho (Gem Trek)

Access: Follow the Trans-Canada Highway to the Ottertail River bridge, 8.5 km (5.5 mi) west of Field. The entrance to the trailhead parking area is on the south side of the highway 300 m east of the bridge.

0.0— Trailhead (1195 m).
N51°20.131' W116°33.015'

— Gradual to moderate uphill.

2.8— Hoodoos viewpoint.

— Gradual uphill above river.

3.5— Giddie Creek bridge.

5.2— Moderately steep downhill next 1.0 km.

6.2— Float Creek bridge.

— Trail climbs away from river and continues gradual ascent of valley.

14.5— Junction. *McArthur Creek* trail left.

14.6— McArthur Creek bridge.

14.9— McArthur Creek Campground (1480 m).

15.1— McArthur Creek Patrol Cabin.

15.5— Ottertail River bridge.

16.2— Junction. Goodsir Pass ahead (see *Helmet Creek*, Kootenay Park chapter). Ottertail Falls left 1.5 km.

(Trail not shown on maps in this book.)

The Ottertail River trail follows an old fire road up a narrow forested valley for 15 km to the to the McArthur Creek Campground and Patrol Cabin. While it's not a particularly inspiring hike, this well-graded trail does provide some views of the river, a small group of hoodoos and, at its culmination, the Goodsirs—Yoho Park's highest peaks.

The trail is mainly used by backpackers as an optional access-exit route for Goodsir Pass and the northern end of Kootenay Park's Rockwall Trail. It is also open to cyclists as far as the McArthur Creek Patrol Cabin.

From a small parking area beside the Trans-Canada Highway, the trail climbs into a dense forest of pine, spruce and aspen. At 1.4 km it emerges onto a bench above the Ottertail River, where views open out across the Kicking Horse Valley to the Van Horne Range and up the Ottertail to Mounts Hurd and Ennis.

At km 2.8 you pass above a steep cutbank where a number of hoodoos have been created by the erosion of calcareous soils and gravels along the river. The exposed soils are also utilized as a mineral lick by local mountain goats.

Beyond Float Creek, the trail swings away from the river and gradually climbs through a subalpine forest of Engelmann spruce and alpine fir. The McArthur Creek trail intersects from the left at 14.5 km (see *McArthur Creek*), and a well-sheltered campground is passed on the right 400 m further along.

Just 200 m beyond the campground, the old roadbed ends at the McArthur Creek Patrol Cabin, which sits on a pleasant, open bench with a commanding view of the twin summits of Mount Goodsir.

The trail runs south from the patrol cabin and crosses the Ottertail River. A 1.5-km trail to Ottertail Falls branches left at km 16.2, while the main trail continues south to Goodsir Pass (see *Helmet Creek*, Kootenay Park chapter).

156 McArthur Creek

Ottertail River to Lake O'Hara—12.4 km (7.7 mi)

Backpack

Allow 4 hours to Lake O'Hara

Elevation gain: 730 m (2,400 ft)
loss: 175 m (570 ft)

Maximum elevation: 2210 m (7,250 ft)

Maps: Lake Louise 82 N/8
Lake Louise & Yoho (Gem Trek)

Access: Follow the *Ottertail River* trail to the McArthur Creek junction at km 14.5–0.4 km downstream from McArthur Creek Campground.

0.0—Ottertail River Junction (1480 m).
N51°16.682' W116°23.246'

—Moderate climb through forest and avalanche paths.

6.0—McArthur Creek crossing.

—Moderate to steep uphill through meadows and forest.

10.0—Junction. Lake McArthur low-route. Keep left.

10.3—McArthur Pass (2210 m).

—Steady descent through forest.

10.8—Schaffer Lake Junction. Intersect with *Lake McArthur* high-route at km 1.6. Keep left.

11.8—Elizabeth Parker Hut Junction. Keep right.

12.4—Lake O'Hara Road (2035 m).
N51°21.454' W116°20.337'

(Trail not fully shown on maps in this book.)

The McArthur Creek trail connects the Ottertail Valley with Lake O'Hara via McArthur Pass. It is usually hiked at the beginning or end of backpacking trips, especially by those following the original Great Divide Trail route. Because the valley is an important wildlife corridor, particularly for grizzly bears, the trail is no longer maintained and there are travel restrictions. However, it can still be used in late summer by special permit.

The trail up the valley starts from a junction with the Ottertail River trail at km 14.5 (see *Ottertail River*). While the trail should still be obvious at this intersection, don't expect that to last. Over the first six km, it climbs through dense forest broken by small meadows and then avalanche paths— expect deadfall and brushy, overgrown track. Stay vigilant for bears and make noise when visibility is limited, which is often.

The route crosses McArthur Creek at km 6.0 and then makes a more serious climb northeast to McArthur Pass. When you reach the Lake McArthur low-route trail, you are only 300 m from the pass. From there, you follow well-travelled trail down through subalpine forest and meadows to Lake O'Hara (see *Lake McArthur* and *Lake O'Hara* introduction).

Restrictions: No travel is permitted in the McArthur Creek valley before August 15. After that, two parties per week may hike the trail after obtaining a permit from a Visitor Centre or Parks Canada's Calgary office. Permits are available three months in advance of departure or, if still available, 24-hours in advance of departure on a first-come, first-served basis at the same locations. No camping is permitted in the valley. Check the Parks Canada website for Yoho Park for full details and current policy (see *Sources—Parks information*).

N

Porcupine

Creek

Field

Horse

River

Kicking

1

Mt▲
Hurd

Mt▲
Vaux

Old
Lookout
Site

160

Mt Hunter
Fire Lookout

Golden

1

Kicking

beaverfoot

Horse

Hoodoos

157

Hoodoo

Creek

Chancellor
▲Pk

River

P

P

Road

159

Wapta
Falls

Beaverfoot

158

River

Ice River

Land above 2300 metres

| 0 | 1 | 2 | 3 | 4km |

Hoodoos

157 Hoodoos

Hoodoo Creek Campground to Hoodoos—2.6 km (1.6 mi)

This short steep trail climbs into a narrow valley containing some of the most extraordinary hoodoo formations in the mountain parks. These sentinel-like pillars of silt, gravel and stone have been formed by erosion, which has eaten away at a slope of partly-consolidated, calcareous glacial debris. Unlike most other hoodoos in the Rockies, cap rocks sit like flat hats on top of the pillars, protecting the material beneath from erosion.

A prescribed burn in 2005 resulted in the closure of most of Hoodoo Creek Campground, and forest surrounding the nearby Deerlodge historic cabin was destroyed. So the most direct route to the trail runs through a section of abandoned campground to a bridge over Hoodoo Creek at 0.9 km (well-signed). After this relatively-flat campground approach, the last 1.7 km climbs quite steeply along the north slope of the Hoodoo Creek valley.

When you near the Hoodoos at km 2.4, the trail splits: the right runs downhill to the base of the formations within 200 m; left is slightly longer and the climb very steep to the superior upper viewpoint. Chancellor Peak is the dramatic mountain rising above the valley to the southeast.

Access: Follow the Trans-Canada Highway to the Hoodoo Creek Campground, 22.5 km (14 mi) west of Field or 7 km (4.5 mi) east of Yoho Park's west boundary. Pass the current campground circle on the left and stay right on paved access road to the entrance to the old A-F campground circles (0.6 km from highway). Park beside the road and start the hike at the cable-barrier. N51°13.336' W116°34.121' *Maps: McMurdo 82 N/2.*

158 Ice River

Hoodoo Creek Campground to Upper Ice River Cabin—25.2 km (15.7 mi)

Backpack

Allow 2 days to Upper Ice River

Elevation gain: 360 m (1,200 ft)

Maximum elevation: 1480 m (4,850 ft)

Maps: McMurdo 82 N/2
Mount Goodsir 82 N/1

Access: Follow the Trans-Canada Highway to the Hoodoo Creek Campground, 22.5 km (14 mi) west of Field or 7 km (4.5 mi) east of Yoho Park's west boundary. Pass the current campground circle on the left and stay right on paved access road to a branch road with cable-barrier on the right (0.5 km from highway). Park beside the road and start the hike at the cable-barrier.

0.0—Trailhead (1120 m).
N51°13.348' W116°34.228'

0.4—Junction. Trail kiosk.
Deerlodge Cabin left. Ice River ahead.

—Gently rolling roadbed along swampy meadows and through heavy forest.

6.0—Steep Creek.

10.0—Tallon Creek.

18.8—Lower Ice River Patrol Cabin (1280 m).

—Trail crosses bridge and park boundary to east side of Ice River.

19.0—Junction. Kootenay River forestry road ahead. Upper Ice River left.

21.2—Mollison Creek.

24.4—Sodalite Creek.

25.2—Upper Ice River Patrol Cabin (1480 m).

Situated on the southern boundary of Yoho Park, the Ice River trail is yet another low elevation valley that is short on scenery but well endowed with peace and solitude. The upper valley lies in the centre of the most important intrusive igneous complex in the Rockies—an area with significant deposits of zinc and blue sodalite.

The roadbed to the Lower Ice River Patrol Cabin is open to cyclists, which is the most popular way to visit the valley. Random camping is permitted along the Beaverfoot Valley, but camping is not permitted on the upper Ice River. The entire trail runs through prime grizzly country.

From the campground access road, the roadbed runs due south and passes a trail kiosk and the short branch trail to Deerlodge Cabin at 0.4 km. After passing the site of the old Leanchoil Warden Cabin on open flats beside the Kicking Horse River, the road turns southwest and, after a short stretch along the river, enters forest and rolls along the east side of the Beaverfoot Valley for nearly 18 km to the Lower Ice River Patrol Cabin.

The road ends at the patrol cabin and, just beyond, crosses a bridge and the park boundary to a junction on the southeast side of the Ice River. The route ahead runs into clearcuts and a logging road that reaches the Beaverfoot Road in another 10 km; the trail up the Ice River branches left.

The Ice River trail makes a gradual ascent along the east side of the river, re-entering Yoho Park approximately 1.5 km beyond the junction. It stays on this side of the river all the way to the Upper Ice River Patrol Cabin. This dubious route is mostly enveloped by forest—a dense mix of Douglas fir, white spruce, poplar and alder. The valley is tight and there are few views worth mentioning.

Wapta Falls

159 Wapta Falls

Wapta Falls Parking Area to Wapta Falls—2.3 km (1.4 mi)

The Wapta Falls trail makes an excellent afternoon outing—it is short, wide and well-defined and, with the exception of a short, steep descent to the lower viewpoint, flat and undemanding. The objective of the hike is a 30-m-high waterfall on the Kicking Horse River—Yoho's largest waterfall by water-volume.

The hike follows an old roadbed for 1.0 km before narrowing to a traditional single-track. You travel through a cool, mossy forest for the last half of the journey—a rich mixture of alder, birch, western red cedar and cottonwood poplar.

You arrive at the fenced upper viewpoint overlooking the falls at 1.9 km. While the view is impressive, we always continue down to the riverside beach below the falls—a steep, switchbacking descent.

The view of the falls from the riverside is partially obscured by a ridge of erosion resistant rock jutting across the river, but at low water you can continue upstream to better vantage points. There is also a nice mountain backdrop created by the Chancellor Range from this angle.

A slightly longer alternate trail climbs back to the upper viewpoint from the riverside. It is more moderately-graded and passes through some incredibly lush vegetation, which includes the insidious devil's-club.

Access: Follow the Trans-Canada Highway to the Wapta Falls access road, 5 km (3 mi) east of Yoho Park's west boundary or 25 km (15.5 mi) west of Field. The gravel access road continues south 1.8 km (1.1 mi) to the trailhead parking area. N51°12.232′ W116°35.095′ *Maps: McMurdo 82 N/2.*

Beaverfoot and Kicking Horse Valleys from Mount Hunter's upper lookout site

between Yoho Park and provincial forest lands. When we first hiked here in 1970, the west side of the Beaverfoot was totally denuded by clearcuts, but they have since been replanted and are hardly noticeable today.

Unfortunately, the Trans-Canada Highway is still visible and audible, even though it lies 400 vertical metres below. Of more interest is the broad swath of downed timber above the highway. No, its not a clearcut, but rather the aftermath of the "Yoho Blow"—a severe windstorm that swept through the valley November 21, 1993. More than 200 hectares of forest on both sides of the highway were flattened by winds exceeding 100 km per hour.

If you still have energy to spare, you can climb along the ridge for another 2.6 km to the upper lookout site, which is twice as high above the valley as the lower lookout. Views are more limited on the upper trail, but the forest becomes noticeably subalpine as you near trail's end. A well-constructed piece of trail with shale reinforcement announces the final 500 m to the lookout keeper's log cabin.

From the cabin you walk out onto the open bluff where the wooden-legged lookout tower once stood. Like most of the fire lookouts in the mountain parks, Mount Hunter was erected in the early 1940s. Though it was later replaced by the lower tower, it stood until the early 1990s when Parks Canada removed it.

Views are similar to those from the lower lookout site, though more expansive and impressive due to the higher elevation.

Kootenay National Park

Kootenay National Park is a 1406-sq-km reserve on the British Columbia side of the Great Divide—the last national park to be created in the Canadian Rockies in 1920. It is bounded on the north by Yoho National Park and on the east by Banff National Park and Mount Assiniboine Provincial Park.

Of the four adjoining mountain national parks, Kootenay is possibly the least known by the average visitor. However, its 200-km trail system runs to some of the most rugged scenery and interesting natural features in the range.

All Kootenay hikes start from Highway 93. Many are short and ideally suited for families or those looking for undemanding walks. Marble Canyon and the Paint Pots, near the north end of the park, are both popular self-guiding nature trails; Stanley Glacier, Dog Lake, and Cobb Lake are rewarding half-day outings; Floe Lake and Kindersley Pass are two of the park's most popular full-day trips.

Though no section of the park seems to be very far from Highway 93, there are several excellent backpacking opportunities on the Tumbling, Helmet, Numa and Floe Creek trails as well as the Rockwall Trail, which connects the headwaters of these four watersheds. These trails can be linked in a variety of ways to make overnight loop trips, or you can complete a classic multi-day trip along the Rockwall. Campgrounds are conveniently spaced along all of these trails, and there is a tent quota for each. Reservations for sites can be made through the Kootenay National Park Information Centre. (See *Sources—Parks information*.)

Information and services. The Kootenay National Park Information Centre is at the south end of Radium village, beside the road leading to Redstreak Campground. The centre is staffed by Parks Canada employees from mid-May until early October, and basic information is provided by Radium Chamber of Commerce staff during the off-season. The Kootenay Park Lodge Visitor Centre provides basic information and interpretive displays during the summer season; the centre is attached to the lodge's general store, which is on Highway 93, 63 km (39 mi) north of the park's west entrance and 31 km (19 mi) south of the Banff-Kootenay Park boundary. A full range of services for Kootenay Park is available off-season from the Yoho National Park Visitor Centre (see *Sources—Parks information*).

McLeod Meadows and Marble Canyon Campgrounds operate along Highway 93 during the summer season. The park's largest and only full-service campground is Redstreak, which is accessed by a road running from the village of Radium.

Radium, B.C., is located just beyond the park's west gate at the intersection of Highways 93 and 95. It is the main service centre for the park and the site of the park administration offices. Services include restaurants, accommodations, grocery stores, service stations, souvenir shops, a post office and a RCMP detachment. Accommodation and dining inside the park is limited to Kootenay Park Lodge at Vermilion Crossing (summer only).

Access: Highway 93 is the only road through the park. The highway intersects the Trans-Canada Highway at Castle Junction in Banff Park and Highway 95 at Radium, B.C. The nearest international airport is at Calgary, Alberta, 264 km east of Radium; commercial flights also operate out of Cranbrook, B.C., 145 km south of Radium on Highway 93/95.

Radium is a stop for Greyhound buses running between Calgary and southeastern B.C., and between Cranbook and Golden, B.C.

Kaufmann
Lake

Mt
Oke

Chimney
Pk

Boom Lake

34

ALBERTA
BRITISH COLUMBIA?

Castle
Junction

Tokumm

Ottertail
Pass

Mt
Whymper

Vermilion
Pass

164

Creek

Vermilion
Pass

Goodsir
Pass

Helmet   Creek

166

165

162

River

161

Limestone
Pk

165

Ochre

163

Creek

Vermilion
Pk

Stanley
Glacier

Stanley Pk

Rockwall
Pass

Creek

Mt
Drysdale

Wolverine
Pass

167

Tumbling

Mt
Haffner

165

Mt
Gray

Tumbling
Pass

169

Creek

The Rockwall

165

93

170

Ball Pass

165

Numa
Mtn

Numa
Pass

Foster
Pk

165

Floe   Creek

Radium

Floe
Lake

168

Land above 2300 metres

0 1 2 3 4 5 6 7 8km

© Andrew Hempstead

Marble Canyon

161 Stanley Glacier

Highway 93 to Stanley Glacier Basin—4.2 km (2.6 mi)

Half-day trip

Allow 1.5 hours one way

Elevation gain: 365 m (1,200 ft)

Maximum elevation: 1950 m (6,400 ft)

Maps: Mount Goodsir 82 N/1

Access: Follow Highway 93 to the Stanley Glacier trailhead parking area, on the southeast side of the road 3.2 km (2.0 mi) west of the Banff-Kootenay Park boundary at Vermilion Pass.

    0.0—Trailhead (1585 m).
        N51°12.331' W116°04.835'

    0.1—Vermilion River bridge.

      —Trail switchbacks up through burn.

    2.4—Stanley Creek bridge.

      —Steady climb above Stanley Creek.

    4.2—Stanley Glacier basin (1950 m).

This easy half-day outing runs from the Vermilion River to a rockbound hanging valley containing Stanley Glacier. The trail is often snow-free in early June, and the hike is very rewarding in the spring and early summer when wildflowers blanket the trailside and numerous waterfalls and avalanches tumble off of Stanley Peak's northeast face.

After crossing the Vermilion River, the trail climbs into burned forest and switchbacks steadily upward across open, blackened slopes for the next 2 km. The fire on this slope was intentionally set by crews on August 16, 2003, to create a fireguard against the spread of the massive Tokumm-Verendrye wildfire. So, now we are back to where we were when we first hiked this trail following the Vermilion Pass burn of 1968—watching the process of forest regeneration and admiring the post-fire profusion of wildflowers, including fireweed, columbine, heart-leaved arnica and asters.

At the top of the slope, the trail angles northeast and crosses Stanley Creek. As you move up this vale beside the creek over the next kilometre, you pass beyond the burn and into a cool, green forest of Engelmann spruce and alpine fir.

The last section of defined trail crosses avalanche paths and climbs a rocky, sparsely-forested slope before ending atop an old moraine in the midst of the basin's boulder fields. From this vantage point you can survey the entire basin, including the tumbled icefall of Stanley Glacier at the head of the valley.

Particularly impressive are the massive Cambrian limestone cliffs beneath Stanley Peak. This wall rises over 450 m, and dozens of waterfalls cascade down its face in late spring. (A few years ago we witnessed a massive avalanche that poured over this precipice and covered much of the wall in a cloud of snow.)

Though the moraine is a fine viewpoint and a pleasant lunch-stop, you can

Stanley Glacier

continue on for another kilometre or so following snippets of trail and cairns to the larch and fir-topped plateau at the head of the valley. Though it is a stiff climb over broken rock, and sometimes snowfields, the stream-fed meadow at the top of the cliff is an outstanding viewpoint for the toe of the Stanley Glacier. Along the way, watch for the hoary marmots, pikas and ptarmigan who make their home in this rocky amphitheatre.

Also look for a pair of small caves at the base of the Stanley Peak cliff about halfway between the end of trail and the upper plateau (approximately 100 m beyond a major waterfall). These shallow caverns were dissolved from the wall at a time when the Stanley Glacier filled this basin. You can reach the caves by making a short climb up a talus slope. Inside you will find the abundant droppings of the cave inhabitants—little brown bats.

162 Marble Canyon

Marble Canyon Circuit—1.4 km (0.9 mi)

Marble Canyon is one of the most popular self-guiding nature walks in Kootenay Park. Well-graded trail follows both sides of the canyon to where Tokumm Creek plunges into the chasm. Seven bridges span the canyon, allowing hikers to travel up one side and back the other, or switch back and forth en route.

The canyon was carved by water flowing through narrow joints in the bedrock. Over many centuries the stream dissolved limestone, widening and deepening the fissures to form the chasm. While distance between canyon walls varies from only 3 to 18 m, it reaches a depth of nearly 60 m (200 ft). In addition to allowing access from one side to the other, the bridges provide dizzying views into the abyss.

In August 2003, forest fires converged on Marble Canyon. The surrounding forest was burned to a crisp, and bridges and guardrails were damaged. The trail has since been totally redesigned with new fencing and bridges, and many burnt trees have been removed. Though the canyon looks naked amidst the remaining blackened spars, it is getting greener every year and a wonderful place to watch the steady process of natural recovery.

Access: Follow Highway 93 to the Marble Canyon parking area, located on the northwest side of the highway 7.0 km (4.3 mi) west of the Banff-Kootenay (Alberta-B.C.) boundary at Vermilion Pass. The trail begins at the trail kiosk sign at the rear of the parking area. N51°11.165' W116°07.378' *Maps: Mount Goodsir 82 N/1.*

163 Paint Pots

Paint Pots Parking Area to Upper Paint Pots—1.0 km (0.6 mi)

The short trail leading to the Paint Pots is a very popular nature walk in the northern region of Kootenay Park. Interpretive signs along the way describe the geology and history of the Ochre Beds—one of the park's unique features.

After descending through the forest and crossing a suspension bridge over the Vermilion River, you enter a meadow where iron-rich mineral waters have stained clay deposits brilliant hues of yellow and red. The trail crosses this colourful meadow and then climbs briefly through the forest to an opening containing the Paint Pots, which have been formed by iron oxide deposits building up around three cold mineral springs.

Before the arrival of the white man, native tribes from both sides of the mountains came here to collect the coloured clays for body paint. These early peoples believed the springs to be sacred places inhabited by animal spirits.

Early white settlers also mined the ochre for a brief period and shipped it to Calgary for use as a base for paint. You will understand why if you get the colourful mud on your boots—it takes some dedicated rinsing to get it off.

Access: Follow Highway 93 to the Paint Pots parking area, located on the northwest side of the highway 9.5 km (6.0 mi) west of the Banff-Kootenay boundary at Vermilion Pass. The trail begins at the trailhead kiosk at the rear of the parking area. N51°10.196' W116°08.853' *Maps: Mount Goodsir 82 N/1.*

164 Tokumm Creek

Marble Canyon Parking Area to Fay Hut Junction—10.4 km (6.5 mi)

Day trip

Allow 2.5 to 3 hours one way

Elevation gain: 185 m (600 ft)

Maximum elevation: 1675 m (5,500 ft)

Maps: Mount Goodsir 82 N/1
Lake Louise 82 N/8

Access: Follow Highway 93 to the Marble Canyon parking area, located on the northwest side of the highway 7.0 km (4.3 mi) west of the Banff-Kootenay Park boundary at Vermilion Pass. Follow the Marble Canyon trail 30 m to a junction and trail sign for Tokumm Valley.

0.0— Trailhead (1490 m).
N51°11.172' W116°07.405'

— Broad gravel path climbs to the right from *Marble Canyon* trail.

0.7— Junction. Upper Marble Canyon left. Continue ahead.

— Trail contours along open, burned slopes.

3.2— Trail descends to flats beside creek.

— Gradual to moderate uphill along creek.

8.5— Tributary stream bridge.

10.3— Tributary stream bridge.

10.4— Fay Hut Junction (1675 m).

The hike along Tokumm Creek once travelled through subalpine forest and occasional meadows and then climbed to Kaufmann Lake—one of the largest and most scenic backcountry lakes in Kootenay Park. But all that ended in 2003, when a lightning-ignited fire consumed the entire valley from Marble Canyon to the lake, including its shoreline campground.

Today hikers are greeted by a valley of wide-open views and fire-blackened trees, standing and fallen. It's an easy trek through fields of wildflowers and a valley in the process of regeneration.

After skirting above Marble Canyon, the track narrows and continues up-valley, contouring well above Tokumm Creek (visible below) and crossing a number of small streams. Fireweed, asters and harebells bloom through to early August, and lodgepole pine trees rise from the ashes.

At the 3-km mark, you descend to dryas-covered flats beside Tokumm Creek, and from this point on you are seldom far from the creek. Views ahead to the Wenkchemna Peaks and Kaufmann Lake cirque tantalize until you reach a tributary-stream crossing and the Fay Hut junction. You are less than 5 km from Kaufmann Lake, but the trail has been so obliterated by deadfall and in-growth, most hikers who have attempted it have lost the way. At this time, Parks Canada has no plans to reconstruct the trail.

Fay Hut. The Alpine Club of Canada built the original Fay Hut high above the valley on the south slope of the Wenkchemna Peaks in 1927. On August 1, 2003, the log structure was destroyed by the Tokumm Creek fire. The ACC built a new log structure on the site in 2005, but that hut accidentally burned in April 2009. There are no plans of replacing the hut, and the steep 2.4-km trail from Tokumm Creek to the site is of little use today.

The Rockwall

Following his epic trek from the U.S.-Canada border to the Yukon in 1988, British author Chris Townsend wrote us to say that the Rockwall Trail was "the best trail I walked in the mountain parks!" How can we disagree? The cover photos for the first three editions of this book came from The Rockwall region.

The Rockwall is the eastern escarpment of Kootenay Park's Vermilion Range. As you drive Highway 93 between the Paint Pots and Vermilion Crossing, there are numerous tantalizing glimpses west to this sheer limestone wall. But The Rockwall is even more impressive close-up—a remarkable combination of high passes, larch forests, wildflower meadows, towering waterfalls, and glaciers. It is quite understandable why it is Kootenay's best-known hiking area.

The Rockwall's recreational history began in 1923 when outfitter Walter Nixon guided a group of visiting dignitaries to Tumbling Pass and the Wolverine Plateau. Included in his party were H.B. Clow, president of the Rand McNally map company, and John Murray Gibbon, publicist for the Canadian Pacific Railway. Before the journey ended, the group concurred that it was the most scenic alpine route they had ever ridden. They also agreed that recreational horseback riders should have the opportunity to do wonderful trips like this annually. With the support of Gibbon and the CPR, the Trail Riders of the Canadian Rockies was formed the following year.

Walter Nixon returned to The Rockwall in the autumn of 1924 to cut the first trail along the escarpment in preparation for the Trail Riders' annual ride the following summer. Over the next four decades, the Trail Riders returned several times to this exceptional area. As trails were established up the short valleys leading to the range, the region became increasingly popular with other horseback parties and, to a lesser extent, hikers and backpackers.

In 1969, Jim Thorsell included the Rockwall Trail in his proposed route for the Great Divide Trail. Though the Great Divide Trail was never formally established, Jim's proposal did draw the attention of a growing number of hikers, and the area soon secured a reputation as one of the finest backcountry destinations in the Rockies.

Four side valleys lead to The Rockwall—Helmet Creek, Tumbling Creek, Numa Creek and Floe Creek, and well-maintained trails along these streams are the primary access routes to the range. Between the headwaters of these four valleys, there are three alpine passes—Rockwall, Tumbling and Numa—which are connected by trails to allow travel along the length of the escarpment.

Options. With such a comprehensive trail system, there are numerous ways to visit The Rockwall and sample its spectacular scenery.

Floe Lake is by far the most popular destination, both for day hikers and backpackers.

The classic backpack is the *Rockwall Trail* circuit, which runs between the *Floe Lake* and *Helmet Creek* trailheads. This four-to-five-day trek crosses all three passes and travels for 30 km beneath The Rockwall's escarpment. The trip can also be extended into Yoho Park utilizing Goodsir Pass, or to Banff Park via the *Hawk Creek-Ball Pass* trail.

Shorter backpacks can be completed over only one or two passes. (All of the single pass loop trips have also been done in a long day by strong hikers.)

Or you can hike to a campground at the headwaters of one of the four valleys and day trip to nearby passes.

Descriptions for the *Rockwall Trail, Helmet Creek, Tumbling Creek, Floe Lake,* and *Numa Creek* are found on the following pages.

Floe Lake and The Rockwall from the Numa Pass trail

165 Rockwall Trail

Paint Pots Parking Area to Floe Lake Parking Area—54.4 km (33.8 mi)

Backpack
Allow 4 to 5 days
Maximum elevation: 2355 m (7,720 ft)
Minimum elevation: 1325 m (4,350 ft)
Maps: Mount Goodsir 82 N/1

Access: To reach the south end of the trail, follow Highway 93 to the *Floe Lake* parking area. The north end of the route starts at the Paint Pots parking area and follows the *Helmet Creek* trail.

0.0—Paint Pots parking area (1450 m). N51°10.196' W116°08.853'

3.7—Junction. *Tumbling Creek* trail left.

6.0—Helmet-Ochre Junction Campground.

14.3—Junction. Goodsir Pass right.

14.9—Helmet Falls Campground (1760 m).

18.1—Limestone Summit (2170 m).

19.1—Helmet Creek south fork bridge (1920 m).

23.0—Rockwall Pass (2240 m).

23.4—Junction. Wolverine Pass right 100 m.

26.5—Tumbling Creek Campground.

26.8—Tumbling Creek Junction (1890 m). Intersection with *Tumbling Creek* trail at km 10.3.

29.1—Tumbling Pass (2210 m).

33.9—Numa Creek Junction (1525 m). Intersection with *Numa Creek* trail at km 6.5.

34.3—Numa Creek Campground.

41.2—Numa Pass (2355 m).

43.9—Floe Lake and Campground (2040 m).

54.4—Floe Lake Parking Area (1325 m). N51°04.877' W116°03.276'

The 30-km trail running beneath The Rockwall between Helmet Falls and Floe Lake is extraordinary for its variety and beauty. It travels beneath massive limestone walls and hanging glaciers and traverses three alpine passes and numerous wildflower meadows. In early summer, waterfalls tumble from the cliffs, including one of Canada's highest—Helmet Falls. In autumn, the passes are bathed in the golden glow of alpine larch.

The only negative aspect of this journey, at least for the overburdened backpacker, is the way the trail rises and falls like a roller-coaster as it ascends passes and plunges into intervening valleys. However, each of these valleys has trail connections to Highway 93, allowing entry or exit at a number of points. (See *Tumbling Creek* and *Numa Creek*.)

The Rockwall circuit, running from the Paint Pots to the Floe Lake trailhead (or visa versa), is the most popular multi-day trip along the range. Some backpackers hike The Rockwall as part of an even longer trip connecting to Banff Park via Ball Pass or Yoho Park via Goodsir Pass, but these options require transportation arrangements between distant trailheads. The beauty of the Rockwall circuit is that, after 4 or 5 days on the trail, you emerge only 13 km from where you started on Highway 93.

It's six-of-one, half-a-dozen of the other whether you start at the north end of the circuit and hike south or visa versa. Our main reason for describing the trail north-to-south is to save Floe Lake until the end of the journey. (There are few sights more inspiring than your first view of Floe Lake from Numa Pass.) However, if the weather forecast is good, and sites are available at Floe Lake Campground, you may want to start south and hike north.

Starting from the Paint Pots, you have a long, gradual climb up Ochre and Helmet Creeks to Helmet Falls (see *Helmet*

Tumbling Pass and Glacier from Rockwall Pass

Creek). If you plan a layover day at Helmet Falls Campground, you can day-trip to nearby Goodsir Pass.

From Helmet Falls you turn south and make a strenuous up-and-down ascent to Rockwall Pass. You gain 410 m over 3.2 km to Limestone Summit—a ridge extending eastward from Limestone Peak. (There are nice views of Helmet Falls as you struggle upwards.) From the summit, you plunge to the south fork of Helmet Creek, then climb steeply again to Rockwall Pass.

Rockwall Pass, with its vast wildflower meadows and far-reaching views, is a wonderful place to linger. And just 0.4 km beyond its summit, you reach a junction beside the narrow gap of Wolverine Pass. A short 100-m walk on this branch trail brings you to the crest of the pass, and a bit further improves westerly views to the Purcell Range and the Bugaboos.

Descending south from Wolverine Pass junction, you see the trail far ahead rising along the Tumbling Glacier to Tumbling Pass—one of The Rockwall's classic views.

You reach Tumbling Creek Campground 300 m before the junction with the Tumbling Creek trail (see *Tumbling Creek*). From this point, the trail climbs beside Tumbling Glacier's terminal moraine to Tumbling Pass, a 2210-m summit with a wonderful view south to your next objective, Numa Pass.

Yet another dramatic loss of elevation across avalanche paths brings you to an intersection with the Numa Creek trail and, 400 m beyond, Numa Creek Campground.

The ascent to Numa Pass is one of the most gruelling of the entire trip, but the sudden appearance of Floe Lake with its Rockwall backdrop makes it all worthwhile. From the 2355-m pass, the trail's high point, you have a pleasant 2.7-km saunter down through meadows and larch groves to the lake and its deluxe campground.

The trip's final 10.5 km descends Floe Creek to Highway 93, which can be hiked in 3 hours or less through the charred remnants of the 2003 Verendrye Creek fire. (See *Floe Lake*.)

166 Helmet Creek

Paint Pots Parking Area to Helmet Falls Campground—14.9 km (9.3 mi)

Backpack

Allow 5 hours to Helmet Falls

Elevation gain: 310 m (1,000 ft)

Maximum elevation: 1760 m (5,775 ft)

Maps: Mount Goodsir 82 N/1

Access: Follow Highway 93 to the Paint Pots parking area, on the northwest side of the highway 9.5 km (5.9 mi) west of the Banff-Kootenay boundary at Vermilion Pass.

  0.0— Trailhead (1450 m).
       N51°10.196' W116°08.853'
    — Follow Paint Pots nature trail.

  0.3— Vermilion River suspension bridge.

  1.0— Paint Pots.
    — Follow trail into forest beyond Paint Pots.

  1.3— Junction. Marble Canyon right 3.2 km. Stay left.

  3.7— Junction. *Tumbling Creek* trail left.

  6.3— Ochre Creek bridge.
       Helmet-Ochre Junction Campground.

  6.6— Helmet Creek suspension bridge.
    — Switchbacks followed by gradual uphill on south side of creek.

  12.0— Helmet Creek suspension bridge.

  14.3— Junction. Goodsir Pass right 4.0 km. Helmet Falls ahead.

  14.9— Helmet Falls Campground (1760 m).

The Helmet Creek trail is the north end of the popular Rockwall Trail circuit. But even if you aren't following this route along the length of the range, the trail accesses some exceptional features at the north end of The Rockwall. These include 352-m Helmet Falls, one of Canada's highest, and the meadows and larch forests of Goodsir Pass, Limestone Summit and Rockwall Pass.

Follow the Paint Pots nature trail for the first 1.0 km. At the end of the nature trail, skirt around the edge of the clay mudflats surrounding the ochre springs and follow the track running into the forest on the opposite side.

After joining the trail from Marble Canyon at km 1.3, you follow nearly level terrain along the east side of Ochre Creek for nearly 5 km. At km 3.7, the Tumbling Creek trail branches left (the trail you will return on if you complete the loop over Rockwall Pass from Helmet Falls).

At km 6.0, you turn left to Helmet-Ochre Junction Campground and cross to the west side of Ochre Creek. Just 200 m beyond the crossing, a suspension bridge takes you to the west side of Helmet Creek and the ascent of Helmet Valley begins.

The trail quickly gains elevation via a series of switchbacks, then it bends to the west and follows upstream along the south side of Helmet Creek. A second suspension bridge takes you to the north side of the creek at km 12.0, and you soon glimpse Helmet Falls ahead through the trees.

The trail to Goodsir Pass branches north at km 14.3. Stay on the left branch for 600 m to reach the Helmet Falls Campground near the patrol cabin.

The highlight of any visit to the Helmet Creek headwaters is undoubtedly Helmet Falls, flowing down through the escarpment enclosing the head of the valley. Limestone Peak (2878 m), Helmet

The Goodsirs from Goodsir Pass

Mountain (3138 m) and Sharp Mountain (3049 m) are the three summits that create the massive amphitheatre, and Sharp Glacier feeds the falls.

Rockwall Pass—8.1 km. One of the best day trips from Helmet Falls Campground follows the *Rockwall Trail* south to Rockwall Pass. From that 2240-m summit you have a classic view south along The Rockwall that includes Tumbling Pass and Glacier. It is a rather steep up-and-down hike that gains a total of 730 m by the time you reach the pass.

You can complete a loop back to the Paint Pots trailhead by continuing over the pass and descending Tumbling Creek to the Ochre Valley junction. We consider this the most scenic single-pass loop trip on The Rockwall, and the only one that brings you back where you started. Total round trip is 37 km. (See *Rockwall Trail* and *Tumbling Creek*.)

Goodsir Pass—4.0 km. Goodsir Pass is a high, long, glorious alpine meadow near the boundary between Kootenay and Yoho Parks. It can be hiked either as a day trip from Helmet Creek Campground or by backpackers bound for Yoho Park.

The trail begins at the junction 0.6 km below the campground and climbs 450 vertical metres to the pass. Despite the rise, the trail is well routed and maintained, and a steady pace will soon take you into a scattered larch forest near treeline.

Once you crest the pass meadows, your attention is immediately drawn to the looming, glaciated spires of Sentry Peak (3267 m) and the twin towers of Mount Goodsir (3561 m)—the highest mountain in Yoho Park.

You cross the park boundary into Yoho Park 1.6 km beyond the summit. The trail makes a steep, steady descent, mainly through heavy forest, to Goodsir Creek and the Ottertail River. The Ottertail bridge and the intersection with the Ottertail River trail lies 8.3 km beyond Goodsir Pass. (See *Ottertail River*, Yoho Park chapter.)

167 Tumbling Creek

Paint Pots Parking Area to Tumbling Creek Campground—10.6 km (6.6 mi)

Day trip or backpack

Allow 3 to 4 hours to Tumbling Creek Campground

Elevation gain: 440 m (1,450 ft)

Maximum elevation: 1890 m (6,200 ft)

Maps: Mount Goodsir 82 N/1

Access: Follow Highway 93 to the Paint Pots parking area, on the northwest side of the highway 9.5 km (5.9 mi) west of the Banff-Kootenay boundary at Vermilion Pass.

0.0— Trailhead (1450 m).
　　N51°10.196' W116°08.853'
　　— Follow Paint Pots nature trail.

0.3— Vermilion River suspension bridge.

1.0— Paint Pots.
　　— Follow trail into forest beyond Paint Pots.

1.3— Junction. Marble Canyon right 3.2 km. Stay left.

3.7— Junction. *Helmet Creek* trail ahead. Turn left.

4.1— Ochre Creek suspension bridge.
　　— Steady climb along north side of Tumbling Creek.

6.6— Tumbling Creek bridge.

9.4— Tumbling Falls viewpoint.

10.3— Junction (1890 m). Intersection with *Rockwall Trail* at km 26.8. Right to Tumbling Creek Campground (0.3 km) and Rockwall Pass (3.8 km). Tumbling Pass ahead 2.3 km.

Notice: At the time of publication this trail was closed due to multiple washed out bridges. Please check Trail Updates at www.canadianrockiestrailguide.com for the latest information.

The Tumbling Creek trail is yet another access route to The Rockwall. While the trail makes a relatively long approach to the head of the Tumbling Valley, it is the most direct route to two of the range's finest alpine meadows on Tumbling and Rockwall Passes. The Tumbling Creek Campground at the head of the valley is a good base for half-day hikes to either of these summits. Or you can continue your backpack south to Numa Pass or north to Helmet Falls as part of an extended circuit along the Rockwall Trail.

The trail follows the Paint Pots nature trail for 1.0 km, then enters heavy forest on the opposite side of the mudflats surrounding these ochre springs. After joining a trail from Marble Canyon at km 1.3, it runs northwest along the east side of Ochre Creek valley.

At km 3.7, the Tumbling Creek trail parts ways with the Ochre Creek trail, which continues northwest to Helmet Creek. From this junction, branch down to the left, cross the creek and begin the long ascent of the Tumbling Valley. (If you complete a loop over Rockwall Pass to Helmet Falls, you will return to this junction on the way home.)

Throughout the remainder of the journey, the turbulent waters of Tumbling Creek are a constant companion. A fine waterfall is passed at km 9.4, and, just a kilometre beyond, you reach the intersection with the Rockwall highline route (see *Rockwall Trail*). Tumbling Creek Campground lies 300 m to the right on the opposite side of the creek.

Tumbling Pass—2.3 km. From the campground junction, it is a short but steep hike to Tumbling Pass (2210 m). The final 2 km to the pass follows a series of steep switchbacks along a high terminal moraine deposited by the Tumbling Glacier. As the trail grinds its way upward, views improve on all sides. Tumbling Glacier and The Rockwall rise

Mount Gray and Tumbling Glacier from the Rockwall Pass meadows

above the trail to the west, while back to the north are the open meadows leading to the Wolverine Plateau and Rockwall Pass.

From the pass, you can see the grey, eastern escarpment of The Rockwall snaking away to the south. The high saddle of Numa Pass lies between the sharp pyramid of Foster Peak and the rounded summit of Numa Mountain. In the foreground, the trail drops away toward the Numa Creek valley, threading its way across a meadow that is filled with wildflowers in summer and bordered by golden larch in late September.

South of the pass, the trail descends to a junction with the Numa Creek trail. By descending that trail you return to Highway 93 at the Numa Falls Picnic Area, or you can continue south along the Rockwall Trail to Numa Pass and Floe Lake. (See *Numa Creek* and *Rockwall Trail*.)

The Tumbling Creek-Tumbling Pass-Numa Creek trip is 24 km, and is often completed as a day trip by hikers who have arranged transportation at the Paint Pots and Numa Falls trailheads.

Rockwall Pass—3.8 km. By following the Rockwall Trail north from Tumbling Creek Campground, you can reach the open meadows of the Wolverine Plateau and Rockwall Pass after 3 km of steady climbing. This summit is every bit as scenic as Tumbling Pass, and the meadows are far more extensive.

The term "Rockwall" takes on new meaning here. In fact, it's not until you reach Wolverine Pass that you realize there is a cleft in the 500-m-high wall. A short, 100-m side trail leads to the actual summit of the pass (2210 m), where views stretch west to the Purcell Range beyond the Columbia Valley.

From Wolverine Pass junction, the Rockwall Trail continues through alpine meadows another 400 m to the true summit of Rockwall Pass. By continuing north on this route, you can complete a loop trip back to the Paint Pots via Helmet Creek or continue over Goodsir Pass to Yoho Park. (See *Rockwall Trail* and *Helmet Creek.*)

168 Floe Lake

Highway 93 to Floe Lake—10.5 km (6.5 mi)

Day trip or backpack

Allow 3 to 4 hours to Floe Lake

Elevation gain: 715 m (2,350 ft)

Maximum elevation: 2040 m (6,700 ft)

Maps: Mount Goodsir 82 N/1

Access: Follow Highway 93 to the Floe Lake-Hawk Creek parking area, located on the west side of the highway 22.5 km (14 mi) south of the Banff-Kootenay boundary at Vermilion Pass and 8.3 km (5.2 mi) north of Kootenay Park Lodge.

0.0— Trailhead (1325 m).
   N51°04.877' W116°03.276'

   — Trail descends to Vermilion River.

0.5— Vermilion River bridge.

   — Trail contours northwest to Floe Valley.

1.8— Floe Creek bridge.

   — Moderate to steep climb along north side of Floe Valley.

5.7— Steep switchbacks next 0.3 km.

8.0— Steep switchbacks next 2 km.

10.1— Trail levels off.

10.5— Floe Lake and Campground (2040 m). Numa Pass north 2.7 km. (See also *Rockwall Trail* and *Numa Creek*.)

Set beneath a 1000-m limestone escarpment and a sprawling necklace of glacial ice, Floe Lake is easily a match for any beauty spot in the Rockies. Beyond its north shore a subalpine forest of alpine fir and larch grades upward to the treeless meadows of Numa Pass—a summit that provides a wonderful high-level view of the entire Floe Lake cirque.

From the parking area, the trail immediately descends to a bridge over the Vermilion River, then climbs and contours into the narrow Floe Valley. What you see along this first stretch is what you get nearly to the lake—the charred remains of the August 2003 Verendrye Creek Fire. The treeless landscape does allow for continuous views ahead to the imposing Rockwall, and typical of recently burned terrain, fireweed, arnica, harebells and asters fill the stark landscape with colour through mid-summer. (When wet, lush overgrowth along sections of trail can soak clothing and gear.)

There are a couple steep, switchbacking sections as you climb toward the lake, the last and longest beginning at km 8.0—an exposed, painfully dry climb on a sunny day. At the top of the grade lush subalpine forest returns and you enter the Floe Lake cirque.

Floe Lake is situated at 2040 m, well into the upper subalpine zone. Trees along its northern shore are scattered and somewhat stunted, and, in mid-summer, many varieties of wildflowers carpet the surrounding meadows. In autumn, the golden needles of alpine larch provide a brilliant foreground for the lake, glacier and The Rockwall.

The Rockwall is composed of a dark grey Cambrian limestone (Ottertail Formation)—the east-facing escarpment forming the backbone of the Vermilion Range for 40 km. A small glacier clings to the base of the wall and plunges to the southern edge of the lake, and the resulting ice floes give the lake its name. There

Floe Lake from Numa Pass

is also a lagoon created by the ridgetop of a terminal moraine, which loops out into the lake and partitions off a section of its waters.

The campground in the forest above the shore is a bit deluxe for some tastes, but it is a wonderful place to relax close to one of the best views in the Rockies. However, it is a busy campground in midsummer, so consider reservations if you want to be assured of a site.

Numa Pass—2.7 km. For strong day hikers, or those camped at Floe Lake, the trail continuing to Numa Pass is a must. Branching away from the lakeshore just before the patrol cabin, the trail rises nearly 300 m to the pass.

Views from Numa Pass are some of the most expansive of any trail in the park. Set between Foster Peak (3204 m) on the west and Numa Mountain (2725 m) to the east, it is by far the best viewpoint for Floe Lake. To the north, set off by sheer walls, limestone pinnacles and hanging glaciers, the long face of The Rockwall runs off toward Yoho Park. The sharp snowy mountains to the far north are the Wenkchemna Peaks, which

rise above the Valley of the Ten Peaks in Banff Park.

Strong day hikers and backpackers can complete a circuit back to Highway 93 by descending the Numa Creek trail north of Numa Pass—an option that emerges at the Numa Falls Picnic Area 8 km north of the Floe Lake trailhead. Total distance for the Floe Lake-Numa Pass-Numa Creek trip is 27 km. (See *Numa Creek.*)

Rockwall Trail. The Floe Lake trail is the southern terminus for the Rockwall Trail—a 55-km route that runs northwest along the face of the Vermilion Range to Helmet Falls and then back to Highway 93 at the Paint Pots trailhead. In addition to crossing three high and very scenic passes, the route intersects three trails running up Numa, Tumbling and Helmet Creeks, which allows for a variety of itineraries. (See *Rockwall Trail.*)

169 Numa Creek

Numa Falls Picnic Area to Rockwall Trail Junction—6.5 km (4.0 mi)

Day trip or backpack
Allow 2 hours one way
Elevation gain: 95 m (310 ft)
Maximum elevation: 1525 m (5,000 ft)
Maps: Mount Goodsir 82/N

Access: Follow Highway 93 to the Numa Falls Picnic Area, located beside the Vermilion River 14 km (8.5 mi) south of the Banff-Kootenay boundary and 16.5 km (10.3 mi) north of Kootenay Park Lodge. Trail begins at the Vermilion River footbridge 100 m beyond the parking area.

0.0— Trailhead (1430 m).
  N51°07.962' W116°07.923'

  —Gradual ascent through forest then descent to Numa Creek.

3.0— Numa Creek bridge.

  —Gradual to rolling ascent alongside of creek.

4.8— Trail climbs above creek and into forest.

6.4— Tributary bridge.

6.5— Junction (1525 m). Intersection with *Rockwall Trail* at km 33.9.
  Right to Tumbling Pass (4.8 km).
  Left to Numa Creek Campground (0.4 km) and Numa Pass (7.3 km).

**Notice: At the time of publication this trail was closed due to multiple washed out bridges.
Please check Trail Updates at www.canadianrockiestrailguide.com for the latest information.**

The Numa Creek trail is the shortest access route to the Rockwall Trail, but there is little reason to use it except as an optional exit. Views along the trail are limited, and once you reach the Rockwall Trail proper, you face steep, long climbs to worthwhile destinations, like Tumbling and Numa Passes. However, the first 3 km do provide an interesting nature walk through a lush western-slope forest, and there is very little elevation gain from the trailhead to the junction with the Rockwall Trail.

From the trailhead bridge over the Vermilion River, you hike downstream briefly before switchbacking right and making a gradual ascent over a rise to Numa Creek. The forest here is very dense, carpeted with feather moss and filled with alder and even the occasional patch of devil's club. At km 1.1, the track flattens out briefly then makes a gradual downhill contour before dropping suddenly into the Numa Creek gorge.

At km 3.0, you cross a bridge over Numa Creek and begin a gradual, uneventful ascent along the northwest side of the creek. For nearly 2 km, the trail skirts beside or near the creek. Several avalanche paths are crossed, but views ahead to the Rockwall are infrequent and limited.

At km 4.8, you climb well above the creek via a double switchback and then travel into dense but pleasant spruce-fir forest carpeted with moss, ferns and bunchberry. A major tributary is crossed at km 6.4 (it feeds Numa Creek 100 m below this bridge), and a few minutes later you reach the junction with the Rockwall Trail. From this junction, which is only 400 m north of Numa Creek Campground, you can continue right to Tumbling Pass or left to Numa Pass. Both options are steep and gruelling. (See *Rockwall Trail*.)

Numa Creek

(169)

Castle Junction

Isabelle Pk

Ball Pass

(33)

(29)

Mt Bourgeau

(170)

Hawk Creek

Haiduk Pk

Whistling Pass

Healy Pass

Egypt Lake

Redearth Pass

(28)

(27)

Vermilion River

Numa Mtn

Ball Range

Verdant Creek

Natalko Lake

Sunshine

ALBERTA
BRITISH COLUMBIA

(165)

Floe Creek

Numa Pass

Hawk Ridge

(25)

Foster Pk

(168)

Floe Lake

93

(171)

Honeymoon Pass

The Monarch

Kootenay Park Lodge

?

The Rockwall

Mt Verendrye

Verendrye Creek

Mt Shanks↑

(172)

Surprise Creek

(172)

Simpson River

Mt Wardle

Vermilion River

(174)

Kootenay River

Spar Mtn

Octopus Mtn

Split Pk

Mt Sam

Kootenay Crossing Station

93

Kootenay River

N

(175)

Dolly Varden Creek

Luxor Pass

Vermilion River

Radium

Mt Daer

Land above 2300 metres

0 1 2 3 4 5 6 7 8km

170 Hawk Creek—Ball Pass

Highway 93 to Ball Pass—10.1 km (6.3 mi)

Day trip or backpack

Allow 3 to 4 hours one way

Elevation gain: 885 m (2,900 ft)

Maximum elevation: 2210 m (7,250 ft)

Maps: Mount Goodsir 82 N/1
Banff 82 0/4
Banff-Egypt Lake (Gem Trek)

Access: Follow Highway 93 to the Floe Lake-Hawk Creek parking area, located on the west side of the highway 22.5 km (14 mi) south of the Banff-Kootenay boundary at Vermilion Pass and 8.3 km (5.2 mi) north of the Kootenay Park Lodge. The trail begins on the east side of the highway opposite the parking area entrance.

0.0— Trailhead (1325 m).
N51°04.905' W116°03.211'

— Trail follows north along highway.

0.4— Hawk Creek highway bridge.

— Trail runs northeast on old roadbed.

1.1— Trail begins climb along northwest side of canyon.

— Steady moderate to steep ascent.

4.4— Tributary stream bridge.

5.0— Avalanche path and upper edge of burn.

7.4— Steep switchbacks begin.

8.8— Trail enters subalpine meadow.

— Steep ascent to pass.

10.1— Ball Pass (2210 m). Banff-Kootenay Park boundary.
Trail connects with *Bow Valley Highline Trail* 2.7 km beyond pass. (See also *Shadow Lake Area Hikes.*)

Straddling the Kootenay-Banff boundary, Ball Pass is a scenic summit set beneath the glaciers of Mount Ball. Despite being a long, strenuous trip, it is often day-hiked from Highway 93 (you'll likely appreciate the scenery more on the way back). It is also popular with backpackers on extended trips between Banff and Kootenay Parks.

From the trail sign opposite the parking area, the trail follows along Highway 93 for 400 m to the Hawk Creek highway bridge. Cross the bridge to the north side and follow trail up into the charred remains of the 2003 Verendrye Creek Fire.

For the next 4 km, you climb steadily through fire-blackened trees, standing and fallen, with Hawk Creek continually visible off to the right. Denuded slopes have been exposed to erosion, so expect trail washouts on side-hills as you gain elevation.

A major tributary is crossed at km 4.4, and 0.6 km beyond, you reach the upper edge of the burn and enter avalanche paths and massive rockslides. There is little relief until you reach the stream-fed meadows just below the pass.

The pass is a narrow notch in the middle of the Ball Range. Rockslides have turned the northern lip of the pass into a rather tumbled, desolate place, but a scattered forest of larch and alpine fir interspersed with patches of meadow soften the rest of the summit. Glacier-capped Mount Ball (3311 m) rises above the pass to the north, while the Haiduk Valley runs away to the northeast toward Shadow Lake.

Banff-bound backpackers will find the first campground 2.7 km to the east, where the trail intersects with the Bow Valley Highline Trail (see *Bow Valley Highline Trail* km 21.0 and *Shadow Lake Area Hikes*, Banff Park chapter).

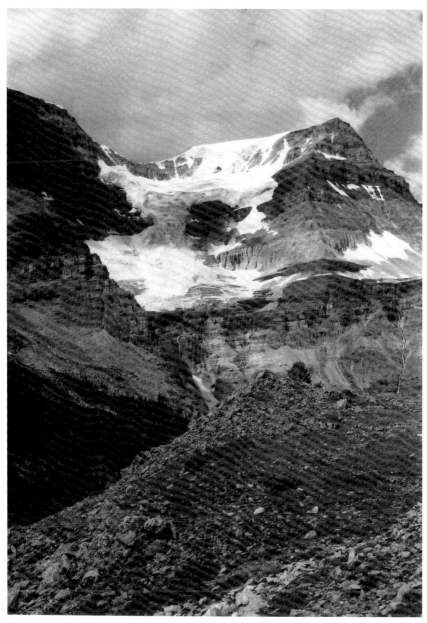

Ball Pass

171 Honeymoon Pass—Verdant Creek

Highway 93 to Honeymoon Pass—5.6 km (3.5 mi)
Highway 93 to Egypt Lake Campground via Verdant Creek—21.5 km (13.4 mi)

Day trip or backpack

Allow 2 hours to Honeymoon Pass

Elevation gain: 730 m (2,400 ft)

Maximum elevation: 1995 m (6,550 ft)

Maps: Banff 82 O/4
Banff-Egypt Lake (Gem Trek)

Access: Follow Highway 93 to the Honeymoon Pass-Verdant Creek parking area, located on the east side of the highway 30.5 km (19 mi) south of the Banff-Kootenay boundary and 300 m north of the Kootenay Park Lodge.

0.0— Trailhead (1325 m).
N51°01.621' W115°59.061'

— Narrow, vague trail through burn followed by steep switchbacks.

4.3— Grade moderates.

5.1— Marshy meadow with stream crossings.

5.6— Honeymoon Pass (1995 m).

— Steady descent to Verdant Creek on vague track.

8.0— Verdant Creek crossing to northeast bank.

8.5— Verdant Creek Campground (1790 m).

9.5— Verdant Creek crossing to southwest bank.

10.7— Verdant Creek crossing to northeast bank.

11.2— Verdant Creek crossing to southwest bank.

11.6— Verdant Creek Patrol Cabin and Junction (1675 m). Verdant Creek crossing (log bridge) to northeast bank.

— Trail ascends along East Verdant Creek (wet and indistinct sections).

18.2— Redearth Pass (2090 m).
Banff-Kootenay boundary.

18.8— Junction. Talc Lake left 1.9 km.

21.3— Junction. Intersection with Healy Pass-Egypt Lake trail at km 12.2. Egypt Lake Campground left 200 m.

The day trip to Honeymoon Pass is still no honeymoon, despite the fire in 2003 that opened up the forest to better views. Sitting well below treeline, the pass is a narrow, cheerless gap sandwiched between a rockslide and trees.

From the trailhead, you immediately enter the Verendrye Creek burn. After the first kilometer, the climb is steady and steep, the track often vague, and don't be surprised if you have to crawl over deadfall. However, there are views back across the valley to the impressive spire of Mount Verendrye (3086 m), albeit filtered through fire-blackened spars. Green forest returns in the pass, but a boggy meadow offers little more than wildflowers and a viewless rest-stop.

Verdant Creek. The trail continues north to Verdant Creek—a difficult route used by adventurous backpackers bound for Redearth Pass and Egypt Lake in Banff Park. The track is often obscure as it makes a quick descent to the creek, where you face the first of several crossings and reach the valley's only campground at km 8.5. All of these crossings are completed on makeshift log bridges or by fording (usually knee-deep).

From the patrol cabin at 11.6 km, the trail to Redearth Pass branches to the northeast side of Verdant Creek one last time (bridged) and begins the ascent along East Verdant Creek. The track is often indistinct, and blazes or flagging tape are frequently the only indication you are on-route. In the upper portion, vague trail crosses East Verdant Creek a number of times (bridged or rock-hop).

Redearth Pass is rather long and undistinguished. After passing the Talc (Natalko) Lake junction beyond the park boundary, the trail continues another 2.7 km to Egypt Lake Campground (see *Egypt Lakes Area Hikes*, Banff Park).

172 Simpson River—Ferro Pass

Highway 93 to Ferro Pass—22.9 km (14.2 mi)
Highway 93 to Lake Magog Campground via Ferro Pass—32.2 km (20.0 mi)

Backpack

Allow 2 days to Lake Magog

Elevation gain: 1020 m (3,350 ft)

Maximum elevation: 2270 m (7,450 ft)

Maps: Mount Assiniboine 82 J/13

Access: Follow Highway 93 to the Simpson River trail parking area, located on east side of the highway 5.9 km (3.7 mi) south of the Kootenay Park Lodge and 57 km (35.5 mi) north of Kootenay Park West Gate at Radium. The parking area is beside a footbridge crossing the Vermilion River.

0.0— Trailhead (1250 m).
    N50°58.702' W115°56.884'

0.2— Junction. Simpson River right.

    — Trail runs through Mt Shanks burn.

1.4— Trail comes abreast of Simpson River.

2.2— River bench viewpoint.

    — Trail angles away from river.

8.8— Kootenay-Mt Assiniboine boundary.

10.9— Junction (1400 m). Upper Simpson River ahead. Ferro Pass right across suspension bridge.

11.0— Surprise Creek Shelter and Campground.

    — Steep climb along Surprise Creek for 2.5 km.

18.4—Rock Lake.

19.2— Campground.

22.9— Ferro Pass (2270 m).

26.5— Nestor Creek bridge (1995 m). Mitchell Meadows Campground.

29.6— Junction. Cerulean Lake west end.

31.3— Sunburst Lake Cabin.

31.8— Junction. Assiniboine Lodge ahead. Magog Campground right.

32.2—Lake Magog Campground (2165 m).

If you're looking for a short, flat walk with lots of wildflowers and peaceful, riverside vistas, the first 2 km of the Simpson River trail should be your cup of tea. From the trailhead footbridge over the Vermilion River, you walk through the scorched remains of the Mount Shanks Fire (2001) to the Simpson River. Continue along its north bank and onto a low bench overlooking the river and the north end of the Mitchell Range. This short walk will be snow-free by May and decorated with fields of fireweed, asters and harebells in mid-summer.

However, the primary purpose of the trail is to transport hikers and riders eastward into the remote wilderness of northern Mount Assiniboine Park. And when extended over Ferro Pass, it is an alternate route to Lake Magog at the foot of Mount Assiniboine.

After the first 2.2 km, the trail swings away from the river and passes through alternating sections of green and burned forest (expect deadfall) until just west of the park boundary. Two km beyond the boundary, you cross the Simpson River on a suspension bridge to the Surprise Creek Campground and shelter cabin— a popular destination for early-season overnight trips.

The ascent to Rock Lake is long, steep and scenically humdrum (dense forest), but above the lake views improve to the massive rock wall of Simpson Ridge and Indian Mountain. At Ferro Pass, views open up to Mount Assiniboine, The Marshall, Mount Watson, and Wedgwood Lake.

Southeast from the pass, you enter the core area of Mount Assiniboine Park, and it's just over 9 km from the pass to Lake Magog Campground via Cerulean Lake and the Sunburst Valley. (See Ferro Pass, *Lake Magog Area Hikes* in Assiniboine Park chapter.)

Kootenay Valley Fire Roads

After a major forest fire swept the Kootenay Valley in 1926, a network of fire roads was constructed to allow wardens and firefighters rapid access to all parts of the valley. Today the roads are no longer used by park service vehicles and they are slowly growing in along their margins.

While these abandoned roads make for humdrum hiking, their low elevation does permit access in early spring and late autumn when other trails are still snow-covered, and easy grades make for comfortable walking. They are also popular with cyclists and cross-country skiers.

Two of these roads, the West Kootenay Trail and East Kootenay Trail, extend beyond park boundaries to B.C. forest lands, eventually connecting to main forestry roads.

173 East Kootenay Trail

McLeod Meadows Picnic Area to Daer Creek—7.3 km (4.5 mi)
McLeod Meadows Picnic Area to Pitts Creek—5.7 km (3.5 mi)

The East Kootenay Fire Road was built to access the east side of the Kootenay Valley during fire emergencies. From a point near the confluence of the Vermilion and Kootenay Rivers, the road runs south for 36 km to the park's southern boundary near the Cross River. Today part of the road's northern section is less accessible due to bridge removal, but an 11-km stretch between Daer and Pitts Creeks is still maintained by trail crews and is often used by cyclists and early-season hikers.

Hikers most often sample the central section of the old fire road on short trips from McLeod Meadows Picnic Area or Campground. The gently graded road-bed makes for undemanding walking, and despite unremarkable scenery, these outings are rewarding in spring when the valley's first flowers are coming into bloom.

Follow the Dog Lake trail from either the McLeod Meadows Picnic Area or the rear of the campground (see *Dog Lake*). After crossing the Kootenay River suspension bridges just beyond the campground, you continue on the Dog Lake trail for another 250 m to its intersection with the fire road. At this point you can turn left and follow the road north 6.4 km to Daer Creek, or turn right and go south 4.8 km to Pitts Creek.

The washout of the Daer Creek bridge limits travel to the north, and the trail is not maintained south of Pitts Creek. While it's possible to travel beyond both of these creeks in either direction, you can expect lots of deadfall.

There is usually a fair amount of bear activity along the floor of the Kootenay Valley in the spring and early summer, so hikers and cyclists should always travel cautiously along this route.

Access: Follow Highway 93 to the McLeod Meadows Picnic Area, located on the east side of the highway 26.5 km (16.5 mi) north of Kootenay Park West Gate at Radium and 0.5 km (0.3 mi) south of McLeod Meadows Campground. The trail begins near the picnic shelter. (Campers start from the rear of the campground.) N50°45.914' W115°56.515' *Maps: Mount Assiniboine 82 J/13, Tangle Peak 82 J/12.*

174 West Kootenay Trail

Kootenay Crossing Station to Park Boundary—9.8 km (6.1 mi)

The West Kootenay Trail is a fairly boring 10-km road walk that is of more interest to cyclists and cross-country skiers than hikers. The trail is well removed from the Kootenay River most of the way, so there is little relief from the tedium of pine and spruce forest. However, a short branch road near the park boundary does lead to the river and, perhaps, some fine fly-fishing.

From the trail sign 300 m southwest of the Kootenay Crossing Station, follow well-graded road 0.9 km to the Dolly Varden Trail split. Stay right and continue northwest onto a benchland above the river.

There are few ups-and-downs as the broad track runs through the forest west of the river. Just before crossing a bridge over a major tributary at km 6.2, the roadbed descends to an interesting marsh environment near the Kootenay River.

At km 9.7, just 100 m before the park boundary, a 0.9-km branch road cuts right and crosses a low hill to the river. The main road continues across the park boundary, where it turns into a rough, wet, brushy track that eventually reaches the Beaverfoot Forestry Road in approximately 12 km.

Access: Follow Highway 93 to Kootenay Crossing Station, on the west side of the highway 42.5 km (26.5 mi) north of the Kootenay Park West Gate and 20.5 km (12.5 mi) south of Kootenay Park Lodge. Park out of the way in the station complex and follow a roadway leading left (southwest) from the compound for 300 m (passing an access gate) to rock barriers and a trail sign. N50°52.924' W116°03.208' *Maps: Spillimacheen 82 K/16.*

175 Dolly Varden Trail

Kootenay Crossing Station to Crook's Meadow—11.2 km (7.0 mi)

This fire road begins at Parks Canada's Kootenay Crossing Station and loops south along the west side of valley before returning to Highway 93 at Crook's Meadow group campground. Though forest-enclosed, it does offer a bit more interest with its ups-and-downs than most of the valley's fire roads. It also accesses the Luxor Pass trail.

From the trail sign 300 m southwest of the station complex, follow the fire road 0.9 km to the Dolly Varden-West Kootenay road split. Stay left and climb over a low, forested ridge before plunging down to the meadows of Dolly Varden Creek. These meadows provide the only open views, and the bridge over the creek (km 3.6) makes a pleasant rest stop.

Beyond the creek, the road climbs past Luxor Pass junction (km 4.1), then rolls through a stream-filled forest. You finally descend to Highway 93 at Crook's Meadow. (Cyclists can complete a 20-km loop by riding back to the station on the highway.)

Luxor Pass—4.3 km. This little used trail branches southwest from the Dolly Varden Trail at km 4.1. It climbs a steep, densely forested slope and exits the park via Luxor Pass (1905 m). Unmaintained trail connects to logging roads on the west slope of the Brisco Range.

Access: Follow Highway 93 to Kootenay Crossing Station, on the west side of the highway 42.5 km (26.5 mi) north of the Kootenay Park West Gate and 20.5 km (12.5 mi) south of Kootenay Park Lodge. Park out of the way in the station complex and follow a roadway leading left (southwest) from the compound 300 m (passing an access gate) to rock barriers and a trail sign. N50°52.924' W116°03.208' *Maps: Spillimacheen 82 K/16.*

Land above 2300 metres

0   1   2   3   4   5   6   7   8km

Dog Lake and the Mitchell Range

176 Dog Lake

McLeod Meadows Picnic Area to Dog Lake—2.6 km (1.6 mi)

Dog Lake is a shallow, marsh-fringed lake with open views of the Kootenay Valley. It is in one of the most temperate valleys in the Canadian Rockies, making it an excellent area for experiencing the montane forest ecosystem. Because of its low elevation, it can be hiked earlier and later in the season than most.

From the picnic area, the trail runs across a meadow and through the middle of the campground, exiting at a trail sign beyond the last campsite access road. Just 200 m beyond the campground, you cross two channels of the Kootenay River on suspension bridges.

Climbing beyond the river, the trail crosses the *East Kootenay Trail* and continues up into a dry forest of Douglas fir, white spruce and lodgepole pine—a slope covered with the brilliant orange blooms of western wood lilies in July.

The wide, well-graded trail reaches its high point at km 1.9, then descends

through a cooler forest carpeted with feather moss and bunchberry.

At km 2.6, you come abreast of the lake's marshy west shore, where you have views across the lake to two prominent peaks of the Mitchell Range—Mounts Daer and Harkin.

Follow the trail leading around to open dryas flats at the lake's north end (stay right at a signed junction). Here there are more open views south and a large lakeside wetland filled with marsh-loving horsetails (*equisetum*).

Access: Follow Highway 93 to the McLeod Meadows Picnic Area, located on the east side of the highway 26.5 km (16.5 mi) north of Kootenay Park West Gate at Radium and 0.5 km (0.3 mi) south of McLeod Meadows Campground. The trail begins near the picnic shelter. (Campers start from the rear of the campground.) N50°45.914′ W115°56.515′ *Maps: Mount Assiniboine 82 J/13 (trail not shown).*

177 Kindersley Pass—Sinclair Creek Circuit

Highway 93 to Kindersley Summit—9.8 km (6.1 mi)
Kindersley Pass-Sinclair Creek Circuit—16.2 km (10.1 mi)

Day trip
Allow 5 to 6 hours for circuit
Elevation gain: 1055 m (3,450 ft)
Maximum elevation: 2395 m (7,850 ft)
Maps: Tangle Peak 82 J/12

Access: Follow Highway 93 to the Kindersley Pass trailhead parking area, located on the south side of the highway 9.5 km (6 mi) east of Kootenay Park West Gate at Radium (trailhead on opposite side of road). The Sinclair Creek trail parking area is on the north side of the highway 1.2 km east of the Kindersley Pass trailhead.

0.0—Kindersley Pass trailhead (1340 m).
   N50°39.930' W115°57.407'

   —Moderate uphill through forest.

2.7—Avalanche slope.

   —Steady climb along avalanche path.

6.1—Lookout Point ridge.

   —Trail crosses avalanche paths.

8.4—Kindersley Pass (2210).
   Park boundary.

   —Trail cuts up to right.
   Steep ascent across open slopes.

9.8—Kindersley Summit (2395 m).

   —Follow markers down to Sinclair Creek headwaters.

11.2—Good trail reappears east side of valley.

11.7—Trail enters forest.

   —Steep switchbacking descent.

14.5—Sinclair Creek bridge to west side.

16.2—Sinclair Creek trailhead (1435 m).
   N50°40.394' W115°56.742'

   —Kindersley Pass trailhead 1.2 km west.

Notice: Travel on this trail often requires a group of four people hiking in close proximity to one another due to the presence of grizzly bears.

The hike to Kindersley Pass and the high, alpine ridges beyond is one of the most scenic day trips in Kootenay Park—and one of the most strenuous. After nearly 10 km of steady climbing, you will be more than happy to relax on the 2395-m crest of Kindersley Summit and enjoy the view. Or perhaps stroll along the high traverse to nearby Nixon Creek Summit and scan the slopes for the flocks of bighorn sheep that summer in this range.

While you can always return from the summit the way you came, the traditional and quickest way is to complete a loop by descending to the Sinclair Creek headwaters and following the 5-km trail down along the creek to the highway. This route brings you back to the highway just east of the Kindersley Pass trail parking area, leaving a quick 1.2-km downhill road walk back to your vehicle.

Though it is 100 m lower than Sinclair Creek, we always start at the Kindersley Pass trailhead to make a longer but more gradual ascent to the summit, and a downhill walk along the highway at the end of the day. (If you have two vehicles to arrange transportation between trailheads, you may prefer doing it in the opposite direction.)

From Kindersley trailhead, you climb steadily up a narrow, densely forested valley, which opens suddenly at km 2.7 into a series of avalanche paths. As you ascend above the first slide area and cross a small divide just west of Lookout Point, you enter cool subalpine forest of Engelmann spruce and alpine fir.

More avalanche paths are crossed near Kindersley Pass, and piles of snow from these slides often linger into late summer. Along the margins of the retreating snowbanks, glacier lilies and western anemones can often be found in bloom, even in August.

Kindersley Pass is a bit of an anti-climax after the stiff 8.4-km climb to its

Climbing to Kindersley Summit

summit, yet a small meadow at the pass makes a pleasant rest stop. It also provides the first good views northward to the long procession of peaks comprising the Brisco Range.

The true glory of the hike begins above the pass. By following the trail ascending the ridge to the north, you soon emerge through the last stands of larch onto open slopes dotted with stunted islands of alpine fir. At km 9.8, you reach Kindersley Summit, the highest point on the trip where the trail crests a ridge between two rocky peaks. From this lofty saddle, views open to the headwaters of Sinclair Creek and an endless sea of peaks stretching away to the northeast.

From Kindersley Summit, you can side-trip along a high path contouring around the head of the Sinclair Creek basin for 2 km to Nixon Creek Summit. This is alpine walking at its best, and though the trail is indistinct at times, there is no problem sighting its trace on the open slope ahead.

At Nixon Creek Summit, new views open along the crest of the Brisco Range and down to the forested headwaters of Nixon Creek. Rock scramblers can ascend the 2530-m peak immediately above this col for an even better view.

Unless you're adverse to very steep descents, you might as well return to the highway on the Sinclair Creek trail and complete the Kindersley-Sinclair Circuit (it's the shortest way back to the highway). Descend due east from the Kindersley Summit saddle, across steep avalanche slopes, to the head of the Sinclair Valley. (Watch for markers and cairns.) Once the valley floor is reached near a series of small cascades, a faint trail materializes. This rough track follows the west side of the creek for 100 m and then crosses to the east side. Not far beyond it turns into good trail and descends from the avalanche-swept basin back into a cool, closed forest.

This steep downhill track brings you back to Highway 93 at the Sinclair Creek trailhead parking area. From there it is an easy walk down along highway to the Kindersley Pass trailhead.

Cobb Lake

178 Cobb Lake

Highway 93 to Cobb Lake—2.7 km (1.7 mi)

This forest-encircled lake on the lower slopes of Mount Sinclair is noted for its mirror reflections and peaceful setting. The trail makes a nice escape from the busyness of Highway 93, but be aware that you lose more elevation than you gain on the way to the lake; be prepared for a bit of climbing on the way out.

While the trail is usually snowfree from early May to late October, it is most rewarding in spring (late May-early June) when many forest wildflowers bloom, including heart-leaved arnica, blue clematis and false solomon seal.

From the roadside pull-out just east of Sinclair Pass, the trail switchbacks down through a heavy forest dominated by lodgepole pine, white spruce and the occasional aspen poplar.

There are also a few old Douglas fir giants. Thanks to their thick, protective bark, these patriarchs survived a forest fire through this section of the Kootenay Valley in 1918. (Look for charred bark around the base of these trees.)

After a steady descent over 1.6 km, you cross Swede Creek and climb for the final kilometre to the lake.

Some folks like to wet their fishing lines in the lake in hopes of hooking the elusive brook trout that are frequently seen leaping from its waters. (A park fishing license is required.)

Access: Follow Highway 93 to a roadside pullout on the south side of the highway 14.5 km (9 mi) from Kootenay Park West Gate and 0.6 km (0.4 mi) west of the Kootenay Valley Viewpoint. N50°40.349′ W115°53.726′ *Maps: Tangle Peak 82 J/12 (trail not shown).*

179 Kimpton Creek

Highway 93 to Trail's End—4.9 km (3.0 mi)

When midsummer heat is beating down on nearby Radium and the Columbia Valley, folks escape to Sinclair Canyon and take a cool walk in the forest along Kimpton Creek.

From the bridge over Sinclair Creek 150 m below the parking area, the trail joins Kimpton Creek and stays along its rushing waters for the next 1.5 km. Along the first 300 m a large limestone cliff rises above the west side of the creek, creating a canyon that traps the cool air generated by the creek.

Douglas fir and white spruce dominate the forest canopy, though deciduous trees, like Douglas maple, white birch and aspen, do grow in areas where sunlight breaks through.

At 1.5 km, four switchbacks lift you above the creek and its cool environment. Other than the occasional avalanche slope to the right, the way up-valley is tedious and forest-enclosed.

At 4.2 km, the trail finally breaks out onto an open slope overlooking a willowy meadow and avalanche slopes. Here you have the only distant views on the entire trip, looking back down-valley to mountains north of Sinclair Creek.

After climbing steeply beneath some shaly bluffs, the trail re-enters forest and descends to an "End of Trail" sign beside a major tributary stream.

Access: Follow Highway 93 to a small roadside parking area on the Sinclair Creek side of the highway 7.0 km (4.3 mi) east of Kootenay Park West Gate. Walk down the highway 150 m on a very narrow berm to the trailhead bridge across Sinclair Creek. N50°38.780' W115°58.179' *Maps: Tangle Peak 82 J/12 (trail not shown).*

180 Redstreak Creek

Highway 93 to Trail's End—2.3 km (1.4 mi)

The Redstreak Creek trail probes the narrow confines of a side-valley intersecting Sinclair Canyon from the south. While there are no open views, the gorge is a unique environment dominated by deciduous trees—a wonderful place in spring when new leaves are unfolding and wildflowers like false solomon seal, arnica and fairybells are blooming on the forest floor.

From the trailhead bridge over Sinclair Creek, you immediately climb above the creek via a series of switchbacks and stay well east of the stream for the remainder of the hike.

The forest floor is well shaded initially and covered with feather moss and bunchberry; where sun filters through, there are wild roses and junipers.

Grades become gradual at 0.5 km and you enter an unusual woodland dominated by Douglas maple along with a scattering of white birch and aspen. At km 1.0 a windstorm has felled hundreds of less flexible lodgepole pine trees, which are piled like kindling beneath the hardwoods.

The trail becomes narrow and rooty before reaching the "end of trail" sign at a small spring-fed streamlet (the only water on the trail).

Access: Follow Highway 93 to the trailhead parking area on the south side of the highway 4.5 km (2.8 mi) east of Kootenay Park West Gate. The trail begins at the bridge across Sinclair Creek. N50°38.479' W116°00.206' *Maps: Tangle Peak 82 J/12 (trail not shown).*

181 Juniper Trail–Sinclair Canyon Circuit

Radium Hot Springs Parking Area to Juniper Trail Summit—0.8 km (0.5 mi)
Sinclair Canyon Circuit—6.2 km (3.9 mi)

Short walk to half-day trip

Allow: 20 minutes to summit
2.5 hours for circuit

Maximum elevation: 1100 m (3,600 ft)

Minimum elevation: 880 m (2,890 ft)

Maps: Radium Hot Springs 82 K/9 †
   † trail not shown

Access: Follow Highway 93 to Radium Hot
Springs Pools, 1.7 km (1.0 mi) east from
Kootenay Park West Gate. Go to the parking
area on the north side of the highway,
opposite the pools complex. The Juniper
Trail kiosk is at the rear of the parking area.
From the kiosk, walk up the Radium Hot
Springs Lodge access road 170 m to the
trail sign.

0.0— Trailhead (1030 m).
   N50°38.145' W116°02.596'
   —Moderate uphill.

0.8— Summit viewpoint (1100 m).
   —Trail descends west from summit.

1.1— Viewpoint.

1.8— Canyon rim viewpoint (fenced).

2.7— Sinclair Creek bridge (880 m).
   Sinclair Falls left (30 m beyond bridge).

2.8— Junction. Canyon Campground ahead.
   Juniper Trail left.
   —Moderate to steep uphill.

3.1— Juniper Trail lower trailhead (920 m).
   N50°37.911' W116°03.561'
   —Follow sidewalk uphill along Hwy 93.

3.3— Trail sign south side of highway
   (cross with care).
   —Moderate to steep uphill.

3.9— Sinclair Canyon viewpoint (left 20 m).

4.0— Junction. Right to Redstreak
   Campground (200 m) and viewing
   platform (30 m).
   Radium Hot Springs ahead.

4.4— South summit (1070 m).
   Begin descent through forest.

5.5— "Place of Silence Peace Park".

5.9— Radium Hot Springs Pools. Pedestrian
   tunnel under Hwy 93 to north-side
   parking area.

The Juniper Trail is the most popular
hike near Radium. In addition to views
of Sinclair Canyon, the Columbia Valley
and the highest summits of the Purcell
Range, it passes through two very distinct west-slope forest environments.
You can also connect with a trail on the
south side of Highway 93 to make a complete loop around Sinclair Canyon. And
the trail enjoys a very long snow-free
season, usually from mid-April through
early November.

Though there are several access points
to the canyon circuit, we prefer the
parking area opposite the Radium Hot
Springs Pools. The trail kiosk-map is at
the rear of the parking lot, but the actual
trailhead is 170 m away, up the paved access road to Radium Hot Springs Lodge
(watch for sign on left).

A 20-minute climb through Douglas
fir and Rocky Mountain juniper leads
to the Juniper Trail summit, where the
Columbia Valley, Radium and the highway snaking out of Sinclair Canyon are
suddenly revealed. On the western horizon are the ice-capped peaks of the Purcell Range—the most distinctive being
smokestack-shaped Farnham Tower
(3353 m) and, further south, the leaning
pyramid of Mount Nelson (3283 m).

If you are only out for a short hike to
the best view on the trail, turn back here.
But completing the circuit around the
canyon is a rewarding trip that should
take less than 3 hours. Beyond the
summit, the trail descends to another
overlook with even better views into
the canyon, and in another 0.7 km, you
reach a viewpoint contained by a chain-
link fence on the canyon rim.

As the trail descends, it switchbacks
through a semi-open Interior Douglas
fir forest—a dry slope with scattered
Rocky Mountain juniper and Douglas
fir, where bluebells and golden-flowered
gaillardia bloom in early summer.

Columbia Valley from the Juniper Trail

Yet another dramatic change occurs when you reach Sinclair Creek. Suddenly you are enclosed by a cool, lush stand of western red cedar, and a forest floor carpeted with feather moss. Just beyond the footbridge, a 200-m trail branches left to a view of Sinclair Falls tumbling from the canyon. Meanwhile, the main trail switchbacks upwards to the lower trailhead for the Juniper Trail on Highway 93, just 200 m from Kootenay Park West Gate.

Follow the sidewalk uphill along the highway toward the mouth of the canyon. You can shorten your hike by following the paved walkway back along the highway to the hot pools parking area (1.4 km). Or you can continue the circuit on the south-side trail to Redstreak Campground.

Sinclair Canyon Circuit. After hiking up the sidewalk 200 m from the lower Juniper trailhead, cross to the trail sign on the south side of the highway at the entrance to Sinclair Canyon (be wary of traffic emerging from the canyon).

After a short climb through Douglas fir, birch and maple, you arrive at another canyon overlook (stairs down to the left). The fenced viewpoint is set on the canyon rim, like that on the Juniper Trail, which is visible across the narrow chasm.

Steep stairs climb to a short trail branching right to Redstreak Campground (an optional access point to the circuit for campers). By following this branch for 30 m, you come to a viewing platform for the Columbia Valley and Purcell Range.

Beyond the campground junction, there is more stair climbing until the trail levels out in thinned forest surrounding the campground's water supply station. From here, it contours along cool, heavily-forested slopes back to the hot springs. The highlight on this section is a grove of magnificent cedars containing a small amphitheatre—the "Place of Silence Peace Park."

A short section of fenced switchbacks leads down to the Radium Hot Springs pools complex. Follow through the courtyard and up stairs to a pedestrian tunnel leading to the trailhead parking area on the north side the highway.

Waterton Lakes National Park

At 518 sq km, Waterton Lakes National Park is the smallest of the five national parks in the Canadian Rockies. Tucked into the southwestern corner of Alberta, it is bounded on the west by British Columbia's Akamina-Kishinena Provincial Park, on the south by the U.S. border and Glacier National Park, and on the north and east by the rolling prairies of southern Alberta.

There are over 170 km of trails in Waterton Lakes National Park and they are the best constructed in the Canadian Rockies—moderately graded, well-marked, scenically routed and, as might be expected, heavily travelled. Most trails in the park can be hiked in a day, and nearly all lead to small subalpine lakes nestled in hanging valleys.

The most popular day trips branch from the park's main roads. Rowe Lakes-Lineham Ridge and the Carthew—Alderson hikes start from the Akamina Parkway, as do two popular day trips to Forum Lake and Wall Lake in British Columbia's Akamina-Kishinena Park (see *Akamina-Kishinena Provincial Park*). The Twin Lakes and Goat Lake are reached via the Snowshoe Trail from the end of the Red Rock Parkway. The Bertha Lake trail, the park's most popular day hike, strikes off from the edge of Waterton townsite, and the unique Crypt Lake trip is initiated from the village marina with a 3-km boat ride.

While there are campgrounds on many of the shorter trails, serious backpacking opportunities are limited in such a small park. The Tamarack Trail, which runs along the Great Divide for 36 km from the Akamina Parkway to Red Rock Canyon, is the park's best known route. Though the Snowshoe-Blakiston Creek Loop can be completed in a long day, it too is often backpacked. And the Waterton Lakeshore trail provides access to wilderness trails in the northern region of Glacier National Park, Montana.

As in other Rocky Mountain national parks, you must obtain a Wilderness Pass for any overnight outing in Waterton's backcountry. Quotas are observed in all campgrounds, and since many of these sites are very popular, particularly on weekends, you should consider reserving space up to three months prior to your trip.

Citizens of the U.S. and Canada may cross the border through Goat Haunt at the southern end of Waterton Lake by presenting a passport to Port of Entry staff at the Goat Haunt Ranger Station (open only during summer season until Labour Day). Citizens of other countries should check with the relevant U.S. or Canadian customs and border agency as part of their trip planning.

If you plan on backpacking into Glacier National Park from Waterton, you can obtain a U.S. Park Service Backcountry Use Permit either at the Waterton Visitor Centre or one of several Glacier Park backcountry permit issuing stations.

Information and services. The Waterton Visitor Centre is on the Park Entrance Road just north of Waterton townsite at the top of the hill opposite the Prince of Wales Hotel. It offers the usual range of park information services and materials, including trail reports, weather forecasts, a variety of free pamphlets concerning park activities and issues, and schedules for interpretive programs and guided walks. It also dispenses Wilderness Passes for backcountry camping and park fishing licenses. A townsite outdoor specialty shop, Tamarack Outdoor Outfitters, sells maps and books that hikers will find useful.

There are two main roadside campgrounds in the park: the Townsite Campground, located just south of the townsite's business district; and the Crandell Mountain Campground on the Red Rock Parkway. The smaller Belly River Campground is located on the Chief Mountain Parkway (Hwy 6) near the U.S. border. The Townsite Campground is the only full service facility (hook-ups and showers).

Waterton townsite is the park's sole service centre. Primarily a seasonal village of 800 summer residents, the townsite comprises summer cottages and a small business district that provides basic services: grocery and gift stores, restaurants, a gas station, a laundromat, an outdoor sport-hiking shop and a number of lodges and motels. There are no banks, but ATM machines are available. Many businesses are closed from early October to mid-May. Pincher Creek (48 km) and Cardston, Alberta (45 km), are the nearest full-service towns to the park.

Access. Two provincial highways provide access to the park entrance: Highway 5 from Cardston and Highway 6 from Pincher Creek. Highway 6 (known as Chief Mountain Parkway where it runs through the park) is the most direct route to and from Glacier National Park, Montana, but is only open in summer.

The nearest Alberta cities serviced by commercial airlines are Lethbridge (130 km) and Calgary (264 km). Greyhound bus service is available to Pincher Creek, 48 km north of the park, but there is no scheduled public transport to the park.

Commercial shuttle services transport hikers to Cameron Lake, Red Rock Canyon and other trailhead locations. Sightseeing cruise boats on Upper Waterton Lake also provide hiker drop-offs at Crypt Landing for the Crypt Lake trail and the Goat Haunt dock for trails into northern Glacier National Park. (See *Sources—Backcountry access.*)

Land above 2000 metres

Upper Waterton Lake from Bear's Hump

182 Bear's Hump

Waterton Visitor Centre to Bear's Hump—1.4 km (0.9 mi)

The Bear's Hump, an aptly-named bulge on Mount Crandell's southern ridge, is the most popular short hike in Waterton Lakes National Park. Its status is easy to account for: aside from its proximity to Waterton townsite, it offers a sweeping aerial view of Waterton Valley, the townsite, and the prairies to the northeast. Be forewarned, however: the vista comes with a price. Climbing a heart-pounding 225 m in 1.4 km, the trail constitutes one of the steepest short hikes in the Canadian Rockies.

Starting from the Waterton Visitor Centre parking area, the hike is all trees and steady, steep climbing until you reach the lofty limestone bluff overlooking Upper Waterton Lake.

There is little to block the view from the top—rock and wind dictate that only a few stunted bonsai grow there—and your gaze is immediately drawn down the lake to the mountains of Montana's Glacier National Park. The prominent peak beyond the end of the lake is Mount Cleveland, which at 3190 m is the highest mountain in the Waterton-Glacier International Peace Park.

Immediately below the toes of your boots, the townsite spreads across an alluvial fan created by Cameron Creek, and the Prince of Wales Hotel perches majestically on a promontory above the narrow strait—called the Bosporus—that connects Upper and Middle Waterton Lakes.

The wind is nearly always blowing on Bear's Hump, so take a windbreaker even if it's sunny and warm. Avoid the hike altogether if it's stormy.

Access: Start at the Waterton Visitor Centre, just north of Waterton townsite on the Park Entrance Road. N49°03.629' W113°54.504' *Maps: Waterton Lakes 82 H/4; Waterton Lakes National Park (Gem Trek).*

183 Bertha Lake

Waterton Townsite to Bertha Lake—5.8 km (3.6 mi)

Day trip or backpack

Allow 1.5 to 2 hours one way

Elevation gain: 460 m (1,500 ft)

Maximum elevation: 1755 m (5,750 ft)

Maps: Waterton Lakes 82 H/4
Waterton Lakes National Park
(Gem Trek)

Access: Follow Evergreen Avenue south along the west side of Waterton townsite. Look for the signed trailhead parking area on the right-hand side of the road 0.4 km south of Cameron Falls.

0.0— Trailhead (1295 m).
N49°02.802' W113°55.013'

— Trail climbs south through forest.

1.5— Junction. *Waterton Lakeshore* trail left. Stay right.

— Trail climbs along north side of Bertha Creek.

2.6— Lower Bertha Falls.

— Trail crosses Bertha Creek and makes switchbacking ascent along south side of valley.

5.1— Bertha Lake view from trail summit (1755 m).

— Stay right at lakeshore.

5.8— Bertha Lake Campground.

— Trail continues around the lake as an unmaintained 4.5-km footpath.

The trail to Bertha Lake is one of the most popular day hikes in Waterton Park. Lying less than 6 km from the townsite yet featuring a campground and cooking shelter, it attracts a mixed bag of day hikers and campers. The number of visitors can be a distraction, but the lake is still one of the prettiest backcountry bodies of water in the park.

Starting from the southwest corner of the townsite, the trail climbs gradually for 2 km through a forest rich with undergrowth and wildflowers.

At the *Waterton Lakeshore* junction, the trail breaks out of the trees onto an open slope with excellent views of Upper Waterton Lake. The stunted, brushy trees on the promontory are limber pine—a species that thrives in dry, rocky locales.

At km 2.6, you cross Bertha Creek beneath Lower Bertha Falls and begin the steep climb to the hanging valley that cradles Bertha Lake. After a steady ascent through the forest you'll catch sight through the trees of a cascade spilling over a staircase of brick-red argillite—Upper Bertha Falls.

At km 5.1 the trail reaches its highest point (1755 m), where you'll be rewarded with your first view of the lake. From the crest, the trail modestly descends for 0.7 km to water's edge. Stay right for the campground.

The trail continues around the lake as an unmaintained footpath, passing beneath a vertical wall connecting Mounts Alderson and Richards. The thin, dark band stretching across the rock face is a diabase sill, created by molten rock intruded between the adjacent layers of grey limestone and dolomite long before the uplift of the Rockies.

The lake was named for Bertha Ekelund, an early local who was reputedly sent to jail for passing counterfeit currency. She never returned to Waterton, but her name lives on.

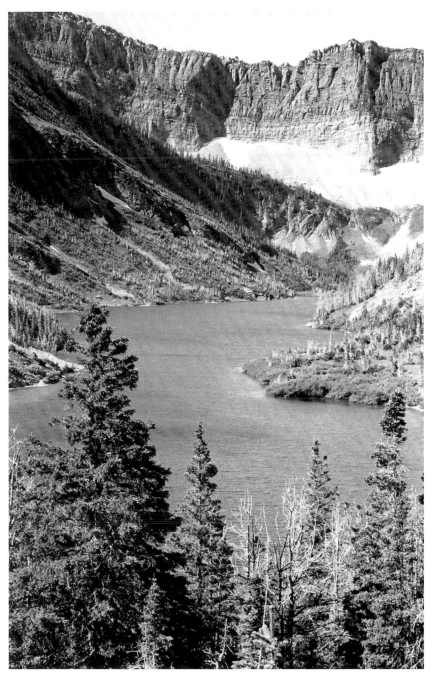

Bertha Lake

Waterton Townsite to Goat Haunt Boat Dock—13.0 km (8.1 mi)

Day trip or backpack
Allow 4 hours one way
Elevation gain: 100 m (350 ft)
       loss: 115 m (375 ft)
Maximum elevation: 1395 m (4,580 ft)
Maps: Waterton Lakes 82 H/4
      Waterton Lakes National Park
      (Gem Trek)

Access: Follow Evergreen Avenue south along the west side of Waterton townsite. Look for the signed Bertha Lake trailhead parking area on the right-hand side of the road 0.4 km south of Cameron Falls.

  0.0— Trailhead (1295 m).
      N49°02.802' W113°55.013'

    — Trail climbs south through forest.

  1.4— Junction. Lake viewpoint left. Keep right.

  1.5— Junction. *Bertha Lake* trail right. Keep left.

    — Trail descends toward lakeshore.

  2.4— Bertha Bay Campground and boat dock.

    — Trail rolls along lakeshore.

  5.8— International boundary monument. Boundary Bay Campground and boat dock.

  6.3— Boundary Creek bridge.

  6.4— Junction. Boundary Creek trail right. Keep left.

    — Trail rolls through forest above lakeshore.

11.5— Junction. Boulder Pass right. Keep left.

12.1— Junction. Rainbow Falls right. Keep left.

    — Waterton River bridge.

12.6— Goat Haunt Ranger Station.

    — Continue around end of lake to boat dock.

13.0— Goat Haunt boat dock (1280 m).

Note: U.S. and Canadian citizens must present valid passports to Port of Entry staff at the Goat Haunt Ranger Station (usually open from Memorial Day to Labour Day). Citizens of other countries should check with the relevant U.S. or Canadian customs and border agency as part of their trip planning.

The 13-km trail running along the west shore of Upper Waterton Lake `offers several options: a short walk to Bertha Bay; a day hike to the international boundary and back; or an extended backpack into the northern wilderness of Glacier National Park. Another popular option is to take a tour boat from Waterton townsite to Goat Haunt and hike back.

The Waterton Lakeshore trail starts as part of the *Bertha Lake* trail and climbs through lush, flower-filled forest for 1.5 km to the Waterton Lakeshore trail junction. There, you branch left and descend to Bertha Bay—one of the prettiest spots along Upper Waterton Lake.

Beyond Bertha Bay, the trail rolls along the rocky lower slopes of Mount Richards to the international boundary and Boundary Bay. Sitting in the quiet lakeside picnic area at Boundary Bay is a unique experience. Across the lake on the slopes of Mount Boswell a distinctive slash line marks the Canada-U.S. border. That line, and the nearby boundary cairn, are the only signs that you are passing from one nation to another.

After crossing Boundary Creek, the trail continues south through enclosed forest above the shoreline, eventually bypassing junctions to Boulder Pass and Rainbow Falls. There are no open views worth mentioning until you cross the Waterton River and branch left to Goat Haunt Ranger Station at the south end of the lake. From the station, paved trail leads east around the shore to the tour boat landing.

If you plan on backpacking into Glacier National Park, obtain a U.S. Park Service Backcountry Use Permit at the Waterton Visitor Centre or one of the Glacier Park backcountry permit issuing stations (information available online). Regardless of whether you are day hiking or backpacking, make sure you present the appropriate documents at the Goat Haunt Ranger Station.

185 Wishbone Trail–Vimy Peak

Chief Mountain Parkway to Crypt Landing—15.2 km (9.4 mi)*
Chief Mountain Parkway to Vimy Basin—11.8 km (7.3 mi)*

Day trip or backpack

Allow 4.5 hours to Crypt Landing

Elevation gain: 70 m (230 ft)
            loss: 90 m (295 ft)

Maximum elevation: 1370 m (4,500 ft)

Maps: Waterton Lakes 82 H/4
         Waterton Lakes National Park
         (Gem Trek)

Access: Follow Highway 5 east from the park entrance junction for 0.9 km to the Chief Mountain Parkway (Hwy 6) intersection. Turn right on to Chief Mountain Parkway and follow it 0.5 km to a gated access road on the right. Park in the pullout on the left (north) side of the highway.

0.0— Trailhead (1300 m).
      N49°06.530' W113°49.580'

    — Trail begins as a reclaimed service road.

2.6— Lower Waterton Lake. Trail becomes a single track.

5.5— Sofa Creek crossing.

7.0— Junction (1295 m). Vimy Peak via Vimy Basin left. Wishbone Trail ahead. End of bike access.

    — Trail climbs above Middle Waterton Lake.

12.0— Loon Lake.

    — Junction. Bosporus right 1.2 km. Crypt Landing left.

14.0— Crypt Landing (1280 m).

*All distances approximate.

Open to cyclists as far as the Vimy Peak trail junction (7.0 km), the Wishbone Trail offers easy, agreeable hiking and great wildflowers early in the season and provides access to the east side of the Waterton Valley and the Vimy Peak trail

Beginning as a reclaimed service road, the trail provides comfortable, essentially flat hiking through aspen-cottonwood woodland for 2.6 km to the shore of Lower Waterton Lake. There, the last vestiges of the old road disappear and the trail continues as a single track, working through more woodland and across open grassy sections (where it can be indistinct in spots).

Soon after passing the Vimy Peak trail junction at km 7.0, the Wishbone reaches Middle Waterton Lake and angles west for 5 km to tiny Loon Lake. From the lake, most hikers take the short Bosporus side-trip—a 1.2-km unmaintained track that leads over the ridge between Middle and Upper Waterton Lakes. Although many hikers turn back at Bosporus, the main Wishbone Trail continues south along Upper Waterton Lake for another 2 km to the Crypt Landing boat dock and the *Crypt Lake* trail.

Vimy Peak. Views from summit of Vimy Peak (2347 m) are spectacular, encompassing Waterton Valley and stretching out to the prairie. Be forewarned, however, that the route to the top is steep, passes through prime grizzly habitat, and includes an hour of rock scrambling from the end of the trail in Vimy Basin. The trail begins its steep ascent from its junction with the Wishbone Trail at km 7.0 and ascends the east side of the mountain to the barren Vimy Basin. At the 4.8-km mark the Vimy Peak trail fizzles out, leaving you to follow the line of least resistance up steep scree and broken rock to the summit.

Crypt Landing to Crypt Lake—8.7 km (5.4 mi)

Day trip or backpack

Allow 2.5 to 3.5 hours one way

Elevation gain: 665 m (2,220 ft)

Maximum elevation: 1955 m (6,420 ft)

Maps: Waterton Lakes 82 H/4
Waterton Lakes National Park
(Gem Trek)

Access: Book passage on the earliest
tour boat crossing Upper Waterton Lake
from Waterton to Crypt Landing dock. (See
Sources—Backcountry access for tour boat
contact information.)

0.0— Trailhead (1280 m).
N49°01.872', W113°53.668'

0.4— Junction. Hell-Roaring Falls lower
cutoff right. Falls 1.0 km.

— Switchbacking ascent through forest.

2.4— Last switchback.

3.0— Junction. Hell-Roaring Falls upper
cutoff.

3.5— Twin Falls viewpoint.

5.6— Burnt Rock Falls.

— Switchbacking climb.

8.1— Tunnel.

8.5— Entrance to Crypt Lake cirque.
Top of Crypt Falls.

8.7— Crypt Lake (1945 m).

Crypt Lake has more tricks and amusements than any other trail in the Rockies. You cross the Rockies' windiest lake by tour boat, ascend a narrow valley past a staircase of waterfalls, climb an iron ladder, crawl through a tunnel, tippy toe along a cliff while clinging to a cable, and skirt a precipice from which a stream bursts forth to plunge 175 m to the rocks below. And if that doesn't satisfy your taste for the bizarre, you can stroll along the shore of the Rockies' most perfect cirque lake and visit another country.

The fun begins at the Waterton town marina by booking the early morning trip to Crypt Landing on the eastern shore of Upper Waterton Lake (see *Sources—Backcountry access* for tour boat contact info). When doing so, make sure to check with the captain about pick-up time in the late afternoon.

From the Crypt Landing dock, the trail climbs directly into dense lakeshore forest. Just 0.4 km into the hike you pass a side trail to Hell-Roaring Falls, which loops south to Hell-Roaring Canyon and its impressive waterfall, then climbs to reconnect with the Crypt trail at km 3.0. (Save the falls for the return trip, and only then if you have time to spare before catching your boat.)

The trail quickly gains elevation through spruce and fir forest via a series of switchbacks, then heads up-valley through more open country and passes a viewpoint for Twin Falls.

Beyond Burnt Rock Falls—a beautiful 15-m waterfall dropping over limestone and red argillite—the trail climbs across open talus slopes and up another series of steep switchbacks.

The last 0.8 km to the lake is not well suited for the claustrophobic, acrophobic or obese. A short jaunt across talus brings you to a sheer wall—an apparent cul de sac but for a ladder leading up to a dark hole in the rock. At the top of the ladder a 20-m tunnel cuts through

Crypt Lake

the mountain spur—a cramped shaft that nearly brings you to your hands-and-knees. At the end of the tunnel, you emerge onto a ledge across an exposed precipice, where a cable offers support for the faint-of-heart.

At the entrance to Crypt Lake cirque, the lake's outlet stream suddenly surfaces from beneath a pile of boulders and leaps over a cliff to form Crypt Falls.

Crypt Lake is certainly no anticlimax to its multi-faceted approach. Its waters are of the deepest green and seldom free of ice, even in mid-summer when ice floes drift on its surface. Surrounded by 600-m cliffs, it is a textbook example of a glacially-carved cirque.

By keeping to the east shore, you can walk to the far end of the lake, which rests precisely on the Canada-U.S. boundary. No immigration officer to greet you here, only the occasional mountain goat patrolling the slopes above. However, the Wilson Range forms one of the most effective barriers anywhere along the 6500-km border.

Allow about two hours to catch the last boat back to Waterton, and please spare this beautiful valley by not short-cutting switchbacks on the way down.

N

Newman
▲Pk

Mt▲
Glendowan

Goat
Lake ▲ (194)

Mt▲
Dungarvan

Castle
River
Divide

Avion Ridge

Bauerman Creek

Lost Lake

Sage
Pass (195)

(191)

Anderson
▲Pk

(191)

Red Rock
Canyon

Twin
Lakes

Mt▲
Bauerman

Blakiston
Falls (193)

Blue Grouse
Basin

Blakiston Creek

South
Kootenay
Pass (195)

Lone
▲Mtn

Mt▲
Blakiston

Waterton

Lone Lake (191)

Mt▲
Hawkins

Ruby Ridge

Crandell
Lake ▲ (192)

Festubert Mtn

ALBERTA
BRITISH COLUMBIA

Lineham Lakes

Lineham
Ridge

(187)

Mt▲
Lineham

Lineham Creek

Waterton

Akamina

Creek

(190) (191)

Rowe Cr.

Creek

Buchanan Ridge

Upper Rowe
Lakes

Lower Rowe
Lake

Carthew Creek

▲Mt
Rowe

Cameron

Mt▲
Carthew

(189)

Alderson
Lake

AKAMINA-KISHINENA
PROVINCIAL PARK

Akamina
Pass

Cameron Lake

Carthew
Lakes

Carthew
Summit

▲Mt
Alderson

Creek

(196) (197)

Forum
Lake

(188)

Summit
Lake

Akamina Ridge

Wall
Lake

Forum
Pk▲

CANADA
UNITED STATES

Boundary Creek

Land above 2000 metres

0 1 2 3 4km

187 Lineham Falls

Akamina Parkway to Lineham Falls—4.2 km (2.6 mi)

The trail to Lineham Falls ascends Lineham Creek, climbing the valley between Mounts Blakiston and Lineham to end in a broad, subalpine meadow where a 100-m waterfall tumbles down a massive cliff. Despite nice open views back down-valley and great early summer wildflower displays, fewer people than might be expected actually make the hike. That's because the real beauties of the valley—a cluster of lakes in a tiny larch-laced basin—lie above the cliff in the Lineham Basin.

The trail begins as a relatively steep but straightforward climb along open, south-facing slopes on the north side of the Lineham Creek Valley. Eventually the grade moderates through mixed forest in the upper valley.

You emerge from the trees at trail's end to see the falls and its imposing cliff 0.5 km beyond. You can extend your outing by following climbers' paths across the meadow toward the cliff and then angling over to the base of the falls. If you're lucky, you may spot mountain goats on the upper valley slopes.

Only experienced climbers who have registered with Parks Canada at the Waterton Visitor Centre should attempt to scale the cliff to reach the Lineham Basin. If you don't climb, we recommend you retreat and hike the trail to Lineham Ridge, which provides an outstanding view of this unique, lake-filled hanging valley (see *Rowe Lakes—Lineham Ridge*).

Access: From Waterton townsite, follow the Akamina Parkway 9.5 km (6.0 mi) to the trailhead parking area, on the right side of the road just east of Lineham Creek bridge. N49°03.956' W113°59.950' *Maps: Sage Creek 82 G/1; Waterton Lakes National Park (Gem Trek).*

188 Cameron Lakeshore

Cameron Lake Parking Area to Trail's End—1.5 km (0.9 mi)

The short Cameron Lakeshore trail, tracing the lake's western shore, is a pleasant outing through cool subalpine forest—a welcome escape from the crowds at the lake's parking area, interpretive kiosk and boat dock. The trail is flat and there are a number of fine gravel beaches for lounging and picnicking along the way.

The trail is broad and level as it passes from the open gravel beach at the north end of the lake into a forest of Engelmann spruce and alpine fir. The forest is typical of Waterton's subalpine—lush and green, filled with cow parsnip, thimbleberry, menziesia and red monkeyflower. Mount Custer, with the Herbst Glacier clinging to its north face, rises beyond the far end of the lake.

The southern end of Cameron Lake lies in Montana's Glacier National Park, but the trail ends about halfway down the lake at a viewing platform with an interpretive sign that explains why there may well be bears foraging close by. While it may be tempting to bushwhack to the end of the lake, the lakeshore is overgrown and the chance of suddenly meeting a grizzly is very real.

Access: From Waterton townsite, follow the Akamina Parkway 16 km (10 mi) to the parking area at Cameron Lake. From the lakeshore interpretive kiosk, follow the shoreline trail to the right. N49°01.183' W114°02.702' *Maps: Sage Creek 82 G/1; Waterton Lakes National Park (Gem Trek).*

189 Carthew–Alderson Trail

Cameron Lake to Carthew Summit—7.9 km (4.9 mi)
Cameron Lake to Waterton townsite—20.1 km (12.5 mi)

Day trip or backpack

Allow 6 to 8 hours

Elevation gain: 650 m (2,135 ft)
loss: 1020 m (3,350 ft)

Maximum elevation: 2311 m (7,582 ft)

Maps: Sage Creek 82 G/1
Waterton Lakes 82 H/4
Waterton Lakes National Park
(Gem Trek)

Access: From Waterton townsite, follow the Akamina Parkway 16 km (10 mi) to its terminus at the Cameron Lake parking area. From the lakeshore interpretive kiosk follow the shoreline trail left to the trailhead at the Cameron Creek bridge.

0.0—Cameron Creek Trailhead (1660 m).
N49°01.177' W114°02.633'

—Steady switchbacking climb through dense forest.

3.0—Trail emerges into subalpine forest.

4.2—Summit Lake (1935 m).

4.3—Junction. Boundary Creek right.
Carthew Summit left.

—Steep climb through dwindling forest.

7.9—Carthew Summit (2311 m).

—Steep descent across scree slopes.

9.3—Upper Carthew Lake.

9.8—Lower Carthew Lake.

—Trail descends steeply into forest.

13.1—Alderson Lake and Campground (1875 m).

—Steady descent along slopes of Bertha Peak.

20.1—Waterton townsite (1290 m).
Cameron Falls.
N49°03.063' W113°54.983'

The 20-km Carthew—Alderson trail between Cameron Lake and Waterton townsite is the most popular one-way hike in the Canadian Rockies. It is a classic Waterton trail that takes you through subalpine forest and meadows, along the shores of four high lakes, and across vast scree slopes of red and green argillite. And at Carthew Summit you stand atop one of the highest trail-accessible viewpoints in the Waterton-Glacier International Peace Park.

Since Cameron Lake is 365 m higher than Waterton townsite, most everyone hikes the trail from west to east. If you have two vehicles at your disposal, you can set-up transportation between trailheads. However, many hikers either bum a ride to Cameron or, better yet, book space on the commercial shuttle to the lake (see *Sources—Backcountry access* for contact information). Or, if you don't want to play the transportation game, you can still experience the best the trail has to offer by hiking round-trip to Carthew Summit from Cameron Lake.

From Cameron Lake, the trail switchbacks up through a lush forest, climbing 275 m in just over 3 km. There are brief glimpses down to Cameron Lake and out to the surrounding mountains, primarily Forum Peak (2415 m) to the west and Mount Custer (2708 m) to the south.

Near the 3-km mark the trail levels off and runs southeast through open forest to tiny Summit Lake. The meadows surrounding the lake are filled with wildflowers throughout mid-summer, including stands of tall, showy beargrass, and often visited by curious mule deer. It is an excellent spot to take a break before tackling the climb ahead.

The downhill trail to Glacier Park's Boundary Creek branches right at Summit Lake, but you stay left and begin the ascent to Carthew Summit—375 m

The peaks of Glacier National Park from Carthew Summit

over the next 3.6 km via a series of steep switchbacks. Views improve rapidly to the south as the trail climbs above treeline and crosses slopes stained red by the broken argillites of the Kintla Formation. (Make sure to pack water—this is a hot, dry climb on a sunny day.)

Though views from Carthew Summit's barren ridge are exceptional, they are even better from the lower summit of Mount Carthew—a 15-minute scramble to the north. A sea of peaks rises from Glacier National Park to the south, including nearby Chapman Peak (2867 m), with the Hudson Glacier and Lakes Nooney and Wurdeman on its northern flank. It is all quite wonderful on a clear day, but not a spot to linger when a storm is moving in.

From Carthew Summit the trail descends across steep scree slopes into the basin containing the Carthew Lakes. The lakes are visible ahead throughout the descent, cradled in the rocky barrens between Mounts Carthew and Alderson. You reach Upper Carthew Lake 1.4 km below the summit, and skirt the north shore of Lower Carthew 0.5 km farther along.

Beyond Lower Carthew Lake the trail drops rapidly across two rock formations to Alderson Lake, lying at the foot of the impressive 700-m north face of Mount Alderson. A campground at the lake, the only one on the route, is most frequently used by backpackers who have hiked in from Waterton townsite.

From Alderson Lake the trail scurries down along the Carthew Valley between Buchanan Ridge and Bertha Peak, descending steadily through a forest of pine, spruce and Douglas fir. Just before reaching Waterton, it joins Cameron Creek, passes the town's hydro station, and soon emerges at the edge of town 50 m south of Cameron Falls.

Akamina Parkway to Upper Rowe Lakes—6.4 km (4.0 mi)
Akamina Parkway to Lineham Ridge—8.6 km (5.3 mi)

Day trip

Allow 3 hours to Lineham Ridge

Elevation gain: 950 m (3,115 ft)

Maximum elevation: 2560 m (8,400 ft)

Maps: Sage Creek 82 G/1
Waterton Lakes National Park
(Gem Trek)

Access: Follow the Akamina Parkway from
Waterton townsite to the Rowe Lakes
trailhead parking area, located on the right
side of the road 10 km (6 mi) from the
townsite.

0.0— Trailhead (1610 m).
N49°03.458' W114°00.684'

0.3— Rowe Creek cascades.

— Steady uphill.

2.3— Avalanche slope.

3.9— Junction (1965 m). Lower Rowe Lake
left 0.2 km. Upper Rowe Lakes ahead.

— Rowe Basin Meadow

5.2— Junction (2010m). *Tamarack Trail* and
Lineham Ridge (3.4 km) right.

— Steep grade with switchbacks.

6.4— Upper Rowe Lakes (2165 m).

The Rowe Lakes trail transports you to
three small lakes at the upper limits of
the subalpine and one of the park's best
wildflower meadows. While you can easily spend the day relaxing beside the lakes
and photographing flowers in the Rowe
Basin Meadow, strong hikers will want to
continue onward and upward to the incredible panoramic view from Lineham
Ridge—the highest trail-accessible point
in Waterton Park.

The trail has a very pretty beginning.
The first 0.3 km follows along the north
side of Rowe Creek, where a series of
cascades slides over one of the most
colourful streambeds imaginable—a
long chute of brilliant red argillite.

Beyond the creek you climb across a
semi-open slope scattered with lodgepole pine, but as you continue up the
valley, the pine grades into a mature forest of spruce and alpine fir.

At km 3.9, a 200-m spur trail branches
left to Lower Rowe Lake. Despite the
lake's diminutive size, the steep walls of
the surrounding amphitheatre enhance
its setting, and the subalpine forest along
its shore is a pleasant place to stop and
relax awhile.

From the junction, the trail continues
its climb to the upper lakes, eventually
emerging into the Rowe Basin Meadow
at the head of the valley. This lush meadow is where many end their hike, pulling
out their cameras in preparation for a rewarding day of wildflower photography.

A bridge at the far edge of the meadow
spans a tributary stream to a junction. At
this split the *Tamarack Trail* branches
right and begins its ascent to Lineham
Ridge, while the trail to Upper Rowe
Lakes cuts left and climbs a steep slope
into a stand of alpine larch.

The larger of the two Upper Rowe
Lakes is backed against the cliffs of the
Great Divide and surrounded by stunted
stands of alpine fir and larch. (Look for

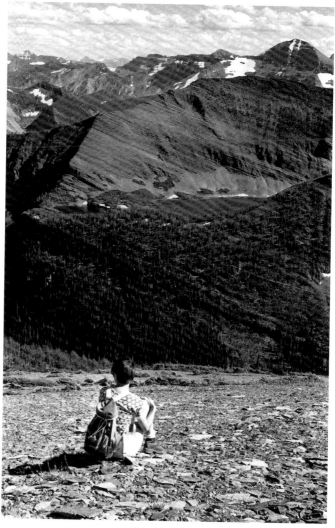

Rowe Lakes Basin from Lineham Ridge

bighorn sheep on the slopes above.) By continuing down to its tiny sister lake, you can peek over the lip of the hanging valley to the waters of Lower Rowe Lake, 150 vertical metres below.

Lineham Ridge. If you get back to the *Tamarack Trail* junction with time and energy to spare, a hike to the top of Lineham Ridge (2560 m) will most certainly be the high point of your day. Follow the *Tamarack Trail* option from the meadow to reach the crest of the ridge in another 3.4 km of steady climbing.

Since the ridge is nearly as high as most of the surrounding mountaintops, the views are magnificent. A sea of mountains stretches out in all directions (we've identified peaks as far away as 50 km), while on the opposite side of the ridge, the beautiful, deep blue Lineham Lakes lie in their verdant basin.

191 Tamarack Trail

Akamina Parkway to Red Rock Canyon—36.4 km (22.6 mi)

Backpack

Allow 2 to 3 days

Maximum elevation: 2560 m (8,400 ft)

Minimum elevation: 1495 m (4,900 ft)

Maps: Sage Creek 82 G/1
Waterton Lakes National Park
(Gem Trek)

Access: Northbound travellers start from the Akamina Parkway on the *Rowe Lakes-Lineham Ridge* trail. Southbound hikers start from the Red Rock Canyon parking area and follow the *Snowshoe Trail.*

- 0.0— Akamina Parkway Trailhead (1610 m). N49°03.458' W114°00.684'
- 3.9— Junction (1965 m). Lower Rowe Lake left. Continue ahead.
- — Rowe Basin Meadow.
- 5.2— Junction (2010m). Upper Rowe Lakes left. Tamarack Trail right.
- 8.6— Lineham Ridge (2560 m).
- 13.8— Blakiston Creek south fork (1890 m).
- 15.7— Festubert Saddle (2225 m).
- 17.7— Lone Lake and Campground (2025 m).
- 21.5— Junction. South Kootenay Pass left 1.7 km. Continue ahead.
- 21.6— (1920 m). Intersection with *Snowshoe-Blakiston Creek Loop.* Red Rock Canyon via Blakiston Creek right 10.1 km. Continue ahead.
- 22.2— Blue Grouse Basin.
- 22.9— Bauerman Divide (2070 m).
- 24.1— Junction. Lower Twin Lake right 0.3 km. Continue ahead.
- 24.7— Upper Twin Lake and Twin Lakes Campground (1950 m).
- 24.8— Junction. Sage Pass left 1.5 km. Continue ahead.
- 27.9— Junction (1720 m). Snowshoe Campground. Lost Lake (1.9 km) and Castle River Divide (3.1 km) left. Follow *Snowshoe Trail* right.
- 31.8— Junction. *Goat Lake* left 2.4 km. Continue ahead.
- 36.4— Red Rock Canyon (1495 m). N49°07.845' W114°01.605'

The Tamarack Trail is the longest backpack in Waterton Park. For nearly 23 of its 36 km, the trail is less than a kilometre from the crest of the Great Divide as it passes over high ridges, through stands of alpine larch and lush meadows, and near several small lakes.

The trail runs from the Akamina Parkway to Red Rock Canyon in the park's northwest corner. While the journey is very rewarding, some of the route's best scenery can be visited on long day trips or shorter backpacks from either end of the trail. (See *Rowe Lakes–Lineham Ridge* and *Snowshoe–Blakiston Creek Loop.*)

There is an elevation advantage to starting the trip from the south end, though you may question the benefit after travelling 17.7 km and climbing nearly 1300 vertical metres on the up-and-down route to the first campground at Lone Lake. The initial 8.6 km of the trip follows the *Rowe Lakes–Lineham Ridge* trail—a steady ascent to 2560-m Lineham Ridge, the highest trail-accessible point in the park.

From Lineham Ridge, the trail makes a long, switchbacking descent to Blakiston Creek's south fork, followed by another tough climb to a 2225-m saddle on Festubert Mountain's east ridge. From this summit, the trail drops rapidly to Lone Lake Campground near the trip's midpoint.

Beyond Lone Lake, the trail levels out through larch forest and subalpine meadows. At km 21.6 it intersects the *Snowshoe-Blakiston Creek Loop* at the Blakiston Valley junction. Continue northwest through Blue Grouse Basin and over Bauerman Divide to Twin Lakes and Upper Twin Lake Campground.

The final 12 km is somewhat anti-climactic as the route descends to the *Snowshoe Trail* and follows its broad track down the Bauerman Valley to Red Rock Canyon.

192 Crandell Lake

Akamina Parkway to Crandell Lake Campground—1.2 km (0.75 mi)
Red Rock Parkway to Crandell Lake Campground—2.0 km (1.2 mi)

Forest-encircled Crandell Lake lies in a narrow saddle between Mount Crandell and Ruby Ridge. While the scenery surrounding the lake is unexceptional, either of two short trails leading to the lake make a pleasant nature walk. It is particularly enjoyable in the fall, when the colours are in full glory.

The lake is a very short walk from the Akamina Parkway to the south, and only a bit longer—and steeper—from the Red Rock Parkway to the north. With hikers, cyclists and anglers sharing the trail, it is little wonder it is well trodden and the lakeshore usually quite busy. From either approach, the trail climbs gently through the forest to cross a low ridge and descend to the lake. There is a small backcountry campsite on the north shore of the lake.

Access: From the south, follow the Akamina Parkway to a parking area on the right side of the road 7 km (4.5 mi) from Waterton townsite. N49°04.608' W113°58.472' From the north, take the Red Rock Parkway for 8 km (5 mi) to the Crandell Lake–Canyon Church Camp Road. Follow the turn-off 0.6 km (.04 mi) to the trail parking lot. N49°06.035' W113°57.915' (A third trailhead, convenient for hikers staying at Crandell Mountain Campground, is located at the campground's southwest corner. *Maps: Waterton Lakes 82 H/4; Waterton Lakes National Park (Gem Trek).*

193 Blakiston Falls

Red Rock Canyon to Blakiston Falls—1.0 km (0.6 mi)

You don't have to hike very far up Blakiston Creek from Red Rock Canyon to discover one the valley's finest features—Blakiston Falls. While quite a few people walk to the falls, the trail is a peaceful contrast to the traffic jams at Red Rock Canyon.

In following the trail, you are walking in the footsteps of one of Waterton's earliest European visitors, Lieutenant Thomas Blakiston. Blakiston was a member of John Palliser's British North American Exploring Expedition when he descended the valley from South Kootenay Pass in September, 1858. He subsequently provided the first detailed description of the region, and named the Waterton Lakes for the noted British naturalist Charles Waterton.

After a short climb through a forest dominated by lodgepole pine, you emerge above a gorge and look down on Blakiston Falls. Viewing platforms that extend out over the canyon provide views from below and immediately above the waterfall.

Access: From its junction with Park Entrance Road 2 km (1.2 km) north of Waterton townsite, follow the Red Rock Parkway 15 km (9 mi) to its terminus at Red Rock Canyon parking area. Cross the footbridge over the canyon, turn left and follow the Red Rock Canyon trail downhill to the Bauerman Creek footbridge, where the trail to Blakiston Falls begins. N49°07.767' W114°01.696' *Maps: Sage Creek 82 G/1; Waterton Lakes National Park (Gem Trek).*

194 Goat Lake

Red Rock Canyon to Goat Lake—7.0 km (4.3 mi)

Day trip or backpack

Allow 2 to 3 hours one way

Elevation gain: 530 m (1,750 ft)

Maximum elevation: 2025 m (6,650 ft)

Maps: Sage Creek 82 G/1
Waterton Lakes National Park
(Gem Trek)

Access: From its junction with the Park Entrance Road 2 km (1.2 mi) north of Waterton townsite, follow Red Rock Parkway 15 km (9 mi) to its terminus at Red Rock Canyon. The trail begins at the canyon footbridge at the west edge of the parking area.

0.0— Trailhead (1495 m).
N49°07.845' W114°01.605'
—Gentle grades on roadbed.

2.4— Side stream crossing.

3.4— Side stream crossing.

4.0— Enter mature forest and begin gradual climb.

4.6— Junction (1570 m). Goat Lake right.
—Steady moderate to steep climb.

5.0— Trail emerges on open slopes.

5.7— First switchbacks.
—Steep climb along open slopes.

6.5— Trail enters Goat Lake cirque. Grades moderate.

6.7— Waterfall.
—Trail follows Goat Lake outlet stream.

7.0— Goat Lake (2025 m).
—Trail continues around north shore.

7.2— Goat Lake Campground.

Goat Lake is a shallow, emerald-hued lake surrounded by subalpine forest, lush wildflower meadows, and high ridges of crimson argillite. The small cirque containing the lake, perched high above the Bauerman Valley, is a textbook example of a hanging valley and, as the name suggests, one of the best places in the park to see mountain goats.

The lake is a good objective for day hikers, even though the last 2.4 km climbs 455 m. Alternately, you can backpack to the pleasant campground in the open forest along its northern shore. Either way, the ascent up the south-facing slope from the Bauerman Valley will wilt even the most enthusiastic on a warm day. (Be sure to pack extra water for day.)

Starting from Red Rock Canyon, the first 4.6 km of the hike traverses the *Snowshoe Trail* along the north side of Bauerman Creek (see *Snowshoe– Blakiston Creek Loop*). It takes a bit over an hour to hike, but since the *Snowshoe Trail* is open to mountain bikes, you can save 30 minutes in, and even more on the way out, by cycling the stretch to the Goat Lake junction. The trail itself is a restored fire road that rolls gently through a pleasant open forest of aspen, cottonwood and pine. Creekside meadows along the way provide fine views of the 700-m north face of Anderson Peak and its distinctive dark band of diabase rock.

From the Goat Lake junction, the climb is steep and dry. Rising from the forest of pine and spruce along Bauerman Creek, the trail gains elevation rapidly and emerges onto open slopes above the valley in less than 0.5 km. Views extend back across the valley to Anderson Peak and west to the Great Divide near Twin Lakes.

As the trail nears the entrance to the Goat Lake cirque, the steep grade moderates. Limestone outcrops along the trail contain fossilized remains

Goat Lake and Avion Ridge

of stromatolites, visible as a series of swirls in the rock. These cyanobacterial colonies were one of the earth's earliest life forms, part of a reef that thrived in Precambrian seas over one billion years ago!

Goat Lake is a quiet body of water reflecting forest and the Avion Ridge headwall. The trail continues around the north shore to a pretty little campground sheltered by scattered stands of alpine fir.

Beyond the campground there is an extensive meadow where yellow glacier lilies bloom along the edges of receding snowbanks in early summer. Later in the season the meadows fill with a wide variety of subalpine flowers, dominated by tall, white-topped beargrass.

The steep scree slope descending to the water's edge on the west shore is etched by the trails of mountain goats, which are commonly seen on the cliffs above. The long crest of Avion Ridge is capped by the brilliant red argillite common throughout Waterton Park. Named for a town in France where Canadians fought in 1917, Avion forms part of the northwestern boundary of the park.

Avion Ridge. This high ridge is a popular objective for strong hikers and rock scramblers since it provides exceptional views out over much of Waterton Park. Though Avion Ridge is often hiked as a circuit that connects the ridge, Castle River Divide and Goat Lake, it can be day-hiked by anyone camping at Goat Lake.

The route to the ridge climbs about 2 km up steep scree slopes beneath Newman Peak (watch for scramblers' trails worn into the loose rock), then traverses to the col west of Newman Peak. Once you've reached the ridge you can wander south and west along its crest for another 3 km. (See *Snowshoe-Blakiston Creek Loop: Castle River Divide–Avion Ridge*.)

195 Snowshoe–Blakiston Creek Loop

Red Rock Canyon to Twin Lakes Campground—11.7 km (7.3 mi)
Snowshoe-Blakiston Creek Loop—24.9 km (15.5 mi)

Day trip or backpack

Allow 3 to 4 hours to Twin Lakes

Elevation gain: 575 m (1,900 ft)

Maximum elevation: 2070 m (6,800 ft)

Maps: Sage Creek 82 G/1
      Waterton Lakes National Park
      (Gem Trek)

Access: From its junction with the Park
Entrance Road 2 km (1.2 mi) north of
Waterton townsite, follow the Red Rock
Parkway 15 km (9 mi) to its terminus at Red
Rock Canyon. The trail begins at the canyon
footbridge at the west edge of the parking
area.

0.0— Trailhead (1495 m).
      N49°07.845' W114°01.605'
   —Gentle grades on roadbed.

2.4— Side stream crossing.

3.4— Side stream crossing.

4.0— Gradual climb into mature forest.

4.6— Junction. *Goat Lake* right 2.4 km.
      Continue ahead.

8.5— Junction (1720 m). Snowshoe
      Campground. *Lost Lake* (1.9 km) and
      Castle River Divide (3.1 km) right.
      Continue ahead to Twin Lakes.

   —Steady climb with sections of
     switchbacks.

11.6— Junction. *Sage Pass* right 1.5 km.
      Continue ahead.

11.7— Upper Twin Lake and Twin Lakes
      Campground (1950 m).

12.3— Junction. Lower Twin Lake left 0.3 km.
      Continue ahead.

13.5— Bauerman Divide (2070 m).

14.2— Blue Grouse Basin.

14.8— Junction (1920 m). *Tamarack Trail*
      ahead. Turn left and descend
      Blakiston Creek.

   —Moderate to steep downhill.

18.4— Blakiston Creek-Lone Creek
      confluence.

   —Gradual descent through forest and
     avalanche paths.

23.9— Blakiston Falls.

24.9— Red Rock Canyon (1495 m).

The Snowshoe Trail and Blakiston Creek
trail both begin at Red Rock Canyon.
While neither of these valley-bottom
routes is terribly exciting, they provide
access to some fine subalpine meadows
and lakes beneath the Great Divide in
the park's northwestern corner. Since
the two trails are linked together at their
far end by a trail paralleling the divide,
you can hike out on one and back on the
other to complete a 25-km loop.

The Snowshoe Trail is an old fire road
that is open to cyclists, so it is quite
popular to peddle to road's end at Snowshoe Campground and then hike to
scenic points of interest like Twin Lakes
or Lost Lake. We have also hiked the
entire circuit in a long day, though this
only allowed time for one short side-trip.
Since there are several rewarding side-
trips along the route, it is worthwhile
backpacking into the Snowshoe or Twin
Lakes Campground and spending a day
or two exploring.

We prefer to hike the circuit counter-
clockwise by starting on the Snowshoe
Trail. This broad track runs through
open montane forest near Bauerman
Creek with little gain or loss of elevation
for the first 4 km. As you roll through
grassy meadows and scattered stands
of poplar and pine, there are continuous views south to the massive cliffs of
Anderson Peak.

Two unbridged tributaries flow across
the trail at km 2.4 and 3.4. While these
streams are easy rock-hops in late summer, you may experience some difficulties early in the season or during periods
of heavy rainfall.

At the 4-km mark, the old road begins climbing gradually into coniferous
forest, which limits your views for the
remainder of the journey to road's end
at Snowshoe Campground.

The trail to *Lost Lake* and *Castle River
Divide* branches northwest from the end

Blue Grouse Basin

of the Snowshoe Trail, but if you are hiking the circuit you will want to cross the nearby bridge and follow the trail southwest toward Twin Lakes. The trail climbs steadily through heavy forest and across avalanche slopes at the foot of Mount Bauerman to reach Upper Twin Lake in just over 3 km.

Upper Twin Lake is a pretty tarn backed against the Great Divide immediately beneath Sage Pass. Along with the smaller Lower Twin Lake, it serves as the headwaters for Bauerman Creek. Meadows near the lakes are filled with wildflowers in midsummer, including tall, spiky stands of beargrass—a member of the lily family that is unique to this section of the Canadian Rockies.

Continuing south from Twin Lakes, the trail makes a short climb along steep scree and rock ledges to a beautiful stand of alpine larch on the crest of the ridge connecting Mount Bauerman to the Great Divide. On the ascent you have a fine view back down the Bauerman Valley to the mountains above Red Rock Canyon.

Beyond the summit, you descend into Blue Grouse Basin (aka Peck's Basin)

and skirt a small pond surrounded by moist meadows and more beargrass.

At km 14.8, you arrive at the Blakiston Creek trail junction. The *Tamarack Trail* runs south from this split, but circuit hikers will turn east and return down the Blakiston Valley to the Red Rock Canyon trailhead.

Other than avalanche paths, which provide views to two of the park's highest peaks, Mount Blakiston (2940 m) to the south and Anderson Peak (2683 m) to the north, the descent of the Blakiston Valley is mostly forest-enclosed and scenically uneventful. When you reach the canyon containing the valley's best feature, Blakiston Falls, you'll know you only have 1.0 km remaining to reach the Red Rock Canyon parking area.

Side-trips from the circuit to *South Kootenay Pass, Sage Pass, Lost Lake* and *Castle River Divide–Avion Ridge* are described on the following page.

Snowshoe—Blakiston Creek Hikes

The Snowshoe-Blakiston Creek Loop provides access to a number of excellent high-country, side-trip destinations. With the exception of Avion Ridge, all are short half-day hikes from either the Snowshoe or Twin Lakes Campground. Distances are listed from junctions on the circuit (*indicates distance approximate).

Castle River Divide–Avion Ridge—8 km*. Although the trail to Castle River Divide has little to recommend it, it redeems itself by serving as an approach to Avion Ridge, which is one the finest ridge hikes in the Rockies. Once you've scrambled to its 2420-m crest, you'll discover views stretching southeast over much of Waterton Park and the Castle River headwaters to the north. Reserve this lofty traverse for blue-sky days; the ridge would be a grim and dangerous place to get caught in a storm.

Follow the Castle River Divide trail northwest from the junction at the end of the Snowshoe Trail. The forested climb is gradual to moderate, but becomes steeper as you near the pass. At km 3.1 you crest the forest-enclosed pass on the park boundary. Here you turn east and climb toward Avion Ridge. There is no defined trail from the divide to Avion Ridge, so take a 1:50,000 topo map as a guide.

Don't expect to find more than snippets of path as you climb through scattered larch and meadows. Use your maps and stay on the high ground that leads upward along the line of the park boundary. Eventually, this becomes a more defined ridge, which you continue along to steep red argillite scree slopes and the crest of Avion Ridge.

At the top of the ridge, follow its crest east and then north, staying near the 2400-m level for nearly 3 km. Eventually you arrive on a col southwest of Newman Peak overlooking Goat Lake.

At this point it is probably easiest to return the way you came. However, some hikers traverse the steep scree on the south slopes of Newman Peak and pick their way down to *Goat Lake*. (Watch for hiker's tracks in the scree and avoid rock bluffs.) At Goat Lake, you can return to the Snowshoe Trail in the Bauerman Valley via the Goat Lake trail.

Lost Lake—1.9 km. As the smallest lake in the park's northwest corner, Lost Lake lies quietly beneath the Great Divide just a stone's throw from the end of the Snowshoe Trail. Backpackers can visit it as an easy, after-dinner walk from Snowshoe Campground.

Starting from the junction at the end of the Snowshoe Trail, follow the Castle River Divide trail northwest. The trail to Lost Lake branches left from the Castle River trail at km 0.8 and follows near the lake's outlet stream to its source.

Sage Pass—1.5 km. From a junction near the shore of Upper Twin Lake, a short steep trail climbs to the 2160-m summit of Sage Pass atop the Great Divide. The sparsely-treed summit provides grand views of Twin Lakes and the Bauerman Creek valley to the east, and not-so-grand views of logging roads on the headwaters of British Columbia's Sage Creek to the west.

South Kootenay Pass—1.7 km. South Kootenay Pass was used by the Kootenay as a route to the plains of southwestern Alberta, and their trail was followed by the Palliser Expedition's Thomas Blakiston when he discovered Waterton Lakes in 1858. Views from the 2260-m pass are limited to the Blakiston Valley, which runs away to the east, and the logging-scarred upper Kishinena Valley to the west.

The trail to the pass begins 100 m south of the Blakiston Creek junction (km 14.8). It switchbacks up the lower slopes of Kishinena Peak, then traverses south onto the lightly forested summit.

Akamina-Kishinena Provincial Park

At 109 sq km, Akamina-Kishinena Provincial Park is one of the smallest parks in the Canadian Rockies. It is snuggled into the southeast corner of British Columbia, sharing a common boundary with Waterton Park along the Great Divide. The international boundary and Montana's Glacier National Park borders it to the south, while B.C. forest lands, with active logging operations, contain the park to the west and north.

Throughout most of its past, the park area was remote wilderness. Before the arrival of Europeans, the Kootenay travelled up Kishinena Creek and over the Great Divide to hunt buffalo on the plains of southwest Alberta. Thomas Blakiston, magnetic observer with the Palliser Expedition, traversed the Kishinena Valley en route to South Kootenay Pass and Waterton Lakes in 1858. In 1860 and 1861 members of the American and British Boundary Commissions camped near Akamina Pass while completing the survey of the international boundary from the Pacific coast to the crest of the Great Divide.

Soon after oil was discovered on Cameron Creek in 1901, a tote road was constructed over Akamina Pass to allow for further drilling on Akamina Creek. Following the completion of the "Akamina Highway" to Waterton Park's Cameron Lake in 1927, Waterton boosters lobbied to have the old tote road improved and extended down the Akamina and Kishinena Valleys to connect to the Flathead North Fork road along the west side of Glacier National Park. However, nothing came of the proposal, and the Akamina-Kishinena remained the domain of a handful of trappers, commercial outfitters, and grizzly bears.

As logging operations began moving up the Kishinena Valley in the 1970s and 80s, the B.C. government moved to protect this special wilderness. In 1986 it was designated a Provincial Recreation Area, and it received full protection as a Class A Provincial Park in 1995.

While there are a number of primitive trails in the park's more remote valleys, the only maintained trails run to Forum and Wall Lakes in the park's southwest corner. Both are reached by hiking into the park on the old roadbed over Akamina Pass and are popular day hikes from the Akamina Parkway in Waterton Lakes Park. Akamina Ridge, which rises above the southern shoreline of both lakes, can be reached from either trail and has emerged as one of the most popular off-trail ridge walks in the mountain parks.

Information and services. An information kiosk at Akamina Pass greets hikers who ascend the 1.5 km trail from Waterton Park. The board displays a map of the park and park rules and regulations. The park's main campground, Akamina Creek, is located 0.9 km from Akamina Pass on the Wall Lake trail. At the time of publication, camping fees were $5 per person per night for all persons six years of age or older.

Access: From Waterton townsite, follow the Akamina Parkway 15 km (9.5 miles) to the Akamina Pass trailhead parking area, on the east side of the road 1.0 km from its termination at Cameron Lake. The trail to Akamina Pass is on the west side of the road. N49°01.830' W114°02.568'.

Akamina Parkway to Wall Lake—5.2 km (3.2 mi)

Day trip

Allow 1.5 hours one way

Elevation gain: 110 m (350 ft)

Maximum elevation: 1780 m (5,850 ft)

Maps: Sage Creek 82 G/1
Waterton Lakes National Park
(Gem Trek)

Access: Follow the Akamina Parkway 15 km (9.5 mi) from Waterton townsite to the Akamina Pass trailhead parking area, located on the east side of the road 1.0 km north of Cameron Lake. The trail begins on the opposite side of the road.

0.0— Trailhead (1670 m).
N49°01.830' W114°02.568'

— Steady uphill on old roadbed.

0.9— Grades level off.

1.5— Akamina Pass (1780 m).
Park information kiosk.
Alberta-B.C. boundary markers.

— Gradual to moderate descent.

2.2— Junction (1770 m). Forum Falls (0.3 km) and Forum Lake (2.2 km) left. Wall Lake ahead.

2.4— Akamina Creek Campground.

2.5— Junction. Wall Lake left across Akamina Creek bridges.

— Single-track trail contours through forest.

3.2— Junction. Horse trail branches right. Hiker trail stays left.

4.8— Major avalanche path.

5.2— Wall Lake (1770 m). Outlet bridge.

— Trail follows lakeshore west.

5.6— Junction. Bennett Pass right 2.5 km.

5.8— Wall Lake west shore.

Wall Lake was a favourite destination for horseback tours led by Waterton's pioneer outfitter Bert Riggall during the 1920s. Today it is the most popular hike in Akamina-Kishinena Park.

The pretty, emerald lake is quite scenically situated beneath the north face of Akamina Ridge. Large snowfields extend out into its waters from the base of this wall into midsummer, adding a brilliant contrast to the shadowed cliffs and deep green of lake and forest.

The hike begins on the moderately-graded tote road that leads from Waterton's Akamina Parkway to the Alberta-B.C. boundary on Akamina Pass. After passing the park's information kiosk on the pass, the roadbed descends through spruce-pine forest to Forum Lake junction and Akamina Creek Campground.

Just 50 m beyond the campground, the Wall Lake trail branches left from the roadbed and crosses log bridges over Akamina Creek. Single-track trail follows around the end of a heavily-forested ridge, staying close to the 1750 m level as it contours into the Wall Lake cirque.

At km 4.7 you enter a stand of old Engelmann spruce trees, some snapped by avalanches descending from Akamina Ridge. Just beyond, the trail crosses a verdant slide path filled with fireweed, sticky geranium and ragwort.

The trail crosses Wall Creek to the northeast end of Wall Lake at km 5.2. While the best overview of the lake is from this point, you will want to follow around the north end of the lake to the site of the old campground at a small lagoon on the west shore.

The forest along the west side of the lake is quite lush, filled with red elderberry, gooseberry, heart-leaved arnica, red monkey flower and black twinberry, and it is often visited by mule deer. It is a pleasant spot to relax, eat your lunch,

Wall Lake and Akamina Ridge

and scan the bluffs of Akamina Ridge for mountain goats.

Trail continues beyond the old campsite for another 300 m to open flats at the south end of the lake, near the headwall snowfield. Be wary of venturing onto this steep snowpatch, particularly early in the season when it extends into the lake. Kay Riggall, the young daughter of outfitter Bert Riggall, got stranded on its icy surface during a trip to the lake in the 1920s and barely escaped a slide into the lake's frigid waters.

Bennett Pass—Akamina Ridge. The 3-km trail to Bennett Pass runs due west from Wall Lake to a 2250-m summit at the northwest end of Akamina Ridge. The climb to the pass includes flower-filled meadows, larch forest and a high, windswept viewpoint for the wild Kintla Creek region of Montana's Glacier National Park.

From where the marked trail branches up into the forest at the northwest corner of Wall Lake, you climb steadily to open stands of alpine larch and avalanche paths. Grades are steady and steep over the final kilometre to the summit ridge, which lies just above the actual pass.

Most who hike to the pass continue the journey by following the crest of Akamina Ridge back to the east. While there is no defined trail, you can easily follow the ridgeline all the way to Forum Peak on the Great Divide—5 km from Bennett Pass. If you stay on the crest of the ridge, you reach an elevation of 2565 m, and along the way you'll overlook Wall and Forum Lakes on the Canadian side of the border and Upper Kintla Lake in Glacier National Park. And if you go as far as Forum Peak, you look straight down a dizzying 2500 vertical metres to Waterton's Cameron Lake.

This is definitely one of the most spectacular ridge walks in this section of the Rockies. However, the hike is a long, strenuous day from the Akamina Parkway trailhead or Akamina Creek Campground. It is strictly for strong hikers and should only be attempted when the weather is good. (See also *Forum Lake*.)

197 Forum Lake

Akamina Parkway to Forum Lake—4.4 km (2.7 mi)

Day trip
Allow 1.5 hours one way
Elevation gain: 350 m (1,150 ft)
Maximum elevation: 2020 m (6,650 ft)
Maps: Sage Creek 82 G/1
      Waterton Lakes National Park
      (Gem Trek)

Access: Follow the Akamina Parkway
15 km (9.5 mi) from Waterton townsite to
the Akamina Pass trailhead parking area,
located on the east side of the road 1.0 km
north of Cameron Lake. The trail begins on
the opposite side of the road.

0.0—Trailhead (1670 m).
     N49°01.830' W114°02.568'

   —Steady uphill on old roadbed.

0.9—Grades level off.

1.5—Akamina Pass (1780 m).
     Park information kiosk.
     Alberta-B.C. boundary markers.

   —Gradual to moderate descent.

2.2—Junction (1780 m). Akamina Creek
     Campground (200 m) and Wall Lake
     (3.0 km) ahead. Forum Lake left.

2.4—Park patrol cabin.

2.5—Junction. Forum Falls right 50 m.

   —Steady climb through forest.

3.6—Forum Creek bridge to west side.

3.8—Grades level off into Forum cirque.

4.4—Forum Lake (2020 m).

Forum Lake lies in a high cirque beneath Akamina Ridge and Forum Peak in the southeast corner of Akamina-Kishinena Park. Unlike the lushly-forested shores of nearby Wall Lake, this small sink lake is cradled in a rocky basin with only a scattering of stunted fir and larch trees nearby. While the distance to Forum is nearly a kilometre shorter than to Wall, you have to climb 250 m over the final 2 km, so the approach takes nearly as long.

The first 2.2 km of the hike runs over the same route as the Wall Lake trail, following an old roadbed to Akamina Pass from the Akamina Parkway in Waterton Park. The Forum Lake trail branches left from the broad track 0.7 km west of the pass and, after passing the park patrol cabin, arrives at Forum Falls junction—a one minute side-trip to a forest-enclosed waterfall on Forum Creek.

The climb to the lake begins just beyond the falls—steep and steady through alpine fir. Grades moderate after 0.3 km and the trees thin as you pass through a series of small meadows. The trail crosses Forum Creek at km 3.6, where you obtain your first views ahead to Forum Peak and Akamina Ridge. The final stretch climbs gradually through beargrass meadows and across lush avalanche paths filled with false hellebore, ragwort and meadow rue.

Though the lake's headwall is formed by grey limestone cliffs, its rocky shoreline is coloured with shards of red and green argillite, some of which preserve the ripple marks of Precambrian shorelines. Today the ancient rocks provide sanctuary for pikas.

Akamina Ridge Circuit—18.5 km. While you can easily reach the summit of Akamina Ridge via trail from Wall Lake to Bennett Pass, adventurous hikers can make a complete circuit that includes Forum Lake, Akamina Ridge and Wall Lake. If you are hiking the circuit, it

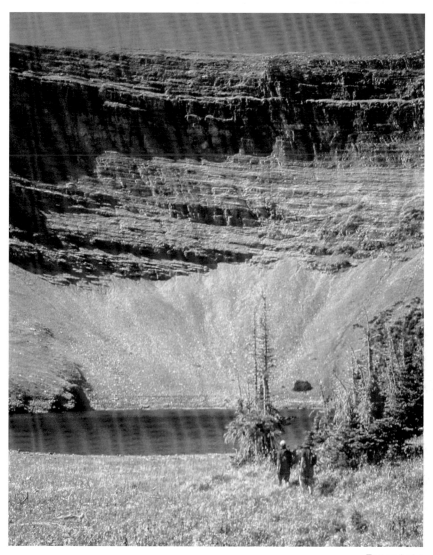

Forum Lake

is better done clockwise, allowing you to climb rather than descend the cliff band above Forum Lake.

When you near the north shore of Forum Lake, watch for a branch track leading due west toward the ridge separating Forum and Wall Lakes. When the track fizzles out, look for breaks in the cliff band above. (Be careful not to kick rocks down on one another as you

scramble through the band.) Once you reach the crest of this ridge, follow it south to Akamina Ridge. From there it is relatively easy hiking west along the ridge to Bennett Pass. (See *Wall Lake.*)

Remember, the section from Forum Lake to the summit of Akamina Ridge is not a trail but rather a scrambler's route that requires experience climbing steep, loose rock.

Peter Lougheed Provincial Park

Lying on the eastern slopes of the Great Divide in Alberta, Peter Lougheed Provincial Park is part of the 4,200 sq km Kananaskis Country multi-use recreation area, created in 1977 to "alleviate congestion in National Parks, and to provide greater recreation opportunities for Albertans." The park is 509 sq km in area and shares boundaries with Banff National Park to the northwest, British Columbia's Height of the Rockies and Elk Lakes Provincial Parks to the west and south, and Alberta's Elbow-Sheep Wildland Provincial Park to the east.

Three major roads provide access to the hiking trails profiled in this guide. Noting that the major roads in the park are also referred to as "Trails," they are: the Kananaskis Trail (Hwy 40), which traverses the park from north to south; the Kananaskis Lakes Trail, which branches from Kananaskis Trail in the heart of the park and provides access to Upper and Lower Kananaskis Lakes; and the Smith-Dorrien/Spray Trail (Hwy 742), which provides access to the Smith-Dorrien Pass region in the park's northwest corner.

There are more than 100 km of official hiking trails in the park, ranging from short interpretive walks to multi-day backpacks. All trails were redeveloped when the park was established in 1977 and they are among the best designed in the mountain parks. Major flooding in 2013 affected many park trails, so check www.canadianrockiestrailguide.com or park visitor centres for the latest information.

Most of the hikes are concentrated near Lower and Upper Kananaskis Lakes, including the park's two premier backpacking routes to North and South Kananaskis Passes. Smith-Dorrien Pass is the starting point for popular hikes to Chester Lake and Burstall Pass. Highwood Pass (2206 m) is the starting point for the Ptarmigan Cirque hike—one of the park's finest short trips.

Backpackers must obtain a permit to stay in any of the park's backcountry campgrounds. Permits cost $12.00 per person, per night, plus a non-refundable reservation charge of $12.00 per party per trip. Reservations can be made online through www.albertaparks.ca, by phone, or through any Kananaskis Country visitor centre or by phone (see *Sources—Parks information*).

Information and services. Peter Lougheed Provincial Park Visitor Information Centre is on Kananaskis Lakes Trail, 3.5 km south of its junction with Kananaskis Trail (Hwy 40). Barrier Lake Visitor Information Centre lies north of the park on the Kananaskis Trail (Hwy 40), 6.5 km south of the Trans-Canada Highway. Both centres are open year round to provide full information services, dispense brochures, maps, books, and issue backcountry permits.

All of the park's roadside campgrounds are near the Kananaskis Lakes and are accessed via Kananaskis Lakes Trail. (Elkwood and Boulton are the largest and both have showers.) Other vehicle-accessible campgrounds are along the Kananaskis Trail (Hwy 40) just north of the park.

Boulton Creek Trading Post, at km 9.7 on Kananaskis Lakes Trail, is a general store and restaurant and the only commercial outlet within the park. A general store and gas station is located at Fortress Mountain junction 2.6 km north of the park boundary on Kananaskis Trail (Hwy 40). The nearest commercial accommodation is at Kananaskis Village, 21 km north of the park boundary on Highway 40. The closest full service town is Canmore.

Access: Primary access to Peter Lougheed Provincial Park is via Kananaskis Trail (Hwy 40), which intersects the Trans-Canada Highway 80 km west of Calgary and 30 km east of Canmore. The park can be reached more directly from Canmore via the Smith-Dorrien/Spray Trail (Hwy 742)—a well-maintained, all-season gravel road.

Land above 2300 metres

0 1 2 3 4 km

198 Upper Kananaskis Lake

Upper Kananaskis Lake Circuit—16.2 km (10.2 mi)

Day hike

Allow 4 to 5 hours

Elevation gain: 60 m (197 ft)

Maximum elevation: 1785 m (5,856 ft)

Maps: Kananaskis Lakes 82 J/11†
Kananaskis Lakes (Gem Trek)
† trail not shown

Access: From the Trans-Canada Highway, follow Kananaskis Trail (Hwy 40) for 50 km (31 mi) and turn right on Kananaskis Lakes Trail. Drive another 15 km (9.5 mi) to the North Interlakes Day Use Area. The trailhead kiosk is at the north end of the parking lot.

- 0.0 – Trailhead (1725 m).
  N50°37.926' W115°08.422'
  - Trail crosses Kananaskis Lakes intake dam and spillway.
  - Trail follows old roadbed.
- 0.5 – Junction. Trail splits. Stay right.
- 0.9 – Junction. *South Kananaskis Pass* and *North Kananaskis Pass* ahead. Upper Kananaskis Lake circuit left.
  - Trail descends to lake and follows shoreline.
- 2.2 – Palliser rockslide.
- 2.4 – Junction. Stay left.
- 3.7 – Point Campground.
- 4.4 – Lower Kananaskis Falls.
- 4.5 – Kananaskis River bridge.
  - Trail ascends above shoreline to hike's high point (1785 m).
- 6.7 – Trail rejoins lakeshore.
- 10.6 – Junction. *Rawson Lake* right.
- 10.7 – Sarrail Creek Falls.
- 11.8 – Junction. Stay left.
  - Trail runs between lake and parking area to boat launch and dam. Proceed across dam.
- 12.7 – North end of dam.
- 14.7 – Junction. Old roadbed to right. Stay left.
- 16.2 – Trailhead (1725 m).
  North Interlakes Day Use Area.

Despite its length, the Upper Kananaskis Lake circuit is an easy trip that offers an ever-changing panorama of the lake and the mountains that ring it. Because it provides access to several other trails, sections of the route can be very busy. The ideal time to hike it is mid-week in mid-September: take a lunch, map, field guides, a reflective turn of mind, and plan to spend a leisurely day with curiosity as your guide.

Moving counterclockwise from the North Interlakes trailhead kiosk, the first leg of the trail traces the north shore of the lake, with views of the glacier-carved mountains to the west and south: Mt. Putnik (2940 m); Mt. Lyautey (3082 m); Mt. Sarrail (3174 m); Mt. Foch (3180 m) and Mt. Fox (2973 m). Just shy of the 1-km mark, the trail veers left, descends to the lake, then climbs over a massive rockslide that in some earlier era spilled down from Mt. Indefatigable and pushed well out into the lake. The resultant spit is now the site of the Point Campground.

Past the campground, the trail skirts a small bay and crosses the Lower Kananaskis Falls via a sturdy wooden bridge. Beyond the bridge it angles southeast and climbs to its high point 60 metres above the lake. Views are limited, but the forest is green and lush, providing great opportunities to sink down in a carpet of feather moss and contemplate the flora at hand.

Trail traffic picks up near the *Rawson Lake* junction, and increases to include cars, dogs and Frisbees as you pass through the Upper Lakes Day Use Area. Pick your way between the parking lots and picnic tables, and head across Upper Kananaskis Lake's main dam, taking advantage of the fine views ahead to Mt. Indefatigable and the Opal Range. Beyond the dam, the Upper Kananaskis Lake circuit wends its way through pleasant open forest back to the starting point.

199 Rawson Lake

Upper Lake Parking Area to Rawson Lake—3.5 km (2.2 mi)

Half-day trip

Allow 1.5 hours one way

Elevation gain: 300 m (1,000 ft)

Maximum elevation: 2025 m (6,650 ft)

Maps: Kananaskis Lakes 82 J/11†
Kananaskis Lakes (Gem Trek)
† trail not shown

Access: From the Trans-Canada Highway, follow the Kananaskis Trail 50 km (31 mi) and turn right on Kananaskis Lakes Trail. Follow the Kananaskis Lakes Trail 12.5 km (7.8 mi) to the Upper Lake Day Use Area. The trail begins at the southwest corner of the parking lot as part of the *Upper Kananaskis Lake* circuit.

0.0— Trailhead (1725 m).
N50°36.585' W115°07.134'

— Trail contours just above Upper Kananaskis Lake.

1.1— Sarrail Creek Falls.

1.2— Junction. *Upper Kananaskis Lake* circuit ahead. Rawson Lake left.

— Trail begins moderate-to-steep climb through forest.

2.7— Trail levels off into cirque.

3.2— First of several sections of log corduroy.

3.3— Trail split (stay left).

3.5— Rawson Lake (2025 m).

3.6— Outhouse.

— Minor trail fork (stay left). Trail runs below cliff bands.

3.9— Park interpretive sign. End of official trail.

The trail to Rawson Lake offers a relaxed half-day trek to a small lake set in a spectacular glacier-carved cirque. Because of the lake's easy access and spectacular setting, the trail can be a busy one in mid-summer, but the lake's perimeter is big enough to offer all visitors a quiet spot of their own. For hikers seeking more of a challenge, some stout vertical scrambling beyond the end of the trail provides both solitude and an inspiring high mountain vista.

The trail begins on the *Upper Kananaskis Lake* circuit, following a wide, pleasant path through a mature subalpine forest of Engelmann spruce and subalpine fir. Small creeks tumble down from the left, and the Upper Kananaskis Lake is a constant companion on the right.

At Sarrail Creek, 1.1 km from the trailhead, the mists rising from a boisterous 10-metre cataract will delight small children and cool overheated parents on hot summer afternoons. The falls herald the Rawson Lake turn-off just 100 m beyond.

The middle section of the trail consists of 1.5 km of switchbacks up through the forest to the Rawson Lake cirque. Hikers who find they are breathing harder than they would like should consider that the trail is a vast improvement over the old access, which involved a vegetation-gripping ascent directly up the outlet stream. Such was certainly the experience of Dr. Donald Rawson, a limnologist who did pioneering fisheries research in the Kananaskis in the late 1930s, and for whom the lake is named.

The end of the steepest part of the climb is signaled by sections of split log that span a boggy section of forest floor. At this point you have reached the lip of the Rawson Lake cirque, and it is only a couple of hundred more metres to the lake's outlet.

The sudden appearance of the lake, accompanied by signs prohibiting fire

Rawson Lake

and camping, may suggest the hike is over. In fact, the best lies ahead: following the trail along the southeast shore for a few hundred metres, you'll encounter small meadows and some cliff bands. It is there you'll begin to feel physically the presence of the curved, soaring headwall that wraps around the western end of the lake.

An intimidating face of 350-million year-old Carboniferous limestone, the headwall drops from the summit of Mount Sarrail (3174 m) over 1200 m to the lake below. Rawson Lake is typical of many of the cirque lakes in the Rockies, but by virtue of the symmetry and height of the headwall it is a particularly impressive example. Even in late July, remnants of last year's snow hug the bottom of the cliffs, and the lakeshore blooms profusely with alpine buttercup, fringed grass-of-Parnassus, and twinberry.

Just shy of the 4-km mark, a park interpretive sign spells out the end of the official trail, warning that the shoreline and surrounding slopes are fragile, and that grizzly bear sightings are common in the area beyond.

If you can ascertain there have not been recent grizzly sightings in the area, you can proceed around the end of the lake on a rough-hewn trail and scramble upslope to the obvious saddle to the northwest. It is a solid 350 vertical metres to the saddle, but the view down the other side to the Kananaskis Lakes is a worthy reward.

200 South Kananaskis Pass

North Interlakes Parking Area to Three Isle Lake—11.7 km (7.3 mi)
North Interlakes Parking Area to South Kananaskis Pass—14.2 km (8.8 mi)

Day hike or backpack
Allow 5 hours to Three Isle Lake
Elevation gain: 565 m (1,850 ft)
Maximum elevation: 2290 m (7,515 ft)
Maps: Kananaskis Lakes 82 J/11
      Kananaskis Lakes (Gem Trek)

Access: From the Trans-Canada Highway, follow the Kananaskis Trail (Hwy 40) for 50 km (31 mi) and turn right on the Kananaskis Lakes Trail. Drive another 15 km (9.5 mi) to the North Interlakes Day Use Area. The trailhead kiosk is at the north end of the parking lot.

0.0— Trailhead (1725 m).
     N50°37.926' W115°08.422'
     — Trail crosses Kananaskis Lakes intake dam and spillway.
     — Trail follows old roadbed.
0.9— Junction. *Upper Kananaskis Lake* circuit left. Stay right.
2.1— Trail crosses Palliser rockslide.
4.0— Invincible Creek bridge.
5.8— Kananaskis River bridge.
7.3— Spring.
     — Gravel outwash flats and small streams (bridged).
8.0— Junction (1790 m) and Forks Campground. *North Kananaskis Pass* ahead. Three Isle Lake-South Kananaskis Pass left.
9.4— Trail enters large avalanche chute.
     — Stone steps.
10.1— Tributary stream bridge.
     — Steep scree, 250-m ascent up valley headwall.
11.5— Top of headwall (2190 m).
     — Gentle descent to Three Isle Lake.
11.7— Three Isle Lake Campground.
     — Trail skirts north shore of Three Isle Lake.
12.8— Trail sign for South Kananaskis Pass.
13.3— North end of Three Isle Lake.
     — Trail climbs moderately through forest.
14.2— South Kananaskis Pass (2290 m).

The trail to Three Isle Lake and South Kananaskis Pass is one of the most popular hikes in Peter Lougheed Provincial Park. While some brave souls attempt it as a day trip, most choose to backpack, with Three Isle Lake Campground as the overnight destination. Others pack in only as far as the Forks Campground, and then day hike from there. The latter approach means a longer second day, but with less weight to carry up a high, steep headwall.

The first leg of the trip traces the north shore of *Upper Kananaskis Lake* via a narrow dirt roadbed, bypassing the trail junction to the Upper Kananaskis Lake circuit. Aside from some wonderful views across the lake up to the hanging valley between Mounts Lyautey and Sarrail, the trail's most interesting offering is the Palliser talus field—a tremendous rockslide that several centuries ago roared down from the upper reaches of Mount Indefatigable and out into the lake.

The roadbed—as well as the mountain bike traffic permitted on it—ends at Invincible Creek. Beyond, the trail becomes an exceptionally pleasant, essentially level, single-width path that runs through some spectacular old growth forest carpeted with moss and horsetails and dappled with sunlight. The forest's stand of 400-year-old lodgepole pine is Alberta's oldest.

Just before the 6-km mark, the trail crosses the cascading Kananaskis River and proceeds along its southern bank between Mount Lyautey and the southern end of the Spray Mountains. The trail twists more, and has more rocks and roots than the previous section, but remains comfortable underfoot. Views ahead, however, reveal a looming headwall that promises travel of a very different nature.

A spring of gin-clear water at km 7.3 heralds a reach of avens-laced gravels and several small streams braiding their way to the Kananaskis River. The Forks Campground, at km 8.0, is perched just above the Kananaskis River in dense forest at the foot of Mount Putnik.

The South Kananaskis Pass trail veers left (west) at the campground, and begins climbing along the north bank of Three Isle Creek. Eventually, the forest is left behind for the willow and alder of some high avalanche chutes (a good place to make some noise to alert any bears in the area). The willow-alder bush then gives way to the high, steep scree slopes and rock bands of the headwall. It is at this point backpackers usually second-guess their decision to hike beyond the Forks with a full pack.

Not far above the rock bands, the trail loses some of its incline, traverses to the top of the headwall, and then wanders down to the Three Isle Lake Campground. In mid-summer, with the water levels up, the lake is the picture of gentle wilderness, framed by forest and the heights of Mount Worthington (2838 m).

From Three Isle Lake it is an easy 2.5-km jaunt to South Kananaskis Pass. The trail snakes along the sinuous northeast shore of the lake, affording views to Mount Worthington and time to contemplate the enduring mystery of Three Isle Lake: Why are there only two Isles?

Beyond the end of the lake, the trail climbs gradually through an open sub-alpine forest peppered with old man's beard, heart-leaved arnica, fleabane, paintbrush, and valerian. Scattered larches signal the approach of treeline, but the trail doesn't actually break free of the forest until it reaches the pass itself, marked by a large cairn and a sign announcing your entry into British Columbia. Beyond, open meadows stretch away to the pyramid of Mount Beatty (2999 m). For those with the time and energy, a 2-km walk down-valley to Beatty Lake is a great addition to an already great hike.

201 North Kananaskis Pass

North Interlakes Parking Area to Turbine Canyon Campground—16.2 km (10.1 mi)
North Interlakes Parking Area to North Kananaskis Pass—18.3 km (11.4 mi)

Backpack

Allow 6.5 hours to Turbine Canyon Campground

Elevation gain: 645 m (2,100 ft)

Maximum elevation: 2370 m (7,775 ft)

Maps: Kananaskis Lakes 82 J/11
Kananaskis Lakes (Gem Trek)

Access: From the Trans-Canada Highway, follow the Kananaskis Trail (Hwy 40) for 50 km (31 mi) and turn right on the Kananaskis Lakes Trail. Drive another 15 km (9.5 mi) to the North Interlakes Day Use Area. The trailhead kiosk is at the north end of the parking lot.

0.0— Trailhead (1725 m).
N50°37.926' W115°08.422'
— Trail crosses Kananaskis Lakes intake dam and spillway.
— Trail follows old roadbed.
0.9— Junction. *Upper Kananaskis Lake* circuit left.
2.1— Trail crosses Palliser rockslide.
4.0— Invincible Creek bridge.
5.8— Kananaskis River bridge.
7.3— Spring.
8.0— Junction (1790 m) and Forks Campground. *South Kananaskis Pass* left. North Kananaskis Pass ahead.
— Trail parallels Kananaskis River then makes switchbacking climb up avalanche slopes.
12.4— Trail tops ridge above Putnik's Pond.
— Trail crosses old moraine.
14.3— Lawson Lake (2220 m).
— Trail skirts west shore of the lake.
16.0— Junction. Park Ranger cabin left.
16.1— Maude Brook bridge.
16.2— Turbine Canyon Campground.
— Trail turns west along north bank of Maude Brook.
17.0— Trail summit (2370 m).
— Maude Lake.
18.3— North Kananaskis Pass (2360 m).

North Kananaskis Pass is a rolling alpine ridge perched on the Great Divide at the boundary of Peter Lougheed Provincial Park and B.C.'s Height of the Rockies Provincial Park. The hike to the pass is notable for the variety of terrain it traverses, and memorable for the scenery along the way. It can be approached as either a trip of two full days with an overnight stay at the Turbine Canyon Campground, or as a trip involving three days, with a short hike to the Forks Campground on day one, a long day hike to the pass and back on the second, and a short trip out on the third.

The first section of the trip duplicates the *South Kananaskis Pass* trail as far as the Forks Campground at km 8.0 (see). From the Forks, however, the North Kananaskis Pass trail swings away to the north. Pick your way through the campground and follow the trail as it traces the pools and riffles of the Kananaskis River along its west bank. Unfortunately, the delightful riverside stretch is soon replaced with a long, sustained climb up an avalanche slope whose only virtue is some impressive views back to Mount Lyautey.

After turning the corner on a number of switchbacks, the trail traverses north into the forest, where the appearance of some treeline-favouring larch trees attest to its altitude. Mount Putnik and Mount Beatty now dominate to the west, and the long, ragged ridge of the Spray Mountains to the east.

At km 12, the trail suddenly pops out of the forest on the crest of a rock ridge and descends toward a small tarn known as Putnik's Pond. The open meadows beyond and glacier-draped Mount Beatty (2999 m) offer a sense of what lies ahead—a long, glorious traverse of a high (2200-m) bench running beneath Beatty.

Maude Lake

The bench walk opens with some spectacular rock gardens and moves on to an open larch forest featuring trees 60 cm or more in diameter, views ahead to Mount Maude (3042 m), the Haig Glacier and Mount Jellicoe (3246 m), and finally the shores of Lawson Lake. (If there aren't a lot of other hikers around, shout hello to the sheer wall of Mount Black Prince across the lake and listen to the double echo bounce back to you—one of the best in the Rockies!)

At the far end of Lawson Lake, you'll pass a sign indicating a ranger cabin (off to the left) and, just beyond, the bridge over Maude Brook and the Turbine Canyon Campground. The campground's namesake, a narrow defile that drops abruptly away toward the Kananaskis River, lies just to the east, downstream, and is well worth investigating.

The trail to North Kananaskis Pass, involving another 2.1 km of hiking and an additional 152 m elevation gain, swings west at the campground and rises through the last dwarfed trees, crossing a high rocky ridge (the high point of the hike at 2370 m) and descending to Maude Lake, a lovely alpine catchment that reflects both the colour of the sky and the austere flanks of Mount Maude that rise directly above it.

A short distance beyond Maude Lake you'll find a sign indicating that you have, indeed, reached North Kananaskis Pass. The trail continues beyond the pass, dropping so precipitously into Leroy Creek and the Height of the Rockies Provincial Park that most hikers won't be tempted to stray beyond the pass. Looking down Leroy Creek, the spectacular Royal Group, featuring Mounts Prince Edward and Prince Henry, dominate the skyline.

Boulton Creek Trading Post to Kananaskis Fire Lookout—6.2 km (3.9 mi)

Day hike

Allow 2 hours one way

Elevation gain: 418 m (1,371 ft)

Maximum elevation: 2118 m (6,949 ft)

Maps: Kananaskis Lakes 82 J/11
Kananaskis Lakes (Gem Trek)

Access: From its junction with the Kananaskis Trail (Hwy 40), follow the Kananaskis Lakes Trail 9.7 km (6 mi) to the Boulton Creek Trading Post. Turn left and find your way to the upper parking lot. The trail begins on the asphalt bicycle path at the southeast corner of the parking lot.

0.0— Trailhead (1700 m).
N50°38.135′ W115°06.415′

— Trail starts south (right) along bicycle path.

0.2— Junction. Amphitheatre ahead (outhouses on the left). Turn left.

— Follow Whiskey Jack trail uphill on wide gravel path, crossing campground loop roads twice.

1.3— Junction. Reclaimed access road veers right. Stay left.

2.5— Small creek and picnic table.

3.8— Junction. Intersection with Pocaterra trail. Turn right.

4.4— Junction. Stay right. Tyrwhitt trail left.

— Trail climbs steeply toward lookout.

6.2— Kananaskis Fire Lookout (2118 m).

The trip to the Kananaskis Fire Lookout should be mandatory for anyone planning to spend much time exploring the Kananaskis Lakes region. The lookout provides an impressive overview of the lakes—the heart of Peter Lougheed Provincial Park—which in turn offers an excellent opportunity to understand the way the tangled topography around the lakes fits together.

There are three approaches to the lookout, of which the most popular is the leisurely climb through the forest from Boulton Creek Trading Post and Campground. Although the hike begins amidst the development associated with the campground, and the trail receives heavy use from mountain bikers, the trip is a pleasant and rewarding experience.

The first leg of the trip, starting at the Trading Post parking lot, follows the Whiskey Jack trail, which takes about a kilometre to shake its campground trappings and establish itself as a gentle climb along an old roadbed through pine-spruce forest featuring gurgling creeks and a lush variety of forest flowers. Just shy of the 4-km mark, the Whiskey Jack trail intersects with the Pocaterra trail. Turn right at the "T" and follow Pocaterra for 0.6 km to its junction with the Tyrwhitt trail, where you should again stay to the right.

Beyond the junction, the Pocaterra trail becomes the Lookout trail proper, a name change that heralds the last leg of the climb. The Pocaterra trail, combined with the Whiskey Jack, Hydroline, and Tyrwhitt trails, provides a network of Nordic skiing trails during the winter. (Fortunately, the trail nomenclature is considerably more confusing than the trail system itself!)

Beyond Tyrwhitt junction, the Lookout trail begins a sustained climb, and most hikers will find themselves shifting from second gear to compound low. Nearing the lookout, the road's incline

Kananaskis Lakes from Kananaskis Fire Lookout

eases and the forest thins to preview the scenery ahead. A sign just below the lookout reminds hikers of their manners: respect the lookout person's work and privacy, and don't ask for water and food.

The lookout sits atop a small, cleared knoll and provides an unimpeded view across the valley to the Kananaskis Lakes. With a map spread out on one of the hilltop picnic tables, you can sort out the peaks, passes and drainages that provide much of the best hiking and scrambling in the park. From the west, the array of mountains that wraps around the lakes includes Mounts Fox (2973 m), Foch (3180 m), Sarrail (3174 m), Lyautey (3082 m), Putnik (2940 m), and Indefatigable (2670 m).

Highway 40 to Kananaskis Fire Lookout—4.5 km. Despite being a shorter approach with less elevation gain, the fire road leading from Kananaskis Trail (Hwy 40) to the lookout is not a good choice owing to limited trailhead parking. The option is best suited to mountain bikers who cycle to the trail or, perhaps, hikers who can arrange a drop-off.

The gated fire road is at an unmarked turn-off on the right side the Kananaskis Trail 59 km (37 mi) south of the Trans-Canada Highway. Follow the roadbed south on a gradual ascent along the west slope of the Elk Range.

The Pocaterra trail joins the road from the right at km 0.5 and intersects the Whiskey Jack trail from Boulton Creek at km 2.2. Complete the final 2.3 km to the lookout as described above.

Hyrdoline Option. For hikers with the luxury of two vehicles and a willingness to work a short shuttle, it is possible to add variety to the trip by descending south from the Lookout on unmaintained trails to the Hydroline trail. Turn right, follow the trail 1.6 km to the Elk Pass junction, turn right again and walk the final 2.0 km to the Elk Pass trailhead. The total distance from the lookout is 6.9 km. Not recommended during periods of wet weather.

203 Boulton Creek

Boulton Creek Loop—3.0 km (1.9 mi)

This short interpretive loop near the Boulton Creek Trading Post and Campground offers a good introduction to the forest environment of the Kananaskis Lakes valley. In midsummer, armed with an interpretive brochure available online from the park's website (see *Sources—Parks information*), you will encounter a wonderful variety of woodland plants and flowers, as well as numerous but not-so-wonderful mosquitoes.

Immediately after crossing the trailhead footbridge, the trail passes the historic Boulton Cabin, which was used by forest rangers in the 1930s. Stay right at the first junction and, for the next 0.5 km, hike through lodgepole pine forest filled with buffaloberry and a scattering of wildflowers. Look for bunchberry, heart-leaved arnica, ragwort and occasional stands of fireweed.

At km 0.7 the trail skirts the edge of the Boulton Campground and follows along an open bluff above Boulton Creek. It soon veers back into the forest, composed here of a dense "doghair" stand of lodgepole pine. At the end of the loop the trail descends to Boulton Creek and crosses a footbridge to the creek's true left bank. It follows the creek back to the trailhead, passing through dense forest and along horsetail bogs.

Access: Follow the Kananaskis Lakes Trail 10 km (6 mi) from its junction with the Kananaskis Trail (Hwy 40) to Boulton Bridge Picnic Area. The parking area is 50 m off the highway to the left. The trail starts at a footbridge over Boulton Creek. N50°37.963' W115°06.502' *Maps: Kananaskis Lakes 82 J/11; Kananaskis Lakes (Gem Trek).*

204 Canadian Mount Everest Expedition Trail

Canadian Mount Everest Expedition Loop—2.2 km (1.4 mi)

Canadian Mount Everest Expedition Trail is an intimidating title for what is actually a short woodland loop to a promontory overlooking Upper and Lower Kananaskis Lakes. Though we are pleased to honour those who made the first Canadian ascent of Everest in 1982, the original name—the Interlakes Trail—better describes this easy hike.

The well-graded trail, featuring numerous interpretive signs and benches, climbs through a typical valley-bottom forest of spruce and pine to the loop split at km 0.2. Stay right and continue through dense forest carpeted with feather moss and lichen.

A staircase assists the climb to the summit viewpoint at km 1.2, where you have a 360-degree panorama of the valley. Though Lower Kananaskis Lake is visible to the north, the best view is west to Upper Kananaskis Lake.

This rocky point is quite open and dry, and harebells, vetches and asters bloom amidst a ground cover of low-growing junipers and kinnikinnick in midsummer.

From the summit, the trail makes a steep descent across open slopes, with continual good views of Upper Kananaskis Lake, then re-enters the forest and completes the loop back to the parking area.

Access: From its junction with Highway 40, follow the Kananaskis Lakes Trail 13 km (8 mi) to the White Spruce parking lot opposite the entrance to Mount Sarrail Campground. The trail starts at the stairs at the west side of the parking lot. N50°36.950' W115°07.399' *Maps: Kananaskis Lakes 82 J/11 (trail not shown); Kananaskis Lakes (Gem Trek).*

Elbow Lake

205 Elbow Lake

Kananaskis Trail (Hwy 40) to Elbow Lake—1.3 km (0.8 mi)

Elbow Lake is a small, serene body of water nestled between subalpine forest and talus fields beneath Mt. Rae. It is not, however, a place of much solitude. Fair game to hikers, bikers and equestrians, the trail is just 1.3 km distant from, and 125 vertical metres higher than the trailhead. Add a 15-site backcountry campground into the mix and you have all the makings of a backcountry social on summer weekends.

The trail begins as an old roadbed that leaves the parking lot with a short, sharp ascent up and around the southern flank of Mount Elpoca. A trailside bench at 0.5 km allows you to catch your breath and enjoy an expansive view back down the Kananaskis Valley to the Spray Mountains and Kananaskis Range.

The trail moderates its climb across a large avalanche runout, and bumps up and over the forested summit of Elbow Pass (2100 m) to arrive at the lake. Most hikers pick their way through the campground and follow the trail around the lake.

The outlet at the far end of the lake is a source of the Elbow River, and marks the boundary between Peter Lougheed Provincial Park and the Elbow-Sheep Wildland Provincial Park.

Day hikers usually turn left after crossing the Elbow and finish the loop by traversing a series of talus slopes, which offer numerous views across the lake to Mount Rae.

Access: From the Trans-Canada Highway, follow the Kananaskis Trail (Hwy 40) for 62 km (38.5 mi) to the Elbow Pass Day Use Area. The trail begins from the parking lot trail kiosk. (Hwy 40 is closed beyond the Kananaskis Trail–Kananaskis Lakes Trail junction from December 1 to June 15.) N50°38.140' W115°01.420' *Maps: Kananaskis Lakes 82 J/11; Kananaskis Lakes (Gem Trek).*

Highwood Meadows to Ptarmigan Cirque summit—1.8 km (1.1 mi)

Half-day trip

Allow 45 minutes one way

Elevation gain: 210 m (700 ft)

Maximum elevation: 2415 m (7,920 ft)

Maps: Mount Rae 82 J/10†
    Kananaskis Lakes (Gem Trek)
    † trail not shown

Access: Follow the Kananaskis Trail (Hwy 40) south from its junction with the Kananaskis Lakes Trail for 17.5 km to the Highwood Meadows Day Use Area. The trailhead is in the day use parking area on the west side of road. (Note: Highway 40 is closed south of the Kananaskis Trail–Kananaskis Lakes Trail junction from December 1 to June 15.)

0.0— Trailhead (2205 m).
    N50°35.771' W114°59.162'

— Trail runs across meadows on west side of highway.

0.4— Junction. Stay right and cross to east side of highway.

— Steady, steep climb through forest.

1.0— Meadow margin viewpoint.

1.1— Junction. Ptarmigan Cirque loop split. Stay left.

1.2— Trail climbs above trees into alpine meadows.

1.5— Grades moderate through rolling meadow.

1.8— Ptarmigan Cirque trail summit (2415 m).

— Trail turns right, crosses stream and descends southeast side of meadows.

2.4— Waterfalls viewpoint.

— Trail descends steeply into forest.

2.5— Junction. Return to Ptarmigan Cirque loop split.

3.6— Highwood Pass parking area (2205 m).

(Trail not shown on maps in this book.)

As one of Peter Lougheed Provincial Park's popular interpretive trails, Ptarmigan Cirque offers one of the quickest routes to the alpine in all the mountain parks, a state owing to the trailhead's location in Highwood Pass—the highest point in Canada accessible by paved road. The amphitheatre is contained by rockslides and the limestone cliffs, but alpine meadows and wildflowers are the area's prize. Wildlife may also be encountered along the way—mountain sheep and grizzly bears are equally common here.

Despite its short length, the trail is no casual stroll. The hike begins at the Highwood Meadows Day Use parking area just south of Highwood Pass and follows the meadow's nature trail back toward the 2206-m summit. The trail splits after 400 m, and the Ptarmigan Cirque trail crosses Kananaskis Trail (Hwy 40) and begins a steady climb to the cirque.

The ascent through the upper reaches of subalpine forest is a bit demanding, but there are many excuses to stop in early summer when the woods are filled with the blooms of glacier lilies, larkspur, heart-leafed arnica, fleabane, and light pink Indian paintbrush.

At km 1.1 the trail splits to create a loop through the meadows above. The left branch immediately climbs above the treeline and then levels out into the rolling meadows of Ptarmigan Cirque.

At the upper end of the loop, the trail reaches a steep, rocky terminal moraine, where it swings right, crosses a small stream, and begins a gradual descent along the east side of the meadows. On this return leg, views open to Pocaterra cirque and the twin summits of Mount Tyrwhitt on the west side of Highwood Pass. Just before re-entering the forest and returning to the loop split, you receive one last reward—a deeply eroded gorge containing a series of waterfalls.

Ptarmigan Cirque

Warspite Lake

207 Black Prince Cirque

Black Prince Day Use Area to Warspite Lake—2.1 km (1.3 mi)

This short interpretive trail takes you to the emerald waters of Warspite Lake beneath the walls of Black Prince Cirque. The trail's reward to effort ratio must be one of the best in the Rockies, just as its name must be one of the most romantic. (Mount Black Prince was named by surveyor Arthur O. Wheeler to honour a British cruiser of the same name that was sunk during WWI.)

Armed with the interpretive brochure available from the park's website (see *Sources—Parks information*), start from the parking lot trailhead (1735 m), cross the Smith-Dorrien Creek and begin a gradual climb into the forest. Interpretive trail markers punctuate the route, providing frequent opportunities to stop and ponder the trail's subalpine environs.

At the 1-km mark, the trail veers right from the road and, 0.4 km beyond, passes the loop split (stay right). The rocky east shore of Warspite Lake (1830 m) is reached at km 2.1.

The lake is a placid tarn, handsomely offset by the dark forest beyond, the glacier-carved amphitheatre of Mount Black Prince, and the incised ridge of Mount Warspite. Numerous large boulders provide comfortable platforms for soaking up sun and solitude.

Loop back down-valley to the approach trail by skirting the southeast corner of the lake and traversing a rockslide.

Access: From its junction with Kananaskis Trail (Hwy 40), follow Kananaskis Lakes Trail 2.2 km (1.4 mi) to the Smith-Dorrien/ Spray Trail (Hwy 742) junction. Follow the Smith-Dorrien/Spray Trail 8.3 km (5.2 mi) to the Mount Black Prince Day Use Area. N50°42.391' W115°11.902' *Maps: Kananaskis Lakes 82 J/11 (trail not fully shown); Kananaskis Lakes (Gem Trek).*

Land above 2300 metres

0 1 2 3 4km

208 Chester Lake

Smith-Dorrien/Spray Trail (Hwy 742) to Chester Lake—4.9 km (3.0 mi)

Half-day trip

Allow 1.5 hours one way

Elevation gain: 315 m (1,030 ft)

Maximum elevation: 2220 m (7,280 ft)

Maps: Spray Lakes Reservoir 82 J/14†
Kananaskis Lakes (Gem Trek)
† trail not fully shown

Access: Follow the Smith-Dorrien/ Spray Trail (Hwy 742) 45 km (28 mi) from downtown Canmore to Smith-Dorrien Summit, or 20 km (12.5 mi) northwest from the road's junction with Kananaskis Lakes Trail. The Chester Lake trailhead parking area is on the east side of the road, opposite the south end of Mud Lake.

0.0— Trailhead (1905 m).
N50°47.460' W115°18.039'

— Gradual to moderate uphill along old roadbed.

0.2— Chester Creek bridge.

0.6— Junction. Go left or right, but most hikers turn left.

— Steady climb through spruce-fir forest.

2.6— Junction. Stay left on single-track trail. End of bike access.
(On the return trip, hikers can turn left here for a shorter route back to the trailhead.)

— Climb through subalpine forest.

3.1— Trail flattens out across meadow.

4.3— Enter extensive meadow below lake.

4.9— Chester Lake (2220 m).

Notice: The trail to Chester Lake is closed annually in May and June to allow the area to dry and prevent damage to the trail and surrounding area.

If you hike to Chester Lake on a summer weekend, you will not travel alone. Hikers and mountain bikers share the trail to the 2.6-km junction, and it often feels as if half of Calgary has descended on this tiny lake beneath the limestone walls of The Fortress and Mount Chester. But if you go during the week, you will find its less-crowded shores and flower-filled meadows well worth the short hike.

For a more gradual ascent, stay left at the 0.6-km junction and climb through second-growth forest into mature Engelmann spruce and alpine fir. Intermittent clearings, filled with alpine buttercups and glacier lilies in late June and early July, provide glimpses ahead to the rugged summits of Mount Galatea (3185 m), The Fortress (3000 m) and Mount Chester (3054 m)—the peaks containing the Chester Lake cirque. The trail levels off around 3 km and alternates between meadow and forest for the rest of the way. One long final meadow leads to the lake.

The cliffs of Mount Chester create a dramatic setting for the lake, while the nearby rockslides are home to a healthy pika population. However, the meadows near the lake's outlet provide most of the colour. Shortly after the last snow has disappeared, usually in late June, the meadow at the west end of the lake turns into a vast field of golden glacier lilies. A rough path circles the lake, offering new views of the surrounding peaks and a waterfall about halfway around.

Three Lakes Valley. A trail skirts the lake's western shore and climbs over a larch-covered rise to the narrow Three Lakes Valley beneath Mount Galatea. Scramble up this tight, rocky vale for another 1.5 km, passing three tiny tarns and enjoying good views back across Smith-Dorrien Summit to the heavily-glaciated peaks of the Great Divide.

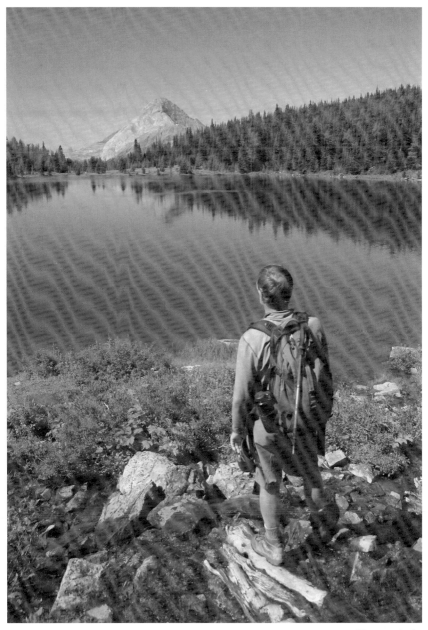

© Andrew Hempstead

Chester Lake

209 Burstall Pass

Smith-Dorrien/Spray Trail (Hwy 742) to Burstall Pass—7.5 km (4.7 mi)

Day trip

Allow 2 to 2.5 hours one way

Elevation gain: 475 m (1,550 ft)

Maximum elevation: 2375 m (7,800 ft)

Maps: Spray Lakes Reservoir 82 J/14†
       Kananaskis Lakes (Gem Trek)
       † trail not fully shown

Access: Follow the Smith-Dorrien/
Spray Trail (Hwy 742) 45 km (28 mi) from
downtown Canmore to Smith-Dorrien
Summit, or 20 km (12.5 mi) northwest from
the road's junction with Kananaskis Lakes
Trail. The Burstall Pass trailhead parking
area is on the west side of the road at the
south end of Mud Lake.

  0.0— Trailhead (1900 m).
       N50°47.456' W115°18.240'

    — Follows old roadbed.

  2.5— Trail passes above Burstall Lakes.

  3.3— Road becomes single-track trail.
       End of bicycle access.

  3.9— Trail crosses Burstall Creek flats
       (ankle deep channel fords).

  4.5— Climb from flats into forest.

  5.5— Trail enters open meadow.

  6.4— Steady climb to pass begins.

  7.5— Burstall Pass (2375 m).
       Park boundary.

    — Trail descends draw to northwest
       (vague track) then contours south
       to avalanche slopes and descends
       steeply.

10.6— Trail levels off and travels north
       through scattered forest.*

12.2— Junction (1905 m).* Intersection with
       Upper Spray River-Palliser Pass trail
       at km 19.8 (see Banff Park chapter).

*distance approximate

Burstall Pass is one of the finest trail-accessible summits in this section of the Rockies—a high, open region of rocky outcrops and alpine meadows on the Peter Lougheed-Banff Park boundary. Views from the 2375-m pass are extensive and encompass some of the highest peaks in Peter Lougheed, Banff, Height of the Rockies and Mount Assiniboine Parks—including Mount Assiniboine.

Understandably, the pass is one of the park's most popular day hikes and is particularly busy on weekends. It can also be quite wet early in the season when the braided flats beyond Burstall Lakes flood, necessitating several ankle-deep fords. Backpackers also use the trail as an "express route" to the upper Spray Valley at the southern end of Banff Park.

The trail begins its journey from a parking area at the south end of Mud Lake on Smith-Dorrien Summit and follows an old logging road for 3.3 km to a point above the Burstall Lakes. Few hikers bother to linger at these lakes that lie just off the trail to the right—their shores are marshy and usually well guarded by armies of mosquitoes. Mountain bikes are permitted on this first stretch of trail and in dry weather are definitely a boon in gaining speedy access to the pass.

The willow flats beyond the lakes provide a good view south to Mount Robertson (3194 m) and the Robertson Glacier, which is responsible for the silty runoff that inundates this section of trail early in the summer. (Later in the season you can tiptoe across the braided channels on rocks or logs.)

From the Burstall Creek flats you begin the climb to the pass, rising steadily through subalpine forest and across avalanche paths. The trail levels off briefly in a long meadow beneath Mount Birdwood before bending south and resuming the heart-pounding ascent to the summit.

Mount Birdwood from Burstall Pass

The rolling summit ridge of the pass is an open invitation to wander and explore, particularly towards South Burstall Pass. The meadows cradled between the summit's rocky bluffs fill with the blooms of wildflowers from early July to mid-August, including western anemone, white mountain avens, golden fleabane, alpine cinquefoil, pearly everlasting and white Indian paintbrush.

Mount Birdwood (3097 m) rises dramatically to the north above the Burstall Creek headwaters, but it loses some of its grandeur when compared to glacier-draped Mount Sir Douglas (3406 m), which forms the crest of the Great Divide 5 km to the south. And both these peaks pale in comparison to the pyramid of Mount Assiniboine (3610 m), the highest mountain in the southern Canadian Rockies, which is visible on clear days just over 20 km away to the northwest.

Upper Spray Valley. By continuing due west through the pass on obvious trail, you will bypass a large sinkhole and then discover a fine viewpoint for Leman Lake and Banff Park's upper Spray Valley. But if you are bound for that remote valley, retreat to the sinkhole, skirt its west side, and look for cairns leading down a large gully to the northwest. Persevere down this vale for 0.5 km or so until good trail re-emerges.

After passing through larch groves and small meadows, the trail turns south along the Spray Valley's western slope and contours onto a major avalanche path. Then it plunges downward, losing more than 200 m of elevation in the space of 2 km.

When you reach the valley bottom at the toe of the avalanche path, the trail turns back to the north and parallels the Spray River trail for nearly 2 km. It eventually breaks through the scattered forest to join that route in open meadow beside the Spray River 0.2 km north of the Leman Lake trail junction (see *Upper Spray River-Palliser Pass*, Banff Park chapter).

Elk Lakes Provincial Park

Elk Lakes is a 173 sq km provincial park at the headwaters of British Columbia's Elk River. The park is bordered on the north by the Great Divide and Alberta's Peter Lougheed Provincial Park, to the west and south by B.C.'s Height of the Rockies Provincial Park, and on the east by B.C. forest lands.

Lower and Upper Elk Lakes form the park's core. The lakes, which are only a kilometre apart, are blessed with a spectacular backdrop of high, heavily-glaciated peaks to the west, including Mounts McCuaig, Nivelle and Castelneau.

The lakes were quite remote and relatively inaccessible until a power line was constructed over Elk Pass in 1951. Soon adventurous motorists and four-wheel drive enthusiasts began accessing the lakes and Elk Pass via the rough, power-line service road connecting Kananaskis Lakes and the Elk Valley.

With increased visitation, the B.C. parks department established a small recreational reserve around the lakes in 1955. In 1973 it was enlarged to 56 sq km to create Elk Lakes Provincial Park. Following a land use review in 1995, the adjacent Elk Lakes Recreation Area to the south was annexed and the park expanded to its present size.

The only regularly maintained trails in the park are in the core area surrounding the Elk Lakes. The lakes can be visited on a backpack or long day hike from Alberta's Peter Lougheed Park via West Elk Pass, or they can be reached in less than an hour from the parking area at the end of B.C.'s Elk River Forest Service Road. The core trail from the forestry road also extends beyond Upper Elk Lake to Pétain Falls and Basin—the only full day trip from the Elk River trailhead or Lower Elk Lake Campground.

Mountain bikes are not permitted on any park trails (see *Access* below).

Information and services. The Elk Lakes Cabin is situated on the Elk Lakes trail just beyond the Elk River road parking area. Formerly a park ranger cabin, it is operated as a dorm-style hut by the Alpine Club of Canada. The cabin sleeps 10 and provides a propane stove and lights along with basic kitchen wares. A custodian is on site throughout the summer season. (See *Sources—Huts* for contact details.)

Since rangers are no longer stationed in the park, visitors should check the trailhead kiosk at the parking area for general information and notices. The custodian at the Elk Lakes Cabin can also provide information about the park and campgrounds.

There are only two developed backcountry campgrounds in the park—at Lower Elk Lake and Pétain Creek. A fee of $5.00 per person per night (six years of age or older) is collected by the Alpine Club of Canada hut custodian.

Access: If you drive to the park entrance at the headwaters of B.C.'s Elk River, the lakes are little more than a short stroll from the trailhead. However, unless you live or are travelling in the Crowsnest Pass region, it is an epic journey to get there.

The first leg of the trip requires reaching Sparwood, B.C. via Highway 3. From Sparwood follow paved Highway 43 north 33 km (21 mi) to the village of Elkford. Beyond Elkford a gravel forestry road continues along the west side of the Elk River for another 44 km (27 mi), then crosses to the east side of the river to join the Kananaskis Power Line road. From this crossing it is another 23 km (14 mi) to the Elk Lakes trailhead parking area at the park's east boundary. Several forest service campgrounds are located on the road between Elkford and the park, including two within 5 km of the park boundary. (Keep a sharp eye out for logging trucks beyond Elkford, particularly on weekdays.)

You can also reach Elk Lakes from Alberta's Peter Lougheed Provincial Park by hiking the *Elk Lakes via West Elk Pass* trail or cycling the limited access Kananaskis Power Line service road over Elk Pass to the park entrance parking lot.

Mount Aosta and Lower Elk Lake

210 Elk Lakes via Elk Valley

Elk Lakes Parking Area to Upper Elk Lake—2.5 km (1.6 mi)
Elk Lakes Parking Area to Pétain Falls—7.5 km (4.7 mi)*

Half-day to day trip

Allow 1 hour to Upper Elk Lake

Elevation gain: 70 m (230 ft)

Maximum elevation: 1800 m (5,900 ft)

Maps: Kananaskis Lakes 82 J/11†
      Kananaskis Lakes (Gem Trek)
      † trail not shown

Access: From Sparwood, B. C., follow Highway 43 and the Elk River Forest Service Road 100 km (62 mi) north to the trailhead parking area for Elk Lakes Provincial Park at road's end. (See also *Access* in Elk Lakes Provincial Park introduction.)

0.0— Trailhead (1740 m).
      N50°33.064' W115°04.262'

0.1— Elk Lakes Cabin.

0.2— Elkan Creek bridge and Junction.
      West Elk Pass via Elkan Creek right
      4.0 km. Stay ahead.

    —Pass along meadows and through
      forest on mainly flat trail.

1.2— Lower Elk Lake (1730 m).
      Lower Elk Lake Campground.

1.7— Elk River bridges.

1.8— Junction. Viewpoint left 1.2 km.
      Upper Elk Lake ahead.

    — Trail climbs gradual to moderate
      through lush forest.

2.5— Upper Elk Lake and Junction (1740 m).
      West Elk Pass right across outlet
      bridge (see *Elk Lakes via West Elk
      Pass*). Pétain Creek and Falls left.

    — Rough trail along east shore of Upper
      Elk Lake.

4.5— South end of Upper Elk Lake.

    — Route crosses alluvial flats beyond
      lake to west edge of flood plain
      (possible fords).

6.0— Pétain Creek Campground.*

    — Trail bends west on brushy flats and
      through forest.

7.5— Pétain Falls Viewpoint (1800 m).*

*distance approximate

If British Columbia's Elk Valley had been connected to Alberta by a good, paved road over Elk Pass, as many valley residents desired, Elk Lakes would rival nearby Kananaskis Lakes in popularity. As it is, these scenic gems with their spectacular backdrop of peaks and glaciers are reserved for those who are willing to make the long, rough drive north from Elkford, B.C., or who hike or bike from Alberta's Peter Lougheed Park.

Regardless of how you get there, the park's core trail to Lower and Upper Elk Lakes is one of the easiest short hikes in the Rockies. You can also continue past the upper lake to Pétain Falls—a series of cascades beneath Mount Castelneau that ranks as one of Canada's highest waterfalls.

The trail begins at the parking lot at the end of the Elk River Forest Service Road and a trailhead kiosk with park map and general information. It passes the Elk Lakes Cabin 100 m beyond the parking area and immediately descends to the Elkan Creek bridge and a junction for the low trail to West Elk Pass.

Beyond the bridge you follow good gravel-fill trail along the edge of some fine willow-dwarf birch meadows, containing the meandering Elk River, and into mossy subalpine forest where glacier lilies, globeflowers, fairybells and heart-leaved arnica bloom in profusion in early summer. Though the trail rolls up and down a bit, there is no significant gain or loss of elevation.

Shortly after coming abreast of the Elk River, you reach Lower Elk Lake and its pleasant campground. Views across the lake are quite stunning, particularly on still mornings when its waters mirror distant pyramid-shaped peaks to the southwest and Mount Aosta (2944 m) near its southern shore.

After skirting the lake's northeast shore, the trail re-enters forest and

Lower Elk Lake

crosses the bridged channels of the Elk River to the Viewpoint trail junction (see below). Stay right and climb gravel track through lush forest to the upper lake.

You reach Upper Elk Lake where the Fox Lake trail intersects via a bridge over the lake's outlet (see *Elk Lakes via West Elk Pass*). The scene is similar to the lower lake, but you get a better overview of the lake and distant peaks by crossing the bridge and following the Fox Lake trail up a scree slope for 100 m or so.

The south-facing cliffs of Mount Fox rise above the northeast end of the lake, and in early summer numerous waterfalls gush down the escarpment to create a "weeping wall."

The gravel-fill trail ends at this point and a rocky and rooty track continues along the lake's east shore for 2 km to its far end. However, it's not worth hiking unless you are bound for Pétain Falls.

Pétain Falls. This impressive waterfall cascades down from the Pétain Glacier at the head of the Upper Elk Lake valley. A viewpoint near the base of the falls can be reached in 1.5 hours or so from the north end of Upper Elk Lake.

Follow the rough trail along the lake's east shore (flooded in spots in early summer) and, at the far end, emerge onto alluvial flats covered by willows and scattered islands of spruce. This area is frequently flooded early in the season, so you may have to route-find and wade channels to the west side of the flats, where you will discover a dry, defined track leading to Pétain Creek Campground at km 6.0.

Beyond the campground, the trail bends west and continues up-valley for approximately 2 km until you emerge from spruce forest into a meadow with the best view of the waterfalls and the Castelneau Glacier. If you wish, you can continue through meadows to a point near the base of the main waterfall.

Viewpoint Trail. This 1.2 km trail branches from the main trail at km 1.8 and, after skirting the west shore of Lower Elk Lake, climbs to the top of a 1860-m promontory overlooking the lower lake and the Elk Valley. You gain 130 m of elevation on this short side-trip and pass above some hazardous cliffs (travel with care).

211 Elk Lakes via West Elk Pass

Kananaskis Lakes Trail to Lower Elk Lake Campground—10.2 km (6.3 mi)

Day trip or backpack

Allow 3 hours one way

Elevation gain: 225 m (750 ft)
loss: 215 m (700 ft)

Maximum elevation: 1945 m (6,380 ft)

Maps: Kananaskis Lakes 82 J/11†
Kananaskis Lakes (Gem Trek)
† trail not shown

Access: Follow Kananaskis Trail (Hwy 40) to its intersection with Kananaskis Lakes Trail. Continue south on the Kananaskis Lakes Trail 12.0 km (7.5 mi) to the Elk Pass trailhead parking area, located on the left side of the road 0.5 km before Upper Lake Day Use Area.

0.0– Trailhead (1720 m).
N50°37.031' W115°06.674'

1.0– Road reaches powerline.

1.3– Road branches right from powerline.

2.0– Fox Creek Junction.
West Elk Pass trail branches right from powerline access road.

3.7– Enter marshy, willow-covered meadow.

4.1– Junction. Branch road to powerline left. Continue ahead.

4.6– Junction. Follow trail branching right from roadbed.

5.1– West Elk Pass (1905 m). Junction. Elk Lakes Cabin via Elkan Creek ahead (4.0 km). Fox Lake right.

5.2– Junction. Frozen Lake route right. Fox Lake left.

6.0– Fox Lake (1945 m).

7.0– Steady downhill begins.

8.9– Upper Elk Lake Junction (1740 m). Intersection with *Elk Lakes via Elk Valley* trail at km 2.5. Stay left.

9.8– Lower Elk Lake.

10.2– Lower Elk Lake Campground (1730 m).

While the Elk Lakes can be reached on a short hike from the trailhead at the end of B.C.'s Elk River Forest Service Road, not many people are willing to make the long drive to get there. A longer but more popular hike to the lakes is from Alberta's Peter Lougheed Park. By following old roadbeds and trail over West Elk Pass, you can reach the lakes on an easy backpack or long day hike.

There are a number of routes over Elk Pass that can be used to reach the lakes. The road beneath the power line between B.C.'s Elk Valley and Kananaskis Lakes is a popular route for mountain bikes, but not an attractive option for hikers. The most direct and scenic hiking route goes by way of West Elk Pass and Fox Lake, an approach that provides fine views of Elk Lakes as it descends along the east slope of Mount Fox.

You have a number of intersecting roads to contend with as you climb from the parking area in Lougheed Park to Elk Pass. The first kilometre follows a service road upwards through a dense forest of lodgepole pine and Engelmann spruce to the powerline. After walking the broad cut beneath the hydro towers for 300 m, you follow roadbed branching right into the forest and descend to cross Fox Creek at km 2.0.

After crossing Fox Creek, the road climbs gradually along the true right (east) side of the creek for the next 2.5 km to willow and dwarf birch-covered meadows on Elk Pass. The cool subalpine forest and meadows beside the revegetating road margins offer a lush display of wildflowers in midsummer, including fireweed, asters, arnica, harebells, and Indian paintbrush.

At km 4.6, you turn right onto single-track trail, which crosses a narrow meadow and runs through forest for 0.5 km to a junction on West Elk Pass. Standing atop the Great Divide and the Alberta-B.C. boundary, you have two options

Upper Elk Lake

for approaching Elk Lakes: the trail ahead descends Elkan Creek for 4.0 km to the Elk Lakes Cabin at the Elk River trailhead; the right branch climbs to Fox Lake and makes a more direct and scenic approach to Upper Elk Lake via the slopes of Mount Fox (our preference).

You follow narrow rooty trail southwest along the Alberta-B.C. boundary briefly before angling south to Fox Lake—a small sink lake beneath the east face of Mount Fox, and the highest point on the hike.

The trail continues south along the slopes of Mount Fox and, a kilometre beyond Fox Lake, begins a steady descent to Elk Lakes. There is a good viewpoint for Lower Elk Lake and the Elk Valley on an avalanche path at km 7.8 and, while crossing a talus slope less than a kilometre beyond, you get your first view of Upper Elk Lake.

The trail completes its descent at Upper Elk Lake's outlet bridge, where you intersect the park's core trail (see *Elk Lakes via Elk Valley*). Day hikers usually linger awhile at Upper Elk Lake, then continue to Lower Elk Lake. Backpackers have a choice of camping at Lower Elk Lake Campground or following the trail along Upper Elk Lake's southeast shore to Pétain Creek Campground, 1.5 km beyond the far end of the lake.

Elkan Creek Option. While the Elkan Creek trail is mainly through forest and a bit longer than the Fox Lake approach, it does provide a different return route to West Elk Pass. Pick-up the trail at its junction with the trail from the Elk River road 1.0 km below Lower Elk Lake (100 m west of Elk Lakes Cabin). After a steady climb of 4.0 km near the course of Elkan Creek, you arrive back at the Fox Lake junction on West Elk Pass.

Mount Assiniboine Provincial Park

Created in 1922, British Columbia's Mount Assiniboine Provincial Park is a 386-sq km reserve bounded on the east by the continental divide and Banff National Park, on the west by Kootenay National Park, and on the south by B.C. Provincial Forest lands.

The focal point of the park is Mount Assiniboine (3618 m)—the highest peak south of the Columbia Icefield. The mountain soars well above nearby peaks and is visible for many kilometres in all directions. It is distinctive not only for its height but for its pyramid shape, which resembles Switzerland's Matterhorn (it is often referred to as "the Matterhorn of the Rockies").

While wilderness trails traverse remote valleys in the northern two-thirds of the park, most visitation is centred on Lake Magog at the base of Mount Assiniboine. Lake Magog lies in a basin at 2165 m directly beneath the mountain's north face, and a vast meadowland scattered with stands of alpine fir and larch extends north and east from its shores. Most visitors stay at Mount Assiniboine Lodge or the rustic Naiset Huts at the northeast end of the lake, or camp at Magog Campground on its west side.

There are many excellent hikes from Lake Magog, ranging from half-day jaunts to Wonder Pass, Nub Ridge and Sunburst Valley to full-day outings to Og Pass, Windy Ridge, Og Lake, and Ferro Pass. You need to spend at least two or three days in the area to begin to appreciate this amazing region.

Campgrounds. Magog Campground is just beyond the lake's west shore (29 gravel tent pads, a cooking shelter and water taps fed by a nearby spring). Og Lake Campground is 5.3 km north of Mount Assiniboine Lodge on the *Mount Assiniboine-Citadel Pass* trail (seven gravel tent pads, food storage boxes and a cooking area). Open fires are prohibited at both of these core-area campgrounds (fuel or propane camp stoves only), and there is a fee of $10 per person per night.

Group camping for up to 25 persons is available at O'Brien Meadows, just off the Assiniboine Pass trail 0.5 km west of the park boundary. Reservations are made through Mount Assiniboine Lodge (403-678-2883).

Naiset Huts. Five small rustic cabins above the east shore of Lake Magog were built by Alpine Club of Canada founder A.O. Wheeler in 1925 for patrons of his Banff-Assiniboine walking tour. Today, these heritage cabins are administered by Mount Assiniboine Lodge for BC Parks as overnight shelters. A more-recently constructed cabin serves as a communal area for preparing meals (well-appointed with propane cook stoves and heater, solar electric lighting, and a sink with running water). While the huts are available on a first-come, first-served basis (be prepared to camp if all beds are occupied), reservations are recommended to guarantee a space. The nightly fee is $20 per person for first-come first-served, or $25 if reservations are made through the lodge (403-678-2883).

Mount Assiniboine Lodge. The original Mount Assiniboine Lodge was constructed above the east shore of Lake Magog during the summer of 1928. It was built by the CPR at the behest of the Marquis degli Albizzi and Erling Strom, who operated it as the first ski lodge in the Canadian Rockies. The small lodge and its six outlying guest cabins soon became a popular summer destination as well, and Strom took sole ownership of the lease in 1936.

The lodge was enlarged to its present configuration between 1958 and 1963, and the Strom family continued to operate it until 1983. Since that time, it as been operated by the Renner family. Mount Assiniboine Lodge is one of the finest backcountry lodges in

Mount Assiniboine and Lake Magog

the Rockies, and the view from the lodge and cabins is beyond compare. (See *Sources—Backcountry lodges.*)

Access: You have two ways of reaching the Lake Magog area of Assiniboine Park—backpack or helicopter.

The shortest and most popular hiking route is via the *Bryant Creek-Assiniboine Pass* trail (see Banff Park). Total distance from the trailhead in Alberta's Spray Valley Provincial Park to Magog Campground is 26.7 km.

If you book the bus to Sunshine Village, the backpack via Citadel Pass and the Valley of the Rocks is not much farther and more scenic. Since you begin the trip at 2200 m, there is also less elevation gain than *Bryant Creek-Assiniboine Pass.* Distance from Sunshine Village to Magog Campground is 28.9 km (see *Assiniboine via Citadel Pass*).

Two other park trails are considerably longer and not nearly as popular. The trail from Kootenay Park via Simpson River and Ferro Pass to Magog Campground is 32.2 km (see *Simpson River-Ferro Pass*, Kootenay Park). You can also follow the historic route used by Albizzi and Strom, which runs from Banff to Assinboine via Brewster Creek, Allenby Pass and Og Pass; total distance to Magog Campground is 41.5 km, but a special group permit is required from August 1 to September 30 (see *Brewster Creek-Allenby Pass*, Banff Park).

Many lodge guests, campers and climbers fly to Lake Magog by helicopter. Flights originate from the Mount Shark helipad in Spray Valley Provincial Park and land at a helipad near Mount Assiniboine Lodge. Anyone overnighting in the park can book flights through Mount Assiniboine Lodge. Flights operate throughout the summer on Wednesdays, Fridays and Sundays (Monday replaces Sunday on holiday weekends). At the time of publication, the cost of helicopter flights for campers is $160 per person/each way, and there is a per-person baggage weight limit of 18 kg (40 lbs). More details and requirements concerning flights are available on the Mount Assiniboine Lodge website (see *Sources—Backcountry access*).

N

Banff

Sunshine Road

Gondola

Sundance
Lodge

Sunshine Village

National

Kootenay

MOUNT

70

Citadel
Pass

Park

93

ASSINIBOINE

212

Halfway
Lodge

172

PROVINCIAL

Allenby
Pass

Radium

Og
Pass

National

Ferro
Pass

Assiniboine
Pass

72

PARK

Mt. Assiniboine
Lodge

Wonder
Pass

Park

73

0   5   10   15km

212 Mount Assiniboine via Citadel Pass

Sunshine Village to Assiniboine Lodge—27.5 km (17.1 mi)

Backpack

Allow 1 to 2 days

Maximum elevation: 2395 m (7,850 ft)

Minimum elevation: 1980 m (6,500 ft)

Maps: Banff 82 O/4
      Mount Assiniboine 82 J/13

Access: Travel to Sunshine Village as described in the *Sunshine Meadows* area introduction. From the day-lodge trailhead, follow the Citadel Pass trail uphill to the southeast. (See *Quartz Hill-Citadel Pass*, Banff Park chapter.)

0.0— Sunshine Village (2200 m).
      N51°04.712' W115°46.942'

1.3— Junction. Rock Isle Lake ahead 0.5 km. Citadel Pass left.

5.2— Quartz Hill (2395 m).

5.8— Howard Douglas Lake and Campground (Su8).

9.3— Citadel Pass (2360 m). Banff-Assiniboine Park boundary.

— Descend into Golden Valley.

12.5— Junction. Porcupine Campground right 1.2 km. Stay left on high route.

— Trail enters rocky, forest terrain at head of Golden Valley.

16.5— Junction. Simpson River trail right. Stay left.

— Trail winds through Valley of the Rocks.

22.2— Og Lake and Campground (2060 m).

— Gradual ascent through Og Meadows.

26.3— Junction. Og Pass left. Continue ahead.

26.5— Junction. Horse trail to Sunburst Lake right. Continue ahead.

27.0— Junction. Intersection with *Bryant Creek-Assiniboine Pass* trail at km 24.8. Lake Magog right.

27.3— Junction. Magog Campground ahead 1.6 km. Assiniboine Lodge left.

27.5— Mount Assiniboine Lodge (2180 m). Naiset Cabins ahead 0.5 km.

The trail from Sunshine Village via Citadel Pass and Valley of the Rocks is undoubtedly the most scenic and varied approach to Mount Assiniboine. While the more popular *Bryant Creek-Assiniboine Pass* trail is shorter, the Citadel Pass approach is only 2 km longer and there is actually a slight net loss of elevation over the course of the journey. The only disadvantage is the lack of water, so make sure you carry an adequate supply.

To enjoy the advantages of the Citadel Pass approach, you must book the shuttle bus to Sunshine Village (see *Sunshine Meadows*, Banff National Park), which costs a bit of money and requires that you arrange your departure to coincide with the bus schedule. If you don't take the bus, add 6 km to the trip by starting at the bottom of the Sunshine Village access road.

The first 9.3 km from Sunshine Village follows the very scenic *Quartz Hill-Citadel Pass* trail. After this wonderful, rolling meadow walk, with occasional views of Mount Assiniboine in the distance, you cross into Assiniboine Park at Citadel Pass and descend steeply into the Golden Valley at the headwaters of the Simpson River.

If you want to spend the night at Porcupine Campground, continue to the bottom of Golden Valley. However, through-hikers should follow the trail branching left on the steep, open slope well above the valley floor and contour southwest into the Valley of the Rocks.

The Valley of the Rocks is a long, dry, forest-enclosed vale that features a wild array of giant boulders—the remains of a gigantic rockslide. Og Lake, with its refurbished campground, marks the end of the valley. From this point on, the trail enters a series of open meadows with continuous views ahead to Mount Assiniboine over the final 5 km to Assiniboine Lodge and Lake Magog. (See also Og Lake, *Lake Magog Area Hikes*.)

Citadel Pass

Valley
Of The
Rocks

212

Windy
Ridge

216

Og Mtn

Og Pass

Og
Lake

Allenby Pass

Nestor
Pk▲

Simpson River

172

Ferro
Pass

Cave Mtn

Nub
▲Pk

Bryant Creek

72

Assiniboine
Pass

215

ALBERTA

Creek

Elizabeth
Lake

BRITISH COLUMBIA

Mitchell
Meadows

Ⓥ

214

▲Nublet

Nestor

Cerulean
Lake

Mt. Assiniboine
Lodge

Wedgwood
Lake

Ranger Cabin

Naiset
Cabins

Mitchell River

Sunburst
Lake

213

Sunburst Pk
▲

Lake Magog

Gog
Lake

Wonder
Pass

Naiset Pt

Wedgwood
▲Pk

Mt▲
Watson

The▲
Marshall

Mt▲
Strom

Mt▲
Assiniboine

Terrapin
Mtn ▲

The
▲Towers

73

Ⓥ

Marvel Lake

Mt▲
Magog

Mt▲
Sturdee

Lake Gloria

Land above 2300 metres

0   1   2   3   4km

Lake Magog Area Hikes

Mount Assiniboine's core area is one of the best hiking locales in the Rockies. On the following pages, we describe four of our favourite trips from Lake Magog—*Wonder Pass, Sunburst Valley, Nub Peak,* and *Og Pass-Windy Ridge.*

Other rewarding hikes follow the area's main access trails. If you're not travelling into or out of the park on one of these routes, consider them as alternate day hikes from Lake Magog. All distances are from the Assiniboine Pass trail junction 0.2 km north of Mount Assiniboine Lodge. N50°54.696', W115°37.299'

Assiniboine Pass—2.1 km. If you are flying to and from the park and staying at Assiniboine Lodge or Naiset Cabins, you might like to hike to Assiniboine Pass and peer down the upper Bryant Creek valley to see how most backpackers reach the park.

From the lodge junction, follow the trail climbing gradually to the northeast. The well-beaten track rolls through scattered subalpine forest and across O'Brien Meadows before reaching the summit. (See also *Bryant Creek-Assiniboine Pass,* Banff National Park.)

Og Lake—5.1 km. The hike to Og Lake retraces the southern end of the access trail from Sunshine Village via Citadel Pass. It is an undemanding trail that descends gradually through a series of meadows to the shores of this rockbound sink lake at the base of Og Mountain.

Follow the Assiniboine Pass trail northwest from the lodge junction for 0.3 km to the Og Lake junction. Turn left and follow the Og Lake trail due north along the valley floor to the vast Og Meadows and the lake. On your return, you have continuous views of Mount Assiniboine. (See also *Assiniboine via Citadel Pass.*)

Ferro Pass—10.7 km. The longest day trip from Lake Magog provides a different perspective of the area. Escaping the confines of the lake and Mount Assiniboine, you travel due west via Sunburst Valley to a 2270 m pass overlooking Wedgwood Lake and a massive, glacier-capped wall formed by Wedgwood Peak, The Marshall and Mount Watson.

Follow the Sunburst Valley trail to the Elizabeth Lake junction at the north end of Cerulean Lake. Continue along Cerulean's northwest shore and pass the junction for Wedgwood Lake at the west end of the lake (stay right). The Ferro Pass trail continues west from Sunburst Valley, making a steady descent through subalpine forest to the Nestor Creek bridge and Mitchell Meadows Campground at km 7.1.

The remainder of the hike is a long, steady ascent. As the trail approaches the pass, it swings across a major avalanche path and then switchbacks up to the summit.

Though the pass provides acceptable views, a short scramble to higher ground west or east of the summit allows a better vista. (See also *Simpson River-Ferro Pass,* Kootenay National Park.)

Wedgwood Lake—7.5 km. Hardly anyone backpacks into the park via the Mitchell River, but the trail does access this forest-enclosed lake beneath the massive cliffs of Wedgwood Peak, The Marshall, and Mount Watson.

The trail branches left from the Ferro Pass route at the west end of Cerulean Lake (km 4.0) and loses 900 m over the next 2.6 km. This section is usually muddy, sometimes overgrown, and there are a couple of minor stream crossings.

Branch left from the Mitchell River trail at km 6.6 and follow boggy track for 0.9 km to Wedgwood's north shore. Views across the lake to the Assiniboine group are quite fine, and you will find more solitude here than on any other area trail.

213 Wonder Pass

Mount Assiniboine Lodge to Wonder Pass—3.1 km (1.9 mi)

Half-day trip

Allow 1 hour one way

Elevation gain: 215 m (700 ft)

Maximum elevation: 2395 m (7,850 ft)

Maps: Mount Assiniboine 82 J/13

Access: Begin hike from Mount Assiniboine Lodge or the Naiset Cabins. (Magog Campground campers reach the lodge via the 1.5 km lakeshore trail skirting around the north end of Lake Magog.)

0.0—Mount Assiniboine Lodge (2180 m).
   N50°54.586', W115°37.201'

0.5—Naiset Cabins.
   Park headquarters cabin.

   — Trail climbs along Gog Creek.

1.1—Gog Creek bridge.

1.5—Junction. Gog Lake right 100 m.

   — Steep pitch followed by steady uphill through larch stands.

2.2—Trail emerges into open meadows.

3.1—Wonder Pass (2395 m).
   Trail intersects with *Wonder Pass* trail from Banff Park.

The hike to Wonder Pass from Lake Magog features Gog Lake, pure stands of alpine larch, vast wildflower meadows, and views that extend over much of the park's core area. And by extending the hike to a viewpoint on the slopes of Wonder Peak, you will discover marvellous views of Marvel Lake.

For backpackers travelling to and from Assiniboine via Bryant Creek, Wonder Pass is an obvious choice on the return journey. For those utilizing other routes, or who flew to the park by helicopter, the pass should rank high on a list of priority hikes from Lake Magog.

The trail begins its ascent to the pass from the park headquarters cabin and Naiset Cabins (500 m south of Assiniboine Lodge) and follows a shallow vale southeast along Gog Creek. After crossing the creek at km 1.1, it comes abreast of Gog Lake. The lake lies beyond a marshy meadow beneath Naiset Point and is a pleasant place to relax on a sunny day. It is also a fine destination for evening walks from the lodge or the Naiset Cabins.

Above the lake, the trail climbs in stages through alpine larch stands interspersed with open meadows. This is a particularly beautiful section during mid-September when the autumn gold of larch needles is most brilliant.

After climbing through the last stunted larch trees, the trail emerges into a vast, rolling alpine meadow leading to the summit of the pass. In the midst of this open landscape, you have your first good views back over the core area of the park—vistas that stretch northward along the course of Og Valley to Citadel Pass and beyond. (You can even see the ski lifts on Lookout Mountain above Sunshine Village.)

Views into Banff Park from the pass are limited by the slopes of Wonder Peak and The Towers, which create a narrow window south to mountains across the

Marvel Lake valley. Backpackers leaving Assiniboine Park on this route descend Banff Park's *Wonder Pass* trail to ever-improving views of the valley and, eventually, Marvel Lake itself.

Wonder Viewpoint. While the views from Wonder Pass are wonderful, the pass takes its name from Wonder Peak, which was christened by interprovincial boundary surveyors who established a station on its summit in 1913. The wondrous view they had from the mountaintop was of Marvel Lake and Lake Gloria in Banff Park—lakes that cannot be seen from Wonder Pass.

While you may not want to climb the peak to confirm the surveyors' awe, you can continue beyond the pass for another 2 km to an open slope on the mountain and approximate their view.

Descend into Banff Park through rocky meadows for 0.7 km to where the trail to the viewpoint angles off to the left (marked by cairns). This narrow track climbs gradually along the southwest slope of Wonder Peak then makes a steep descent to the viewpoint.

This is a grand vantage point for Marvel Lake and Lake Gloria, lying between your toes over 500 vertical metres below. The extensive icefield stretching between Aye and Eon Mountains feeds these two lakes, but since Gloria filters out most of the silt from this glacier before it reaches Marvel, its colour is a milky turquoise compared to the darker blue of Marvel.

The ice-clad summits of the Assiniboine group create an impressive amphitheatre at the head of the Marvel Valley, while the lightly forested summit of Marvel Pass can be seen southwest of Marvel Lake and Peak.

214 Sunburst Valley

Mount Assiniboine Lodge to Elizabeth Lake—3.9 km (2.4 mi)

Half-day trip

Allow 1 to 1.5 hours one way

Elevation gain: 120 m (400 ft)

Minimum elevation: 2300 m (7,550 ft)

Maps: Mount Assiniboine 82 J/13

Access: The hike begins from Mount Assiniboine Lodge junction, 0.2 km north of the lodge. Starting from Magog Campground, follow the Sunburst Lake shortcut trail that branches left at the north edge of the campground for 0.4 km to intersect the hike at km 1.8 (subtract 1.4 km from all distances below).

0.0—Mt Assiniboine Lodge junction (2180 m).
N50°54.696', W115°37.299'

0.1—Junction. Nub Ridge right. Continue ahead.

—Flat trail through meadows above Lake Magog.

1.4—Junction. Magog Campground left (0.2 km). Continue ahead.

1.8—Junction. Magog Campground left (0.4 km). Continue ahead.

2.2—Sunburst Lake.

—Trail follows northeast shoreline.

2.3—Sunburst Cabin.

2.8—Cerulean Lake.

3.0—Junction (2210 m).
Ferro Pass and Wedgwood Lake left. Elizabeth Lake right.

—Steady uphill along shallow valley.

3.5—Junction (2300 m).
Nub Ridge uphill to right 0.9 km. Continue ahead.

—Trail descends to Elizabeth Lake.

3.9—Elizabeth Lake outlet (2270 m). Junction. Chuck's Ridge ahead 0.8 km. Ferro Pass trail left 1.4 km.

Sunburst Valley lies a short distance west of Lake Magog. The valley contains Sunburst and Cerulean Lakes and is reached on flat, undemanding trail from either Assiniboine Lodge or Magog Campground. Most hikers include nearby Elizabeth Lake in their itinerary, and those looking for a longer outing continue up Nub Ridge.

From Assiniboine Lodge, follow the area's core trail southwest along a plateau above Lake Magog. At km 1.4 the campground trail splits left, but you continue to the right through the forested vale leading to Sunburst Lake.

Sunburst Lake is a sparkling little gem set beneath the cliffs of Sunburst Peak. The trail follows its shoreline and immediately passes Sunburst Cabin, which was built by Banff outfitter Pat Brewster in the mid-1930s. It was operated as a guest camp from 1951 to 1970 by Elizabeth "Lizzie" Rummel, and though it has been used as a residence for BC Parks staff in recent years, for those who knew this warm-hearted hostess, it will always belong to Lizzie.

Only a narrow band of forest separates Sunburst from its larger neighbour Cerulean Lake. The trail stays near Cerulean's northeast shore to a junction at its north end. While you can continue to the west end of the lake from this intersection, most hikers turn right and complete a short climb over a forested divide to tiny Elizabeth Lake—a pretty lake surrounded by alpine fir and larch that is named for Lizzie Rummel.

From Elizabeth Lake's outlet, you can continue in a westerly direction for 1.4 km to a junction with the Ferro Pass trail west of Cerulean Lake, then return to Cerulean to complete a circuit of the Sunburst Valley. However, there isn't much to see, so we suggest a side trip to Chuck's Ridge or extending your hike to Nub Ridge.

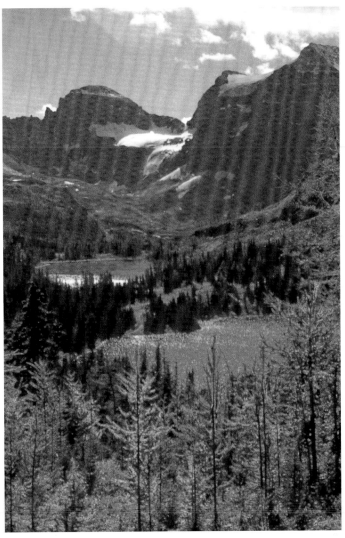

Sunburst and Cerulean Lakes from Elizabeth Lake trail

Chuck's Ridge. This 0.8-km trail branches right from the main trail on the opposite side of the Elizabeth Lake outlet bridge and climbs steeply to a ridge extending southwest from Nub Peak. The ridge, which overlooks the headwaters of the Mitchell River and Wedgwood Lake, was named for Charles "Chuck" Millar, an early guide employed by Erling Strom at Assiniboine Lodge.

Nub Ridge. Without adding a lot of distance to your day, you can climb to the crest of Nub Ridge and the Nublet for the classic high-angle view of Lake Magog and Mount Assiniboine. The connector trail to the ridge branches northeast from the Elizabeth Lake trail at km 3.5. After 0.9 km of steady uphill, it intersects the ridge trail at km 2.4 (see *Nub Ridge*).

215 Nub Ridge

Mount Assiniboine Lodge to Nublet—2.9 km (1.8 mi)

Half-day trip
Allow 1.5 hours one way
Elevation gain: 350 m (1,150 ft)
Maximum elevation: 2530 m (8,300 ft)
Maps: Mount Assiniboine 82 J/13

Access: Begin hike from the junction 0.2 km north of Mount Assiniboine Lodge.

0.0— Mt Assiniboine Lodge junction (2180 m).
N50°54.696', W115°37.299'

0.1— Junction. Nub Ridge right.

0.5— Junction. Horse trail to Og Meadows right. Continue ahead.

1.0— Junction. Horse trail to Sunburst Lake left. Nub Ridge right.

— Steady uphill through subalpine forest.

2.1— Trail crests Nub Ridge.

— Trail ascends crest of ridge.

2.3— Nub Ridge Summit (2390 m).

— Gradual descent along ridgetop.

2.4— Junction. Elizabeth Lake trail downhill to left 0.9 km. Nublet ahead.

— Steep narrow trail climbs through rocky bluffs.

2.9— Nublet (2530 m).

One of the finest views of Mount Assiniboine is from the crest of the ridge leading to Nub Peak. The promontory is strategically situated just north of the Assiniboine group to provide a perfect panorama of all the peaks surrounding this magnificent pyramid and the lakes scattered near its base.

While a short 2.3-km hike to the ridge will reveal the classic, much-photographed view of Mount Assiniboine with Magog, Sunburst and Cerulean lakes, you can get an even higher perspective by continuing another 0.6 km to the Nublet—a 2530-m alpine platform immediately above the ridge to the north. And if you are really looking for a workout, scramble up the last step to the summit of Nub Peak (2743 m) for the full 360-degree overview of the park's core area.

If you are staying at Assiniboine Lodge or the Naiset Cabins, start the hike from the Assiniboine Pass trail junction 0.2 km north of the lodge. Follow the trail west 100 m and branch right onto the trail angling across the meadows toward Nub Ridge. You soon leave the meadows and begin a gradual climb through a forest of Engelmann spruce, alpine fir and scattered alpine larch.

At km 1.0, the horse trail to Sunburst Lake branches left. Stay right and begin the climb to the ridge in a shallow draw. This vale is bordered by lots of small larch trees, which form a golden corridor in mid-September. As you near the upper end of the draw, views begin to open ahead to the rocky slopes of Nub Ridge.

The trail reaches the crest of the ridge at km 2.1 and follows up along its backbone for another 0.2 km to its highest point. From this viewpoint the Assiniboine environs are spread like a map at your feet: a great wall formed by Wedgwood Peak, The Marshall and Mount Watson looms above the heavily forested shores of Wedgwood Lake to the

Mount Assiniboine basin from Nub Ridge

southwest; Sunburst and Cerulean Lakes are wrapped around the rocky promontory of Sunburst Peak directly beneath the ridge to the south; and the sparkling waters of Lake Magog, the park's largest lake, stretch beneath the incomparable "horn" of Mount Assiniboine.

Continuing north, the trail makes a slight descent to the junction for the connector trail down to Elizabeth Lake. A less-defined track continues ahead to the top of the Nublet, ascending through rocky bluffs and eventually entering a large alpine meadow. The Nublet isn't really a peak but more of an extensive platform that allows a loftier view of Mount Assiniboine and the Lake Magog basin.

While defined trail ends on the Nublet plateau, strong hikers can extend the journey upwards for another 1.5 km to the summit of Nub Peak—a steep but obvious scramble. While the foreground for Mount Assiniboine is not nearly as balanced and interesting from the peak as the ridge, views are more expansive, particularly to the Og Meadows–Og Lake environs immediately below the summit to the east.

Elizabeth Lake–Sunburst Valley. If you haven't already hiked to Sunburst Valley and Elizabeth Lake, this is a logical way to return from Nub Ridge. The option only adds 2.0 km to the return trip and allows you to visit all the lakes on the Sunburst Valley route.

From the 2.4-km junction on Nub Ridge, follow the 0.9-km connector trail that switchbacks down to the summit of the Sunburst Valley trail (km 3.5). Elizabeth Lake is just 0.4 km downhill to the right from this junction. After paying a visit to this tiny lake among the larches, return to the junction and descend to Cerulean and Sunburst Lakes. (See *Sunburst Valley*.)

If you are staying at Lake Magog Campground, the Sunburst Valley trail is a shorter, more direct approach to Nub Ridge, saving the 1.5-km detour back to the trailhead near the lodge.

216 Og Pass—Windy Ridge

Mount Assiniboine Lodge to Windy Ridge—7.2 km (4.5 mi)

Day trip

Allow 2.5 to 3 hours to Windy Ridge

Elevation gain: 470 m (1,550 ft)

Maximum elevation: 2650 m (8,700 ft)

Maps: Mount Assiniboine 82 J/13

Access: Begin the hike from the Mount Assiniboine Lodge junction, 0.2 km north of the lodge and 1.6 km east of Magog Campground on the *Assiniboine Pass* trail.

0.0— Mt Assiniboine Lodge junction (2180 m).
N50°54.696', W115°37.299'

— Follow *Assiniboine Pass* trail northeast.

0.3— Junction. Assiniboine Pass ahead. Og Pass left.

0.8— Junction. Horse trail to Sunburst Lake left. Continue ahead.

1.1— Junction. Og Lake ahead. Og Pass right.

— Trail angles north across Og Meadows.

1.4— Junction. Assiniboine Pass horse trail right. Og Pass left.

3.2— Trail climbs from meadows into forest.

— Steady climb through forest.

4.7— Trail levels out into Og Pass.

5.0— Junction (2300 m). Ahead to Og Pass summit (0.3 km) and *Brewster Creek-Allenby Pass* trail (5.8 km). Windy Ridge left.

5.3— Trail passes above treeline.

— Moderately steep climb across rocky meadows.

6.4— Trail levels out briefly on alpine meadow.

— Steep ascent of scree slope.

7.2— Windy Ridge (2650 m).

The trail to Windy Ridge via Og Pass is one of the most rewarding day trips in Assiniboine Park. No other trail provides such an expansive panorama of Mount Assiniboine and the Lake Magog basin, and the wildflower meadow on the slopes below Windy Ridge is one of the finest in the Rockies. And once you reach the trail's 2650-m summit, you will have attained one of the highest points in the mountain parks accessible by defined trail.

Begin the hike on the Assiniboine Pass trail 0.2 km north of Assiniboine Lodge. (You will have to hike 0.7 km to reach this junction if you are staying at Naiset Cabins or 1.6 km from Magog Campground.) Follow the trail northeast toward the pass 0.3 km before branching left on the Og Lake trail. After descending a shallow vale and passing through a draw, you emerge onto the vast, open expanse of Og Meadows, where the trail to Og Pass and Windy Ridge splits right and continues north toward Og Mountain.

After leaving the meadows, the trail ascends steadily for 1.5 km through a subalpine forest of Engelmann spruce, alpine fir and, eventually, larch. At km 4.7, it levels off into the kilometre-long Og Pass. In another 300 m you arrive at the Assiniboine-Banff Park boundary and the junction for the Windy Ridge trail.

While you may be eager to continue your climb to Windy Ridge, a short side-trip to the east will bring you to the true summit of Og Pass and, not far beyond, a pretty lake backed against the rocky north slope of Cave Mountain. The moist meadows surrounding the lake support a luxuriant growth of wildflowers in midsummer, including ragwort, purple fleabane, valerian, fringed grass-of-Parnassus, red-stemmed saxifrage and white paintbrush.

If the weather is reasonable, you will

Mount Assiniboine from the Windy Ridge trail

most certainly want to continue your journey to Windy Ridge from the junction near the park boundary. While the trip becomes more strenuous beyond the Og Pass junction, the views are increasingly rewarding as you ascend the west slope of Og Mountain.

Just 2.4 km above the junction, the climb moderates briefly as the trail traverses a grassy ridge. At a lofty 2515 m, this open slope provides a fantastic panorama that stretches from the peaks of the Assiniboine group on the south to Kootenay Park's Rockwall and Yoho Park's twin-towered Goodsir Peak on the northwestern horizon.

If you have any doubts about how much higher Mount Assiniboine is than its neighbouring peaks, they will be dispelled from this viewpoint. Every other summit in the vicinity lies at least 300 m beneath this towering 3618-m pyramid.

This slope is one of the finest alpine wildflower meadows in the Rockies. In late July and early August it is covered with the colourful blooms of forget-me-nots, arnica, contorted lousewort, golden fleabane, alpine speedwell, red-stemmed saxifrage and moss campion.

After one last uphill grunt over a steep scree slope, the trail crests a high saddle just below Og Mountain's summit. From this crest, you have a mountaineer's-eye view of the ranges to the east and the upper Brewster Creek valley (you can see Halfway Lodge on the edge of a meadow near the head of the valley). A dizzy precipice drops away from the eastern lip of Windy Ridge, where you can peer warily down between your toes for 400 vertical metres to a beautiful hanging valley cradling a tiny azure lake.

Mount Robson Provincial Park

With an area of 2249 sq km, British Columbia's Mount Robson is the largest provincial park in the Canadian Rockies. The park's eastern boundary is formed by a 200-km stretch of the Great Divide, a border it shares with Jasper National Park. With the exception of tiny Mount Terry Fox Provincial Park on its western border, the park is bounded on all other sides by B.C. forest lands.

Despite the park's relatively large size, most visitation is centred around Mount Robson—the highest mountain in the Canadian Rockies at 3954 m (12,972 ft). This giant remained unclimbed until an Alpine Club of Canada party led by the Austrian-born guide Conrad Kain reached its summit in 1913—the same year that the B.C. Legislature created Mount Robson Provincial Park. Even today it is considered a difficult and dangerous ascent, mostly due to the heavy weather created by its lofty summit. (Over the years, around 10% of parties attempting the climb have reached the summit.)

The park's first recreational trail was built along the Robson River to Berg Lake in the spring of 1913 by Jasper outfitter Donald "Curly" Phillips in preparation for the Alpine Club of Canada camp. Sections of the trail have been relocated and upgraded over the years, but it remains the most heavily travelled trail in the park. The initial 4.5 km to Kinney Lake is the park's most popular day hike.

Shorter walks near Mount Robson Viewpoint include Overlander Falls and the Lookout Trail (a higher vantage point for Mount Robson). The short hike to Yellowhead Mountain Viewpoint and a longer, more demanding trip to Mount Fitzwilliam basin are the two most frequently hiked routes in the east section of the park. The only multi-day backpack is Moose River—a remote wilderness track that is only completed by a handful of experienced backpackers each season. Berg Lake is the only trail requiring a camping permit (see *Berg Lake*).

Information and services. Headquarters for the park are in the Mount Robson Visitor Information Centre at Mount Robson Viewpoint, 60 km west of the B.C.-Alberta border on Highway 16. The visitor centre operates from May to September 30, dispensing a full range of information on the park and BC Tourism opportunities as well as registering hikers and collecting overnight fees for the Berg Lake trail. Off-season information is available through the park headquarters office (250-566-4325) or the BC Parks website (www.bcparks.ca).

Two of the park's three road-accessible campgrounds are at Mount Robson Viewpoint: Robson Meadows (125 sites) and Robson River (19 sites). Lucerne Campground (36 sites) is 10 km west of the B.C.–Alberta boundary on Highway 16.

A restaurant-service station-camp store complex adjacent to the Visitor Centre provides meals, gasoline, basic groceries, refreshments and souvenirs. Several lodge and cabin-style accommodations are located nearby in the valley. The nearest towns to Mount Robson Viewpoint are Valemount, B.C. (36 km), McBride, B.C. (79 km) and Jasper, Alberta (87 km). All three towns provide accommodation and a full variety of services, plus McBride and Jasper have hospitals.

Access: The only highway access through the park is the Yellowhead Highway (Hwy 16). Though VIA Rail passenger trains traverse the park daily on the CNR line, the nearest stations are beyond the park at Jasper, Alberta, and Valemount, B.C. (a flag stop). Greyhound buses make daily runs east and west on the Yellowhead Highway with scheduled stops at Valemount and flag stops (arranged in advance) at Mount Robson Viewpoint.

217 Lookout Trail

Mount Robson Viewpoint Parking Area to Lookout—3.3 km (2.1 mi)

The Mount Robson Lookout Trail climbs to a lofty and peaceful vantage point for the Rockies' highest mountain. The steep climb to this forested promontory also provides a good introduction to the unique flora of the upper Robson Valley.

Start on the service road running east into the forest from the end of the Visitor Centre parking lot. At km 0.4 you pass a water storage tank and follow an old roadbed uphill, climbing at a moderate grade through a mixed forest of western red cedar, Douglas fir, white spruce, aspen, Douglas maple, alder, thimbleberry and occasional devil's club.

At km 1.2 the Lookout Trail branches left from the roadbed and, 200 m beyond, begins a steep, switchbacking ascent. A viewpoint with a bench at km 2.7 allows you to catch your breath and look down upon the Yellowhead Highway and Fraser Valley.

The trail crests the Lookout summit at 3.3 km—425 m above your starting point. To the northeast the forest opens to a fine view of the south face of Mount Robson. On the south side of the promontory, there are views down to the Fraser River and Overlander Falls and to the distant Cariboo Mountains.

Access: Hike begins on a service road at the east end of Mount Robson Visitor Centre parking lot. N53°02.091' W119°13.599' *Maps: Mount Robson 83 E/3 (trail not shown).*

218 Overlander Falls

Overlander Falls Parking Area to Overlander Falls—0.5 km (0.3 mi)
Overlander Falls-Fraser River Circuit—6.0 km (3.7 mi)

A short trail descends to a viewpoint for this broad waterfall on the Fraser River. The falls are named for the "Overlanders"—fortune-seekers who bushwhacked down-valley en route to the Cariboo gold fields in 1862.

You can also extend the trip to the falls into a half-day outing by completing a circuit that begins and ends at the Visitor Centre parking area. In addition to the falls, you will experience the area's rich and varied forest environment and a 2-km stretch of the Fraser River.

The circuit follows the Lookout Trail for 1.2 km to where the trail to the lookout branches left. You can side-trip to the lookout at this junction (add 4.2 km to the trip), or simply continue on the circuit by following the roadbed east. In another kilometre you cross the Yellowhead Highway to the Overlander Falls parking area and descend the 0.5-km trail to the falls.

After visiting the falls, return to a junction 100 m above the viewpoint and follow the trail branching left. It descends above the Fraser River for approximately 2 km, passing an old cabin built by Dennis Hogan, a contractor involved in the construction of the original rail lines down the valley between 1912 and 1914.

You emerge on the Hargreaves Road where it crosses the Fraser River. After peering into the river's gorge from the bridge, follow the road north back to the Visitor Centre parking area.

Access: The direct trail to the falls begins from a parking area on the south side of the Yellowhead Highway (Hwy 16) 1.4 km (0.9 mi) east of Mount Robson Viewpoint. N53°01.880' W119°12.480' The circuit trip begins at the east end of Mount Robson Visitor Centre parking area. N53°02.091' W119°13.599' *Maps: Mount Robson 83 E/3 (trail not shown).*

Land above 2300 metres

0 1 2 3 4 km

219 Kinney Lake

Berg Lake Trail Parking Area to Kinney Lake—4.5 km (2.8 mi)
Berg Lake Trail Parking Area to Kinney Lake Campground—6.8 km (4.2 mi)

Day hike or backpack

Allow 1.5 hours one way

Elevation gain: 130 m (425 ft)

Maximum elevation: 985 m (3,230 ft)

Maps: Mount Robson 83 E/3

Access: From Mount Robson Viewpoint junction, follow the Kinney Lake Road north from the service station and restaurant for 2 km to the Kinney Lake/Berg Lake parking area. The hike begins across the Robson River bridge at the far end of the parking area.

0.0— Trailhead (855 m).
N53°03.047' W119°12.870'

— Flat travel on roadbed near Robson River.

0.8— Cinnamon Rockslide.

— Trail climbs over open rockslide.

1.4— Trail enters cedar-hemlock forest.

2.7— Trail emerges from cedar-hemlock forest.

— Steady, moderate ascent.

3.3— Robson River cascades.

4.4— Kinney Lake outlet bridge (985 m).

4.5— Junction. Kinney Lake Picnic Area left 150 m.

— Follow gravel trail around southeast end of lake.

5.0— Kinney Lake viewing platform.

5.7— Trail crosses alluvial outwash along east shore.

— Trail follows eastern shoreline.

6.8— Kinney Lake Campground (985 m).

7.2— Mountain bike access limit (bike rack). Berg Lake trail continues up into forest (see *Berg Lake*).

Berg Lake is the most popular backpack in the Rockies, and the initial 4.5 km of that route to Kinney Lake is the park's most popular day hike. While this large, glacier-fed lake beneath Mount Robson is an attractive destination, the forest you travel through to get there is very special—a rainforest in the Rockies.

The hike follows an old roadbed all the way to the lake, but the track is quite natural and enjoyable to walk. Most of the first kilometre is flat and easy, travelling through lush forest and seldom far from the Robson River.

At 0.8 km you emerge from the forest and climb over a rockslide. This large slide sloughed down from a gully on the east slope of Cinnamon Peak in May, 1986. It has been slowly revegetating ever since and is covered with a colourful display of wildflowers in early summer, including red-stemmed saxifrage, harebells and red columbine.

On the opposite side of the slide, the trail runs into a wonderful forest of western red cedar and western hemlock. The cool, well-shaded understorey is carpeted with feather moss, bunchberry, ferns, thimbleberry and some humongous devil's club. You feel like you've suddenly entered B.C.'s coastal rainforest, and, indeed, this is the farthest east in the province that this forest type appears. This unique forest results from a microclimate created by the mass of nearby Mount Robson, which "catches" weather systems and deposits moisture in this valley.

Near the 3-km mark you climb from the cedar-hemlock forest and come abreast of the Robson River again at a series of cascades. The trail continues its ascent to a bridge across the river, where you have your first view of Kinney Lake and the glaciated pyramid of Whitehorn Mountain beyond. (Before you cross the bridge, scan the nearby rocks for

Kinney Lake and Mount Whitehorn

pikas, this being one of the lowest locales where these tiny members of the hare family are seen in the Rockies.)

As soon as you cross the Robson River, a side-trail branches left to Kinney Lake Picnic Area. The small gravel beaches at this site are pleasant spots to relax and eat your lunch in late summer, but they are often flooded by high lake levels earlier in the season.

The lake is named for the Reverend George Kinney, who made several desperate attempts to climb Mount Robson between 1907 and 1909. On the final expedition, Kinney and his inexperienced companion, Donald "Curly" Phillips, reached a point very near the summit.

Though most hikers end their trip at the picnic area, it is tempting to follow the main trail around to the lake's eastern shoreline. There is a bit of a climb before you descend to the east shore, and in the midst of this forested traverse, there is an elevated platform overlooking the lake.

Once the trail returns to the lakeshore, you cross an alluvial wash that fingers down through the cottonwoods to form a broad gravel beach. Continue along the lake, passing a number of rocky beaches, until you reach Kinney Lake Campground.

The campground is situated on the shoreline not far from the north end of the lake. It is a pleasant site with a substantial, log picnic shelter— a fine destination for families or anyone who doesn't want to work too hard to enjoy a backcountry camp-out.

While the campground is a busy place in midsummer, we will always remember stopping there on a warm evening at the end of September while hiking out from Berg Lake. There was nary a soul around as we rested and watched the last rays of sun illuminate the golden cottonwoods and aspen along the shore, and the lake was a shimmering layer of glass beneath the shadowed slope of Cinnamon Peak.

220 Berg Lake

Robson River Parking Area to Berg Lake Campground—20.2 km (12.6 mi)

Backpack

Allow 7 to 10 hours one way

Elevation gain: 790 m (2,600 ft)

Maximum elevation: 1640 m (5,380 ft)

Maps: Mount Robson 83 E/3

Access: From Mount Robson Viewpoint junction, follow the Kinney Lake Road north from the service station and restaurant for 2 km to the Kinney Lake/Berg Lake parking area. The hike begins across the Robson River bridge at the far end of the parking area.

0.0— Trailhead (850 m).
 N53°03.047' W119°12.870'

4.4— Kinney Lake outlet bridge.

6.8— Kinney Lake Campground (985 m).

7.2— Mountain bike access limit (bike rack).

8.7— Robson River bridge to alluvial flats.

9.0— Bottom of Whitehorn Hill.

10.8— Robson River bridge.
 Whitehorn Ranger Station left 150 m.

10.9— Whitehorn Campground (1115 m).

11.8— Robson River bridge.

12.3— White Falls Viewpoint.

13.4— Falls of the Pool Viewpoint.

14.8— Junction. Emperor Falls right 0.2 km.

15.4— Emperor Falls Campground (1630 m).

17.8— Hargreaves Creek bridges.

18.1— Marmot Campground.

18.4— Junction. *Hargreaves Glacier* left.

20.2— Berg Lake Campground (1640 m).

20.3— Toboggan Creek bridge and junction.
 Toboggan Falls trail left.

21.3— Rearguard Campground.

21.7— Junction. Snowbird Pass right. Berg Lake Ranger Station left. Stay ahead.

22.3— Junction. Left to Robson Pass Campground (100 m) and *Mumm Basin*.

22.7— Robson Pass (1652 m). Robson-Jasper Park boundary. Connects to Jasper's *North Boundary Trail* at km 156.7.

The Berg Lake trail is one of the most popular backpacking trips in the mountain parks. Little wonder. This turquoise lake, dotted with icebergs and backdropped by the ice-bound north wall of the Canadian Rockies' highest peak is one of the wonders of the mountain world.

Hikers attack the 790-m ascent to Berg Lake with a variety of strategies: traditionalists backpack to one of four campgrounds at the lake in a day; the realists stage the trip over two days by camping at Kinney Lake or Whitehorn before assaulting the steep Valley of a Thousand Falls; the masochists hike to Berg and back in a day, often using mountain bikes over the first 7.2 km to facilitate their marathon; and the "sissies" helicopter to Robson Pass on one of two days each week when landings are allowed. Whichever strategy you use, read the information at the end of this description concerning fees and quotas.

From the Robson River bridge at the trailhead parking area, a broad, road-width track climbs gradually along the Robson River through a micro-rainforest to Kinney Lake (see *Kinney Lake*). After crossing the lake's outlet bridge, single-track trail continues around the eastern shoreline to Kinney Lake Campground, where you are greeted with fine lakeside views.

At km 7.2 the trail branches up into the forest to avoid flooding river channels on the alluvial plain north of Kinney Lake. This section rolls up and down for 1.5 km before descending to an aluminum bridge over the Robson River. (Late-season hikers can usually avoid this rolling forested section by staying on the flats between km 7.2 and 8.7. Check at Visitor Centre for conditions.)

After crossing the alluvial flats, the trail begins a steady climb of Whitehorn Hill—the first major step on the journey

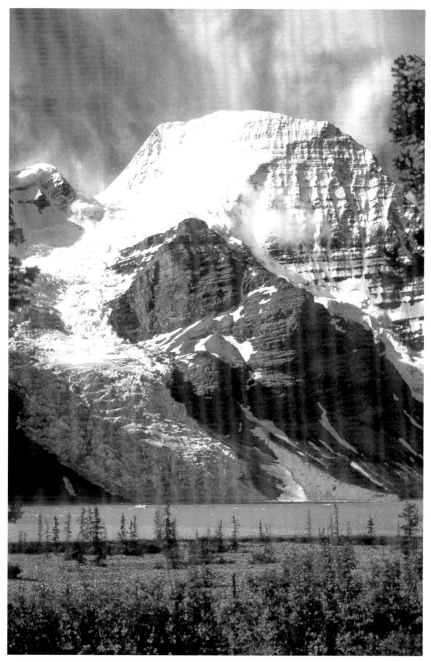

Berg Lake and Mount Robson

to Berg Lake. After gaining nearly 150 m, you descend to the Robson River beneath Whitehorn Mountain where a suspension bridge spans the river to Whitehorn Campground.

Enjoy the short, flat walk beyond Whitehorn Campground to a second bridge back across the river, because the real work is about to begin—a steady, steep 450-m climb along the Valley of a Thousand Falls. Three major waterfalls are passed on the ascent—White Falls, Falls-of-the-Pool and the magnificent Emperor Falls—and each viewpoint provides a welcome respite from the gruelling climb.

The trail finally levels off at Emperor Falls Campground then rolls along the open, braided channels of the Robson River, where you get your first glimpse of the majestic north wall of Mount Robson. Views of the mountain and its glaciers become increasingly grand as you near Berg Lake.

After passing Marmot Campground at the southwest end of the lake, the trail rolls along above the northwest shoreline to Berg Lake, Rearguard and Robson Pass Campgrounds. Views across the lake's powder-blue waters to Mount Robson are exceptional. Two rivers of ice, Mist and Berg Glacier, tumble down from the mountain's uppermost reaches, the latter terminating at the edge of the lake. The groan and rumble of these two overburdened bodies of ice is constant, and chunks of ice calving from Berg Glacier often drift into the lake.

The 3954-m summit of Mount Robson lies more than two vertical kilometres above the lake. First climbed in 1913 by Albert MacCarthy, William Foster and their guide Conrad Kain, it has been the object of many subsequent expeditions. It is still considered one of the most difficult ascents in Canada, mainly due to the mountain's unpredictable weather. The mountain also displays the greatest section of Cambrian rock known in Canada—some 4000 metres thick.

Berg Lake Campground is the most popular of four campgrounds near the lake, thanks in part to the old Berg Lake Chalet situated in its midst. The chalet was constructed in 1927 by outfitter Roy Hargreaves and was used by commercial horse parties until the late 1970s. BC Parks has restored the heritage cabin for day use and renamed it the Hargreaves Shelter. While you cannot overnight inside, it is a cozy and welcome refuge during inclement weather.

Rearguard, Robson Pass and Marmot Campgrounds can also be quite busy during high season, so be flexible about where you camp or make a reservation in advance of your trip.

Robson Pass lies just over 2 km beyond the northeast end of the lake and at virtually the same elevation. The pass is a gateway to the remote northwest corner of Jasper National Park and a good approach to Robson's Moose Pass region. Adolphus Lake is less than a kilometre beyond the pass—a short and easy trip from any of Berg's northeast campgrounds. (See *North Boundary Trail* and *Moose Pass* in the Jasper Park chapter and *Moose River* in this chapter.)

There are a number of fine day trips within easy reach of any of the Berg Lake campgrounds, including *Toboggan Falls*, *Mumm Basin-Hargreaves Glacier*, and *Snowbird Pass*.

Emperor Falls

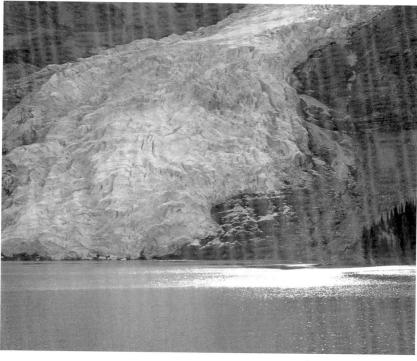

Berg Lake and Glacier

Berg Lake trail information

The Berg Lake trail is renowned as the best managed trail in the Rockies. With the exception of a short section of rough terrain beyond Kinney Lake, and the grunt up the Valley of a Thousand Falls, the trail is broad, easily graded and well maintained. Mountain bikes are allowed to km 7.2 (0.4 km beyond Kinney Lake Campground).

As of this writing, and despite cutbacks in funding, a B.C. Park Ranger is still stationed at Berg Lake (cabin near Robson Pass) and occasionally at Whitehorn throughout the hiking season. If an emergency occurs while the ranger is absent, visitors can use two-way radios mounted outside ranger cabins to call for assistance.

There are seven campgrounds along the trail with large tent pads and bear-proof storage lockers. Large open-air shelters at Kinney Lake and Whitehorn and the enclosed Hargreaves Shelter at Berg Lake are available for day use. Robson Pass is the only campground where open fires are permitted.

There are quotas and a camping fee of $10 per person per night to overnight at any of the campgrounds on the trail. Reservations for campsites can be made from January 2 onwards each year by calling the BC Parks campground reservation line (1-800-689-9025) or online at www.discovercamping.ca.

There is also helicopter access to Robson Pass for anyone overnighting at Berg Lake. The service is available on Fridays and Mondays (Tuesday replaces Monday on holiday weekends) throughout the summer. At the time of publication, the cost of the flight to Robson Pass is $250 per person (minimum 4 passengers). See Robson Heli-Magic, *Sources—Backcountry access.*

Mumm Basin–Toboggan Falls Circuit—8.1 km (5.0 mi)
Mumm Basin–Hargreaves Glacier Circuit—11.6 km (7.2 mi)

Day trip

Allow 4 hours for Mumm-Hargreaves circuit

Elevation gain: 500 m (1,650 ft)

Maximum elevation: 2150 m (7,050 ft)

Maps: Mount Robson 83 E/3†
      †trail not shown

Access: Follow the *Berg Lake* trail to Robson Pass Campground Junction at km 22.

0.0—Robson Pass Campground Jct (1650 m). N53°09.837' W119°07.964'

0.1—Robson Pass Campground.

— Steep ascent on defined track.

0.6—Stream bridge.

1.0—First views of Berg Lake-Robson Pass.

1.7—Alberta-B.C. boundary marker.

— Steep ascent over rocky terrain.

2.0—Rock cairn viewpoint (2100 m).

— Faint track. Cairns and markers.

2.5—Stream crossing.

3.0—Mumm Basin Summit (2150 m).

3.4—Stream crossing in rocky gorge.

— Steep descent across scree slope.

4.9—Junction (1920 m). Intersection with *Toboggan Falls* trail at km 1.2: Toboggan Falls left; Toboggan Creek Cave right 1.0 km; Hargreaves Glacier ahead.

5.1—Toboggan Creek bridge.

— Climb over ridge.

6.3—Hargreaves Glacier lateral moraine.

6.6—Junction. Hargreaves Lake viewpoint right 300 m. Berg Lake left.

— Steep descent.

7.7—Berg Lake Trail Junction (1640 m). N53°08.620' W119°10.204'

Intersection with *Berg Lake* trail at km 18.4.

Mumm Basin provides the classic, much-photographed overview of Berg Lake and Mount Robson. It is one of the most popular day trips from campgrounds in the Berg Lake vicinity and a must for anyone who has a day to spare at the lake. And if the weather is good, you should consider extending the high traverse to Hargreaves Lake at the toe of the Hargreaves Glacier. Otherwise, shorten the loop and return to Berg Lake on the Toboggan Falls trail.

Rough trails to Mumm Basin and Hargreaves Glacier evolved over several decades as campers and guests at Berg Lake Chalet scrambled to these viewpoints. However, it wasn't until the late 1980s that park rangers tied the snippets of trail together with cairns, markers and a bit of trail work to define the routes. But make no mistake, the Mumm Basin–Hargreaves Glacier traverse is steep and demanding, and in many sections you must watch carefully for cairns and markers to stay on route.

We like to begin the circuit from the Robson Pass Campground junction. This approach travels across the basin's high slopes from northeast to southwest, keeping the best views ahead rather than back over your shoulder.

From the rear of the Robson Pass Campground, follow the Mumm trail into a forest of lodgepole pine and spruce. The track leads steadily upwards and, after crossing a small stream, continues gaining elevation across steep side slopes and rocky terrain at a heart-throbbing rate.

After passing an Alberta-B.C. boundary marker at km 1.7, the trail climbs to a rocky promontory with a large rock cairn. This 2100-m platform is a great place to stop for a breather since it provides an exceptional 180-degree panorama stretching from Adolphus Lake in Jasper Park to the mountains west of

Berg Lake and Mt. Robson from Mumm Basin trail

Mount Robson—and your first unfettered view of Mount Robson, Berg Lake, Robson Pass and Glacier.

Beyond the cairn viewpoint, the trail angles left and climbs toward Mumm Basin. Grades moderate as you follow snippets of trail, cairns and yellow markers along the lip of the basin, traversing slab rocks, heather meadows and crossing a small stream. The trail summit is reached on a high meadow at km 3.0, where Berg Lake and Mount Robson dominate the scene.

From the summit, you begin a steady 2-km descent to Toboggan Creek. There are several steep plunges as you "step" down across scree slopes and over the largest of the basin's outlet streams in a boulder-filled gully (you must look carefully for cairns and markers on this trackless descent). Defined trail re-emerges just before you re-enter forest, and soon you reach the Toboggan Falls trail at a four-way junction above Toboggan Creek (see *Toboggan Falls*).

Hargreaves Glacier. If you continue to Hargreaves Glacier, stay straight ahead at the four-way Toboggan Creek junction and descend to a bridge across the creek. From this crossing, the trail climbs over a ridge and approaches a large lateral moraine deposited by the Hargreaves Glacier. Not long after the trail begins its descent toward Berg Lake, you reach a junction where a 300-m side-trail leads right to the viewpoint for the rocky moonscape of Hargreaves Lake and Glacier.

After returning to the main trail, continue straight and steeply downslope through scattered forest to intersect the Berg Lake trail near the southwest end of Berg Lake (0.3 km east of Marmot Campground). Regardless of which campground you started from, total distance for the combined Mumm Basin–Hargreaves Glacier circuit is 11.6 km.

© Don Beers   *Looking out from the cave beneath Mt. Anne-Alice*

222 Toboggan Falls

Toboggan Creek Junction to Toboggan Creek Cave—2.0 km (1.2 mi)

This short, steep trail leads to a series of cataracts sluicing over limestone slabs to create a remarkable natural waterslide. You can continue up along Toboggan Creek for another kilometre to a small cave near the creek's headwaters, or use the trail as an access or exit route for the *Mumm Basin–Hargreaves Glacier* traverse.

The hike up Toboggan Creek begins from a junction 100 m beyond Berg Lake Campground on the Berg Lake trail. After a short steep climb to the lower end of the Toboggan Creek canyon, the trail detours east into the forest briefly before returning to the creek, where you find it sliding merrily down over the limestone bedrock. Climb along this waterslide for the next 0.5 km, but stay back from its edge: if you slipped, you would not enjoy the ride.

The trail reaches the lower end of Toboggan Falls at km 0.9. Another 100

m of steep climbing brings you to a wooden bench and a viewpoint for the upper section of the falls and Mount Robson's north face.

If you continue up Toboggan Creek another 0.2 km, you reach a four-way intersection with the *Mumm Basin–Hargreaves Glacier* trail. While some hikers branch off to one of these high destinations, you can continue along the east side of the creek for another kilometre to a 30-m deep cave beneath the south ridge of Mount Anne-Alice (take a headlamp if you plan on entering the cavern).

Access: Hike the Berg Lake trail to the Toboggan Falls trail junction 100 m east of Berg Lake Campground (east side of Toboggan Creek bridge). N53°09.338' W119°09.224' *Maps: Mount Robson 83 E/3 (trail not shown).*

© Don Beers

Resplendent Mountain from Snowbird Pass

223 Snowbird Pass

Snowbird Pass Junction to Snowbird Pass—9.2 km (5.7 mi)*

Snowbird Pass provides some of the finest mountain scenery in North America—the heavily-crevassed Robson Glacier, the ice-draped northeast face of Mount Robson and the vast Reef Icefield. Extensive, marmot-infested meadows only enhance its reputation as one of the finest day trips in the Rockies.

The trip to Snowbird is long and demanding, and a traverse atop Robson Glacier's lateral moraine requires sturdy footwear. The trail has been improved over the years, but be prepared for exposure and a gain of 780 m, most of it over the last half of the trip.

From its junction with the Berg Lake trail near the ranger cabin, the trail runs southeast across alluvial flats near Robson Glacier's outlet stream. Passing east of a lake at the glacier toe, it ascends a lateral moraine via several short, steep pitches, including one exposed location with a chain guardrail.

You come abreast of the Robson Glacier at km 2.4 and continue south along the rocky crest of the moraine. When you near the main stream draining Snowbird Meadows (km 5.6), the trail branches east and switchbacks upwards into this vast meadowland. It follows near this outlet stream as it climbs steadily toward the pass, but eventually the track disappears into rocky terrain.

The final ascent to the gap between Titkana Peak and Lynx Mountain is quite steep over broken rock and scree, but cairns lead the way to the 2425-m pass and its sudden horizon-filling view of the Reef Icefield.

Access: Hike the *Berg Lake* trail to Snowbird Pass Junction at km 21.7 (1.0 km west of Robson Pass). N53°09.584′ W119°08.237′ *Maps: Mount Robson 83 E/3 (trail not shown).*
*distances approximate

224 Moose River

Yellowhead Highway to Moose Pass—48.9 km (30.4 mi)

Backpack

Allow 3 days to Moose Pass

Elevation gain: 945 m (3,100 ft)

Maximum elevation: 2025 m (6,650 ft)

Maps: Rainbow 83 D/15
      Resplendent Creek 83 E/2
      Mount Robson 83 E/3

Access: Follow the Yellowhead Hwy (#16) to the trailhead access road on the north side of the highway 3 km (2 mi) east of the Moose Lake Boat Launch and 0.5 west of the Moose River highway bridge. Follow access road to the trailhead kiosk.

0.0— Trailhead (1080 m).
     N52°55.467' W118°48.487'

3.6— Trail reaches Moose River.

4.2— Campsite.

11.1— Resplendent Creek cascades.

15.3— Resplendent Campground.
     Ford Resplendent Creek to east bank.

17.8— Trail branches northeast from Resplendent Creek.

20.1— Trail reaches Moose River.

24.7— Junction. Route to Colonel Creek right. Stay left.

26.0— Trio Mountain Campground.

30.8— Moose River fords (four crossings next 2.5 km).

34.7— Moose River ford to east side.

36.4— Moose River ford to west side.

    — Two crossings of Steppe Creek.

38.3— Steppe Creek Campground. Steppe Creek ford.

40.6— Moose River ford to east side.

43.8— Slide Lake Campground.

48.9— Moose Pass (2025 m).
     Mt Robson-Jasper Park boundary.
     Intersection with *Moose Pass* trail, Jasper National Park.

(Trail not shown on maps in this book.)

Moose River is major tributary for the upper Fraser River. A 49-km trail runs up the valley from near the river's confluence with the Fraser to the summit of Moose Pass. After crossing the pass into Jasper Park, it descends through extensive meadows and along Calumet Creek to intersect Jasper's *North Boundary Trail* 5.4 km north of Robson Pass.

Moose River is one of the most demanding trips in the mountain parks, mainly due to numerous fords. Yet, it is still fairly popular, probably because it can be linked with the Berg Lake trail to create a partial circuit around the Mount Robson massif. (Some backpackers descend the valley after visiting Berg Lake.) It is a route reserved for experienced wilderness travellers and usually hiked late in the season when river levels are lower.

Much of the lower Moose Valley was scorched by a prescribed burn in 2003, so expect open, fire-scarred landscape for the first 20 km or so. From the trailhead, you cross the CNR tracks on a gravel road then branch left onto well-defined trail. After crossing a ridge at the end of the Rainbow Range, the trail descends to the Moose River at km 3.6.

The 7-km stretch along the Moose to Resplendent Creek is rather flat and uneventful except for sections of trail that are muddy and overgrown. Views along the river flats stretch northwest to Lynx Mountain and the Reef Icefield near the head of the Resplendent Valley.

The trail passes the confluence of the Moose River and Resplendent Creek near the 10 km mark and starts ascending the latter valley above a series of cascades. The Resplendent Creek detour may appear unreasonable on the map, but not when you encounter this stream. Fed by the Reef Icefield, Resplendent is a major tributary that contributes much of the water volume of the lower Moose. You must travel upstream nearly 5 km to reach a reasonable ford.

© Mike McReynolds

Wildflower meadows below Moose Pass

At km 15.3 you reach Resplendent Campground, where you should ford this silty stream to its east bank. The hiker trail continues up along the east side of the creek for 2.5 km before reuniting with the horse trail. At that point, you turn northeast and cross a ridge to return to the Moose River at km 20.1.

You continue up the valley at a distance from the river, but rejoin it at km 24.3, shortly before coming abreast of the mouth of Colonel Creek. A short distance upstream is the crossing for the Colonel Creek trail leading east to Colonel Pass and Jasper Park. All of this country was burned by a lightning-ignited fire in 1998, but park personnel have cleared and re-established the route from the crossing to the top of the burn on Colonel Creek. (See *Miette River*, Jasper Park.)

At a point nearly 5 km beyond Trio Mountain Campground, you reach the first of four fords of the Moose over the next 2.5 km. There are two more fords of the river at km 34.7 and 36.4, followed by two crossings of Steppe Creek before you arrive at Steppe Creek Campground.

Slosh across Steppe Creek again as you depart the campground and, just over 2 km beyond, ford the Moose River one last time. From this crossing the trail climbs steadily to higher and drier ground on its final ascent through gradually thinning forest to Moose Pass.

Slide Lake Campground is beautifully situated near a small lake amidst islands of stunted alpine fir. It is the last campground before the pass, which can be seen beyond the treeless meadows and a large rockslide to the northwest. (This is prime grizzly territory, so take extra care if you camp here.)

While the final approach to the 2025-m summit is rocky and barren, the true reward comes on the Jasper Park side—a descent through one of the finest wildflower meadows in the Rockies. (See *Moose Pass*, Jasper Park chapter, for details on the 9.5 km section connecting to the North Boundary Trail.)

Note: check at the park visitor centre for the latest info on trail conditions and pick-up a copy of the park's trail brochure-sketch map, which will help you find your way on this difficult trail.

225 Mount Fitzwilliam

Yellowhead Highway to Mount Fitzwilliam Basin—13.0 km (8.1 mi)

Day trip or backpack
Allow 4 to 5 hours one way
Elevation gain: 945 m (3,100 ft)
Maximum elevation: 2060 m (6,750 ft)
Maps: Rainbow 83 D/15
      Jasper 83 D/16

Access: Follow the Yellowhead Highway (Hwy 16) to the Yellowhead Lake Picnic Area and boat launch parking area, located on the north side of the highway 7 km (4.5 mi) west of the Alberta-B.C. boundary and 3 km (2 mi) east of Lucerne Campground. The trailhead is on the south side of the highway opposite the boat launch parking area.

0.0— Trailhead (1115 m).
    N52°51.629' W118°32.007'

  — Trail follows pipeline right-of-way west above highway.

0.7— Junction.
    Trail branches left from roadbed.

  — Steady switchbacking ascent.

2.7— Trail crests forested ridge (1370 m).

  — Steep switchbacking ascent.

3.3— Underground stream.
    Trail begins to climb again.

6.3— Rockingham Creek Campground (1605). Bridge.

  — Rocky, rooty trail.

10.1— Rockslide area. Trail bends due south toward Fitzwilliam Basin.

  — Faint trail through forest above marshy meadow and lake.

11.7— Fitzwilliam Basin headwall.

  — Route follows tributary stream to left. Steep ascent along east side of headwall.

13.0— Fitzwilliam Basin (2060 m). Campsite.

(Trail not shown on maps in this book.)

This alpine basin containing a number of small lakes on the east slope of Mount Fitzwilliam is the most rewarding destination near Yellowhead Pass. However, the last 7 km are unmaintained and so rough that only the strongest hikers can reach the basin and return in a day. The trip is ideal as a light overnight backpack, which allows time to explore the entire basin—the only justification for such a grim approach.

The trip begins somewhat inauspiciously on a pipeline right-of-way above the Yellowhead Highway. While it might not seem so, this cutline through the forest is an important piece of history for the people of the Robson Valley. When the Trans Mountain Oil Pipeline was constructed through Yellowhead Pass in 1952—the first pipeline across the Rockies—it heralded the coming of the Yellowhead Highway nearly 20 years later.

Once you break free from this broad reminder of the park's industrial past, you start to gain elevation along well-graded trail. The trail switchbacks steadily upward through a mixed forest of lodgepole pine, white birch, aspen and a few old Douglas fir, which limits views to a few brief glimpses of the Yellowhead Pass environs.

The uphill grades relent once you top a 1370-m ridge at km 2.7, but dense "doghair" stands of lodgepole pine totally enclose the track. The climb soon resumes and continues through forest to Rockingham Creek Campground.

The campground is set at the north end of an extensive meadow beneath the western wall of Mount Fitzwilliam. On the east side of Rockingham Creek, the superhighway trail suddenly turns into a rocky, rooty wilderness track that contours above Fitzwilliam Creek through scattered forest and willow meadows. (Watch for markers on trees when the trail becomes faint.) Frequent muddy

Kataka Mountain from the Mount Fitzwilliam trail

sections reveal the tracks of the mountain's inhabitants, including deer, moose and, occasionally, bear.

When the valley bends south around the slopes of Fitzwilliam, defined trail all but disappears. As you near the base of the headwall guarding the lakes, you stay left and follow the stream flowing from the largest of the basin's lakes above. This stream descends along the eastern side of the headwall, and the hike is completed by scrambling up along its course to the basin.

At the top of the headwall you suddenly emerge near the north end of the basin's largest lake, which is a scenic highlight along the eastern edge of this wonderful little plateau contained by Mount Fitzwilliam, Bucephalus Peak, Mount Clairvaux and Kataka Mountain. The Jasper topo map (83 D/16) is handy for orienting yourself to the basin, which can be explored rather thoroughly in a half-day from the largest lake on the east side to a small tarn 2 km to the west beneath Mount Fitzwilliam.

There is a small primitive campsite with a bear pole and privy near the point where you emerge into the basin. While it is a scenic spot to overnight, some backpackers prefer to camp at Rockingham Creek and attack the final 7 km of rough trail, and the very steep scramble along the basin headwall, with a light daypack.

Viscount Milton of Fitzwilliam named Mount Fitzwilliam for himself at the suggestion of his Stoney guide when he crossed Yellowhead Pass in 1863 with his travelling companion Dr. Walter B. Cheadle. Reputed to be the first trans-Canadian tourists, Milton and Cheadle later published a book about their difficult journey, which celebrated the heroics of Cheadle's ungainly steed Bucephalus during the crossing of the Rockies. In 1917, boundary surveyors bestowed the horse's name on the peak near Fitzwilliam.

226 Yellowhead Mountain Viewpoint

Yellowhead Lake Parking Area to Yellowhead Mountain Viewpoint—1.5 km (0.9 mi)

One of the best places to view the historic Yellowhead Pass is from the slopes of Yellowhead Mountain. This short hike is particularly rewarding in late September when aspen and birch leaves turn to gold and the first snows dust the ramparts of Mount Fitzwilliam across the valley.

The hike begins from a parking area beneath the railway tracks on the north side of Yellowhead Lake. Cross the tracks and follow the service road 100 m to where the trail branches right into a forest of aspen mixed with pine and birch.

The grade is initially steep, but moderates as the trail contours to the right across the slope to the viewpoint—an opening in the trees with a bench that overlooks Yellowhead Lake, Mount Fitzwilliam and the peaks of the Selwyn Range to the west.

The trail continues beyond the viewpoint, climbing through the forest to an avalanche slope around the 5 km mark. Though the track becomes vague, it is possible to continue even farther up the mountain. Views are limited, however, and since the route climbs through prime bear habitat, it is seldom hiked.

Access: Follow the Yellowhead Highway (Hwy 16) to the junction with a gravel access road on the north side of the highway 1.7 km (1.1 mi) east of Lucerne Campground and 8.5 km (5.5 mi) west of the Alberta-B.C. boundary. Follow gravel road for 1.0 km to the trailhead parking area below the CNR tracks. N52°51.616' W118°33.216' *Maps: Rainbow 83 D/15 (trail not shown).*

(Trail not shown on maps in this book.)

227 Portal Lake

Portal Lake Circuit—1.0 km (0.6 mi)

The trail around Portal Lake, a tiny tarn just west of the Alberta-British Columbia boundary, allows you an opportunity to stretch your legs on the backbone of the continent.

From the parking area, where interpretive displays commemorate the Yellowhead Pass National Historic Site, follow the trail running along the east shore of the lake for 300 m to a point near its north end. The dark, precipitous bluffs containing the lake are composed of some of the oldest rock in this section of the Rockies—Precambrian shales of the Middle Miette Group.

As you near the end of the lake, the trail branches right and climbs steeply through a dense, stunted forest of lodgepole pine. After a vertical ascent of 30 m, it reaches the interprovincial boundary cutline and the Great Divide. Descend steeply along this broad cut for 150 m before following trail back into British Columbia. The forest floor is quite lush in early summer, when it is carpeted with the blooms of bunchberry and heart-leaved arnica.

The trail runs flat for the final 0.2 km, completing the circuit back to the parking area through a boggy spruce forest filled with equisetum (horsetails).

Access: Follow the Yellowhead Highway (Hwy 16) to the Yellowhead Pass Picnic Area, located on the north side of the highway at the Alberta-British Columbia boundary (3.2 km west of Jasper Park West Gate). N52°52.940' W118°27.062' *Maps: Jasper 83 D/16 (trail not shown).*

(Trail not shown on maps in this book.)

Sources

PARKS INFORMATION

Following is a list of parks with phone numbers and website addresses (email addresses for parks are listed on websites). With the exception of BC Parks, phone and fax numbers are for park visitor centres.

Websites are always your best bet for complete information on any of these parks, including fees, trail conditions, restrictions and closures, and in many cases regularly updated backcountry campground vacancy reports. And when looking for information on BC Parks, they are virtually your only source.

Banff National Park
Phone: 403-762-1550
Web: www.pc.gc.ca/banff
Backcountry campsite reservations:
403-762-1556 or 403-522-1264

Jasper National Park
Phone: 780-852-6176
Web: www.pc.gc.ca/jasper
Backcountry campsite reservations:
780-852-6177

Yoho National Park
Phone: 250-343-6783
Web: www.pc.gc.ca/yoho
Lake O'Hara campsite reservations:
250-343-6433

Kootenay National Park
Phone: 250-347-9505
Web: www.pc.gc.ca/kootenay

Waterton Lakes National Park
Phone: 403-859-2224
Web: www.pc.gc.ca/waterton

BC Parks
Web: www.bcparks.ca
Links on the website home page take you to individual park pages for Akamina-Kishinena, Elk Lakes, Mt Assiniboine and Mt Robson.
Berg Lake reservations: 519-826-6850 or 800-689-9025;
www.discovercamping.ca

Peter Lougheed Provincial Park
Phone: 403-591-7226
Web: www.albertaparks.ca
Backcountry campsite reservations:
403-678-3136

WEATHER

Environment Canada
Meteorological Service of Canada
Web: www.weather.gc.ca
Banff weather phone: 403-762-2088
Jasper weather phone: 780-852-3185
The website displays weather maps and forecasts for mountain parks and specific communities. Several stations report conditions on an hourly basis: select Alberta to check Banff, Jasper and Waterton Lakes; select British Columbia to check Yoho National Park (an automatic station situated at 1615 m near Kicking Horse Pass). Weather phones provide recorded current conditions and forecasts and are updated throughout the day.

Friends of Jasper National Park
500 Connaught Ave, Jasper
Phone: 780-852-4767
Web: www.friendsofjasper.com
Non-profit organization selling books and maps specific to Jasper National Park. Retail outlet in the Jasper Visitor Centre.

Friends of Yoho National Park
Trans-Canada Hwy, Field
Phone: 250-343-6393
Web: www.friendsofyoho.ca
Non-profit organization selling books and maps specific to Yoho National Park. Retail outlet in Yoho Visitor Centre, at the entrance to Field townsite.

Friends of Kootenay National Park
7556 Main St. East, Radium Hot Springs
Phone: 250-347-6525
Web: www.friendsofkootenay.ca
Non-profit organization selling books and maps specific to Kootenay National Park. Retail outlet in Radium Hot Springs Visitor Centre.

Friends of Kananaskis Country
Phone: 403-678-5593
Web: www.kananaskis.org
Non-profit organization selling books, trail brochures and maps specific to Peter Lougheed Provincial Park and Kananaskis Country. Retail outlets in Kananaskis Country visitor centres.

Mountain Equipment Co-op
Phone: 604-876-6221 or 888-847-0770
Web: www.mec.ca
One of the largest outlets for outdoor recreation gear in Canada, with stores in major cities across the country. Retail outlets in Calgary and Edmonton carry an excellent selection of maps and guidebooks for the Canadian Rockies.

Map Town
#100, 400 5th Avenue SW
Phone: 403-266-2241 or 877-921-6277
Web: www.maptown.com
A good source for government topographical maps. Also carries guidebooks, the full line of Gem Trek maps, and GPS digital maps.

BACKCOUNTRY LODGES

Brewster's Shadow Lake Lodge
Phone: 403-762-0116 or 866-762-0114
Web: www.shadowlakelodge.com
Located near Shadow Lake,
Banff National Park.
Summer season:
mid-June to late September.

Skoki Lodge
Phone: 403-522-1347 or 888-997-5654
Web: www.skoki.com
Located in the Skoki Valley east of
Lake Louise, Banff National Park.
Summer season:
mid-June to mid-September.

Shovel Pass Lodge
Phone: 780-852-4215 or 888-852-7787
Web: www.skylinetrail.com
Shovel Pass Lodge provides midway
accommodation for hikers traversing
Jasper's Skyline Trail.
Summer season: July to late September.

Tonquin-Amethyst Lake Lodge
Phone: 780-852-1188
Web: www.tonquinadventures.com
Located along the east side of Amethyst
Lakes (near the Narrows) in the
Tonquin Valley, Jasper National Park.
Summer season:
mid-July to early September.

Tonquin Valley Backcountry Lodge
Phone: 780-852-3909
Web: www.tonquinvalley.com
Located at the north end of
Amethyst Lakes in the Tonquin Valley,
Jasper National Park.
Summer season:
July 1 to September 30.

Lake O'Hara Lodge
Phone: 250-343-6418 or 403-678-4110
(off-season)
Web: www.lakeohara.com
Located at Lake O'Hara, Yoho National Park.
Summer season: mid-June to early October.

Twin Falls Chalet
Phone/fax: 403-228-7079
Web: www.twinfallschalet.ca
Located at the base of Twin Falls in the
Yoho Valley, Yoho National Park.
Season: July to early September.

Amiskwi Lodge
Phone: 403-678-1800
Web: www.amiskwi.com
Located above Amiskwi Pass just
beyond the northwest boundary of
Yoho National Park.
Hut-style accommodation.
Summer season: July to October.

Mount Assiniboine Lodge
Phone: 403-678-2883
Web: www.assiniboinelodge.com
Located at Lake Magog,
Mount Assiniboine Provincial Park.
Summer season: mid-June to early October.

HUTS

Alpine Club of Canada
Phone: 403-678-3200
Web: www.alpineclubofcanada.ca
Operates a network of alpine huts throughout the Canadian Rockies. The Stanley Mitchell and Elizabeth Parker Huts in Yoho Park, Wates-Gibson Hut in Jasper Park, and Elk Lakes Cabin in Elk Lakes Provincial Park are accessible by hiking trails. Reservations are required (by phone or e-mail) and accepted up to one year in advance for members, 30 days in advance for non-members.

HOSTELS

Hostelling International—Canada
Phone: 613-237-7884
Web: www.hihostels.ca
Operates hostels throughout the mountain parks, many near hiking trails. Make reservations online or call 778-328-2220.

GUIDED WALKS

Interpreters in the five national parks offer a variety of guided walks from late June to early September (check with park visitor centres for locations and schedules). A number of private operators offer guided walking tours.

Of specific interest to Yoho Park visitors are the guided hikes to the Burgess Shale Beds organized by the Burgess Shale Geoscience Foundation, which are the only way to visit this lofty World Heritage Site. For schedules, rates and mandatory reservations contact:

Burgess Shale Geoscience Foundation
Phone: 250-343-6006 or 800-343-3006
Web: www.burgess-shale.bc.ca

White Mountain Adventures
Phone: 403-762-7889
Web: www.sunshinemeadowsbanff.com
Provides shuttle bus service to
Sunshine Meadows, Banff National Park.
Operating from Sunshine Village base
station (hourly) and Banff (once a day)
from mid-June to September 30.

Jasper-Maligne Shuttle
616 Patricia Street, Jasper
Phone: 780-852-3370
Web: www.malignelake.com
Shuttle bus between Jasper and
Maligne Lake; late June to late September
up to three round-trips daily. Provides
hikers with trailhead drop-offs and pick-ups
along Maligne Lake Road. It is popular with
backpackers hiking the Skyline Trail from
Maligne Lake back to Jasper.
Reservations recommended.

Mount Assiniboine Lodge
Phone: 403-678-2883
Web: www.assiniboinelodge.com
Books flights from Mt. Shark Heliport in
the Spray Lakes valley to the Lake Magog
area of Mt. Assiniboine Provincial Park for
campers as well as lodge guests.
Helicopter access on Wednesdays, Fridays
and Sundays (Monday replaces Sunday
on long weekends), mid-June to late
September. Helicopter transport of luggage
also available.

Robson Helimagic
Phone: 250-566-4700 or 877-454-4700
Web: www.robsonhelimagic.com
Books flights for campers and climbers to
Robson Pass near Berg Lake.
Access available on Fridays and Mondays
(Tuesday replaces Monday on long
weekends).
Advance reservations recommended.

Waterton Shoreline Cruise Co.
Phone: 403-859-2362
Web: www.watertoncruise.com
Operates sightseeing tours on Upper
Waterton Lake, Waterton Lakes National
Park, and offers hiker drop-off and pick-up
to Crypt Landing for the Crypt Lake Trail and
Goat Haunt in the US. Visitors planning to
stay and hike in Glacier National Park must
have proper international documentation.
Cruise tickets are available from the marina
office at the Waterton townsite docks with
recommended purchase at least one hour
before departure. Operations begin in late
May and continue into October.

Tamarack Outdoor Outfitters
Phone: 403-859-2378
Web: www.watertonvisitorservices.com
Located at 214 Mount View Road in
Waterton townsite. Aside from being one
of the best outdoor shops in the Canadian
Rockies, Tamarack operates a highly useful
park shuttle service for hikers needing
drop-off or pick-up along the Akamina or Red
Rock Parkways. The Cameron Express, used
by those bound for the Carthew-Alderson
trail, is particularly popular. Shuttles run
daily during the peak season. Seats are
limited, so try to reserve a spot one or two
days ahead.

RECOMMENDED READING

Following are books we endorse for anyone spending time in the Canadian Rockies and who wants to explore the trails and natural history of the region more completely. All of these titles are available in regional bookstores, outdoor sports shops, and through parks' "Friends" shops and websites.

Banff-Assiniboine: A Beautiful World
Jasper-Robson: A Taste of Heaven
by Don Beers
(Calgary: Highline Publishing)
The above hiking guides deal with specific areas within the mountain parks and are written and illustrated by veteran hiker-photographer Don Beers. In the same series, *The Wonder of Yoho* and *The World of Lake Louise* can be found at used bookstores. The four titles cover these areas in much more detail than is possible in our guidebook—including main trails and many side routes. Filled with excellent colour photography and entertaining historical anecdotes. A true labour of love.

Kananaskis Country Trail Guide:
Volume 1 (4th edition)
by Gillean Daffern
(Calgary: Rocky Mountain Books, 2010)
The most complete coverage of trails in Alberta's Peter Lougheed Provincial Park, as well as Kananaskis Valley and Smith-Dorrien regions. Also describes many popular off-trail routes. Additional volumes cover other sections of Kananaskis Country.

Hiking Canada's Great Divide Trail
(2nd edition)
by Dustin Lynx
(Calgary: Rocky Mountain Books, 2007)
The Great Divide Trail is the most popular long-distance backpacking route in the Canadian Rockies. It is an unofficial trail that runs north along the Great Divide for approximately 1200 km from Waterton Lakes National Park to British Columbia's Kakwa Lake Provincial Park. This guidebook provides the most detailed description of the route.

Handbook of the Canadian Rockies
(3rd edition)
by Ben Gadd
(Canmore: Corax Press, 2009)
One of the most comprehensive natural history guides ever published in North America. Covers everything—geology, weather and climate, plants, insects, fish, amphibians, reptiles, birds, mammals, etc. Also a condensed historical chronology and brief introduction to recreational activities. "The bible" for Canadian Rockies' naturalists.

The Canadian Hiker's and Backpacker's
Handbook
by Ben Gadd
(Vancouver: Whitecap Books, 2008)
An essential how-to guide for anyone planning on hiking or backcountry camping in the Canadian Rockies. Includes everything from tips for choosing the best boots to emergency preparation.

Fire Lookout Hikes in the Canadian
Rockies (2nd edition)
by Mike Potter
(Calgary: Luminous Compositions, 2008)
A hiking guidebook to over 100 fire lookouts in the Canadian Rockies. Includes historical notes, maps, and colour photos.

Parkways of the Canadian Rockies
(5th edition)
by Brian Patton
(Banff: Summerthought Publishing, 2008)
Canadian Rockies Trail Guide co-author Brian Patton brings a wealth of experience to this user-friendly and fact-filled driving guide to the Canadian Rockies. First published in 1975, it was the first comprehensive guide to roads in the mountain national parks of Banff, Jasper, Yoho, and Kootenay.

Index

Names and pages in **bold** type refer to main trail headings used in this book.

About the Authors

Bart Robinson (with trail wheel) and Brian Patton on Molar Pass,
Banff National Park

For the past 40 years, **Brian Patton** has interpreted the natural and human history of the Canadian Rockies, including stints with CBC Radio, The Banff Centre, the Whyte Museum of the Canadian Rockies, and as a park naturalist at Banff, Saskatchewan River Crossing and Mount Robson. He has also appeared as an historical interpreter and storyteller in five documentary films about the region. His other books include *Parkways of the Canadian Rockies*, *Tales from the Canadian Rockies*, *Mountain Chronicles: Jon Whyte* and *Bear Tales from the Canadian Rockies*. He continues to work on a variety projects from his home in Invermere, British Columbia.

Following the publication of the *Canadian Rockies Trail Guide*, **Bart Robinson** authored several books on the Canadian Rockies: *Banff Springs: The Story of a Hotel*, *Columbia Icefield: A Solitude of Ice* and *Great Days in the Rockies: The Photographs of Byron Harmon*. Subsequently, he has enjoyed a long career as a journalist, editor, and conservationist. He was an editor with *Equinox* magazine from 1982 to 1994, and the Executive Director of the Yellowstone to Yukon Conservation Initiative from 1996 to 2003. He currently lives in Canmore, Alberta, and works for the Alberta Ecotrust Foundation.